# Lecture Notes in Artificial Intelligence 13310

Subseries of Lecture Notes in Computer Science

More information about this subseries at https://link.springer.com/bookseries/1244

Dylan D. Schmorrow · Cali M. Fidopiastis (Eds.)

# Augmented Cognition

16th International Conference, AC 2022
Held as Part of the 24th HCI International Conference, HCII 2022
Virtual Event, June 26 – July 1, 2022
Proceedings

 Springer

*Editors*
Dylan D. Schmorrow
Soar Technology Inc.
Orlando, FL, USA

Cali M. Fidopiastis
Katmai Government Services
Orlando, FL, USA

ISSN 0302-9743                    ISSN 1611-3349 (electronic)
Lecture Notes in Artificial Intelligence
ISBN 978-3-031-05456-3           ISBN 978-3-031-05457-0 (eBook)
https://doi.org/10.1007/978-3-031-05457-0

LNCS Sublibrary: SL7 – Artificial Intelligence

This Springer imprint is published by the registered company Springer Nature Switzerland AG
The registered company address is: Gewerbestrasse 11, 6330 Cham, Switzerland

# Foreword

Human-computer interaction (HCI) is acquiring an ever-increasing scientific and industrial importance, as well as having more impact on people's everyday life, as an ever-growing number of human activities are progressively moving from the physical to the digital world. This process, which has been ongoing for some time now, has been dramatically accelerated by the COVID-19 pandemic. The HCI International (HCII) conference series, held yearly, aims to respond to the compelling need to advance the exchange of knowledge and research and development efforts on the human aspects of design and use of computing systems.

The 24th International Conference on Human-Computer Interaction, HCI International 2022 (HCII 2022), was planned to be held at the Gothia Towers Hotel and Swedish Exhibition & Congress Centre, Göteborg, Sweden, during June 26 to July 1, 2022. Due to the COVID-19 pandemic and with everyone's health and safety in mind, HCII 2022 was organized and run as a virtual conference. It incorporated the 21 thematic areas and affiliated conferences listed on the following page.

A total of 5583 individuals from academia, research institutes, industry, and governmental agencies from 88 countries submitted contributions, and 1276 papers and 275 posters were included in the proceedings to appear just before the start of the conference. The contributions thoroughly cover the entire field of human-computer interaction, addressing major advances in knowledge and effective use of computers in a variety of application areas. These papers provide academics, researchers, engineers, scientists, practitioners, and students with state-of-the-art information on the most recent advances in HCI. The volumes constituting the set of proceedings to appear before the start of the conference are listed in the following pages.

The HCI International (HCII) conference also offers the option of 'Late Breaking Work' which applies both for papers and posters, and the corresponding volume(s) of the proceedings will appear after the conference. Full papers will be included in the 'HCII 2022 - Late Breaking Papers' volumes of the proceedings to be published in the Springer LNCS series, while 'Poster Extended Abstracts' will be included as short research papers in the 'HCII 2022 - Late Breaking Posters' volumes to be published in the Springer CCIS series.

I would like to thank the Program Board Chairs and the members of the Program Boards of all thematic areas and affiliated conferences for their contribution and support towards the highest scientific quality and overall success of the HCI International 2022 conference; they have helped in so many ways, including session organization, paper reviewing (single-blind review process, with a minimum of two reviews per submission) and, more generally, acting as goodwill ambassadors for the HCII conference.

This conference would not have been possible without the continuous and unwavering support and advice of Gavriel Salvendy, founder, General Chair Emeritus, and Scientific Advisor. For his outstanding efforts, I would like to express my appreciation to Abbas Moallem, Communications Chair and Editor of HCI International News.

June 2022                                                                    Constantine Stephanidis

# HCI International 2022 Thematic Areas and Affiliated Conferences

**Thematic Areas**

- HCI: Human-Computer Interaction
- HIMI: Human Interface and the Management of Information

**Affiliated Conferences**

- EPCE: 19th International Conference on Engineering Psychology and Cognitive Ergonomics
- AC: 16th International Conference on Augmented Cognition
- UAHCI: 16th International Conference on Universal Access in Human-Computer Interaction
- CCD: 14th International Conference on Cross-Cultural Design
- SCSM: 14th International Conference on Social Computing and Social Media
- VAMR: 14th International Conference on Virtual, Augmented and Mixed Reality
- DHM: 13th International Conference on Digital Human Modeling and Applications in Health, Safety, Ergonomics and Risk Management
- DUXU: 11th International Conference on Design, User Experience and Usability
- C&C: 10th International Conference on Culture and Computing
- DAPI: 10th International Conference on Distributed, Ambient and Pervasive Interactions
- HCIBGO: 9th International Conference on HCI in Business, Government and Organizations
- LCT: 9th International Conference on Learning and Collaboration Technologies
- ITAP: 8th International Conference on Human Aspects of IT for the Aged Population
- AIS: 4th International Conference on Adaptive Instructional Systems
- HCI-CPT: 4th International Conference on HCI for Cybersecurity, Privacy and Trust
- HCI-Games: 4th International Conference on HCI in Games
- MobiTAS: 4th International Conference on HCI in Mobility, Transport and Automotive Systems
- AI-HCI: 3rd International Conference on Artificial Intelligence in HCI
- MOBILE: 3rd International Conference on Design, Operation and Evaluation of Mobile Communications

# List of Conference Proceedings Volumes Appearing Before the Conference

1. LNCS 13302, Human-Computer Interaction: Theoretical Approaches and Design Methods (Part I), edited by Masaaki Kurosu
2. LNCS 13303, Human-Computer Interaction: Technological Innovation (Part II), edited by Masaaki Kurosu
3. LNCS 13304, Human-Computer Interaction: User Experience and Behavior (Part III), edited by Masaaki Kurosu
4. LNCS 13305, Human Interface and the Management of Information: Visual and Information Design (Part I), edited by Sakae Yamamoto and Hirohiko Mori
5. LNCS 13306, Human Interface and the Management of Information: Applications in Complex Technological Environments (Part II), edited by Sakae Yamamoto and Hirohiko Mori
6. LNAI 13307, Engineering Psychology and Cognitive Ergonomics, edited by Don Harris and Wen-Chin Li
7. LNCS 13308, Universal Access in Human-Computer Interaction: Novel Design Approaches and Technologies (Part I), edited by Margherita Antona and Constantine Stephanidis
8. LNCS 13309, Universal Access in Human-Computer Interaction: User and Context Diversity (Part II), edited by Margherita Antona and Constantine Stephanidis
9. LNAI 13310, Augmented Cognition, edited by Dylan D. Schmorrow and Cali M. Fidopiastis
10. LNCS 13311, Cross-Cultural Design: Interaction Design Across Cultures (Part I), edited by Pei-Luen Patrick Rau
11. LNCS 13312, Cross-Cultural Design: Applications in Learning, Arts, Cultural Heritage, Creative Industries, and Virtual Reality (Part II), edited by Pei-Luen Patrick Rau
12. LNCS 13313, Cross-Cultural Design: Applications in Business, Communication, Health, Well-being, and Inclusiveness (Part III), edited by Pei-Luen Patrick Rau
13. LNCS 13314, Cross-Cultural Design: Product and Service Design, Mobility and Automotive Design, Cities, Urban Areas, and Intelligent Environments Design (Part IV), edited by Pei-Luen Patrick Rau
14. LNCS 13315, Social Computing and Social Media: Design, User Experience and Impact (Part I), edited by Gabriele Meiselwitz
15. LNCS 13316, Social Computing and Social Media: Applications in Education and Commerce (Part II), edited by Gabriele Meiselwitz
16. LNCS 13317, Virtual, Augmented and Mixed Reality: Design and Development (Part I), edited by Jessie Y. C. Chen and Gino Fragomeni
17. LNCS 13318, Virtual, Augmented and Mixed Reality: Applications in Education, Aviation and Industry (Part II), edited by Jessie Y. C. Chen and Gino Fragomeni

**http://2022.hci.international/proceedings**

# Preface

The main goal of the field of augmented cognition is to research and develop adaptive systems capable of extending the information management capacity of individuals through computing technologies. Augmented cognition research and development is therefore focused on accelerating the production of novel concepts in human-system integration and includes the study of methods for addressing cognitive bottlenecks (e.g., limitations in attention, memory, learning, comprehension, visualization abilities, and decision making) via technologies that assess the user's cognitive status in real time. A computational interaction employing such novel system concepts monitors the state of the user, through behavioral, psychophysiological, and neurophysiological data acquired from the user in real time, and then adapts or augments the computational interface to significantly improve their performance on the task at hand.

The International Conference on Augmented Cognition (AC), an affiliated conference of the HCI International (HCII) conference, arrived at its 16th edition and encouraged papers from academics, researchers, industry, and professionals, on a broad range of theoretical and applied issues related to augmented cognition and its applications.

The field of augmented cognition has matured over the years to solve enduring issues such as portable, wearable neurosensing technologies and data fusion strategies in operational environments. These innovations coupled with better understanding of brain and behavior, improved measures of brain state change, and improved artificial intelligence algorithms have helped expand the augmented cognition focus areas to rehabilitation, brain-computer interfaces, and training and education. The burgeoning field of human-machine interfaces such as drones and autonomous agents are also benefitting from augmented cognition research.

This volume of the HCII 2022 proceedings is dedicated to this year's edition of the AC conference and focuses on topics related to understanding human cognition and behavior, brain activity measurement and electroencephalography, human and machine learning, and augmented cognition in extended reality.

Papers of this one volume are included for publication after a minimum of two single-blind reviews from the members of the AC Program Board or, in some cases, from members of the Program Boards of other affiliated conferences. We would like to thank all of them for their invaluable contribution, support, and efforts.

June 2022

Dylan D. Schmorrow
Cali M. Fidopiastis

# 16th International Conference on Augmented Cognition (AC 2022)

The full list with the Program Board Chairs and the members of the Program Boards of all thematic areas and affiliated conferences is available online at

**http://www.hci.international/board-members-2022.php**

# HCI International 2023

The 25th International Conference on Human-Computer Interaction, HCI International 2023, will be held jointly with the affiliated conferences at the AC Bella Sky Hotel and Bella Center, Copenhagen, Denmark, 23–28 July 2023. It will cover a broad spectrum of themes related to human-computer interaction, including theoretical issues, methods, tools, processes, and case studies in HCI design, as well as novel interaction techniques, interfaces, and applications. The proceedings will be published by Springer. More information will be available on the conference website: http://2023.hci.international/.

General Chair
Constantine Stephanidis
University of Crete and ICS-FORTH
Heraklion, Crete, Greece
Email: general_chair@hcii2023.org

**http://2023.hci.international/**

# Contents

**Brain Activity Measurement and Electroencephalography**

## Human and Machine Learning

## Extended Reality and Augmented Cognition

# Understanding Human Cognition
# and Behavior

# Examining the Impact of Chronic Pain on Information Processing Behavior: An Exploratory Eye-Tracking Study

Doaa Alrefaei[✉], Gaayathri Sankar, Javad Norouzi Nia, Soussan Djamasbi, and Diane Strong

User Experience and Decision Making (UXDM) Laboratory, Worcester Polytechnic Institute, Worcester, MA, USA
{dalrefaei,gsankar,jnorouzinia,djamasbi,dstrong}@wpi.edu

**Abstract.** Chronic pain is a multifaceted complex experience that is often captured with self-reported measures. While subjective self-reported measures capture pain from a patient's point of view, they are limited in information richness. Collecting eye movements when completing self-reported subjective pain measures provides valuable insight about information processing and decision behavior. This information can improve the information richness of self-reported pain measures by providing a broader view of an individual's pain experience. How people process information and make decisions when completing pain measures can also help to investigate the cognitive-evaluative aspects of chronic pain, which in turn can provide insight for developing eye-tracking biomarkers of chronic pain, and by doing so help develop smart clinician support technologies. Our preliminary results show that people with chronic pain expended significantly more cognitive effort than their pain-free counterparts when completing three self-reported pain measures that are widely used in clinical settings. These results are promising because they suggest that eye movements may serve as valuable information to accompany self-reported pain scores and thus enable effective assessment and management of chronic pain. The results also suggest that eye movements may serve as suitable biomarkers of chronic pain.

**Keywords:** Gaze behavior · Chronic pain · Visual attention · Attentional bias · Information processing · Decision behavior · PROMIS-29

## 1 Introduction

Chronic pain, defined as pain that persists for at least three months (Merskey 1986), is a major public health problem. In the United States, chronic pain is one of the most commonly experienced chronic conditions, afflicting about 50 million (1 out of 5) adults (CDC 2020; Yong et al. 2022). Pain refers to "a distressing experience associated with actual or potential tissue damage with sensory, emotional, cognitive, and social components" (Crofford 2015). Chronic pain occurs when that pain persists over months.

© The Author(s), under exclusive license to Springer Nature Switzerland AG 2022
D. D. Schmorrow and C. M. Fidopiastis (Eds.): HCII 2022, LNAI 13310, pp. 3–19, 2022.
https://doi.org/10.1007/978-3-031-05457-0_1

Chronic pain impacts quality of life by limiting work and life activities; it often negatively affects individuals' physical and mental health as well as their family and social relationships. In addition to having a negative impact on quality of life, chronic pain also has negative economic costs including reduced productivity levels, increased compensatory payments due to disabilities caused by persistent pain, and increased health care costs and medical expenses (CDC 2020; Phillips 2006; Yong et al. 2022).

Effective treatment and management of chronic pain starts with comprehensive assessment of pain experience and impact. Currently, chronic pain is assessed by capturing self-reported level of pain intensity and level of interference that chronic pain has on one's daily function (McCahon et al. 2005; Rose et al. 2018). Such self-reported measures are instrumental in capturing chronic pain experience from the patients' point of view.

Self-reported measures, by their nature, provide only a narrow view of pain experience because they require patients to summarize a multifaceted complex experience into a single subjective score (Xu and Huang 2020). Because they are subjective and lack rich information, they are limited in providing physicians with the information they need for effective treatment.

Information about how people go about providing such a score when completing a self-reported measure (i.e., how they process the provided information to decide which single score best represents their pain experience) may help to broaden the inherently narrow view of pain experience that is captured by such process. For example, capturing the type and range of information when a patient is choosing a response may help to reveal the extent (low-high boundaries) of pain experience by that patient. Similarly, identifying visual elements that received the most intense attention can reveal pieces of information that served as anchors for decision making. These insights gained from information processing and decision behavior when completing self-reported measures provide a more comprehensive and dynamic understanding of pain experience, which in turn can help develop guidelines for more effective pain assessment, management, and treatment.

In this study, we take a first step towards the larger project of building such smart clinician support technologies, by examining the differences in viewing behavior and patterns of people with and without chronic pain when they summarize their pain experience into single scores in three pain-related scales in the Patient-Reported Outcomes Measurement Information System (PROMIS) 29+ profile measure: pain intensity, pain interference, and physical function.

To examine viewing behavior and patterns of people summarizing their pain experience, we conduct an eye-tracking study. Eye-tracking research shows that machine learning engines using only eye movements can automatically and reliably detect whether a user is experiencing higher/lower cognitive load (Shojaeizadeh et al. 2019). These studies, which show the reliability and predictive quality of eye movements in detecting a user's experience of cognitive load, suggest that other experiences, such as chronic pain, may also be reflected in eye movements.

Identifying eye movement behavior and/or patterns that are affected by chronic pain not only provides a more comprehensive picture of pain experience and the effect it has on cognition and decision behavior, but also can help identify ocular behavior that can serve as effective biomarkers for chronic pain. Such biomarkers can in turn be used in designing machine learning engines that can detect the presence and intensity of chronic pain in real-time to support health professionals in the development of personalized pain treatment and management solutions.

## 2 Background

Our approach to developing richer and more objective assessments of chronic pain is based on two results from the pain literature, that those experiencing pain differ in their allocation of attention to pain stimuli and they differ in their cognitive processes such as those involved in decision making. These results, which are briefly discussed below, basically suggest that pain affects how people process information and how they use that information to make decisions. Because eye-tracking provides unobtrusive insights into attention and cognition related to decision making, we conjecture that eye-tracking could be used to differentiate between those who are experiencing chronic pain and those who are pain free, and thus provide biomarkers of pain.

### 2.1 Pain and Attention

The pain literature suggests that allocation of attention to pain stimuli can reveal the presence of pain experience (Chan et al. 2020). For example, studies show that people in chronic pain often gravitate towards pain stimuli. This phenomenon is referred to as pain-related attentional bias and is a major focus of chronic pain literature. Pain-related attentional bias is typically studied via stimulus presentation methods that measure attention by reaction time to pain/non-pain pairs of stimuli, such as sensory words and images (Chan et al. 2020).

More recently, chronic pain studies have used eye tracking to directly measure how attention is allocated to such pairs of stimuli (Fashler and Katz 2014; Franklin et al. 2019; Lee et al. 2018; Vervoort et al. 2013). These studies are grounded in the "eye-mind" assumption (Just and Carpenter 1980), which has led to wide agreement that eye gaze serves as a reliable measure of attention. Eye gaze is measured with eye trackers, which record moment-to-moment ocular behavior, providing a continuous record for when, for how long, and how many times a person paid attention to a stimulus (Djamasbi 2014).

### 2.2 Pain and Decision Making

Chronic pain affects cognitive processes (e.g., attention, perception, and evaluation) that are fundamental in judgment and decision making (Moriarty et al. 2011). Hence, chronic pain studies may benefit from extending their investigations from examining attentional biases to pain related stimulus to examining how stimuli are used to make pain related decisions. We take this approach in this study by examining the impact of chronic pain on information processing and decision behavior of individuals when they complete a pain measure.

Self-reported pain measures provide suitable stimuli for investigating how chronic pain impacts decision behavior. These subjective measures assess chronic pain by ask- ing people to select the response that best summarizes their pain experience among a set of available responses. By doing so, these subjective measures provide an excellent opportunity for observing differences in attention to information that is needed for making judgments and decisions between people with or without chronic pain. Additionally, because self-reported pain measures are widely used in clinical settings, they provide an ecological valid paradigm of investigation that increases confidence in the generalizability of the results.

## 2.3 Pain Assessment with PROMIS

Through an initiative by the National Institutes of Health (NIH), PROMIS measures were developed to provide a standardized national resource for clinicians and scholars to assess and/or monitor an individual's physical, mental, and social well-being (Cella et al. 2010; Rose et al. 2018). The PROMIS profile includes measures in a number of health domains such as physical function, anxiety, fatigue, depression, cognitive function, ability to participate in social roles, sleep disturbance, pain interference, and pain intensity. In this study, we used three measures from the PROMISE 29+ profile, namely pain intensity, pain interference, and physical function, because these are the most direct measures of chronic pain and the ones of initial concern by physicians. That is, the starting point in chronic pain assessment is evaluating the intensity of one's pain, how much the pain interferes with one's daily life, and how much the pain affects one's physical functioning.

The pain interference and physical function measures used in our study, each included four items that were scored on a 5-point numeric rating scale. Larger scores for these two measures indicated higher levels of interference with daily activities and more difficulty with physical functioning. The pain intensity measure included one item that was scored on an 11-point numeric rating scale from 0–10, where 0 indicated no pain at all and 10 indicated worst pain imaginable.

In this study, we compare the information processing and decision behavior of people with and without chronic pain. To do so, we first categorized the data from individuals who participated in our study into two groups (chronic pain and pain free groups) based on participants' own self-identification as suffering from chronic pain or being pain free.

In this study we use the pain intensity, pain interference, and physical function measures in two ways. First, we use the self-reported scores obtained from these measures to assess the differences in pain experience levels of participants in the chronic pain and pain free groups. This comparison allows us to see whether there were major differences in the degree to which these two groups experienced pain. Understanding the difference in pain experience between the groups could potentially help with interpreting the eye tracking results. The more pronounced the difference in pain experience between the two groups the more likely we will find differences in information processing and decision behavior in this initial step of our project.

In addition to using the scores of the self-reported pain intensity, pain interference, and physical function measures to assess differences in level of pain experience between the two groups, we use the items, and response scales of these measures as the stimuli for an eye-tracking experiment to assess whether eye gaze data, as indicators of visual information processing and decision behavior, differ for participants with and without chronic pain.

# 3   Methodology

Our study is an IRB-approved eye-tracking experiment using two groups of subjects, those who are pain-free and those with chronic pain. Participants in our study complete the pain intensity, pain interference, and physical function measures in the PROMISE 29+ profile while their eye movements are captured by an eye-tracking machine. The scores for the three aforementioned measures as well as the eye-tracking data captured while these measures were completed by study participants, were analyzed to produce the results reported in the next section.

## 3.1   Participants

Thirty-nine graduate and undergraduate students participated in our study which took place over a seven-week period. Each participant received a $20 gift card as a token of our appreciation. It is often the case that the eye tracker cannot be calibrated for a small percentage of participants in a study (Fehrenbacher and Djamasbi 2017). In our experiment, we encountered one such case. Hence, the data for this participant was excluded from the analysis reported in this paper.

The remaining 38 sets of data were then grouped into chronic pain (n = 12), pain free (n = 22), and in-between (n = 4) categories based on participants' self-identification as suffering from chronic pain, being free of chronic pain, or being somewhere in-between these two conditions. Because in this study we were interested in comparing the ocular behavior of people with and without chronic pain, we removed the recordings for those four individuals who self-identified as "in-between" condition from the analysis. This process resulted in a dataset with gaze movement recordings for a total of 34 participants.

## 3.2   Task

To study information processing and decision behavior, we used three self-reported pain measures (i.e., pain intensity, pain interference, and physical function) as the visual stimuli in our study. The primary task in our study required participants to process the stimuli by providing responses to the items of these three self-reported measures. The task was presented to participants via a desktop computer while their eye movements were being captured unobtrusively by an eye-tracking machine attached to the monitor.

## 3.3   Data Collection Procedure

The eye movements of each participant were collected individually in the eye-tracking lab in a northeastern U.S. university. We used the Tobii Pro Spectrum 600 Hz to collect participants' eye movements. We used the IVT filter provided by Tobii Pro Lab software to identify fixations and saccades in the raw gaze stream. The IVT filter threshold was set on 30°/s and the minimum fixation duration was defined as 100 ms (Liu et al. 2021).

After calibrating the eye tracker for participants, they were asked to complete the task (complete the three pain self-reported measures). After participants competed the task, we conducted an exit interview, during which we provided participants with the definition of chronic pain and asked them to self-identify their pain status.

## 3.4 Measures

We used four subjective self-report and four objective eye-tracking measures in our study. One of the subjective measures was used to categorize participants into two pain-status (chronic pain and pain free) groups. The other three subjective measures were used to determine the degree to which the two groups differed in pain experience. These measures are explained below.

**Subjective Pain Status (1 Measure).** We used this measure to categorize participants into chronic pain and pain free groups. We provided participants with the definition of chronic pain, i.e., a pain experience that is rated as 4 or higher on a 0–10 low to high scale and lasts more than 3 months. Then, we asked participants to tell us how they would describe their pain status: would they self-identify as 1) someone who is suffering from chronic pain, 2) someone who is pain free, 3) or someone who has a pain experience that is somewhat in-between the chronic pain and pain free conditions. Only the data for chronic pain and pain free groups were used in the analysis reported in this study.

**Subjective Pain Measure (3 Measures).** The experimental task in our study required participants to complete three subjective pain measures. In addition to using these pain measures as visual stimuli for the task, we used their ratings to investigate the degree to which participants in the chronic pain and pain free groups differed in pain experience. For example, we used ratings for the pain intensity measure to examine the differences in the severity of experienced pain between the chronic pain and pain free groups. Similarly, we used ratings for the pain interference and the physical function measures to assess differences between the two groups in the degree to which pain interfered with their daily life and the degree to which pain impacted their physical function.

**Objective Measures of Eye Movements (4 Measures).** We computed three quantitative metrics for eye movement behavior that capture attention: fixation count, fixation duration, and visit count. Fixation count refers to the number of moments when the eye remains still on a stimulus. Fixation duration refers to total processing time for viewing a stimulus. Visit count refers to the number of times a given stimulus is visited by a viewer.

   We used the relative fixation duration heatmap, a qualitative measure of attention, to explore differences in viewing patterns, e.g., the dispersion of fixations on various parts of a stimulus. Because eye-tracking heatmaps overlay the aggregated gaze data on stimulus, they provide an excellent tool for detecting patterns of visual attention. In addition to patterns, heatmaps reveal intensity of attention by using colors (e.g., using red, yellow, and green to visualize high to low fixation intensity). The relative fixation duration heatmap that we use in our analysis, depicts the intensity of each participant's attention to various areas of a stimulus relative to the participant's total attention to the entire stimulus.

## 3.5 Analysis

The subjective self-identified pain status (chronic pain", "pain free", or "in-between") will be used to group datasets into chronic pain and pain free categories. The data for participants who self-identified as having an "in-between" pain status will not be included in the analysis in this study.

We will use the scores that were obtained from the self-reported pain measures during the experimental task (i.e., subjective ratings for pain intensity, pain interference, and physical function) to test whether differences in pain experience between participants in the chronic pain and pain free groups is significant or not. Because pain affects cognition, lack or presence of significant differences in pain experience can provide better explanations for the eye-tracking results. For example, the more pronounced the differences in pain experience between the two groups the more likely we will observe differences in information processing and decision behavior of participants with and without chronic pain.

For eye movement analysis, as customary in eye-tracking research (Djamasbi 2014), we will define areas of investigations or interest (AOIs) that are relevant to the visual stimuli used in our study. The task in our study requires participants to complete three self-reported pain measures, each of which requires participants to read a set of pain related questions and respond to those questions by selecting an option on a numeric scale. Hence, visual stimuli used in our study contains three essential AOIs. The first AOI is the part of the stimulus, or self-reported measure, that contains the questions (Question AOI) to be answered. This question region is separate from the answer region of the stimulus that contains possible answers to those questions. The second and third AOIs separate the answer region on the stimulus into two separate AOIs: one that contains the labels for the numeric scale (Label AOI) and one that contains the response options (Response AOI). We will use the quantitative and qualitative eye tracking metrics explained in the previous section to compare differences in viewing behavior and patterns in the AOIs between the two groups.

## 4   Results

### 4.1   Findings from Self-reported Measures

To prepare the datasets for analysis, we grouped them into chronic pain and pain free groups based on participants' self-reported pain status, i.e., participant's self-identification as suffering from chronic pain or being free of chronic pain. Next, we compared participants' scores for the three self-reported pain measures (pain intensity, pain interference, physical function) between the two groups. Participants in the chronic pain group provided significantly ($p < 0.01$) higher scores for pain intensity (5.42 vs. 0.68), pain interference in daily function (2.67 vs. 1.12), and difficulty in physical function (1.79 vs. 1.10). Based on these results, which are displayed in Fig. 1, we conclude that participants in the chronic pain group had a significantly heightened pain experience as compared to participants in the pain free group.

Next, we analyzed the eye movement data captured during the completion of the three pain measures (i.e., pain intensity, pain interference, and physical function measures) to examine differences in information processing and decision behavior between the two groups.

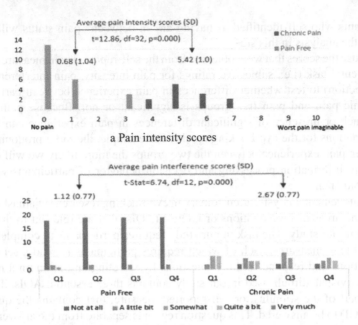

a Pain intensity scores

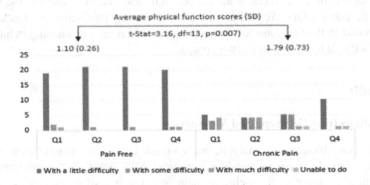

b Pain interference scores

c Physical function scores

**Fig. 1.** Ratings for pain experience self-reported measures.

## 4.2 Findings from Eye Movement Metrics

The eye movement analysis in this section is organized in three separate parts, each reporting the results for one of the three stimuli, i.e., pain intensity, pain interference, and physical measures. The results reported in each part are summarized by a table that is organized first by eye movement metrics and then by the defined AOIs. Each part also provides a heatmap for the analysis of fixation patterns within the defined AOIs. Fixation patterns on these heatmaps are visualized with colors red, yellow, and green representing high, medium, and low levels of fixation intensity. The combination of quantitative and qualitative eye tracking data has been shown to extend the explanatory power of eye tracking analysis (Djamasbi et al. 2011).

**Pain Intensity.** The results of t-tests did not show significant differences between the two groups in fixation and visit metrics for the Question AOI on this stimulus. There were also no significant differences between the groups in fixation durations in any of the AOIs. The results, however, showed that people in the chronic pain group had significantly (p = 0.04) fewer fixations (3.58 vs. 6.36) in the Label AOI and visited this AOI significantly (p = 0.01) less frequently (1.92 vs. 3.14) than people in the pain free group. People in the chronic pain group had almost significantly (p = 0.07) more fixations in the Response AOI (Table 1).

**Table 1.** t-test results for the pain intensity measure

| Fixation count | Pain free | Chronic pain | |
|---|---|---|---|
| Question AOI | 6.09 (3.84) | 6.00 (2.49) | t = 0.08, df = 32, p = 0.94 |
| Response AOI | 7.5 (3.83) | 10.58(5.57) | t = 1.90, df = 32, p = 0.07* |
| Label AOI | 6.36 (4.09) | 3.58 (2.81) | **t = 2.09, df = 32, p = 0.04** |
| Fixation duration (ms) | | | |
| Question AOI | 1256.41 (1010.26) | 1130.92 (475.60) | t = 0.49, df = 32, p = 0.62 |
| Response AOI | 2356.96 (1596.68) | 3135.42 (1794.32) | t = 1.30, df = 32, p = 0.20 |
| Label AOI | 1177.14 (823.72) | 756 (833.15) | t = 1.41, df = 32, p = 0.17 |
| Visit count | | | |
| Question AOI | 2.36 (1.62) | 2.00 (0.60) | t = 0.75, df = 32, p = 0.46 |
| Response AOI | 3.14 (1.13) | 3.5 (1.00) | t = 0.93, df = 32, p = 0.36 |
| Label AOI | 3.14 (1.32) | 1.92 (1.24) | **t = 2.63, df = 32, p = 0.01** |

*Almost significant

Viewing patterns shown in the Question AOI were dispersed covering the entirety of the textual information (Fig. 2). This behavior represents careful processing of text-based communication (Djamasbi et al. 2011). Viewing patterns in the Response and Label AOIs, which supported the results displayed in Table 1, show that the two groups differed in how their fixations were distributed when they were deciding on a response to represent their experience. People in the chronic pain group looked at the last 8 last numeric options in the Response AOI to make decisions. Even though no one in the chronic pain group selected responses 3, 8, and 10 (see Fig. 1.a), these response options received relatively intense fixations (Fig. 2a). People in the pain free group looked at the first 6 and the last 2 response options (Fig. 2.b) while the majority of participants in this group chose the first two responses (Fig. 1.a). Another notable difference in fixation patterns between the two groups is the way they viewed the Label AOI. Fixation patterns in Fig. 2 show that people in the chronic pain group considered only the "worst pain imaginable" label when trying to assess their pain experience while people in the pain free group used both labels to make the same decision.

These results together show that people in the pain group summarized their pain experience into a single value by gauging how their experience faired against "worst pain imaginable". They processed the Label AOI with significantly less effort than the pain free group, but processed the Response AOI with almost significantly (p = 0.07) more effort than the pain free group.

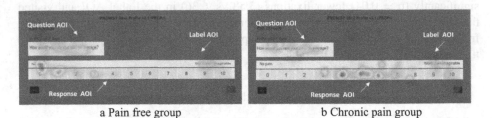

a Pain free group                      b Chronic pain group

**Fig. 2.** Relative fixation duration heatmaps for pain intensity.

**Pain Interference.** The results of t-tests were not significant for differences in fixation/visit intensity between the two groups in the Question and Label AOIs for this self-reported measure. The intensity of fixations between the two groups, however, was significantly different when participants were processing the Response AOI of the pain interference measure. People in the chronic pain group had significantly (p = 0.000) more (15.92 vs. 8.77) and longer fixations (3919.92 ms vs. 2144.36 ms) in this AOI and visited it significantly (p = 0.002) more frequently (8.17 vs. 5.55) than people in the pain free group (Table 2).

Figure 3 displays the relative fixation duration heatmaps for the pain interference measure. These heatmaps show that both groups exhibited similar thorough processing patterns for the Question AOI evidenced by the dispersed fixation patterns covering the entirety of the textual information in this area. The heatmaps, however, show that the two groups had notable differences in viewing patterns in the Response and Label AOIs. People in the chronic pain group had more dispersed fixations in the Response AOI than people in the pain free group (evidenced by larger colorful areas). They also showed a more dispersed viewing pattern in the Label AOI. People in the chronic pain group looked at more labels, in particular the first four labels, to choose a response while people in the pain free group viewed the first three labels for decision making. The most intense fixations of people in the chronic pain group were on labels "a little bit", "somewhat", and "quite a bit". The most intense fixations of people in the pain free group were on labels "not at all" and "a little bit". These results reveal labels that were mostly considered for decision making by each group.

The results displayed in Table 2 and the more dispersed pattern of fixations in the heatmap in Fig. 3.a vs. the heatmap in Fig. 3.b, together show that people in the chronic pain group expended significantly more cognitive effort to decide which response to choose.

**Table 2.** t-test results for the pain interference measure

| Fixation count | Pain free | Chronic pain | |
|---|---|---|---|
| Question AOI | 38.77 (1689) | 38.5 (13.14) | t = -0.05, df = 32, p = 0.96 |
| Response AOI | 8.77 (3.94) | 15.92 (3.20) | **t = 5.38, df = 32, p = 0.000** |
| Label AOI | 5.2 (3.02) | 7 (3.41) | t = 1.51, df = 29, p = 0.14 |
| Fixation duration (ms) | | | |
| Question AOI | 7659.73 (4085.30) | 7422.92 (3094.07) | t = 0.17, df = 32, p = 0.86 |
| Response AOI | 2144.36 (1123.06) | 3919.92(1252.42) | **t = 4.23, df = 32, p = 0.000** |
| Label AOI | 1245.3 (884.97) | 1593.91 (806.04) | t = 1.08, df = 29, p = 0.29 |
| Visit count | | | |
| Question AOI | 5.91 (1.69) | 6.00 (1.41) | t = 0.16, df = 32, p = 0.88 |
| Response AOI | 5.55 (2.48) | 8.17 (1.53) | **t = 3.32, df = 32, p = 0.002** |
| Label AOI | 2.77 (1.77) | 3.92 (2.23) | t = 1.64, df = 32, p = 0.11 |

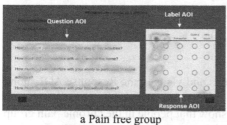 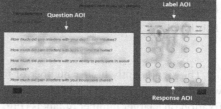

a Pain free group                    b Chronic pain group

**Fig. 3.** Relative fixation duration heatmaps for pain interference.

**Physical Function Stimulus.** Once again, we found no significant differences between the two groups in how intensely they processed or how frequently they visited the Question AOI when completing the physical function measure. While we found no significant differences between the two groups in fixation and visit metrics in the Label AOI, our analysis showed that the chronic pain group processed the Response AOI with significantly (p = 0.049) more fixations (12.42 vs. 9.23) and visited this AOI significantly (p = 0.02) more frequently (8.83 vs. 6.32) than the pain free group.

Figure 4 displays the relative fixation duration heatmaps for the chronic pain and pain free groups when they were completing the physical function measure. As in previous heatmaps displayed in Figs. 2 and 3, the heatmaps in Fig. 4 show that both groups processed the Questions AOI with similarly dispersed fixation patterns that is representative of thorough information processing behavior (Djamasbi et al. 2011). Both groups viewed all of the labels in the Label AOI, but people in chronic pain had more intense fixations on the first four labels ("without any difficulty", "with a little difficulty", "with some difficulty", "with much difficulty"). The most intense fixation of people in the pain free group was on the first label ("without any difficulty"). Fixation patterns of people in the chronic pain group were more dispersed covering the first four columns in the Response AOI. Fixation patterns of people in the pain free group were more focused covering mainly the first column of the Response AOI (Fig. 4 and Table 3).

**Table 3.** t-test results for the physical function survey

| Fixation count | Pain free | Chronic pain | |
| --- | --- | --- | --- |
| Question AOI | 39.27 (17.06) | 39.67 (12.94) | t = 0.07, df = 32, p = 0.95 |
| Response AOI | 9.23(3.60) | 12.42 (5.50) | **t = 2.04, df = 32, p = 0.049** |
| Label AOI | 17.5 (9.88) | 23.83 (10.72) | t = 1.73, df = 3, p = 0.09 |
| Fixation duration (ms) | | | |
| Question AOI | 7775.64(4111.79) | 7297.58(2505.20) | t = 0.37, df = 32, p = 0.72 |
| Response AOI | 2332.86 (1011.83) | 2912.67(1348.79) | t = 1.42, df = 32, p = 0.17 |
| Label AOI | 4204.96 (2990.81) | 5219.25(2193.48) | t = 1.03, df = 32, p = 0.31 |
| Visit count | | | |
| Question AOI | 6.55 (2.60) | 7.33 (2.31) | t = 0.88, df = 32, p = 0.39 |
| Response AOI | 6.32 (2.50) | 8.83 (3.43) | **t = 2.46, df = 32, p = 0.02** |
| Label AOI | 5.64 (3.03) | 7.33 (3.17) | t = 1.54, df = 32, p = 0.14 |

The significantly higher number of fixations and visits in the Response AOI, along with the more dispersed fixation patterns in the Response AOI and having more intense fixation on a larger number of labels (Fig. 4), show that people in the chronic pain group went through a more cognitively effortful decision process than those in the pain free group.

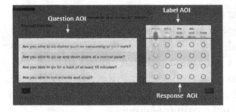 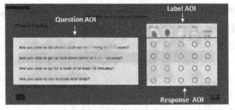

a Pain free group                                          b Chronic pain group

**Fig. 4.** Relative fixation duration heatmaps for physical function.

## 5   Discussion

We used eye tracking to compare information processing and decision behavior of people with and without chronic pain when they were summarizing their pain experience into a single score via responding to three pain related measures that are included in the PROMIS 29+ profile. We investigated information processing and decision behavior by examining attention on three complementary AOIs that were necessary for decision making: 1) Question AOIs delineating questions in pain measures, 2) Label AOIs labeling response options (e.g., "not at all", "quite a bit", etc.), and 3) Response AOI delineating the response options that were available for selection. Differences in attention to these AOIs between the two groups were determined by comparing how many times an AOI was viewed (visit count), how many fixations (fixation count) were used to process it, and how long those fixations lasted (fixation duration) in each AOI. To increase the explanatory power of this preliminary analysis, we used relative fixation duration heatmaps to examine fixation patterns and intensity on various parts of the AOI.

The qualitative and quantitative analysis of eye movements showed that questions in all three self-reported pain measures were processed thoroughly by both groups. No significant differences were detected between the two groups when they were reading the questions in the aforementioned pain measures (processing Question AOIs). The fixation pattern in both groups exhibited a thorough reading behavior by showing that fixations covered the entire text in the Question AOI.

When summarizing pain experience into scores along the given scales, however, our results showed that people with and without chronic pain had major differences in information processing and decision behavior. For example, the chronic pain group exhibited almost significantly more fixations than the pain free group in the Response AOI of the pain intensity measure. When making decisions about pain interference, the chronic pain group, significantly more than the pain free group, expended cognitive effort to process the Response AOI as evidenced by their significantly more visits and significantly more and longer fixations on this AOI. Similarly, the chronic pain group exhibited a higher level of cognitive effort when processing the Response AOI of the physical function measure by exhibiting significantly more frequent visits and significantly more fixations on this AOI than the pain free group.

The higher level of cognitive effort in the chronic pain group when responding to questions was also evidenced by their eye movement patterns. For example, the relative pain intensity heatmaps developed for the chronic pain group showed more red-colored clusters in the Response/Label AOI than those developed for the pain free group. Similarly, the number of red and bright yellow clusters in heatmaps for pain interference and physical function measures showed that the pain group had more relative intense fixations in the Response and Label AOIs than the pain free group. In these heatmaps, fixations of the chronic pain group covered a larger area of the Response/Label AOI than fixations of the pain free group, which is yet another indication of expending more cognitive effort (Djamasbi et al. 2011).

Heatmaps also revealed which labels were more heavily used in selecting responses. For example, the heatmaps in Fig. 2 show that the chronic pain summarized their experience of pain intensity by focusing mainly on the "worst pain imaginable" label, while the pain free group considered both "no pain" and "worst pain imaginable" labels. The heatmaps for the pain interference measure (Fig. 3) show that the pain group viewed the labels in the middle range of spectrum (labels in 2nd, 3rd, and 4th place) more intensely than labels in the outer edges of the spectrum. The pain free group more intensely focused on the low end of the spectrum (the first two labels). The viewing pattern for the physical function measure (Fig. 4) shows that both groups viewed all five labels. These heatmaps, however, show that the pain group fixated more intensely on the first four labels while the pain free group focused more on the first two labels. The pattern of focus on labels not only suggests differences in cognitive effort between the two groups (the more labels used to choose responses, the more effortful the decision making process) but also reveals notable differences in low-high range of label boundaries that they were used for decision by the two groups (e.g., "a little bit" to " quite a bit" vs. "not at all" and " a little bit" in Fig. 3).

These differences can provide a more comprehensive picture of pain experience to help assess how intensely a person suffers from chronic pain. It can also potentially be used in developing objective markers of chronic pain. For example, Fig. 2 shows that the pain group visited the label area significantly less frequently, with significantly fewer fixations, and focused only on the "worst pain experience" label when deciding which response best represented their pain intensity. The narrowly focused (using only one label) and decisive decision process (fewer fixations on the label) represents the pain experience reality of people who live with chronic pain. Suffering from chronic pain naturally excludes "no pain" from one's experience palette. This interpretation also explains the fixation patterns of the pain free group for the same measure. While the pain free group viewed both labels of the pain intensity measure, the red color on the "no pain" label (Fig. 2.b) suggests that this label, which is representative of their dominant pain experience, had a larger weight in their decision making.

The observed differences in information processing and decision behavior of people with and without chronic pain in our study suggest that eye movements may serve as reliable objective (physiological) biomarkers for chronic pain. Our results, showing the sensitivity of eye movement data in detecting differences in cognitive effort unobtrusively without additional burden to users, are promising for developing eye tracking machine learning engines that can detect in real-time whether and how intensely a person suffers from chronic pain.

Our results also suggest that the insight gained from eye movements may help provide more personalized interventions. Pain is a complex phenomenon that benefits from multi-dimensional assessments (van Boekel et al. 2017). Augmenting self-reported pain measures with the insight revealed by the objective eye movement data (e.g., the range of labels and anchors used in decision making) may help develop guidelines that more successfully can meet the unique needs of individual patients for pain treatment and/or management (NSW 2021).

Advances in eye-tracking technology increasingly and positively affect the affordability of high-quality eye trackers (Djamasbi 2014). This trend makes it increasingly realistic and practical to collect eye-movement data when patients complete pain measures at clinics or office visits. The additional insight provided by eye movements when patients complete pain measures can be coded along the self-reported scores in a user-friendly decision support feedback for practitioners in real-time. This feedback in turn can help practitioners gain a more comprehensive view of their patients' pain experience and thus be able to have more effective visits with their patients and develop more successful treatment options for them.

## 5.1 Theoretical and Practical Implications

From a theoretical point of view, our study contributes to human computer interaction literature in two ways: 1) by examining a user attribute (chronic pain) that may affect how decision support systems are used (Djamasbi 2007) and 2) by examining eye movement behavior that can contribute to developing smart user-centered systems for supporting chronic pain healthcare professionals. Our study also contributes to chronic pain literature in two ways: 1) by investigating the potential of eye movements as a biomarker for chronic pain and 2) by using the more context rich and ecologically valid decision-making paradigm of pain measures to study information processing and decision behavior.

From a practical point of view, our results show that collecting eye movements during completion of pain measures at clinics can augment the self-reported pain scores with user-friendly visual report (e.g., fixation duration heatmap) and/or coded visual feedback developed from eye-movement data (Jain et al. 2020; Jain and Djamasbi 2019). Such augmented self-reported measures can provide clinicians with a more comprehensive picture of pain experience, which in turn can lead to more successful office visits and more effective personalized chronic pain treatment solutions. Advances in video-based eye tracking make it possible to capture eye movements unobtrusively and without any additional burden on users. Eye trackers can easily be attached to computer monitors, laptops, kiosks, and other digital screens. Hence, they can easily be added to computerized systems that are used for administering self-reported pain measures at clinics typically immediately before an office visit.

As more and more high-quality eye-tracking technologies are embedded in consumer grade laptops and mobile devices, such information can also be collected during remote office visits which sometimes are the only practical and/or cost-effective option for clinicians to treat their patients (e.g., during pandemics, natural disasters, and/or patients' mobility issues).

## 5.2 Limitations and Future Studies

As with any experiment, our study has limitations. For example, we had a relatively small sample size. While small sample sizes are common in exploratory eye-tracking research, future studies with larger sample sizes may help to detect more significant differences in information processing behavior of people with and without chronic pain. The significant results obtained in our study, however, support the sensitivity and potential power of eye movements in detecting user experience (Shojaeizadeh et al. 2019), which is promising for developing eye tracking biomarkers of chronic pain.

The analysis of viewing behavior in our study was limited to three AOIs reflecting three major components of the pain intensity, pain interference, and physical function measures. Future studies can refine this analysis by creating more AIOs, e.g., a separate AOI for each question and its respective response area. Our preliminary analysis mainly focused on fixation and visit metrics, using saccadic and/or pupillometry metrics may provide additional insight.

## 6 Conclusion

The analysis of eye-tracking data showed differences in information processing and decision behavior for people with and without chronic pain when they were responding to three self-reported pain-related measures. The results showed that people with chronic pain, compared to those who did not suffer from chronic pain, exhibited eye movement behaviors and patterns that were representative of expending more cognitive effort. These preliminary results are promising because they suggest that eye movements may serve as suitable biomarkers of chronic pain, which can help in developing systems that can detect pain experience automatically and unobtrusively. The results also suggest that collecting eye movements when completing a clinical pain measure provides additional useful information that can help practitioners have a more comprehensive view of their patients' pain experience.

## References

CDC: Chronic Pain and High-impact Chronic Pain Among U.S. Adults, 2019. NCHS (2020). https://www.cdc.gov/nchs/products/databriefs/db390.htm#ref1

Cella, D., et al.: The patient-reported outcomes measurement information system (PROMIS) developed and tested its first wave of adult self-reported health outcome item banks: 2005–2008. J. Clin. Epidemiol. **63**(11), 1179–1194 (2010)

Chan, F.H.F., Suen, H., Jackson, T., Vlaeyen, J.W.S., Barry, T.J.: Pain-related attentional processes: a systematic review of eye-tracking research. Clin. Psychol. Rev. **80**, 101884 (2020)

Crofford, L.J.: Chronic pain: where the body meets the brain. Trans. Am. Clin. Climatol. Assoc. **126**, 167–183 (2015)

Djamasbi, S.: Does positive affect influence the effective usage of a decision support system? Decis. Support Syst. **43**(4), 1707–1717 (2007)

Djamasbi, S.: Eye tracking and web experience. AIS Trans. Hum.-Comput. Interact. **6**(2), 37–54 (2014)

Djamasbi, S., Siegel, M., Tullis, T.: Visual hierarchy and viewing behavior: an eye tracking study. In: Jacko, J.A. (ed.) HCI 2011. LNCS, vol. 6761, pp. 331–340. Springer, Heidelberg (2011). https://doi.org/10.1007/978-3-642-21602-2_36

Fashler, S.R., Katz, J.: More than meets the eye: visual attention biases in individuals reporting chronic pain. J. Pain Res. **7**, 557–570 (2014)

Fehrenbacher, D.D., Djamasbi, S.: Information systems and task demand: an exploratory pupillometry study of computerized decision making. Decis. Support Syst. **97**, 1–11 (2017)

Franklin, Z.C., Holmes, P.S., Fowler, N.E.: Eye gaze markers indicate visual attention to threatening images in individuals with chronic back pain. J. Clin. Med. **8**(1), 1–14 (2019)

Jain, P., Djamasbi, S.: Transforming user experience of nutrition facts label - an exploratory service innovation study. In: Nah, F.-H., Siau, K. (eds.) HCII 2019. LNCS, vol. 11588, pp. 225–237. Springer, Cham (2019). https://doi.org/10.1007/978-3-030-22335-9_15

Jain, P., Djamasbi, S., Hall-Phillips, A.: The impact of feedback design on cognitive effort, usability, and the impact of feedback design on cognitive effort, usability, and technology use technology use. In: Americas Conference on Information Systems (AMCIS) (2020)

Just, M.A., Carpenter, P.A.: A theory of reading: from eye fixations to comprehension. Psychol. Rev. **87**(4), 329–354 (1980)

Lee, J.E., Kim, S.H., Shin, S.K., Wachholtz, A., Lee, J.H.: Attentional engagement for pain-related information among individuals with chronic pain: the role of pain catastrophizing. Pain Res. Manag. **2018**, 1–9 (2018)

Liu, W., Trapp, A.C., Djamasbi, S.: Outlier-Aware, Density-Based Gaze Fixation Identification. Omega (United Kingdom), p. 102 (2021)

McCahon, S., Strong, J., Sharry, R., Cramond, T.: Self-report and pain behavior among patients with chronic pain. Clin. J. Pain 21(3), 223–231 (2005)

Merskey, H.: Pain - classification of chronic pain - descriptions of chronic pain syndromes and definitions of pain terms. Pain (Suppl.3) (1986)

Moriarty, O., McGuire, B.E., Finn, D.P.: The effect of pain on cognitive function: a review of clinical and preclinical research. Progr. Neurobiol. 93(3), 385–404 (2011)

New South Wales (NSW) Government. Chronic Pain Screening Guide to PROMIS29+ (2021). https://doi.org/10.1037/hea0000685

Phillips, C.J.: Economic burden of chronic pain. Expert Rev. Pharmacoecon. Outcomes Res. 6(5), 591–601 (2006)

Rose, A.J., et al.: Evaluating the PROMIS-29 v2.0 for use among older adults with multiple chronic conditions. Qual. Life Res. 27(11), 2935–2944 (2018). https://doi.org/10.1007/s11136-018-1958-5

Shojaeizadeh, M., Djamasbi, S., Paffenroth, R.C., Trapp, A.C.: Detecting task demand via an eye tracking machine learning system. Decis. Support Syst. 116, 91–101 (2019)

van Boekel, R.L.M., Vissers, K.C.P., van der Sande, R., Bronkhorst, E., Lerou, J.G.C., Steegers, M.A.H.: Moving beyond pain scores: multidimensional pain assessment is essential for adequate pain management after surgery. PLoS ONE 12(5), 1–16 (2017)

Vervoort, T., Trost, Z., Prkachin, K.M., Mueller, S.C.: Attentional processing of other's facial display of pain: an eye tracking study. Pain 154(6), 836–844 (2013)

Xu, X., Huang, Y.: Objective pain assessment: a key for the management of chronic pain. F1000 Res. (9), F1000 Faculty Rev-35 (2020). https://doi.org/10.12688/f1000research.20441.1

Yong, R.J., Mullins, P.M., Bhattacharyya, N.: Prevalence of chronic pain among adults in the United States. Pain 163(2), e328–e332 (2022)

# Improved Psychological Health Through a Remote Behavioral Intervention: A Telehealth Pilot Study for Veterans with Chronic Multi-symptom Illness

Charity B. Breneman[1,2] , Immanuel Samuel[1,2] , Arghavan Hamedi[2] ,
Timothy J. Chun[2] , Walter Jachimowicz[2], Kamila U. Pollin[2] ,
Rebecca A. McCullers[1,2] , Lucas Crock[2] , Ryan C. Brewster[2] , Adil Alaoui[3],
Michael J. Roy[4] , Matthew J. Reinhard[2,5] , and Michelle E. Costanzo[2,4(✉)] 

[1] Henry M. Jackson Foundation for the Advancement of Military Medicine, Inc., Bethesda,
MD, USA
`Charity.Breneman@va.gov`
[2] Department of Veterans Affairs, War Related Illness and Injury Study Center (WRIISC),
Washington, DC, USA
`Michelle.Costanzo@va.gov`
[3] Innovation Center for Biomedical Informatics (ICBI), Georgetown University Medical Center,
Washington, DC, USA
[4] Department of Medicine, Uniformed Services University of the Health Sciences, Bethesda,
MD, USA
[5] Department of Psychiatry, Georgetown University Medical School, Washington, DC, USA

**Abstract.** Cognitive control enables individuals to imagine future events and develop personal goals, which are critical for sense of purpose. For Veterans with chronic multi-symptom illness (CMI), augmenting cognitive control and other factors related to brain health may improve symptom management and quality of life (QoL). This pilot study utilizes neuroscience evidence to enhance psychological health, with a combination of remote meditation and aerobic exercise (mental and physical [MAP] training) to evaluate what type of distance-based instruction is optimal for Veterans engaged in these health behaviors. Twenty-five Veterans with CMI were randomized to either an eight-week directed MAP (dMAP; n = 12) group where specific instructions were provided via text messaging or an eight-week self-guided MAP (sgMAP; n = 13) group where they received the goals of the MAP intervention without weekly guidance. Participants also completed health coaching weekly. Self-report health measures were collected during baseline, post-treatment, and three-month follow-up, with the primary outcome assessed using the Behavior Rating Inventory of Executive Function - Adult Version (BRIEF-A). A significant group-by-time interaction was observed for the BRIEF-A subscales: inhibit and task monitor, both demonstrating differences in the direction of change between the groups. A significant overall time effect was observed for depression, sleep quality, and mental health-related QoL, each demonstrating improvement. MAP training significantly improved multiple symptoms in Veterans with CMI. This suggests that empowering Veterans with goals and support through health

D. D. Schmorrow and C. M. Fidopiastis (Eds.): HCII 2022, LNAI 13310, pp. 20–33, 2022.
https://doi.org/10.1007/978-3-031-05457-0_2

coaching may be a viable approach to improving health in those suffering from chronic illness.

**Keywords:** Meditation · Aerobic exercise · CMI · Executive function · Distance-based

# 1 Introduction

Chronic multi-symptom illness (CMI) is a complex symptom-based condition characterized by the clustering of persistent symptoms that are medically unexplainable [1]. Given the heterogeneous presentation of symptoms, cases are identified based on the predominance of subjective combinations of chronic symptoms from different symptom categories/domains (e.g., fatigue, mood/cognition, musculoskeletal) [2]. Many Veterans suffer from CMI, with prevalence estimates ranging from 25–60% depending on deployment history (Gulf War versus more recent conflicts), and case definitions [1, 3], thus representing a critical healthcare issue.

The Department of Veterans Affairs (VA) and the Department of Defense have recently updated their clinical practice guidelines for managing CMI, which includes recommendations to maximize non-pharmacologic therapies [4]. These guidelines are in alignment with the VA's healthcare organizational vision that moves from a problem-based disease care system to one that is patient-centered and focused on whole health. This offers an exciting clinical approach to engaging patients in a meaningful manner and holds promise for sustainable health. The success of such an important program requires that patients efficaciously engage in high-level executive functioning such as decision making, working memory, attention, and planning, meditated by an intact cognitive control capability [5]. In order for Veterans to succeed in the self-care needed to foster their path towards healing, the cognitive control capacity required for self-regulatory behavior relies on intact function of neural systems that mediate internally-focused (i.e., self-monitoring, evaluations of self) and goal-directed (i.e., problem solving, modulation of affect and attention) processing. Yet, converging evidence suggests that disturbance in neural networks involved in cognition and emotion may underpin a range of neuropsychiatric conditions and persistent health problems commonly experienced by Veterans [6, 7].

Behavioral health approaches such as mindfulness meditation and aerobic exercise are two non-pharmacologic therapies mentioned in the clinical practice guidelines for CMI [4], which are often prescribed individually within a treatment plan. However, recent findings demonstrate that the combination of meditation with aerobic exercise, performed one right after the other, known as mental and physical (MAP) training, produces a synergistic effect on several health outcomes (e.g., improvements in depression, anxiety, and ruminative thoughts) compared to either modality alone [8–11]. Although the positive benefits of MAP training have been demonstrated in different clinical populations, it has yet to be examined among Veterans with CMI.

MAP training is traditionally administered in a group setting which limits accessibility, especially during the COVID pandemic [8–10, 12]. A recent study has demonstrated the feasibility of combining one in-person group session with one home-based practice of MAP training among medical students [10]; however, additional research is needed to evaluate the translation of MAP training from an in-person program to a completely distance-based program. Therefore, we evaluated the feasibility of a telehealth MAP training program that utilizes distance-based technology and health coaching among Veterans with CMI. We predicted improved health outcomes, with expected benefit particularly observed in executive function, in those who received more guidance on how to implement the MAP training from home compared to those that were only provided with the general goals of the intervention. While recruitment was impacted during the COVID pandemic, the present analysis was performed to generate preliminary results to identify trends and discuss implications of findings.

## 2   Methods

This pilot study was a two-arm, randomized trial evaluating the feasibility of an eight-week telehealth MAP intervention with two groups: 1) directed MAP (dMAP) and 2) self-guided MAP (sgMAP). The study was approved by the Institutional Review Board of the Washington, DC Veterans Affairs Medical Center (DC VAMC). Informed consent was obtained from all participants prior to taking part in the study.

### 2.1   Participants

Participants were recruited between October 2018 and May 2021 from Veterans undergoing a comprehensive clinical evaluation at the War Related Illness and Injury Study Center (WRIISC), a VA tertiary care center located at the DC VAMC. Veterans are referred to the WRIISC when they have exhausted their treatment/evaluation options at their local VA for conditions that are complex, medically unexplained, or difficult to diagnosis. Veterans were provided with a study brochure prior to their scheduled clinical evaluation, and anyone expressing interest was screened for eligibility during the week of their clinical evaluation. Inclusion criteria included: 1) > 18 years of age; 2) deployed U.S. Veteran; 3) had a smart phone; and 4) met the Fukuda case definition for CMI (one or more chronic symptoms from at least two symptom categories [fatigue, musculoskeletal, mood-cognition]) [13]. Exclusion criteria included: 1) excessive alcohol consumption; 2) current drug use, abuse, or dependence within the previous 90 days; 3) current suicidal or homicidal ideation; 4) acute or unstable chronic illness; 5) recent trauma within the past month; and 6) dementia or significant cognitive impairment.

### 2.2   Procedures

Prior to the COVID pandemic, the consenting process and baseline study procedures occurred in-person while all other study-related visits occurred remotely from home. After the start of the COVID pandemic, these in-person baseline study procedures were modified to be completely distance-based using video conferencing and were separated into two remote visits to provide time for study materials to be shipped to the participant. As part of their baseline procedures, all participants received instruction on how to use the study devices and apps.

**Study Devices and Apps.** Participants in both groups received a Fitbit Charge 2 (Fitbit, LLC, San Francisco, CA, USA) for logging their exercise sessions and a tablet (Samsung Galaxy Tab A; Samsung Electronics America, Inc., Ridgefield Park, NJ, USA) preinstalled with three web-based applications: 1) Daily Workouts Fitness Trainer app (Daily Workout Apps, LLC); 2) Fitbit: Health & Fitness app (Fitbit, LLC, San Francisco, CA, USA); and 3) Brain Health app (custom-developed). The Daily Workouts Fitness Trainer app contained a library of workout routines. The Fitbit: Health & Fitness app served as a portal for participants to transfer data collected during their exercise sessions using their Charge 2 device to their Fitbit dashboard, where it was downloaded by research staff. The Brain Health app was custom developed by the Innovation Center for Biomedical Informatics at Georgetown University (Washington, DC, USA) for administering the online surveys at each timepoint (baseline, post-treatment, and three-month follow-up) and the pre-recorded meditation sessions.

## 2.3 Intervention

The telehealth MAP intervention was eight weeks long and consisted of two home-based MAP training sessions and one health coaching session per week. Participants were randomized to either the dMAP or the sgMAP group in a 1:1 allocation ratio using a simple randomization procedure (computerized random numbers) and bias was minimized through allocation concealment. Blinding was not feasible for this pilot given the small number of staff dedicated to the project, but self-report measures were administrated via the Brain Health app thus minimizing risk of measure implementation bias. The dMAP group received specific instructions via text messaging using the VA's Annie mobile application for Veterans (app) [14], a Short Message Service (SMS), to complete certain meditation and workout sessions using the pre-installed apps on their assigned tablet on specific days of the week. The sgMAP group served as an active control in which the same apps/devices were provided and the intervention goals (e.g., target HR, duration of guided meditation) were communicated at the beginning of the study. No further guidance was provided to the sgMAP during the eight-week intervention.

Each MAP training session consisted of 30 min of guided meditation and 30 min of aerobic exercise at moderate-to-vigorous intensity. To facilitate self-practice, guided meditation scripts from iRest® Yoga Nidra were audio recorded and uploaded to the Brain Health app for participants to access. iRest® is a guided meditation practice that is used clinically at numerous VAMCs and has been developed into an eight-week training protocol for clinical research. For the purposes of this study, only the meditation exercises from the training protocol were audio recorded to shorten each session from one hour to approximately 30 min. Remote adherence measures were collected by the Brain Health app through timestamps of when the iRest® sessions were completed. The physical activity component of MAP training utilized the Fitbit Charge 2 for logging each aerobic exercise session and for monitoring heart rate within 50 to 85% of their age-predicted maximal heart rate (calculated as 220 minus their age) and these data were also collected for remote monitoring of intervention compliance.

Health coaching was added to the MAP training intervention to provide a motivational check in about physical activity levels and support for meditative practice. Each health coaching session was 30 min and consisted of meeting with a nurse health educator telephonically or through video conferencing every week for the duration of the intervention. The coaches were trained in administering the health coaching by completing the Veterans Health Administration Office of Patient Centered Care and Cultural Transformation health coaching course. The coaches utilized the remotely acquired adherence data from the Brain Health app and Fitbit dashboard to address barriers to achieving goals using primarily a self-discovery approach. These could range from thoughts and beliefs, lack of skills and knowledge, conflicts and competing priorities, relationships, and outside influences, such as work, weather, and illness. The weekly check-in aimed to foster the development of contingency plans and working within these barriers to create accountability and maximize the likelihood that participants will engage in these practices. Participants were given the option of continuing sessions during the three-month follow-up period by joining the WRIISC Health Coaching program, which entailed entering into a coaching relationship focused on a range of health topics and committing to creating a vision, goals, and action steps over the next three months. The goal of providing follow-up health coaching was to extend discussions to domains beyond those of meditation and physical activity to areas identified as priorities for the Veteran, consistent with the VA Whole Health Model of patient-centered care [15].

## 2.4 Outcomes

Participants completed online surveys at baseline, post-treatment, and three-month follow-up via the Brain Health app.

**Primary Outcome.** The primary outcome was executive function which was assessed using the Behavior Rating Inventory of Executive Function – Adult Version (BRIEF-A) [16]. The BRIEF-A is a 75-item self-report measure that captures nine non-overlapping domains of executive function in adults, including Emotional Control, Initiate, Inhibit, Organization of Materials, Plan/Organize, Self-Monitor, Shift, Task Monitor, and Working Memory. In addition to examining each subscale separately, two summary index scores (Behavioral Regulation Index and Metacognition Index) and a collective Global Executive Composite score were calculated and examined.

**Secondary Outcomes.** Psychological distress was measured using the Brief Symptom Inventory (BSI), a 53-item questionnaire that asks participants to rate the degree to which they were bothered by various psychological and psychiatric symptoms across nine dimensions: somatization, obsessiveness, interpersonal sensitivity, depression, anxiety, hostility, phobic anxiety, paranoia, and psychoticism [17]. Subjective memory and general cognitive complaints were measured using the Cognitive Difficulties Scale (CDS), a 39-item self-report measure across seven factors: Distraction, Activities of Daily Living, Prospective Memory, Long-term Memory, Orientation, Language, and Fine Motor Control [18]. Mindfulness was measured using the Five-Factor Mindfulness Questionnaire (FFMQ), a 39-item questionnaire that focuses on thoughts, experiences, and actions in daily life across five facets of mindfulness: Acting with Awareness, Describing, Non-judging of Inner Experience, Non-reactivity to Inner Experience, and Observing [19]. Each facet of mindfulness was examined separately. Posttraumatic stress disorder

(PTSD) symptoms and severity were measured using the PTSD Checklist – Military version (PCL-M), a 17-item self-report measure that asks participants to rate the extent to which a particular symptom bothered them over the previous month [20]. Depression was measured using the Patient Health Questionnaire – 9 (PHQ-9), a nine-item measure used for screening, diagnosing, and monitoring depression [21]. Subjective sleep quality was quantified using the Pittsburgh Sleep Quality Index (PSQI), a 19-item questionnaire with seven domains: subjective sleep quality, sleep latency, sleep duration, habitual sleep efficiency, sleep disturbances, use of sleep medications, and daytime dysfunction over the last month [22]. Stress was measured using the Perceived Stress Scale (PSS-10), a 10-item self-report measure used to assess one's perception of stress at the global level [23]. Health-related quality of life (QoL) was measured using the Medical Outcomes Study Short-Form-36 version 2 (SF-36v2), a 36-item self-report measure that yields two summary health component scores – one for mental health-related QoL (Mental Component Score) and one for physical health-related QoL (Physical Component Score) [24]. Total scores for BSI (Global Severity Index), CDS, PCL-M, PHQ-9, PSQI, PSS, and each SF-36v2 component score were used in the analyses.

## 2.5  Statistical Analysis

All analyses were conducted using SPSS Statistics software – version 27 (IBM Corp., Armonk, NY, USA). Descriptive statistics were reported as frequencies, means, and standard deviations. Linear mixed-effects models were used to examine if there were any differences between groups over time in each of the self-reported measures, controlling for age. A group-by-time interaction was tested for each self-reported measure. If found to be statistically significant, between- and within-groups differences were examined to determine if the groups differed at post-treatment and follow-up as well as if there were any significant changes over time within each group. If the group-by-time interaction was nonsignificant, this term was removed, and the main effect of time was examined to determine if significant changes occurred over time while controlling for age and group. Given that both groups received the same MAP training and health coaching minus differences in the delivery, the main effect of time was examined by collapsing across the groups to increase the sample size. An intention-to-treat analysis was conducted in which all participants were included regardless of their level of compliance to the intervention and significance was set at $\alpha < 0.05$.

# 3  Results

Baseline characteristics are summarized by group assignment in Table 1. There was a total of 25 participants who met study criteria, consented, and were randomized to either the dMAP (n = 12) or sgMAP (n = 13). Of the 25 participants, 19 completed the post-treatment assessment (dMAP:sgMAP = 9:10; ~76% retention rate) and 15 completed the three-month follow-up assessment (dMAP:sgMAP = 7:8; ~60% retention rate). Overall, participants were middle aged ($M_{age}$: 49.2 years) and predominantly male (92%) and white (96%). Most were married (80%), had greater than a high school education (76%),

**Table 1.** Demographic characteristics by MAP training group

| Characteristic | Total (n=25) | dMAP (n=12) | sgMAP (n=13) |
|---|---|---|---|
| Age, Mean ± SD | 49.2 ± 8.9 | 48.2 ± 11.5 | 50.2 ± 6.0 |
| Gender, # (%) | | | |
| Male | 23 (92.0) | 12 (100.0) | 11 (84.6) |
| Female | 2 (8.0) | 0 (0.0) | 2 (15.4) |
| Race, # (%) | | | |
| White | 24 (96.0) | 12 (100.0) | 12 (92.3) |
| Non-White | 1 (4.0) | 0 (0.0) | 1 (7.7) |
| Marital Status, # (%) | | | |
| Married | 20 (80.0) | 9 (75.0) | 11 (84.6) |
| Separated/divorced | 4 (16.0) | 2 (16.7) | 2 (15.4) |
| Living with a partner | 1 (4.0) | 1 (8.3) | 0 (0.0) |
| Education, # (%) | | | |
| HS/GED | 6 (24.0) | 2 (16.7) | 4 (30.8) |
| > HS/GED | 19 (76.0) | 10 (83.3) | 9 (69.2) |
| Employment Status, # (%) | | | |
| Unemployed | 1 (4.0) | 0 (0.0) | 1 (7.7) |
| Student | 1 (4.0) | 1 (8.3) | 0 (0.0) |
| Employed at least part-time | 16 (64.0) | 9 (75.0) | 7 (53.8) |
| Retired | 7 (28.0) | 2 (16.7) | 5 (38.5) |

Note: No significant differences were observed between the two intervention arms. dMAP = directed mental and physical training; GED = General Education Development; HS = high school; SD = standard deviation; sgMAP = self-guided mental and physical training

and were working at least part-time (64%). There were no significant differences between the two intervention arms at baseline.

Figure 1 summarizes the adjusted mean scores for the health outcomes with a significant group-by-time interaction. There were only two health outcomes meeting this criterion, both of which were executive function subscales (BRIEF-A): inhibit and task monitor. There were no between-group differences observed at post-treatment or follow-up for either subscale; however, there were significant within-group differences observed for each. For the inhibit subscale, the dMAP group was observed to have significantly higher scores at follow-up compared to baseline and post-treatment, demonstrating greater difficulty. When adjusting for multiple comparisons, only the difference between post-treatment and follow-up remained significant for the dMAP group. No within-group differences were observed for the sgMAP group for the inhibit subscale. As for the task monitor subscale, both groups were observed to have significant within-group differences. Specifically, the scores for task monitor were significantly higher at follow-up compared to post-treatment for the dMAP group, demonstrating greater difficulty. Contrary, the scores for task monitor in the sgMAP group were significantly lower at follow-up compared to baseline, demonstrating lesser difficulty. However, when adjusting for multiple comparisons, both within-group differences become non-significant.

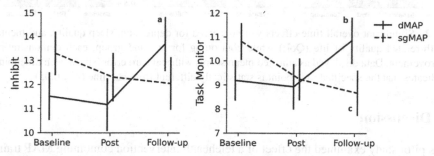

**Fig. 1.** Significant group-by-time interaction terms were observed for the Inhibit and Task Monitor subscales of the executive function questionnaire – BRIEF-A. Planned comparisons revealed no between-group differences for either subscale but did reveal significant within-group differences. Data displayed as adjusted mean scores with standard error bars at each timepoint. dMAP = directed mental and physical training; sgMAP = self-guided mental and physical training. [a]Indicates a significant within-group difference between follow-up and the other two timepoints. However, only the within-group difference between follow-up and post-treatment remained after adjusting for multiple comparisons. [b]Indicates a significant within-group difference between follow-up and post-treatment that became non-significant after adjusting for multiple comparisons. [c]Indicates a significant within-group difference between follow-up and baseline that became non-significant after adjusting for multiple comparisons.

For the remaining measures, the group-by-time interaction was non-significant and therefore, removed to examine the main effect of time with the two groups collapsed (see Fig. 2). In the reduced models, a significant overall time effect was observed for depression, sleep quality, and mental health-related QoL (SF-36v2 Mental Health Component Summary score) while controlling for age and group. Specifically, depression symptoms were significantly lower at post-treatment and follow-up compared to baseline, but no difference was observed between post-treatment and follow-up values ($p = 0.89$). Additionally, PSQI scores were observed to be significantly lower at post-treatment compared to baseline, indicating an improvement in subjective sleep quality. The Mental Component Summary scores were observed to be significantly higher at follow-up compared to baseline, demonstrating a significant improvement in mental health-related QoL. No other significant time effects were observed for the remaining health outcomes (data not shown).

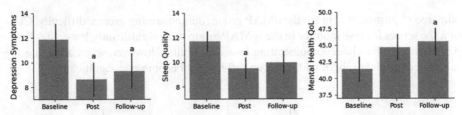

**Fig. 2.** Significant overall time effects were observed for depression, sleep quality, and mental health-related quality of life (QoL) while controlling for age and group, each demonstrating improvement. Data displayed as adjusted mean scores with standard error bars at each timepoint. [a]Indicates that the specified time point is statistically different from baseline (p < 0.05)

## 4 Discussion

This pilot study examined the effect of a telehealth intervention combining MAP training and health coaching on several health outcomes in a group of Veterans with CMI. Participants were randomized to either the directed MAP group where specific instructions of the MAP training were provided via text messaging or the self-guided MAP group in which the intervention goals were communicated without detailed instruction. The findings of this pilot study are preliminary given the small sample size but demonstrate important trends in two of the executive function (BRIEF-A) subscales: inhibit and task monitor. Additionally, there was suggestive evidence demonstrating significant improvement in depression, perceived sleep quality, and mental health-related QoL, possibly indicating that the delivery of the training (directed versus self-guided) may not be as important a predictor for these measures.

The direction of change for the BRIEF-A subscales demonstrates some differences between the intervention arms. We originally hypothesized that those receiving directed guidance on how to implement the MAP training (dMAP group) would have greater improvement in the self-reported cognitive control outcomes. However, counter to predictions of a dose-response benefit related to the level of instruction, the dMAP group was observed to have some difficulties on two subscales for executive function at follow-up. Specifically, the dMAP group had a significant within-group difference for the inhibit subscale in which follow-up scores were significantly higher compared to post-treatment even after adjusting for multiple comparisons, an indication of greater difficulty with inhibition. Although not statistically significant, the sgMAP group was observed to have lower scores at follow-up compared to post-treatment for the inhibit subscale. A similar trend was observed for the task monitor subscale where follow-up scores were significantly higher for the dMAP group, an indication of greater difficulty self-monitoring performance on tasks, and significantly lower for the sgMAP group (less difficulty) compared to their respective post-treatment scores. Both within-group differences for the task monitor subscale became non-significant after adjusting for multiple comparisons. Further examination of the remaining executive function subscales reveals additional differences in the direction of change between the intervention arms (results not shown). Specifically, the dMAP group was observed to self-report increasing difficulty overtime for five of the remaining seven BRIEF-A subscales (Initiate, Organization of Materials, Plan/Organize, Shift, Working Memory); while the sgMAP group either saw a continual decrease overtime (Shift) or a decrease at post-treatment followed by a slight increase at follow-up that was always below baseline scores (Initiate, Organization of Materials, Plan/Organize, Working Memory). While these observed trends were not significant, they suggest that executive function may be influenced by the delivery of MAP training; however, additional research is needed to confirm this observation in a larger sample.

One possible explanation is that the self-guided MAP training protocol provided opportunities for initiating and choosing how to implement the intervention goals which when combined with health coaching likely created an autonomy-supportive environment [25, 26]. The literature documents several benefits of autonomy-supportive environments compared to controlling ones including greater improvements in autonomous motivation and self-regulation, performance (e.g., academic), persistence, and well-being [27–30]. Disruption of such autonomy garnered by detailed instruction may have unexpectedly produced a burden on executive function that can modulate self-regulatory failure [31]. In addition to autonomy, self-regulation is necessary for sustaining behavioral change especially when those health-promoting behaviors may be perceived as aversive (e.g., exercise) [32]. This is particularly important for individuals with CMI because post-exertional malaise is a commonly reported complaint that manifests as an exacerbation of symptoms appearing after a mentally challenging task or an acute physiological stressor [33–35]. This indicates that the combined efforts of mental and physical training may be especially challenging among individuals with CMI; however, this pilot study provides initial evidence suggesting that the use of a self-guided delivery approach when empowered with clear goals and support may lead to sustained participation. In the present study, participants were given the option of joining the WRIISC Health Coaching program after completing the eight-week intervention which enabled Veterans to customize their behavioral health goals further (e.g., increase exercise, practice mindfulness daily, etc.). A closer examination of those with follow-up data revealed that participants in the sgMAP group were more likely to continue with health coaching (dMAP = 5 out of 7; sgMAP = 7 out of 8) and with the MAP training program (dMAP = 3 out of 7; sgMAP = 6 out of 8) for an additional three months, possibly indicating greater self-regulatory efficacy.

After eight weeks of MAP training, participants also self-reported significant improvements in three health outcomes: depression, sleep quality, and mental health-related QoL. Improvements were observed in both groups for each of these health outcomes at post-treatment which may partly explain why the group-by-time interaction was not statistically significant and therefore, was removed from the statistical models so that the overall time effect could be examined. Although the interpretation of the overall time effect does not allow for group differences to be examined, these suggestive findings may either indicate that the sample size was too small to detect differences or that the delivery of the training (directed versus self-guided) may not be as important a predictor for these outcomes. With respect to depression, participants, on average, self-reported significantly less symptoms of depression at post-treatment and follow-up compared to baseline, suggesting a drop in severity from moderate (PHQ-9: 10–14) at baseline to mild depression (PHQ-9: 5–9) at follow-up [21]. This finding is supported by previous research which demonstrated a significant reduction in symptoms of depression following eight weeks of in-person MAP training [9, 12]. With respect to sleep quality, the application of the PSQI cut point for military samples (PSQI total score $\geq$ 10; [36]) suggests that, on average, participants had a higher likelihood of meeting the diagnostic criteria for insomnia at baseline. After the intervention, participants self-reported significant improvements to their perceived sleep quality with their overall PSQI scores falling below the cut point for probable insomnia. Although perceived sleep quality has not been assessed in previous MAP training studies, there is evidence demonstrating a positive association between PSQI scores and depression symptoms [37], indicating that improvement in sleep quality may lead to improvement in depression symptoms or vice versa. On average, mental health-related QoL also improved with total scores at follow-up being significantly higher compared to baseline, indicating enhanced mental health. The improvements in mental health-related QoL may stem from reductions in depression symptoms and/or improvements in perceived sleep quality. Another study also observed significant improvements to overall QoL among healthy medical students after completing an eight-week in-person MAP training program [10].

Although not assessed in this pilot study, previous studies examining the effects of MAP training also have demonstrated significant improvements in trauma-related thoughts and rumination, self-worth, anxiety, mindfulness, chronic low back pain, and brain activity [8, 9, 38]. There is some evidence suggesting that the effect of MAP training on different health outcomes appears to be dependent on the level of severity self-reported at baseline. For example, MAP training has beneficial effects on mental health in both healthy and clinical populations; however, those with a clinical diagnosis of depression were found to have a significantly greater improvement in depression symptoms compared to healthy individuals who also saw significant improvement but to a lesser extent [9]. Others have speculated that the lack of significant improvement in a health outcome previously found to improve in a different population is likely due to lower baseline levels in their cohort of participants [38], indicating that the beneficial effect of MAP training may be less potent at lower levels of severity for a given health outcome.

## 4.1 Limitations

This study has limitations warranting acknowledgment including a small sample size. Recruitment goals were impacted by the temporary suspension of study enrollment during the beginning of the COVID pandemic in 2020. Additionally, the primary aim of the pilot study was to assess the feasibility of administering an eight-week telehealth MAP training intervention rather than the efficacy, which means that the study was slightly underpowered from the beginning. Therefore, the results should be interpreted with caution and validated in a larger sample. Another limitation of the study is that our sample consisted primarily of white, middle-aged males, which limits the applicability of the findings to other populations. However, the MAP training protocol is generalizable to anyone who is physically able to exercise aerobically and has access to a guided meditation mobile app. Furthermore, the synergistic effects of MAP training and health coaching could not be examined given that both groups received the same intervention but with a different delivery format. Also, the use of self-report questionnaires for assessing each health outcome is another limitation of the study and are subject to bias; however, they were remotely administered which has benefits for distance-based research. Lastly, participation in MAP training during the three months of follow-up was self-reported and not objectively measured using the study devices and apps.

## 4.2 Conclusion

In summary, the suggestive findings of this pilot study indicate that the combination of a telehealth MAP training program with health coaching improves depression symptoms, perceived sleep quality, and mental health-related QoL among Veterans with CMI. Additionally, this study provides initial evidence suggesting that the delivery of MAP training may influence different aspects of executive function with the self-guided protocol demonstrating some additional benefits over directed. The telehealth version of MAP training also demonstrates the feasibility and value of harnessing remote technology to deliver an intervention and collect both objective and subjective data, with emphasis on being able to continue research when there are restrictions on in-person interactions during a global pandemic. These findings also suggest that empowering Veterans with goals and support through the use of health coaching may be a feasible approach to improving health in those suffering from chronic illness. Additional research is needed to determine the synergistic effect of telehealth MAP training with health coaching in a larger, more generalizable sample.

**Funding Sources.** This pilot study was funded by the Georgetown-Howard Universities Center for Clinical and Translational Science: Pilot Translational and Clinical Studies Program.

**Conflicts of Interest.** Authors report no conflicts of interest. The opinions presented in this article are those of the authors and do not reflect the views of any institution/agency of the U.S. government, Georgetown University, Uniformed Services University of the Health Sciences, or the Henry M. Jackson Foundation for the Advancement of Military Medicine, Inc.

## References

1. McAndrew, L., Helmer, D., Phillips, L., Chandler, H., Ray, K., Quigley, K.: Iraq and Afghanistan Veterans report symptoms consistent with chronic multisymptom illness one year after deployment. J. Rehabil. Res. Dev. **53**(1), 59–70 (2016)
2. Institute of Medicine: Chronic multisymptom Illness in Gulf War Veterans: Case Definitions Reexamined. The National Academies Press, Washington, D.C. (2014). https://doi.org/10.17226/18623
3. Porter, B., Long, K., Rull, R., Dursa, E.: Millennium cohort study team: prevalence of chronic multisymptom illness/gulf war illness over time among millennium cohort participants, 2001 to 2016. J. Occup. Environ. Med. **62**(1), 4–10 (2020)
4. Department of Veterans Affairs and Department of Defense: VA/DoD clinical practice guideline for the management of chronic multisymptom illness (2021). https://www.healthquality.va.gov/guidelines/MR/cmi/VADoDCMICPG508.pdf
5. Niendam, T., Laird, A., Ray, K., Dean, Y., Glahn, D., Carter, C.: Meta-analytic evidence for a superordinate cognitive control network subserving diverse executive functions. Cogn. Affect. Behav. Neurosci. **12**(2), 241–268 (2012)
6. Cole, M.W., Repovs, G., Anticevic, A.: The frontoparietal control system: a central role in mental health. Neuroscientist **20**(6), 652–664 (2014)

7. Allan, J.L., McMinn, D., Daly, M.A.: Bidirectional relationship between executive function and health behavior: evidence, implications, and future directions. Front. Neurosci. **10**(386) (2016)
8. Shors, T., Chang, H., Millon, E.: MAP training my BrainTM: meditation plus aerobic exercise lessens trauma of sexual violence more than either activity alone. Front. Neurosci. **12**, 211 (2018)
9. Alderman, B., Olson, R., Brush, C., Shors, T.: MAP training: combining meditation and aerobic exercise reduces depression and rumination while enhancing synchronized brain activity. Transl. Psychiatry **6**, e726 (2016)
10. Lavadera, P., Millon, E., Shors, T.: MAP train my brain: meditation combined with aerobic exercise reduces stress and rumination while enhancing quality of life in medical students. J. Altern. Complement. Med. **26**(5) (2020)
11. Millon, E.M., Shors, T.: Taking neurogenesis out of the lab and into the world with MAP train my BrainTM. Behav. Brain Res. **376**, Epub (2019)
12. Shors, T., Olson, R., Bates, M., Selby, E., Alderman, B.: Mental and physical (MAP) training: a neurogenesis-inspired intervention that enhances health in humans. Neurobiol. Learn. Mem. **115**, 3–9 (2014)
13. Fukuda, K., Nisenbaum, R., Stewart, G., et al.: Chronic multisymptom illness affecting air force veterans of the gulf war. JAMA **280**(11), 981–988 (1998)
14. U.S. Department of Veteran Affairs: Annie App for Veterans. https://mobile.va.gov/app/annie-app-veterans
15. U.S. Department of Veteran Affairs: Whole Health, 26 July 2021. https://www.va.gov/WHOLEHEALTH/veteran-resources/whole-health-basics.asp. Accessed 14 Jan 2022
16. Roth, R., Isquith, P., Gioia, G.: Behavioral Rating Inventory of Executive Function—Adult Version. Psychological Assessment Resources, Inc., Lutz (2005)
17. Derogatis, L., Spencer, P.: Brief Symptom Inventory: BSI. Pearson, Upple Saddle River (1993)
18. Derouesné, C., Dealberto, M., Boyer, P., et al.: Empirical evaluation of the 'cognitive difficulties scale' for assessment of memory complaints in general practice: a study of 1628 cognitively normal subjects aged 45–75 years. Int. J. Geriatr. Psychiatry **8**(7), 599–607 (1993)
19. Baer, R., Smith, G., Lykins, E., et al.: Construct validity of the five facet mindfulness questionnaire in meditating and nonmeditating samples. Assessment **15**(3), 329–342 (2008)
20. Wilkins, K., Lang, A., Norman, S.: Synthesis of the psychometric properties of the PTSD checklist (PCL) military, civilian, and specific versions. Depress. Anxiety **28**(7), 596–606 (2011)
21. Kroenke, K., Spitzer, R., Williams, J.: The PHQ-9: validity of a brief depression severity measure. J. Gen. Intern. Med. **16**, 606–613 (2001)
22. Buysse, D.J., Reynolds, C.F., Monk, T.H., Berman, S.R., Kupfer, D.J.: The Pittsburgh sleep quality index: a new instrument for psychiatric practice and research. Psychiatry Res. **28**(2), 193–213 (1989)
23. Cohen, S., Kamarck, T., Mermelstein, R.: A global measure of perceived stress. J. Health Soc. Behav. **24**(4), 385–396 (1983)
24. Ware, J., Sherbourne, C.: The MOS 36-item short-form health survey (SF-36): I. Coneptual framework and item selection. Med. Care **30**(6), 473–483 (1992)
25. Oliver, E.J., Markland, D., Hardy, J., Petherick, C.M.: The effects of autonomy-supportive versus controlling environments on self-talk. Motiv. Emot. **32**(3), 200–212 (2008)
26. Hagger, M.S., Hardcastle, S.J., Chater, A., Mallett, C., Pal, S., Chatzisarantis, N.L.: Autonomous and controlled motivational regulations for multiple health-related behaviors: between- and within-participants analyses. Health Psychol. Behav. Med. **2**(1), 565–601 (2014)
27. Gagne, M., Ryan, R.M., Bargmann, K.: Autonomy support and need satisfaction in the motivation and well-being of gymnasts. J. Appl. Sport Psychol. **15**(4), 372–390 (2003)

28. Grolnick, W.S., Ryan, R.M., Deci, E.L.: Inner resources for school achievement: motivational mediators of children's perceptions of their parents. J. Educ. Psychol. **83**(4), 508–517 (1991)
29. Vansteenkiste, M., Simons, J., Lens, W., Sheldon, K.M., Deci, E.L.: Motivating learning, performance, and persistence: the synergistic effects of intrinsic goal contents and autonomy-supportive contexts. J. Pers. Soc. Psychol. **87**(2), 246–260 (2004)
30. Vansteenkiste, M., Simons, J., Lens, W., Soenens, B., Matos, L.: Examining the motivational impact of intrinsic versus extrinsic goal framing and autonomy-supportive versus internally controlling communication style on early adolescents' academic achievement. Child Dev. **76**(2), 483–501 (2005)
31. Hofmann, W., Schmeichel, B.J., Baddeley, A.D.: Executive functions and self-regulation. Trends Cogn. Sci. **16**(3), 174–180 (2012)
32. Kelley, N.J., Gallucci, A., Riva, P., Romero Lauro, L.J., Schmeichel, B.J.: Stimulating self-regulation: a review of non-invasive brain stimulation studies of goal-directed behavior. Front. Behav. Neurosci. **12**(337) (2019)
33. Cook, D.B., Stegner, A.J., Ellingson, L.D.: Exercise alters pain sensitivity in Gulf War Veterans with chronic musculoskeletal pain. J. Pain **11**(8), 764–772 (2010)
34. Rayhan, R.U., Stevens, B.W., Raksit, M.P., et al.: Exercise challenge in Gulf War Illness reveals two subgroups with altered brain structure and function. PLoS ONE **8**(6), e63903 (2013)
35. Li, M., Xu, C., Yao, W., et al.: Self-reported post-exertional fatigue in Gulf War veterans: roles of autonomic testing. Front. Neurosci. **7**(269) (2014)
36. Matsangas, P., Mysliwiec, V.: The utility of the Pittsburgh sleep quality index in US military personnel. Mil. Psychol. **30**(4), 360–369 (2018)
37. Huang, Y., Zhu, M.: Increased global PSQI score is associated with depressive symptoms in an adult population from the United States. Nat. Sci. Sleep **12**, 487–495 (2020)
38. Polaski, A., Phelps, A.L., Smith, T.J., et al.: Integrated meditation and exercise therapy: a randomized controlled pilot of a combined nonpharmacological intervention focused on reducing disability and pain in patients with chronic low back pain. Pain Med. **23**(2), 444–458 (2021)

# An Eye Tracking Analysis
# of Conversational Violations in Dyadic
# and Collaborative Interaction

Bengisu Cagiltay[1] and Cengiz Acarturk[1,2(✉)]

[1] Department of Cognitive Science, Middle East Technical University,
Ankara, Turkey
acarturk@metu.edu.tr
[2] Department of Cognitive Science, Jagiellonian University, Kraków, Poland

**Abstract.** Linguistic principles are crucial in maintaining reliable and
transparent communication for dyadic interactions. However, violating
these principles might result in unwieldy and problematic communications. We use gaze as a medium to explore how visual attention and
task performance changes when conversational violations occur. We conducted an eye-tracking study (N = 17) measuring changes in visual patterns in response to social communication errors, specifically Grice's
Maxims violations. Our study investigates how social-communicative
errors influence task performance and gaze during dyadic and collaborative social interactions. The results suggest participants' visual exploration patterns shift towards the violator when the maxim of Relation
is violated in a task instruction. Gaze stays mainly within the task area
after receiving instructions with Quantity, Quality, and Manner violations. Moreover, it takes longer to respond to task instructions that
include Quantity and Quality violations, than the Manner and Relation
violations. Finally, our qualitative analysis revealed participants' adaptive and non-adaptive strategies in response to the Quality violation. Our
findings contribute to the design space of human performance in dyadic
and collaborative interactions, with future work implications exploring
human performance in joint system-human interactions.

**Keywords:** Eye tracking · Conversational violations · Cooperative
principle

## 1 Introduction

To maintain a well-functioning conversation in daily life settings, humans follow
basic conversational norms. By trial and error, we learn to follow these rules
in social communication. However, it is likely that these conversational principles are violated in daily conversations, which may negatively influence the
interaction by causing dissatisfaction, confusion, or even a failure in the communication. In workplaces, these negative influences caused by conversational

D. D. Schmorrow and C. M. Fidopiastis (Eds.): HCII 2022, LNAI 13310, pp. 34–47, 2022.
https://doi.org/10.1007/978-3-031-05457-0_3

violations might decrease human performance, efficiency, and success in socially collaborative tasks. Grice [1] introduced the Cooperative Principle, identifying four types of conversational violations. The Gricean principles suggest a mutual expectation of contribution to the conversation between interlocutors. In particular, Grice categorizes four ways in which the conversational implicature can be identified (i.e., the maxims of Quantity, Quality, Relation, Manner). These principles apply in various conversational settings, including interactions with conversational agents such as chatbots, voice interfaces, or social robots (e.g., [3–8]). As conversational agents become more prevalent in daily-life settings such as workplaces and homes, it is key to understand how conversational violations impact task performance.

Human-centered approaches, including discourse analysis, gaze modeling, and social norms inform social agent designs for speech interfaces or social robots. In discourse analysis, machine learning algorithms are utilized to identify social norm violations [9]. Gaze is a medium to understand how people's visual attention is shaped. Like humans, gaze is a unique channel for representing allocated attention in embodied agents, such as social robots. Previous work investigated modeling human-like gaze behavior or conversational roles for social robots (e.g., [10–13]). By investigating how humans' visual attention is shaped in the presence of conversational violations, our motivation for the present study is to lay the groundwork for informing the future design of gaze (including visual exploration patterns, fixation durations, and visual attention patterns) for modeling social and embodied agents' interactions that include conversational violations.

Overall, we aim to address the following research question, *RQ: How do conversational violations affect gaze patterns, visual exploration, and task performance in dyadic and collaborative interactions?*

## 2   Background and Related Work

### 2.1   Linguistic Principles in Conversational Violations

Grice introduced the Cooperative Principle of linguistic guidance for a productive and successful conversation between participants. The four conversational maxims that Grice presented are as follows:

*Maxim of Quantity:* The quantity of the provided information should not be more than required.
*Maxim of Quality:* The provided information should be correct and evident.
*Maxim of Relation:* The provided information should be relevant.
*Maxim of Manner:* The provided information should be clear, brief, non-ambiguous, and orderly.

These conversational principles have been applied in studies investigating the daily life applicability of Grice's Maxims concerning humor, writings, conversations, and technologies such as chatbots or customer service agents (e.g., [2,3,7,15–19]). Other lines of work focus on the developmental aspects of the cooperative principle by investigating the stage of development when children detect violations of Gricean maxims (e.g., [20–23]). Similar studies focus on understanding children's awareness on information quality, speaker preference, sensitivity, or understanding of the maxim violations (e.g., [24–28]).

## 2.2  Linguistic Utterances and Gaze in Conversational Settings

Hemforth et al. [29] utilized eye-tracking to compare English, French, and German speakers' preferences by focusing on the linguistic attributes that include Gricean Maxim of Manner. The participants matched sentences that violated the maxim of Manner with their corresponding visual representation, while the fixation patterns and preferences of participants were recorded. The results suggest that English, French, and German speakers focused on different visual regions when they encountered sentences violating the maxim of Manner. Another eye-tracking study [30] investigated whether participants were sensitive to the violations of Gricean maxim of Quantity. The results suggest that the violation of the maxim of Quantity might have a moderate effect on communication success, such that people are sensitive to undershared information but not to overshared information. They report that the eye movements may suggest a state of confusion when information is overshared. However, Davies and Katsos [31] found that people are sensitive to both dimensions of the maxim of Quantity. Similarly, another study that utilized cognitively inspired cooperative language tasks demonstrated that task performance improves in the presence of the cooperative principle [32]. Previous work also reported that the personalities of human partners in an interaction might influence gazing towards faces. By utilizing eye-tracking to investigate dyadic communications, the personality dimension agreeableness is correlated with an increased gaze towards faces [14].

## 2.3  Flexibility and Subjectivity of the Interpretation of Communication

Communication principles discussed above focused primarily on literal information transfer, which does not include subjective interpretations of communication and conversational principles. However, humans transfer information by multiple non-verbal modalities in communication. Non-verbal information transfer leads to flexibility in people's perception of communicative principles due to subjective interpretation. For example, it can be perceived as being "deceptive" (e.g., [33–35]). Martin and Rubin [36] proposed that communication flexibility is related to social desirability, communication adaptability, and behavioral flexibility.

Additionally, the flexibility of communication influences the interpretation of conversational violations. This flexibility leads to conversational violations being perceived differently based on people's culture, language, the content of the communication, and the neurodiversity of people involved within the communication (e.g., [37–40]). As an example of how culture relates to flexible interpretations of conversational violations, Yeung [41] investigated the conversational violations perceived as "deceptive" in Hong Kong Chinese culture. A replication [42] tested the differences in the cultural perception of conversational violations in

Americans. They mainly followed the Information Manipulation Theory, which describes "deception" as an appeared result of the violations of any Gricean maxims. The results showed that Hong Kong Chinese participants experienced deception from Grice's maxim violations differently from U.S. Americans. The maxims of Quality and Relation were perceived most deceptive by Hong Kong Chinese. However, Quantity and Manner were not perceived as deceptive compared to U.S. Americans.

## 3  Method

To investigate gaze, visual attention, and exploration patterns of interlocutors in the presence of conversational violations, we designed an experiment to measure the participants' eye movements and task performance in response to task instructions that violate Gricean Maxims.

### 3.1  Design and Stimuli

We created a LEGO© building task and conducted a within-subjects study. For the independent variable, we manipulated the presence of maxim violations in instructions. The dependent variables were the participants' eye-tracking measures (i.e., fixation duration) and task performance (i.e., time spent on completing instructions). The study consisted of six trial sets, and every trial had four tasks. Overall, the study presented a total of 24 tasks. The order of trials was randomized. Each task included three instructions that informed the participants about which pieces they needed for the task by providing information about the color, shape, and the order it's placed. Participants received 72 instructions (i.e., six trials, four tasks, three instructions each). One out of three of the instructions deliberately demonstrated a violation of Grice's Maxims for each task. The order of the violation was balanced to reduce the order effect.

**Fig. 1.** *Experimental Setup*: The figure visualizes the distribution of color and shapes of the pieces. Grey, green, brown, beige, blue, and white-colored square pieces were followed by green and brown colored rectangle pieces. A larger rectangular platform was placed below the pieces. (Color figure online)

## 3.2   Measures

We measured the participants' eye movements (fixation duration and interval duration) using a wearable Tobii Pro Glasses 2 eye-tracker with a sampling rate 100 Hz. We also measured participants' personality traits in five dimensions (extraversion, agreeableness, conscientiousness, neuroticism, openness) with the Ten Item Personality measure (TIPI) scale [43]. We conducted a semi-structured qualitative interview after the study was completed.

## 3.3   Participants

Seventeen adults (eleven females) were recruited through canvassing at a university campus, which participants volunteered to attend the study. The ages of the participants ranged between 22 and 35 years (M = 23.16, SD = 4.89). All participants had normal or corrected vision, and they did not use glasses during data recording. Participants reported their familiarity with LEGO© pieces as M = 3.3, SD = 0.6 (1 = Not familiar, 5 = Very familiar). Participants reported their last interaction with LEGO©'s ranged between 2 months to 15 years (M = 9.2, SD = 5.9 years). Participants' TIPI scores from a 7-point scale (1 = low, 7 = high) were: extroversion M = 5.05, SD = 1.67, agreeableness M = 5.58, SD = 0.84, conscientiousness M = 5.38, SD = 1.23, emotional stability M = 3.7, SD = 1.57, and openness M = 5.41, SD = 1.30.

## 3.4   Procedure

The study procedure started as the experimenter greeted the participants and provided informed consent. Next, the participant wore the eye-tracking device calibrated by the experimenter. The experimenter and the participant were seated approximately one meter apart (see Fig 2). The experimenter verbally informed the participants about the study setup and experiment procedure and started the recording. To reduce the familiarity effect, the participant ran two test trials. The test trials had neutral instructions and did not contain any variable manipulations. After answering any questions about the test trials, the experimenter initiated the study. The experimenter read the task instructions to the participant from a printed copy, then the participants verbally expressed when they completed the instruction. After completing the trials, the experimenter conducted a semi-structured post-study interview. Each session took approximately 30 min.

## 3.5   Analysis

We used Tobii Pro Lab (version 1.123) to analyze the eye-tracking data and excluded the gaze data of two participants, due to having gaze samples less than 60%. We used the default Tobii I-VT (Attention) gaze filter (velocity parameter set to 100°/s). All Time of Interest (TOI) points and dynamic Area of Interests (AOI) were manually annotated using the Tobii Pro Lab software. We specified four AOI regions (Person Area, Task Area, Peripheral (Left), Peripheral (Right)) and annotated them using the dynamic AOI tool. Participants' fixation duration and task duration measurements were analyzed using a one-way analysis of variance (ANOVA).

Qualitative data analysis on the interview transcripts was conducted to identify themes in participant responses to conversation violations. The qualitative analysis was conducted by the first author and followed the five steps of Thematic Analysis (TA) including familiarizing with the data to identify the potential items of interest, generating initial codes, searching for the themes, reviewing themes, defining and naming the themes, and producing the report [44].

## 4   Results

### 4.1   Eye Tracking Results

The results (see Table 1) show that the violation type has a significant effect on fixation duration, $F(2.07, 33.07) = 33.29, p < .001$. The total fixation duration compared between the person and task AOI's are significantly different within the overall study duration, $F(1, 16) = 94.66, p < .001$. The total fixation duration was longer in the task area ($M = 6.47$ s) than the person area ($M = 0.63$ s). The combined effects for both the violation type and the AOI were significant, $F(3, 48) = 29.95, p < .001$. The fixation duration was most prolonged in person area for the maxim of Relation ($M = 1.09$ s), followed by the maxim of Quality ($M = 0.56$ s), the maxim of Quantity ($M = 0.53$ s), and maxim of Manner ($M = 0.32$ s). The fixation duration was longest in the task area for the maxim of Quantity ($M = 9.19$ s), followed by the maxim of Quality ($M = 7.85$ s), the maxim of Manner ($M = 4.9, 7$ s), and the maxim of Relation ($M = 3.85$ s). Overall, the most prolonged fixation duration in the person area ($M = 1.09$ s) and the shortest fixation duration in the task area ($M = 3.85$ s) was for the violations of the maxim of Relation.

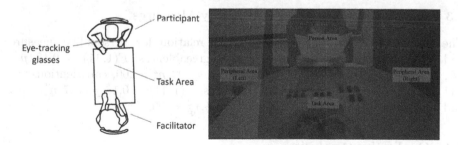

**Fig. 2.** Illustration of the experimental setup (left). The setup for the dynamic AOI regions is displayed from the participant's field of view (right)

**Table 1.** Mean fixation duration, in seconds, for each AOI and violation type

| AOI | Violation Type | Mean | Std. Error | 95% Confidence Interval | |
|---|---|---|---|---|---|
| | | | | Lower Bound | Upper Bound |
| Person Area | Quantity | 0.539 | 0.151 | 0.219 | 0.859 |
| | Quality | 0.568 | 0.240 | 0.060 | 1.076 |
| | Relation | 1.098 | 0.367 | 0.319 | 1.877 |
| | Manner | 0.329 | 0.118 | 0.079 | 0.579 |
| Task Area | Quantity | 9.191 | 0.690 | 7.728 | 10.6530 |
| | Quality | 7.852 | 0.904 | 5.935 | 9.769 |
| | Relation | 3.859 | 0.443 | 2.920 | 4.798 |
| | Manner | 4.979 | 0.551 | 3.810 | 6.148 |

## 4.2   Response Duration

We define task performance as the fixation duration participants spent attempting to solve the given instructions. To measure the influence of maxim violations on task performance, each task's response time within a violation was analyzed (see Table 2). Mauchly's test indicated that the sphericity assumption was violated, $\chi2(5) = 22.35, p < .001$, and a greenhouse Geisser sphericity correction was conducted. The violation type had a significant effect on response time, $F(1.681, 26.898) = 12.48, p < .001, \eta_p^2 = .43$. The average response time was longest for the maxim of Quantity (M = 26.79 s), followed by the maxim of Quality (M = 24.66 s), Manner (M = 22.30 s), and Relation (M = 21.89 s).

## 4.3   Task Performance and Personality Measures

The results did not show any significant relation for personality measures and task performance between subjects: Agreeableness, $F(1, 11) = 0.19, p = .68, \eta_p^2 = .016$, extroversion, $F(1, 11) = .0, p = .99, \eta_p^2 = .00$, conscientiousness, $F(1, 11) = 0.04, p = .84, \eta_p^2 = .004$, openness, $F(1, 11) = 0.16, p = .7, \eta_p^2 = .01$, and emotional stability, $(1, 11) = 0.6, p = .45, \eta_p^2 = .05$.

## 4.4   Qualitative Analysis

The thematic analysis results highlighted contrasting responses between participants. All participants displayed one of two contrasting behaviors in response to the maxim of Quality violation condition (i.e., an instruction that contains

**Table 2.** Mean response time, in seconds, for completing the tasks with each violation

| Violation Type | Mean | Std. Error | 95% Confidence Interval | |
|---|---|---|---|---|
| | | | Lower Bound | Upper Bound |
| Quantity | 26.79 | 0.912 | 24.86 | 28.73 |
| Quality | 24.66 | 1.573 | 21.33 | 28.00 |
| Relation | 21.89 | 0.851 | 20.09 | 23.70 |
| Manner | 22.31 | 1.018 | 20.15 | 24.47 |

incorrect information), categorised as (1) *adaptive*, i.e., seen to attempt picking up an alternative piece even though it does not fit the description of the instruction, and (2) *non-adaptive*, i.e., refused to pick up any piece, faked the hand movement of picking up a piece without actually picking up a piece, and behaved as if they followed the instruction and requested to continue to the next set of instructions. Nearly half of the participants (8 out of 17) were coded under the adaptive condition, and more than half of participants (9 out of 17) were coded under the non-adaptive condition. The adaptive and non-adaptive responses were not significantly associated with any demographic information (i.e., gender, age, or personality measures). Participants who employed adaptive responses stated that they did not think much about their responses, interpreted the instruction, and generally preferred the most relevant pieces to the original instruction. Participants categorized under the non-adaptive response type generally expressed that they usually ignored the instruction because the required piece "did not exist." Furthermore, some participants expressed that they sometimes felt "confused when they were instructed with unrelated tasks." For example, one participant in the adaptive category expressed their frustration by stating, *"the instructions asked for non-existing pieces. You deceived me! ... I had a task in front of me, but the instruction did not exist; this was confusing."* Overall, the semi-structured interviews showed that participants had some perception of a violation within the instructions, i.e., they stated that they experienced incorrect or unrelated instructions and expressed how they perceived or responded to the instructions that violated their expectations. When asked about the reasoning behind their responses to the unexpected instructions with violations, participants stated that they either ignored, skipped, or interpreted the instruction based on their perceptions and adapted their response by completing the task in a semi-related way.

## 5    Discussion

Here we discuss the implications of conversational principle violations on fixation duration and response times, evaluated through eye-tracking and qualitative analyses. The eye-tracking findings suggest that maxim violations impacts gaze. Our findings reveal that the participants spent longer duration to visually explore the tasks that violate the maxims of Quantity and Quality. Besides, participants had shorter visual exploration for the tasks that violated the maxims of Manner and Relation. The eye-tracking results partially support that maxim violations influence visual exploration towards the violator (i.e., person area). The findings show that the mean fixation duration in the person area is the most evident for the maxim of Relation and unrelated instructions in this condition tend to shift visual exploration from the task area towards the experimenter suggesting that maxim violations influence visual exploration. However, the violations for the maxims of Quantity, Quality, and Manner have less of an influence on visual exploration towards the person, as the fixations stay mainly within the task area and rarely shift to the person area.

The fixation duration was highest in the task area for the maxim of Quantity violation, suggesting that the excessive amount of information provided for these instructions influences visual exploration. Participants tend to keep their attention in the task area but partake in visual exploration to compare and evaluate the given information for the task equipment. Our results add on to the related work, which suggests that the presence of overshared information due to the maxim of Quantity might result in confusion [30]. A similar effect was visible but less effective in the Quantity, Quality, and Manner violation conditions. For the maxim of Quality, the fixations were mainly located in the task area than the person area, suggesting that when incorrect instructions were presented, participants tend to keep their attention in the task area while processing the information. The fixation amount in the task area was lower for the violations of Manner and Relation, which suggests that ambiguous and unrelated instructions have a lower influence in keeping the participants' visual exploration in the task area.

Our results regarding response time support the existing literature related to the decreased task performance as an effect of the maxim of Quality and Quantity [3]. Through the results of our study, we observed that the participants demonstrate a longer response time for the tasks that violate the maxim of Quality and Quantity. This suggests that conversational violations have substantial effects on task performance. Specifically, excessive amount of information (i.e., quantity violation) or incorrect information (i.e., quality violation) decreases task performance. Besides, participants' response time was shorter for the tasks that violate the Relation and Manner maxims. These results suggest that task instructions including unrelated information (i.e., relation violation) or ambiguous information (i.e., manner violation) have less influence on task performance.

Prior work in the literature shows a correlation between agreeableness scores and the percentage of time that participants spend for mutual gaze [14]. However, our results do not reflect this correlation between the agreeableness personality measure nor the rest of the personality measures (i.e., extroversion, conscientiousness, openness, emotional stability) for gaze and visual exploration towards the interlocutor. Our results suggest that personality measures may not be a factor in task performance with conversational violations. However, future work is needed to investigate the possible connections between personality measures and visual exploration patterns in the context of conversational violations.

The qualitative observational analysis yielded some interesting findings concerning participant responses to conversational violations. One interesting finding was that for maxim of Quality violations (i.e., when participants were presented with an incorrect instruction), the thematic analysis highlighted two distinct behaviors of participants, categorized as (1) *adaptive*, i.e., seen to attempt picking up an alternative piece even though it does not fit the description of the instruction, and (2) *non-adaptive*, i.e., rejected picking up any piece, faked the hand movement of picking up a piece without actually picking up a piece, and behaved as if they followed the instruction and requested to continue to the next set of instructions. These two responses contrast each other. While in both responses participants have attempted to deceive the instructor to an extent, it can be argued that the adaptive response is a coping strategy that participants used to "maintain cooperation via gamification." In contrast, the non-adaptive response is a deceptive strategy used to "maintain cooperation via attempting a fake perception of success." This contrast suggests a flexibility component to the interaction. This flexibility could be interpreted as cooperation approaches with gamification and attempted deception, or in other words, attempting to rig the task to achieve success. Due to the nature of the task one may suggest that when incorrect information was instructed some participants decided to step in and adapt their response based on their interpretations, rather than obeying and following what the instructions clearly stated. Concerning the participant responses to the semi-structured interviews, participants who performed an adaptive response to Quality violations, i.e., picked up an alternative piece, stated that they interpreted the instruction and decided to select the pieces most relevant or closest to the original instruction. Participants who performed a non-adaptive response to Quality violations, i.e., ignored the incorrect information, did not pick up a piece and asked for the next instruction, stated that their preference to ignore the instruction was because they thought it would be incorrect to take an alternative approach since that was not instructed. In sum, when people encounter instructions that violate the maxim of Quality, there are two opposite interpretations observed.

Although the exact reasoning behind the adaptive and non-adaptive responses was not investigated within this study, future work can enlighten the factors that weigh the differences in response types of participants. Future research questions may address why participants tend to gamify the task or deceive the instructor when presented with conversational violations or further investigate the flexibility in interpretations of conversational violations. Furthermore, it would also be interesting to see how this flexibility component in communication might be influential in a study replicated with a conversational agent or social robot acting as the task instructor. Particularly, the results of this study highlight an opportunity to investigate the reasoning behind people's tendencies to gamify tasks, deceive the instructor, and try to adapt their responses based on their interpretation of a task when presented with conversational violations (i.e., specifically in the case of incorrect instructions).

### 5.1 Limitations and Future Work

This work was limited by the study design and sample size. Future work should extend the study design to evaluate different effects of Gricean Maxim violations within task instructions. One example extension can be to have the participant read the instructions that include Gricean Maxim violations and investigate their task performance and gaze responses in this setting. Future work should also investigate how participant responses would differ if the instructor were a robot. A study design that replicates the same set of instructions and tasks but replaces the human instructor with a robot could address research questions related to trust and tolerance of humans when a conversational agent violates Gricean Maxims. Overall, in future work, the number of participants recruited in the study should be increased to offer generalizable results.

This work was limited by relying only on eye-tracking analysis as a quantitative measurement of visual attention. The work can be extended by applying different measurements, such as analyzing proximity while conversational violations occur in a less structured environment or measuring the affective responses speakers and addressees express within conversational violations.

Furthermore, the current analysis method focused on the participant responses after the instructions were presented. An alternative analysis should include a holistic approach that includes pre- and post-condition responses of the participants to the conversational violations. This alternative analysis would entail observation of the gaze behavior of the participant while the instruction is provided, followed by the visual inspection of the participant and the moment they completed the task.

## 6    Conclusion

Linguistic principles provide a guideline in the design of new technology related to conversational agents and voice interfaces. Paul Grice presents four principles influential on the value of dyadic conversations: maxims of Quantity, Quality, Relation, and Manner. In HCI and social robotics, Grice's cooperative principles provide a useful paradigm to implement and evaluate conversational agents. Our work explored how conversational violations influence visual attention. To observe the responses to conversational violations, an experimental task was designed, including a set of instructions that violate Gricean maxims and evaluated how participants respond to the violations via eye-tracking methods. The results suggest that all four Gricean maxims influence visual exploration and fixation durations. Specifically, the maxim of Relation violation causes the participants' visual exploration to shift away from the task area towards the violator. Overall, the violations decrease task performance by increasing response time, most significantly for the maxims of Quality and Quantity, followed by the maxims of Manner and Relation. The qualitative analyses show that participants adapt two contrasting behaviors when presented with incorrect instructions (i.e., violation of the maxim of Quality), categorized as adaptive and non-adaptive responses. Overall, in our work, we have investigated conversational violations by following simple but well-established principle of Gricean Maxims. However, we believe our approach presented in this work can be extended in future work to explore visual attention patterns through the focus of contemporary conversational violation principles. Similarly, our analysis is mainly motivated by investigating whether our approach can be operationalized, thus lacks a critical technological approach. We aim to extend our work to the human-robot interaction and conversational agents' domain to design appropriate gaze cues and visual attention models when conversational violations are present in interactions with embodied social robots.

**Acknowledgement.** This work was partially supported by TUBITAK (The Scientific and Technological Research Council of Turkey) Grant No 117E021.

# References

1. Grice, H.P.: Logic and conversation. In: Cole, P., Morgan, J.L. (eds.) Speech Acts, pp. 41–58 (1975)
2. Jacquet, B., Baratgin, J., Jamet, F.: The Gricean maxims of quantity and of relation in the turing test. In: The Proceedings of the 11th International Conference on Human System Interaction (HSI), pp. 332–338. IEEE (2018)
3. Jacquet, B., Hullin, A., Baratgin, J., Jamet, F.: The impact of the Gricean maxims of quality, quantity and manner in chatbots. In: Proceedings of the International Conference on Information and Digital Technologies (IDT), pp. 180–189. IEEE (2019)
4. Knepper, R. A., Tellex, S., Li, A., Roy, N., Rus, D.: Single assembly robot in search of human partner: versatile grounded language generation. In: Proceedings of the 8th ACM/IEEE International Conference on Human-Robot Interaction (HRI), pp. 167–168. IEEE (2013)
5. Briggs, G., Scheutz, M.: Multi-modal belief updates in multi-robot human-robot dialogue interactions. In: Proceedings of the AISB/IACAP Symposium on Linguistic and Cognitive Approaches to Dialogue Agents (LaCATODA), pp. 67–72 (2012)
6. En, L.Q., Lan, S.S.: The applicability of Gricean maxims in social robotics polite dialogue. In: Proceedings of the 6th ACM/IEEE International Conference on Human-Robot Interaction (HRI), pp. 195–196. IEEE (2011)
7. Kleinke, S.: Speaker activity and Grice's maxims of conversation at the interface of pragmatics and cognitive linguistics. J. Pragmat. **42**(12), 3345–3366 (2010)
8. Saygin, A.P., ÇiçSekli, I.: Pragmatics in human-computer conversations. J. Pragmat. **34**(3), 227–258 (2002)

9. Zhao, T., Zhao, R., Meng, Z., Cassell, J.: Leveraging recurrent neural networks for multimodal recognition of social norm violation in dialog. arXiv preprint:1610.03112 (2016)
10. Jokinen, K.: Conversational gaze modelling in first encounter robot dialogues. In: Proceedings of the LREC Workshop on Language and Body in Real Life and Multimodal Corpora. European Language Resources Association (ELRA) (2018)
11. Admoni, H., Scassellati, B.: Social eye gaze in human-robot interaction: a review. J. Hum.-Robot Interact. **6**(1), 25–63 (2017)
12. Mutlu, B., Kanda, T., Forlizzi, J., Hodgins, J., Ishiguro, H.: Conversational gaze mechanisms for humanlike robots. ACM Trans. Interact. Intell. Syst. (TiiS) **1**(2), 1–33 (2012)
13. Broz, F., Kose-Bagci, H., Nehaniv, C.L., Dautenhahn, K., Hatfield, U.K.: Towards automated human-robot mutual gaze. In: Proceedings of ACHI, the International Conference on Advances in Computer-Human Interactions, pp. 222–227 (2011)
14. Broz, F., Lehmann, H., Nehaniv, C.L., Dautenhahn, K.: Mutual gaze, personality, and familiarity: dual eye-tracking during conversation. In IEEE RO-MAN: The 21st IEEE International Symposium on Robot and Human Interactive Communication, pp. 858–864. IEEE (2012)
15. Kassel, J.F., Rohs, M.: Talk to me intelligibly: investigating an answer space to match the user's language in visual analysis. In: Proceedings of the Designing Interactive Systems Conference, pp. 1517–1529 (2019)
16. Xiao, Z., et al.: Tell me about yourself: using an AI-powered chatbot to conduct conversational surveys. arXiv preprint:1905.10700 (2019)
17. Gnewuch, U., Morana, S., Maedche, A.: Towards designing cooperative and social conversational agents for customer service. In: Proceedings of the 38th International Conference on Information Systems (ICIS) (2017)
18. White, R.: Adapting Grice's maxims in the teaching of writing. ELT J. **55**(1), 62–69 (2001)
19. Attardo, S.: The violation of Grice's maxims in jokes. In: Proceedings of the Annual Meeting of the Berkeley Linguistics Society, vol. 16, no. 1, pp. 355–362 (1990)
20. Nordmeyer, A.E., Frank, M.C.: Early understanding of pragmatic principles in children's judgments of negative sentences. Lang. Learn. Dev. **14**(4), 262–278 (2018)
21. Gweon, H., Shafto, P., Schulz, L.: Development of children's sensitivity to overinformativeness in learning and teaching. Dev. Psychol. **54**(11), 2113 (2018)
22. Okanda, M., Asada, K., Moriguchi, Y., Itakura, S.: Understanding violations of Gricean maxims in preschoolers and adults. Front. Psychol. **6**, 901 (2015). https://doi.org/10.3389/fpsyg.2015.00901
23. Siegal, M., Iozzi, L., Surian, L.: Bilingualism and conversational understanding in young children. Cognition **110**(1), 115–122 (2009)
24. Antoniou, K., Taguchi, N.: Multilingual pragmatics: implicature comprehension in adult L2 learners and multilingual children. In: Taguchi, N. (ed.) The Routledge Handbook of Pragmatics and Second Language Acquisition. Routledge, Abingdon (2019)
25. Gillis, R.L., Nilsen, E.S.: Children's use of information quality to establish speaker preferences. Dev. Psychol. **49**(3), 480–490 (2013). https://doi.org/10.1037/a0029479
26. Ferrier, S., Dunham, P., Dunham, F.: The confused robot: Two-olds' responses to breakdowns in conversation. Soc. Dev. **9**(3), 337–347 (2000)
27. Surian, L., Tedoldi, M., Siegal, M.: Sensitivity to conversational maxims in deaf and hearing children. J. Child Lang. **37**(4), 929–943 (2010)

28. Eskritt, M., Whalen, J., Lee, K.: Preschoolers can recognize violations of the Gricean maxims. Br. J. Dev. Psychol. **26**(3), 435–443 (2008). https://doi.org/10.1348/026151007X253260
29. Hemforth, B., et al.: Language specific preferences in anaphor resolution: exposure or Gricean maxims? In: Proceedings of the 32nd Annual Conference of the Cognitive Science Society, pp. 2218–2223 (2010)
30. Engelhardt, P.E., Bailey, K.G., Ferreira, F.: Do speakers and listeners observe the Gricean maxim of quantity? J. Mem. Lang. **54**(4), 554–573 (2006)
31. Davies, C., Katsos, N.: Are speakers and listeners 'only moderately Gricean'? An empirical response to Engelhardt et al. (2006). J. Pragmat. **49**(1), 78–106 (2013)
32. Vogel, A., Bodoia, M., Potts, C., Jurafsky, D.: Emergence of Gricean maxims from multi-agent decision theory. In: Proceedings of the Conference of the North American Chapter of the Association for Computational Linguistics: Human Language Technologies, pp. 1072–1081 (2013)
33. Zuckerman, M., DePaulo, B.M., Rosenthal, R.: Verbal and nonverbal communication of deception. In: Berkowitz, L. (ed.) Advances in Experimental Social Psychology, vol. 14, pp. 1–59. Academic Press (1981)
34. Edwards, C.C.: Detecting deception in conversation: a comparative analysis of communication theories. Thesis report. Texas Tech University (1997)
35. Buller, D.B., Burgoon, J.K.: Interpersonal deception theory. Commun. Theory **6**(3), 203–242 (1996)
36. Martin, M.M., Rubin, R.B.: Development of a communication flexibility measure. South. J. Commun. **59**(2), 171–178 (1994)
37. Bilmes, J.: Ethnomethodology, culture, and implicature: toward an empirical pragmatics. Pragmatics **3**(4), 387–409 (1993)
38. Danziger, E.: On trying and lying: cultural configurations of Grice's maxim of quality. Intercult. Pragmat. **7**(2), 199–219 (2010)
39. Dewaele, J.M.: Interpreting Grice's maxim of quantity: interindividual and situational variation in discourse styles of non-native speakers. In: Cognition in Language Use: Selected Papers from the 7th International Pragmatics Conference, vol. 1, pp. 85–99 (2001)
40. Surian, L.: Are children with autism deaf to Gricean maxims? Cogn. Neuropsychiatry **1**(1), 55–72 (1996)
41. Yeung, L.N., Levine, T.R., Nishiyama, K.: Information manipulation theory and perceptions of deception in Hong Kong. Commun. Rep. **12**(1), 1–11 (1999)
42. McCornack, S.A., Levine, T.R., Solowczuk, K.A., Torres, H.I., Campbell, D.M.: When the alteration of information is viewed as deception: an empirical test of information manipulation theory. Commun. Monogr. **59**, 17–29 (1992)
43. Gosling, S.D., Rentfrow, P.J., Swann, W.B., Jr.: A very brief measure of the big five personality domains. J. Res. Pers. **37**, 504–528 (2003)
44. Braun, V., Clarke, V.: What can "thematic analysis" offer health and wellbeing researchers? Int. J. Qual. Stud. Health Well Being **9**(1), 26152 (2014)

# Planting a Poison SEAD: Using Social Engineering Active Defense (SEAD) to Counter Cybercriminals

Matthew Canham[1](✉) and Juliet Tuthill[2]

[1] Beyond Layer Seven, LLC, Oviedo, FL, USA
mcanham@belay7.com

[2] University of Central Florida, Orlando, FL, USA

**Abstract.** By nearly every metric, the status quo of information security is not working. The interaction matrix of attacker-defender dynamics strongly favors the attacker who only needs to be lucky once. We argue that employing social engineering active defense (SEAD) will be more effective to countering malicious actors than maintaining the traditional passive defensive strategy. The Offensive Countermeasures (OCM) approach to defense advocates for three categories of countermeasures: annoyance, attribution, and attack. Annoyance aims to waste the attacker's time and resources with the objective of not only deterrence but also to increase the probability of detection and attribution. Attribution attempts to identify who is launching the attack. Gathering as much threat intelligence on who the attacker is, provides the best possible defense against future attacks. Finally, attack involves running code on the attacker's system for the purpose of deterrence and attribution. In this work, we advocate for utilizing similar approaches to deny, degrade, and de-anonymize malicious actors by using social engineering tools, tactics, and procedures against the attackers. Rather than fearing the threats posed by synthetic media, cyber defenders should embrace these capabilities by turning these against criminals. Future research should explore ways to implement synthetic media and automated SEAD methods to degrade the capabilities of online malicious actors.

**Keywords:** Social engineering active defense · Offensive countermeasures · Synthetic media · Deep fakes · Cybercrime

## 1 The Security Status Quo is not Working

Over the past five years, the FBI's Internet Crime Complaint Center (IC3) logged over two million cybercrime complaints [1]. Only a very small fraction of these complaints will ever result in an arrest, much less a conviction. One of the many reasons these criminals are rarely convicted is that they generally reside outside the legal jurisdictions of the nations in which their victims are located. Another factor to consider is that humans are consistently the primary vectors targeted by cyber criminals [2]. The current state of information security can therefore be simplified as follows; high numbers of cybercrimes

© The Author(s), under exclusive license to Springer Nature Switzerland AG 2022
D. D. Schmorrow and C. M. Fidopiastis (Eds.): HCII 2022, LNAI 13310, pp. 48–57, 2022.
https://doi.org/10.1007/978-3-031-05457-0_4

are committed, extremely low arrest and conviction rates present little to no deterrence to threat actors, and humans continue to be the attack vector of choice. The traditional models of information protection do not appear to be working. Perhaps it is time for the security community to assume a new approach to these rapidly developing problems.

## 1.1 Remote Online Social Engineering (ROSE) Attacks

Social engineering is the primary method of exploiting the human attack surface. Chris Hadnagy defines social engineering as "any act that influences a person to take an action that may, or may not, be in his or her best interests" [3]. Malicious actors use social engineering tactics, techniques, and procedures (TTPs), to manipulate human targets into taking actions that help the attackers achieve their objectives. Attacker TTPs commonly involve impersonating fellow employees, superiors, and persons in need, as a means of emotionally appealing to the target's psychological processes to circumvent critical thinking or evaluation of the attacker's pretext. Attackers simultaneously leverage known psychological phenomena such as social influence principles to manipulate their targets. Such TTPs may include, but are not limited to, inducing stress through threats or time pressure, inducing sympathy through assistance ploys, appeals to ego through aggrandizement, and exploitation of security policy ignorance. The risk-reward ratio for remote online social engineering (ROSE) ploys such as phishing (email-based attacks), vishing (voice-based attacks), and smishing (SMS text-based attacks) is so favorable for cybercriminals that this remains their preferred mode of operation [4]. By launching these attacks from remote locations, often from beyond legal jurisdiction, threat actors assume little risk even if their attack is detected. Technologically mediated communication affords attackers the ability to shape the attack environment and impersonate known associates while exerting a significant degree of perception management against their targets. For example, lateral phishing leverages the saved contact list of a compromised account to launch a "pivot attack" toward a previous contact. by assuming the identity of the compromised account, the attacker shapes the perception of the target to convince them that the phishing email is originating from the trusted contact, thus substantially increasing the chances of a successful attack.

## 1.2 Automated Social Engineering

Automation is a significant ROSE force multiplier because it both increases the attacker's ability to scale and adds capabilities for shaping target perceptions. [5]. Researchers have demonstrated these enhanced capabilities through several projects, examples include the following. The Social Engineering eXposure Index demonstrates the feasibility of automating the reconnaissance stage in social engineering attacks through scripted collection of open-source intelligence [6, 7]. Automated Twitter bots capable of launching spear-phishing attacks demonstrate automated social engineering attack capabilities [8]. Chatbot social engineering has progressed beyond proof-of-concept as there has been an 820% increase in chatbot-enabled gift-card scams since the COVID-19 pandemic shift to working from home [9]. The sophistication of these attacks is increasing as recently shown by GPT-3 generation of spear-phishing emails which are more effective than those generated by humans in some cases [10].

The emergence, prevalence, and incorporation of synthetic media into ROSE attacks is a recent trend that is causing concern among the security community [11]. Synthetic media is broadly defined as the artificial manipulation, modification, and production of information and includes a wide spectrum of communications media from audio-video deepfakes to text-based chatbots [5]. This new capability massively increases ROSE attacker capability by significantly increasing their ability to impersonate others, thus substantially increasing the number of attacks that they can launch while also elevating pretext believability. Among the growing capabilities and complexities synthetic media presents, deepfake audio and video are perhaps the most concerning. This technology repurposes existing audio or video clips to create digital puppets that can be manipulated through an actor's movements and speech. Using an existing file, a generative adversarial network (GAN) creates a synthetic visual or auditory puppet (synpuppet) that can be manipulated by a human puppet master's movements or speech. This technology has been employed in cinematic entertainment for many years and is used in special effects; however, the recent proliferation of this technology on open-source software repositories means that sophisticated deepfake audio and video are becoming more accessible, therefore deepfake content can be easily generated by threat actors seeking to impersonate unique targets. Recent examples include an attempt to falsify evidence during a custody hearing [12], and multiple uses of deepfake audio to impersonate executives during vishing attacks [13, 14].

### 1.3 Is the Best Defense a Good Offense?

John Strand, the CEO of Black Hills Security, advocates for the employment of Offensive Countermeasures (OCM) in his book by that name [15]. The authors argue that the "old strategies of security have failed us and will continue to fail us unless we start becoming more offensive in our defensive tactics." To these ends, they present three categories of Offensive Countermeasures (OCM): annoyance, attribution, and attack. Annoyance aims to waste the attacker's time and resources with the objective of not only deterrence but also to increase the probability of detection and attribution. The next category, attribution, attempts to identify who is launching the attack. Gathering as much threat intelligence on who is behind the attack provides the best possible defense against future attacks. Attack is the final category of OCM and involves running code on the attacker's system for the purpose of deterrence and attribution. Offensive countermeasures raise many legitimate concerns among skeptics and critics, not the least of which are legality and collateral damage. By "counter-hacking" a defender runs the risk of crossing legal boundaries that can put them and their organizations in jeopardy. Considering cybercriminals often utilize third-party proxies to launch their attacks, collateral damage is another serious consideration. The owners of the systems launching attacks are often themselves victims of the attackers, unaware of their systems being compromised. Hacking against these systems with the intention of causing some degree of damage has the potential to inflict harm on innocent third parties. Accounting for this, the authors advocate for poison (a dangerous substance used defensively against predators) rather than venom (a dangerous substance injected into prey by a predator).

The above considerations apply to information technology and the employment technology-based defenses and actions. This poses the question of what degree these considerations apply to social engineering (human-focused) attacks. An in-depth discussion of the domestic and international legal implications of offensive countermeasures is beyond the scope of this work; however, we propose that automated and synthetic social engineering TTPs may be used counter-offensively by defenders as a more effective counter to cyber threat actors.

## 2 Social Engineering Active Defense (SEAD)

The emergence of synthetic media has generated a significant level of anxiety within the security community around how these technologies will be used by attackers [5]. Rather than fearing these technologies, defenders should embrace them as additional capabilities to be employed proactively as a defense against ROSE attacks. We propose employing social engineering active defense (SEAD) to deter ROSE attacks, by leveraging synthetic media technology enabled active countermeasures. A SEAD approach leverages one or more of the OCM approaches of annoyance, attribution, and attack to deny, disrupt, and deter cyber threat actors in their efforts. Furthermore, this approach differs from traditional cyber deception in that SEAD deliberately seeks to exploit the cognitive vulnerabilities of attackers for the purposes of annoyance, attribution, and attack.

It should be noted that when employing any variation of active defense, defenders should be mindful of any and all legal regulations and statutes to avoid crossing into criminal territory. This point of caution withstanding, SEAD assumes less potential to cause third-party collateral damage than technologically implemented OCM because SEAD directly engages the attacker.

### 2.1 SEAD Annoyance

If you have ever received an unsolicited phone call from a scammer, you may have wished to impose all manner of ill will upon them. Roger Anderson took this to a new level when he developed the Jolly Roger Bot (JRB). The JRB uses a series of pre-recorded voice clips to respond to a scam caller. From the user's perspective, the interaction occurs in the form of an unrecognized call, which the user then redirects to the JRB app. Jolly Roger users have the option of listening to call recordings later to ensure the bots have accurately detected spammers. From the caller's perspective, the app answers the phone appearing to be a human. The bot responds to the sound of the caller's voice with pre-recorded sound clips of random statements. Since the software uses human voice recordings, the responses effectively appear to be human, rather than synthetic. This voice bot has been so effective at wasting scam callers' time that some have remained on the phone conversing with the bot for 20 min or more [16]. One recorded interaction captured the caller in conversation with an apparent supervisor, during which the supervisor made the statement "Whenever we get these (voice chatbots)… we have to write the phone number down and then we get them sent to our dialer guy so that we don't get charged for it" [17]. Such outcomes advocate for the effectiveness of this approach in countering voice-based scams.

As Strand et al. (2017) state that annoyance "is about wasting the attacker's time" and resources. Some security-minded individuals have turned this into a sport, known as "scambaiting". Comedian James Veitch has given a series of TED talks about his interactions with email and phone scammers and his efforts to hilariously waste their time [18]. He has been so successful in his efforts that scammers have pleaded with him to stop emailing them [19]. These examples illustrate the potential for SEAD techniques to consume malicious actor resources; however, these countermeasures are being carried out mostly for the entertainment of the researchers. We ask, what might be possible if such OCMs are taken to the next level through AI-driven exploitation of attacker cognitive biases?

Some researchers have proposed employing Oppositional Human Factors as a means of leveraging known design principles against attackers to degrade their efforts [20]. This work explored how cognitive bias influences the perceptions and performance of red team security auditors. Researchers discovered that informing research participants that deception would be used in the study environment not only degraded red teamers' performance but did so in specific and predictable ways. For example, researchers exploited the confirmation bias of red teamers by informing them that a subset of systems were honey pots when in truth all the systems were legitimate. Presented with this information, the red teamers uncovered several false positives, which were systems that they suspected to be illegitimate. The participants even went to great lengths in collecting evidence that these resources were false, thus diverting their attention away from legitimate targets [20]. Covert Impairments have also been proposed as intentional mechanisms to deter and degrade attackers through the employment of subtle forcing functions to "guide" attacker actions in directions that are advantageous for the defenders [21].

We propose that leveraging existent technologies such as the JRB, combined with covert impairments that deliberately target the cognitive biases of attackers, could be a highly effective deterrent against human hackers that use social engineering tactics to compromise their targets. Such an approach would also present a likely counter to automated attacks in a manner demonstrated by a video depicting two chatbots in a conversation [22]. Furthermore, if such techniques are employed strategically, they could provide valuable threat intelligence about the attackers.

## 2.2  SEAD Attribution

Several researchers have proposed that honey pots could be repurposed to infer personality traits and other individual characteristics of attackers [23]. Employing a series of forced actions, similar in nature to those techniques used by magicians, defenders may be able to create an illusion of choice for the attackers that causes them to reveal individually attributable characteristics [24]. Sometimes referred to as 'inference attacks', behavioral actions [25], or cognitive preferences [26] can reveal characteristics of an unidentified individual. Malin (2021) argues that Locard's Exchange Principle applies to digital artifacts and that every interaction within and across digital space will necessarily leave behind digital trace evidence which can be later analyzed. Aggregated, these digital traces give way to the Watanabe Principle of Digital Artifact Exchange which posits that these can be leveraged to derive attribution to a particular offender [27, 28]. If such exchanges can be deliberately manipulated or induced, it may be possible to create 'Cognitive Fingerprints' through a series of 'covert games', as some suggest [26]. Wixey refers to this process as finding the person behind the machine [29]. While there is still much work to be done within this domain, these SEAD tactics focus on actions taken within the defender's perimeter, a more aggressive posture might carry the fight beyond friendly territory by taking actions against criminal-controlled assets.

## 2.3 SEAD Attack

An excellent example of a successful SEAD attack is the Honey Phish Project. In this project, researcher Robbie Gallagher, set up several fake email addresses to act as mailbox honey pots for phishing scammers. These Honey Phish would automatically reply to phishing emails with an email containing a uniquely generated link, that when clicked, generated client-side browser fingerprinting, sending identifiable information back to the researcher [30]. Another example can be found in the scambaiting community with a researcher going by the handle Engineer Man, who used a Python bot to insert false usernames and passwords into a malicious website to the point of filling up the scammer's database [31].

Gift-card scams have increased substantially since the remote working trend due to the COVID pandemic. These scams often follow a similar script of the criminal employing a pretext to convince the victim to purchase gift cards, scratch off the coating obscuring the redemption code on the back and sending an image of this code to the scammer, who uses this code to obtain the funds on the card. A potential SEAD attack to counter these gift card scams might include embedding a tracking pixel that relays attributable information about the attacker's device, location, and possibly their identity back to defenders. One reason these examples are likely to enjoy a high level of success is that the attackers do not expect that they themselves will become victims of an attack. We again strongly advise any researchers exploring these lines of SEAD to consult with legal experts before conducting this type of research.

# 3   Future Directions, Research Questions and Challenges

We posit that active defense against malicious social engineering attacks will be more effective in countering malicious attacks than the status quo approach of continuing to rely on passive defense strategies. To shift the balance of power back in favor of the defenders, future research into SEAD should pursue the following research avenues.

## 3.1   Identifying an Attack

Among the more formidable challenges to implementing automated SEAD approach will be detecting that a malicious social engineering attack is occurring, as opposed to a benign interaction. Indeed, the overarching challenge of countering social engineering is that successful attacks are frequently not recognized as malicious attacks. This makes automating the identification process extremely challenging. Some researchers have identified a potential bottleneck that all social engineering attacks must pass through, by either asking for private information or directing the target to take an adverse action [32]. Understanding that this conversational bottleneck exists allows automated natural language processing (NLP) algorithms to constrain focus on conversational features within this scope. Other researchers have explored incorporating NLP with other algorithms to detect grammar anomalies and check for the presence of social influence principles [33]. Another approach may be to create digital cognitive clones of human operators to emulate human responses to social engineering attempts [34]. A significant amount of work remains to be explored within this field.

## 3.2 Annoyance

Once a potential attack is identified, the question of how to best degrade attacker capabilities comes in focus. Future research in this area should ask to what extent can automated SEAD bots waste the time and resources of attackers through social engineering and covert impairments? What factors will most degrade attacker capabilities? To what extent can voice-bots deceive attackers into believing that the bots are humans? Which characteristics of the voice-bots most contribute to this deception? In this effort, more investigative efforts should explore ways in which Cialdini's principles of influence and magnetizers (mysterious, self-relevant, and unfinished) may enhance the efficacy of SEAD annoyance efforts [35]. A recent study on phishing susceptibility found that simulated phishing emails which included a greater number of these magnetizer techniques resulted in substantially higher click-rates than did emails employing fewer magnetizers [36]. We suggest that these same techniques might be employed against attackers to consume more of their attention, time, and resources, and potentially lead them to reveal attributable characteristics about themselves.

## 3.3 Attribution

Previous work in human side-channel attacks and forensic linguistics reveals that significant insights may be derived from data that appears to be innocuous [4]. Future work should seek to maximize attributable inferences and identify which types of data are most likely to reveal crucial insights. A few questions that researchers might explore include the following. Which attacker attributes are most likely to be uncovered by various SEAD measures? To what extent can the attacker's psychological characteristics and cognitive biases be used against them to reveal critical threat intelligence? Which TTPs will most effectively allow defenders to cognitively fingerprint attackers? Which forms of digital trace evidence are most likely to be uncovered by SEAD bots? Beyond identifying who potential attackers are, it might be possible to reveal more about them by utilizing TTPs that go "beyond the perimeter" of defenders' systems.

## 3.4 Attack

Future work on SEAD attacks could potentially move in two parallel tracks, one which focuses on improving technological capabilities, and another which focuses on legal and regulatory questions. Improving technical countermeasures that will interfere with criminal activities without causing collateral damage to innocent third parties should be the priority for technology focused research. Legal research should clarify how existing domestic and international legal frameworks might better accommodate offensive countermeasures, or alternatively how legislation can be passed to better accommodate SEAD actions that extend into criminal systems to deter future malicious actions and to assist law enforcement. Questions to be answered include, to what extent will SEAD methodologies fall within the scope of computer abuse regulations? How can SEAD TTPs stay within the boundaries of being legal while still presenting an effective counter to malicious cyber actors?

The status quo of information security appears to be failing. It is time for the security community to adopt new approaches. Social Engineering Active Defense (SEAD) represents such an approach. Exploring these lines of research will allow the security community to proactively mitigate malicious attacks and potentially tilt the balance of power in the defenders' favor.

# References

1. FBI: Internet Crime Complaint Center (IC3). Internet Crime Report 2020. Washington, DC (2021b)
2. Verizon: DBIR 2021 Data Breach Investigations Report. Verizon, New York (2021)
3. Hadnagy, C.: Social Engineering: The Science of Human Hacking. John Wiley & Sons, New York (2018)
4. Wixey, M.: Every ROSE has its Thorn: The Dark Art of Remote Online Social Engineering. Black Hat USA, Las Vegas (2018)
5. Canham, M.: Deepfake Social Engineering: Creating a Framework for Synthetic Media Social Engineering. Black Hat USA, Las Vegas (2021)
6. Wilkerson, W.S., Levy, Y., Kiper, J.R., Snyder, M.: Towards a development of a Social Engineering eXposure Index (SEXI) Using Publicly Available Personal Information. In: 2017 KSU Conference on Cybersecurity Education, Research, and Practice. Kennesaw State University, Kennesaw (2017)
7. Wilkerson, W.S.: Development of a Social Engineering eXposure Index (SEXI) Using Open-Source Personal Information. Doctoral Dissertation, Nova Southeastern University, Fort Lauderdale-Davie (2021)
8. Seymour, J., Tully, P.: Generative models for spear phishing posts on social media. arXiv preprint arXiv:1802.05196 (2018)
9. % Jump in E-Gift Card Bot Attacks since COVID-19 Lockdowns began. https://www.techrepublic.com/article/820-jump-in-e-gift-card-bot-attacks-since-covid-19-lockdownsbegan/. Accessed 21 Mar 2021
10. Lim, E., Tan, G., Hock, T., Lee, T.: Turing in a Box: Applying Artificial Intelligence as a Service to Targeted Phishing and Defending Against AI-Generated Attacks. Black Hat USA, Las Vegas (2021)
11. FBI: Malicious Actors Almost Certainly Will Leverage Synthetic Content for Cyber and Foreign Influence Operations. Federal Bureau of Investigations Private Industry Notification. Washington, DC (2021a)
12. 'Deepfake' Audio Evidence Used in UK Court to Discredit Dubai Dad, 26 October 2021. https://www.thenationalnews.com/uae/courts/deepfake-audio-evidence-used-in-uk-court-to-discredit-dubai-dad-1.975764
13. Fraudsters Used AI to Mimic CEO's Voice in Unusual Cybercrime Case. https://www.wsj.com/articles/fraudsters-use-ai-to-mimic-ceos-voice-in-unusual-cybercrime-case-115671 57402. Accessed 29 July 2020

14. Fraudsters Cloned Company Director's Voice in $35 Million Bank Heist, Police Find. https://www.forbes.com/sites/thomasbrewster/2021/10/14/huge-bank-fraud-uses-deep-fake-voice-tech-to-steal-millions/?sh=35955ba77559. Accessed 14 Oct 2021

15. Strand, J., Asadoorian, P., Robish, E., Donnelly, B., Galbraith, B.: Offensive Countermeasures: The Art of Active Defense. CreateSpace Independent Publishing Platform, Scotts Valley (2017)

16. Telephone Spam/Scam Problem? Bring in the Robots. https://www.youtube.com/watch?v=UXVJ4JQ3SUw. Accessed 02 Jan 2022

17. Absolute Proof that Jolly Roger Telephone is Disrupting the Vacation Cruise Telemarketers. https://www.youtube.com/watch?v=ezZ2V1CH32E. Accessed 02 Jan 2022

18. This is What Happens When You Reply to Spam Email. TED Global Geneva. https://www.ted.com/talks/james_veitch_this_is_what_happens_when_you_reply_to_spam_email?language=sc#t-149006. Accessed 07 Dec 2021

19. Ultimate troll. https://www.youtube.com/watch?v=3MHDDSekvcE. Accessed 22 Dec 2021

20. Gutzwiller, R., Ferguson-Walter, K., Fugate, S., Rogers, A.: "Oh, Look, A Butterfly!" A framework for distracting attackers to improve cyber defense. In: Proceedings of the Human Factors and Ergonomics Society Annual Meeting, vol. 62, no. 1, pp. 272–276. Sage Publications, Los Angeles (2018)

21. Monaco, J.V.: Bug or feature? Covert impairments to human computer interaction. In: Proceedings of the 2020 CHI Conference on Human Factors in Computing Systems, pp. 1–15 (2020)

22. AI vs. AI. Two Chatbots Talking to Each Other. https://www.youtube.com/watch?v=WnzlbyTZsQY. Accessed 22 Dec 2021

23. Odemis, M., Yucel, C., Koltuksuz, A., Ozbilgin, G.: Suggesting a honeypot design to capture hacker psychology, personality and sophistication. In: 13th International Conference on Cyber Warfare and Security. Academic Conferences, Washington, DC (2018)

24. Macknik, S., Martinez-Conde, S., Blakeslee, S.: Sleights of Mind: What the Neuroscience of Magic Reveals about our Everyday Deceptions. Henry Holt and Company, New York (2010)

25. Naini, F.M., Unnikrishnan, J., Thiran, P., Vetterli, M.: Where you are is who you are: user identification by matching statistics. IEEE Trans. Inf. Forensics Secur. 11(2), 358–372 (2015)

26. Abramson, M.: Cognitive fingerprints. In: 2015 AAAI Spring Symposium Series. Palo Alto (2015)

27. Watanabe, D.: Digital behavioral criminalistics: the art and science. In: Proceedings of the 9th Annual Mid-Atlantic INLETS: Violent Crimes and Terrorism Trends, Washington, DC (2018)

28. Malin, C.: Digital behavioral criminalistics to elucidate the cyber pathway to intended violence. In: Meloy, J.R., Hoffmann, J. (eds.) International Handbook of Threat Assessment, 2nd edn. Oxford University Press, Oxford (2021)

29. Wixey, M.: Betrayed by the Keyboard: How What You Type Can Give You Away

30. Where Do the Phishers Live? Collecting Phishers' Geographic Locations from Automated Honeypots. ShmooCon 2016. https://shmoo.gitbook.io/2016-shmoocon-proceedings/one_track_mind/06_where_do_the_phishers_live. Accessed 07 Dec 2021

31. Showing, A.: Craigslist Scammer Who's Boss Using Python. https://www.youtube.com/watch?v=UtNYzv8gLbs. Accessed 07 Dec 2021

32. Sawa, Y., Bhakta, R., Harris, I.G., Hadnagy, C.: Detection of social engineering attacks through natural language processing of conversations. In: 2016 IEEE Tenth International Conference on Semantic Computing (ICSC), pp. 262–265. IEEE, New York (2016)

33. Lansley, M., Mouton, F., Kapetanakis, S., Polatidis, N.: SEADer++: social engineering attack detection in online environments using machine learning. J. Inf. Telecommun. 4(3), 346–362 (2020)

34. Golovianko, M., Gryshko, S., Terziyan, V., Tuunanen, T.: Towards digital cognitive clones for the decision-makers: adversarial training experiments. Procedia Comput. Sci. **180**, 180–189 (2021)
35. Cialdini, R.: Pre-Suasion: A Revolutionary Way to Influence and Persuade. Simon and Schuster, New York (2016)
36. Canham, M., Dawkins, S., Jacobs, J.: Manuscript Under Review

# Using Augmented Cognition to Examine Differences in Online Handwriting Recognition for Native and Non-native Writers

Mariam Doliashvili[✉], Michael-Brian C. Ogawa, and Martha E. Crosby

University of Hawaii at Manoa, Honolulu, HI 96822, USA
{mariamd,ogawam,crosby}@hawaii.edu

**Abstract.** The handwritten recognition (HWR) is a complex task with variety of challenges associated with natural language, variety in the styles of writing, variety and nuances of alphabets etc. The core research in handwritten recognition focuses around Latin alphabet and corresponding languages. However, differences between the languages using Latin as their main script are still major: from changed letter frequencies to additional letters. Additionally, handwriting practices and styles are not developed consistently within the same language; for example - cursive vs print calligraphy. As a result of globalization estimated 50% of world's population speaks second language [1]. Researching characteristics of non-native handwriting has been done by various educational and second language research purposes but remains largely unaddressed in the context of augmented cognition using online handwritten recognition. We researched differences and similarities of online handwriting between native and non-native speakers of English, Georgian, Chinese and Korean speakers. We have also examined related research for Arabic, Italian and Malay handwritings. As a result, we have identified key characteristics of non-native speakers' distinguishing from the native ones. In addition, we have identified differences based on writers' individual maturity with the second language.

**Keywords:** Handwritten recognition · Dynamic handwriting · Natural language processing

## 1 Introduction

For the world's languages, there are four broad classes of writing systems [2], also known as - orthographies. An "alphabet" is a type of writing system that includes a symbol for each sound in a language that is, for both consonants and vowels. European languages utilize the Greek, Cyrillic - Ukrainian, Bulgarian, etc., or Latin (Roman) alphabets - English, German, French, etc. The Latin alphabet is exceptionally broad and is used for numerous languages all over the world, not simply those spoken in Europe. The name "alphabet" itself is derived from the first two letters of the Greek alphabet, alpha and beta. Which are derived from Phoenician/Arabic words for "ox" and "home" respectively [3].

Second category of languages just depict the language's consonants. Abjad is a form of writing system that belongs to this category. Two well-known examples with numerous

D. D. Schmorrow and C. M. Fidopiastis (Eds.): HCII 2022, LNAI 13310, pp. 58–68, 2022.
https://doi.org/10.1007/978-3-031-05457-0_5

speakers are Hebrew and Arabic. In truth, vowels are only partially represented in these systems, and they are derived by additional constructions. These systems came to form the limitations on representation of vowels because most languages have a limited or smaller number of vowels compared to consonants.

Third type of writing system include languages that use a single symbol to indicate syllables. For example, a symbol for groups of consonant and vowel (CV), a consonant followed with a vowel and a consonant (CVC), a consonant followed with a vowel that's followed with two consonants (CVCC), etc. This type of system is known as a syllabary. The most well-known are Japanese and Korean. For example, in Korean 뉴스(news) contains two CV syllables, 꽃(flower) contains one CVC syllable, etc. As a matter of fact, Japanese uses two such writing systems, Hiragana and Katakana. In addition, Japanese is based on number of Chinese-derived characters known as Kanji. Syllabaries operate effectively given that such languages tend to have a small number of syllables. These languages do not enable complicated consonant clusters at the beginning or end of a syllable, the writing system usually cannot accommodate such complications [4]. In addition, there are less number of vowels and consonants used overall (Fig. 1).

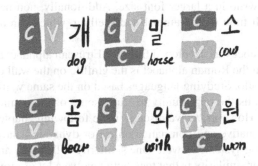

**Fig. 1.** Syllable creation in Korean language

As for the fourth category of writing systems - Chinese is the best example to describe this type. This form of system is known as logographic, from "logo" which in Greek means "word". Logographic writing system expresses each word with a symbol. A logographic system, used for a language expression, comprises thousands of symbols - also referred to as "characters". Chinese letters, in fact, are a blend of word meaning and pronunciation (Fig. 2).

**Fig. 2.** The evolution of the Chinese writing system [5]

Latin alphabet, also called Roman alphabet, is the most widely used alphabetic writing system in the world. It is the standard script of the English language and is used in more than 100 other languages [6].

Non-native handwriting is a term used to describe writing that does not originate from the country in which the language being written is spoken. In many cases, non-native handwriting can be difficult to read for native speakers of the language. This is often due to differences in spelling conventions and grammar usage between the two languages.

There are several differences between native and non-native handwriting when it comes to people being native to different writing systems from their second language proficiency. One of the most noticeable differences is the way that people write letters. Non-native writers often have a tendency to write letters that are more block-like, while native writers have a tendency to write letters that are more connected and fluid [7]. Another difference is the way that people form letters. Non-native writers often have a tendency to form letters that are more rigid and angular, while native writers have a tendency to form letters that are more curved and flowing. Additionally, non-native writers often have a tendency to write in a smaller font size, while native writers often have a tendency to write in a larger font size. Additionally, non-native speakers may have a more difficult time with grammar and spelling, which can also be reflected in their handwriting.

The Roman alphabet was developed from the Etruscan alphabet about 500 BC. The earliest inscription in the Roman alphabet is the graffito on the wall of a men's lavatory at the Temple of Apollo. Studying languages based on the same writing system and the same alphabet gives us the opportunity to study some of the common characteristics of bilingual writers. However, as we discuss in the following chapters, there are some similarities between native and non-native online or dynamic handwriting for writers using different writing systems as well. One similarity is that they are both written in a cursive style. Another similarity is that they both involve a lot of movement and are not very precise. There are many similarities in writing different languages using the same alphabet. For example, the letter "a" is always written as "a" in any language and the letter "z" is always written as "z" in most languages. Additionally, there are slight or no variations for majority of the letters from the Latin alphabet. Occasionally, new letters are introduced.

Advantages of analyzing the differences for native and non-native writers come from the various factors regarding online handwriting that records and provides more information to analyze compared to static handwriting:

1. Static handwriting recognition is performed by scanning a physical piece of paper with a hand-written note on it. Online handwriting recognition is performed by a tablet, mobile phone, or another digital device.
2. Online/Dynamic (performed on an electronic device) handwriting recognition is a more accurate recognition process because it takes into account the features describing the individuals writing style, by capturing the angle and inclination of the pen, and the pressure of the pen on the device [8]. Static handwriting recognition is not as accurate because it does not take into account all of these factors and there

could be additional factors about the physical conditions of the paper hindering the recognition process.

3. Static handwriting recognition can only recognize handwritten notes that are written on a specific type of paper. Online handwriting recognition can recognize handwritten notes that are written on any type of device.

4. Static handwriting recognition is a slower recognition process, as it needs pre-processing for extracting the relevant data [9].

To sum up, there are drastic differences between different writing systems indicating vastly different expected behavior of writers. However, given that the writers have unique individual habits there are still similarities between their handwriting in different writing systems. Additionally, even though some of the languages use same type of writing systems, the variety of the alphabets within the writing system poses additional challenge for handwritten recognition. The later also helps to study important similarities of non-native and native writing that we can utilize for better performance of recognition algorithms. As a part of the novel augmented cognition research, we utilize the advantages of researching online handwriting over static handwriting to recognize the key factors useful for handwriting recognition.

## 2  Background

Online handwritten recognition can be influenced various factors, especially regarding the writing style and speed of the process. Observations show that these factors are influenced by:

1. How long the writer has been practicing writing using this specific language
2. The complexity of transition from the previous language
3. The difficulty level of the language acquisition for the specific language, etc.

Given that examining native vs non-native speakers' writing style is a novel direction there is still need for researching the individual nuances of the way each language affects to the writers' style development. However, we can examine the similarities across several languages utilizing different alphabets and/or writing systems. To achieve this goal, we have surveyed the research related to differences in native vs. non-native speakers pronunciation and the way they form sentences [10]. Additionally we have examined handwritten character recognition methods for Arabic [11], Chinese [12], Pashto [13] and English languages.

Children learn languages with no prior experience. In the early stage of language learning when children start speaking about 50 words are acquired. At this point there is no syntax (word order) or grammar (plurals, verb tenses, etc.) being expressed yet. Some languages have more complex syntax or morphology that takes longer for children to master. For example Danish children learn language much slower compared to other languages [14]. Similarly, the impact of a non-native language on the writing process may be greater for students who are less proficient in the target language. Therefore, to understand the effect of second language or non-native behavior on writing diverse experience group of writers as well as cross-language examination is necessary.

Native                                    Foreigner

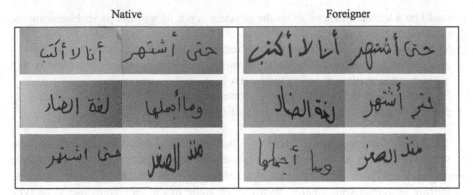

**Fig. 3.** Arabic handwriting of native vs non-native writers [11]

Arabic alphabet and calligraphy are a good example to study, as its uniqueness makes the learners go through various steps for developing their handwriting style (Fig. 3) [15].

The stages of written language learning and handwriting acquisition place different demands on the writer, and the relationship between body functions and handwriting performance varies between languages and stages of learning. The paper - "Relationship between body functions and Arabic handwriting performance at different acquisition stages" investigated the link between linguistic, visual-motor integration (VMI), and motor coordination (MC) functions and Arabic handwriting by analyzing two levels of handwriting acquisition [15]. The variation in handwriting speed in both grades was explained by handwriting automaticity. Improved VMI performance increased the likelihood of having good legibility in second grade but not in fourth grade. The body functions associated with Arabic handwriting differ depending on the stage of acquisition. As a result, the handwriting evaluation should be tailored to the students' developmental stage [15].

A research paper from 2005 investigated the class characteristics in English handwriting of three ethnic groups in Singapore: Chinese, Malay, and Indian. They looked at letter designs, letter spacing, pen lifts, and decorative elements, among other factors. They used a two-by-three chi-square analysis to compare the frequency with which each feature occurred in the groups in order to identify the distinctive features unique to each group. Their findings confirmed the influence of the native language writing system on English handwriting [16]. Six class factors have been recognized, and they were attributed to the habitual effect of writing in their own native language: Chinese, Tamil, and Arabic. Not only they were able to determine the class characteristics in English handwriting of different groups, they have implicated the ability of identifying nationality or ethnic origins of writers.

## 3 Motivation

Researching differences and similarities for native and non-native writers can substantially aid in online handwriting recognition. Handwriting recognition is a complex task with numerous variables affecting the accuracy of the outcome. Factors such as the size, stroke directions, shapes, and slant of letters; the spacing between letters and words; and the presence or absence of flourishes can all affect how well a handwriting recognition system works.

Nowadays common method used to improve the accuracy of handwriting recognition is to use a large database of handwritten samples to train the system. Most of the recent solutions are based on deep learning algorithms. This allows the system to learn the specific characteristics of the writer's handwriting. There are also various hybrid methods of using deep learning with more traditional natural language processing methods [17].

Latest developments in technology made tablets, phones and other widely available devices equipped with pen and other writing means. There is also significant amount of software offering online handwriting services. Therefore, there are more and more opportunities for studying handwriting characteristics that were not available just for static writing (pen on paper). The study of fine motor movements is carried out using intrinsic properties that measure precise motion features extracted from digitally recorded phrases. For hand motor performance quantification, we factor the basic elements of writing, such as strokes, letters and components.

Enriching the databases with additional descriptive information about the writers writing history and affiliation with other languages, gives an excellent opportunity for improving the model outcome with less information to be extracted by the HWR systems. Considering that our previous study on handwriting signature showed that there is significant information to gain whether the writing is done by the original signature author or it is a learned behavior for performing a skilled forgery, this study also focuses on analyzing the pen pressure as writing second language can be considered in the same angle of learned behaviors to imitate others' writing [8].

Additionally, to aiding with HWR task, differences between writing styles of non-native speakers and native speakers is standalone fascinating research topic for Augmented cognition. Given the fact that there are numerous studies focusing on speech/accent differences for native and non-native speakers and its demonstrated applicability to a diverse set of tasks from speech recognition to aiding with improving clarity for non-native speakers. Non-native accents can pose a challenge for listeners when trying to understand what is being said. Non-native accents have been demonstrated in studies to have a negative impact on speech recognition accuracy [18], speech comprehension [19], and listener perceptions of speakers' comprehensibility [20]. Non-native accents are generally less understandable than native accents due to more pronunciation problems and unfamiliar phonetic elements. According to the research, there are a number of factors that contribute to listeners' difficulties comprehending non-native speakers. This provides us with a strong incentive to search for such elements in handwriting, characterize them, and indicate their influence levels on handwriting recognition.

Moreover, the paper about "Detecting English Writing Styles For Non Native Speakers" [10] shows some interesting observations on the similarity between different languages measured by the similarity of their users English typing styles. This technique could be used to show some well-known facts about languages as in grouping them into families, which our experiments also include.

## 4  Analysis/Methodology

Examining the online handwriting of population including languages from the all three writing systems as well as the ones belonging to the same writing system but different alphabets is not possible by currently available dynamic handwriting datasets. We are anticipating that the wide distribution and popularity of technological devices like tablets and phones will naturally lead to making more samples of online handwriting available for research. For this preliminary study we opt in to collect dataset from wider range of writing styles, rather than collecting more samples for the same popular languages that are already widely studied for handwritten recognition tasks.

For this study we have managed to collect dataset for four different languages both from native and non-native speakers: English, Chinese, Korean and Georgian.

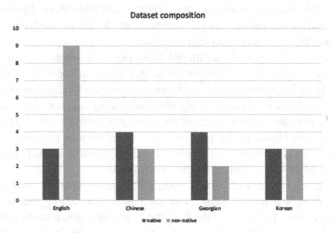

**Fig. 4.**  Sample population

On Fig. 4 the size of population sample is shown. It includes three writing systems. Additionally Georgian and English both use alphabets though Georgian writing system is based on Georgian alphabet while English is based on Latin.

It is also worth mentioning that the writers of different language had different experiences and maturity with their non-native languages.

## 5  Results

We discussed in the analysis section the advantages given by analyzing dynamic handwriting over static handwriting. Therefore, we measured the features available for the online handwriting component: speed, pen pressure, letter/character size, pen ups, stroke count.

We compared the native and non-native speakers on two tasks:

1. Writing a simple word (<5 letters length or 1 character)
2. Writing a simple paragraph (<5 lines length, <25 words)

A stroke is the basic component of writing movements, defined by points of minimal curvilinear velocity [21], a component is the segment between two successive pen lifts, letter does not need a definition for alphabet and for the sake of this experiment we also considered one kanji character as a letter. The dynamic handwriting parameters associated with strokes, components, and letters - such as duration, length, pen pressure, and so on - may also reveal information about a writer's level of automation and fluency.

The three main types of online handwriting differences for second language speakers: speed, pen ups, stroke count. We have also included letter or character size in our measurements.

The first task showed similar results for all the characteristics besides the speed, by Chinese being slower to perform for all the non-native writers. 1.6 speed of the native writer.

Second task results are shown in the Fig. 5. Each number on the y scale represents the ratio of non-native speakers' measurement over the native speakers measurement.

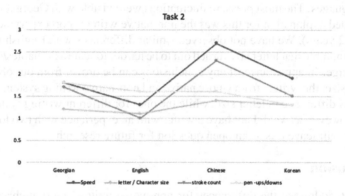

**Fig. 5.** Comparison of the handwriting characteristics of (non-native writers)/(native writers)

The most drastically difference is shown for non-native speakers writing speed against the native speakers of Chinese – 2.7, however the ratio between the stroke amount is 1.5. This can be explained with Kanji being based on short strokes. The native speakers also have to use the equal amount of pen ups, if they follow the writing rules. However, because of the speed of writing sometimes they omit a few pen-ups. It is important to notice that Handwriting recognition systems for Chinese do take into account the stroke count. Therefore, knowing the writer is non-native and given the ratio, we can accurately calculate the stroke count that otherwise would be obscured.

Korean being was the second language by having the most differences between the native and non-native writers speed - 1.9. This could be explained by using both letters, and syllables made of letters in Korean writing system. Stroke count and difference in speed can be explained with similar reasons as the ones for Chinese. Though Korean native writers used less strokes compared to non-natives per syllable. It did not show as much difference as the Chinese writers overall, as one Korean syllable needs significantly less strokes than a Chinese character.

Georgian had the most difference between pen-ups. Georgian writing system is taught through alphabet at first and as a second step cursive handwriting is introduced. The native writers in our sample had an influence of the cursive writing, however the non-native speakers have not.

English had the least difference in ratios that can also be biased since most of the individuals from our experiment sample had the longest experience with English as a second language.

For each language in our sample population non-native speakers used larger letters and characters, which leads us to conclude that scaling should be done separately for native and non-native handwriting for it to not affect the recognition task negatively.

The only scenario where there was no noticeable difference between native and non-native speakers was for the 1st task and from writers of the same writing system (Georgian and English).

We have also examined pen pressure graphs between native and non-native writers. For the languages based on short strokes like Chinese and Korean, the pressure value is high in the beginning of the stroke and decreases gradually. The flow was natural for both of these languages. The most pressure fluctuations were visible with Georgian language. Our implicated explanation for this was the non-native writers short experience with the alphabet (<2 years). We have not observed similar differences with English writing.

It is also notable that letter size turned out to be harder to scale as syllables/Characters tend to be larger in appearance. If any conclusions can be drown from our observations of the letter size, the writers from whose native and non-native writing system is same do not show any difference in letter size, while the ones for different writing system tend to be larger. However, as we did not have a writer with an experience with two logographic systems, we will leave this as an open question for future research.

## 6   Conclusion

Our research addressed the differences for non-native writers' motion characteristics, opposed to the ones of the native writers of a language. We have approached the problem from Augmented Cognition perspective, and we have used the features of online/dynamic handwriting performed on a tablet. There are three main types of online handwriting differences for second language speakers: speed, pen ups, stroke count. Since these features are used in handwriting recognition, we conclude that speakers' origin (native vs non-native) can affect the handwriting recognition process negatively if not being processed separately. As we examined the pen pressure, pen inclination, etc. does not affect in the context of second language writing skills. The most difference between the writing speed distinguished the native speakers of logographic writing system from the non-native ones. The least differences were shown for the languages in alphabetic group. As the handwritten datasets are becoming more available in different corners of the world, we expect to have more resources to continue researching the differences for non-native speakers of the languages that are not yet studied.

**Acknowledgement.** This material is based upon work supported by the National Science Foundation (NSF) under Grant No. 1662487. Any opinions, findings, and conclusions or recommendations expressed in this material are those of the authors and do not necessarily reflect the views of the NSF.

We would like to express our gratitude to the volunteered participants for contributing to the development of the handwriting dataset.

# References

1. Ansaldo, A.I., Marcotte, K., Scherer, L., Raboyeau, G.: Language therapy and bilingual aphasia: clinical implications of psycholinguistic and neuroimaging research. J. Neurolinguistics **21**, 539–557 (2008). https://doi.org/10.1016/j.jneuroling.2008.02.001
2. Daniels, P.T., Bright, W.: The World's Writing Systems. Oxford University Press, Oxford (1996)
3. Carpenter, R.: The antiquity of the Greek alphabet. Am. J. Archaeol. **37**, 8–29 (1933). https://doi.org/10.2307/498037
4. Taylor, I.: The Korean writing system: an alphabet? A syllabary? a logography? In: Kolers, P.A., Wrolstad, M.E., Bouma, H. (eds.) Processing of Visible Language. Nato Conference Series, vol. 13, pp. 67–82. Springer, Boston (1980). https://doi.org/10.1007/978-1-4684-106 8-6_5
5. Tian, F., et al.: Let's play Chinese characters: Mobile learning approaches via culturally inspired group games (2010). https://doi.org/10.1145/1753326.1753565
6. Presutti, S.: The development of Latin alphabet identity markers: a comparison among three romance graphemes. Lingua **259**, 103118 (2021). https://doi.org/10.1016/j.lingua.2021.103118
7. MacInnis, S.E.: Adolescent handwriting—native versus non-native. Can. Soc. Forensic Sci. J. **27**, 5–14 (1994). https://doi.org/10.1080/00085030.1994.10757020
8. Doliashvili, M., Jeffrey, D., Ogawa, M.-B., Crosby, M.E.: Pressure analysis in dynamic handwriting for forgery detection. In: Schmorrow, D.D., Fidopiastis, C.M. (eds.) HCII 2021. LNCS (LNAI), vol. 12776, pp. 134–146. Springer, Cham (2021). https://doi.org/10.1007/978-3-030-78114-9_10
9. Techniques for static handwriting trajectory recovery | Proceedings of the 9th IAPR International Workshop on Document Analysis Systems. https://dl.acm.org/doi/abs/10.1145/181 5330.1815390. Accessed 26 Feb 2022
10. Chen, Y., Al-Rfou', R., Choi, Y.: Detecting English Writing Styles For Non Native Speakers. arXiv:1704.07441 (2017)
11. Almisreb, A., Tahir, N., Turaev, S., Saleh, M.A., Junid, S.: Arabic handwriting classification using deep transfer learning techniques. Pertanika J. Sci. Technol. **30**, 641–654 (2022). https://doi.org/10.47836/pjst.30.1.35
12. Impedovo, D., Pirlo, G.: On-line signature verification by stroke-dependent representation domains. In: 2010 12th International Conference on Frontiers in Handwriting Recognition, pp. 623–627 (2010). https://doi.org/10.1109/ICFHR.2010.102
13. Amin, M.S., Yasir, S.M., Ahn, H.: Recognition of Pashto handwritten characters based on deep learning. Sensors **20**, 5884 (2020). https://doi.org/10.3390/s20205884
14. Bleses, D., et al.: Early vocabulary development in Danish and other languages: a CDI-based comparison. J. Child Lang. **35**, 619–650 (2008). https://doi.org/10.1017/S0305000908008714
15. Salameh-Matar, A., Basal, N., Weintraub, N.: Relationship between body functions and Arabic handwriting performance at different acquisition stages. Can. J. Occup. Ther. **85**, 418–427 (2018). https://doi.org/10.1177/0008417419826114

16. Cheng, N., Lee, G.K., Yap, B.S., Lee, L.T., Tan, S.K., Tan, K.P.: Investigation of class characteristics in English handwriting of the three main racial groups: Chinese, Malay and Indian in Singapore. J. Forensic Sci. **50**, 177–184 (2005)

17. Camastra, F., Vinciarelli, A. (eds.): Speech and handwriting recognition. In: Machine Learning for Audio, Image and Video Analysis: Theory and Applications, pp. 345–379. Springer, London (2008). https://doi.org/10.1007/978-1-84800-007-0_12

18. Munro, M., Derwing, T.: The foundations of accent and intelligibility in pronunciation research. Lang. Teach. **44**, 316–327 (2011). https://doi.org/10.1017/S0261444811000103

19. (PDF) Speaking Clearly for Children with Learning Disabilities, https://www.researchgate.net/publication/10846339_Speaking_Clearly_for_Children_With_Learning_Disabilities. Accessed 26 Feb 2022

20. Varonis, E.M., Gass, S.: The comprehensibility of non-native speech*. Stud. Second. Lang. Acquis. **4**, 114–136 (1982). https://doi.org/10.1017/S027226310000437X

21. Influence of Mother Tongue on Dynamic Handwriting Features in Primary School | SpringerLink. https://link.springer.com/chapter/10.1007/978-3-319-13117-7_141. Accessed 25 Feb 2022

# Phishing Susceptibility Across Industries

Thea Mannix[1]([✉]), Gregor Petrič[2], Anita-Catrin Eriksen[1], Jacopo Paglia[1], and Kai Roer[1]

[1] KnowBe4 Research AS, Kristian Augustsgate, 13, Oslo, Norway
{theau,research}@knowbe4.com
[2] Faculty of Social Sciences, University of Ljubljana,
Kardeljeva ploscad 5, 1000 Ljubljana, Slovenia

**Abstract.** Research into the human factors of cyber security is becoming increasingly important in helping to understand how human behaviour can be influenced in the modern age of human targeted cyber-attacks. Phishing is one of the most prevalent methods used to socially engineer human targets, and as such it is important to establish which factors may influence susceptibility to phishing emails. The majority of research has thus far been dedicated to individual level and semantic factors of susceptibility, while other important issues such as organisational context have been largely absent. This paper explores whether industry type influences behaviours resulting from phishing simulations. Here we present a large sample of real-world data from phishing simulations deployed to employees from banking, education, healthcare and pharmaceutical organisations and construction. Analyses were conducted across multiple potential responses - opening an email, clicking a link, replying to the email, entering data, and reporting the email as suspicious. The results revealed significant differences in susceptibility to phishing depending on which industry type employees belonged to. Consistent with previous work, the banking industry had the fewest number of employees engaged in opening phishing emails and clicking links. Implications for future work and industry professionals are discussed.

**Keywords:** Phishing · Social engineering · Industry · Security culture

## 1 Introduction

An ever-increasing global reliance on technology in the collection, storage and sharing of essential information has resulted in an increased threat of it being accessed, modified, stolen, destroyed or otherwise compromised by bad actors. Traditionally considered an IT problem, much of the research in the field of cyber security has been devoted to assessing and developing technological based defences. While maintaining technological defenses is still vital to the protection of information, the role of human factors in data breaches has become increasingly prevalent, with the most recent reports of information security incidents

Supported by KnowBe4, inc.

resulting from intentional or unintentional human negligence ranging from 43% to up to 95% [1,13,23].

Phishing attacks are one of the primary methods used to socially engineer human targets [13]. The term phishing in this context refers to fraudulent emails that appear to be from legitimate sources, but are in reality sent by bad actors with the intention of making the recipient perform an action against their own best interests. This is often done with the aim of eliciting personal information or for illicit financial gain, or to install malware, and may include inducing individuals to reveal personal information such as credentials or payment card information. Phishing is a popular choice for those wishing to access IT systems and protected information illegitimately, as e-mail is a cheap and effective means of infiltration. The attack procedure can be implemented repeatedly and across multiple targets, and as e-mails are a common method of legitimately requesting action in both work and personal life, targets are already primed to trust requests.

Understanding factors under which vulnerability to phishing varies is an important task. The number of human-targeted phishing attacks has consistently increased in recent years [14], while organisational resources to implement security measures are finite. Research is needed to help security leaders focus their security measures in a dynamic way to create the most effective defence relative to funding available. These issues, in conjunction with the shift in the attack landscape to human targets, is reflected in an increased focus of research in investigating the human factors of cyber security.

Establishing which factors influence phishing behaviour is key to determining how risk of human-factor data breaches can vary by circumstance. Research also shows that many psycho-social variables are important factors of susceptibility to phishing, such as perception of risk, propensity to trust, security knowledge, neuroticism and other variables. However, contextual variables are also important. While still in its infancy, investigations examining phishing have highlighted a number of potential candidates. For example, researchers have reported specific age ranges as a factor in determining target vulnerability to phishing attacks. Both [10] and [8] report those in the range of 18–25 are most likely to act on phishing attempts through phishing simulations that measured click rates. Another possible factor is gender. [10] report that their female participants were more likely to fall for phishing attempts. These results were replicated by [17], who also found that female participants were more likely to act on requests from phishing emails than males. In addition to personal demographics, other factors such as historical employment and degree of IT literacy have also been evidenced to influence how an individual will respond to phishing attempts.

Phishing vulnerability may also be influenced by culture [3,5,11]. Flores et al. (2015) report that correlations between factors determining phishing behaviour and phishing behaviour varied based on national culture in a comparison between Sweden, USA, and India. Tembe et al. (2013) report significant differences between participant phishing vulnerability depending on whether they were from USA, India or China.

There are also conflicting outcomes across investigations [24]. For example, while [10] and [8] report individuals between 18 and 25 as most vulnerable, others suggest older individuals are less able to distinguish real vs phishing emails, potentially because they are less likely to be suspicious [2]. Findings on gender as a contributing factor are also less clear, as [25] report males to be more vulnerable to act on phishing attacks, but only during the secondary stage of the attack, while [6] and [9] report no statistically significant differences related to gender at all. Determining contextual factors from phishing simulations is a complex task. Factors may co-occur and interact, while limited sample sizes from laboratory based experiments may be more vulnerable to undetermined confounding factors. Variability in the impact of individual-level factors suggests that the contexts in which studies are conducted are important and should be considered. It is also important to establish what potential influencing factors there may be, preferably using large real world data sets, in order to accurately identify the circumstances under which factors maintain or alter their influence on behaviours.

One potential factor in phishing vulnerability that requires further, more comprehensive investigation is industry type. Evidence that IT literacy, and to a lesser extent, age and gender, may influence vulnerability to phishing provides indirect evidence to support a hypothesis that industry type is more general mediator of phishing vulnerability. This is because these factors are distributed differently among different industry types. For example, statistical assessments demonstrate that women make up only 9.1% of the construction workforce in the USA [15], while skill sets and education typically required for a given field will differ across industries.

Industry reports also suggest differences in phishing susceptibility among various industries. Comparisons of surveys on cyber security knowledge and security culture suggest variations in security related behaviours across industries with employees from finance based organisations such as banking typically performing best in secure behaviours by industry set metrics [18,19]. Such reports suggest that this may be influenced by the commodity a particular industry is concerned with, with other 'high value' industries such as insurance and technology also typically ranking highly, potentially because they typically have greater investment in cyber attack prevention, as well as a typically greater proportion of employees with higher IT literacy. Finance based industries have also been examined in scientific literature, where [7] report that the success of different phishing techniques varied by whether an employee was affiliated with finance or non-finance related industries. While finance industries have been specifically examined, they have yet to be comprehensively compared to other specific industries, and while many papers focus on employees of a specific industry type (e.g. [20]), little field data is currently available directly comparing different industries.

This paper implements an exploratory investigation of how phishing susceptibility varies across industry type. To do so we employ a comparison of phishing response behaviour across 4 industries on employees' responses to large scale phishing simulations. The use of simulated phishing attacks is a popular vehicle by which research evaluates vulnerability. Simulations can refer both to data collected from in-laboratory environments where participants are shown phishing e-mails, often interspersed with legitimate e-mails, and also to field collected data where groups respond to simulated phishing e-mails received in real world environments, such as the workplace. Simulations are particularly useful as they provide a greater degree of ecological validity than other measures that gather first person reports of phishing behaviour. In addition, they circumvent an evidenced bias in phishing behaviour reports that individuals can display overconfidence in their abilities to detect phishing attempts [12,16], which may impact the validity of findings from experiments that measure intentions or self reported behaviour alone.

Due to the regular use of participants from populations in higher education, we have included organisations from the education industry as one of the four industries. We further include responses from those in healthcare and pharmaceutical organisations considering the critical role of this industry in society. As employees from banking are often highlighted in industry reports as demonstrating the most secure behaviour in responses to phishing, we also include this industry to observe whether this is replicated in a large real world data set. The fourth selected industry is construction, both because it is underrepresented in the literature and in order to offer a greater range of skill sets for comparison. The main aim of this study is thus to explore the extent of differences in susceptibility to phishing among banking, construction, education and healthcare and pharmaceutical industries.

## 2    Methods

### 2.1    Participants and Data Collection

Data was collected via simulated phishing campaigns that were implemented by organisations via KnowBe4's security awareness training platform. Data used in the analysis was gathered from organisations exclusively in the United States of America. Participants were sent the simulated phishing emails during campaigns initiated by their organisation which were delivered to their work email accounts. Their response, if any, was then recorded. An overview of the number (N) of respondents per industry can be found in Table 1. As the number of phishing emails received by an individual is evidenced to influence their abilities to recognise the e-mail as suspicious, data selected for analysis were exclusively from the first simulated phishing campaign launched per organisation for the calendar year 2020, where only the first simulation phishing e-mail per user was analysed in the data set.

### 2.2    Stimuli

The simulated phishing emails used in the campaigns were created by using genuine email templates. The quality of the emails varied by 5 stages of complexity and difficulty which were evenly distributed across organisations.

## 2.3   Pre-processing

Categorisation of an organisation to an industry type was taken from self-reported data provided by organisations during on-boarding to KnowBe4's security awareness training program, where each organisation selected their appropriate industry. Included in the analysis were the following industry categories: Healthcare & Pharmaceuticals, Banking, Construction and Education (see Table 1 for overview).

There were 5 potential actions email recipients could take that were selected for analysis - email opened ('Opened'), link in email clicked ('Clicked'), email replied to ('Replied'), data entered ('Data entered'), and suspicious email reported to the organisation ('Reported'). The mean percentage ratio for each dependent variable (Opened, Clicked, Replied, Data entered, Reported) were calculated per individual, and then aggregated to mean percentage ratio per organisation. These data were then aggregated again by industry type ($N = 4$). Actions are not mutually exclusive, such that a single email may potentially be both be opened, clicked, replied, have data entered and reported.

# 3   Results

Table 1. Overview of descriptive data by industry category.

| Industry | N (Employees) | N (Organisations) | Opened (%) | Clicked (%) | Replied (%) | Data entered (%) | Reported (%) |
|---|---|---|---|---|---|---|---|
| Banking | 49 918 | 649 | 15.67 | 4.60 | 0.12 | 0.42 | 11.71 |
| Construction | 25 639 | 253 | 33.78 | 8.35 | 0.08 | 1.46 | 9.94 |
| Education | 94 890 | 461 | 44.19 | 11.51 | 0.38 | 1.27 | 5.97 |
| Health & Pharm. | 124 508 | 621 | 30.27 | 8.95 | 0.31 | 1.40 | 9.42 |

Data were analyzed using one way analysis of variance comparing the four selected industries (Banking, Construction, Education, Healthcare and Pharmaceutical) across the five action variables (Opened, Clicked, Data entered, Replied, Reported). The results revealed significant differences for all action variables with the exception of Replied ($F(3, 1960) = 1.026$, $p = 0.38$, $\eta^2 = 0.01$). An overview of ANOVA outcomes can be found in Table 2. All post hoc tests were performed using Tukey HSD. The significant main effect for Opened ($F(3, 1960) = 103.5$, $p < 0.01$, $\eta^2 = 0.14$). Was revealed to be driven by significant differences between all industries for e-mails opened. Employees from the banking industry demonstrated the fewest number of employees opening phishing emails (Mean (M) = 15.6, Standard Deviation (SD) = 21.2), while those affiliated with education had the most (M = 44.1, SD = 32.8). A main effect was also found for click rates, ($F(3, 1960) = 17.34$, $p < 0.01$, $\eta^2 = 0.03$), where post hoc testing revealed again significant differences between all industries.

**Table 2.** ANOVA outcomes for each of the behaviour variables. $P$-values significant (*) at 0.05.

|          | Opened  | Clicked | Data entered | Replied | Reported |
|----------|---------|---------|--------------|---------|----------|
| F        | 103.5   | 17.34   | 3.847        | 1.026   | 6.673    |
| p-value  | <0.01*  | <0.01*  | 0.02*        | 0.38    | <0.01*   |
| $\eta^2$ | 0.14    | 0.03    | 0.004        | 0.01    | 0.01     |

The main effect found for data entered ($F(3, 1960) = 3.047$, $p = 0.02$, $\eta^2 = 0.04$) was found to be driven by a significant difference between banking (M = 0.42, SD = 4.3) and healthcare and pharmaceuticals (M = 1.40, SD = 7.3). No other significant differences for data entered were found. Post hoc analysis for rates of reporting revealed significant differences between banking (M = 11.7, SD = 23.4) and education (M = 5.9, SD = 18.1) and education and healthcare and pharmaceutical organisations (M = 9.4, SD = 20.8). No other significant differences were found for Report ($ps > 0.09$). All pairwise comparisons can be viewed in Table 3 in the appendix.

## 4   Discussion

This paper presents an exploratory analysis of responses to phishing simulations by employees across banking, construction, education and healthcare and pharmaceutical industries. The results revealed significant differences in behaviours dependent on industry type. The banking industry had the fewest number of employees engaged in opening phishing emails and clicking links. Finance based industries have previously been reported as the most secure with regards to their employees security related knowledge and behaviours, a result replicated here [18, 19]. Banking also had the largest proportion of employees reporting suspicious emails, which was significant when compared with the worst performing industry in this category, education. Future research should consider exploring whether higher rates of reporting are causally related with more secure phishing behaviours, where higher rates of report have the potential to encourage fewer negative phishing response behaviours. This is supported by evidence that self efficacy, self monitoring and expectation of negative outcomes have a positive effect on likelihood of reporting [22].

Scientific research has previously suggested that vulnerabilities based on phishing technique may be causally related to the types of individuals that tend towards specific industries [7]. Specifically, that finance based employees were differently inclined to engage with phishing requests based on their industry characteristics. This was not controlled for here, however it may be the case that phishing techniques more likely to elicit negative behaviours from finance based employees are less common methods of attack, and this is why they tend to outperform other industries in industry reports and here. More research is needed to replicate this outcome.

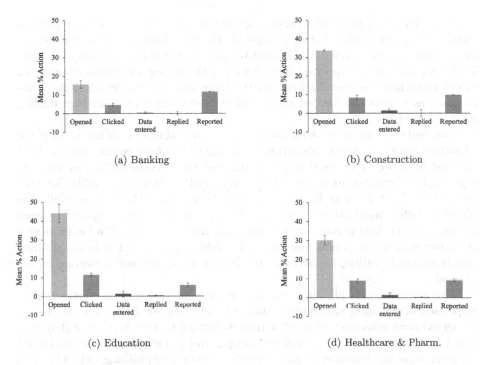

**Fig. 1.** Overview of mean percentage ratio of responses to phishing simulations per industry compared. Bars represent 1 standard error (*SE*)

It is important to note that no industry examined presented risk free behaviour. When interpreted, statistics from employees from the banking industry translate to 4 in every 100 emails resulting in clicking a potentially malicious link, and 1 in 1000 entering credentials. Considering statistics regarding the number of phishing attacks on the finance sector, reaching 30,000 attempted attacks a week [21], the finding that banking performs better in terms of security behaviours than other industries does not equate to a reduced risk consideration for that industry.

Previously, little research has been conducted specifically examining phishing behaviours within the construction industry. Behavioural responses from those in the construction here demonstrated similar outcomes as those from education and healthcare and pharmaceutical industries. Construction further had the second highest rate of reporting suspicious emails. This is not in line with the limited number of industry reports that have reported on this industry [18, 19], where it has typically ranked low in employees security awareness and knowledge. This suggests a that the correlation between positive security behaviours and knowledge is not linear, and requires further investigation.

The largest number of employees sharing credentials on simulated fraudulent websites were from the construction and the healthcare and pharmaceutical industries, where the latter was significantly different when compared with

Banking. This is of particular concern given the critical role healthcare plays in society, where credential sharing is arguably the most high risk behaviour resulting in ransomware or release of important personal or otherwise sensitive data. This is a particularly important finding for healthcare organisations, where other recent investigations have highlighted the large scale of attacks on such organisations, as well as the limited awareness of healthcare professionals in dealing with threats [20].

The highest rate of clicking links were from employees affiliated with the education industry. Across industries, replying to phishing emails was the least enacted response. The consistency of this outcome across industries suggests replying has factors common to individuals regardless of industry affiliation that make it the least likely of insecure phishing behaviours. This is potentially the additional effort required, cognitively and behaviourally, when compared to other actions such as clicking links or entering data, that may demand a higher degree of sophistication from a phishing attack. It could also be linked to many phishing emails explicitly calling for actions like clicking links, and not providing replies to mails.

These results also highlight the importance for research to consider more responses in phishing simulations than just clicking on links. The landscape of behavioural responses differed across industries in the data presented here (see Fig. 1), and behaviours such as opening and reporting are also important considerations in obtaining a comprehensive overview of phishing risk. This may also help guide industry professionals when reducing risk of human oriented cyber-attacks, where training efforts can be focused on specific behaviors to which employees are most vulnerable.

Understanding the contextual factors for phishing behaviour is not only important with regards to practical applications in industry, it is also important for future research to assist with the design and interpretations of data from laboratory settings. While all types of data used in the context of phishing suffer from some degree of limitation in its generalisability, in-lab environments may lack the reliability of real-world data as behaviours are often subject to change based on environmental context, and there is a need for large real-world data to bolster findings from more controlled studies.

It is important to mention that despite the large sample size, effect sizes for some of the analyses conducted here are relatively low. In order to remove potential confounds from the number of phishing emails received by individual users, as well as controlling for known security awareness training from within the organisation, the experimental design used only the first phishing simulation. This sample heterogeneity may have contributed to the large standard deviation and low power observed in some of our results. However, it is important to note that small differences are relevant when examining phishing responses, where even 4 in 1000 sharing credentials as was observed with banking employees is still meaningful. Future research should consider focusing on replication and exploration of causal factors behind findings presented here.

Due to privacy considerations we are unable to report whether employees were aware their organisations implemented simulated phishing campaigns. As only the first ever campaign per user was examined in the data set, we expect this has made little impact on the results. However, it would be a future topic of interest to investigate whether prior knowledge of the use of simulated phishing campaigns influences behavioural outcomes.

## 5 Conclusion

The comparison of phishing behaviour by industry type revealed organisations affiliated with banking as engaging least with phishing emails, and reporting the most suspicious emails. The largest number of employees entering data were from Construction and Healthcare and Pharmaceutical industries. Those from Education reported the fewest suspicious emails. This variance in responses to phishing emails demonstrates industry type as a consideration in phishing susceptibility outcomes. They also highlight industry specific behavioral considerations when reducing risk of human oriented cyber-attacks, which may assist industries in focusing on training specific behaviors to which they are most vulnerable.

## 6 Appendix

**Table 3.** Pairwise comparisons between industries by dependent action variable. $P$-values significant (*) at 0.05.

| Action | Difference (Mean %) | $p$-value | CI (95%) |
|---|---|---|---|
| *Opened* | | | |
| Construction-Banking | 18.1 | <0.01* | 12.7, 23.4 |
| Education-Banking | 28.5 | <0.01* | 24.2, 32.7 |
| Health & Pharm.-Banking | 14.5 | <0.01* | 10.6, 18.5 |
| Education-Construction | 10.4 | <0.01* | 4.8, 16.0 |
| Health & Pharm.-Construction | −3.5 | <0.01* | −8.8, 1.8 |
| Health & Pharm.-Education | −13.9 | <0.01* | −18.2, −9.6 |
| *Clicked* | | | |
| Construction-Banking | 3.75 | <0.01* | 0.56, 6.95 |
| Education-Banking | 6.91 | <0.01* | 4.36, 9.45 |
| Health & Pharm.-Banking | 4.35 | <0.01* | 2.00, 6.70 |
| Education-Construction | 3.15 | <0.01* | −0.21, 6.51 |
| Health & Pharm.-Construction | 0.59 | <0.01* | −2.61, 3.81 |
| Health & Pharm.-Education | −2.55 | <0.01* | −5.12, 0.02 |

*(continued)*

**Table 3.** (*continued*)

| Action | Difference (Mean %) | p-value | CI (95%) |
|---|---|---|---|
| *Data Entered* | | | |
| Construction-Banking | 1.01 | 0.16 | −0.24, 2.31 |
| Education-Banking | 0.84 | 0.14 | −0.17, 1.86 |
| Health & Pharm.-Banking | 0.97 | 0.03* | 0.03, 1.91 |
| Education-Construction | −0.19 | 0.98 | −1.53, 1.15 |
| Health & Pharm.-Construction | −0.06 | 0.99 | −1.34, 1.22 |
| Health & Pharm.-Education | 0.12 | 0.98 | −0.90, 1.15 |
| *Replied* | | | |
| Construction-Banking | −0.03 | 0.98 | −0.62, 0.54 |
| Education-Banking | 0.26 | 0.46 | −0.20, 0.73 |
| Health & Pharm.-Banking | 0.18 | 0.67 | −0.24,0.61 |
| Education-Construction | 0.30 | 0.59 | −0.31, 0.91 |
| Health & Pharm.-Construction | 0.22 | 0.75 | −0.36, 0.75 |
| Health & Pharm.-Education | −0.07 | 0.97 | −0.54, 0.39 |
| *Reported* | | | |
| Construction-Banking | 3.45 | 0.04* | 0.11, 6.78 |
| Education-Banking | −0.52 | 0.98 | −4.69, 3.64 |
| Health & Pharm.-Banking | −2.28 | 0.21 | −5.33, 0.76 |
| Education-Construction | −1.76 | 0.69 | −5.91, 2.38 |
| Health & Pharm.-Construction | −3.96 | 0.09 | −8.33, 0.39 |
| Health & Pharm.-Education | −5.73 | <0.01* | −9.04, 2.42 |

# References

1. Ali, R.F., Dominic, P.D.D., Ali, K.: Organizational governance, social bonds and information security policy compliance: a perspective towards oil and gas employees. Sustainability **1220**, 8576 (2020)
2. Grilli, M.D., et al.: Is this phishing? Older age is associated with greater difficulty discriminating between safe and malicious emails. J. Gerontol. Ser. B **76**(9), 1711–1715 (2021)
3. Flores, W.R., Holm, H., Nohlberg, M., Ekstedt, M.: Investigating personal determinants of phishing and the effect of national culture. Inf. Comput. Secur. (2015)
4. Bailey, P.E., Leon, T.: A systematic review and meta-analysis of age-related differences in trust. Psychol. Aging **345**, 674 (2019)
5. Aleroud, A., Abu-Shanab, E., Al-Aiad, A., Alshboul, Y.: An examination of susceptibility to spear phishing cyber attacks in non-English speaking communities. J. Inf. Secur. Appl. **55**, 102614 (2020)
6. Diaz, A., Sherman, A.T., Joshi, A.: Phishing in an academic community: a study of user susceptibility and behavior. Cryptologia **441**, 53–67 (2020)
7. Tian, C., Jensen, M.L., Durcikova, A: Phishing susceptibility across industries: the differential impact of influence techniques. In: Proceedings of the 13th Pre-ICIS Workshop on Information Security and Privacy, vol. 11, pp. 1–20 (2018)

8. Kumaraguru, P., et al.: School of phish: a real-world evaluation of anti-phishing training. In: Proceedings of the 5th Symposium on Usable Privacy and Security, pp. 1–12 (2009)
9. Li, W., Lee, J., Purl, J., Greitzer, F., Yousefi, B., Laskey, K.: Experimental investigation of demographic factors related to phishing susceptibility. In: Proceedings of the 53rd Hawaii International Conference on System Sciences (2020)
10. Sheng, S., Holbrook, M., Kumaraguru, P., Cranor, L.F., Downs, J: Who falls for phish? A demographic analysis of phishing susceptibility and effectiveness of interventions. In: Proceedings of the SIGCHI Conference on Human Factors in Computing Systems (2020)
11. Tembe, R., Hong, K.W., Murphy-Hill, E., Mayhorn, C.B., Kelley, C.M.: American and Indian conceptualizations of phishing. In: 2013 Third Workshop on Socio-Technical Aspects in Security and Trust, pp. 37–45. IEEE (2013)
12. Canfield, C.I., Fischhoff, B., Davis, A.: Better beware: comparing metacognition for phishing and legitimate emails. Metacogn. Learn. **1433**, 343–362 (2019)
13. Verizon RISK Team et al. 2021: DBIR 2021. https://www.verizon.com/business/en-sg/resources/reports/dbir/2021/masters-guide/summary-of-findings. Accessed 15 Dec 2021
14. Barracuda 2020. https://www.oodaloop.com/briefs/2020/03/27/667-spike-in-email-phishing-attacks-due-to-coronavirus-fears/. Accessed 01 Dec 2021
15. National Association of Women in Construction. https://www.nawic.org/nawic/Statistics.asp. Accessed 01 Jan 2021
16. Wang, J., Li, Y., Rao, H.R.: Overconfidence in phishing email detection. J. Assoc. Inf. Syst. **17**(11), 2 (2016)
17. Halevi, T., Lewis, J., Memon, N: Phishing, Personality Traits and Facebook. Cornell University Library. https://arxiv.org/abs/1301.7643 (2013)
18. Roer, K., Eriksen, A., Pterič, G: The Security Culture Report 2020. KnowBe4 Research (2020). https://www.knowbe4.com/hubfs/Security-Culture-Report.pdf
19. Roer, K., Eriksen, A., Pterič, G: The Security Culture Report 2021. KnowBe4 Research (2021). https://www.knowbe4.com/organizational-cyber-security-culture-research-report
20. Priestman, W., Anstis, T., Sebire, I.G., Sridharan, S., Sebire, N.J.: Phishing in healthcare organisations: threats, mitigation and approaches. BMJ Health Care Inform. **26**(1) (2019)
21. Singh, N: Online frauds in banks with phishing. J. Internet Banking Commer. 1–27 (2007)
22. Kwak, Y., Lee, S., Damiano, A., Vishwanath, A.: Why do users not report spear phishing emails? Telemat. Inform. **48**, 101343 (2020)
23. Services, S.: IBM Infographic: Cyber Security Intelligence Index. IBM: Armonk, NY, USA 2014. http://www.935IBM.com/services/us/en/it-services/2014-cyber-security-index-infographic. Accessed 10 Jan 2022
24. Sommestad, T. and Karlzén, H: A meta-analysis of field experiments on phishing susceptibility. In: 2019 APWG Symposium on Electronic Crime Research (eCrime), pp. 1–14 (2019)
25. Mohebzada, J.G., El Zarka, A., BHojani, A.H., Darwish, A.: Phishing in a university community: two large scale phishing experiments. In: 2012 International Conference on Innovations in Information Technology (IIT), pp. 249–254 (2012)

# Home-Based Assessment of Sleep Quality and Post Concussive Symptoms in Veterans with Mild Traumatic Brain Injury

Kamila U. Pollin[1] , Immanuel Samuel[1,2] , Charity B. Breneman[1,2] ,
Mary M. Valmas[1] , Ryan C. Brewster[1] , Matthew J. Reinhard[1] ,
and Michelle E. Costanzo[1(✉)]

[1] Washington DC VA Medical Center,
War Related Illness and Injury Study Center, Washington DC 20422, USA
{Kamila.Pollin,Michelle.Costanzo}@va.gov
[2] Henry M Jackson Foundation for the Advancement of Military Medicine, Inc., Bethesda,
MD 20817, USA

**Abstract.** Military Veterans report sleep complaints which can be exacerbated by traumatic brain injuries (TBIs) contributing to poor health outcomes. The aim of this study is to examine the relation between sleep quality and postconcussive symptoms, cognitive performance, behavior, and physical activity using home-based remote measures in Veterans with a history of mild TBIs. **Methods:** Participants completed online questionnaires (Neurobehavioral Symptom Inventory [NSI], Five Facet Mindfulness Questionnaire-39 [FFMQ], and Pittsburgh Sleep Quality Index [PSQI]). The Oral Trail Making test and Ohio State University TBI Identification Method (OSU TBI-ID) were administered by a licensed psychologist. Actigraphy (wGT3X-BT) was monitored to measure sleep and step count over 7 days. During three-month follow up the NSI and PSQI were repeated, and sleep and step count was reassessed for 7-days (using a Fitbit). Data were analyzed using Pearson's correlations. **Results:** Eight (8 Males; age: $55 \pm 7$ yrs, Body Mass Index (BMI): $32 \pm 7$ kg/m$^2$ mean $\pm$ SD) Veterans with mild TBI completed the baseline. Six Veterans completed during the three month follow up. There were no significant relations between sleep and FFMQ, or step count. There was a significant relation between sleep duration and processing speed ($r^2 = 0.76$, $P = 0.01$) and between the PSQI and NSI ($r^2 = 0.69$, $P = 0.02$). During the follow up, there were no relations between sleep and NSI, FFMQ, or step count. **Conclusion:** This preliminary analysis suggests evaluating sleep remotely is achievable and valuable information can be gathered to evaluate sleep and health in Veterans with mild TBI. Our work supports the usefulness of home-based assessments and wearable devices.

**Keywords:** Sleep · Traumatic brain injury · Physical activity

## 1 Introduction

Sleep disorders amongst Veterans are increasing in prevalence [1]. Traumatic brain injuries (TBIs) are also common in military members and while most individuals recover,

© The Author(s), under exclusive license to Springer Nature Switzerland AG 2022
D. D. Schmorrow and C. M. Fidopiastis (Eds.): HCII 2022, LNAI 13310, pp. 80–90, 2022.
https://doi.org/10.1007/978-3-031-05457-0_7

many continue to experience post concussive symptoms [2], which include sleep problems [3]. Indeed, 30–70% of patients with a history of TBI report sleep difficulty in the first few weeks post injury and individuals with mild TBIs report greater sleep disturbances compared to those with a moderate or severe brain injury [4, 5]. Sleep problems can contribute to poor cognitive recovery [6] and impaired executive function [7]. Behavioral health approaches may be critical tools to consider for Veterans, given findings that increased mindfulness can predict better subjective sleep quality [8] and those with greater physical activity tend to have better sleep health [9]. However, the bidirectional relation between sleep and physical activity, such that sleep disturbances may reduce exercise capacity [10] and good sleep contributes to increased physical activity [11], is important to consider. This is particularly relevant to Veterans with a history of mild TBI and postconcussive symptoms that report elevated sleep problems [12]. Improved understanding of the connection between sleep quality and health metrics could aid in improving perpetuating factors that maintain impaired sleep.

Sleeping schedules are strongly regulated by the circadian clock and the maintenance of sleep is primarily regulated by homeostatic mechanisms [13]. Evaluation of sleep is typically done in clinical settings, but such sleep studies are resource-intensive and may not reveal the spectrum of sleep disruption encountered at home. Using home-based remote measures allows for data to be collected during free-living conditions and may offer insight into the real-world sleep habits of individuals. Moreover, remote evaluation offers an advantage of convenience for Veterans, thus studying the value of using remote measures effectively and understanding the relation between sleep and these health outcomes is critical for offering improved services for a common Veteran complaint. Home sleep monitoring can be done using multiple methods such as objective actigraphy and the subjective Pittsburgh Quality Sleep Index (PSQI). These methods offer several indices of sleep health such as sleep variability (a higher sleep variability is associated with negative health outcomes [14]) and sleep duration [15] that can be correlated with different health behaviors and symptoms.

The aim of this study is to use remote technology to examine the relation between objective and subjective sleep quality, subjective postconcussive symptoms, cognitive performance, behavioral trait measures and physical activity in a cohort of Veterans with a history of mild TBI. We hypothesize that individuals with worse sleep quality will have greater postconcussive symptoms, impaired performance on a cognitive task, lower behavioral trait scores, and lower physical activity. The present report describes preliminary data of an ongoing study that will help evaluate remote assessments to advance awareness of the relation between sleep disturbances and postconcussive symptoms to develop future interventions to improve sleep quality.

## 2 Methods

### 2.1 Study Participants

This study was approved by the Institutional Review Board at the Washington, DC Veteran Affairs Medical Center. Participants enrolled in the clinical National Referral Program (NRP) at the War Related Illness & Injury Study Center (WRIISC) were recruited for the study. All participants provided informed consent. Participants were excluded if they 1) had a history of moderate or severe TBI, 2) have any psychiatric conditions that were contraindications for remote assessment (e.g., bipolar disorder, psychiatric disorder with primary psychotic features, or current suicidal or homicidal ideation), or 3) have any medical condition that would make it medically unsafe to participate such as unstable chronic illnesses (e.g., congestive heart failure or uncontrolled thyroid disease) or neurological disorders (ex. Alzheimer's or Parkinson's disease).

## 2.2  Remote Protocol

We developed an innovative remote research protocol that allows acquisition of free-living data using wearable devices. Following the virtual (via VA Video Connect Call) consent (using DocuSign), participants were mailed all required devices to their home (Fig. 1). Video tutorials explaining each remote measure were sent to the participants and a tutorial session was scheduled to explain and set up each device. Following the tutorial session, participants wore an actigraph (wGT3X-BT, ActiGraph L.L.C, Pensacola, FL) for 7 days. This monitor was worn on the wrist of the non-dominant hand and is designed to detect movement using an accelerometer. The actigraph uses a validated algorithm to set thresholds where high levels of activity are classified as "wake" and activities below that threshold are classified as "sleep." This actigraph can also detect when lights are turned off. Participants logged their nightly sleep and morning awake times in a sleep diary. We used the sleep diaries to validate the auto sleep period detection algorithm from the actigraph. Additionally, we assessed physical activity through step count and moderate-to-vigorous physical activity (MVPA) captured by the actigraph. MVPA is measured with metabolic equivalents which is the ratio of a person's working metabolic rate compared to their resting metabolic rate. A person at rest has 1 metabolic equivalent and MVPA is defined as 3–6 metabolic equivalents. Actigraphy data were analyzed using ActiLife v6.13.4 software (ActiGraph; Penasacola, Fl).

Participants completed questionnaires on the Qualtrics platform. Questionnaires included the Neurobehavioral Symptom Inventory (NSI; [16]) a symptom-severity assessment following TBI to measure postconcussive syndrome symptoms and the Five Facet Mindfulness Questionnaire-39 (FFMQ; [17]), a measurement of the tendency to practice mindfulness in daily life. The FFMQ is a 39-item self-report questionnaire that uses a 5-point Likert Scale. Participants also completed the PSQI which is a subjective measurement of sleep quality. The PSQI measures seven domains over the past month including sleep quality, sleep latency, sleep duration, sleep efficiency, sleep disturbances, use of sleep medication and daytime dysfunction [18]. Each domain is individually scored, and a global sum is calculated. The global sum ranges from 0–21, where 5 or greater is associated with poor sleep quality. In military populations, a cutoff score of $\geq 10$ is suggested for determining clinically significant insomnia [19].

During each participant's clinical NRP evaluation week at the WRIISC, they met with a neurophysiologist through VA Video Connect and completed the Oral Trial Making Test (OTMT; an assessment of processing speed [part A] and executive function [part B]). The neuropsychologist or neuropsychology postdoctoral fellow under supervision of the neuropsychologist applied the Ohio State University TBI identification method [20] to determine if participant's had a history of mTBI (Fig. 1). A mild TBI exposure was defined as a head injury event, characterized by one or more of the following, 1) a loss of consciousness between 0–30 min, 2) an alteration of consciousness between 0–24 h or 3) posttraumatic amnesia between 0–24 h. Body mass index (BMI) was obtained from medical records. We acquired the clinical records through approved data sharing methods and with consent from the Veteran.

Following the baseline evaluation, participants repeated the questionnaires (NSI, FFMQ, and PSQI) via Qualtrics at a three month follow up. Participants also wore a Fitbit (Charge 2 or 4) for 7 days to measure sleep and step count. These metrics are automatically provided by Fitbit and are not available for data processing.

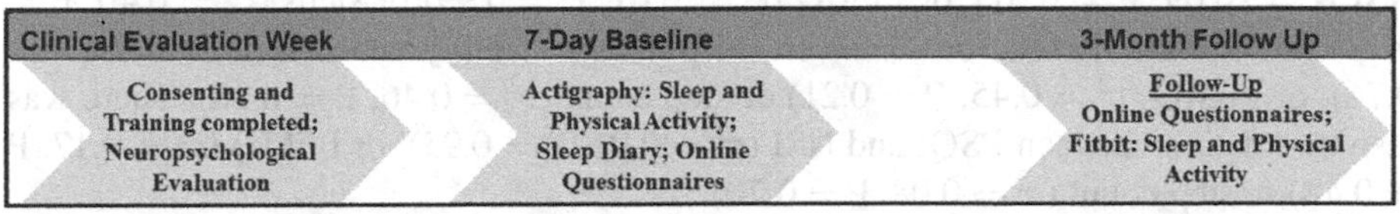

| Clinical Evaluation Week | 7-Day Baseline | 3-Month Follow Up |
|---|---|---|
| Consenting and Training completed; Neuropsychological Evaluation | Actigraphy: Sleep and Physical Activity; Sleep Diary; Online Questionnaires | Follow-Up Online Questionnaires; Fitbit: Sleep and Physical Activity |

**Fig. 1.** Experimental timeline: following the virtual consent and training visit, participants are mailed all required equipment. Participants complete a 7-day baseline where they wear the actigraph and complete questionnaires. Participants repeat questionnaires and wear a Fitbit at the 3-month follow up.

## 2.3 Data Analysis

Using the Actilife v6.13.4 software, we first validated wear vs. non-wear periods manually. Then, we used the auto sleep period detection option using the Tudor-Locke algorithm [21] to detect daily sleep and awake times. Sleep duration is the total time spent asleep from sleep onset to wake onset and was quantified for each night that the actigraph was worn. We averaged sleep duration over the 7 nights for the analysis. We measured the standard deviation (SD) of total sleep time to calculate day-to-day sleep variability. We measured average step count to quantify physical activity levels for 6-days. We excluded the first day for the current cohort because participants wore the actigraphy for only half a day. Data from the OTMT were scored according to recommendations and normative data previously described [31]. Briefly, the Oral Trail Making Test is scored by how long it takes to complete the test. Due to the small sample size at the three-month follow up and the use of different devices, we separately examined the relation between sleep and health metrics at the three-month interval instead of examining the changes over time. We calculated average step count using 7-days (Fitbit) and sleep metrics using 7-nights (Fitbit) during the 3-month follow up. We analyzed the relation between sleep and each metric using Pearson's correlations. Data was analyzed using GraphPad Prism (Graphpad Software LLC, San Diego, CA). Significance was set at $\alpha \leq 0.05$.

## 3 Results

Eight (8 males; age: $55 \pm 7$ yrs, BMI: $32 \pm 7$ kg/m$^2$ mean $\pm$ SD) Veterans with mild TBI completed the baseline evaluation and six Veterans completed the three-month follow-up. Participant demographics are presented in Table 1. Sleep metrics, self-report measures, cognitive evaluations, and physical activity are presented in Table 2. Veterans slept on average $6.9 \pm 1.4$ h per night during their baseline visit. Average sleep time was similar during the 3-month follow up ($7.0 \pm 0.08$ h per night). Table 3 presents the associations between the objective assessment of sleep and health metrics. There was a significant positive relation between total sleep time and processing speed (Table 3) and between the PSQI and NSI (Fig. 2) at baseline. Table 4 presents the associations between the subjective assessment of sleep and health metrics. Due to missing data, sample sizes for each metric are included in Tables 3 and 4.

During the 3-month follow up, there were no relations between total time asleep and NSI ($r^2 = 0.09$, P $= 0.61$), or FFMQ ($r^2 = 0.01$, P $= 0.99$) or steps ($r^2 = 0.40$, P $= 0.17$). There were no relations between sleep time variability and NSI ($r^2 = 0.03$, P $= 0.76$), or FFMQ ($r^2 = 0.45$, P $= 0.21$) or step count ($r^2 = 0.46$, P $= 0.20$). There was also no relation between PSQI and NSI ($r^2 = 0.01$, P $= 0.95$), or FFMQ ($r^2 = 0.17$, P $= 0.48$) or step count ($r^2 = 0.08$, P $= 0.70$).

**Table 1.** Participant demographics

|  | Average | Range |
| --- | --- | --- |
| Sex (M/F) | 8/0 | – |
| Age, y | $55 \pm 7$ | 42–64 |
| Race (W/A/B) | 8/0/0 | – |
| Body mass index (kg/m$^2$) | $32 \pm 7$ | 19–50 |
| Years since military separation (y) | $17 \pm 9$ | 6–34 |
| Years since last head injury (y) | $23 \pm 9$ | 10–35 |
| Approximate age of last head injury | $32 \pm 10$ | 16–50 |

Data are presented as mean $\pm$ SD; W: white; A: Asian; B: Black

**Table 2.** Subject characteristics at baseline and 3-month follow up

|  | Baseline | 3-month follow up** |
| --- | --- | --- |
| Sleep metrics |  |  |
| Sleep duration, min/night | $442.3 \pm 43.9$ | $420 \pm 47.8$ |
| Sleep duration SD, h | $58.0 \pm 11$ | $62 \pm 43$ |
| Global PSQI score | $9.5 \pm 2.5$ | $9.2 \pm 2.5$ |
| Postconcussive symptoms |  |  |
| NSI | $40 \pm 15$ | $31 \pm 11$ |

(*continued*)

**Table 2.** (*continued*)

|  | Baseline | 3-month follow up** |
|---|---|---|
| Cognitive assessment |  |  |
| Part A: processing speed, sec | 13 ± 8 | N/A |
| Part B: executive function, sec | 51 ± 29 | N/A |
| Behavioral trait |  |  |
| FFMQ | 114 ± 19 | 125 ± 12 |
| Physical activity |  |  |
| Total step count, steps/day | 8389 ± 1542 | 6692 ± 4040 |
| MVPA, min/week | 202 ± 53 | N/A |

Data are presented as mean ± SD; **Sleep metrics and physical activity were obtained with a research-grade actigraph during baseline and using the Fitbit during the 3-Month Follow up; FFMQ: Five-Facet Mindfulness Questionnaire; H: hours; Min: minutes; MVPA: moderate-to-vigorous physical activity; N/A: Not Applicable; NSI: Neurobehavioral symptom inventory; PSQI: Pittsburgh Quality Sleep Index; Sec: Seconds

**Table 3.** Associations between objective assessment of sleep metrics at baseline

| Dependent variable | Sleep duration, h | | Sleep variability SD, h | |
|---|---|---|---|---|
|  | $r^2$ | P | $r^2$ | P |
| Body Mass Index (n = 8) | 0.42 | 0.08 | 0.05 | 0.58 |
| NSI (n = 8) | 0.06 | 0.56 | 0.11 | 0.42 |
| PSQI (n = 7) | 0.01 | 0.91 | 0.01 | 0.99 |
| Processing Speed (n = 7) | 0.76 | 0.01* | 0.11 | 0.47 |
| Executive Function (n = 7) | 0.10 | 0.43 | 0.09 | 0.50 |
| FFMQ (n = 8) | 0.08 | 0.51 | 0.12 | 0.39 |
| Step Count (n = 8) | 0.04 | 0.64 | 0.09 | 0.47 |

FFMQ: Five-Facet Mindfulness Questionnaire; NSI: Neurobehavioral symptom inventory; PSQI: Pittsburgh Quality Sleep Index. * Indicates $P < 0.05$

**Table 4.** Associations between subjective assessment of sleep at baseline

| Dependent variable | Global PSQI | |
|---|---|---|
|  | $r^2$ | P |
| Body mass index (n = 6) | 0.01 | 0.98 |
| Processing speed (n = 6) | 0.06 | 0.61 |

(*continued*)

**Table 4.** (*continued*)

| Dependent variable | Global PSQI | |
|---|---|---|
| | $r^2$ | P |
| Executive function (n = 6) | 0.23 | 0.33 |
| FFMQ (n = 7) | 0.53 | 0.07 |
| Step count (n = 7) | 0.01 | 0.97 |

FFMQ: Five-Facet Mindfulness Questionnaire; NSI: Neurobehavioral symptom inventory PSQI: Pittsburgh Quality Sleep Index.

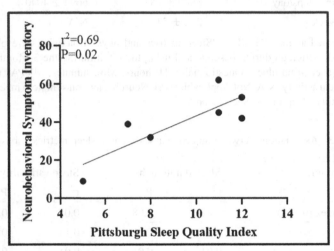

**Fig. 2.** A positive relation exists between the subjective assessment of sleep and postconcussive symptoms (i.e., neurobehavioral symptoms inventory).

## 4    Discussion

This study demonstrates the feasibility of conducting a completely remote observational study in Veterans with a history of mild TBI. We evaluated objective and subjective assessments of sleep in free-living conditions using wearable technologies, virtual neuropsychological assessments and online questionnaires. Our preliminary analysis of this ongoing study did not detect the expected relationship between the objective sleep metrics and postconcussive symptoms, trait mindfulness or step count at rest. We did, however, observe a significant positive relation between objective sleep time and processing speed (cognitive performance) at baseline where greater sleep time was associated with slower processing speed. We also found a significant positive relation between the subjective sleep assessment and postconcussive symptoms, such that those who reported overall worse sleep also endorsed elevated postconcussive symptom severity. In addition, during the 3-month follow up, we did not observe any associations between the sleep metrics and health outcomes.

Previous studies have found a high prevalence of sleep disorders in individuals with mild TBIs [22] and a high prevalence of sleep disorders amongst Veterans in general [1]. Our analysis, however, did not detect a significant relation between objective sleep measures and postconcussive symptoms in our small Veteran cohort. We did, however, observe a positive significant relation between the PSQI and NSI. This is consistent with previous findings suggesting a link between sleep disturbances and postconcussive syndrome [23]. It is unclear why we did not observe a similar association with the objective assessment of sleep. One reason for this discrepancy is our small sample size. Additionally, the PSQI collects additional information compared to actigraphy including sleep disturbances and the use of sleep aids [18] which could influence the results. It is interesting that on average, the Veterans in this cohort were sleeping about 7 h indicating that they met the appropriate sleep duration for their age group [24]. However, sleep duration variability is an emerging sleep metric that may have additive value in sleep health [14] where greater sleep variability is associated with poor metabolic outcomes [25]. Therefore, we also assessed sleep timing variability as well and although we did not observe any strong associations in our current sample, we intend to evaluate this metric as we continue to enroll participants.

Sleep disturbances in patients with TBI have been shown to be predictive of cognitive processing speed [5]. Indeed, sleep was found to be important for executive function in young and older adults [26]. Contrary to what we expected, we observed a positive relation between sleep duration and processing speed such that Veterans with more sleep had slower performance on a measure of processing speed. However, our sample size is small with one Veteran having an average sleep duration of ~9 h and the greatest processing speed, potentially skewing our findings. Although previous work has found sleep deprivation degrades central processing in healthy individuals [27], a U-shaped curve exists between sleep duration and all-cause mortality [28] suggesting that too little and too much sleep can have negative health consequences. Given these unexpected findings, additional review of clinical records of these Veterans revealed that all enrolled have minimal to severe depression which may explain the association observed. Specifically, the prevalence of cognitive disorders in various domains including processing speed is prominent in major depressive disorder [29]. Additional data are needed to confirm these findings.

Given the multiple sequelae of mild TBIs, we also examined how sleep relates to other health outcomes. For example, sleep is also related to mindfulness in that mindfulness can improve sleep health [30]. In a group of students, average total FFMQ was 129.55 while mediators had a score of 148.94. Although we did not detect a relation between sleep and the FFMQ, the Veterans in our cohort had a score of 114 at baseline suggesting that they are less mindful which could be relatively easy way to intervene and improve sleep quality. In addition, we did not observe a relation between sleep and physical activity metrics in our cohort, however exercise still offers an important tool to achieve better sleep health [11]. As we continue to enroll, we will evaluate if these results change.

In summary, technological improvements have been increasing including wearable and nonwearable devices providing physiological data. In this study, we are conducting a remote observational study to evaluate sleep and health outcomes in Veterans. The trajectory of sleep health in military Veterans with a range of military exposures and with aging concerns may present some unique differences and thus, needs further evaluation. Remote clinical research protocols are imperative in collecting real-world data that is not influenced by strict control measures of a laboratory. This study will set the foundation for a remote health intervention protocol which can be an effective means of improving sleep and overall quality of life in Veterans with mild TBI.

## 4.1 Limitations

While the findings presented demonstrate the reliability of conducting a remote clinical research protocol, there are a few limitations to note. First, our sample size is small, however, this is an ongoing research protocol. With a greater sample size, we will have more confidence in the results presented and will use additional statistical models to identify significant relations. Further, due to our assessment being completely remote, tests available to assess cognitive processing speed were significantly limited. We selected the OTMT due to its common use in clinical settings and administration efficiency, but there are limitations with this assessment. Weak correlations are observed between the OTMT Part A (processing speed) and the traditional written version of the Trail Making Test suggesting that the two versions of the test may be less analogous measures of processing speed than intended [31]. Next, there are limitations with our sleep assessments. Polysomnography is the gold standard for sleep assessment; however, it is an expensive, laboratory-based assessment of sleep that requires specialized equipment and technicians. Additionally, polysomnography is conducted in a highly controlled environment and does not reflect the habitual sleep patterns at home. Although actigraphy can overestimate sleep and underestimate awake times compared with polysomnography [32], it is still useful as it represents at home sleep habits and can be used remotely. The PSQI is subject to biases and inaccuracies, however, it is a validated sleep questionnaire [33] that can provide additional information to the objective assessment of sleep and can be administered remotely. There are also limitations with consumer wearables (i.e., Fitbit) in that there is still insufficient evidence to support the validity of this sleep tracer in comparison to an accelerometer based device [34]. Finally, these findings do not provide information regarding causal associations between any of the metrics and thus, future studies are needed to determine the directionality of these relations.

## 5 Conclusion

The aim of this study was to use remote measures to examine how sleep influences postconcussive symptoms, cognitive performance, behavioral traits and physical activity in a cohort of Veterans that have a history of mild TBI. To corroborate our findings, increased enrollment in the present study and future cross-sectional studies designed to evaluate directionality of our results could increase the generalizability of the current observed trends. Such insight could guide the development of interventional studies to enhance sleep health in Veterans.

**Conflicts of Interest.** Authors report no conflicts of interest. the opinions presented in this article are those of the authors and do not reflect the views of any institution/agency of the U.S. government or the Henry M. Jackson Foundation for the Advancement of Military Medicine, Inc.

# References

1. Folmer, R.L., et al.: Prevalence and management of sleep disorders in the Veterans health administration. Sleep Med. Rev. **54**, 101358 (2020)
2. O'Neil, M.E., et al.: Complications of mild traumatic brain injury in veterans and military personnel: a systematic review. In: VA Evidence Synthesis Program Reports (2013)
3. Lu, L.H., Reid, M.W., Cooper, D.B., Kennedy, J.E.: Sleep problems contribute to post-concussive symptoms in service members with a history of mild traumatic brain injury without posttraumatic stress disorder or major depressive disorder. NeuroRehabilitation **44**, 511–521 (2019)
4. Orff, H.J., Ayalon, L., Drummond, S.P.A.: Traumatic brain injury and sleep disturbance: a review of current research. J. Head Trauma Rehabil. **24**, 155–165 (2009)
5. Mahmood, O., Rapport, L.J., Hanks, R.A., Fichtenberg, N.L.: Neuropsychological performance and sleep disturbance following traumatic brain injury. J. Head Trauma Rehabil. **19**, 378–390 (2004)
6. Holcomb, E., et al.: The relationship between sleep-wake cycle disturbance and trajectory of cognitive recovery during acute traumatic brain injury. J. Head Trauma Rehabil. **31**, 108–116 (2016)
7. Lehtonen, S., et al.: Neuropsychological outcome and community re-integration following traumatic brain injury: the impact of frontal and non-frontal lesions. Brain Inj. **19**, 239–256 (2009)
8. Fong, T.C., Ho, R.T.: Mindfulness facets predict quality of life and sleep disturbance via physical and emotional distresses in Chinese cancer patients: a moderated mediation analysis. Psychooncology **29**, 894–901 (2020)
9. Dolezal, B.A., Neufeld, E.V., Boland, D.M., Martin, Cooper, C.B.: Interrelationship between sleep and exercise: a systematic review. Adv. Prev. Med. 1364387 (2017)
10. Chennaoui, M., Arnal, P.J., Sauvet, F., Eger, D.L.: Sleep and exercise: a reciprocal issue? Sleep Med. Rev. **20**, 59–72 (2014)
11. Baron, K.G., Reid, K.J., Zee, P.C.: Exercise to improve sleep in insomnia: exploration of the bidirectional effects. J. Clin. Sleep Med. **9** (2013)
12. Grima, N., Ponsford, J., Rajaratnam, S.M., Mansfield, D., Pase, M.P.: Sleep disturbances in traumatic brain injury: a meta-analysis. J. Clin. Sleep Med. **12**, 419–428 (2016)
13. Deboer, T.: Sleep homeostasis and the circadian clock: do the circadian pacemaker and the sleep homeostat influence each other's functioning? Neurobiol. Sleep Circadian Rhythm **5**, 68–77 (2018)
14. Bei, B., Wiley, J.F., Trinder, J., Manber, R.: Beyond the mean: a systematic review on the correlates of daily intraindividual variability of sleep/wake patterns. Sleep Med. Rev. **28**, 108–124 (2016)
15. Watson, N.F., et al.: Recommended amount of sleep for a healthy adult: a joint consensus statement of the American academy of sleep medicine and sleep research society. Sleep **38**, 843 (2015)
16. Vanderploeg, R.D., et al.: Screening for postdeployment conditions: development and cross-validation of an embedded validity scale in the neurobehavioral symptom inventory. J. Head Trauma Rehabil. **29**, 1–10 (2014)
17. Carpenter, J.K., Conroy, K., Gomez, A.F., Curren, L.C., Hofmann, S.G.: The relationship between trait mindfulness and affective symptoms: a meta-analysis of the five facet mindfulnessquestionnaire (FFMQ). Clin. Psychol. Rev. **74**, 101785 (2019)
18. Buysse, D.J., Reynolds, C.F.I., Monk, T.H., Berman, S.R., Kupfer, D.J.: The Pittsburgh sleep quality index: a new instrument for psychiatric practice and research. Psychiatry Res. **28**(2), 193–213 (1989)

19. Matsangas, P., Mysliwiec, V.: The utility of the Pittsburgh sleep quality index in US military personnel. Mil. Psychol. **30**, 360–369 (2018)
20. Corrigan, J.D., Bogner, J.: Initial reliability and validity of the Ohio State University TBI identification method. J. Head Trauma Rehabil. **22**, 318–329 (2007)
21. Tudor-Locke, C., Barreira, T.V., Schuna, J.M., Mire, E.F., Katzmarzyk, P.T.: Fully automated waist-worn accelerometer algorithm for detecting children's sleep-period time separate from 24-h physical activity or sedentary behaviors. Appl. Physiol. Nutr. Metab. **39**, 53–57 (2014)
22. Castriotta, R.J., Wilde, M.C., Lai, J.M., Atanasov, S., Masel, B.E., Kuna, S.T.: Prevalence and consequences of sleep disorders in traumatic brain injury. J. Clin. Sleep Med. **3**, 349–356 (2007)
23. Minen, M.T., Boubour, A., Walia, H., Barr, W.: Post-concussive syndrome: a focus on post-traumatic headache and related cognitive, psychiatric, and sleep issues. Curr. Neurol. Neurosci. Rep. **16**(11), 1–12 (2016). https://doi.org/10.1007/s11910-016-0697-7
24. Hirshkowitz, M., et al.: National sleep foundation's sleep time duration recommendations: methodology and results summary. Sleep Heal. **1**, 40–43 (2015)
25. Zuraikat, F.M., Makarem, N., Redline, S., Aggarwal, B., Jelic, S., St-Onge, M.P.: Sleep regularity and cardiometabolic health: is variability in sleep patterns a risk factor for excess adiposity and glycemic dysregulation? Curr. Diab. Rep. **20** (2020)
26. Wilckens, K.A., Woo, S.G., Kirk, A.R., Erickson, K.I., Wheeler, M.E.: The role of sleep continuity and total sleep time in executive function across the adult lifespan. Psychol. Aging. **29**, 658 (2014)
27. Ratcliff, R., van Dongen, H.P.A.: Sleep deprivation affects multiple distinct cognitive processes. Psychon. Bull. Rev. **16**, 742 (2009)
28. Yin, J., et al.: Relationship of sleep duration with all-cause mortality and cardiovascular events: a systematic review and dose-response meta-analysis of prospective cohort studies. J. Am. Heart Assoc. **6**(9), e005947 (2017)
29. McIntyre, R.S., et al.: The prevalence, measurement, and treatment of the cognitive dimension/domain in major depressive disorder. CNS Drugs **29**, 577–589 (2015)
30. Ong, J.C., Ulmer, C.S., Manber, R.: Improving sleep with mindfulness and acceptance: a metacognitive model of Insomnia. Behav. Res. Ther. **50** (651) (2012)
31. Mrazik, M., Millis, S., Drane, D.L.: The oral trail making test: effects of age and concurrent validity. Arch. Clin. Neuropsychol. **25**, 236–243 (2010)
32. Ancoli-Israel, S., Cole, R., Alessi, C., Chambers, M., Moorcroft, W., Pollak, C.P.: The role of actigraphy in the study of sleep and circadian rhythms. Sleep **26**, 342–392 (2003)
33. Ibáñez, V., Silva, J., Cauli, O.: A survey on sleep assessment methods. PeerJ **6**, e4849 (2018)
34. Depner, C.M., et al.: Wearable technologies for developing sleep and circadian biomarkers: a summary of workshop discussions. Sleep **43**(1–13), 1–13 (2020)

# Effects of Military Occupational Exposures on Home-Based Assessment of Veterans' Self-reported Health, Sleep and Cognitive Performance Measures

Immanuel Samuel[1,2](✉) ⓘ, Kamila U. Pollin[1] ⓘ, Charity B. Breneman[1,2] ⓘ,
Timothy Chun[1] ⓘ, Mary M. Valmas[1] ⓘ, Ryan C. Brewster[1] ⓘ, Michelle Prisco[1] ⓘ,
John Barrett[1] ⓘ, Matthew J. Reinhard[1] ⓘ, and Michelle E. Costanzo[1] ⓘ

[1] War Related Illness and Injury Study Center,
Washington DC VA Medical Center, Washington DC 20422, USA
Immanuel.Samuel@va.gov
[2] Henry M Jackson Foundation for the Advancement of Military Medicine, Inc., Bethesda,
MD 20817, USA

**Abstract.** Military occupational exposures are varied and the health effects from these exposures may accumulate over time, causing health concerns in Veterans. However, there are currently no comprehensive exposure assessment tools to assess these military exposures. In this report, we present findings from an ongoing study conducted remotely using telehealth technologies to assess the associations between military exposures and health measures. Veterans were recruited for the study and following enrollment, study participants completed remote data collection by (1) completing web surveys, (2) undergoing remote cognitive performance assessment and (3) wearing a wrist actigraphy device for seven days to examine sleep measures. Past military exposures were assessed using the Veteran-Military Occupational Assessment Tool (V-MOAT) which is a detailed survey that assesses military occupational exposures across well-defined occupational and environmental medicine domains of chemical, physical, biological, ergonomic/injury, and psychosocial hazards. Preliminary findings reveal that while longer military service duration and exposure duration were associated with better self-reported health measures and cognitive performance, military exposure frequency was more associated with poor self-reported health measures. Additionally, the exposure duration and service duration were negatively associated with the sleep efficiency and total sleep time respectively. These findings suggest that longer periods of military occupational exposures may not be as detrimental to health as higher exposure frequency.

**Keywords:** Environmental exposure · Military exposure assessment · Remote assessment · Telehealth · Veteran health · Military health · Sleep quality

D. D. Schmorrow and C. M. Fidopiastis (Eds.): HCII 2022, LNAI 13310, pp. 91–102, 2022.
https://doi.org/10.1007/978-3-031-05457-0_8

# 1  Introduction

## 1.1  Background

Military occupational exposures are varied, ranging from chemical, biological, physical, ergonomic/injury and psychological [1–3]. Due to repeated exposure during military training and deployments, health effects from these exposures may accumulate over time, causing health concerns in the Veteran population [4, 5]. Thus, to identify exposure-related health outcomes, we assessed military occupational exposures and health-related measures remotely across domains such as sleep, psychological well-being and cognitive performance in a Veteran cohort. Leveraging such novel technology to develop distance-bridging approaches reduces barriers for patient care and represents an exciting and innovative approach to serve Veterans. During the emergency and continuation of COVID-19, telehealth became an essential component of health care [6], indeed mental telehealth services have previously proven efficacious in reducing psychiatric hospitalizations by as much as 25% for US Veterans [7]. In another study of rural Veterans with PTSD, a video-conference-delivered (telehealth) anger management program was as effective in reducing reported anger [8], and more cost effective, than the same program delivered in-person [9]. The current study is thus part of a programmatic effort to foster practices that will support current methods of in-person clinical treatment and assessment through distance-based programs reaching Veterans where they are best able to actively engage, through an innovative, resource multiplying and promising way to offer a realistic form of care to Veterans across the country. This study utilized such innovation methods in the context of critical and poorly understood topic: health effects of military occupational exposures.

## 1.2  Military Occupational Exposure Assessment

Currently, existing exposure assessment tools are designed to characterize occupational exposures in specific domains rather than providing a comprehensive exposure overview across multiple exposure domains [10]. Many of these exposure assessment tools also are not tailored to the unique concerns of the Veteran population. For this reason, a Veteran-Military Occupational Exposure Tool (V-MOAT) was developed by the Veterans Affairs (VA) War Related Illness and Injury Study Center, in Washington, DC (WRIISC-DC) and subsequently underwent peer review by physician and doctoral associates in the Department of Defense (DoD), the VA, and academia. The V-MOAT was created to capture a comprehensive exposure history that can then be used to assess exposure-related health effects at the individual and population health levels. The V-MOAT draws on well-recognized principles of clinical exposure assessment and asks Veterans about military occupational hazards across the commonly accepted occupational and environmental medicine domains of chemical, physical, biological, ergonomic/injury, and psychosocial hazards. If a Veteran endorses an exposure, the V-MOAT includes other key occupational and environmental medicine principles and asks questions about the duration of exposure, the route of exposure, exposure frequency, and dose-related health effects. Moreover, the V-MOAT queries the use of personal protective equipment at time of exposure and level of concern about the exposure. Thus, Veterans were asked about

64 types of exposures that were drawn from review of the military exposure literature and prior clinical experience of the study team. Additional exposure categories that are of particular concern for military and Veteran populations (ex. anthrax vaccinations, pyridostigmine bromide tablets) also were included in the V-MOAT. Military job duties, deployments, and non-occupational and hobby exposure concerns also were included in the V-MOAT. Additionally, the questionnaire was designed to allow addition of individual characteristics and exposures not specifically tied to military service, thereby allowing the V-MOAT to be used outside of Veteran/military populations and characterize non-military sources of exposures. Establishing a comprehensive, standardized and structured narrative of military exposure history represents a significant advancement in a topic of critical concern for Veterans.

## 1.3 Exposure Related Health Outcomes

Prior research on military exposure and its effects on health have revealed increased risk to adverse mental health in domains like anxiety, mood, memory, post-traumatic stress and substance use [11, 12]. Similarly, military exposures like blast exposure and traumatic brain injury have also been associated with reduction in cognitive performance [13–15]. Such decline in behavioral outcomes have also been supported by changes in hormonal levels [16], inflammatory markers [17] and brain imaging [18]. These relationships are also moderated by levels of resilience [19, 20] and social connectedness [21, 22] which could act as protective factors to adverse health. Thus, establishing a comprehensive approach of evaluation could aide in understanding the dynamics between these factors of health.

A particularly salient health concern for Veterans is poor sleep which has been shown to be worse in Veterans than in civilians due to multiple contributing factors [23] and can increased depressive, post-concussive and post-traumatic stress disorder symptomatology [24]. While subjective sleep assessment using online questionnaires is one method of assessing sleep remotely, wrist-worn actigraphy provides another remote tool that helps to further characterize sleep quantity and quality [25, 26]. Prior studies have shown that actigraphy-based sleep efficiency changes predict next-day stress levels [27] and blood pressure recovery [28] making it a viable tool to remotely characterize sleep related metrics. In summary, this study applied such considerations in the selection of distance-based modalities of evaluation focusing on sleep metrics, self-report behavioral symptoms and quantitative cognitive performance. The general expectation was that greater military occupational exposure would lead to worse outcomes. Consequently, we hypothesized that higher military exposure scores obtained from the V-MOAT would be associated with poor self-reported behavioral measures and poor sleep metrics.

## 1.4 Summary

The goal of this remote study was to assess the role military occupational exposures may have on Veteran health using remote data acquisition methods such as web-based surveys, remote cognitive performance assessments and home-based wearable and non-wearable sensors for collecting physiological measures. In this report, we present preliminary findings from this ongoing study to begin to evaluate the relationships between military-occupational exposures and sleep, behavioral symptoms, psychological traits and cognitive performance. We further discuss methodological considerations incorporated into the study to facilitate remote data acquisition, improve data quality and reduce participant burden.

## 2 Methods

The study was conducted by the War Related Illness and Injury Study Center at the Washington DC Veterans Affairs Medical Center (WRIISC-DC). WRIISC-DC is a national program dedicated to Veterans' post-deployment health concerns and unique health care needs including those related to a history of traumatic brain injury and potentially toxic military occupational exposures. Veterans referred to the WRIISC-DC for clinical evaluation were recruited for the study. Following study enrollment, study participants completed baseline assessment in a completely remote setting by (1) filling remote web surveys, (2) completing cognitive performance assessments with a neuropsychologist through a video teleconference portal; and (3) wearing a wrist actigraphy device (ActiGraph wGT3X-BT) for a minimum of seven days to examine sleep. Study devices and materials were mailed to participants after enrollment and participants then mailed these devices to the study team after completing the remote data collection. To ensure participants understood how to use the actigraphy device, pre-recorded video tutorials, videoconference-based tutorial sessions and consolidated text document with step-by-step directions were provided and follow up calls were made to improve data quality and ensure that study participants understood proper use of data collection tools.

### 2.1 Measures and Analysis

To identify relationships between exposure measures and health outcomes, in this report, a subset of the baseline data as detailed below was analyzed.

1) **Military Exposures**: Scores were derived from the V-MOAT which categorizes exposures into 64 different categories under the five recognized occupational and environmental medicine exposure domains of chemical (e.g., asbestos), physical (e.g. heat), biological (e.g. infections), ergonomic/injuries (e.g.: back injury), psychological (e.g. Post-Traumatic Stress). Based on our clinical experience with Veterans and review of the military occupational exposure literature, a sixth domain was added to include protective health measures such as anthrax vaccinations and pyridostigmine bromide since many deployed Veterans express exposure concerns about these exposures. For each of the exposures, the start and end dates were acquired to estimate exposure duration and the frequency of exposures was estimated on a 4-point scale. The responses across exposure types were averaged to obtain the mean (1) exposure duration and (2) exposure frequency. Total time in military service was also included as measure of exposure.
2) **Self-report behavioral measures**: Web surveys included the following self-report questionnaires to assess resilience, behavioral traits and psychological well-being: Connor-Davidson Resilience Scale (CD-RISC) [29], a measure that assesses one's

perception of their ability to "thrive in the face of adversity, Social Connectedness Scale (SCS) [30], a measure of one's feelings of belongingness and relations with others, Neurobehavioral Symptom Inventory (NSI) [31], a measure of physical, cognitive and emotional symptoms that occur after a mild traumatic brain injury, PTSD Checklist 5 (PCL-5) [32], a screening measure used to assess the 20 DSM-5 symptoms of PTSD, Pittsburg Sleep Quality Index (PSQI) [33], a measure that assesses sleep quality over a 1-month time interval, Patient Health Questionnaire (PHQ-9) [34], a screening measure that assessed the presence and severity of cognitive and somatic symptoms of depression, Neuro-Quality of Life (NQOL) [35], an inventory of symptoms related to general cognitive concerns, and General Anxiety Disorder (GAD) [36], a screening measure of anxiety symptoms.

3) **Cognitive performance**: Oral Trail Making Test [37, 38], a speeded measure of auditory processing speed for overlearned information was administered remotely over video tele-conference. The scores for Part A (Executive function) and Part B (Processing speed) were calculated [39] and the inverse was obtained so that the higher the score implied better performance.

4) **Sleep Outcomes**: Wrist-worn actigraph was used for a minimum of 7 days to obtain quantitative sleep metrics. The average Sleep Efficiency (SE), Total Sleep Time (TST) and Wake After Sleep Onset (WASO) were calculated using ActiLife Software v6.13.

The preliminary analysis included Non-parametric Spearman correlation coefficients between military occupational exposures and the health measures. only associations where $r > 0.5$ (high effect size) [40] were considered and p-values were not considered to account for non-normality of measures and the small sample size.

## 3 Results

Currently, eight Veterans (Age: $55 \pm 7$; Race: 8 White, Sex: 8 Male) completed the baseline evaluation and their average scores are reported in Table 1. Not all participants completed all aspects of the remote data acquisition phase. For this reason, the total sample size for each of the assessed measures also are reported. Preliminary results revealed that age was not highly associated with any of the health measures. However, service duration, exposure duration and exposure frequency were highly associated with the health measures (Fig. 1).

**Table 1.** Summary of measures used in this report including exposure scores, self-report behavioral measures, cognitive performance and sleep metrics.

| Variables | N | Mean | Std |
|---|---|---|---|
| Age (yrs) | 8 | 55.38 | 6.97 |
| Service Duration (yrs) | 8 | 19.09 | 7.21 |

*(continued)*

**Table 1.** (*continued*)

| Variables | N | Mean | Std |
|---|---|---|---|
| Veteran Military Occupation Assessment Tool (V-MOAT) | | | |
| Exposure Duration (yrs) | 8 | 12.83 | 4.31 |
| Exposure Frequency | 8 | 1.87 | 0.38 |
| Self-report behavioral measures | | | |
| Connor-Davidson Resilience Scale (CD-RISC) | 7 | 53.71 | 22.1 |
| Neuro-Quality of Life (NQOL) | 8 | 46.62 | 18.81 |
| Social Connectedness Scale (SCS) | 8 | 67.12 | 4.22 |
| Neurobehavioral Symptom Inventory (NSI) | 8 | 40.62 | 15.65 |
| Pittsburg Sleep Quality Index (PSQI) | 7 | 8.57 | 2.99 |
| Patient Health Questionnaire (PHQ-9) | 7 | 12 | 7.3 |
| PTSD Checklist 5 (PCL-5) | 8 | 40.38 | 21.16 |
| General Anxiety Disorder (GAD-7) | 8 | 11.75 | 3.99 |
| Cognitive Performance (OTMT) | | | |
| Processing Speed (1/s) | 7 | 0.1 | 0.05 |
| Executive Function (1/s) | 7 | 0.03 | 0.01 |
| Actigraphy Sleep Metrics | | | |
| Sleep Efficiency (SE) | 8 | 94.59 | 7.18 |
| Total Sleep Time (TST) | 8 | 442.3 | 43.91 |
| Wake After Sleep Onset (WASO) | 8 | 33.14 | 18.86 |

We observed that higher exposure frequency was more strongly associated with poor self-reported health outcomes (eg. lower CD-RISC, NQOL, SCS; higher NSI, PSQI, PHQ-9, PCL-5). Similarly, longer military service duration and exposure duration were also positively associated with cognitive performance scores (OTMT - Processing speed and executive function). When looking at the Actigraphy-based sleep metrics, the exposure duration and service duration were negatively associated with the sleep efficiency and total sleep time respectively.

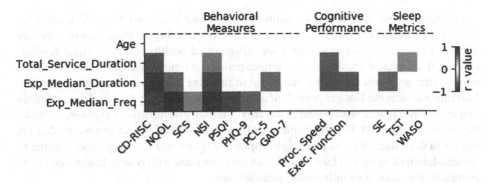

**Fig. 1.** Correlation matrix showing pairwise correlations (|r-values| > 0.5 reflecting high effect size) between age and exposures (y-axis; obtained from V-MOAT) and health measures (x-axis) namely: (1) self-report behavioral measures such as Connor-Davidson Resilience Scale (CD-RISC), Social Connectedness Scale (SCS), Neurobehavioral Symptom Inventory (NSI), PTSD Checklist 5 (PCL-5), Pittsburg Sleep Quality Index (PSQI), Patient Health Questionnaire (PHQ-9), Neuro-Quality of Life (NQOL) and General Anxiety Disorder (GAD) (2) Cognitive performance measures like Processing Speed and Executive Function scores obtained using Oral-Trail Making Test (OTMT) and (3) Sleep metrics such as Sleep Efficiency (SE), Total Sleep Time (TST) and Wake After Sleep Onset (WASO) obtained using Actigraphy.

## 4   Discussion

Preliminary findings from the initial cohort enrolled in this ongoing remote study reveal that while longer military service duration and exposure duration were associated with better self-reported health measures as well as cognitive performance scores, high exposure frequency was generally associated with poor self-reported health measures. This suggests that poor health measures were associated with more frequent exposures as opposed to longer periods of exposures. Lastly, sleep efficiency and total sleep time were negatively associated with exposure and service durations and did not seem to be similarly influenced by the exposure frequency. These findings suggest distinct relationships between exposure metrics and highlights the importance of detailed exposure characterization to identify relationships and possible mechanisms underlying exposure related health changes.

### 4.1   Exposure and Health Outcomes

Although the general notion is that military occupational exposures may act as a detrimental causal factor to Veteran health, we cannot assume such causality in this scenario since it may be that individuals with higher resilience characteristics at the time-of-service entry could enable them to stay in service for longer durations [41]. Likewise, Veterans with increased resilience and/or fewer health conditions-concerns, may remain in the military for longer durations, and thereby have increased occupational exposures, including both deployment and non-deployment related events [41]. Indeed, our findings contradict the general notion that longer exposure duration and service duration is associated with worse outcomes. This also aligns with prior research which showed positive associations between duration of military service and improved patients' knowledge about their medical concerns [42]. However, in this study, higher frequency of exposure appears to be more associated with poor self-reported health measures. These findings suggest that repeated exposures over longer periods of time may enable development of coping strategies which may be beneficial in reducing the exposure effects on health. Veterans who reported longer periods of military service also may have had more training and experience to deal with potential hazards of military occupational exposures. Unlike the exposure duration, higher frequency of exposures could reflect exposures that are higher in dose intensity and possibly complicated by shorter recovery times leading to accumulation of symptom burden and thus are associated with poorer health outcomes. Future studies should examine these associations.

## 4.2 Remote Study Assessment Considerations

This ongoing pilot study demonstrates that the effects of military exposure on Veteran health can be studied in a completely remote setting. Due to the high symptom burden of the participants, many methodological considerations were accounted for to ensure high study data quality while reducing time and effort demands on participants during the study data acquisition. As mentioned in the methods section, both pre-recorded and web-conference based video tutorials along with a brief text document containing clear, step-by-step instructions were provided. Information about all possible discomforts also was repeatedly conveyed to participants starting from informed consent and throughout the remote data acquisition period. Common technical issues and possible solutions were discussed proactively during the training phase to reduce frustration while using the data collection devices. Two follow-up calls also were done (1) at day 2 of the 7-day baseline assessment and (2) at day 7 before participants were asked to mail back the study devices to answer any questions study participants may have. Furthermore, web-surveys were restricted to weekdays (any time Monday-Thursday and Friday until 2 pm) to ensure immediate follow-up by mental health staff if participants endorsed suicidal ideation on the PHQ-9 questionnaire.

## 4.3 Study Limitations

In this study, the exposure evaluation was based on subjective, retrospective surveys and not objective measures obtained at the time of exposure which increases the possibility of recall bias [43]. Given the complexities of military environmental exposures, objective military occupational exposure data for this cohort were not available. While the findings presented in this report are preliminary, this study revealed new relationships between comprehensive exposure metrics assessed using a newly developed exposure assessment tool (V-MOAT) and the study's health outcomes describe above. These relationships, though novel, require more methodological inquiry to explore potential links between military occupational exposures and the Veteran reported health concerns outlined. Because the exposure evaluation conducted in this study was retrospective in nature and the health outcome evaluation reflected current functioning, it is not possible to establish causal relationships between these findings. However, this study does raise the question about whether past military occupational exposures could act as a causal agent for changes in present health.

Another limitation in the exposure characterization is that exposure severity for the exposure types assessed in V-MOAT are not known quantitatively. For this reason, when averaging exposure duration and exposure in the current analysis all the exposure categories were weighted the same since there is no prior empirical characterization of exposure severity. With higher sample size, logistic regression-based odds ratios would enable data driven weight assignment for the exposures in terms of contributing to increased risk for adverse health outcomes. Ranking of exposures based on expert review and objective military data sources (e.g. Individual Longitudinal Exposure Record (ILER)) is also possible and will be explored in future analysis. While the current sample size is low, leading to some of the analytical considerations such as non-parametric testing and interpretation of high-effect associations, further recruitment is planned and will enable regression-based analysis with statistical significance testing with a larger sample size.

## 5  Conclusion

The preliminary findings from this ongoing remote study reveals the importance of comprehensive military-occupational exposure evaluation when exploring health outcomes commonly reported by Veterans. This study also reveals associations between military occupational exposure metrics and Veteran health outcomes assessed across domains such as sleep, psychological well-being and cognitive performance. Furthermore, important remote data acquisition lessons were learned during this study and these considerations may provide a template for telehealth research for future studies in Veteran cohorts.

## References

1. Taylor, M.G., Ureña, S., Kail, B.L.: Service-related exposures and physical health trajectories among aging veteran men. Gerontologist **56**(1), 92–103 (2016). https://doi.org/10.1093/ger ont/gnv662
2. Karl, J.P., et al.: Effects of psychological, environmental and physical stressors on the gut microbiota. Front. Microbiol. **9**, 2013 (2018). https://doi.org/10.3389/fmicb.2018.02013
3. Sajja, V.S.S.S., et al.: The role of very low level blast overpressure in symptomatology. Front. Neurol. **10**, 891 (2019). https://doi.org/10.3389/fneur.2019.00891
4. Kamimori, G.H., Reilly, L.A., LaValle, C.R., Olaghere Da Silva, U.B.: Occupational over-pressure exposure of breachers and military personnel. Shock Waves **27**(6), 837–847 (2017). https://doi.org/10.1007/s00193-017-0738-4
5. Kubli, L., Pinto, R., Burrows, H., Littlefield, P., Brungart, D.: The effects of repeated low-level blast exposure on hearing in marines. Noise Health **19**(90), 227 (2017). https://doi.org/10. 4103/nah.NAH_58_16
6. Thomas, E.E., et al.: Building on the momentum: sustaining telehealth beyond COVID-19. J. Telemed. Telecare 1357633X2096063 (2020). https://doi.org/10.1177/1357633X20960638
7. Godleski, L., Cervone, D., Vogel, D., Rooney, M.: Home telemental health implementation and outcomes using electronic messaging. J. Telemed. Telecare **18**(1), 17–19 (2012). https:// doi.org/10.1258/jtt.2011.100919

8. Morland, L.A., et al.: Telemedicine for anger management therapy in a rural population of combat veterans with posttraumatic stress disorder: a randomized noninferiority trial. J. Clin. Psychiatry **71**(7), 20772 (2010). https://doi.org/10.4088/JCP.09m05604blu

9. Morland, L.A., et al.: Telemedicine: a cost-reducing means of delivering psychotherapy to rural combat veterans with ptsd. Telemed. E-Health **19**(10), 754–759 (2013). https://doi.org/10.1089/tmj.2012.0298

10. Glass, D.C., Sim, M.R.: The challenges of exposure assessment in health studies of Gulf War veterans. Philos. Trans. Roy. Soc. B Biol. Sci. **361**(1468), 627–637 (2006). https://doi.org/10.1098/rstb.2006.1822

11. Campbell, M.S., et al.: Longitudinal relationship of combat exposure with mental health diagnoses in the military health system. Mil. Med. **186**(Supplement_1), 160–166 (2021). https://doi.org/10.1093/milmed/usaa301

12. Elder, G.A., Ehrlich, M.E., Gandy, S.: Relationship of traumatic brain injury to chronic mental health problems and dementia in military veterans. Neurosci. Lett. **707**, 134294 (2019). https://doi.org/10.1016/j.neulet.2019.134294

13. LaValle, C.R., et al.: Neurocognitive performance deficits related to immediate and acute blast overpressure exposure. Front. Neurol. **10**, 949 (2019). https://doi.org/10.3389/fneur.2019.00949

14. Rakers, S.E., et al.: Executive functioning in relation to coping in mild versus moderate-severe traumatic brain injury. Neuropsychology **32**(2), 213–219 (2018). https://doi.org/10.1037/neu0000399

15. Spitz, G., Schönberger, M., Ponsford, J.: The relations among cognitive impairment, coping style, and emotional adjustment following traumatic brain injury. J. Head Trauma Rehabil. **28**(2), 116–125 (2013). https://doi.org/10.1097/HTR.0b013e3182452f4f

16. Morgan, C.A., et al.: Hormone profiles in humans experiencing military survival training. Biol. Psychiat. **47**(10), 891–901 (2000). https://doi.org/10.1016/S0006-3223(99)00307-8

17. Sikkeland, L.I.B., et al.: Systemic and airway inflammation after exposure to fumes from military small arms. Am. J. Respir. Crit. Care Med. **197**(10), 1349–1353 (2018). https://doi.org/10.1164/rccm.201709-1857LE

18. Admon, R., et al.: Stress-induced reduction in hippocampal volume and connectivity with the ventromedial prefrontal cortex are related to maladaptive responses to stressful military service: hippocampal deficits following military stress. Hum. Brain Mapp. **34**(11), 2808–2816 (2012). https://doi.org/10.1002/hbm.22100

19. Sheerin, C.M., et al.: The association of resilience on psychiatric, substance use, and physical health outcomes in combat trauma-exposed military service members and veterans. Eur. J. Psychotraumatol. **10**(1), 1625700 (2019). https://doi.org/10.1080/20008198.2019.1625700

20. Isaacs, K., et al.: Psychological resilience in U.S. military veterans: a 2-year, nationally representative prospective cohort study. J. Psychiatr. Res. **84**, 301–309 (2017). https://doi.org/10.1016/j.jpsychires.2016.10.017

21. Kintzle, S., Barr, N., Corletto, G., Castro, C.: PTSD in U. S. Veterans: the role of social connectedness, combat experience and discharge. Healthcare **6**(3), 102 (2018). https://doi.org/10.3390/healthcare6030102

22. Sippel, L.M., Watkins, L.E., Pietrzak, R.H., Hoff, R., Harpaz-Rotem, I.: Heterogeneity of posttraumatic stress symptomatology and social connectedness in treatment-seeking military veterans: a longitudinal examination. Eur. J. Psychotraumatol. **10**(1), 1646091 (2019). https://doi.org/10.1080/20008198.2019.1646091

23. Babu Henry Samuel, I., Breneman, C.B., Chun, T., Hamedi, A., Murphy, R., Barrett, J.P.: Compounding effects of traumatic brain injury, military status, and other factors on Pittsburgh sleep quality index: a meta-analysis. Mil. Med. usab377 (2021). https://doi.org/10.1093/milmed/usab377

24. Mantua, J., Helms, S.M., Weymann, K.B., Capaldi, V.F., Lim, M.M.: Sleep quality and emotion regulation interact to predict anxiety in veterans with PTSD. Behav. Neurol. **2018**, 1–10 (2018). https://doi.org/10.1155/2018/7940832

25. Razjouyan, J., et al.: Wearable sensors and the assessment of frailty among vulnerable older adults: an observational cohort study. Sensors **18**(5), 1336 (2018). https://doi.org/10.3390/s18051336

26. McDevitt, B., Moore, L., Akhtar, N., Connolly, J., Doherty, R., Scott, W.: Validity of a novel research-grade physical activity and sleep monitor for continuous remote patient monitoring. Sensors **21**(6), 2034 (2021). https://doi.org/10.3390/s21062034

27. Yap, Y., Slavish, D.C., Taylor, D.J., Bei, B., Wiley, J.F.: Bi-directional relations between stress and self-reported and actigraphy-assessed sleep: a daily intensive longitudinal study. Sleep **43**(3), zsz250 (2020). https://doi.org/10.1093/sleep/zsz250

28. Eiman, M.N., Pomeroy, J., Weinstein, A.A.: Relationship of actigraphy-assessed sleep efficiency and sleep duration to reactivity to stress. Sleep Sci. (Sao Paulo, Brazil) **12**(4), 257–264 (2019). https://doi.org/10.5935/1984-0063.20190090

29. Connor, K.M., Davidson, J.R.T.: Development of a new resilience scale: the connor-davidson resilience scale(Cd-risc). Depress. Anxiety **18**(2), 76–82 (2003). https://doi.org/10.1002/da.10113

30. Lee, R.M., Draper, M., Lee, S.: Social connectedness, dysfunctional interpersonal behaviors, and psychological distress: testing a mediator model. J. Couns. Psychol. **48**(3), 310–318 (2001). https://doi.org/10.1037/0022-0167.48.3.310

31. Cicerone, K.D., Kalmar, K.: Persistent postconcussion syndrome: the structure of subjective complaints after mild traumatic brain injury. J. Head Trauma Rehabil. **10**(3), 1–17 (1995). https://doi.org/10.1097/00001199-199510030-00002

32. Weathers, F.W., Litz, B.T., Keane, T.M., Palmieri, P.A., Marx, B.P., Schnurr, P.P.: The PTSD Checklist for DSM-5 (PCL-5) (2013)

33. Buysse, D.J., Reynolds, C.F., Monk, T.H., Berman, S.R., Kupfer, D.J.: The Pittsburgh sleep quality index: a new instrument for psychiatric practice and research. Psychiatry Res. **28**(2), 193–213 (1989). https://doi.org/10.1016/0165-1781(89)90047-4

34. Kroenke, K., Spitzer, R.L.: The PHQ-9: a new depression diagnostic and severity measure. Psychiatr. Ann. **32**(9), 509–515 (2002). https://doi.org/10.3928/0048-5713-20020901-06

35. Cella, D., et al.: Neuro-QOL: brief measures of health-related quality of life for clinical research in neurology. Neurology **78**(23), 1860–1867 (2012). https://doi.org/10.1212/WNL.0b013e318258f744

36. Spitzer, R.L., Kroenke, K., Williams, J.B.W., Löwe, B.: A brief measure for assessing generalized anxiety disorder: the GAD-7. Arch. Intern. Med. **166**(10), 1092 (2006). https://doi.org/10.1001/archinte.166.10.1092

37. Jaywant, A., Barredo, J., Ahern, D.C., Resnik, L.: Neuropsychological assessment without upper limb involvement: a systematic review of oral versions of the trail making test and symbol-digit modalities test. Neuropsychol. Rehabil. **28**(7), 1055–1077 (2018). https://doi.org/10.1080/09602011.2016.1240699

38. Fett, A.-K.J., et al.: Long-term changes in cognitive functioning in individuals with psychotic disorders: findings from the suffolk county mental health project. JAMA Psychiat. **77**(4), 387 (2020). https://doi.org/10.1001/jamapsychiatry.2019.3993

39. Ricker, J.H., Axelrod, B.N.: Analysis of an oral paradigm for the trail making test. Assessment **1**(1), 47–51 (1994). https://doi.org/10.1177/1073191194001001007

40. Rosenthal, R., Rosnow, R.L.: Essentials of Behavioral Research: Methods and data Analysis, Chapter 12. McGraw-Hill Humanities Social, New York (1991)
41. Seelig, A.D., Jacobson, I.G., Donoho, C.J., Trone, D.W., Crum-Cianflone, N.F., Balkin, T.J.: Sleep and health resilience metrics in a large military cohort. Sleep **39**(5), 1111–1120 (2016). https://doi.org/10.5665/sleep.5766
42. Sabatino, M.J., et al.: Duration of military service is associated with decision quality in Veterans considering total knee replacement: case series. Patient Relat. Outcome Meas. **10**, 209–215 (2019). https://doi.org/10.2147/PROM.S163691
43. Coughlin, S.S.: Recall bias in epidemiologic studies. J. Clin. Epidemiol. **43**(1), 87–91 (1990). https://doi.org/10.1016/0895-4356(90)90060-3

# The Role of IT Background for Metacognitive Accuracy, Confidence and Overestimation of Deep Fake Recognition Skills

Stefan Sütterlin[1,2(✉)], Ricardo G. Lugo[2,3], Torvald F. Ask[2,3], Karl Veng[1], Jonathan Eck[1], Jonas Fritschi[1], Muhammed-Talha Özmen[1], Basil Bärreiter[1], and Benjamin J. Knox[2,3,4]

[1] Faculty of Computer Science, Albstadt-Sigmaringen University, Sigmaringen, Germany
stefan.suetterlin@hs-albsig.de
[2] Faculty of Health, Welfare and Organisation, Østfold University College, Halden, Norway
[3] Centre for Cyber and Information Security, Norwegian University of Science and Technology, Trondheim, Norway
[4] Cyber Warfare Centre, Norwegian Armed Forces Cyber Defence, Oslo, Norway

**Abstract.** The emergence of synthetic media such as deep fakes is considered to be a disruptive technology shaping the fight against cybercrime as well as enabling political disinformation. Deep faked material exploits humans' interpersonal trust and is usually applied where technical solutions of deep fake authentication are not in place, unknown, or unaffordable. Improving the individual's ability to recognise deep fakes where they are not perfectly produced requires training and the incorporation of deep fake-based attacks into social engineering resilience training. Individualised or tailored approaches as part of cybersecurity awareness campaigns are superior to a one-size-fits-all approach, and need to identify persons in particular need for improvement. Research conducted in phishing simulations reported that persons with educational and/or professional background in information technology frequently underperform in social engineering simulations. In this study, we propose a method and metric to detect overconfident individuals in regards to deep fake recognition. The proposed overconfidence score flags individuals overestimating their performance and thus posing a previously unconsidered cybersecurity risk. In this study, and in line with comparable research from phishing simulations, individuals with IT background were particularly prone to overconfidence. We argue that this data-driven approach to identifying persons at risk enables educators to provide a more targeted education, evoke insight into own judgement deficiencies, and help to avoid the self-selection bias typical for voluntary participation.

**Keywords:** Metacognition · Deep fake · Cybersecurity · Social engineering

## 1 Introduction

In times of ever increasing Cyber Security (CS) threats and evolving CS defence technology, the resource-intensive arm's race between those intending to exploit technological weaknesses and those dedicated to protecting them, often leads to attack vectors

© The Author(s), under exclusive license to Springer Nature Switzerland AG 2022
D. D. Schmorrow and C. M. Fidopiastis (Eds.): HCII 2022, LNAI 13310, pp. 103–119, 2022.
https://doi.org/10.1007/978-3-031-05457-0_9

circumventing technological defence structures by applying social engineering techniques. According to recent surveys, up to 98% of all cyberattacks in 2020 were social-engineering-enabled [1], with increasing tendencies [2, 3]. The term Social Engineering has been defined as "any act that influences a person to take an action that may or may not be in their best interest" [4, 5]. Cybercriminals consider the exploitation of stable human traits such as interpersonal trust, agreeableness and conscientiousness [6] as cheap, sufficiently reliable and sufficiently riskless to exploit. They do this by applying well established tactics of persuasion [7], such as social proof or reciprocity, depending on the target [8].

Persuasion tactics often aim to induce an emotional reaction (e.g. a sense of urgency, relatedness, compassion, sadness, fear, responsibility or duty) in the target. This will make them direct their attention towards internal processes such as the significance of emotional reactions or gut-feelings that lead to impulsive decision-making [9]. When attention is directed inwards, less attentional resources are directed externally to critically examine the details of the persuasion attempt, such as whether the information that is presented is plausible and warrants immediate action. One such example could be a cybercriminal pretending to be a relative or the superior of a target person while contacting them through a fake email or a fake profile on social media. The cybercriminal might be claiming that they are in trouble and that there is an urgent need for the target to transfer money from the company account or their own, to an account provided by the cybercriminal. If the cybercriminal is successful in instilling a sense of urgency in the target then the target may act without considering the scenario's actual probability. With the vast majority of cybercrime entailing some type of Social Engineering, and with political messaging relying on the spread of fake news that is often emotionally-laden, new and potentially disruptive technologies such as synthetic media (e.g. deep fakes (DF)) have raised attention both in the forensic as well as the political domain [10].

DF technology provides cybercriminals with a unique opportunity to impersonate other individuals with a degree of realism that is hard to falsify with human eyes [11, 12]. In a Social Engineering context, this is (broadly) achieved through 1) manipulating the facial expressions, lip movements, and voice of an individual that is known to the target by using DF technology on an existing video, 2) recording oneself while swapping faces with an individual that is known to the target, or 3) some combination of the two methods. In other words, DFs can be used in a Social Engineering attack through manipulation of facial expression or facial identity [13, 14]. The associated cost of DF scams was estimated to exceed 250 million USD in 2020 [15]. With the continuously increasing sophistication of AI-generated DF technology, the defence technology required to effectively detect and flag DFs may already be too advanced to be used by individuals from non-technical backgrounds [12, 16]. Social Engineering is more effective when aimed at unprepared and unaware individuals thus making them richer targets for Social Engineering attacks. Targeting unsuspecting victims with low levels of awareness of technological aids may effectively render technological solutions irrelevant in contexts where they are unknown, unavailable, or not likely to be applied by the user.

The lack of technological solutions in settings where DFs are most likely to occur highlights an urgent demand for education of users across societal settings and should therefore be integrated in future CS awareness training programs. It has been argued that, just as in other educational contexts, CS awareness training must follow individualised approaches to be most efficient [17, 18]. This tailored approach is required to avoid that participants are unmotivated due to inappropriate demands and difficulty levels. Comprehensive research efforts to map individual and cognitive-emotional factors affecting susceptibility to- and resilience against Social Engineering attacks have only recently started to emerge [19]. To successfully incorporate Social Engineering and DF detection skills in individualised CS awareness training, research must first address the current unanswered questions related to understanding how individual differences and related cognitive processes influence Social Engineering and particularly DF detection skills. The answers to these questions will be the basis for developing individualised approaches targeting cognitive processes on various levels. We argue that understanding trait-like precursors of underperformance in DF recognition can inform educational programs in CS awareness by identifying persons in need of feedback and particular attention. Consequently, these precursors may complement or to some extent, even substitute self-reported perceived competence and the self-selection to training schemes.

Metacognition is the cognitive ability to observe (or be aware of) one's own internal processes, such as thoughts and emotions, through two processes: (1) having knowledge about cognition and (2) how to regulate cognition [20]. Metacognitive awareness and accuracy vary between individuals, and may be a common denominator in both an individual's ability to be aware of- and think critically about their emotional and cognitive reactions during a Social Engineering attack. As well as possessing the requisite amount of self-knowledge about how accurately they are able to evaluate their ability to detect DFs. Previous research shows that having a technical or non-technical professional background does not differentiate susceptibility to phishing attacks. Even when having relevant education and coming from an Information Technology (IT) background, people are still overconfident in their abilities to detect Social Engineering attacks such as phishing emails [21, 22]. The non-differential ability of individuals with and without IT backgrounds to detect Social Engineering attacks may in part be explained by a lack of cognitive involvement, influenced by overconfidence rather than lacking detection abilities [22]. This matters because decisions in risky and uncertain situations are made based on a self-assessment of one's own perceived mastery, and not on actual performance which can only be known after the action has been performed and where there is the chance to receive an objective feedback on the outcomes.

There is a growing field of CS research on human-machine and human-human interactions in cyber-physical contexts (in the Hybrid Space) [23] aiming to improve decision-making that is based on how humans perceive and communicate their awareness of cyber threats. This research indicates that self-regulation and metacognitive skills are predictors of performance in such hybrid contexts [24–26]. While metacognitive awareness may allow individuals to detect when they are having emotional and cognitive reactions to DF-mediated Social Engineering attacks, self-regulation skills may allow individuals to divert attention away from the internal processes and towards critical examination of details such as DF artefacts. An individual with good metacognitive skills that knows their limitations may be more prone to seek out assistance or relevant information rather than making decisions based on an insufficient information basis. Conversely, people with lower levels of metacognition may not accurately judge their abilities to detect DF-mediated Social Engineering attacks, which may lead to overconfidence, thus being unprepared and at increased risk for victimisation. While metacognition has been researched extensively for performance in a cyber context in recent years, few studies have looked at metacognition (the confidence into one's performance and into the accuracy of one's self-assessment) in Social Engineering attacks. They find that participants can accurately judge legitimate emails, but the same participants displayed overconfidence in assessing phishing emails [27]. Accurate confidence judgments were only weakly associated with phishing identification [28].

This study investigated the role of metacognition in identifying DF social engineering attacks. We suggest the calculation of an overconfidence score may allow for the elimination of self-selection effects to cybersecurity awareness education, to ensure that training is delivered where it is needed most, and not only to those that are least confident. We hypothesise that overconfidence can have detrimental effects on DF recognition and that overconfidence is particularly pronounced in persons with IT-Backgrounds and self-reported IT-affinity.

- Hypothesis 1 (H1): IT background and/or self-reported IT-affinity are not associated with higher DF recognition skills.
- Hypothesis 2 (H2): IT background and/or self-reported IT-affinity are associated with higher *perceived* DF recognition skills.

## 2 Methods

### 2.1 Design

Data collection was done via the online platform Google Forms. All questions and instructions were presented in English. On the first page of the form, participants received instructions about the nature and purpose of the study. Upon study commencement, demographic information regarding participant characteristics were collected. Participants were asked to indicate whether they were using a PC, tablet, or smartphone, as well as their age, gender, country of residence, and level of educational attainment ranging from not having attended any education up to doctoral-level education. To collect information about IT and non-IT backgrounds, participants were asked to indicate whether they currently or previously worked in IT, or had received any formal IT education, and to indicate whether they previously or currently worked in CS/IT security. Participants also answered questions regarding their affinity to technology, prior DF knowledge and experience, and were asked to estimate their DF recognition skill level, the confidence they had in their skill level estimates, and how well they would perform on a DF recognition task. They were also asked to provide a number from 0 to 10 of how many clips they expected to correctly classify if shown 10 short clips that were either authentic or fake. Participants were also tested in the Group Embedded Figures Test which will be reported elsewhere. After all baseline information was collected, participants were taken to the task page in the online form. On the task page they were presented with 21 short videos where six of the videos were authentic and 15 of the videos were DFs. All clips were on average 15 s long and were retrieved from publicly available databases (github.com; kaggle.com). Participants were instructed to view each clip only once and

DF videos were presented first. For each clip they rated if the video was authentic or faked. For each clip they rated as fake or authentic they were also asked to rate how certain they were about their individual judgements. After they finished rating the videos they were asked again to rate their DF recognition skills and how confident they were in their opinion about their skills. After finishing the study, participants were given the opportunity to express their opinions about how it was to participate, and also provide feedback for improvement. Participants were given a maximum of 55 min to complete the study including answering the questionnaires. A timer showing how much time they had left to complete the form was visible at the top of the page at all times. The average response time was approximately 20 min.

## 2.2  Questionnaires

**Affinity for Technology Interaction (ATI) Scale.** The ATI scale [29] was used to assess individual differences in affinity for interacting with technology. The ATI scale presents participants with nine statements about their technology habits such as "When I have a new technical system in front of me, I try it out intensively" and "It is enough for me to know the basic functions of a technical system". The statements are judged on a 6-point scale, with responses ranging from 'Completely disagree' to 'Completely agree'. Reliability for the ATI was acceptable (Cronbach's $\alpha = .60$).

**Confidence in Abilities (CIA) Scale.** To assess how confident participants were in their DF recognition abilities, the CIA questions were asked prior to and after the DF recognition task. The CIA scale asks participants to estimate confidence in their abilities on a 6-point scale ranging from 'Very Good' to 'Very Poor'. Prior to the DF recognition task, participants were asked "How would you rate your skills to recognise deep fakes?". After the DF recognition task, participants were asked "How would you rate your skills to recognize deep fakes now?". Very high CIA scores and poor actual DF recognition performance indicate overconfidence, perhaps due to low metacognitive awareness and resulting metacognitive inaccuracy. Very low scores and good DF recognition performance indicate underconfidence due to low metacognitive awareness and accuracy. Judgement scores that match performance indicate good metacognitive awareness and accuracy.

**Judgement of Confidence (JOC) Scale.** JOC questions were used prior to and after the DF recognition task. The JOC scale asks participants to judge how accurate they think their confidence in their abilities are on a 6-point scale ranging from 'Very Good' to 'Very Poor'. Prior to the DF recognition task and following the CIA ratings, participants were asked "How confident are you that your rating above in which you describe your deep fake recognition skills, is accurate?". After the DF recognition task and following the CIA ratings, participants were asked "How confident are you about this opinion about your recognition skill?".

**Certainty in Video Rating (CIVR) Score.** To assess participants' certainty about individual video ratings during the DF recognition task, participants were asked for each video they judged to also rate how certain they were about each ratings on a 4-point scale ranging from 'Very unsure' to 'Very sure'. This requires processing of task difficulty, thus representing a task-oriented judgement of performance. Certainty in DF ratings were averaged as a CIVR DF score. Certainty in authentic ratings were averaged as a CIVR Real score. Total certainty ratings were averaged as a CIVR Overall score.

**Overconfidence Scale (OCS).** OCS was computed using the following formula:

$$OCS = \frac{\left(\frac{CIA\, pre \times 100}{6}\right)}{\% \text{ of correct ratings} + 1}$$

To avoid dividing by zero, a constant (+1) was added on both sides of the fraction. Because the pre-task CIA score is divided by correct ratings, CIA estimates that were correct returned an OCS score of 1, while any CIA score that overestimated DF detection abilities returned an OCS score above 1. Thus, any OCS score above 1 represents an overconfidence in DF detection abilities. Likewise, values below 1 indicate an underestimation of detection skills.

### 2.3  Participants, Recruitment, and Ethical Considerations

A total of 247 participants (92 females; 37.2%) were recruited via the online platform Amazon mTurk and financially compensated for their time. this study complies with the Declaration of Helsinki and is in line with the Recommendations for the Conduct, Reporting, Editing and Publication of Scholarly Work in Medical Journals. Informed consent was obtained from all participants prior to the study and they were all briefed about the purpose of the study prior to participation. Information was given to participants that they could withdraw from participation at any time. Participation was completely anonymous; neither IP address nor any personal information that could lead to identification of participants was registered. No methods of deception were applied in the study and all participants were informed that some of the videos would be faked.

### 2.4  Data Reduction and Analysis.

Participant characteristics were summarised as means (M) and standard deviations (SD) for continuous variables and number (count) and percentage (%) for ordinal variables and presented in tables. Visual inspection of variables showed that they were not normally distributed. Non-parametric tests were therefore used in all subsequent analyses.

Kruskal-Wallis H test was used to assess relationships between ordinal variables and DF detection skills. Results were reported as H statistics (degrees of freedom), p-values, and η2 (effect size). Dunn's Post-hoc test with Bonferroni adjustment was used to assess between-group differences. Results of post hoc tests were reported as Z statistics and Bonferroni adjusted p-values. Spearman correlations were performed to assess relationships between continuous variables and DF detection skills. Results were reported as Spearman's rho ($\rho$) and p-values and presented in a table. Separate linear regressions were performed for significant correlations.

In the first part of the analysis, Kruskal-Wallis tests were used to assess the relationships between IT and CS Background (grouping variables) and DF recognition performance (outcome variables). Spearman correlations were used to assess the relationship between ATI scale score and DF recognition performance. Additional Kruskal-Wallis tests were performed for IT and CS background with DF recognition performance (outcome variables) while weighting on ATI scores to see if technology affinity affected results. In the second part of the analysis, Kruskal-Wallis tests were used to assess differences in CIA, JOC, CIVR, and OCS scores (outcome variables) between IT/non-IT, and CS/non-CS groups (grouping variables). Spearman correlations were used to assess the relationship between ATI scale score and CIA, JOC, CIVR, and OCS scores. Additional Kruskal-Wallis tests were performed for IT and CS background with CIA and JOC scores (outcome variables) while weighting on ATI scores to see if technology affinity affected results. In the third part of the analysis, Kruskal-Wallis tests were used to assess differences in DF recognition performance, CIA, JOC, CIVR, and OCS scores between genders. Interval plots were generated for DF task performance, CIA scores, and OCS scores between IT and non-IT professionals and between genders and presented in tables. $\alpha$ level was set to .05 for all comparisons. All analyses were performed using JASP v0.16 [30].

## 3    Results

### 3.1    Participant Characteristics

Sample background statistics can be found in Table 1.

**Table 1.** Sample characteristics (N = 247).

| Demography | Count (%) | IT background and Device used | Count (%) |
|---|---|---|---|
| Male | 155 (62.7) | IT professional | 214 (86.6) |
| Higher education | 216 (87.5) | CS professional | 193 (78.1) |
| **Country** | | Familiar with DF term | 218 (88.2) |
| USA | 120 (48.5) | Have seen a DF | 214 (86.6) |
| India | 104 (42.1) | **Device used** | |
| Other | 23 (9.3) | PC | 233 (94.3) |
| | | Tablet | 7 (2.8) |
| | | Smartphone | 6 (2.4) |

*Notes.* IT = Information technology. CS = Cyber security. DF = Deep fakey

### 3.2    Descriptive Statistics

Descriptive statistics for age, scale and test scores for IT and non-IT professionals, males and females, and for the total sample can be found in Table 2.

**Table 2.** Descriptive Statistics (N = 247).

| Variables | IT | | Non-IT | | Male | | Female | | Total | |
|---|---|---|---|---|---|---|---|---|---|---|
| | M | SD | M | SD | M | SD | M | SD | M | SD |
| Age | 34.2 | 10.3 | 40.8 | 13.4 | 35 | 11.1 | 34.9 | 10.6 | 35 | 10.9 |
| ATI Scale | 3.9 | 0.4 | 3.9 | 0.4 | 3.9 | 0.5 | 3.9 | 0.5 | 3.9 | 0.5 |
| CIA Pre task | 4.3 | 1.0 | 3.5 | 1.2 | 4.3 | 1.0 | 4.1 | 1.2 | 4.2 | 1.1 |
| CIA Post task | 4.4 | 1.0 | 3.8 | 1.2 | 4.5 | 0.9 | 4.1 | 1.2 | 4.4 | 1.0 |
| JOC Pre task | 4.5 | 1.0 | 4.5 | 1.2 | 4.6 | 1.0 | 4.4 | 1.2 | 4.5 | 1.0 |
| JOC Post-task | 4.6 | 1.0 | 4.4 | 0.9 | 4.7 | 0.9 | 4.4 | 1.1 | 4.6 | 1.0 |
| CIVR DF | 2.9 | 0.3 | 2.9 | 0.4 | 2.9 | 0.3 | 2.9 | 0.3 | 2.9 | 0.3 |
| CIVR Real | 2.9 | 0.3 | 3.0 | 0.5 | 2.9 | 0.3 | 2.9 | 0.4 | 2.9 | 0.4 |
| CIVR Overall | 2.9 | 0.3 | 3.0 | 04 | 2.9 | 0.3 | 2.9 | 0.3 | 2.9 | 0.3 |
| OCS | 1.7 | 5.7 | 1.2 | 0.8 | 1.8 | 6.7 | 1.2 | 0.6 | 1.6 | 5.3 |
| DF rated real (%) | 28.5 | 20.1 | 31.3 | 21.3 | 30 | 20.1 | 26.9 | 20.7 | 28.9 | 20.3 |
| Real rated DF (%) | 71.2 | 27.8 | 76.7 | 19.9 | 72.6 | 26.5 | 70.9 | 27.6 | 72 | 26.9 |
| Correct ratings (%) | 59.2 | 16.7 | 55.6 | 14.9 | 57.7 | 16.6 | 60.3 | 16.8 | 58.7 | 16.7 |

*Notes.* DF = Deep fake. ATI = Affinity for technology interaction. CIA = Confidence in abilities. JOC = Judgment of confidence. Pre task = Pre DF task. Post task = Post DF task. CIVR = Certainty in video rating. OCS = Overconfidence score

### H1: IT background and/or self-reported IT-affinity are not associated with higher DF recognition skills.

Spearman correlations for age, and scale and test scores can be found in Table 3. To test the hypothesis that IT background ($H_1$) does not influence DF recognition skills, Kruskal-Wallis tests were performed using IT and CS background as grouping variables and DF performance variables as outcomes. Spearman correlations were performed on ATI scores and DF recognition variables. All correlations can be found in Table 3. There were no significant differences in DF recognition (DF videos rated as authentic) for IT and non-IT ($H = 0.08(2)$, $p = .774$, $\eta^2 = -.003$) or CS and non-CS professionals ($H = .21(1)$, $p = .649$, $\eta^2 = -.003$).

There were no significant differences in rate of false positives (authentic videos rated as DFs) for IT and non-IT ($H = 0.22(1)$, $p = .638$, $\eta^2 = -.003$) or CS and non-CS professionals ($H = 0.42(1)$, $p = .519$, $\eta^2 = -.002$). There were no significant differences in overall DF task performance (correct ratings) for IT and non-IT ($H = 1.41(1)$, $p = .234$, $\eta^2 = .001$) or CS and non-CS professionals ($H = 0.09(1)$, $p = .769$, $\eta^2 = -.003$). ATI score was not associated with DF recognition ($\rho = -.042$, $p = .509$), false positive ratings ($\rho = -.108$, $p = .092$), or overall DF task performance ($\rho = .090$, $p = .159$). Figure 1 shows interval plots for DF detection performance between IT and non-IT- and CS and non-CS professionals.

**Table 3.** Descriptive Statistics and Spearman Correlations (ρ) (N = 247)

| Variables | 1 | 2 | 3 | 4 | 5 | 6 | 7 | 8 | 9 | 10 | 11 | 12 | 13 |
|---|---|---|---|---|---|---|---|---|---|---|---|---|---|
| 1. Age | — | | | | | | | | | | | | |
| 2. Correct ratings | .095 | — | | | | | | | | | | | |
| 3. Real rated DF | -.181** | -.489*** | — | | | | | | | | | | |
| 4. DF rated real | -.017 | -.872*** | .038 | — | | | | | | | | | |
| 5. ATI | .211*** | .090 | -.108 | -.042 | — | | | | | | | | |
| 6. CIA Pre | .027 | .015 | -.117 | .058 | .145* | — | | | | | | | |
| 7. CIA Post | .040 | -.038 | -.166* | .124 | .138* | .652*** | — | | | | | | |
| 8. JOC Pre | -.150* | -.089 | -.056 | .152* | .233*** | .466*** | .461*** | — | | | | | |
| 9. JOC Post | -.078 | -.094 | -.092 | .170** | .160* | .359*** | .451*** | .561*** | — | | | | |
| 10. CIVR Overall | .126* | -.033 | -.038 | .057 | .460*** | .185** | .253*** | .292*** | .213*** | — | | | |
| 11. CIVR Real | .061 | -.100 | .064 | .075 | .350*** | .204** | .205** | .229*** | .182** | .840*** | — | | |
| 12. CIVR DF | .132* | -.010 | -.069 | .047 | .464*** | .168** | .260*** | .282*** | .201** | .969*** | .708*** | — | |
| 13. OCS | -.100 | -.699*** | .661*** | .287*** | .033 | .632*** | .292*** | .381*** | .292*** | .076 | .169** | .101 | — |

*Notes.* All correlations are 2-tailed. $* p < .05$. $** p < .01$. $*** p < .001$.
DF = Deep fake. ATI = Affinity for technology interaction scale. CIA = Confidence in Abilities score. JOC = Judgement of confidence. CIVR = Certainty in video rating. OCS = Overconfidence score

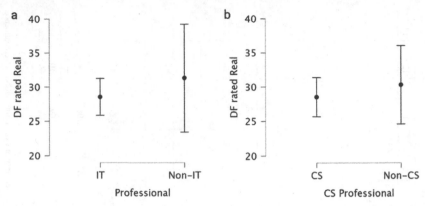

**Fig. 1.** Interval plots for DF detection performance between IT and non-IT professionals. **a** IT background. **b** CS background.

The Kruskal-Wallis test was repeated using IT and CS background as grouping variables and DF performance variables as outcomes while weighting on ATI scores. This did not affect results.

**H2: IT background and/or self-reported IT-affinity are associated with higher perceived DF recognition skills.**

**CIA Scores and IT Background.** To test the hypothesis that IT background influences belief in DF recognition abilities ($H_2$), Kruskal-Wallis tests were performed using IT and CS backgrounds as grouping variables and pre-task and post-task CIA scores as outcome variables. Spearman correlations were performed for ATI scores and pre- and post-task CIA scores (Table 3). There was a significant difference in pre-task CIA scores for IT ($H = 9.53(1), p = .002, \eta^2 = .034$) and CS backgrounds ($H = 14.84(1), p < .001$, $\eta^2 = .064$). Dunn's post hoc test showed that there was a significant difference between IT and non-IT professionals ($z = 3.09, p = .001$), and CS and non-CS professionals ($z = 3.85, p < .001$) with professionals having higher pre-task CIA scores than non-IT and non-CS professionals. There was a significant difference in post-task CIA scores for IT ($H = 8.08(1), p = .004, \eta^2 = .028$) and CS backgrounds ($H = 13.10(1), p < .001, \eta^2 = .049$). Dunn's post hoc test showed that there was a significant difference between IT and non-IT professionals ($z = 2.84, p = .002$), and CS and non-CS professionals ($z = 3.61, p < .001$) with professionals having higher post-task CIA scores than non-IT and non-CS professionals.

ATI scores were positively associated with pre-task CIA ($\rho = .145, p = .023$) and post-task CIA ($\rho = .138, p = .031$) scores ($\rho = .160, p = .012$). Post-task CIA was negatively associated with rating DFs as real ($\rho = -.666, p = .009$).

Linear regression analysis showed that ATI was a significant predictor of pre-task CIA score ($\beta = .136, p = .034, R^2_{Adj} = .014, F = 4.55$) but not post-task CIA scores.

Additional Kruskal-Wallis tests using IT and CS backgrounds as grouping variables and CIA scores as outcome variables while weighting on ATI scores did not affect results.

**JOC Scores and IT Background.** Kruskal-Wallis tests were performed using IT and CS backgrounds as grouping variables and pre-task and post-task JOC scores as outcome variables. Spearman correlations were performed for ATI scores and pre- and post-task JOC scores (Table 2). There was not a significant difference in pre-task JOC scores for IT and non-IT ($H = 0.02(1)$, $p = .891$, $\eta^2 = -.004$) and CS and non-CS professionals ($H = 3.70(1)$, $p = .055$, $\eta^2 = .011$). There was a significant difference in post-task JOC scores for CS and non-CS ($H = 5.50(1)$, $p = .019$, $\eta^2 = .018$) backgrounds, but not for IT and non-IT backgrounds ($H = 1.59(1)$, $p = .207$, $\eta^2 = .002$). Dunn's post hoc test showed that there was a significant difference between CS and non-CS professionals ($z = 2.34$, $p = .009$) with CS professionals having higher post-task JOC scores than non-professionals.

ATI scores were positively associated with pre-task JOC ($\rho = .233$, $p < .001$) and post-task JOC scores ($\rho = .160$, $p = .012$). Post-task JOC scores was positively associated with rating DFs as real ($\rho = .152$, $p = .017$). Linear regression analysis showed that ATI was a significant predictor of pre-task ($\beta = .185$, $p = .004$, $R^2_{Adj} = .030$, $F = 8.65$) and post-task JOC scores ($\beta = .160$, $p = .012$, $R^2_{Adj} = .021$, $F = 6.34$).
Additional Kruskal-Wallis tests using IT and CS backgrounds as grouping variables and JOC scores as outcome variables while weighting on ATI scores did not affect results.

**CIVR Scores and IT Background.** Kruskal-Wallis tests were performed using IT and CS backgrounds as grouping variables and CIVR scores as outcome variables. Spearman correlations were performed for ATI scores and CIVR scores (Table 3). Significant differences in CIVR DF scores were found for CS and non-CS groups ($H = 13.38(1)$, $p < .001$, $\eta^2 = .050$) but not for IT and non-IT groups ($H = 0.68(1)$, $p = .410$, $\eta^2 = -.001$). Dunn's post hoc test showed that CS professionals scored significantly lower on CIVR DF ratings than non-professionals ($z = -3.658$, $p < .001$). There was not a significant difference in CIVR Real scores for IT and non-IT professionals ($H = .45(1)$, $p = .500$, $\eta2 = -.002$) or CS and non-CS ($H = 3.69(1)$, $p = .055$, $\eta^2 = .010$) professionals. There was not a significant difference in CIVR Overall scores for IT and non-IT ($H = 1.53(1)$, $p = .216$, $\eta^2 = .002$) professionals. There was a significant difference in CIVR Overall scores for CS and non-CS ($H = 13.17(1)$, $p < .001$, $\eta^2 = .049$) professionals. Dunn's post hoc test showed that CS professionals scored significantly lower on CIVR Overall scores than non-professionals ($z = -3.63$, $p < .001$).

ATI scores were positively associated with CIVR DF scores ($\rho = .464$, $p < .001$), CIVR Real scores ($\rho = .350$, $p < .001$), and CIVR Overall scores ($\rho = .460$, $p < .001$). CIVR scores were not associated with DF task performance variables.
Linear regression analysis showed that ATI was a significant predictor of CIVR DF scores ($\beta = .392$, $p = < .001$, $R^2_{Adj} = .151$, $F = 44.41$), CIVR Real scores ($\beta = .287$, $p < .001$, $R^2_{Adj} = .079$, $F = 21.89$), and CIVR Overall scores ($\beta = .379$, $p < .001$, $R^2_{Adj} = .140$, $F = 40.85$).
Additional Kruskal-Wallis tests using IT and CS backgrounds as grouping variables and CIVR scores as outcome variables while weighting on ATI scores did not affect results.

**OCS Scores and IT Background.** Kruskal-Wallis tests were performed using IT and CS backgrounds as grouping variables and OCS as outcome variable. Significant differences in OCS scores were found for CS and non-CS groups ($H = 5.56(1)$, $p = .018$, $\eta^2 = .018$) but not for IT and non-IT groups ($H = 2.06(1)$, $p = .151$, $\eta^2 = .004$). Dunn's post hoc test showed that CS professionals scored significantly higher on OCS than non-professionals ($z = 2.36$, $p = .009$). Figure 2 shows interval plots for DF task performance and OCS scores between IT and non-IT professionals. Figure 3 shows interval plots for DF task performance and OCS scores between CS and non-CS professionals.

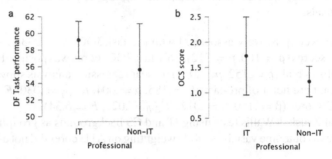

**Fig. 2.** Interval plots for DF task performance and OCS scores between IT and non-IT professionals. **a** DF task performance. **b** OCS score. An OCS score > 1 means overestimation of DF detection skills; an OCS score < 1 means underestimation of DF detection skills.

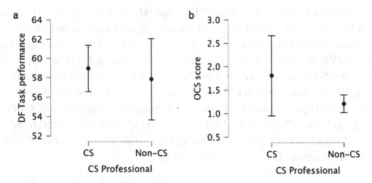

**Fig. 3.** Interval plots for DF task performance and OCS scores between CS and non-CS professionals. **a** DF task performance. **b** OCS score. An OCS score > 1 means overestimation of DF detection skills; an OCS score < 1 means underestimation of DF detection skills.

Additional Kruskal-Wallis tests using IT and CS backgrounds as grouping variables and OCS scores as outcome variable while weighting on ATI scores did not affect results.

**Gender Differences.** Kruskal-Wallis tests for differences in CIA scores, JOC scores, CIVR scores, DF task performance scores, and OCS scores for genders showed that there was only a significant difference for post-task CIA ($H = 5.94(1)$, $p = .015$, $\eta^2 = .020$) and post-task JOC scores ($H = 5.28(1)$, $p = .022$, $\eta^2 = .017$). Dunn's post hoc test showed that males had higher scores than females on post-task CIA ($z = 2.43, p = .007$) and JOC ($z = 2.29, p = .011$) scores.

Additional Kruskal-Wallis tests using gender as grouping variable and OCS scores as outcome variable while weighting on ATI scores did not affect results. Figure 4 shows interval plots for OCS and DF Task performance between genders.

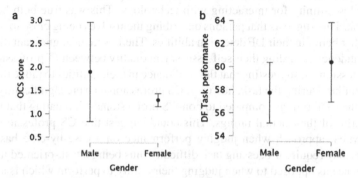

**Fig. 4.** Interval plots for OCS and DF task performance between genders. **a** OCS score. An OCS score > 1 means overestimation of DF detection skills; an OCS score < 1 means underestimation of DF detection skills. **b** DF task performance.

## 4 Discussion

Developing skills that make individuals resilient against Social Engineering attacks requires individualised approaches to be effective [17]. However the field of research inquiring about the cognitive factors influencing individual Social Engineering susceptibility is currently in its infancy [19]. Recent research indicates that having relevant education or an IT background is not a protective factor against Social Engineering [21, 22]. It has been suggested that cognitive factors prevent targets of Social Engineering from engaging with details in a critical manner [22]. Advances in DF generation technology provide cybercriminals with a unique opportunity to impersonate individuals with high credibility, which could be weaponized in Social Engineering attacks against unsuspecting victims. As with the Social Engineering field in general, little is known about the cognitive factors influencing DF recognition skills. Previous research on human-machine interactions in CS contexts suggest that skills related to self-assessment accuracy such as metacognition is relevant for performance [23, 25, 26]. Overconfidence due to poor metacognitive abilities may serve as a possible explanation for why formal education or an IT professional employment does not guarantee resilience against Social Engineering attacks. Thus, in this study we aimed to assess the influence of overconfidence and IT backgrounds on DF recognition skills.

In line with previous research on phishing email susceptibility [22], and in support of our hypothesis that having an IT background does not influence DF detection skills, we found that individuals with an IT background were no better than non-professionals at judging DFs as authentic. This was true for both IT and CS professionals, and for individuals with an affinity for interacting with technology. Weighting results on ATI scores did not influence DF detection abilities between professionals and non-professionals.

We found support for our second hypothesis that having an IT background influences belief in own abilities to detect DFs. Individuals with an IT background, CS background, and individuals who had an affinity for interacting with technology all scored higher on confidence into their DF detection skills compared to participants without an IT background, or low affinity for interacting with technology. This was true both before and after the task. This suggests that persons describing themselves being close to the IT sector had higher belief in their DF detection abilities. There were no significant differences in their confidence regarding their self-assessment quality between IT professionals and non-IT professionals, suggesting that the confidence in their abilities to judge themselves was very similar. During the task, however, CS professionals were significantly less certain about their DF ratings compared to non-CS professionals, indicating that they were more doubtful of their actual ratings. This could suggest that CS professionals had a more analytical approach when judging performance on a case-by-case basis. These judgements may require processing task difficulty thus being a task-oriented judgement of performance as opposed to when judging their ability to perform which is arguably a more self-oriented judgment of performance. Despite this increased insecurity into their self-assessment, having an IT background, did not influence confidence into their perceived skills. Post-task confidence into their self-assessment were significantly higher for CS professionals compared to non-professionals. People with a higher affinity for interacting with technology had higher confidence in their abilities, were more certain about their task performance, and also had a higher belief that their confidence was accurate, suggesting that people with higher affinity are more confident in their abilities.

These findings could be explained by a lack of cognitive involvement, rather than inability, and are in line with elaboration likelihood models such as the Suspicion, Cognition, Automaticity Model (SCAM; Fig. 5, a) [31]. Alternatively, it could be argued the effect may not be the result of a lack of cognitive involvement (i.e., motivation to elaborate the stimulus systematically), but that an IT Background does not provide superior skills in DF recognition. Following this thought, it can be argued that the presented tasks of visual perception and discrimination constituting a DF recognition paradigm are per se based on neuropsychological performance but are not technical tasks. The fact that DF are created and presented on devices with which persons working in the IT domain feel familiar with and show competencies in using, does add to a sense of familiarity and may thus result in overconfidence - even though the task (the systematic processing of a visual or audio-visual stimulus) is perceptual-psychological, rather than technical. The fact that CS professionals were less certain about their performance than non-professionals during task-oriented judgements but had higher belief in their performance for self-oriented judgements could indicate that this latter interpretation might be true at least for CS professionals. On the other hand, people with a higher affinity for interacting with technology were more certain of their case-by-case ratings despite not performing better, possibly indicating a lack of task-oriented judgement of performance which could indeed be reflective of a lack of cognitive engagement with the task.

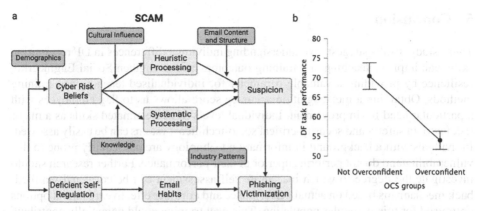

**Fig. 5.** How overconfidence relates to Social Engineering susceptibility in the SCAM. **a** The SCAM. Adapted from [31]. **b** Performance differences between the Overconfident and Not over-confident groups. OCS = Overconfidence scale. SCAM = Suspicion, Cognition, Automaticity Model.

The present study does not determine whether the underlying mechanisms contributing to our findings are due to a lack of engagement or neuropsychological factors related to perceptual processing abilities. Previous research into the neuropsychological correlates of performance on metacognitive and perceptual tasks suggest that they rely on a common neural substrate [32–34]. This could suggest that measuring metacognitive accuracy is indicative of perceptual processing abilities; conversely it could mean that measuring metacognitive accuracy is only indicative of knowing how or when to apply the abilities but not the motivation to do so. Future research measuring confidence judgments and motivation to perform well while applying eye-tracking and EEG (e.g., to record event-related potentials related to perceptual processes and stimuli detection) will be needed to further assess how DF recognition performance relates to engagement and perceptual processes. This could also show whether these underlying mechanisms can be dissociated. Comparing how much time participants spend on individual task items to EEG data may be useful to indicate task engagement relative to perceptual abilities.

Based on these initial findings, we argue that the OCS is an easily obtainable indicator identifying individuals with particular need for systematic feedback and training for improved Social Engineering resilience. OCS assessment can easily be combined with a DF recognition task as demonstrated or be used in classical phishing simulation as they are common practice pre and post cybersecurity awareness interventions. While OCS may uncover persons at heightened risk for failures caused by overestimation of their performance in all sections of an organisation, persons with IT background and related job profiles may be of particular interest. This is due to their demonstrated vulnerability towards overestimation and potentially also due to increased likelihood of access to technical infrastructure and services allowing for a more efficient privilege escalation post-intrusion.

# 5  Conclusion

These study results suggest that understanding individual differences in DF recognition skills can improve teaching and training outcomes and strengthen Social Engineering resilience by providing a valuable parameter for individualised teaching and training methods. Obtaining a metacognition accuracy score allows us to flag employees with a particular need for improvement. Individual levels of overestimated skills as a major risk factor in safety- and security-critical socio-technical systems can be easily assessed. Individuals with a background in information technology are particularly prone to this vulnerability and do not perform superior in their performance. Further research should investigate the degree to which inaccurate self-assessment can be corrected via feedback mechanisms based on actual performance and consider effective treatment options optimised for this particular population. This way training could potentially contribute to better metacognitive awareness and thus better decision-making.

**Acknowledgements.** This study was supported by the Norwegian Research Council (project number 302941).

# References

1. Purplesec, Cyber Security Statistics (2021)
2. IBM Security, Cost of a Data Breach Report 2021 (2021)
3. Verizon, 2021 Data Breach Investigations Report (2021)
4. Hadnagy, C.: Social Engineering: The Art of Human Hacking. Wiley, New York (2010)
5. Mouton, F., Leenen, L., Malan, M., Venter, H. S.: Towards an ontological model defining the social engineering domain. In: Kimppa, K., Whitehouse, D., Kuusela, T., Phahlamohlaka, J. (eds.) HCC 2014. IAICT, vol. 431, pp. 266–279. Springer, Heidelberg (2014). https://doi.org/10.1007/978-3-662-44208-1_22
6. Uebelacker, S., Quiel, S.: The social engineering personality framework. In: 2014 Workshop on Socio-Technical Aspects in Security and Trust. IEEE (2014)
7. Cialdini, R.: Influence: Science and Practice, 3rd edn. Harper Collins College Publishers, New York (1993)
8. Parsons, K., et al.: Predicting susceptibility to social influence in phishing emails. Int. J. Hum Comput Stud. **128**, 17–26 (2019)
9. Baek, E.C., Falk, E.B.: Persuasion and influence: what makes a successful persuader? Curr. Opin. Psychol. **24**, 53–57 (2018)
10. Schick, N.: Deep Fakes and the Infocalypse: What You Urgently Need to Know. Hachette UK (2020)
11. Korshunov, P., Marcel, S.: Deepfake detection: humans vs. machines. arXiv preprint arXiv: 2009.03155 (2020)
12. Rossler, A., et al. Faceforensics++: Learning to detect manipulated facial images. In: Proceedings of the IEEE/CVF International Conference on Computer Vision (2019)
13. Masood, M., et al.: Deepfakes Generation and Detection: State-of-the-art, open challenges, countermeasures, and way forward. arXiv preprint arXiv:2103.00484 (2021)
14. Zollhöfer, M., et al.: State of the art on monocular 3D face reconstruction, tracking, and applications. In: Computer Graphics Forum. Wiley Online Library (2018)

15. iProov: The Threat of Deepfakes. The consumer view of deepfakes and the role of biometric authentication in protecting against their misuse (2020)
16. Hu, S., Li, Y., Lyu, S.: Exposing GAN-generated faces using inconsistent corneal specular highlights. In: ICASSP 2021–2021 IEEE International Conference on Acoustics, Speech and Signal Processing (ICASSP). IEEE (2021)
17. Drogkaris, P., Bourka, A.: Cybersecurity culture guidelines: Behavioural aspects of cybersecurity. European Union Agency for Network and Information Security (ENISA) (2019)
18. Egelman, S., Peer, E.: The myth of the average user: Improving privacy and security systems through individualization. In: Proceedings of the 2015 New Security Paradigms Workshop (2015)
19. Montañez, R., Golob, E., Xu, S.: Human cognition through the lens of social engineering cyberattacks. Front. Psychol. **11**, 1755 (2020)
20. Schraw, G.: Promoting general metacognitive awareness. Instr. Sci. **26**(1), 113–125 (1998)
21. Butavicius, M., et al.: Breaching the human firewall: Social engineering in phishing and spear-phishing emails. arXiv preprint arXiv:1606.00887 (2016)
22. Jampen, D., Gür, G., Sutter, T., Tellenbach, B.: Don't click: towards an effective anti-phishing training. A comparative literature review. HCIS **10**(1), 1–41 (2020). https://doi.org/10.1186/s13673-020-00237-7
23. Jøsok, Øyvind., Knox, B., Helkala, K., Lugo, R., Sütterlin, S., Ward, P.: Exploring the hybrid space. In: Schmorrow, D.D.D., Fidopiastis, C.M.M. (eds.) AC 2016. LNCS (LNAI), vol. 9744, pp. 178–188. Springer, Cham (2016). https://doi.org/10.1007/978-3-319-39952-2_18
24. Jøsok, Ø., et al. Macrocognition applied to the hybrid space: team environment, functions and processes in cyber operations. in International Conference on Augmented Cognition. 2017. Springer
25. Knox, B.J., et al.: Socio-technical communication: the hybrid space and the OLB model for science-based cyber education. Mil. Psychol. **30**(4), 350–359 (2018)
26. Knox, B., Lugo, R., Jøsok, Øyvind., Helkala, K., Sütterlin, S.: Towards a cognitive agility index: the role of metacognition in human computer interaction. In: Stephanidis, C. (ed.) HCI 2017. CCIS, vol. 713, pp. 330–338. Springer, Cham (2017). https://doi.org/10.1007/978-3-319-58750-9_46
27. Canfield, C.I., Fischhoff, B., Davis, A.: Better beware: comparing metacognition for phishing and legitimate emails. Metacognition and Learning **14**(3), 343–362 (2019). https://doi.org/10.1007/s11409-019-09197-5
28. Kleitman, S., Law, M.K., Kay, J.: It's the deceiver and the receiver: Individual differences in phishing susceptibility and false positives with item profiling. PLoS ONE **13**(10), e0205089 (2018)
29. Franke, T., Attig, C., Wessel, D.: A personal resource for technology interaction: development and validation of the affinity for technology interaction (ATI) scale. International Journal of Human-Computer Interaction **35**(6), 456–467 (2019)
30. JASP, JASP-Statistics. 2021
31. Vishwanath, A., Harrison, B., Ng, Y.J.: Suspicion, cognition, and automaticity model of phishing susceptibility. Commun. Res. **45**(8), 1146–1166 (2018)
32. Chechlacz, M., et al.: Structural variability within frontoparietal networks and individual differences in attentional functions: an approach using the theory of visual attention. J. Neurosci. **35**(30), 10647–10658 (2015)
33. Shekhar, M., Rahnev, D.: Distinguishing the roles of dorsolateral and anterior PFC in visual metacognition. J. Neurosci. **38**(22), 5078–5087 (2018)
34. Zanto, T.P., et al.: Causal role of the prefrontal cortex in top-down modulation of visual processing and working memory. Nat. Neurosci. **14**(5), 656–661 (2011)

# When Choice is (not) an Option: Nudging and Techno-Regulation Approaches to Behavioural Cybersecurity

Tommy van Steen(✉) (iD)

Institute of Security and Global Affairs, Leiden University, Turfmarkt 99, 2511DP The Hague, The Netherlands
t.van.steen@fgga.leidenuniv.nl

**Abstract.** The field of behavioural cybersecurity, with a focus on the behaviour of end-users when working to improve the overall cybersecurity of a system or organisation, is gaining ground. As the field is still relatively small, most of the focus lies on awareness campaigns, or the occasional behavioural change intervention. Another way of looking at improving cybersecurity behaviour is by taking a closer look at the way systems present options and choices to end-users. The selection, design, and presentation of these options can strongly influence end-users' behaviour, thereby hindering or supporting the security of systems. These options can be categorised under two approaches: nudging and techno-regulation. The former aims to gently push end-users towards a preferred (safer) course of action, while the latter forcefully removes any unwanted (riskier) options, thereby improving cybersecurity at the cost of freedom of choice. The current paper outlines and compares these two approaches in terms of mechanisms, effectiveness, and potential unwanted side effects. Furthermore, the applicability of these methods to improve cybersecurity behaviour and the ethical dilemmas associated with applying these methods are discussed.

**Keywords:** Behavioural cybersecurity · Nudging · Techno-regulation · Behavioural change

## 1 Introduction

The cost of data breaches is steadily rising [1]. While the focus is often on technical solutions to prevent data breaches, attention is slowly moving towards the behaviour of end-users as they can help prevent breaches and secure the data and systems they work with. Behavioural cybersecurity studies how the behaviour of end-users can be changed to better support the cybersecurity of individuals, organisations, and the wider society. Popular approaches to behavioural cybersecurity include the use of awareness campaigns and end-user training. Even though they are used widely, there is no hard evidence that awareness campaigns sort any effect. For instance, in the case of governmental awareness campaigns, the evidence that these campaigns are effective in persuading people to behave more securely is missing [2]. End-user training seems more successful

© The Author(s), under exclusive license to Springer Nature Switzerland AG 2022
D. D. Schmorrow and C. M. Fidopiastis (Eds.): HCII 2022, LNAI 13310, pp. 120–130, 2022.
https://doi.org/10.1007/978-3-031-05457-0_10

through various approaches such as e-learning and serious games [3]. Training end-users, however, requires the training to be adapted to specific organisational and individual needs for maximum effectivity. Furthermore, it assumes that people are understanding the systems they work with and can – and want to – make informed decisions on how to act and which options to choose. This raises the question whether people should be in control of which options are available to them, or that systems should be designed in such a way that the riskier, and therefore undesirable options from a security perspective, are disabled or discouraged.

While the end-user is often kept in mind when designing new technology in terms of user interface and experience, this usually focuses on the ease of use of the technology, rather than how the level of security can be affected by the behaviour of these users. To address this issue, this paper describes two distinct approaches to behavioural cybersecurity that relate to the design of systems and software: nudging and techno-regulation. First, both approaches are conceptualised, then we turn to their application in the field of behavioural cybersecurity and a comparison of the consequences of these two approaches. Finally, the ethical aspects of using nudging and techno-regulation are discussed.

## 1.1 Nudging

Nudging is popularised by Richard Thaler and Cass Sunstein in their book *Nudge* where they define it as: "any aspect of the choice architecture that alters people's behaviour in a predicable way without forbidding any options or significantly changing their economic incentives"(p.8) [4]. There are various techniques to alter the choices that are presented so that people are more likely to choose the preferred option while maintaining individual freedom of choice. The most important methods are selecting which options to include, defaulting, using opt-ins and opt-outs, and making social norms salient.

The basis of choice architecture lies in deciding which options to include in the first place. What do we want end-users to be able to do and how do we categories options so that people are more likely to choose what is considered the most appropriate setting, and how is this setting defined? These questions usually lead to a focus on commercial gains, or user-friendly settings, rather than focusing on the consequences of choices on cybersecurity. A simple example of choice architecture can be found when withdrawing cash from a typical ATM. The stereotypical ATM design enables users to quickly choose from a limited number of options or put in more effort to get exactly what they want. For instance, ATMs often have a 'quick withdraw' function offering a pre-specified amount or provide a series of pre-set options ranging from a small withdrawal to a larger one. Having these settings optimised means that users can withdraw cash more quickly, improving the user experience, as well as the time spent at the ATM, where shorter engagement times result in more people being able to use the ATM within a specific timeframe.

Once the range of options has been established, the next step is to decide what the default should be. Defaulting is the practice of deciding what option will be acted upon if people do not actively choose one of the presented options. This can include defaults on privacy settings and data sharing practices, but also the presence or absence of multi-factor authentication, or a pre-defined set of user permissions when creating a new account. Defaulting steers behaviour by using the inertia of people, where people who do not have a strong opinion regarding the various options are more likely to go with the default as they might find it too much effort to change the default into their preferred option.

A subcategory of defaulting is the use of opt-in versus opt-out systems. Opt-in systems have as a default that users are not taking part or are not consenting automatically and need to take conscious action to change that. The opposite is true for opt-out systems. They automatically sign people up or assume consent, and people need to act to not take part or voice their objections. The implementation and consequences of changing the default from opt-in to opt-out can be seen in the way countries approach organ donation. In recent years, some countries have moved from an opt-in system, where citizens would need to sign up to become an organ donor in the case of their death, to an opt-out system where citizens are automatically an organ donor, or at least do not object. In Wales, organ donation signup moved to an opt-out system in 2015, whereas England did not. A study examining the effects of this change in default showed that over time, people in Wales were more likely to donate organs compared to people in England [5]. The authors note that this change was not immediate and that significant differences only became apparent over time. Effectively, opt-out systems might not only be about inertia of a large part of the target group, but also about setting a new social norm that takes time to materialise. The use of opt-out systems instead of asking people to sign up can be highly controversial. There are ethical issues surrounding its use, as it is up for debate whether people can be asked to take action when they do *not* want to engage in the newly set default behaviour. One often used method to overcome this criticism is to make the process of opting out as easy as possible, so that the inertia that must be overcome is kept to a minimum.

In addition to deciding which options to offer and which defaults to choose, one of the most successful ways to change behaviour to make social norms salient [6]. Social norms refer to the views and behaviours of peers. There is a vast amount of research showing that presenting people with information on the behaviour of their peers results in them changing their behaviour accordingly. More recent studies have shown that even when the majority does not perform the behaviour yet, the use of social norms can positively influence people's behaviour when the norm shows an upward trend of people adopting the required behaviour [7]. The downside of using social norms is that people who are already performing the behaviour and are perhaps doing better than the behaviour of peers, can also change their behaviour to be more in line with the social norm, thereby reducing the occurrence or intensity of the positive behaviour they performed [8].

## 1.2    Techno-Regulation

Techno-regulation is the idea that systems can be designed in such a way that the techno-logical options regulate the behaviour of users [9]. This notion was further explored by Lawrence Lessig who wrote about 'code as law', where the decisions made by software engineers effectively dictate the possibilities and limits of the interaction a user can have with a system [10, 11]. His argument is that because the Internet is a designed system that is built from scratch, the community can decide on what the Internet looks like, how it works and what is or is not possible when interacting with systems and software.

Implementations of techno-regulation lie not only in the digital realm. For instance, the absence of doorhandles on push doors are a simple method to preclude people from accidentally trying to open the door by pulling a handle, thereby increasing the ease with which people can move from one area to the next. Less altruistic examples contain the design and inclusion of armrests to mark individual seats in park benches, which prevent homeless people from using them as beds. The distinction between nudging and techno-regulation is that with the former, people are still able to choose a course of action that is suboptimal and that perhaps increases cyber risks, whereas techno-regulation removes the option to behave in an unwanted manner altogether.

The use of techno-regulation for societal benefit can also be seen by turning again to the ATM discussed in the previous section. It is easy to see how techno-regulation can limit the freedom of users when they withdraw cash. For example, banks can decide on a hard upper limit regarding how much cash can be withdrawn on a single occasion or within a specified timeframe. Setting such a limit can be frustrating to customers who want to withdraw large sums of cash to buy a luxury product, but at the same time offers help to customers whose bank details got stolen, or who are forced by others to withdraw cash for them. A more direct form of techno-regulation is used in the design of the withdrawal procedure at ATMs, aimed at improving customers security. In ATMs, the order in which you receive your cash and card has consequences for the number of people who lose their bank card when withdrawing cash. In some ATMs, when withdrawing money, the notes come out first, and after that your bank card is returned to you. This leads to people taking their money and leaving, as they forget to wait for their bank card. Banks, realizing the security issues and costs of having to issue new cards, have been changing this procedure to one where you must take out your card first, and only after physically removing the card from the ATM, does the money become available. This method is one of many ways in which ATMs can be designed to include techno-regulation and nudging techniques to improve the user experience and the security of their bank account [12]. While techno-regulation is highly restrictive of users' individual choices, it can lead to improved security and wellbeing when applied for the benefit of customers, general users, and wider society.

## 2 Application in Behavioural Cybersecurity

### 2.1 Nudging in Behavioural Cybersecurity

Nudging is used extensively by technology companies to drive users to spend more time, and therefore attention, on the platform that they have developed. This ranges from Facebook determining how to present the updates of friends on a personalised timeline, sometimes with detrimental consequences to mental health [13], to the way websites design their user interface, and the practice of smartphone apps to use notifications and badges to attract attention and incentivise opening the app and sharing more personal information. Examples where nudging is used for the benefit of the company providing the service rather than the end-user interacting with the technology are widespread. One example is the now infamous cookie wall that websites present to ensure that all users provide consent to tracking, collecting, and storing personal data, so that they comply with the European General Data Protection Regulation (GDPR). These cookie walls are designed in such a way that rejecting all cookies in one click is improbable, such as through using a smaller, less visible button for the 'reject all cookies' option, hiding this option in a submenu, or making it unclear which button to click to reject all unwanted cookies. A further complication exists when end-users need to understand the difference between 'consent' and 'legitimate interest', both of which are separate forms of consent according to some of the most used cookie walls, and both need to be disabled to reduce the unwanted tracking and data collection from the end-user's point of view. These forms of using nudging to remove 'unwanted' options from the technology company's point of view are also known under the name 'Dark Patterns', as coined by Harry Brignull, who created a website that covers the most common dark patterns used by organisations to trick end-users into behaviours by using methods that resemble nudges but without the promise of doing so in the best interest of the end-user [14]. Another form of nudging in cybersecurity is how privacy settings are presented, what their default is, and how easily they can be adjusted. A few years ago, it came to light that Google was storing Android users' location data, even when they had turned off the 'location history' option [15]. Even though it is perhaps possible to turn this function off completely in all settings, purposefully obscuring where these functions are located, and confusing users and tricking them into thinking they have adjusted all settings to fit their personal preferences while they have not makes this a clear example of a Dark Pattern as coined by Brignull.

As we see, nudging is used extensively by technology companies to steer end-user behaviour towards reduced privacy options and increased data sharing. However, there are various ways in which nudging can be used to improve cybersecurity, rather than hinder it. While a range of cybersecurity behaviours has been studied by researchers interested in improving cybersecurity with the help of nudges, most focus on privacy settings and stronger passwords.

For example, one study measured the effects of defaulting on privacy settings in a mock-up of a social networking site [16]. In this study, the default and order of the various options that users had when deciding who could see their future posts were altered between conditions. Users could choose between 'only me', close friends', 'friends', 'friends of friends', or 'everyone'. The difference between the conditions was the default, which was set to 'only me' in the privacy condition and 'everyone' in the non-privacy condition. Furthermore, the order of the other options was reversed in the non-privacy condition, so that the second option there was 'friends of friends' etcetera. Not only did they find that users were likely to stick to the default that was set by the system, but also that people who did change their setting, stayed close to the default. This shows that not only the default itself matters, but also the order in which the other options are presented.

An example of successful nudging to create stronger passwords is a study by Peer and colleagues [17]. They created a range of nudges such as a password meter that showed the strength of the password that was being created in real time, a social comparison nudge where the strength of the password was depicted relative to the passwords created by others, and an average crack-time for the created password. Not only were these nudges effective in persuading participants to create stronger passwords but Peer et al. also showed that the effectiveness of these nudges could be enhanced when some personal characteristics of the users are known. Choosing which nudge to implement for each participant by considering the individual's decision-making style showed to be even more effective than presenting participants with a randomly chosen nudge. These findings can easily be translated into successful real-world applications by analysing the interactions of the user with the system or software and adjust how nudges are presented in line with the individual's decision style or other characteristics.

## 2.2 Techno-Regulation in Behavioural Cybersecurity

Removing unwanted options altogether is a practice that can be found in many social media settings. For instance, the decision of Facebook to at first only include a 'like' button and no dislike button is a form of techno-regulation to push end-users towards more positive interactions on their platform. When the platform grew, and liking messages and posts became unwanted (e.g., when pets and relatives passed away or other negative events happened), Facebook added several other quick-reply options, but still avoided the dislike button. In a similar move in 2021, YouTube removed the number of downvotes on videos, so that regular users could not see how many others disliked the video they were watching [18].

On a more basic level, various technology companies are setting the rules for what users can do while using their products by not implementing options or restricting their use in certain situations. Apple does not allow users to download apps from the web and install them on their iOS devices, as apps can only be installed through Apple's own App Store. Similarly, dating apps such as Tinder limit the information people can share on their platform by not adding photo sharing options in chats, and improve safety by allowing every user to completely delete a chat history for both users in the chat, rather than only on their own device, an approach also taken by Telegram in their messaging app. Furthermore, techno-regulation is also used for good by automatically offering end-to-end encryption for personal messaging as offered by Signal and others, which improves cybersecurity compared to a system where end-to-end encryption is merely optional. In terms of privacy, techno-regulation could be used to improve end-users' privacy by simply not collecting data that is not required for the working of the system, or to automatically restrict who has access to that data. For password strength, it is easy to see how techno-regulation adds to nudging solutions, as requirements for the password such as length, composition and password expiration time are all factors that can be forced on users by using techno-regulation rather than nudging.

Empirical testing of the effectiveness of techno-regulation does not seem to be very useful. As the unwanted options are completely removed, the effectiveness of techno-regulation is high. However, perhaps more than in the case of nudging, there are potential side-effects that cannot be ignored. The two most important side-effects are the potential for reduced productivity and/or use, and the potential increase of shadow security behaviours. Some options that are removed due to a focus on security can be necessary or desirable from a productivity point of view. Removing these options altogether can mean that people need to use a slower, yet more secure, method, or need to ask the helpdesk or a manager how to proceed, all acts that would hinder the productivity of an individual employee or department. Outside of organisations, the lack of options could lead to users abandoning the software and looking for alternative vendors for products that do more or less the same but without the unwanted restrictions.

The second side-effect is that using techno-regulation can lead to shadow security. Shadow security is the idea that people start working around the existing software and systems to complete tasks that are more difficult, or even impossible, to complete when adhering to all security policies and the limitations posed by systems and software [19, 20]. While shadow security is not always riskier than completing tasks using the desired approach, monitoring and ensuring the security of the system becomes more difficult, if at all possible. Empirical tests of these side-effects of techno-regulation could inform the use and limitations of techno-regulation as a behavioural change mechanism where regular training and nudging approaches are seemingly insufficient or less effective. But even with more knowledge on these side effects of techno-regulation, it remains the question where the balance lies. When do you opt for nudging people towards better cybersecurity and when do you decide to enforce security options, perhaps at the expense of productivity or unwanted side effects?

## 3   When is Choice an Option?

We have seen various examples of how nudging and techno-regulation can be applied in the digital realm to improve cybersecurity. While nudging has proven to be effective in changing cybersecurity behaviours, it still allows for individuals to decide to behave in a non-secure manner. The opposite is the case for techno-regulation solutions where these unwanted options are simply taken out. While there are inherent differences between these two approaches, it is difficult in practice to decide whether what we do can be seen as nudging, or whether it is effectively techno-regulation. For example, when deciding which options to include in a drop-down menu on privacy settings, this can effectively limit users to a set of options, of which every option is deemed safe. In those instances, the mere selection of only safe options for users to choose from, and eliminating all other options, could be viewed as using techno-regulation to determine the final set of options available to users. This can then be combined with nudges to further attempt to influence behaviour by highlighting a specific option from the reduced list.

The question remains when to use these approaches to improve cybersecurity behaviour. While the answer is not clear-cut, there are a few things to consider when implementing nudges and techno-regulation to improve cybersecurity behaviours. Firstly, the question is whether nudging and techno-regulation are always the appropriate methods to solve security issues. In terms of risk management, the focus is often on addressing the most pressing risk in terms of probability of a cyberattack and the severity of the consequences once a cyberattack takes place. This form of risk estimation is key in the Protection Motivation Theory (PMT) that postulates that the decision to act is based around the perception of the vulnerability to – and severity of – any given risk, the perceived effectiveness of a proposed solution and the ease with which the solution can be implemented [21, 22]. Not all risks might warrant tightly restricting the freedom of choice of users, making techno-regulation too strong a technique in such cases. On the other hand, some risks might be so consequential that merely nudging people towards more secure behaviour is simply not sufficient. Determining which risks are suitable for nudging and techno-regulation solutions, rather than, for example, end-user training or technical solutions that do not involve changing people's behaviour, needs to be done on a case-by-case basis.

One tool that can be used to determine the applicability of both nudging and techno-regulation in cybersecurity settings is BJ Fogg's Behaviour Grid [23, 24]. In this grid, different types of behaviour are represented along two axes, the familiarity of the behaviour and the behavioural change goal on one axis, and the timeframe on the other. For example, On the first axis, Fogg makes distinctions between behaviours that are completely new to the user, or that they might be familiar with. Furthermore, he makes the distinction between whether these behaviours need to be started, stopped, or increased/decreased compared to a baseline measurement. On the timeframe axis, the distinction is made between three timeframes: a one-time behaviour, a behaviour that needs to be displayed for a specific duration, and a behaviour that should be performed permanently.

As techno-regulation and nudging work in their own unique way and have different uses, the Behavioural Grid can be used to determine which method is most applicable. For example, a behaviour that merely needs to be increased or decreased could be addressed using nudging techniques. This would also be a sensible approach to behaviours that can be considered familiar to users that need to be performed only a single time, such as when setting up a new account, or when installing new software. However, for behaviours that need to be changed permanently and for behaviours that are completely new to users, techno-regulation might be more sensible, as this would reduce the risk of unwanted behaviours in the future and reduces the necessity to educate the users on what the new behaviour would entail and why it is important to adopt this behaviour.

A final aspect that needs to be considered is that of balancing side-effects. As discussed earlier, techno-regulation can lead to shadow security practices, as options, services, and technology that are required to complete tasks are made unavailable. The side-effects of nudging are that people still have the choice to behave in a less secure fashion, as the freedom of choice is larger than with techno-regulation. While both side-effects can be acceptable risks, it is important to not overlook these potential consequences of choosing nudging or techno-regulation as solution to behavioural cybersecurity risks and to measure the extent to which these side-effects occur before rolling out these solutions on a large scale.

## 4  Ethical Considerations

As we have seen, both nudging and techno-regulation are being used by technology companies to influence the behaviour of end-users. In some cases, this might be to improve the user experience, while in other cases these companies use influence techniques to grow their business at the cost of the end-user. It would be an oversimplification to say that, merely because tech-companies use nudging and techno-regulation for profit, we should not think twice and apply everything that is known about nudging and techno-regulation to improve cybersecurity. While there are good reasons to apply these techniques, there are three ethical considerations that cannot be ignored.

The first consideration is the freedom to make choices. While nudging allows for more freedom of choice than techno-regulation, both are effectively restricting the freedom to do whatever the user would want to do. While the restrictive nature of techno-regulation might be clear, nudging also restricts the freedom of choice as the set of options that is presented is often still limited. Furthermore, knowing the power of defaulting and creating opt-in/opt-out systems, the question remains whether the application of choice architecture can still be considered a free choice. After all, using inertia to nudge people towards a specified choice also entails adding barriers to the other choices an individual could make. Especially with opt-out systems, the ethical considerations cannot be understated. As mentioned before, the ethical aspect of opt-out systems is normally countered by making opting-out as easy as possible, but it is unclear who decides when this level of ease is achieved and how people should be supported to opt-out when they so desire.

The second ethical consideration is centred around who decides when and how to use nudging and techno-regulation in their software design. Is this the developer who is implementing a privacy menu? Is it the project leader who oversees the bigger picture? Or is it a companywide board that draws up policies on the use of these techniques in their software? And is the person or body that makes these decisions able to do so in an impartial and objective manner? Where scientists are held to high ethical standards by Institutional Review Boards when they propose a new study, the same does not hold for corporate approaches to software design and the design choices made by User Experience (UX) developers. A wide, societal, discussion on the use, implementation, and ethical limits of using nudging and techno-regulation to steer cybersecurity behaviour could help solve this issue.

The third and final consideration is whether we as society are comfortable with influencing unknowing users into changing their behaviour. While some argue that it is acceptable when attempting to make people change their behaviour in their own interest or that of society, another perspective is that using nudging, people are 'fooled' into making decisions they would not have made had they been given a free choice. The fact that some organisations use the same techniques for commercial gain is perhaps not a good enough argument to support nudging in other areas. And what about nudges that primarily serve the commercial interests of organisations, but also have a small altruistic component, or vice versa? To balance the various needs and stakes, and to ensure that individuals can resist behavioural change attempts when they want to, more education on the existence and workings of these techniques would be useful. These materials could be included in curricula on digital literacy and made available to the wider public through existing channels. For example, national 'nudge units' – as they are colloquially called – could collect and disseminate not only findings of successful nudging projects, but also share educational materials about the workings of nudges to the wider public. A better understanding of what drives people and how they might be influenced by a range of stakeholders, both commercially and for the benefit of society, could help educate people to make more informed decisions and perhaps reduce the need for restrictive human-computer interaction.

# 5  Conclusion

Both nudging and techno-regulation are effective approaches to improve cybersecurity for end-users and the organisations they work in. Both approaches are already widely used for commercial gain by technology companies and the use of these methods to improve cybersecurity is gaining ground. Some interesting empirical findings have emerged surrounding the effectiveness of nudging, and the potential for tailored nudging. However, the long-term effects, and the negative consequences of nudging and techno-regulation in terms of productivity and the occurrence of shadow security practices require more research. While ethical considerations are not to be underestimated, the role of security specialists, software designers and broader society is now to consider where the balance lies and how these methods can be sensibly adopted to increase the security of users, organisations, and society. Do we want to be cybersecure at all costs and sacrifice some individual freedom, which might also produce unwanted side effects, or do we want to nudge people in the right direction, but allow them to make mistakes and suboptimal choices? The field of behavioural cybersecurity will benefit from a deepened understanding of nudging and techno-regulation, its application to improve cybersecurity and how best to implement these practices in real-world applications.

# References

1. IBM Security: Cost of a Data Breach Report 2021. IBM, Armonk, NY (2021)
2. van Steen, T., Norris, E., Atha, K., Joinson, A.: What (if any) behaviour change techniques do government-led cybersecurity awareness campaigns use? J. Cybersecur. **6** (2020). https://doi.org/10.1093/cybsec/tyaa019
3. van Steen, T., Deeleman, J.R.: Successful gamification of cybersecurity training. Cyberpsychol. Behav. Soc. Netw. **24**, 593–598 (2021)
4. Thaler, R.H., Sunstein, C.R.: Nudge. Yale University Press (2021)
5. Madden, S., et al.: The effect on consent rates for deceased organ donation in Wales after the introduction of an opt-out system. Anaesthesia **75**, 1146–1152 (2020)
6. Cialdini, R.B., Trost, M.R.: Social influence: Social norms, conformity and compliance (1998)
7. Mortensen, C.R., Neel, R., Cialdini, R.B., Jaeger, C.M., Jacobson, R.P., Ringel, M.M.: Trending norms: a lever for encouraging behaviors performed by the minority. Soc. Psychol. Person. Sci. **10**, 201–210 (2019)
8. Schultz, P.W., Nolan, J.M., Cialdini, R.B., Goldstein, N.J., Griskevicius, V.: The constructive, destructive, and reconstructive power of social norms. Psychol. Sci. **18**, 429–434 (2007)
9. Brownsword, R.: So what does the world need now? Reflections on regulating technologies. In: Regulating Technologies: Legal Futures, Regulatory Frames and Technological Fixes, pp. 23–48. Hart (2008)
10. Lessig, L.: Code v2.0. Basic Books, New York, NY (2006)
11. Lessig, L.: The new Chicago school. J. Leg. Stud. **27**, 661–691 (1998)
12. Lockton, D., Harrison, D., Stanton, N.A.: The design with intent method: a design tool for influencing user behaviour. Appl. Ergon. **41**, 382–392 (2010)
13. Kramer, A.D., Guillory, J.E., Hancock, J.T.: Experimental evidence of massive-scale emotional contagion through social networks. Proc. Natl. Acad. Sci. **111**, 8788–8790 (2014)
14. Brignull, H.: About this site, https://www.darkpatterns.org/about-us. Accessed 11 Feb 2022

15. Associated Press: Google records your location even when you tell it not to (2018). https://www.theguardian.com/technology/2018/aug/13/google-location-tracking-android-iphone-mobile

16. Cho, H., Roh, S., Park, B.: Of promoting networking and protecting privacy: effects of defaults and regulatory focus on social media users' preference settings. Comput. Hum. Behav. **101**, 1–13 (2019)

17. Peer, E., Egelman, S., Harbach, M., Malkin, N., Mathur, A., Frik, A.: Nudge me right: personalizing online security nudges to people's decision-making styles. Comput. Hum. Behav. **109** (2020)

18. The YouTube Team: An update to dislikes on YouTube. https://blog.youtube/news-and-events/update-to-youtube/. Accessed 11 Feb 2022

19. Kirlappos, I., Parkin, S., Sasse, M.A.: Learning from "Shadow Security": why understanding non-compliance provides the basis for effective security. In: USEC 2014 (2014)

20. Kirlappos, I., Parkin, S., Sasse, M.A.: "Shadow security" as a tool for the learning organization. ACM Sigcas Comput. Soc. **45**, 29–37 (2015)

21. Rogers, R.W.: A protection motivation theory of fear appeals and attitude change. J. Psychol. **91**, 93–114 (1975)

22. Rogers, R.W.: Cognitive and psychological processes in fear appeals and attitude change: a revised theory of protection motivation. In: Social Psychophysiology, pp. 153–176. Guilford Press, New York, NY (1983)

23. Fogg, B.J.: The behavior grid: 35 ways behavior can change. In: Proceedings of the 4th international Conference on Persuasive Technology, pp. 1–5 (2009)

24. Fogg, B.: Fogg Behavior Grid. https://behaviordesign.stanford.edu/fogg-behavior-grid. Accessed 11 Feb 2022

# Brain Activity Measurement
# and Electroencephalography

# Multi-class Task Classification Using Functional Near-Infrared Spectroscopy

Danushka Bandara(✉) (iD)

Fairfield University, Fairfield, CT 06824, USA
dbandara@fairfield.edu

**Abstract.** Task classification is an important step towards brain-computer interfaces (BCI). A reliable task classifier could help build better user models and help the BCI to adapt to the user task. This paper reports on a study conducted with nine human subjects on six different cognitive tasks. The study collected brain activity data from the participants using a 52 channel functional Near-Infrared Spectroscopy (fNIRS) sensor. The resulting dataset was labeled with the task type administered to the subject. After analyzing the across subject dataset using a multi-class decision tree classifier, the results show a promising F1 score of 0.94. The most predictive features for the classification are reported to guide future research into this area. The implications of this work include a generalizable task classifier based on brain activity data.

**Keywords:** fNIRS · Multi-class task classification · Brain-computer interfaces

## 1 Introduction

The human brain drives our behavior and interactions with the world, which are reflected in our brain activity patterns. Numerous studies have used this brain activity data to infer the underlying cognitive state of a computer user. Brain activity measurement methods include Electroencephalography (EEG), Magnetic Resonance Imaging (MRI), Magnetoencephalography (MEG), and Functional Near-infrared spectroscopy (fNIRS). The fNIRS sensor is of great interest in this area due to its non-invasive nature, portability, high spatial resolution, and being less prone to electrical noise than the comparable Electroencephalography (EEG) devices.

Task classification is fundamental in human-computer interaction because it can be used to build better user models and for computers to adapt to the nature of the user's tasks. By understanding the nature of the user's task, the interface can change its presentation so that task usability is improved. Thus, task classification can be a first step towards better Brain-Computer Interfaces.

Previous fNIRS studies have shown that it is possible to discriminate between rest and tasks [1–3] with high accuracy. Other research into classification of discrete tasks via fNIRS data includes driver cognitive state detection [7], physical posture and walking tasks [7], and motor execution [8]. Herff et al. [4] achieved a binary classification accuracy of 71% between two tasks. Hong et al. conducted a three-class task classification

© The Author(s), under exclusive license to Springer Nature Switzerland AG 2022
D. D. Schmorrow and C. M. Fidopiastis (Eds.): HCII 2022, LNAI 13310, pp. 133–141, 2022.
https://doi.org/10.1007/978-3-031-05457-0_11

[6] where they achieved 75.6% classification accuracy for a three-task, within-subject classification study. This study attempts to build on the above approaches for multi-class cognitive task classification and achieve generalizability via across-subject classification.

Nine subjects took part in this fNIRS study in which they were instructed to perform six different cognitive tasks designed to induce various cognitive processes. Each task was conducted in multiple trials, approximately 8 s in length. The number of trials ranged from 15 to 60. The tasks were selected to span a wide range of cognitive processing [5].

1.  Adaptive words (visual lexical processing): adaptive words task was developed to induce workload on participants' visual-lexical processing resources. The words for the numerical values of the digits one through eight were displayed in this task. The words were displayed vertically for a variable amount of time in the center of the screen. The participant's goal was to determine whether the word on the screen corresponded to either an odd or even numerical value
2.  Visual Search (Visual processing): A circular array of nine letters consisting of a distractor (backward Ns) and a target (normal facing Ns) was displayed to the participant for a variable amount of time. The participant's task was to determine whether or not the target was displayed within the array
3.  Go no go (Response inhibition): Involved one target stimuli (a large blue circle) and one distractor stimuli (a large blue square). The participant was asked to respond if the target was presented and not respond when the distractor was presented.
4.  N back (working memory): The N-Back task was designed to cause cognitive load on people's working memory resources. The task required participants to hold a stream of characters in their working memory and respond when a new character presented to them matches one of the characters they are currently holding.
5.  Posner cueing task (visual attention): This task involved the participant fixating on a point in the middle of the screen. After this, a visual cue was provided to the participant pointing towards the left or the right. This cue indicated where the stimulus shape would appear in the next step.
6.  Simple reaction time task (perception and response execution): This task activates the basic cognitive processes of perception and response execution—the task involved participants pressing the spacebar whenever the stimulus shape appeared on the screen.

## 2 Methodology

### 2.1 Signal Acquisition

The brain activity data was collected by a Hitachi ETG-4000 fNIRS device which can capture 52 channels of Oxygenated hemoglobin (HbO) and Deoxygenated hemoglobin (HbR) concentration data at a sampling rate of 0.1 Hz. The optodes were arranged in a 3 × 11 formation and placed over the participants' forehead area. The fNIRS sensor captured the brain activity in the prefrontal cortex at 10 Hz frequency. The fNIRS system uses near-infrared light of two wavelengths (760 and 830 nm) to detect concentration changes of oxygenated hemoglobin (HbO) and deoxygenated hemoglobin (HbR) molecules in the brain cortex. The molecules (HbO and HbR) absorb photons with different absorption coefficients. The reflected light intensity can be used along with Beer-Lambert Law [9] to calculate the change in HbO and HbR concentration in that region of the brain. The HbO data is a proxy for brain activity because increased brain activity results in increased blood flow to those areas. HbR is negatively correlated with brain activity because HbR flows out of the brain area when HbO flows in. Both of these measures are proxy indicators of brain activity. Furthermore, because of the locality of the near-infrared light, fNIRS data provides high spatial resolution.

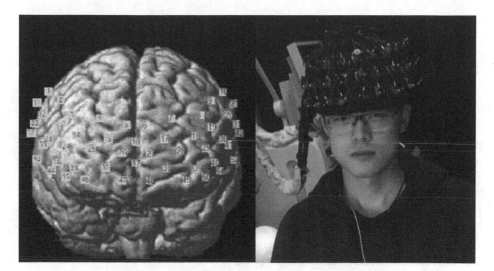

**Fig. 1.** A participant wearing fNIRS system used in the lab

## 2.2  Subjects

A total of nine subjects took part in the experiment; all of them were college-age students from a university in the northeast united states. None of them had a history of any psychiatric or neurological disorder. The experimental procedure was explained to all of them in detail before providing their informed consent.

## 2.3  Experiment Setup

The subjects were asked to sit in a comfortable chair facing a 22-inch monitor (1280 × 1024 pixel resolution) located at approximately 65 cm apart from their eyes in a dimly lighted room.

## 2.4  Experiment Protocol

1. Consent
2. Participant sits in front of the computer

3. fNIRS sensor set up and calibrated
4. Cognitive benchmark tasks presented to the participant in randomized order with a variable interstimulus interval (ISI) between the offset of a trial and the onset of a new trial. During the ISI, a cross-fixation point in the center of the screen was displayed. The length of the ISI was an exponential distribution (mean = 4 s, min = 2 s, max = 8 s).

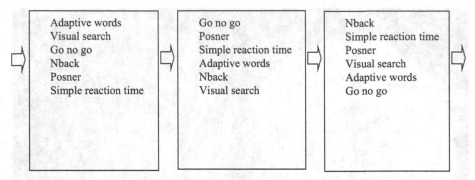

**Fig. 2.** Flow chart of experiment protocol with pseudo randomization

### 2.5 Feature Generation and Classification

The HbO and HbR data for the duration of each trial was extracted by synchronizing the data with experiment log files. The extracted HbO and HbR data were then labeled using the task name for each trial. The brain activity data were first preprocessed into statistical features, mean, minimum, maximum, standard deviation. These features were calculated on a per-trial basis. Along with the labels, these features constitute the complete dataset. The dataset contained 2996 trials representing the six cognitive tasks.

The dataset was analyzed in both within-subject and across-subject scenarios. The machine learning analysis used a 70: 30 train test split.

### 2.6 Decision Tree Classifier

A decision tree classifier was used for this analysis due to the interpretability of the decision tree classifier and the ability to handle multi-class classification. Decision trees are machine learning models that split the dataset at multiple levels, choosing the split with the highest information gain at each level. The features that occur in the splits towards the tree's root are higher in predictive power due to the higher information gain in those splits.

Information gain for split i = $I.G._1$ = Entropy of parent - Average entropy of the child nodes.

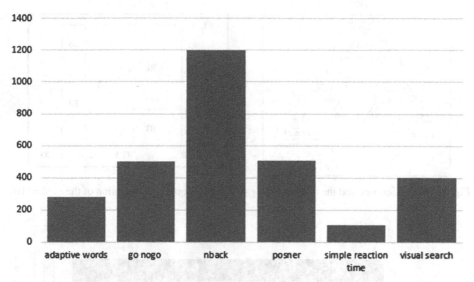

**Fig. 3.** The number of instances of each cognitive task in the dataset

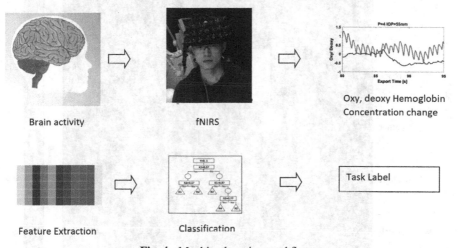

**Fig. 4.** Machine learning workflow

## 3   Results and Discussion

The confusion matrix for the six-class classification using decision tree classifier is shown in Fig. 6. Since there is a class imbalance, the F1 score was used to measure classifier performance. The theoretical chance level in our paradigm was 16.6%. The classification performance as shown in the confusion matrix is well above this.

An F1 score of 0.94 was achieved for the multi-class classification, which is very encouraging compared to the state-of-the-art.

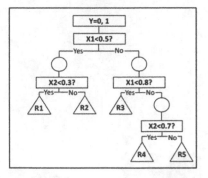
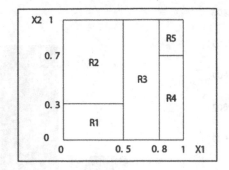

**Fig. 5.** A decision tree and the corresponding two-dimensional representation of the model [10].

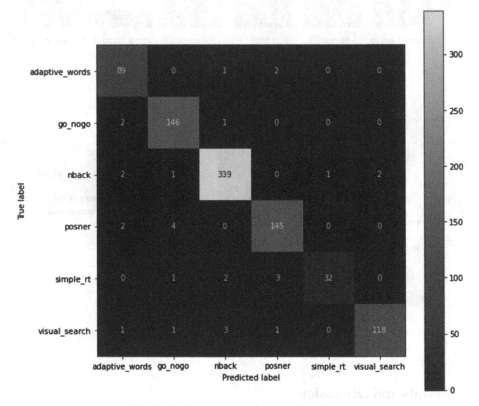

**Fig. 6.** Confusion matrix for task classification

Figure 7 shows the most predictive features of task classification as they are spacially located on the forehead of a participant. Note that the fNIRS channels shown in Fig. 1 have been projected onto a rectangular shape for display simplicity. The top edge of the rectangular areas corresponds to the top of the forehead area, and the bottom edge corresponds to the area just above the eye line of the participant.

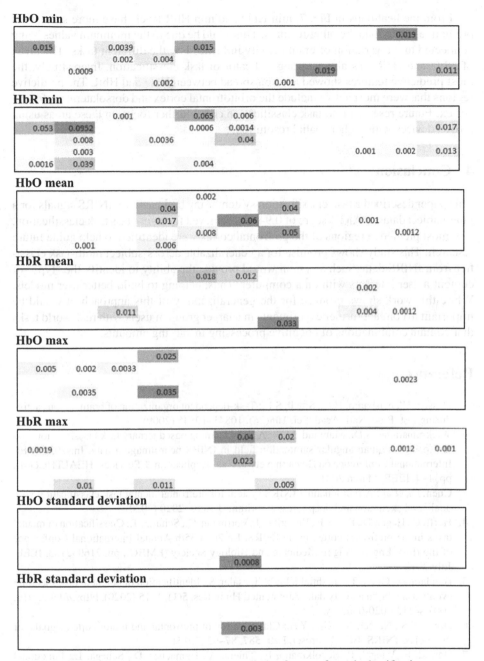

**Fig. 7.** Heatmaps showing the most predictive features for task classification.

From the heatmaps in Fig. 7, min HbO and min HbR levels have more substantial predictive power than the other features. This could be due to the minimum values being connected to the variation of brain activity influenced by the different tasks. The mean of HbO and HbR was also a strong indicator of task classification. Interestingly, the most predictive features showed an even spread between HbO and HbR. The predictive regions that were most active include the orbitofrontal cortex and dorsolateral prefrontal cortex. Future research into task classification could further focus on these areas using fNIRS devices with higher spatial resolution.

## 4   Conclusion

This paper described a task classification system using brain activity fNIRS signals for a nine-subject dataset. An F1 score of 0.94 was achieved for a six-class task classification. The most predictive regions of the prefrontal cortex were identified to help guide future research. This study shows promise for a generalizable across-subject multi-task classifier from fNIRS data. Such a system would provide the ability to identify the "type" of content a user interacts with on a computer. Thus, helping to build better user models. While this work shows promise for the generalizability of this approach, it would be important to conduct further experiments in a larger group of users with real-world tasks that contain combinations of cognitive processing in varying amounts.

## References

1. Hasson, U., Nusbaum, H.C., Small, S.L.: Task-dependent organization of brain regions active during rest. Proc. Natl. Acad. Sci. **106**(26), 10841–10846 (2009)
2. Wickramaratne, S.D., Mahmud, M.S.: A deep learning based ternary task classification system using Gramian angular summation field in fNIRS neuroimaging data. In: 2020 IEEE International Conference on E-health Networking, Application & Services (HEALTHCOM), pp. 1–4. IEEE, March 2021
3. Chen, C., et al.: A multichannel fNIRS system for prefrontal mental task classification with dual-level excitation and deep forest algorithm. J. Sens. **2020** (2020)
4. Herff, C., Heger, D., Putze, F., Hennrich, J., Fortmann, O., Schultz, T.: Classification of mental tasks in the prefrontal cortex using fNIRS. In: 2013 35th Annual International Conference of the IEEE Engineering in Medicine and Biology Society (EMBC), pp. 2160–2163. IEEE, July 2013
5. Bandara, D., Grant, T., Hirshfield, L., Velipasalar, S.: Identification of potential task shedding events using brain activity data. Augmented Hum. Res. **5**(1), 1–15 (2020). https://doi.org/10.1007/s41133-020-00034-y
6. Hong, K.S., Naseer, N., Kim, Y.H.: Classification of prefrontal and motor cortex signals for three-class fNIRS–BCI. Neurosci. Lett. **587**, 87–92 (2015)
7. Herold, F., Wiegel, P., Scholkmann, F., Thiers, A., Hamacher, D., Schega, L.: Functional near-infrared spectroscopy in movement science: a systematic review on cortical activity in postural and walking tasks. Neurophotonics **4**(4), 041403 (2017)

8. Shamsi, F., Najafizadeh, L.: Multi-class classification of motor execution tasks using fNIRS. In: 2019 IEEE Signal Processing in Medicine and Biology Symposium (SPMB), pp. 1–5. IEEE, December 2019

9. Kocsis, L., Herman, P., Eke, A.: The modified Beer-Lambert law revisited. Phys. Med. Biol. **51**(5), N91 (2006)

10. Song, Y.Y., Ying, L.U.: Decision tree methods: applications for classification and prediction. Shanghai Arch. Psychiatry **27**(2), 130 (2015)

# Transfer Blocks Method on Multi-degrees Mental Workload Assessment with EEG

Lipeng Gao[1], Tao Wang[3], Xingwei An[1,2(✉)], and Yufeng Ke[1,2(✉)]

[1] Academy of Medical Engineering and Translational Medicine,
Tianjin University, Tianjin 300072, China
{anxingwei,clarenceke}@tju.edu.cn

[2] Tianjin Key Laboratory of Brain Science and Neural Engineering, Tianjin 300072, China

[3] College of Precision Instruments and Optoelectronics Engineering,
Tianjin University, Tianjin 300072, China

**Abstract.** Mental workload (MW) could be described as the cognitive resource that the human required to perform a specific task. An appropriate MW could increase the task performance, however, mental overload or underload would cause adverse effect. This paper recruited sixteen subjects in the experiment under four degrees workload tasks and Electroencephalogram (EEG) signals were recorded. Furthermore, in this work, the multi-degrees mental workload assessment was performed using Shannon entropy and power spectral density (PSD) with theta (4–7 Hz), alpha (8–13 Hz), beta1 (14–20 Hz) and beta2 (20–30 Hz) bands. Afterwards, the exploration of cross-block classification with transfer blocks was conducted. The results revealed that the energy of theta, beta1 and beta2 bands increased as MW degrees increased, while was obvious in theta band, and the multi-degrees mental workload assessment achieved an accuracy of 80% ± 7.6% using SVM model. For cross-block classification, the Transfer Blocks method increased 23% accuracy for two-degrees mental workload assessment in comparison with the accuracy achieved by directly cross blocks method. It was concluded that the proposed Transfer Blocks method has better classification performance for mental workload assessment during cross blocks condition.

**Keywords:** Mental workload · Electroencephalography · Power spectral density · Shannon entropy · Transfer Blocks

## 1 Introduction

Mental workload (MW) could affect the working abilities of humans during they performed any cognitive task and cause adverse effect on the task performance at an adequate workload [1, 2]. The key premise was to evaluate the MW efficiently, which could detect the status of human and allocate the human-machine task dynamically [3, 4]. MW could be measured by the physiological signals, task performance and subjective scales of the human, while the physiological signals were more popular among these methods.

D. D. Schmorrow and C. M. Fidopiastis (Eds.): HCII 2022, LNAI 13310, pp. 142–150, 2022.
https://doi.org/10.1007/978-3-031-05457-0_12

In the early years, the perspective of evaluating MW was mainly from the psychology, and the research methods used were mainly subjective scales [5] (e.g. NASA-TLX) or behavioral responses during various mental task degree [6]. With the widespread application of automation technology, the role of human factor in human-machine system received more attention. Emerged many evaluation methods for MW, including electroencephalography (EEG), electrocardiography (ECG) and Functional near-infrared spectroscopy (fNIRS) et al. [7–9], reflect the workload changes during the cognotive task. The EEG had been used efficiently to monitor the workload changes of changing degrees of mental task difficulty. Power spectral density (PSD) was the most popular method for feature extraction. The energy of frequency bands was extracted as features, and ratio of the energy could be used as a feature similarly. As the task difficulty improved, the energy of theta band increased significantly [10, 11]. When human performed difficult tasks, alpha rhythm would be suppressed, and the energy of beta band increased [12]. Research indicated that ratio between the energy of frequency bands was related to the MW, which could be used as a feature [10, 13].

In the current research, most literature focused on the binary classification, and rarely involved multi-class. Among them, the classification results needed to be further verified and cross-block classification remained a challenge. In this study, we designed four levels workload tasks, using the multi-attribute task battery (MATB) design software, a multi-task platform for simulating pilot tasks [14], in order to evaluate the multi-degrees mental workload. Afterwards, the exploration of cross-block classification with transfer blocks was conducted.

The rest of this paper is organized as follows. In part 2, the experimental design and data processing is described. In part 3, the experimental results are discussed. In part 4, we conclude this paper and propose the future work.

## 2 Materials and Methods

### 2.1 Participants

Sixteen volunteers (22.6 ± 0.88 years old) were recruited for this study, including 10 males and 6 females. None of them had ever suffered from neurological diseases and all of them had normal or corrected-to-normal vision. Participants were required to take adequate rest before the experiment. Moreover, they had signed the informed consent of EEG experiment.

### 2.2 Experiment Design

In this experiment, we designed four-degrees workload tasks (Easy [E], Medium [M], Hard [H] and Very Hard [VH]) using the multi-attribute task battery (MATB) design software, which contained four sub-tasks (Fig. 1): (1) system monitoring task, (2) tracking task [14], (3) communication task and (4) resource management task. And four-class task difficulty levels based on MATB was first introduced.

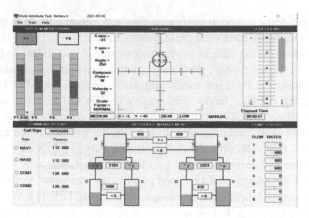

**Fig. 1.** The MATB task interface

In the system monitoring task, participants needed to pay attention to the changes of F1-F6 indicators. Under normal conditions, F5 was displayed in green, F6 was in white, and the dark blue bar of F1-F4 was shaking up and down in the central area. When an error occurs in any indicator, participants should immediately press the button of that indicator to bring it back to its normal state. In the tracking task, participants controlled the moving circle within the square by manipulating the joystick. In the communication task, participants heard the voice announcement from time to time. When the current call sign (e.g. NASA504) appeared, they pressed the "up/down" key to select the correct radio channel, and the "left/right" key to tune to the specific frequency. In the resource management task, A and B were fuel consumption tanks, C-F were fuel storage tanks, and 1–8 were pipeline switches that control fuel transmission. The switch off state was gray, on state was green, and fault state was red. Participants controlled the switches to maintain the fuel volume of A and B tanks at around 2500.

The overall task level was altered by a single task difficulty and the number of tasks processed in parallel. Among them, the difficulty of tracking task was controlled by adjusting the sensitivity of joystick, and the other tasks were altered by the number and frequency of events that occurred.

## 2.3  Procedure

The experimental procedure was shown in Fig. 2(a). The day before the formal experiment, participants were trained for 20 min. In the formal experiment, four blocks (each block lasted 15 min) were involved and the interval of two blocks was five minutes. Each block contained the eyes-open rest as the baseline and four-degrees mental workload tasks (Fig. 2(b)). Participants needed to fill out the NASA-TLX questionnaire after each block.

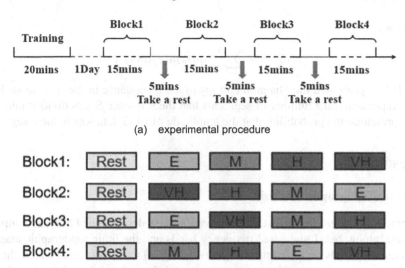

(a)   experimental procedure

(b)   experimental design of each block

(Rest represents eyes-open rest; E, M, H and VH represent Easy, Medium, Hard and Very Hard level, respectively)

**Fig. 2.**  Experimental introduction

### 2.4   Data Acquisition and Analysis

The EEG signals were recorded with 64 electrodes by the 10–20 international standard lead system and were amplified by the amplifier of Neuroscan. The M1 and M2 electrodes placed on the mastoid were used as reference, and the 50 Hz notch filter was used to eliminate power frequency interference. The sampling rate was 1000 Hz. The electrode impedance remained below 10 KΩ. Following methods on the recorded data were performed.

1) **Data Pre-processing:** First, the artifacts with obviously eye-movement were removed manually. Second, a band-pass filter (1–45 Hz) was used for filtering. Finally, independent component analysis (ICA) was used to decompose the raw EEG data to remove the eye-blink components [15].

2) **Feature Extraction:** The artifact-free EEG signals were segmented the artifact-free EEG data into 10-s epochs, with an overlap of 5 s at first. Then the power spectral density (PSD) of each epoch was calculated, and the energy of all channels in theta (4–7 Hz), alpha (8–13 Hz), beta1 (14–20 Hz) and beta2 (20–30 Hz) frequency bands were extracted as features. The non-parametric estimation method based on periodogram (welch power spectrum estimation) was selected. The method was calculated by the pwelch function in the MATLAB 2016a toolbox with a 500 sampling points hamming window.

Shannon entropy, also known as information entropy, represented the change of information complexity over time in the cognitive process of brain [16]. This paper introduced the time-dependent Shannon entropy as another feature, and the calculation formula was:

$$H(S) = -\sum\nolimits_{n=1}^{N} p(s_n)log_2(p(s_n)) \tag{1}$$

where $H(S)$ represented the Shannon entropy of the S sequence in the continuous EEG data, $N$ represented the number of segments that the sequence S was divided into, and $p(sn)$ represented the probability that the amplitude of EEG data was in the n segment.

## 3  Results

### 3.1  Brain Topography Analysis

In order to estimate the mental workload of various task degrees, the PSD was computed with theta, alpha, beta1 and beta2 frequency bands and the brain topographic maps of four frequency bands on different MW degrees (Fig. 3) was performed, which showed that the energy is mainly concentrated in prefrontal, frontal and dorsolateral prefrontal regions. Each frequency band in these maps used a different spectrum energy scale, in order to demonstrate the variation of spectral energy for different MW degrees in the same frequency band. The energy of theta, beta1 and beta2 bands increased as MW degrees increased, while was obvious in theta band, but no significant change in alpha bands.

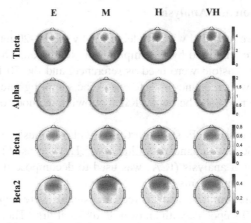

**Fig. 3.** Brain topographic map in each frequency band at each level (E, M, H and VH represent easy, medium, hard and very hard level, respectively)

### 3.2  Channel Energy Analysis

With the analysis of Brain Topography, we knowed that the energy is mainly concentrated in prefrontal, frontal and dorsolateral prefrontal regions, therefore, the channel energy maps was plotted particularly. The channels on the centerline of scalp (FPZ, FZ, FCZ,

CZ) were selected, which were significant changed in the theta bands (P < 0.05) during the MW tasks performed. The spectrum energy of these channels under rest and four difficulty levels state was shown in Fig. 4.

It could be illustrated that the spectrum energy in prefrontal (FPZ) and frontal (FZ) channels could effectively distinguish the task difficulty levels, whose energy was more obvious in the theta (4–7 Hz) and beta2 (20–30 Hz) frequency bands. Moreover, the figure indicated that the alpha (8–14 Hz) frequency band showed similar response for all mental states, and other frequency bands gave the discriminative sequential responses. The spectrum energy was the highest in the VH state, low in the H and M states, and the lowest in the E state. The Rest (baseline) state generated the lowest spectrum energy as compared to other mental states.

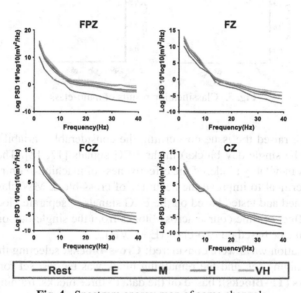

**Fig. 4.** Spectrum energy map of some channels

### 3.3 Classification

The classification result contained two parts: multi-class and cross-block classification. For multi-class classification (Fig. 4), the data of all blocks were selected and performed 10-fold cross-validation by four models, including support vector machines (SVM), linear discriminant analysis (LDA), random forest (RF) and k-nearest neighbor (KNN) models. In each condition, the accuracy of SVM model was the highest. For two-class, the classification accuracy was the highest among the other conditions and the accuracy of the SVM model was 92% ± 3.7%. Moreover, for the four-class, the accuracy of the SVM model was 80% ± 7.6%. It demonstrated that our experimental design was reasonable and distinguishable (Fig. 5).

In the case of multi-class, the classification accuracy was found exceed 70%. Yet, one inescapable aspect of EEG signals was the temporal factors associated during data

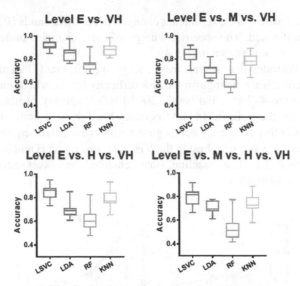

**Fig. 5.** Classification results of multi-class

recording, which raised the issue concerning the considerable variability of inter-day (even between the single-day blocks) in the EEG signals [17, 18]. The variability in the EEG signals inevitably hindered the effectiveness of machine learning classifiers. It was thus quite critical to improve the accuracy of cross-block MW classification task which were trained and tested based on the EEG signals of separate blocks. This study examined the effect of time course across blocks from the single-day on classification model's performance based on two-class (E vs. VH).

Two combination ways were considered: **Cross-Blocks:** selecting the data of three blocks as the training set, and the remaining block was the test set for classification. **Transfer-Blocks (TF-Blocks):** based on the data of three blocks, training set combines the two-minute data of the remaining block (each degree MW extracted one-minute data). Then, comparing with the classification of all blocks (**All-Blocks**). The **Cross-Blocks** method performed a classification across blocks and the proposed **TF-Blocks** method used to verify that the classification accuracy had improved. The **TF-Blocks** method, training the data from available blocks that adding a portion data of the remaining block as calibration and testing on the unseen data, could provide some enlightenment on developing an online MW-classification analytical framework accounting for the EEG variability of inter-day. In this subsection, level E and level VH was used as two-class. The classification result was shown in Fig. 6.

Comparing with the result of All-Blocks, the accuracy of Cross-Blocks and TF-Blocks significantly decreased, while was more obvious in Cross-Blocks. By mixing part of the test set data, TF-Blocks accuracy increases 23% for SVM model, comparing with Cross-Blocks. It can be concluded that by combining a small amount of target data, the TF method has better classification performance. This research provided a good foundation for our further research based on across blocks.

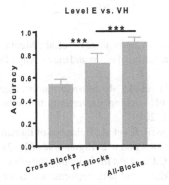

**Fig. 6.** Classification Results of cross blocks

## 4 Conclusion

This paper aimed to evaluate multi-degrees mental workload by performing four-degrees workload tasks, which contained four sub-tasks. Power spectral density was computed with theta, alpha, beta1 and beta2 frequency bands, at the same time, the brain topographic maps of four frequency bands on different MW degrees was performed, which demonstrated that the energy is mainly concentrated in prefrontal, frontal and dorsolateral prefrontal regions and the energy of theta bands increased obviously as MW degrees increased. Moreover, the Shannon entropy was calculated and selected as raw features with Power spectral density, performing multi-class classification using four diffierent classifier. The results of multi-class classification demonstrate that using the data of all blocks, we could get a relatively high accuracy of 4-class. Futher, this study examined the effect of temporal factors across blocks on classification model's performance based on two-class (E vs. VH). It could be found that the accuracy of across blocks is relatively low comparing with using all blocks. Therefore, we proposed the concept of Transfer-Blocks and found that this method can improve the classification accuracy of across blocks.

This research provided a good foundation for further research with the stability of MW over time and the dynamic adjustment of the model as an initial exploration. Future work focus on solving the problem of temporal factor in cross-day research. In addition, combining the other indicators, such as behavioral performance and eye movement to further enhance the feasibility of constantly monitoring of MW in the complex and changeable working condition.

**Acknowledgments.** The authors sincerely thank all participants for their voluntary participation. This work was supported in part by National Natural Science Foundation Of China (grant 81925020, 81630051), Tianjin Science and Technology Project of China (grant 20JCZDJC00620) and Space Medical Experiment Project of China Manned Space Program (grant HYZHXM03009).

# References

1. Jacquet, T., Lepers, R., Poulin-Charronnat, B., et al.: Mental fatigue induced by prolonged motor imagery increases perception of effort and the activity of motor areas. Neuropsychologia **150**, 107701 (2021)
2. Shuggi, I.M., Oh, H., Wu, H., et al.: Motor performance, mental workload and self-efficacy dynamics during learning of reaching movements throughout multiple practice sessions. Neuroscience **423**, 232–248 (2019)
3. Navarro, J., Heuveline, L., Avril, E., et al.: Influence of human-machine interactions and task demand on automation selection and use. Ergonomics **61**(12), 1601–1612 (2018)
4. Wang, X., Li, D., Menassa, C.C., et al.: Investigating the effect of indoor thermal environment on occupants' mental workload and task performance using electroencephalogram. Build. Environ. **158**, 120–132 (2019)
5. Aghajani, H., Garbey, M., Omurtag, A.: Measuring mental workload with EEG+fNIRS. Front. Hum. Neurosci. **11**, 359 (2017)
6. Zokaei, M., Jafari, M.J., Khosrowabadi, R., et al.: Tracing the physiological response and behavioral performance of drivers at different levels of mental workload using driving simulators. J. Saf. Res. **72**, 213–223 (2020)
7. Parent, M., Peysakhovich, V., Mandrick, K., et al.: The diagnosticity of psychophysiological signatures: can we disentangle mental workload from acute stress with ECG and fNIRS? Int. J. Psychophysiol. **146**, 139–147 (2019)
8. Iqbal, M.U., Srinivasan, B., Srinivasan, R.: Dynamic assessment of control room operator's cognitive workload using Electroencephalography (EEG). Comput. Chem. Eng. **141**, 106726 (2020)
9. Dimitrakopoulos, G.N., Kakkos, I., Dai, Z., et al.: Task-independent mental workload classification based upon common multiband EEG cortical connectivity. IEEE Trans. Neural Syst. Rehabil. Eng. **25**(11), 1940–1949 (2017)
10. Ahn, S., Nguyen, T., Jang, H., et al.: Exploring neuro-physiological correlates of drivers' mental fatigue caused by sleep deprivation using simultaneous EEG, ECG, and fNIRS data. Front. Hum. Neurosci. **10**, 219 (2016)
11. van Gog, T., Paas, F., et al.: Effects of process-oriented worked examples on troubleshooting transfer performance. Learn. Instr. **16**(2), 154–164 (2006)
12. Mohanavelu, K., et al.: Dynamic cognitive workload assessment for fighter pilots in simulated fighter aircraft environment using EEG. Biomed. Sig. Process. Control **61**, 102018 (2020)
13. Puma, S., Matton, N., Paubel, P.V., et al.: Using theta and alpha band power to assess cognitive workload in multitasking environments. Int. J. Psychophysiol. **123**, 111–120 (2018)
14. Cegarra, J., Valéry, B., Avril, E., Calmettes, C., Navarro, J.: OpenMATB: a multi-attribute task battery promoting task customization, software extensibility and experiment replicability. Behav. Res. Methods **52**(5), 1980–1990 (2020). https://doi.org/10.3758/s13428-020-01364-w
15. Minguillon, J., Lopez-Gordo, M.A., Pelayo, F.: Trends in EEG-BCI for daily-life: requirements for artifact removal. Biomed. Signal Process. Control **31**, 407–418 (2017)
16. Zhang, Z., Wang, J., Dai, J.: Different bands of sleep EEG analysis based on the multiscale Jenson-Shannon divergence. In: International Congress on Image and Signal Processing, BioMedical Engineering and Informatics (2017)
17. Lin, Y.P., Jao, P.K., Yang, Y.H.: Improving cross-day EEG-based emotion classification using robust principal component analysis. Front. Hum. Neurosci. **11**, 64 (2017)
18. Yin, Z., Zhang, J.H.: Cross-session classification of mental workload levels using EEG and an adaptive deep learning model. Biomed. Signal Process. Control **33**, 30–47 (2017)

# Study of Different Classifiers and Multi-modal Sensors in Assessment of Workload

Emma MacNeil, Ashley Bishop, and Kurtulus Izzetoglu(✉)

School of Biomedical Engineering, Science and Health Systems, Drexel University,
Philadelphia, PA 19104, USA
ki25@drexel.edu

**Abstract.** Cognitive workload changes in the assessment of human performance have long been monitored through the use of subjective self-reports, physiological, or neuro-physiological measures. The purpose of this study is to use multi-modal sensors and machine learning (ML) approach as an assessment method and to investigate which set of biometrics serves as the best objective predictor of cognitive workload. Several biometrics, including prefrontal cortex oxygenation changes, heart rate, and respiratory rate, were collected in both 5-screen and 1-screen immersion conditions to induce high and low task load in simulated use of force (UOF) scenarios. These biometrics were then used to train logistic regression and feature mapping classifiers. Performance of these classifiers was assessed through measures of F1-score and accuracy in order to determine which feature set lends itself to the best prediction power. The classifier trained with left anterior medial prefrontal cortex oxygenation changes performed the best out of individual biometrics, with an accuracy of 0.68 and a f1-score of 0.67. The accuracy of this model was marginally improved to 0.69 when heart rate and oxygenation changes from the other prefrontal cortex quadrants were included, however, the f1-score decreased to 0.51. These results suggest that the logistic regression model underfit the data, necessitating an increase of training data set and exploration of alternative ML approaches in order to use these sensor-driven biometrics effectively and reliably to assess cognitive workload.

**Keywords:** Human performance · Training · Cognitive workload · Machine learning · fNIRS · Heart rate · Respiratory rate

## 1 Introduction

### 1.1 Background

Measurement of cognitive workload changes during training could offer additional insight to the monitoring of trainees' expertise development toward operational readiness. One way to define cognitive workload is an interaction between task requirements and human capabilities or resources [1, 2]. In this interaction, workload involves the objective effects of task difficulty on the participant, and the participant's effort while engaged in maintaining performance. That is, workload can be defined in terms of some

© The Author(s), under exclusive license to Springer Nature Switzerland AG 2022
D. D. Schmorrow and C. M. Fidopiastis (Eds.): HCII 2022, LNAI 13310, pp. 151–161, 2022.
https://doi.org/10.1007/978-3-031-05457-0_13

objective criteria for task difficulty (e.g., an air traffic controller managing 6 versus 12 planes), or in terms of the participant's capability to perform the identified task. Another perspective of cognitive workload is a conglomeration of demands placed on cognitive, perceptual, and neurophysiological processes [3]. Such demands elicit activation of these neurophysiological pathways that can then be measured. Objective criteria for task difficulty and task demand also call for reliable assessment of the performance that is required to execute a particular mission. Measurement of mental load or neural reserve is key in such an objective assessment as simply observed performance may not reflect the true cognitive workload. For instance, two operators can complete the same task with similar observed performance. However, one of them may have utilized significant cognitive resources to reach that level of performance and has less resources left to allocate compared to the other operator. Advances in the measurement of physiological and neurological phenomena, such as local oxygenation changes in the brain bring promising new assessment alternatives for these true cognitive workload measures. Hence, our study aims to use multi-modal sensors and machine learning approach as an assessment method and to investigate which set of biometrics serves as the best objective predictor of cognitive workload.

Machine learning (ML) provides the opportunity to model how these biomarkers correlate with changes in cognitive workload. Classification models have been used in other studies to model changes in cognitive workload. For example, features from electroencephalogram (EEG) signals have been used in classical machine learning models with moderately successful accuracies [4]. Improved accuracies, approaching ninety percent, have been achieved in studies which applied deep learning models to EEG features [5]. Supervised machine learning methods have also been applied to brain imaging data from functional near infrared spectroscopy (fNIRS) with varying levels of success [6, 7]. Furthermore, studies have assessed the use of eye-tracking features [8] and pupillometry data [9] in classification models for cognitive workload level. These eye tracking studies have resulted in a rather large range of accuracies.

Despite the fair number of studies that have looked at quantifying cognitive workload through ML models trained on biometric data, few studies have taken a multimodal approach to these models. Additionally, applications of these models have not fully explored the field of law enforcement training. By leveraging these models, training paradigms can be created in which the training could be personalized in real time based on individual's experienced workload at the moment.

## 2 Methodology

### 2.1 Participants

Nine trainees between the ages of 21 to 31 volunteered to participate in the study. These trainees were recruited with the help of the Federal Law Enforcement Training Centers.

## 2.2 Multimodal Sensors

Advances in functional brain activity monitoring techniques have taken place over the last two decades, and in particular their deployment in simulation-based training and real-world field studies to support performance assessment metrics in both aerospace and medical domains [10–12]. In general, increased brain activity raises the metabolic demand of neurons, leading to local increases in oxygenated hemoglobin. Near-infrared light can be utilized to measure concentration changes in oxygenated and deoxygenated blood hemoglobin levels by applying a modified Beer-Lambert Law [13]. The modified Beer-Lambert law provides an empirical description of how light propagates differentially in tissue, depending on relative hemoglobin concentrations. These principles are applied when using a continuous wave fNIRS device to quantify brain activity in the prefrontal cortex (PFC). Studies have utilized fNIRS to demonstrate hemodynamic responses in the PFC due to cognitive workload in multitasking environments, such as unmanned aerial pilot training or medical personnel training [11, 14].

Heart rate (HR), and more specifically heart rate variability (HRV), has been implicated as an indicator of psychological and emotional stress [15]. While more research needs to be conducted to further explore and explain the use of HRV as a measure of cognitive load, Thayer et al. [16] report the possibility of measurable HR changes as a result of PFC activation.

Extensive research has also been conducted on the effects that cognitive load has on respiration-based biomarkers such as respiration rate (RR). For example, a review paper reported 54 journal articles containing some component linking cognitive workload to respiration factors [17]. The consensus of the reviewed papers showed that respiration rate tended to rise with increasing cognitive workload.

Combining these biomarkers in the form of wearable sensors could give an in-depth analysis of the cognitive load of trainees' experience during training, such as when practicing use of force (UOF) scenarios. In fact, our previous study demonstrated statistically significant increases in both PFC activation and HR during higher immersion conditions when compared to lower immersion conditions [18].

## 2.3 Experimental Design

The UOF training task was displayed to participants using the MILORange Theater 300 system (FAAC Incorporated, Ann Arbor, Michigan). UOF scenarios were pre-recorded, branching videos streamed on HD screens. The scenarios are included with the MILO-Range Theater system. Participants were equipped with a duty belt holding a holstered laser-emitting pistol and were instructed to respond to the scenarios according to their training as if in real life. Depending on the scenario, they could engage verbally to deescalate the situation, give commands, or respond to sudden threats using the simulation pistol. The simulation pistol emits a coded infrared laser pulse when fired. Shots, including locations, are tracked by sensors calibrated to each screen. An instructor was present to operate the simulator and control the scenario branching depending on each participant's actions. Two screening conditions were used to maximize the difference in the amount of audiovisual immersion and information presented to the participants. The first screening configuration consisted of a singular screen in front of the participant with a single hidden speaker behind the screen. The second arrangement entailed the use of five screens, each with its own hidden speaker and audio channel, as shown in Fig. 1.

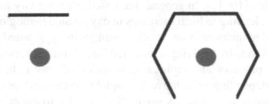

**Fig. 1.** Diagram of the screen layout for one screen (left) and five screen (right) conditions. The red circle indicates the location of the subject relative to the UOF simulator screen(s). (Color figure online)

Two wearable sensors were used for physiological data collection. Neurological data, monitoring oxygenation in the prefrontal cortex, was captured by an 18-optode fNIR Devices 2000M (fNIR Devices LLC, Potomac, MD) headband operated with LED wavelengths at 730 nm and 850 nm and a sampling frequency of 10 Hz. A Hexoskin wearable garment measured both heart rate and respiration at 1 Hz. Prior to use, the textile electrodes found on the shirt were moistened with a water-based gel. Participants were instructed to wear the garment snug so that the electrodes had close skin contact. Figure 2 displays the collection of sensors used.

Participants were given two questionnaires after each screening condition to gauge subjective measures of cognitive load and feeling of psychological flow. The NASA TLX questionnaire was used to address self-reported cognitive load and produced an

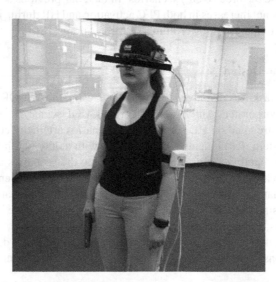

**Fig. 2.** Example of how the physiological sensors were positioned on each participant.

overall score based on six scoring factors: mental demand, physical demand, temporal demand, performance, effort, and frustration [19]. Participants were also instructed to fill out a flow state scale [20] to measure subjective feelings of psychological flow for potential use as a discriminant measure.

Figure 3 shows the approximate timeline for the experimental protocol of each subject. Prior to each screening condition, a baseline recording of at least two minutes was acquired to attenuate the effects of the previous condition and for initial sensor calibration. During the screening conditions, participants responded to three or four UOF scenarios to interact with by verbally responding to live action prompts or through engagement with a simulation pistol. The scenarios ranged from simple trespassing to persons in crisis to homicide and were grouped to provide similar total session lengths. The scenarios were not repeated for any participant, ensuring novelty of content regardless of screening condition. The order of screening conditions was counterbalanced among participants. The simulator was operated in a darkened environment to control ambient light conditions and increase salience of the simulator environment. After each screening condition, participants were instructed to complete a series of self-report questionnaires to subjectively report sense of immersion.

| Baseline | Condition 1 | Questionnaire | Baseline | Condition 2 | Questionnaire |
|---|---|---|---|---|---|

Minute  0          2                    10              20        25              35              45

**Fig. 3.** Timeline of the experimental protocol. Condition 1 corresponds to one screen, and Condition 2 corresponds to the five-screen trial.

## 2.4  Data Analysis

The data analysis capitalizes on the same data set recorded from the aforementioned four sensors and analysis reported in [18]. This study focused solely on the HR and RR data collected from the Hexoskin Smart shirt and the neurological data collected from the fNIRS device as these were the most complete data sets. Outliers of 2.5 standard deviations away from the mean were removed from HR and RR data for each screening condition.

Oxygenation changes from fNIRS were calculated for each quadrant of the PFC from left to right: left dorsolateral PFC (DLPFC), left anterior medial PFC (AMPFC), right AMPFC, right DLPFC (see Fig. 4).

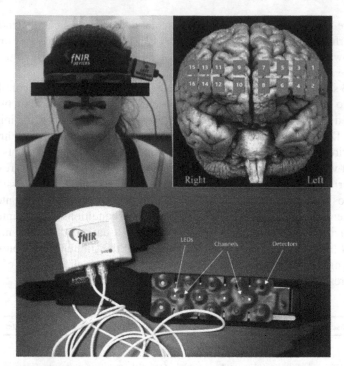

**Fig. 4.** 18-channel fNIRS sensor with sensor placement of LEDs, detectors, and optode locations on participant PFC areas. Left Dorsolateral PFC (Left DLPFC: optodes 1–4). Left Anterior Medial PFC (Left AMPFC: optodes 5–8). Right Anterior Medial PFC (Right AMPFC: optodes 9–12). Right Dorsolateral PFC (Right DLPFC: optodes 13–16). Image of optode locations (1–16; top right) is adapted from [19].

## 2.5 Classifier Training

Data from five of the subjects was used to train a logistic regression classifier, the approach of which is shown in Fig. 5. A logistic regression model was chosen for its low computational demand compared to other machine learning methods, as well as its lower tendency to overfit on small datasets. This last part was especially important for this study as we were limited to data from only five of the subjects. The other four subjects were excluded due to incomplete data sets. This data set included 2228 data points labeled as 5-screen and 2243 data points labeled as 1-screen. Table 1 shows the breakdown of these data points by subject. A k-fold cross-validation method was employed, with each subject serving as a data subset, in order to improve the generalizability of the resulting models. After training on each subset, average test accuracy and average f1-score were calculated for the logistic regression model. Test accuracy was included because it is one of the more intuitive measures of classifier performance, however it weights true cases the same as false cases. F1-score was included as it is the harmonic mean of precision and recall and thus serves as a better evaluation metric when false cases carry a greater weight than true cases.

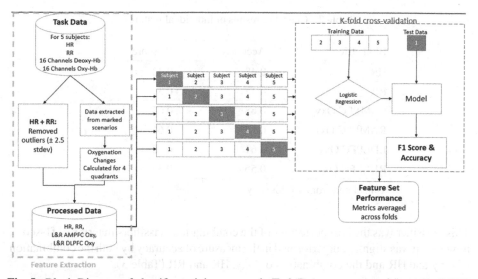

**Fig. 5.** Block Diagram of classifier training approach. Task Data was extracted from the fNIRS signal and used to calculate oxygenation changes from the L&R AMPFC and DLPFC. Outliers were removed from the HR and RR data. The extracted features were used to train a logistic regression classifier model, using a k-fold cross validation strategy in which each subject in turn serves as the test set for the trained model. Mean of f1-core and Accuracy were taken across the folds for each model to serve as performance metrics for the feature set used.

**Table 1.** Breakdown of screening-condition-labeled points by subject

|          | 1   | 2   | 3   | 4   | 5   | Totals |
|----------|-----|-----|-----|-----|-----|--------|
| 1-screen | 453 | 443 | 446 | 453 | 448 | 2243   |
| 5-screen | 438 | 448 | 450 | 444 | 448 | 2228   |

## 3  Results

### 3.1  Individual Features

Mean test accuracy and f1-score were calculated for classifiers trained on each biometric feature (See Table 2). F1 score for the right AMPFC had to be calculated from only four folds of the cross-validation as one of the folds classified every test point as low workload, and thus could not be used to calculate f1-score. The classifier trained on the left AMPFC data performed better than the other features in terms of both accuracy and f1-score.

### 3.2  Combinations of Biometrics

Mean test accuracy and f1-score were calculated for classifiers trained on all combinations of data from the sensor groups. The Oxy classifier was trained on a four-dimensional data set of oxygenation changes from the LAMPFC, LDLPFC, RDLPFC, and RAMPFC.

**Table 2.** Classifier results of individual features

| Biometric | Accuracy | F1 score |
|-----------|----------|----------|
| HR | 0.48 | 0.42 |
| RR | 0.47 | 0.37 |
| LAMPFC Oxy | 0.68 | 0.67 |
| RAMPFC Oxy | 0.57 | 0.61* |
| LDLPFC Oxy | 0.61 | 0.58 |
| RDLPFC Oxy | 0.56 | 0.34 |

*Calculated from 4 folds only

This classifier was the best performer of the combination classifiers in terms of f1-score, however, it was slightly outperformed in the measure of accuracy by both the combination of Oxy and HR and the combination of Oxy, HR and RR (Table 3).

**Table 3.** Classifier results for all combinations of sensor groups. Oxy referes to oxygenation changes from all four quadrents of the PFC.

| Feature Set | Accuracy | F1 score |
|-------------|----------|----------|
| Oxy | 0.66 | 0.64 |
| HR + RR | 0.48 | 0.46 |
| Oxy + HR | 0.69 | 0.51 |
| Oxy + RR | 0.63 | 0.46 |
| Oxy + HR + RR | 0.68 | 0.49 |

## 4    Discussion

Classifier performance results revealed that oxygenation changes in the PFC overall serve as better predictors of cognitive workload than both HR and RR. Interestingly, previous analysis of this data [18] showed significant changes between the 5-screen and 1-screen conditions in all quadrants of the PFC, except the LAMPFC. However, this was the quadrant that demonstrated the best outcomes from the individual classifier models. This may simply indicate that the data from the LAMPFC is better linearly separable than the data from the other quadrants. The logistic regression algorithm assumes the data used is linearly separable, but that is unlikely to be the case with the biometric data. Further investigation into the performance of the individual biomarkers in classification models for non-linear problems should be conducted. One solution to this would be to transform the feature space into higher order dimensions through the application of feature mapping in the hope that the data is linearly separable in these higher dimensions. Another approach that is used commonly [4, 6–9] is the supervised classification algorithm support vector machine (SVM). Similar to feature mapping, this method uses kernels to increase the dimensionality of the feature set in order to differentiate classes that are not linearly separable.

Combining the oxygenation changes with HR did show a comparable result in classifier test accuracy. However, this case resulted in a lower f1-score than the LAMPFC alone. This indicates that the classifier did a better job of predicting one screen condtion over the other. Since the data used is close to a fifty percent split between 1-screen and 5-screen, this likely indicates that the logistic regression model is under-fitting the biometric data. Once again, this is probably due to the non-linearity of these features.

The accuracy of the well performing models in this study is greater than random chance, which is promising. However, the achieved accuracies are likely not high enough to provide a significant benefit in adaptive training scenarios. Further investigation into the performance of these features sets in other machine learning algorithms such as SVM is necessary to further understand how these biometrics and their various combinations perform as predictors of cognitive workload. Furthermore, a larger data set with a greater number of subjects would allow for better confidence in how well these models would generalize to the population of law enforcement trainees. Overall, the results of this study are promising for the use of a multimodal approach and the biometrics as predictors of different levels of cognitive workload. However, this study also indicates the critical need for future research with more data set and training paradigms allowing to manipulate various level of workload.

# References

1. Hancock, P.A., Chignell, M.H.: Toward a theory of mental workload: stress and adaptability in human-machine systems. In: Proceedings of the International IEEE Conference on Systems, Man and Cybernetics, pp. 378–383 (1986)
2. Welford, A.T.: Forty years of experimental psychology in relation to age: retrospect and prospect. Exp. Gerontol. **21**, 469–481 (1986)
3. Baldwin, C.L., Coyne, J.T.: Mental workload as a function of traffic density: Comparison of physiological, behavioral, and subjective indices (2003)
4. Gerjets, P., Walter, C., Rosenstiel, W., Bogdan, M., Zander, T.O.: Cognitive state monitoring and the design of adaptive instruction in digital environments: lessons learned from cognitive workload assessment using a passive brain-computer interface approach. Front. Neurosci. **8**(DEC), 1–22 (2014). https://doi.org/10.3389/fnins.2014.00385
5. Zhou, Y., Huang, S., Xu, Z., Wang, P., Wu, X., Zhang, D.: Cognitive workload recognition using EEG signals and machine learning: a review. IEEE Trans. Cogn. Dev. Syst. **8920**(c), 1–21 (2021). https://doi.org/10.1109/tcds.2021.3090217
6. Hincks, S.W., Afergan, D., Jacob, R.J.K.: Using fNIRS for real-time cognitive workload assessment. In: Schmorrow, D.D.D., Fidopiastis, C.M.M. (eds.) AC 2016. LNCS (LNAI), vol. 9743, pp. 198–208. Springer, Cham (2016). https://doi.org/10.1007/978-3-319-39955-3_19
7. Siddiquee, M.R., Atri, R., Marquez, J.S., Hasan, S.M.S., Ramon, R., Bai, O.: Sensor location optimization of wireless wearable fnirs system for cognitive workload monitoring using a data-driven approach for improved wearability. Sensors (Switzerland) **20**(18), 1–15 (2020). https://doi.org/10.3390/s20185082

8. Kaczorowska, M., Plechawska-Wójcik, M., Tokovarov, M.: Interpretable machine learning models for three-way classification of cognitive workload levels for eye-tracking features. Brain Sci. **11**(2), 1–22 (2021). https://doi.org/10.3390/brainsci11020210

9. Sharma, H., Drukker, L., Papageorghiou, A.T., Noble, J.A.: Machine learning-based analysis of operator pupillary response to assess cognitive workload in clinical ultrasound imaging. Comput. Biol. Med. **135**, 104589 (2021). https://doi.org/10.1016/j.compbiomed.2021.104589

10. Aksoy, E., Izzetoglu, K., Baysoy, E., Agrali, A., Kitapcioglu, D., Onaral, B.: Performance monitoring via functional near infrared spectroscopy for virtual reality based basic life support training. Front. Neurosci. **13**, 1336 (2019). https://doi.org/10.3389/fnins.2019.01336

11. Izzetoglu, K., Aksoy, M.E., Agrali, A., et al.: Studying brain activation during skill acquisition via robot-assisted surgery training. Brain Sci. **11**, 937 (2021). https://doi.org/10.3390/BRA INSCI11070937

12. Izzetoglu, K., et al.: The evolution of field deployable fNIR spectroscopy from bench to clinical settings. J. Innov. Opt. Health Sci. **4**(3), 239–250 (2011). https://doi.org/10.1142/S17 93545811001587

13. Strangman, G., Boas, D., Sutton, J.: Non-invasive neuroimaging using near-infrared light. Biol. Psychiat. **52**(7), 679–693 (2002). https://doi.org/10.1016/S0006-3223(02)01550-0

14. Izzetoglu, K., et al.: UAV operators workload assessment by optical brain imaging technology (fNIR). In: Valavanis, K.P., Vachtsevanos, G.J. (eds.) Handbook of Unmanned Aerial Vehicles, pp. 2475–2500. Springer, Dordrecht (2015). https://doi.org/10.1007/978-90-481-9707-1_22

15. Thayer, J.F., Åhs, F., Fredrikson, M., Sollers, J.J., Wager, T.D.: A meta-analysis of heart rate variability and neuroimaging studies: implications for heart rate variability as a marker of stress and health. Neurosci. Biobehav. Rev. **36**(2), 747–756 (2012). https://doi.org/10.1016/j.neubiorev.2011.11.009

16. Thayer, J.F., Hansen, A.L., Saus-Rose, E., Johnsen, B.H.: Heart rate variability, prefrontal neural function, and cognitive performance: the neurovisceral integration perspective on self-regulation, adaptation, and health. Ann. Behav. Med. **37**(2), 141–153 (2009). https://doi.org/10.1007/s12160-009-9101-z

17. Grassmann, M., Vlemincx, E., Von Leupoldt, A., Mittelstädt, J., Den Bergh, O.: Respiratory changes in response to cognitive load: a systematic review (2016)

18. Bishop, A., MacNeil, E., Izzetoglu, K.: Cognitive workload quantified by physiological sensors in realistic immersive settings. In: Schmorrow, D.D., Fidopiastis, C.M. (eds.) HCII 2021. LNCS (LNAI), vol. 12776, pp. 119–133. Springer, Cham (2021). https://doi.org/10.1007/978-3-030-78114-9_9

19. National Aeronautics and Space Administration. https://humansystems.arc.nasa.gov/groups/tlx/

20. Jackson, S.A., Marsh, H.W.: Development and validation of a scale to measure optimal experience: the flow state scale. J. Sport Exerc. Psychol. **18**(1), 17–35 (1996). https://doi.org/10.1123/jsep.18.1.17

21. Reddy, P., Richards, D., Izzetoglu, K.: Cognitive performance assessment of UAS sensor operators via neurophysiological measures. Front. Hum. Neurosci. **12** (2018). https://doi.org/10.3389/conf.fnhum.2018.227.00032

22. Kerr, J., Reddy, P., Kosti, S., Izzetoglu, K.: UAS operator workload assessment during search and surveillance tasks through simulated fluctuations in environmental visibility. In: Schmorrow, D.D., Fidopiastis, C.M. (eds.) HCII 2019. LNCS (LNAI), vol. 11580, pp. 394–406. Springer, Cham (2019). https://doi.org/10.1007/978-3-030-22419-6_28

23. Izzetoglu, K., Bunce, S., Onaral, B., Pourrezaei, K., Chance, B.: Functional optical brain imaging using near-infrared during cognitive tasks. Int. J. Hum.-Comput. Interact. **17**(2), 211–227 (2004). https://doi.org/10.1207/s15327590ijhc1702_6
24. Izzetoglu, K., et al.: Applications of functional near infrared imaging: case study on UAV ground controller. In: Schmorrow, D.D., Fidopiastis, C.M. (eds.) FAC 2011. LNCS (LNAI), vol. 6780, pp. 608–617. Springer, Heidelberg (2011). https://doi.org/10.1007/978-3-642-21852-1_70

# EEG4Home: A Human-In-The-Loop Machine Learning Model for EEG-Based BCI

Xiaodong Qu[1,2](✉) [iD] and Timothy J. Hickey[1]

[1] Brandeis University, Waltham, MA 02453, USA
{xiqu,tjhickey}@brandeis.edu
[2] Swarthmore College, Swarthmore, PA 19081, USA

**Abstract.** Using Machine Learning and Deep Learning to predict cognitive tasks from electroencephalography (EEG) signals has been a fast-developing area in Brain-Computer Interfaces (BCI). Yet, one fundamental challenge is that EEG signals are vulnerable to various noises. This paper identifies two types of noise: external noise and internal noise. External noises are caused by subjects' movement or sensors' instability, and internal noises result from the subjects' random mental activities due to the subjects' mind wandering during the experiment. When the participants conduct other mental activities researchers cannot infer, it will result in data corresponding to' unknown' tasks. We pioneer a Human-In-The-Loop (HITL) machine learning model, EEG4Home, to handle both types of noise and increase the accuracy of predicting known tasks. We introduce a plateau threshold to remove external noise and an unknown threshold set to detect unknown tasks to remove internal noise. Both unsupervised (such as K-Means) and supervised (Such as Random Forests, CNN, and RNN) learning algorithms are implemented in this HITL approach. We use the Thinking1 BCI experiments dataset with sixty subjects (available to academic researchers by request). The average prediction accuracy of known tasks has increased from 56.8% to 65.1%. Overall, this EEG4Home model enables researchers or end-users to gain higher prediction accuracy and more interpretable results.

**Keywords:** Brain machine interface · Machine learning · Interpretability · BCI for everyone · Human-centered computing

## 1 Introduction

Researchers from both clinical and non-clinical fields have applied EEG-based Brain Computer Interaction (BCI) techniques in many different ways [4,13], such as diagnosis of abnormal states, evaluating the effect of the treatments, seizure detection, motor imagery tasks [5], and developing BCI-based games [3]. Previous studies have reviewed existing machine learning and deep learning algorithms [11,14,15,24,27,30] for classifying EEG-based BCI tasks.

© The Author(s), under exclusive license to Springer Nature Switzerland AG 2022
D. D. Schmorrow and C. M. Fidopiastis (Eds.): HCII 2022, LNAI 13310, pp. 162–172, 2022.
https://doi.org/10.1007/978-3-031-05457-0_14

However, EEG-based BCI remains an expensive and time-consuming app-roach, more for research or clinical settings than for non-expert users to use at home. Also, EEG signals have a relatively low signal-to-noise ratio, mainly because of the contact of sensors and skin for several current consumer-grade devices. The outlier issue is also a concern for the EEG data. Some participants have had difficulties generating stable EEG signals for various reasons, such as head shape, hairstyle, and the EEG headsets electrodes. Current EEG-based BCI algorithms and frameworks are more for clinical-style devices and less for an affordable instrument with at-home settings.

Can we develop an easy-to-use machine learning EEG framework for non-expert end-users to classify their everyday learning tasks better? This paper proposed a framework, EEG4Home, to eliminate these disturbing artifacts by utilizing a Human-In-The-Loop (HITP) machine learning approach. We eval-uated this approach on four EEG data sets and presented the main results with increased prediction accuracy and more interpretable feedback to both researchers and end-users.

## 2   Related Work

There are several existing frameworks for analyzing EEG data, such as BCI2000 [27]; OpenVibe [23]; USC Brainstorm [28]; Harvard HAPPE [6]; Stanford EEG-BIDS [18]; and JHU BCI2000web [16]. These frameworks are more for EEG data with clinical devices, usually 128 or 64 electrodes.

Since 2015, several consumer-grade EEG-based BCI headsets have been released, which are more affordable for researchers and non-expert end-users, as shown in Fig. 1.

After comparing different non-invasive, easy-to-use options [10,26], We selected Muse and (Muse 2) headsets to collect EEG data for our experiments

| Device Name | Manufacturer | Price* | Channels | Main Functions advertised |
|---|---|---|---|---|
| Muse 2 | InteraXon(Canada) | $220 | 4 | Meditation, self-assessment |
| Muse S | InteraXon(Canada) | $300 | 4 | Meditation, self-assessment, Sleep |
| Insight | Emotiv Systems | $300 | 5 | Self-assessment, device control |
| Epoc+ | Emotiv Systems | $700 | 14 | Self-assessment, device control |
| MindWave Mobile 2 | Neurosky | $100 | 1 | Meditation,Self-assessment, Gaming, device control |
| 'Mark IV' | Open BCI | $500 to 600 | 8 to 16 | (unassembled), self-assessment open-development, |

* price, as of Jun 20, 2020. From the Manufacturers' official websites.

**Fig. 1.** EEG head sets

**Table 1.** Tasks in experiments

| Exp (Task) | (1) | (2) | (3) | (4) | (5) |
|---|---|---|---|---|---|
| [19] | Math | Close-eye Relax | Read | Open-eye Relax | None |
| [22] | Python Passive | Math Passive | Python Active | Math Active | None |
| [21] | Read | Write Copy | Write Answer | Type Copy | Type Answer |
| [20] | Think | Count | Recall | Breathe | Draw |

[19–22]. After getting approval from the IRB, we invited more than a hundred college students to participate in four EEG recording experiments, mainly asking them to conduct learning-related cognitive tasks, such as reading, writing, and typing. Table 1 is a summary of the activities in these experiments. Each row is an experiment mentioned in a paper. Each of the first two experiments has four tasks. So the fifth task in the table is labeled as 'None'. Each of the last two experiments has five tasks. The researchers and end-users co-developed these tasks. The goal is to make the experimental tasks as similar as possible to the frequently conducted tasks at home.

## 3  Methods

Researchers continue to develop new algorithms for EEG-based BCI, such as [1,2,7–9,12,17,25,29]. However, the quality of the results heavily rely on the quality of the datasets. We proposed a human-centered framework to collect data faster, with less noise, and provide participants with more interpretable results.

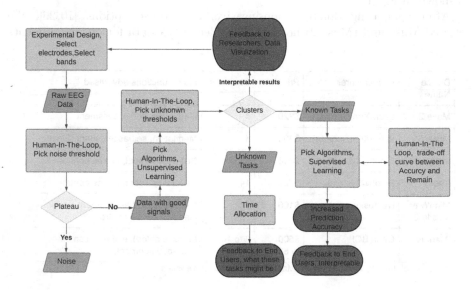

**Fig. 2.** Experiment and data analysis flow chart.

### 3.1  Framework

Figure 2 demonstrated our closed-loop framework, EEG4Home. The starting point is the experimental design on the top left. Here the researchers from computer science and neuroscience discussed the selection of electrodes. We talked about what EEG devices we use and which electrodes we care about the most. For example, we chose the four-electrode Muse headsets in the four experiments above. And we pay more attention to the AF7 and AF8 electrodes.

Then we collected the raw EEG data. For Muse 2016, we used the research software provided by the Muse manufacturer, InteraXon. For Muse 2018 and later, because InteraXon no longer supports the research software, we switched to Mind Monitor, a third-party application. We used Matlab and Python 3 for data analysis.

Next, we implemented the Human-In-The-Loop approach. Figure 3 is an example of a five-minute session from the Read-Write-Type (RWT) experiment. The plateaus of the EEG signal the noise (5.4%), and researchers decided how long a meaningful noise threshold should be for this experiment. For example, we chose 1.4 s as the noise threshold in these four experiments. If a plateau lasts more than that, we marked this time range of signals as the noise.

After removing the noise, we picked algorithms to identify the tasks. First, we used unsupervised learning to figure out the natural clusters of the tasks. We tested unsupervised clustering algorithms, such as DBSCAN, K-Means and GMM. K-Means provided the most interpretable results for our experiments. When we presented the clustering results from k-means to the end-users, they

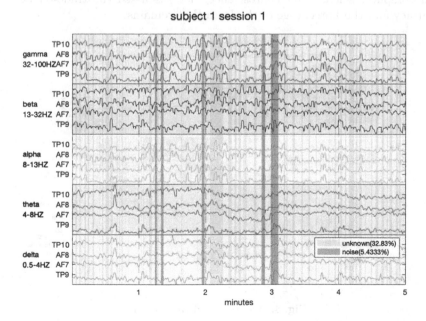

**Fig. 3.** Noise, unknown, and known tasks, experiment RWT: subject one, session one.

could recall the difference between known and unknown tasks for more than 80% of the experiment time. Typically, they described a 'mind wandering' state that was not the task in the experimental design.

For the unknown tasks, we marked it on the feedback images to the end-user and started an investigation about what it could be. The 'mind wandering' state is the leading reason for such unknown tasks.

For the known tasks, we then picked the supervised learning algorithms. The Random Forest and LSTM beat most other machine learning and deep learning algorithms, and combining them using the Time-Continuity-Voting algorithm outperformed others. After removing the noise and unknown tasks, the prediction accuracy increased substantially, with increased interpretability to the end-users.

Then the researchers and the end-users reviewed the noise, the unknown tasks, and known tasks together. Based on this discussion, the researchers and end-users developed the next version of the experiment. This closed-loop approach generated less noise and unknown tasks during each iteration.

## 3.2   Algorithms

Figure 4 is an overview of how the pair of cluster number K in K-means and unknown threshold co-determined the prediction accuracy and the percentage of data remains for the known tasks. We recognized the pattern that, both indicators contribute to the results, and there is an intersection line of the two surfaces of Accuracy, and the Percentage of the Data remains. The researchers from computer science and neuroscience then discussed the trade-off between Accuracy and the Percentage of the Data that remains.

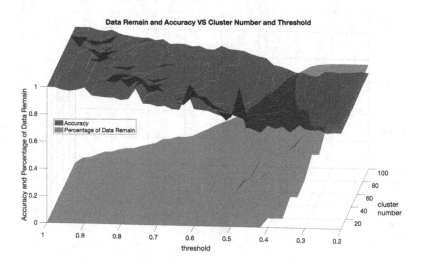

**Fig. 4.** Accuracy and Remain, 3D

One crucial innovation here is the Human-In-The-Loop approach. The pattern is when the percentage of data remains decreased. We can get a higher prediction accuracy for the known tasks using this approach. But how to decide the best threshold? Is the intersection line necessarily the best? After several rounds of discussion from computer scientists, neuroscientists, and end-users, we agree that interpretability is also essential in such an approach. We eventually selected the threshold to link the end-users reflection best to the machine learning clustering and prediction results.

## 4    Results

We found the following machine learning results with this framework.

Figure 5 demonstrated the trade-off between prediction accuracy and the percentage of data remains. The X-Axis ranks threshold pairs (cluster number K in K-means and the unknown threshold). We included the top 150 pairs, corresponding to 0.87 to 0.74 for the known tasks. Compared with the random of 0.2 (because we predict a task from five possible tasks), this accuracy provides meaningful feedback to the end-users.

The Y-Axis is the prediction accuracy for the blue line. It also shows the percentage of data-remaining using the orange line. As we can observe from this figure, when the accuracy decreased from 0.87 to 0.74, the data-remaining increased from 0.37 to 0.94.

During our Human-In-The-Loop discussions, the neuroscientists preferred to keep more data remaining as it represents more experiment time. Computer scientists prefer high accuracy. The end-users prefer a model that can classify

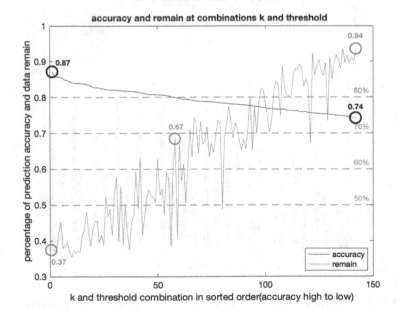

**Fig. 5.** Accuracy and Remain, 2D

```
noiseRemoved_data = readcsv("subjID.csv");

for threshold = 0.3:0.02:0.6
    % removed unknown using kmeans
    unknownRemoved_data = Kmeans(noiseRemoved_data,threshold);
    % calulate REMAIN
    REMAIN = size(unknownRemoved_data)/size(original_data);
    % use randomforest to predict tasks
    prediction = RandomForest.fit(unknownRemoved_data);
    % calulate ACCURACY
    ACCURACY = compare(prediction,label);
end

plot2D(ACCURACY,REMAIN,"sort","descend ACCURACY ");
```

**Fig. 6.** Pseudo code

their experience – the noise, unknown tasks, and known tasks. The model is expected to match the end-users reflection about the experiment. Ideally, when the results show the end-user was doing an unknown task from 3 min and 5 s to 3 min and 15 s, the end-user might remember and agree with that type of classification.

Although the individual difference is significant, the trade-off pattern between accuracy and data-remaining is the same for more than 90% of the end-users in these experiments. Figure 6 is the pseudo code to generate the results in Fig. 5 for each end-users. Figure 7 is the results of the noise, unknown tasks, and known tasks for different participants in the same experiment.

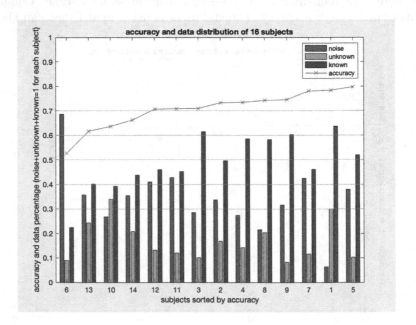

**Fig. 7.** Experiment RWT: noise, unknown, and known tasks percentage.

The X-axis in Fig. 7 is the subject ID of the experiment, ordered by prediction accuracy, from low to high. The Y-axis is the prediction accuracy for that accuracy line. And the percentage of the data for the colored bars. As we can see, subject 5 has about 35% of noise, 10% of unknown tasks, and 55% of the known tasks. Using this approach, the prediction accuracy for the known task for this subject 1 is close to 80%. While subject 6 has almost 70% of noise, that implies the improvement for the recording of this Subject's EEG could be more focused on how to avoid such a high noise level.

Figure 8 is the summary of prediction accuracy and data-remaining for different end-users. The X-axis is the subject ID ordered by the prediction accuracy of the known task. The Y-axis is the percentage. The blue bar for the prediction accuracy. After removing the noise and unknown tasks, the orange bar for the data-remaining is the known tasks. The Yellow bar and purple bar on the right are the averages of all the participants in this experiment.

Figure 9 is an example of the visual feedback to each end-user. The X-axis is the predicted task in this experiment. The Y-axis is the actual task. The diagonal cells represent the accuracy of successfully predicting a certain task. For example, Task 5, as T5 in this figure, is classified with 89% accuracy and is not confused with other tasks. While task 2 is 69% successfully predicted, it has an 11% chance to be misclassified as Task 1 or Task 4.

## 5   Discussion

This paper presents an EEG4Home framework, which aims to be a fast and more interpretable solution for non-expert BCI end-users at home. The short-term goal of this EEG4Home algorithm development is to inspire new machine

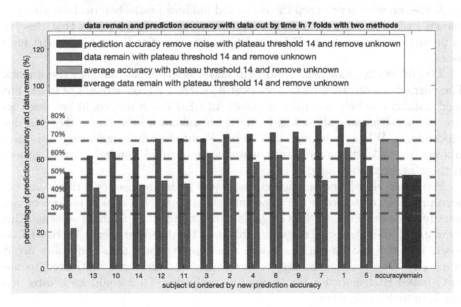

**Fig. 8.** Experiment RWT: prediction accuracy.

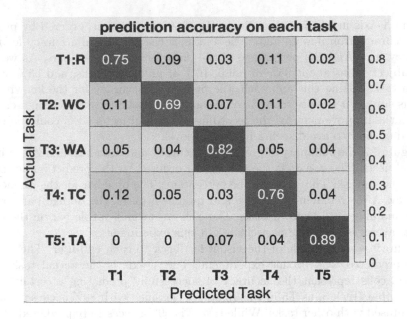

**Fig. 9.** Feedback to end-users

learning and deep learning approaches for decoding such cognitive tasks from the Human Brain. The long-term goal of this research is to get more end-users involved in using EEG-based BCI. Eventually, using EEG-based BCI could be as common and simple as using a smartphone nowadays.

Based on the research we have reviewed in this paper, we identified some guidelines on whether to keep the noise and unknown tasks before classifying the known tasks. We also recognized several open research questions that deserve to be answered to make EEG-based BCI more user-friendly to non-expert end-users.

The following guidelines could help end-users conduct similar experiments. The current non-invasive EEG devices still generate a large amount of noise, but user training can help control this noise. An EEG coach role could be constructive in this situation. Mind-wandering is an unknown everyday activity in our experiments. When designing tasks, think about the mind-wandering activities, and assume at least one more task as unknown or mind-wandering could appear in the classification results.

Providing visual feedback to end-users and gathering user experience are the best practices to improve the experimental design. Non-expert end-users can usually record meaningful EEG signals with two to three training sessions. But some individuals struggled to get reliable data for the experiments. So this EEG-based BCI still has limitations before most smartphone users can easily use it every day. One exciting finding is that many end-users are motivated to use EEG-based BCI more for fun, game-like activities. That could be a direction worth more investigation.

# 6   Conclusion

In this paper, we presented the EEG4Home model. Four existing experiments were used in this research. Human-In-The-Loop Machine learning and deep learning approaches have been implemented in data analysis. The results showed a reasonable high prediction accuracy and interpretable task types for most end-users. This framework could be a building block towards the future of everyone using non-invasive, wireless, and affordable EEG-based BCI systems every day at home, similar to current smartphone usage.

# References

1. Bashivan, P., Rish, I., Yeasin, M., Codella, N.: Learning representations from EEG with deep recurrent-convolutional neural networks. arXiv preprint arXiv:1511.06448 (2015)
2. Chevalier, J.A., Gramfort, A., Salmon, J., Thirion, B.: Statistical control for spatio-temporal MEG/EEG source imaging with desparsified multi-task Lasso. arXiv preprint arXiv:2009.14310 (2020)
3. Coyle, D., Principe, J., Lotte, F., Nijholt, A.: Guest editorial: brain/neuronal-computer game interfaces and interaction. IEEE Trans. Comput. Intell. AI Games 5(2), 77–81 (2013)
4. Craik, A., He, Y., Contreras-Vidal, J.L.: Deep learning for electroencephalogram (EEG) classification tasks: a review. J. Neural Eng. 16(3), 031001 (2019)
5. Devlaminck, D., Waegeman, W., Bauwens, B., Wyns, B., Santens, P., Otte, G.: From circular ordinal regression to multilabel classification. In: Proceedings of the 2010 Workshop on Preference Learning (European Conference on Machine Learning, ECML), p. 15 (2010)
6. Gabard-Durnam, L.J., Mendez Leal, A.S., Wilkinson, C.L., Levin, A.R.: The Harvard automated processing pipeline for electroencephalography (HAPPE): standardized processing software for developmental and high-artifact data. Front. Neurosci. 12, 97 (2018)
7. Hersche, M., Millán, J.d.R., Benini, L., Rahimi, A.: Exploring embedding methods in binary hyperdimensional computing: a case study for motor-imagery based brain-computer interfaces. arXiv preprint arXiv:1812.05705 (2018)
8. Hersche, M., Rellstab, T., Schiavone, P.D., Cavigelli, L., Benini, L., Rahimi, A.: Fast and accurate multiclass inference for MI-BCIs using large multiscale temporal and spectral features. In: 2018 26th European Signal Processing Conference (EUSIPCO), pp. 1690–1694. IEEE (2018)
9. Hosseini, M.P., Hosseini, A., Ahi, K.: A review on machine learning for EEG signal processing in bioengineering. IEEE Rev. Biomed. Eng. 14, 204–218 (2020)
10. Ienca, M., Haselager, P., Emanuel, E.J.: Brain leaks and consumer neurotechnology. Nat. Biotechnol. 36(9), 805–810 (2018)
11. Kaya, M., Binli, M.K., Ozbay, E., Yanar, H., Mishchenko, Y.: A large electroencephalographic motor imagery dataset for electroencephalographic brain computer interfaces. Sci. Data 5(1), 1–16 (2018)
12. Li, G., Lee, C.H., Jung, J.J., Youn, Y.C., Camacho, D.: Deep learning for EEG data analytics: a survey. Concurr. Comput. Pract. Exp. 32(18), e5199 (2020)
13. Lotte, F., et al.: A review of classification algorithms for EEG-based brain-computer interfaces: a 10 year update. J. Neural Eng. 15(3), 031005 (2018)

14. Lotte, F., Congedo, M., Lécuyer, A., Lamarche, F., Arnaldi, B.: A review of classification algorithms for EEG-based brain-computer interfaces. J. Neural Eng. **4**(2), R1 (2007)
15. Miller, K.J.: A library of human electrocorticographic data and analyses. Nat. Hum. Behav. **3**(11), 1225–1235 (2019)
16. Milsap, G., Collard, M., Coogan, C., Crone, N.E.: BCI2000Web and WebFM: browser-based tools for brain computer interfaces and functional brain mapping. Front. Neurosci. **12**, 1030 (2019)
17. Orsborn, A.L., Moorman, H.G., Overduin, S.A., Shanechi, M.M., Dimitrov, D.F., Carmena, J.M.: Closed-loop decoder adaptation shapes neural plasticity for skillful neuroprosthetic control. Neuron **82**(6), 1380–1393 (2014)
18. Pernet, C.R., et al.: EEG-BIDS, an extension to the brain imaging data structure for electroencephalography. Sci. Data **6**(1), 1–5 (2019)
19. Qu, X., Hall, M., Sun, Y., Sekuler, R., Hickey, T.J.: A personalized reading coach using wearable EEG sensors-a pilot study of brainwave learning analytics. In: CSEDU, no. 2, pp. 501–507 (2018)
20. Qu, X., Liu, P., Li, Z., Hickey, T.: Multi-class time continuity voting for EEG classification. In: Frasson, C., Bamidis, P., Vlamos, P. (eds.) BFAL 2020. LNCS (LNAI), vol. 12462, pp. 24–33. Springer, Cham (2020). https://doi.org/10.1007/978-3-030-60735-7_3
21. Qu, X., Mei, Q., Liu, P., Hickey, T.: Using EEG to distinguish between writing and typing for the same cognitive task. In: Frasson, C., Bamidis, P., Vlamos, P. (eds.) BFAL 2020. LNCS (LNAI), vol. 12462, pp. 66–74. Springer, Cham (2020). https://doi.org/10.1007/978-3-030-60735-7_7
22. Qu, X., Sun, Y., Sekuler, R., Hickey, T.: EEG markers of stem learning. In: 2018 IEEE Frontiers in Education Conference (FIE), pp. 1–9. IEEE (2018)
23. Renard, Y., et al.: OpenViBE: an open-source software platform to design, test, and use brain-computer interfaces in real and virtual environments. Presence **19**(1), 35–53 (2010)
24. Roy, Y., Banville, H., Albuquerque, I., Gramfort, A., Falk, T.H., Faubert, J.: Deep learning-based electroencephalography analysis: a systematic review. J. Neural Eng. **16**(5), 051001 (2019)
25. Sabbagh, D., Ablin, P., Varoquaux, G., Gramfort, A., Engemann, D.A.: Manifold-regression to predict from MEG/EEG brain signals without source modeling. arXiv preprint arXiv:1906.02687 (2019)
26. Sawangjai, P., Hompoonsup, S., Leelaarporn, P., Kongwudhikunakorn, S., Wilaiprasitporn, T.: Consumer grade EEG measuring sensors as research tools: a review. IEEE Sens. J. **20**(8), 3996–4024 (2019)
27. Schalk, G., McFarland, D.J., Hinterberger, T., Birbaumer, N., Wolpaw, J.R.: BCI 2000: a general-purpose brain-computer interface (BCI) system. IEEE Trans. Biomed. Eng. **51**(6), 1034–1043 (2004)
28. Tadel, F., Baillet, S., Mosher, J.C., Pantazis, D., Leahy, R.M.: Brainstorm: a user-friendly application for MEG/EEG analysis. Comput. Intell. Neurosci. **2011**, 1–13 (2011). https://doi.org/10.1155/2011/879716. Article ID 879716
29. Tu, T., Paisley, J., Haufe, S., Sajda, P.: A state-space model for inferring effective connectivity of latent neural dynamics from simultaneous EEG/fMRI. Adv. Neural. Inf. Process. Syst. **32**, 4662–4671 (2019)
30. Zhang, X., Yao, L., Wang, X., Monaghan, J.J., Mcalpine, D., Zhang, Y.: A survey on deep learning-based non-invasive brain signals: recent advances and new frontiers. J. Neural Eng. **18**, 1–42 (2020). https://iopscience.iop.org/article/10.1088/1741-2552/abc902/meta

# Wavelet-Based Analysis of fNIRS Measures Enable Assessment of Workload

Pratusha Reddy[1], Kurtulus Izzetoglu[1], and Patricia A. Shewokis[1,2(✉)]

[1] School of Biomedical Engineering, Science and Health Systems, Drexel University,
Philadelphia, PA 19104, USA
{ki25,pas38}@drexel.edu
[2] Nutrition Science Department, College of Nursing and Health Professions, Drexel University,
Philadelphia, PA 19104, USA

**Abstract.** Functional near infrared spectroscopy (fNIRS) measurements are confounded by signals originating from different physiological causes (i.e., neuronal, Mayer wave, respiratory, and cardiac), whose time-frequency characteristics are modulated by the experimental task. Most fNIRS research reports workload measures from very low frequency (VLF) band as it correlates to neuronal activity and considers systemic factors (i.e., Mayer wave, respiratory, and cardiac) as noise. However, studies using the physiological sensors have extensively shown that inclusion of systemic factors improve assessment of workload. Wavelet analysis enables investigation of physiological factors of varying temporal and frequency characteristics within the same plane. Therefore, this study aims to investigates task-evoked effects on the fNIRS measurements originating from different physiological sources using wavelet-based analysis. To accomplish this objective, we used the data collected from 13 novice participants who underwent a realistic training protocol that consisted of two easy sessions and one hard session. We extracted time-averaged wavelet-features (relative energy density and relative amplitude) from different physiological bands (cardiac, respiratory, Mayer wave, and neuronal) and hemispheres (right and left). Firstly, results indicated that wavelet-features increased across sessions within VLF bands and decreased within cardiac bands. No changes were observed in Mayer wave and respiratory bands. Secondly, interaction between task load and hemisphere was only observed in VLF band. In conclusion, these results indicate that wavelet-based analysis of fNIRS signals is not only sensitive in detecting workload changes but can also provide complimentary information regarding physiological changes.

**Keywords:** Functional near infrared spectroscopy · fNIRS · Wavelet · Human performance · Workload · Training

## 1 Introduction

Cognitive workload refers to the collective demands induced by the task, environment and an individuals' expertise level on their performance and mental effort [1]. Assessment of cognitive workload has major implications in not only understanding human machine

D. D. Schmorrow and C. M. Fidopiastis (Eds.): HCII 2022, LNAI 13310, pp. 173–182, 2022.
https://doi.org/10.1007/978-3-031-05457-0_15

teaming to prevent human error, but also in creating training programs intended for optimal transfer of appropriate skills. Cognitive workload can be measured using subjective self-reports, performance-based measures, physiological, or neurophysiological measures [2]. Of these measures, those derived from functional near-infrared spectroscopy (fNIRS) are becoming increasingly ubiquitous due to advantages of being non-invasive, affordable, portable, and allowing for real-time safe and continuous monitoring.

Studies assessing cognitive workload using fNIRS, typically apply low pass filters to remove signal components arising from systemic factors (i.e., Mayer wave, respiratory, and cardiac) and extract signals originating from very low frequency band (VLF, 0.01 to 0.06 Hz) as it corresponds to neuronal factor [3, 4]. Although, the general trend is to deem systemic effects as noise, an expanding literature is suggesting that inclusion of these factors may improve assessment of cognitive workload. For example, one study added features of cardiac oscillations (0.4 to 2 Hz) extracted from fNIRS signals to a machine learning architecture and reported increases in classification accuracy of stress by at least 10% when compared against standard model containing only the neuronal activity related information [5]. Furthermore, use of physiological measures (e.g., heart rate variability) have long been used to evaluate cognitive workload [6]. Therefore, this study aims to investigate how workload changes manipulated by task load effect neuronal and systemic factors.

To accomplish this aim, we plan on using wavelet transform (WT) on data collected from a realistic training scenario (consisting of initial training, last training and first transfer sessions). WT is advantageous as it enables simultaneous assessment of signals originating from different physiological causes that vary in time-frequency characteristics [7]. In a study comparing WT against Fourier transform, results indicated distinct low frequency peaks only when WT was applied [8]. WT has been used on fNIRS signals for removing motion artifacts, understanding the interaction between cerebrovascular and cardiovascular dynamic in healthy and diseases populations, and studying social interaction [9–12]. To a limited extent WT has been used to assess training and workload [13–16]. However, all these studies have only focused on effects of changes in task load on brain connectivity features (i.e., coherence between channels, individuals, etc.) extracted from VLF band and not amplitude and energy density features from systemic bands (i.e., cardiac, respiratory, Mayer wave). Therefore, we hypothesize that amplitude and energy density features extracted from different physiological bands are sensitive to changes in task load.

## 2    Materials and Methods

### 2.1    Participants

Data for thirteen right-handed participants ranging from 19 to 40 years, consisting of nine males and four females, was used in this study. The original study was approved by the Drexel University Human Subjects Institution Review Board and further details are reported in [17].

## 2.2 Functional Near Infrared Spectroscopy Sensor

A continuous wave fNIRS device (fNIRS Imager 1200; fNIR Devices LLC, Potomac, MD) was used to measure hemodynamic changes from the PFC. The sensor emits light at peak wavelengths of 730 and 850 nm, samples every 100 ms, has 12 detectors and 4 light sources. The detector and light source combination result in a total of 16 cerebral and 2 extracerebral measurement locations.

## 2.3 Experimental Protocol

In the original study, participants underwent three easy and two hard 12-min-long sessions, during which they engaged in scan and target find tasks. The easy sessions occurred during high visibility conditions, while the hard sessions occurred during low visibility conditions. Each session consisted of six 2-min-long blocks. Since the scope of this study is to show changes in task load, analysis was performed on data from easy session 1, easy session 3 and hard session 1. More details regarding the tasks and experimental protocol are discussed in [17].

## 2.4 Pre-processing fNIRS Signals

First, we employed visual inspection to remove saturated signals [18, 19]. Second, we applied wavelet-based motion artifact removal algorithm to correct abrupt spikes [9]. Third, we converted optical density data into the relative concentration changes of oxy-hemoglobin (HbO) and deoxy-hemoglobin using modified beer lambert law, with the baseline period defined as ten seconds prior to the onset of tasks and age-correction of depth penetration factor [20, 21] Fourth, we used spline interpolation method to correct for abrupt signal shifts [22]. Lastly, we averaged HbO and HbR measures across left (channels 3 to 6) and right (channels 11 to 14) hemispheres.

## 2.5 Wavelet Feature Extraction

Time-Frequency Analysis in Multiscale Oscillatory Dynamics Analysis toolbox was used to extract wavelet coefficients [23]. The Morlet wavelet function with a central frequency of 1 Hz was used to extract the wavelet coefficients [7, 24]. The wavelet coefficients were then partitioned into cardiac [0.4, 2] Hz, respiratory [0.15, 0.4] Hz, Mayer wave [0.06, 0.15] Hz, and very low frequency [0.009, 0.06] Hz bands [25]. Like previous studies we calculated time-averaged relative amplitude (relA) and energy density (rel$\varepsilon$) within each frequency band [7].

## 2.6 Statistics

Linear mixed effects regression (LMER) modelling was performed using R (R Core Team, 2019). Specifically, *lme4*, *lmerTest* and *emmeans* packages were used [26–28]. Models generated investigated the main and interaction effects of Session (Easy 1, Easy 3, and Hard 1) and Hemisphere (Left and Right) on relA and rel $\varepsilon$ per biomarker (HbO and HbR), and band (VLF, Mayer wave, respiratory, and cardiac). The specific model used to evaluate the features is given in Eq. 1.

$$DV \sim 1 + Session + Session : Hemisphere + (1|ID) \tag{1}$$

Homogeneity of variance, and normality of residuals and random effects were conducted using visual inspection. If model predictions showed heteroscedasticity or nonnormal distribution, then log10 transformations were performed on the response variables. Significance of fixed effect terms were evaluated using likelihood ratio tests, where the full effects model was compared against a model without the effect in question. Maximum likelihood estimation was used to conduct likelihood ratio tests, while restricted maximum likelihood was used to evaluate post hoc comparisons. If "Session" or "Session: Hemisphere" terms were significant, then post hoc analyses were performed. Specifically, if "Session: Hemisphere" term was found to be significant, then three comparisons between hemispheres per session (e.g., Easy 1: Left - Right) and two comparisons between sessions per hemisphere (i.e., Left: Easy 1 – Easy 3, and Easy 3 – Hard 1) were performed. A total of seven planned post hoc comparisons were conducted. If the interaction term was not significant, then post hoc analysis of the main effect term was conducted. Specifically, two post hoc comparisons (Easy 1 – Easy 3, and Easy 3 – Hard 1) were performed. Satterthwaite approximation of degrees of freedom was used in post hoc analyses [29]. For all statistical analyses, the level of significance was set at $\alpha = 0.05$. Adjustments using false discovery rate (FDR) were made on p-values to account for Type I error inflation per dependent variable. Cohen's $d$ was used to examine post hoc effects [30]. $d$ of 0.2 is considered a small effect, while 0.5 and 0.8 represent medium and large effects, respectively.

## 3   Results

Wavelet transform of fNIRS signals averaged across subarea, session, hemisphere, and subjects per biomarker (see Fig. 1). Peaks can be observed in VLF and cardiac bands of both HbO and HbR biomarkers with HbR displaying greater peak in VLF band and HbO displaying greater peak in cardiac band.

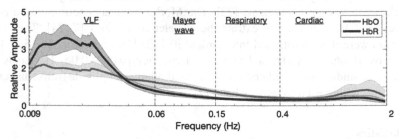

**Fig. 1.** Time-averaged relative amplitude across frequency per fNIRS measure. Solid lines represent mean, while shaded portion represents standard error of mean.

Interaction between Session and Hemisphere were significant in only VLF (relA: $\chi^2(3) = 13.15$, p = 0.004), Mayer wave (relA: $\chi^2(3) = 41.80$, p < 0.001; rel$\varepsilon$: $\chi^2(3)$

= 39.57, p < 0.001) and respiratory (rel$\varepsilon$: $\chi^2(3) = 11.47$, p = 0.009) bands of HbR biomarker. Post hoc comparisons between hemispheres per session and across sessions per hemisphere for relA of HbR biomarker is shown in Table 1. Post hoc comparisons were only significant within VLF and Mayer wave band. Results from within session comparisons (between hemispheres per session) indicated significant differences in (i) only Easy 1 for VLF band, where wavelet-features were greater in left hemisphere; and (ii) all three sessions for Mayer wave band, where wavelet-features were greater in left hemisphere during easy sessions and right hemisphere during hard session. Results from across sessions per hemisphere comparisons, indicated significant changes from Easy 1 to Easy 3 to Hard within VLF band, and Easy 3 to Hard session within Mayer wave band. Specifically, within VLF band wavelet-features decreased in left hemisphere and increased in right hemisphere from Easy 1 to Easy 3, while they decreased in left hemisphere and did not change in right hemisphere from Easy 1 to Hard. Within Mayer wave band wavelet-features increased in only left hemisphere from Easy 3 to Hard.

**Table 1.** Post hoc differences in HbR-relA measures between hemispheres per session and across sessions per hemisphere for bands where interaction between session and hemisphere was significant. adj.p and d are false discovery rate adjusted p values and effect sizes, respectively. If d is positive then the first term in the contrast has a greater value, and vice versa.

| Band | Within session (left - right) | | | Across sessions | | | | |
| | | | | | Left | | Right | |
| Band | Session | adj.p | d | Contrast | adj.p | d | adj.p | d |
|---|---|---|---|---|---|---|---|---|
| VLF | E1 | 0.029 | 0.80 | E1 – E3 | 0.008 | 2.70 | 0.013 | −1.97 |
| | E3 | 0.064 | −2.77 | E1 – H | 0.026 | 1.35 | 0.171 | −0.21 |
| | H | 0.183 | 1.90 | E3 – H | 0.435 | −1.56 | 0.171 | −0.89 |
| Mayer wave | E1 | 0.002 | 1.22 | E1 – E3 | 0.097 | 0.33 | 0.100 | 1.45 |
| | E3 | 0.002 | 0.23 | E1 – H | 0.645 | 0.19 | 0.346 | −0.12 |
| | H | 0.045 | −0.89 | E3 – H | 0.045 | −0.26 | 0.489 | 0.28 |
| Respiratory | E1 | 0.241 | −0.01 | E1 – E3 | 0.241 | −0.16 | 0.241 | 0.20 |
| | E3 | 0.241 | 0.21 | E1 – H | 0.241 | −0.15 | 0.241 | 0.05 |
| | H | 0.241 | −0.16 | E3 – H | 0.989 | 0.07 | 0.989 | 0.06 |

Session had a significant effect on VLF (HbO-relA: $\chi^2(2) = 45.78$, p < 0.001; HbR-relA: ($\chi^2(2) = 21.51$, p < 0.001; HbO-rel $\varepsilon$: $\chi^2(2) = 30.65$, p < 0.001; HbO-rel $\varepsilon$: $\chi^2(2) = 6.53$, p = 0.038), Mayer wave (HbR-relA: $\chi^2(2) = 8.20$, p < 0.017), respiratory (HbO-relA: $\chi^2(2) = 9.07$, p = 0.01; HbR-relA: $\chi^2(2) = 7.09$, p = 0.029; HbO-rel $\varepsilon$: $\chi^2(2) = 14.00$, p = 0.001; HbO-rel $\varepsilon$: $\chi^2(2) = 7.30$, p = 0.026), and cardiac (HbO-relA: $\chi^2(2) = 115.65$, p < 0.001; HbR-relA: $\chi^2(2) = 62.77$, p < 0.001; HbO-rel $\varepsilon$: $\chi^2(2) = 116.20$, p < 0.001; HbR-rel $\varepsilon$: $\chi^2(2) = 56.23$, p < 0.001) bands.

Results from post hoc comparisons between sessions per band, biomarker and feature are provided in Table 2. Within VLF band, wavelet-features significantly increased from

Easy 1 to Easy 3 to Hard. Within Mayer wave and respiratory bands, significant changes were observed only from Easy 1 to Easy 3. Specifically, wavelet-features increased in Mayer wave band and decreased in respiratory band. Lastly, within cardiac band, wavelet-features decreased from Easy 1 to Easy 3 to Hard.

**Table 2.** Post hoc differences across sessions per band, biomarker, and wavelet-feature. adj.p and d are false discovery rate adjusted p values and effect sizes, respectively. If d is positive then the first term in the contrast has a higher value, and vice versa.

| | | HbO | | | | HbR | | | |
|---|---|---|---|---|---|---|---|---|---|
| | | relA | | rel $\varepsilon$ | | relA | | rel $\varepsilon$ | |
| Band | Contrast | adj.p | $d$ | adj.p | $d$ | adj.p | $d$ | adj.p | $D$ |
| VLF | E1 – E3 | 0.000 | −1.05 | 0.000 | −0.66 | 0.000 | −1.00 | 0.047 | −0.50 |
| | E1 – H | 0.001 | −4.02 | 0.001 | −3.57 | 0.008 | −3.81 | 0.104 | −2.40 |
| | E3 – H | 0.036 | −2.97 | 0.267 | −2.90 | 0.114 | −2.80 | 0.529 | −1.91 |
| Mayer wave | E1 – E3 | 0.625 | −0.53 | 0.372 | −0.17 | 0.039 | −0.32 | 0.191 | −0.06 |
| | E1 – H | 0.204 | −0.66 | 0.240 | 0.02 | 0.644 | −0.71 | 0.910 | −0.12 |
| | E3 – H | 0.168 | −0.13 | 0.372 | 0.19 | 0.050 | −0.38 | 0.191 | −0.06 |
| Respiratory | E1 – E3 | 0.028 | 0.17 | 0.010 | 0.08 | 0.054 | 0.01 | 0.058 | 0.00 |
| | E1 – H | 0.149 | 0.58 | 0.062 | 0.30 | 0.054 | 0.20 | 0.058 | 0.03 |
| | E3 – H | 0.235 | 0.42 | 0.176 | 0.22 | 0.935 | 0.19 | 0.917 | 0.03 |
| Cardiac | E1 – E3 | 0.000 | 0.73 | 0.002 | 0.26 | 0.000 | 0.37 | 0.000 | 0.05 |
| | E1 – H | 0.000 | 2.27 | 0.003 | 0.97 | 0.004 | 1.04 | 0.005 | 0.16 |
| | E3 – H | 0.000 | 1.55 | 0.003 | 0.71 | 0.000 | 0.67 | 0.001 | 0.11 |

## 4  Discussion

In this paper, we investigated whether wavelet-based analysis of fNIRS signals can provide further insight into changes in workload during training. The wavelet-features (relative energy density and relative amplitude) from different physiological bands and each hemisphere were extracted. Firstly, these time-averaged features indicated that fNIRS signals have varying time-frequency characteristics in different physiological bands (i.e., VLF, Mayer wave, Respiratory, and Cardiac). Secondly, the wavelet-features within VLF and Cardiac bands appeared to be modulated by task load, while other bands were not. Specifically, wavelet-features within VLF band increased across sessions, while they decreased within the cardiac band. Lastly, only wavelet-features within VLF band varied between hemispheres, with decreases observed in left hemisphere and increases observed in right hemisphere.

Results from VLF band demonstrated that wavelet-features increased across sessions (from beginning to end of training and end of training to transfer condition), when effect of hemisphere was not accounted for. These changes in wavelet-features observed from beginning to end of training are opposite of what was observed from temporal analysis of the same dataset, where intensity of brain activity decreased with practice [17]. These results are not supportive of neural plasticity theory, which states that practice results in schema construction and automation [2, 31]. Accounting for hemisphere demonstrated opposite changes in wavelet-features from beginning to end of training per hemisphere, with wavelet features decreasing in left hemisphere and increasing in right hemisphere. Therefore, results from left hemisphere are supportive of neural plasticity theory. However the changes observed in right hemisphere could be due to task prioritization [32]. Specifically, the task employed in this study is a scan and target find dual task, which requires simultaneous utilization of attention (processed in anterior medial prefrontal cortex) and spatial working memory resources (processed in left dorsolateral prefrontal cortex), respectively [33, 34]. However, since this is the first-time individuals in this study were exposed to such a task environment, individuals may have prioritized a particular task. This prioritization is supported by the results that higher values were observed in left hemisphere at the beginning of training, which suggests that individuals prioritized target find task. Changes observed from end of training to transfer condition are similar to that of the temporal analysis of the same dataset, where increases in task load increased intensity of brain activity [17]. These results, support transfer theory, which states that increasing task load of a learned task via a lower acquisition training environment (i.e., sequential or blocked order) increases brain activity, but not to the same extent as that of an unlearned or insufficiently practiced task [1, 35].

Although, results from Mayer wave and respiratory bands demonstrated effect of task load on wavelet-features, the effects were significant only for HbR measures. Previous research has indicted that HbR is not as highly influenced by systemic factors as HbO [4, 24]. Therefore, since no task-evoked effect was seen on HbO, the detected changes can be interpreted to be not due to a task-evoked effect. Furthermore, these results are supported by the lack of a peak within the Mayer wave and respiratory bands for neither HbO nor HbR biomarker in Fig. 1.

Results from the cardiac band demonstrated decreases in wavelet-features across sessions. The decrease in wavelet-features may be due to stress relief with increased familiarization of the task. Similar effects of task load on stress and changes in stress with practice have been reported from measures extracted via physiological sensors [36–38].

In conclusion, this study demonstrates the use of wavelet analysis in assessment of cognitive workload changes during training on a realistic task. Furthermore, the results indicate high sensitivity of wavelet-features from very low frequency and cardiac bands to changes in task load. Although the results presented in this paper are novel, the interpretations of the results are preliminary. Future studies should include more training sessions and physiological measures to confirm the interpretations.

# References

1. Paas, F., Tuovinen, J.E., Tabbers, H., Van Gerven, P.W.M.: Cognitive load measurement as a means to advance cognitive load theory. Educ. Psychol. **38**, 63–71 (2003). https://doi.org/10.1207/S15326985EP3801_8

2. Curtin, A., Ayaz, H.: The age of neuroergonomics: towards ubiquitous and continuous measurement of brain function with fNIRS. Jpn. Psychol. Res. **60**, 374–386 (2018). https://doi.org/10.1111/jpr.12227

3. Pinti, P., Scholkmann, F., Hamilton, A., et al.: Current status and issues regarding preprocessing of fNIRS neuroimaging data: an investigation of diverse signal filtering methods within a general linear model framework. Front. Hum. Neurosci. **12**, 505 (2019). https://doi.org/10.3389/fnhum.2018.00505

4. Reddy, P., Izzetoglu, M., Shewokis, P.A., et al.: Evaluation of fNIRS signal components elicited by cognitive and hypercapnic stimuli. Sci. Rep. **111**(11), 1–15 (2021). https://doi.org/10.1038/s41598-021-02076-7

5. Hakimi, N., Jodeiri, A., Mirbagheri, M., Kamaledin Setarehdan, S.: Proposing a convolutional neural network for stress assessment by means of derived heart rate from functional near infrared spectroscopy. Comput. Biol. Med. **121**, 103810 (2020). https://doi.org/10.1016/j.compbiomed.2020.103810

6. Charles, R.L., Nixon, J.: Measuring mental workload using physiological measures: a systematic review. Appl. Ergon. **74**, 221–232 (2019). https://doi.org/10.1016/J.APERGO.2018.08.028

7. Stefanovska, A., Bracic, M., Kvernmo, H.: Wavelet analysis of oscillations in the peripheral blood circulation measured by laser doppler technique. IEEE Trans. Biomed. Eng. **46**, 1230–1239 (1999). https://doi.org/10.1109/10.790500

8. Kvandal, P., Landsverk, S.A., Bernjak, A., et al.: Low-frequency oscillations of the laser Doppler perfusion signal in human skin. Microvasc. Res. **72**, 120–127 (2006). https://doi.org/10.1016/J.MVR.2006.05.006

9. Molavi, B., Dumont, G.A.: Wavelet-based motion artifact removal for functional near-infrared spectroscopy. Physiol. Meas. **33**, 259–270 (2012). https://doi.org/10.1088/0967-3334/33/2/259

10. Holper, L., Scholkmann, F., Seifritz, E.: Prefrontal hemodynamic after-effects caused by rebreathing may predict affective states – a multimodal functional near-infrared spectroscopy study. Brain Imaging Behav. **11**(2), 461–472 (2016). https://doi.org/10.1007/s11682-016-9527-4

11. Highton, D., Ghosh, A., Tachtsidis, I., et al.: Monitoring cerebral autoregulation after brain injury: multimodal assessment of cerebral slow-wave oscillations using near-infrared spectroscopy. Anesth. Analg. **121**, 198 (2015). https://doi.org/10.1213/ANE.0000000000000790

12. Xu, J., Slagle, J.M., Banerjee, A., et al.: Use of a portable functional near-infrared spectroscopy (fNIRS) system to examine team experience during crisis event management in clinical simulations. Front. Hum. Neurosci. **13**, 85 (2019). https://doi.org/10.3389/FNHUM.2019.00085/BIBTEX

13. Wang, F., Jiang, Z., Li, X., et al.: Functional brain network analysis of knowledge transfer while engineering problem-solving. Front. Hum. Neurosci. **15** (2021). https://doi.org/10.3389/FNHUM.2021.713692

14. Xu, L., Wang, B., Xu, G., et al.: Functional connectivity analysis using fNIRS in healthy subjects during prolonged simulated driving. Neurosci. Lett. **640**, 21–28 (2017). https://doi.org/10.1016/J.NEULET.2017.01.018

15. Zhang, L., Sun, J., Sun, B., et al.: Studying hemispheric lateralization during a Stroop task through near-infrared spectroscopy-based connectivity. **19**, 057012 (2014) . https://doi.org/10.1117/1.JBO.19.5.057012

16. Verdière, K.J., Roy, R.N., Dehais, F.: Detecting pilot's engagement using fnirs connectivity features in an automated vs. Manual landing scenario. Front. Hum. Neurosci. **12**, 6 (2018). https://doi.org/10.3389/FNHUM.2018.00006/BIBTEX

17. Reddy, P., Kerr, J., Shewokis, P.A., Izzetoglu, K.: Brain activity changes elicited through multi-session training assessment in the prefrontal cortex by fNIRS. In: Schmorrow, D.D., Fidopiastis, C.M. (eds.) HCII 2021. LNCS (LNAI), vol. 12776, pp. 63–73. Springer, Cham (2021). https://doi.org/10.1007/978-3-030-78114-9_5

18. Ayaz, H., Shewokis, P.A., Curtin, A., et al.: Using MazeSuite and functional near infrared spectroscopy to study learning in spatial navigation. J. Vis. Exp. **8**, 3443 (2011). https://doi.org/10.3791/3443

19. Izzetoglu, M., Izzetoglu, K.: Real time artifact removal. 1–9 (2014)

20. Villringer, A., Chance, B.: Non invasive optical spectroscopy and imaging of human brain function. Trends Neurosci. **20**, 435–442 (1997). https://doi.org/10.1016/S0166-2236(97)011 32-6

21. Scholkmann, F., Wolf, M.: General equation for the differential pathlength factor of the frontal human head depending on wavelength and age. J. Biomed. Opt. **18**, 105004 (2013). https://doi.org/10.1117/1.jbo.18.10.105004

22. Scholkmann, F., Spichtig, S., Muehlemann, T., Wolf, M.: How to detect and reduce movement artifacts in near-infrared imaging using moving standard deviation and spline interpolation. Physiol. Meas. **31**, 649–662 (2010). https://doi.org/10.1088/0967-3334/31/5/004

23. Iatsenko, D., McClintock, P.V.E., Stefanovska, A.: Linear and synchrosqueezed time-frequency representations revisited: overview, standards of use, resolution, reconstruction, concentration, and algorithms. Digit. Signal Process. A Rev. J. **42**, 1–26 (2015). https://doi.org/10.1016/j.dsp.2015.03.004

24. Kirilina, E., Yu, N., Jelzow, A., et al.: Identifying and quantifying main components of phys-iological noise in functional near infrared spectroscopy on the prefrontal cortex. Front. Hum. Neurosci. **7**, 864 (2013). https://doi.org/10.3389/fnhum.2013.00864

25. Yücel, M.A., Selb, J., Aasted, C.M., et al.: Mayer waves reduce the accuracy of estimated hemodynamic response functions in functional near-infrared spectroscopy. Biomed. Opt. Express **7**, 3078–3088 (2016). https://doi.org/10.1364/boe.7.003078

26. Bates, D., Mächler, M., Bolker, B.M., Walker, S.C.: Fitting linear mixed-effects models using lme4. J. Stat. Softw. **67**, 1–48 (2015). https://doi.org/10.18637/jss.v067.i01

27. Kuznetsova, A., Brockhoff, P.B., Christensen, R.H.B.: lmerTest package: tests in linear mixed effects models lmertest package: tests in linear mixed effects models. J. Stat. Softw. **82** (2017). https://doi.org/10.18637/jss.v082.i13

28. length, R.: emmeans: Estimated Marginal Means, aka LeastSquares Means (2020)

29. Friston, K.J.: Statistical Parametric Mapping. In: Kötter, R. (eds.) Neuroscience Databases, pp. 237–250. Springer, Boston (2003). https://doi.org/10.1007/978-1-4615-1079-6_16

30. Westfall, J., Kenny, D.A., Judd, C.M.: Statistical power and optimal design in experiments in which samples of participants respond to samples of stimuli. J. Exp. Psychol. Gen. **143**, 2020–2045 (2014). https://doi.org/10.1037/xge0000014

31. Izzetoglu, K., Aksoy, M.E., Agrali, A., et al.: Studying brain activation during skill acquisition via robot-assisted surgery training. Brain Sci. **11**, 937 (2021). https://doi.org/10.3390/BRA INSCI11070937

32. Seghier, M.L., Price, C.J.: Interpreting and utilising intersubject variability in brain function. Trends Cogn. Sci. **22**, 517–530 (2018). https://doi.org/10.1016/j.tics.2018.03.003

33. Izzetoglu, K., Ayaz, H., Hing, J.T., et al.: UAV operators workload assessment by optical brain imaging technology (fNIR). In: Valavanis, K., Vachtsevanos, G. (eds.) Handbook of Unmanned Aerial Vehicles, pp. 2475–2500. Springer, Dordrecht (2015). https://doi.org/10.1007/978-90-481-9707-1_22

34. Izzetoglu, M., Bunce, S.C., Izzetoglu, K., et al.: Functional brain imaging using near-infrared technology. IEEE Eng. Med. Biol. Mag. **26**, 38–46 (2007)

35. Shewokis, P.A., Shariff, F.U., Liu, Y., et al.: Acquisition, retention and transfer of simulated laparoscopic tasks using fNIR and a contextual interference paradigm. Am. J. Surg. **213**, 336–345 (2017). https://doi.org/10.1016/j.amjsurg.2016.11.043

36. Mandrick, K., Peysakhovich, V., Rémy, F., et al.: Neural and psychophysiological correlates of human performance under stress and high mental workload. Biol. Psychol. **121**, 62–73 (2016). https://doi.org/10.1016/j.biopsycho.2016.10.002

37. Liu, Y., Ayaz, H., Shewokis, P.A.: Multisubject "learning" for mental workload classification using concurrent EEG, fNIRS, and physiological measures. Front. Hum. Neurosci. **11**, 389 (2017). https://doi.org/10.3389/fnhum.2017.00389

38. Palma Fraga, R., Reddy, P., Kang, Z., Izzetoglu, K.: Multimodal analysis using neuroimaging and eye movements to assess cognitive workload. In: Schmorrow, D.D., Fidopiastis, C.M. (eds.) HCII 2020. LNCS (LNAI), vol. 12196, pp. 50–63. Springer, Cham (2020). https://doi.org/10.1007/978-3-030-50353-6_4

# A Method of Developing Video Stimuli that Are Amenable to Neuroimaging Analysis: An EEG Pilot Study

Michael C. Trumbo[✉], Aaron P. Jones, Bradley M. Robert, Derek Trumbo, and Laura E. Matzen

Sandia National Laboratories, Albuquerque, USA
{mctrumb,ajones3,bmrober,dtrumbo,lematze}@sandia.gov

**Abstract.** Creation of streaming video stimuli that allow for strict experimental control while providing ease of scene manipulation is difficult to achieve but desired by researchers seeking to approach ecological validity in contexts that involve processing streaming visual information. To that end, we propose leveraging video game modding tools as a method of creating research quality stimuli. As a pilot effort, we used a video game sandbox tool (Garry's Mod) to create three steaming video scenarios designed to mimic video feeds that physical security personnel might observe. All scenarios required participants to identify the presences of a threat appearing during the video feed. Each scenario differed in level of complexity, in that one scenario required only location monitoring, one required location and action monitoring, and one required location, action, and conjunction monitoring in that when an action was performed it was only considered a threat when performed by a certain character model. While there was no behavioral effect of scenario in terms of accuracy or response times, in all scenarios we found evidence of a P300 when comparing response to threatening stimuli to that of standard stimuli. Results therefore indicate that sufficient levels of experimental control may be achieved to allow for the precise timing required for ERP analysis. Thus, we demonstrate the feasibility of using existing modding tools to create video scenarios amenable to neuroimaging analysis.

**Keywords:** EEG · ERP · Ecological Validity · P300

## 1 Introduction

Traditionally, visual search experiments rely primarily on static images of stimuli such as letters and basic shapes [1] which may not be ecologically valid for analysts who examine streaming data feeds such as security personnel monitoring video feeds of security cameras. Behavioral research using stimuli in motion has suggested that factors such as the number of moving objects, the number of video feeds, the motion of both the camera and of the target, the scene complexity, and the area of coverage influence the percentage of missed targets [2–4]. In addition, biological motion appears to have a

© National Technology & Engineering Solutions of Sandia, LLC 2022
D. D. Schmorrow and C. M. Fidopiastis (Eds.): HCII 2022, LNAI 13310, pp. 183–201, 2022.
https://doi.org/10.1007/978-3-031-05457-0_16

particular influence on salience and interpretation of the scene – including discernment of the intentions of the actors [5].

Development of stimuli in this domain should allow for manipulation and implementation of these factors, as well as factors that drive human attention such as the frequency of events of interest and distractor events, the timing and duration of the events, the perceptibility of the events, and the overall length of the task [6]. It can be difficult, however, to develop such stimuli. The use of motion-capture, professional animations, or live-action video can be expensive, time-consuming, difficult to alter, or have a steep learning curve that acts as a barrier to entry.

As a ubiquitous activity, video game playing has attracted the attention of cognitive scientists who seek to understand who plays video games and why they do so [7, 8] as well as the impact of video games on attention, memory, and other cognitive faculties [9–11]. Conversely, other researchers have focused on the opposite direction – how video game players influence the nature of the games they play.

The term "modding" is used as a slang term in reference to the act of making modifications to the existing aesthetics, experience, or structure of a video game [12; see 13 for a history of modding]. The goals of modding may be to improve the interactivity of a game, adjust the graphics or responsiveness, control the difficulty, create additional content, develop programming skills, or to satisfy various psychological needs such as the need for self-expression, co-operation, and involvement in a community with a shared interest [12, 14, 15]. From a game developer perspective, successful engagement with modding communities can result in new features and content that strengthen the brand-name, add to the shelf-life of the game, increase customer loyalty, improve sales of and spark interest in the original game (as mods often require the original software to run), serve as a method of identifying and recruiting skilled developers, and reduce research & development as well as marketing costs by providing insight into the types of features that are desired by and popular with the gaming community [12, 13, 16].

Therefore, many game development companies encourage the gaming community to act as prosumers engaged in participatory design via the release of tools to make modding easier [14, 17, 18]. Thus, there is a demand for tools that assist in game modifications, and developers may benefit from providing such tools. The result of mutual interest between video game players and video game developers in accessible modding presents an opportunity for educators and researchers to leverage readily available tools to adapt game scenarios to serve an educational [19–21] or a research function [22].

One niche within the modding community is the use of game engines to create cinematic productions, referred to as "machinima" – a misspelled portmanteaux of "machine" and "cinema." There are four primary methods of accomplishing this type of production, including reliance on the AI of the game engine, digital puppetry, manipulation of the in-game camera, and – critically for neuroimaging considerations – precise scripting of actions [23]. This has previously been suggested as a method of creating educational materials [24]. We therefore propose to use these tools as a method of creating ecologically valid streaming stimuli amenable to neuroimaging analysis.

In the current study, we consider the feasibility of using modding tools to develop stimuli that have an attentional profile similar to streaming sensor data, such as full-motion video (i.e., a continuous stream of irrelevant events with important events interspersed at unpredictable intervals) and provide experimenters with full control of variables of interest. Furthermore, we propose that stimuli developed in this fashion can be made amenable to neuroimaging analysis via strict control over the timing and duration of events. Electroencephalography (EEG) records millisecond-level information about the electrical activity of the brain, and the relationships between specific patterns in EEG data and neural processes related to attention are well established in the cognitive neuroscience literature [see 25 and 26 for reviews]. EEG data can be used to determine the depth of encoding of stimuli [27–29], to determine whether the processing was automatic or controlled [30, 31], and even to detect leading indicators of an analyst's decision [32, 33].

A common paradigm designed to elicit an EEG response is the so-called 'oddball' paradigm, in which (typically) two stimuli are presented in a random order with one occurring less frequently than the other (the infrequent stimulus thus being the oddball); participants are required to identify the rare target stimulus. A variation of this paradigm, the three-stimulus oddball, involves the addition of an infrequent non-target stimulus along with the infrequent target stimulus and frequent standard stimulus [34]. We chose to model our creation of streaming video stimuli after this 3-stimulus implementation of the oddball paradigm, reasoning that in the context of physical security there may be instances in which rare non-threatening events occur alongside rare threatening events and frequent banal events. With this consideration in mind, three video scenarios were created, replacing the static-letter stimuli used in previous research [34]. with streaming events that represent more ecologically-valid scenarios for physical security operators. EEG was recorded while participants watched the videos and responded to events they were instructed to view as threatening.

## 2 Method

### 2.1 Scenario Development

Given the above requirements regarding need for experimental control and the limitations of previous methods, we used "Garry's Mod" [35]. Garry's Mod is a physics-based sandbox game with no set objectives that allows users to create simulated environments that contain both static and dynamic elements. Simulations take place on maps that define the physical space for the simulation, where terrain has been sculpted, buildings and structures have been placed, and other objects have been arranged in the environment. Several default maps and numerous other objects are provided with the initial install of the game, but it allows custom maps and objects to be created and loaded as well. The game allows players to spawn and manipulate elements in the environment ranging from furniture, weapons, vehicles, and other non-player controlled (NPC), AI-driven characters. Game engines, including the one selected for this study, often include a physics engine [16], and games are often designed to mimic our intuitive mental representations of how physical objects should move and interact with each other, further allowing for the development of ecologically valid stimuli [36].

Critically, Garry's Mod allows programmatic control over actions of characters, such as spawn location, movement path, and movement speed, enabling precise control over timing of situations. There were three scripts required to create a framework to automate scenarios:

1. A script to start a scenario.
2. A script to stop a scenario.
3. A script representing a custom NPC type that executes a series of tasks each with a given duration.

Beyond that, for each scenario we tested in this experiment, we had to create a single scenario definition script. This script defines how many NPCs will be in the scenario, what models are used to represent them visually, and the tasks each NPC is to execute during that scenario. These scripts were developed to match the experimental design and are specific to a given map.

To start a scenario, a given scenario definition script that corresponds to the current map is loaded and then the start scenario script is executed. The latter reads the scenario definition, sorts the defined NPCs by when they should first appear in the simulation, and then uses what is called a *hook* in Garry's Mod to spawn the NPCs at the times requested in the scenario's definition. Hooks allow the scripts to respond to certain events that happen in the simulation, like the user pressing a key. The hook used here is Garry Mod's "Think" hook, which fires on every game frame, allowing our script to repeatedly check whether the next NPC should be spawned yet.

These NPCs are defined by a script based off the "NextBot" entity type available in Garry's Mod. Once spawned, each NPC will follow the list of tasks given to it. Each task defined in the scenario definition script will contain parameters specific to that task's type. For example, movement tasks will have destination coordinates, speed, and acceleration provided.

Finally, to stop a scenario the stop scenario script is executed. This script removes the "Think" hook and removes all custom NPCs that are still loaded in the scenario. This small handful of Garry's Mod Lua scripts allowed us to quickly and flexibly define the scenarios placed before our subjects. Within this development framework, video can be captured as scenarios play out, and subsequently can be presented as stimuli, as in the current pilot experiment.

## 2.2 Scenarios

Stimuli EEG signals can be time-locked to events such as the onset of a stimulus, resulting in event-related potentials (ERPs) that provide information about the brain's processing in relation to those events [37]. The so-called P300 ERP refers to activity that occurs roughly 300 ms following an event and is thought to reflect processes such as attention allocation and categorization [38]. The P300 is often studied in the context of the 'oddball' paradigm we modeled the video scenarios after for this study [34]. With Three video scenarios were created to reflect common types of monitoring tasks in the physical security domain, including identification of a hazardous situation (Scenario 1:

Hallway), potential theft (Scenario 2: Parking Lot), and suspicious behavior (Scenario 3: Fence).

**Scenario 1 (Hallway):** In the first scenario, participants were presented with scientist character models entering a fictional research facility (see Fig. 1, below). Participants were told that scientists walking into the building was a normal activity that did not require a response. Scientists running into the building represented an anomaly worth noting (via a button press), but did not constitute a threat (e.g., perhaps they are just late to a meeting). Scientists running out of the building should be considered a threat as they may be fleeing a hazardous scenario, and the participant should sound an alarm by pressing a "threat detected" button. There were 140 stimuli total; 100 common stimuli (walkers), 20 non-threat distractors (runners into the building), and 20 threats (runners out of the building). Non-threat and threat stimuli could co-occur with common stimuli, but did not co-occur with each other. Common stimuli were spaced an average of 6 s apart, with up to 500 ms of jitter on either side (5.5 s–6.5 s); the 40 runners were spaced an average of 15 s apart, with up to 1250 ms of jitter on either side (13.75 s–16.25 s). As runners co-occurred with walkers, the total duration of the video scenario was 10 min (100 walkers with an average of 6 s in between).

**Fig. 1.** An image of Scenario 1 (Hallway). Scientist character models are seen entering and exiting a research facility.

**Scenario 2 (Parking Lot):** In the second video scenario, civilian character models were seen entering or exiting a convenience store (see Fig. 2 below). Participants were instructed to ignore characters entering the store, but to indicate via a non-threat button press characters who exited the store, went into the parking lot, and passed between vehicles. They were asked to press the "threat detected" button when characters whom paused to peer into a car window, as this could indicate a potential car theft. Distribution (100 entering the store, 20 non-threats exiting, 20 threats exiting) and timing (an average of 6 s with up to 500 ms jitter in between common stimuli; an average of 15 s with up to 1250 ms of jitter for the uncommon stimuli) was the same as in the hallway scenario.

**Fig. 2.** An image of Scenario 2 (Parking Lot). Civilian character models are seen entering and exiting a convenience store.

**Scenario 3 (Fence):** In a third scenario, participants were presented with a depiction of a military installation with a fence separating the installation from public space (see Fig. 3 below). Participants were told that soldiers were performing their morning exercises, and soldiers running inside of the fence could be safely ignored. The fence may be approached from the outside by both civilians and security guards. Civilians walking

**Fig. 3.** An image of Scenario 3 (Fence). A military installation is displayed with soldier character models inside the fence and security guard and civilian models outside of the fence.

by the fence without stopping were a notable (button-press) non-threat event, as were security guards stopping to check the fence as per their duties. Conversely, participants were told that civilians stopping at the fence were a threat, as were security guards failing to stop at the fence (see Figs. 4 and 5 below for guard and civilian models, respectively).

Therefore, this scenario required a conjunction consideration (character model + action) in order for a given character to be deemed a threat or non-threat. Timing was the same as the first two scenarios (6 s on average in between with up to 500 ms jitter on either side for the common soldier stimuli; an average of 15 s in between for civilian and guard stimuli with up to 1250 ms jitter on either side). Distribution of stimuli was similar as well, though with conjunction considerations, as follows: 100 common soldier stimuli, 10 civilian threats, 10 civilian non-threats, 10 guard threats, 10 guard non-threats.

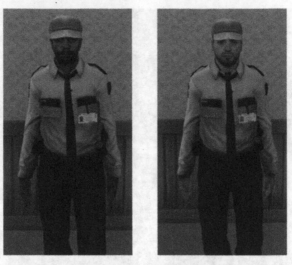

**Fig. 4.** Security guard models used in the third (Fence) video scenario.

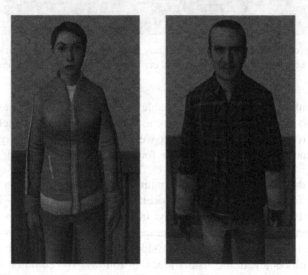

**Fig. 5.** Civilian models used in the third (Fence) video scenario.

## 2.3 Participants

Eight employees (five female; age 24–59) of Sandia National Laboratories participated in data collection.

## 2.4  Procedure

EEG data were collected using an Advanced Neuro Technologies (ANT) system with a 128-channel, Duke layout cap and digitized at 250 Hz. Participants were tested individually in a sound-attenuated booth. Participants sat 90 cm away from the computer monitor. Scenarios were presented electronically in a random order using the E-Prime 3.0 software [39]. Scenarios were presented in randomized order as three separate video files (i.e., one video file of approximately 10-min duration each for Scenario 1, 2, and 3), with a short break given after completion of each scenario. E-Prime presented the stimuli such that the onset of each trial or video was synchronized with a refresh of the stimulus presentation monitor.

E-Prime sent triggers related to the onset of specific stimuli and participants' responses to the EEG amplifier via parallel port. For Scenario 1 (Hallway), trigger timing corresponded with the first frame at which pixels of a scientist character model became visible, as participants were able to determine the categorization of stimuli based on the screen location onset of the character model. In Scenario 2 (Parking Lot), triggers for standard stimuli were sent corresponding to first frame of onset of the character model. For rare threat and rate non-threat stimuli, triggers were sent corresponding to a critical action. Rare non-threat and rare threat character models would both stop near a car, then either continue walking (non-threat) or duck near the vehicle door (threat). The trigger was sent at the first frame of this critical action, as that represented the point at which the participant was able to categorize the stimuli. For Scenario 3 (Fence), triggers were sent in a similar fashion as in Scenario 2 (Parking Lot); standard models generated triggers at onset, while rare threat stimuli and rare non-threat stimuli generated triggers at the first frame of a critical decision point (continuing to walk past a security gate or stopping at the gate).

Participants responded using button presses on a controller that were recorded via E-Prime. As in previous ERP research using the oddball paradigm, participants were asked to respond to both rare types of stimuli (threat and non-threat) in order to avoid motor contamination [40]. This allowed for a clean comparison between rare events that were framed as threats and rare events that were framed as benign.

**EEG Preprocessing/P300 Measurement:** EEG data were preprocessed in EEGLAB v2019.1 [41], using the FASTER toolbox [42], all in MATLAB 2017b [43]. Raw data were bandpass filtered from 1–50 Hz, and Independent Components Analysis (ICA; runICA.m function) was used for artifact rejection. Automatic artifactual rejection was accomplished within the FASTER toolbox using a 3 Z threshold for median gradient, spectral slope, spatial kurtosis, Hurst exponent, and EOG correlation. Data were then re-referenced to the average of all channels. After running ICA artifact rejection procedures, no trials were rejected based on artifact, using a 3 Z threshold for deviation from mean, variance, and amplitude range. Using ERPLAB [44], the data were then epoched into 1 s bins, from −200 ms to 800 ms post-stimulus, and baseline corrected from −100 ms to 0 ms pre-stimulus. Averaged event-related potentials (ERPs) were then generated and lowpass filtered to 30 Hz for analysis. P300 amplitude values were calculated as the peak amplitude between a 250 ms to 500 ms post-stimulus latency range over 15 channels (45; see Fig. 6 for the analogous channels used from the ANT Duke layout). Finally, ERPs were grand averaged across subjects for visualization in the form of topographical scalp maps. In addition, a representative waveform was produced for each scenario separately for visualization purposes.

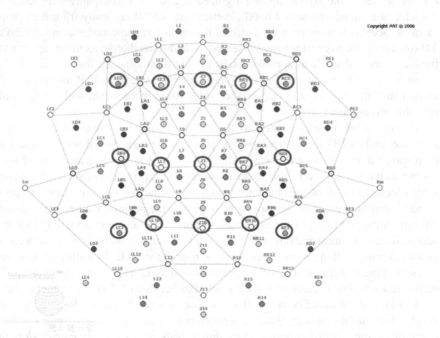

**Fig. 6.** Advanced Neuro Technologies (ANT) system 128-channel, Duke layout. Channels used for P300 analysis are circled in red and correspond to the 15 channels used in [45].

## 3 Results

### 3.1 Behavioral

Target accuracy data for each scenario (1 – Hallway; 2 – Fence; 3 – Parking Lot) were investigated using a mixed effects ANOVA (subject entered as a random factor and scenario [3-levels; hallway, fence and parking lot] entered as a fixed factor). Data were subjected to outlier analysis. Data for one participant was removed from the Fence and the Parking Lot scenarios due to confusion regarding the correct response button, resulting in abnormally low accuracy, leaving a total of eight participants for the hallway scenario and seven participants each for the Fence and Parking Lot scenarios. Analysis of hit rate did not reveal any significant effect of scenario ($F_{(2\ 19)} = 1.24, p = 0.313$, see Fig. 7).

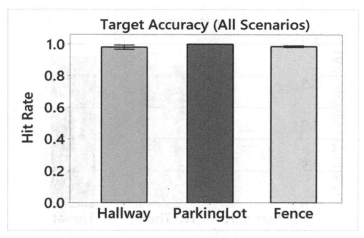

**Fig. 7.** Average target accuracy reported as hit rate for each scenario; no significant effects were observed. Error bars = ± 1 SEM.

### 3.2 P300 Amplitude

EEG data from one participant was removed due to poor data quality leaving seven participants to be included in the P300 analysis. The participant for whom behavioral data was excluded was included in the EEG analysis because they understood the task, but merely pressed the wrong response button, presumably leaving the P300 intact for this participant. The data for each scenario (1 – Hallway; 2 – Fence; 3 – Parking Lot) were investigated individually using a linear mixed effects model, with subject specified as a random factor, and stimulus type (3 levels – standard, rare threat, rare no-threat) as a fixed factor. Amplitude data from the 15 EEG channels were averaged, such that each participant had one value for each stimulus type. Variance estimation was accomplished with restricted maximum likelihood (REML) estimation. Post-Hoc pairwise comparisons between stimulus types were Bonferroni corrected. Data were analyzed in Minitab 19.2020 [46].

**Scenario 1 (Hallway):** The effect of stimulus type was significant, $F_{(2, 12)} = 37.09$, $p < 0.001$, where amplitudes for standard stimuli ($M = 0.826$ uV) were significantly lower than rare threat ($M = 1.828$ uV) and rare no threat ($M = 1.713$ uV) stimuli (see Fig. 8). No significant difference was found between rare stimulus types. The topographical maps for the Hallway scenario can be found in the top row of Fig. 11, and a waveform from a representative participant can be found in Fig. 12a.

**Scenario 2 (Parking Lot):** The effect of stimulus type was significant, $F_{(2, 12)} = 17.80$, $p < 0.001$. P300 amplitude for standard stimuli ($M = 0.777$ uV) were significantly lower than rare no threat ($M = 1.385$ uV) or rare threat ($M = 1.883$ uV) stimuli (see Fig. 9). A trend effect ($t_{(12)} = 2.68$, $p = 0.06$) was found between rare stimulus types, where amplitude for threat stimuli was larger than no threat stimuli. The topographical maps for the Parking Lot scenario can be found in the middle row of Fig. 11, and a waveform from a representative participant can be found in Fig. 12b.

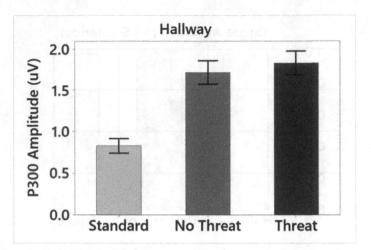

**Fig. 8.** Average mean amplitude for the Hallway scenario P300 for Standard, Rare No Threat, and Rare Threat stimuli. Rare stimuli showed significantly greater amplitude compared to standard, but no difference between rare stimulus types. Error bars = + \− 1 SEM.

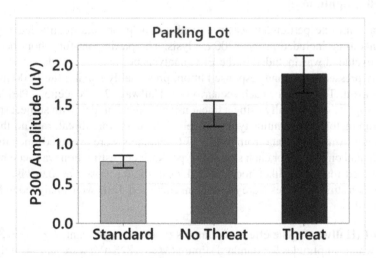

**Fig. 9.** Average mean amplitude for the Parking Lot scenario P300 for Standard, Rare No Threat, and Rare Threat stimuli. Rare stimuli showed significantly greater amplitude compared to standard, and a trend effect ($p = 0.06$) was found between rare stimulus types. Error bars = + \−1 SEM.

**Scenario 3 (Fence):** The effect of stimulus type was significant, $F_{(2,\ 12)} = 31.15$, $p < 0.001$. P300 amplitude was significantly lower for standard stimuli ($M = 0.917\,\text{uV}$), than rare no threat ($M = 1.702\,\text{uV}$) or rare threat ($M = 1.559\,\text{uV}$) stimuli (see Fig. 10). No significant difference was found between rare stimulus types. The topographical maps for the Fence scenario can be found in the bottom row of Fig. 11, and a waveform from a representative participant can be found in Fig. 12c.

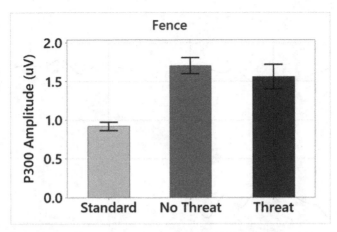

**Fig. 10.** Average mean amplitude for the Fence scenario P300 for Standard, Rare No Threat, and Rare Threat stimuli. Rare stimuli showed significantly greater amplitude compared to standard, but no difference between rare stimulus types. Error bars = + \−1 SEM.

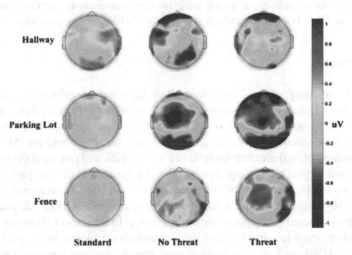

**Fig. 11.** Topographical maps for each scenario and stimulus type. Maps were derived by taking the mean peak amplitude across participants for each stimulus type in each scenario occurring between 250–500 ms post-stimulus. Note in all three scenarios, there is a much larger response to both rare (threat and no threat) stimuli compared to the standard stimuli. Specifically, for the Parking Lot scenario, a trend level effect was observed between rare no threat and rare threat stimuli, where a stronger response was observed for threat stimuli. The scale is ±1 uV.

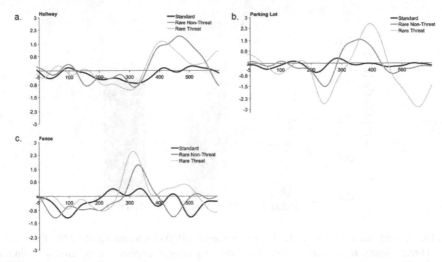

**Fig. 12.** Waveforms for a representative participant and channel for the Hallway Scenario (a), Fence Scenario (b), and Parking Lot Scenario (c). P300 Responses to standard stimuli are in black, responses to rare non-threat stimuli are in blue, and responses to rare threat stimuli are in red. ERPs were filtered (infinite impulse response) from 1–10 Hz for visualization.

## 4   Discussion

Creation of streaming video stimuli that allow for strict experimental control while providing ease of scene manipulation is difficult to achieve. In this effort, we propose leveraging video game modding tools as a method of creating research quality stimuli. To this end, three steaming video scenarios were created, following the three-stimulus oddball paradigm of frequent non-targets, rare non-targets, and rare-targets [34], with the targets and non-targets having equal probability. In the current design, participants saw frequent non-targets, and two types of rare target stimuli (threat and non-threat). These scenarios were designed to mimic situations that operators monitoring video surveillance feeds for physical security purposes might experience. In Scenario 1 (Hallway; scientists entering and exiting a facility) location information was sufficient to categorize stimuli. In Scenario 2 (Parking Lot; convenience store patrons passing through a parking lot) participants had to monitor a particular location for a particular action by a character model in order to distinguish between target and non-target stimuli. In Scenario 3 (Fence; security personnel and civilians passing alongside a fence within which military exercises were occurring), participants had to monitor a particular location (a gate) for a particular action (pausing or continuing to walk without stopping) that was only considered a threat if performed by a certain character model. In all scenarios we found evidence of a P300 for comparisons between standard stimuli and both types of rare stimuli (threat and non-threat), though the amplitudes observed were on average smaller than other studies.

The amplitude of the P300 can be influenced by numerous variables, including age, where a reduction in amplitude was observed as participants advanced in age [47], as well as attentional load (the tasks in the current experiment likely require a higher degree of attention than more traditional P300 experiments which could lead to reduction in amplitude; see [48]). In addition, the P300 is known to exhibit significant inter-individual variability in amplitude [49]. Any of these factors, and likely others, could have contributed to the lower-than-average amplitudes observed in the current experiment. Though this finding suggests that the proposed method of stimuli creation results in sufficient experimental control to allow for ERP analysis, there are several limitations to this pilot work that should be addressed in subsequent efforts. As a pilot study emphasizing the method of stimuli creation, the number of participants is quite small and therefore results should be interpreted with caution.

For Scenario 2 (Parking Lot), there was an additional finding of a trend effect for a larger P300 when comparing rare threat stimuli to rare no-threat stimuli. This is consistent with a prior finding in the context of a three-stimulus oddball paradigm in which targets elicited a larger P300 than non-targets when probability of occurrence was equal [45]. It is possible that a similar effect was not observed in the other two scenarios due to the ambiguous nature of the so-called "threatening" stimuli; a model crouched behind a vehicle may be more clearly identified as suspicious than a person exiting a building quickly or the impact of a character model pausing or not pausing at a gated entrance. Future research could benefit from inclusion of ratings of stimuli to determine threat ambiguity and intensity.

Prior work has established that P300 amplitude is inversely related to stimulus probability [45]. In the current work, we did not vary the probability of occurrence for the different stimuli types, and the probability of targets and non-targets was equal. Other factors found to influence P300 amplitude, such as the number of non-targets preceding a target and the target-to-target interval [50] were also not systematically manipulated in this study. This is notable because while this method *could* theoretically produce scenarios that are ecologically valid, the target-to-target intervals, number of targets, and ratio of targets to non-targets used in this pilot study were almost certainly not an accurate representation of what an analyst monitoring a security feed experiences in the world. While the current study likely overrepresented number of targets within a brief time frame due to time considerations, the P300 amplitude has previously been found to be sensitive to level of fatigue, and may therefore serve as an indication of flagging attention in tasks that require sustained attention [38]. Our method of creating streaming video stimuli could therefore be used to emulate the number and types of video feeds that operators in domains such as physical security may be exposed to and thereby characterize the time course of fatigue onset.

Additionally, Garry's Mod was released in 2006, making it a relatively old game with dated graphics at the time of this study. Over time, video game realism has increased via improved graphics and game engines more capable of paralleling human mental representations [51]. With advances in virtual reality gaming tools, increasing levels of immersion may be possible and offer much greater ecological validity as the ability to approximate realistic environments increases. Therefore, this pilot study does not constitute an endorsement of Garry's Mod in particular, and does not include a direct comparison to other modding tools or methods of creating streaming stimuli. Popular games such as Roblox and Minecraft offer modding capabilities, but these were deemed not realistic enough for the physical security scenarios desired in the current study.

While modding may be possible for a number of games, support and accessibility might differ dramatically (e.g., Sims 4, while offering powerful modding abilities, is sometimes derided by community members as lacking support from the developer [52]. Other tools should therefore be evaluated in future work to determine their pros and cons and allow researchers to select the optimal tool for their needs.

It is also worth noting that creating video stimuli using video game tools can range from simple to complex contingent on the tool selected and the nature of the desired scenario. There are four main methods of creating machinima [23]. From most simple to most difficult these are: using the game's inherent AI to control actions, digital puppetry (capturing the manual manipulation of digital characters/objects – "playing" the scenario), recamming (adjusting camera locations), and precise scripting of actions. It is likely that the most difficult method – precise scripting of actions – is necessary if the study goal involves the timing necessary for ERP analysis. Another option, as per [16], is to take an existing scenario and adjust it to suit the goals of the research. For instance, adjustment of the character models used in the scenarios described in the current work may be accomplished via a trivial replacement of filenames that could be performed in a manner of minutes, allowing adjustment along dimensions such as the size, gender, and skin color of character models.

Regarding analysis considerations, often P300 paradigms ask participants to fixate their gaze on the center of a screen while static stimuli are presented, allowing researchers to be relatively certain about what participants are looking at and when [53]. However, when using streaming stimuli with the possibility of co-occurrence of different stimuli types as in the current study, researchers may know when certain events are presented by virtue of having scripted the timing of those events, but it may not be clear where participants are directing their gaze at a given time. To this end, in the current study P300 amplitude values were calculated as the peak amplitude during a latency range of 250 ms to 500 ms [45] following an event of interest. This assumes that the highest amplitude wave in this timeframe reflects participant processing of the event of interest (e.g., a character model ducking near a car in the Parking Lot scenario), but without eye tracking data to verify gaze location this remains an assumption. The addition of eye tracking data would allow for calculation of fixation-related potentials that clearly time-lock neuroimaging data to timepoints during which participants were looking at events of interest [53] and is recommended as a future direction for purposes of verifying data quality.

As a general limitation of creating video stimuli that reflect real-world circumstances, allowing for the timing of events to play out (e.g., having character models walk over distances) results in a reduced number of trials over a given timeframe relative to presentation of simple static stimuli that may be flashed on a screen for short durations. This could be mitigated by a longer experimental session (which may risk fatiguing a participant) to accumulate a reasonable number of trials, or by running a greater number of participants (note that the number of participants in the current study is quite small). While these factors may be difficult for researchers to work around, they are necessary if one wishes to study human behavior and brain responses using stimuli that closer approximate real-world situations.

# 5 Conclusion

Mutual interest between game developers and game players in ease of modding has created a situation that may be leveraged by researchers interested in creating video stimuli. Here we demonstrate the feasibility of using existing modding tools to create video scenarios amenable to neuroimaging analysis. The results indicate that sufficient levels of experimental control may be achieved to allow for the precise timing required for ERP analysis. The variety of tools available allows for a vast range of video stimuli to be created using this method, which also allows for relative ease of adjustment. While the emphasis of the current study was on scenarios relevant to physical security, the general method of stimuli creations could be implemented by researchers operating in a wide variety of domains. This method of creating realistic streaming stimuli may assist in adding to the body of literature representing research with stimuli in motion [54, 55].

**Acknowledgements.** Sandia National Laboratories is a multimission laboratory managed and operated by National Technology and Engineering Solutions of Sandia, LLC, a wholly owned subsidiary of Honeywell International Inc., for the U.S. Department of Energy's National Nuclear Security Administration under contract DE-NA0003525. This work was funded by Sandia National Laboratories' Laboratory-Directed Research and Development program. SAND2022-2063 C. *This paper describes objective technical results and analysis. Any subjective views or opinions that might be expressed in the paper do not necessarily represent the views of the U.S. Department of Energy or the United States Government.*

# References

1. Wolfe, J.M., Võ, M.L.H., Evans, K.K., Greene, M.R.: Visual search in scenes involves selective and nonselective pathways. Trends Cogn. Sci. **15**(2), 77–84 (2011)
2. Eziolisa, O.N.: Investigation of capabilities of observers in a watch window study. (Master of Science in Engineering), Wright State University, Dayton, OH (2014). http://rave.ohiolink.edu/etdc/view?acc_num=wright1401889055
3. Irvine, J.M., et al.: Development of a motion imagery quality metric. In: Proceedings of the American Society for Photogrammetry and Remote Sensing (ASPRS) Annual Meeting, pp. 1–5 (2006)
4. Sulman, N., Sanocki, T., Goldgof, D., Kasturi, R.: How effective is human video surveillance performance? In: 2008 19th International Conference on Pattern Recognition, pp. 1–3. IEEE, December 2008
5. Steel, K., Ellem, E., Baxter, D.: The application of biological motion research: biometrics, sport, and the military. Psychonomic Bull. Rev. **22**(1), 78–87 (2015)
6. Wolfe, J.M., Horowitz, T.S.: Five factors that guide attention in visual search. Nat. Hum. Behav. **1**(3), 1–8 (2017)
7. Williams, D., Yee, N., Caplan, S.E.: Who plays, how much, and why? debunking the stereotypical gamer profile. J. Comput.-Mediat. Commun. **13**(4), 993–1018 (2008)
8. Yee, N.: Motivations for play in online games. Cyberpsychol. Behav. **9**(6), 772–775 (2006)
9. Green, C.S., Seitz, A.R.: The impacts of video games on cognition (and how the government can guide the industry). Policy Insights Behav. Brain Sci. **2**(1), 101–110 (2015)
10. Spence, I., Feng, J.: Video games and spatial cognition. Rev. Gen. Psychol. **14**(2), 92–104 (2010)

11. Toril, P., Reales, J.M., Ballesteros, S.: Video game training enhances cognition of older adults: a meta-analytic study. Psychol. Aging **29**(3), 706–716 (2014)
12. Bostan, B., Kaplancali, U.: Explorations in player motivations: game mods. In: Proceedings of GAMEON-ASIA (2010)
13. Kücklich, J.: Precarious playbour: modders and the digital games industry. Fibreculture **5**(1), 1–5 (2005)
14. Hofman-Kohlmeyer, M.: Players as a prosumer. Individual motives for engaging in game modding. World Sci. News **133**, 191–203 (2019)
15. Sotamaa, O.: When the game is not enough: Motivations and practices among computer game modding culture. Games Culture **5**(3), 239–255 (2010)
16. Wallace, R.: Modding: Amateur authorship and how the video game industry is actually getting it right. BYu L. Rev **219**, 219–256 (2014)
17. Bostan, B.: Game Modding and TES: New Way to Design Virtual Worlds, 3rd International Symposium of Interactive Media Design. Yeditepe University, Turkey (2005)
18. Newman, J.: Playing with videogames. Routledge (2008)
19. McClarty, K.L., Orr, A., Frey, P.M., Dolan, R.P., Vassileva, V., McVay, A.: A literature review of gaming in education. Gaming in Education, 1–35 (2012)
20. Moshirnia, A.: The educational potential of modified video games. Issues Inf. Sci. Inf. Technol. **4**, 511–521 (2007)
21. Paul, N., Hansen, K.: Disaster at Harperville: The modding of Neverwinter Nights to teach journalism students the strategic steps in information gathering. In: Pearson, E., Bohman, P. (eds.) Proceedings of ED-MEDIA 2006–World Conference on Educational Multimedia, Hypermedia & Telecommunications, pp. 1954–1959. Association for the Advancement of Computing in Education (AACE), Orlando (2006)
22. Mohseni, M.R., Liebold, B., Pietschmann, D.: Extensive modding for experimental game research. In: Lankoski, P., Björk, S. (eds.) Game Research Methods, pp. 323–340. ETC Press, Pittsburgh, PA (2015)
23. Kelland, M., Morris, D., Lloyd, D.: Machinima: Making Movies in 3D Virtual Environments. The Ilex Press, Cambridge (2005)
24. Gawlik-Kobylińska, M.: Machinima in education for security and safety. IJRET: Int. J. Res. Eng. Technol. **6**, 42–46 (2017)
25. Fabiani, M., Gratton, G., Coles, M.G.H.: Event-related brain potentials: methods, theory, and applications. In: Cacioppo, J.T., Tassinary, L.G., Berntson, G.G. (eds.) Handbook of psychophysiology, 2nd edn., pp. 53–84. Cambridge University Press, Cambridge, England (2000)
26. Herrmann, C.S., Knight, R.T.: Mechanisms of human attention: event-related potentials and oscillations. Neurosci. Biobehav. Rev. **25**(6), 465–476 (2001)
27. Haass, M.J., Matzen, L.E.: Using computational modeling to assess use of cognitive strategies. In: International Conference on Foundations of Augmented Cognition, pp. 77–86. Springer, Heidelberg, July 2011
28. Hanslmayr, S., Spitzer, B., Bäuml, K.H.: Brain oscillations dissociate between semantic and nonsemantic encoding of episodic memories. Cereb. Cortex **19**(7), 1631–1640 (2009)
29. Rugg, M.D., Curran, T.: Event-related potentials and recognition memory. Trends Cogn. Sci. **11**(6), 251–257 (2007)
30. Hoffman, J.E., Simons, R.F., Houck, M.R.: Event-related potentials during controlled and automatic target detection. Psychophysiology **20**(6), 625–632 (1983)
31. Strayer, D.L., Kramer, A.F.: Attentional requirements of automatic and controlled processing. J. Exp. Psychol. Learn. Mem. Cogn. **16**(1), 67–82 (1990)
32. Gratton, G., Bosco, C.M., Kramer, A.F., Coles, M.G., Wickens, C.D., Donchin, E.: Event-related brain potentials as indices of information extraction and response priming. Electroencephalogr. Clin. Neurophysiol. **75**(5), 419–432 (1990)

33. Leuthold, H., Sommer, W., Ulrich, R.: Partial advance information and response preparation: inferences from the lateralized readiness potential. J. Exp. Psychol. Gen. **125**(3), 307–323 (1996)
34. Katayama, J.I., Polich, J.: Auditory and visual P300 topography from a 3 stimulus paradigm. Clin. Neurophysiol. **110**(3), 463–468 (1999)
35. Facepunch Studies, Inc. [Garry's Mod] (2006). https://gmod.facepunch.com/
36. Ullman, T.D., Spelke, E., Battaglia, P., Tenenbaum, J.B.: Mind games: game engines as an architecture for intuitive physics. Trends Cogn. Sci. **21**(9), 649–665 (2017)
37. Luck, S.J.: An introduction to the event-related potential technique. MIT Press (2014)
38. Polich, J., Kok, A.: Cognitive and biological determinants of P300: an integrative review. Biol. Psychol. **41**(2), 103–146 (1995)
39. Psychology Software Tools, Inc. [E-Prime 3.0]. (2016). https://www.pstnet.com
40. Yuan, J., He, Y., Qinglin, Z., Chen, A., Li, H.: Gender differences in behavioral inhibitory control: ERP evidence from a two-choice oddball task. Psychophysiology **45**(6), 986–993 (2008)
41. Delorme, A., Makeig, S.: EEGLAB: an open source toolbox for analysis of single-trial EEG dynamics including independent component analysis. J. Neurosci. Methods **134**(1), 9–21 (2004)
42. Nolan, H., Whelan, R., Reilly, R.B.: FASTER: fully automated statistical thresholding for EEG artifact rejection. J. Neurosci. Methods **192**(1), 152–162 (2010)
43. MATLAB. version 9.3.0.713579 (R2017b). Natick, Massachusetts: The MathWorks Inc. (2017)
44. Lopez-Calderon, J., Luck, S.J.: ERPLAB: An open-source toolbox for the analysis of event-related potentials. Front. Hum. Neurosci. **8**, 213 (2014)
45. Katayama, J.I., Polich, J.: P300, probability, and the three-tone paradigm. Electroencephalography Clin. Neurophysiol./Evoked Potentials Sect. **100**(6), 555–562 (1996)
46. Minitab 19 Statistical Software (2020). [Computer software]. State College, PA: Minitab, Inc. www.minitab.com
47. van Dinteren, R., Arns, M., Jongsma, M.L., Kessels, R.P.: P300 development across the lifespan: a systematic review and meta-analysis. PLoS ONE **9**(2), e87347 (2014)
48. Watter, S., Geffen, G.M., Geffen, L.B.: The n-back as a dual-task: P300 morphology under divided attention. Psychophysiology **38**(6), 998–1003 (2001)
49. Li, F., et al.: Inter-subject P300 variability relates to the efficiency of brain networks reconfigured from resting-to task-state: evidence from a simultaneous event-related EEG-fMRI study. Neuroimage **205**, 116285 (2020)
50. Gonsalvez, C.J., Polich, J.: P300 amplitude is determined by target-to-target interval. Psychophysiology **39**(3), 388–396 (2002)
51. Barlett, C.P., Rodeheffer, C.: Effects of realism on extended violent and nonviolent video game play on aggressive thoughts, feelings, and physiological arousal. Aggressive Behav. Official J. Int. Soc. Res. Aggression **35**(3), 213–224 (2009). https://doi.org/10.1002/ab.20279
52. Hanabi, J.: The Sims 4 modern Python modding. Gitconnected, 20 September 2020. https://levelup.gitconnected.com/the-sims-4-modern-python-modding-part-1-setup-83d1a100c5f6
53. Brouwer, A.M., Reuderink, B., Vincent, J., van Gerven, M.A., van Erp, J.B.: Distinguishing between target and nontarget fixations in a visual search task using fixation-related potentials. J. Vis. **13**(3), 17 (2013)
54. Hirai, M., Hiraki, K.: The relative importance of spatial versus temporal structure in the perception of biological motion: an event-related potential study. Cognition **99**(1), B15–B29 (2006)
55. Steel, K.A., Baxter, D., Dogramaci, S., Cobley, S., Ellem, E.: Can biological motion research provide insight on how to reduce friendly fire incidents? Psychon. Bull. Rev. **23**(5), 1429–1439 (2016). https://doi.org/10.3758/s13423-016-1006-9

# EEG Daydreaming, A Machine Learning Approach to Detect Daydreaming Activities

Ruyang Wang[1(✉)] and Xiaodong Qu[2]

[1] Brandeis University, Waltham, MA 02453, USA
ruyangwang@brandeis.edu
[2] Swarthmore College, Swarthmore, PA 19081, USA
xqu1@swarthmore.edu

**Abstract.** In this paper, we propose a new method to detect noise hindrances in Electroencephalographic (EEG) signals caused by mental distractions, which we named "daydreaming signals." Our approach is based on sliding windows and aims to detect and locate these daydreaming signals to specific points in time. We expect to get cleaner data and, therefore, higher prediction accuracy in current available EEG datasets by removing these daydreaming signals. Beyond these improvements to existing data, this approach also has the potential to improve the quality of future data collection, as researchers can discover the pattern of daydreaming signals in trial rounds and deal with these signals accordingly.

**Keywords:** Design methods and techniques · Machine learning · Supervised learning · Electroencephalography (EEG) · Sliding windows · EEG signal classification

## 1 Introduction

Electroencephalography (EEG) is widely used in Brain-Machine Interfaces research [15]. The classification of cognitive tasks using EEG signals has been the focus of discussion in the past few decades [16]. The low signal-to-noise ratio is a common hindrance in EEG signal classification. While multiple types of machine learning and deep learning algorithms have been used for cognitive task classification [4,12,23], the accuracy of EEG signal classification can hit a bottleneck without a proper separation of noise. Noise in EEG data could come from a variety of sources, which can be identified as two main types: i) noise from the outside, including factors like environmental noise, noise caused by experimental settings, and noise caused by static electricity; and ii) noise from the human body, including physical activity such as blinking and breathing, and mental activity such as distracting thoughts [25]. Although large quantities of research have been conducted and shown success in removing the external noise [14], the problem of detecting and removing internal noise remains an area in

D. D. Schmorrow and C. M. Fidopiastis (Eds.): HCII 2022, LNAI 13310, pp. 202–212, 2022.
https://doi.org/10.1007/978-3-031-05457-0_17

need of more exploration. This paper focuses on the latter source of noise, noise from mental activity, and aims to design an algorithm to detect and remove noise caused by mental distractions.

In experiments, subjects sometimes lose focus on the task assigned to them. Instead of performing the designated tasks, they may engage in other activities intentionally or unintentionally. Such distractions can lead to noise in EEG signals that is different from expected signals of expected activities. We designed an algorithm to detect and remove this kind of noise, which we have named "daydreaming signals." Our approach first removed the environmental noise with plateau threshold [19], then analyzed the cleaned data by two rounds of baseline classification analysis combined with sliding windows. We implemented this algorithm with the publicly available Thinking1 BCI experiments dataset.

Since the Thinking1 BCI experiments dataset is a relatively small dataset, we focused on classifiers that work well with EEG data and small datasets. We chose three classifiers for baseline classification: Random Forest (RF), Support Vector Machines (SVM), and Long Short-Term Memory (LSTM). Random Forest is a classifier that combines numerous randomized decision trees [6]. Random Forest has shown outstanding performance when there is a larger number of variables compared with the number of observations [3]. It was also proved in EEG dataset that the Random Forest classifier outperforms other classifiers when the sample set is small [16]. Support Vector Machines is a linear classifier that implements a hyperplane to identify classes [8]. General advantages of using SVM include good generalization properties, as well as their resistance to overtraining and the curse of dimensionality [17]. Support Vector Machines are commonly employed in human-computer interaction to identify physiological patterns, and have shown high performance in prediction accuracy of EEG data [22]. Long Short-Term Memory is a deep learning architecture that uses an artificial Recurrent Neural Network (RNN) [10]. Long Short-Term Memory has been widely used on EEG signal classification and showed high accuracy when combined with other classification techniques [2,9]. Neural Networks usually work well on large datasets, yet Long Short-Term Memory can show high accuracy with small datasets [7,13,20,24].

As for results, Table 1 shows the old (without sliding windows analysis) and new (with sliding windows analysis) prediction accuracy of three baseline methods. Compared with traditional Random Forest, Support Vector Machines, and Long Short-Term Memory classifications, this approach increased the average prediction accuracy from 55.0% to 66.1%, from 41.2% to 65.5%, and from 46.0% to 56.3%, respectively.

**Table 1.** Average prediction accuracy for baseline methods

|  | RM | SVM | LSTM |
|---|---|---|---|
| Prediction Accuracy (old) | 55.0 | 41.2 | 46.0 |
| Prediction Accuracy (new) | **66.1** | **65.5** | **56.3** |

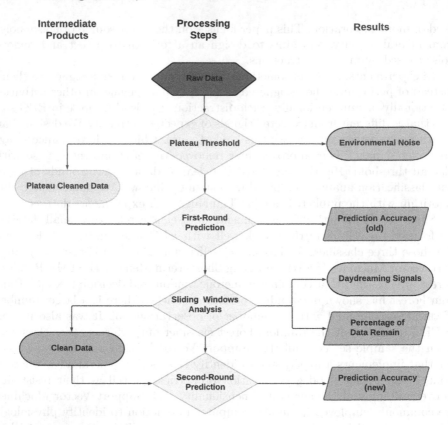

**Fig. 1.** Workflow chart for the proposed method that detects and removes daydreaming signals. After removing the environmental noise with plateau threshold, the cleaned data is analyzed by two rounds of baseline method analysis combined with sliding windows. Three types of EEG signals are identified: environmental noise (e), daydreaming signals (d), and clean data (c); data remaining percentage, old and new prediction accuracy are recorded.

## 2    Proposed Method

Figure 1 shows the workflow of our algorithm with four significant steps contained: Plateau Threshold, First-Round Prediction, Sliding Windows Analysis, and Second-Round Prediction. The detailed method is described in this section.

### 2.1    Data Source and Preprocess

The Thinking1 BCI experiments dataset contains 16 health non-expert subjects. Signals are captured using Muse neuromonitoring headset, which are suggested for meditation evaluations and non-medical usages [11]. Despite having a smaller number of available electrodes compared with medical-use devices (4 electrodes

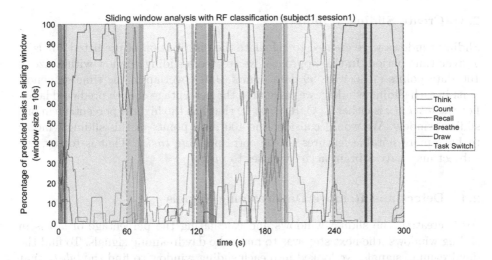

**Fig. 2.** Result of sliding window analysis on subject 1 session 1 using Random Forest as baseline method. Each task is represented by one color. Environmental noise, daydreaming signals, and clean data are marked with different degrees of background color saturation within each task. Environmental noise has the largest degree of saturation, daydreaming signals have a middle degree of saturation, and clean data has the smallest degree of saturation.

vs. 16 electrodes), Muse neuromonitoring headset can collect accurate data at a lower cost [1,5]. In Thinking1 BCI experiments dataset, each subject conducted a 30-minute experiment that contained six sessions on five tasks (Think [T], Count [C], Recall [R], Breathe [B], Draw [D]) in a random sequence. Before conducting our proposed algorithm, all EEG data for analysis were pre-processed to remove external noise. In the analysis of this experiment, environmental noise (e) caused by poor contact was removed using the "plateau threshold method." For more details, please refer to the previous work [19].

## 2.2  Baseline Prediction

For the baseline prediction, We divided each session into ten folds chronologically. Fold 1 represents the first one-tenth of recorded data in the time sequence, fold 2 represents the second one-tenth of recorded data in the time sequence, and so forth. We conducted 10-fold cross-validation with the baseline prediction method (RF, SVM, or LSTM) and recorded the classification results for each EEG data point as $label_X$. According to the experiment setup, there are five possible labels for each data point, representing five cognitive tasks: $label_T$, $label_C$, $label_R$, $label_B$ are $label_D$. Prediction accuracy and the percent of data remaining for each subject were also recorded for future comparison.

## 2.3    Create Sliding Windows

Sliding windows were created to calculate the distribution of predicted labels in a given time period. In this approach, we created a sliding window with a size of 100 data points (10 s) with 99 data points (9.9 s) overlap in the time sequence. Within each sliding window, we calculated the percentage of each predicted label. For the $label_x$ (x is either T, C, R, B, or D) that has the highest percentage in one sliding window, We would consider the 100 data points in this sliding window to have more notable features to the corresponding $task_x$. That is to say, the subject may have a brain activity closer to $task_x$.

## 2.4    Detect and Remove Daydreaming Signals

After creating the sliding windows and calculating the percentage of labels in sliding windows, the next step was to mark the daydreaming signals. To find the daydreaming signals, we looked into each sliding window to find the $label_x$ that had the highest percentage among the 100 labels; each window is then marked as $label_x$ as a whole. We took the designed $task_x$ in each session as the ground truth to compare with $label_x$. If $label_x$ were different from the ground truth, we would mark the first data point in this sliding window as a "daydreaming signal (d)" and remove this data point. The data remaining after this step is identified as "clean data (c)." Fig. 2 shows an example of sliding window percentage and distribution of daydreaming signals in subject 1 session 1.

## 2.5    Second-Round Prediction

After removing the daydreaming signals, we repeated step 2 (10-fold cross-validation with the same baseline classification method) for the rest of the clean data and calculated the final prediction accuracy and percent of data remaining. The result was compared with prediction accuracy and the percentage of data remaining in the first-round prediction.

# 3    Results

## 3.1    Prediction Accuracy and Data Remaining

In Fig. 3, we show the prediction accuracy of baseline methods and the improved prediction accuracy after removing daydreaming signals. Three baseline classification algorithms are marked in three different colors. The baseline accuracy is represented in dashed lines, and the new prediction accuracy by implementing our algorithm is represented in solid lines. Compared with traditional Random Forest classification (red dashed line), our algorithm (red solid line) improved the average accuracy from 55.0% to 66.1%. Compared with traditional Support Vector Machines classification (green dashed line), our algorithm (green solid line) improved the average accuracy from 41.2% to 65.5%. And compared with traditional Long Short-Term Memory classification (blue dashed line), our algorithm (blue solid line) improved the average accuracy from 46.0% to 56.3%. Our algorithm has significantly increased prediction accuracy compared with all three baseline classification algorithms.

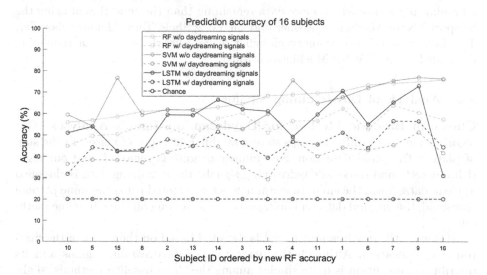

**Fig. 3.** Prediction accuracy of 16 subjects: baseline classification algorithms (dashed lines) vs. our improved algorithm (solid lines) (Color figure online)

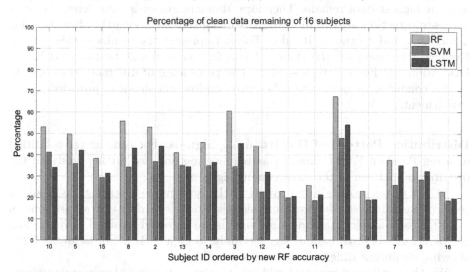

**Fig. 4.** Percentage of clean data remaining of 16 subjects after removing environmental noise and daydreaming signals for three baseline methods: Random Forest (red bars), Support Vector Machines (green bars), Long Short-Term Memory (blue bars) (Color figure online)

We also provide the data remaining condition for three baseline algorithms after removing daydreaming signals in Fig. 4. Compared with Support Vector Machines (with an average of data remaining of 30.2%) and Long Short-Term Memory (with an average of data remaining of 34.1%), RF classifier has a higher average data remaining percent (42.2%). On average, using the RF classifier as a baseline algorithm leaves more data remaining than the condition of using the Support Vector Machines classifier and the Long Short-Term Memory classifier. The Long Short-Term Memory classifier leaves slightly more data remaining than the Support Vector Machines classifier.

### 3.2    Analysis of Daydreaming Signals

**Choice of Baseline Method for Daydreaming Signals Analyses.** Our algorithm includes different steps to remove different types of noises. In the step of plateau threshold detection, environmental noise is removed, and our algorithm detects and removes daydreaming signals; the remaining data is classified as clean data. Since the environmental noises are detected using the same plateau threshold, the original data remaining is the same among all three baseline methods.

However, the daydreaming signal is detected based on the result of the first-round classification. Although the percentage of daydreaming signals and its distribution condition is quite similar among the three baseline methods, slight differences exist among different baseline conditions. According to the result of our experiment, the Random Forest classifier has the highest prediction accuracy, and the highest data remain. Therefore, Random Forest is considered the most accurate detection algorithm for daydreaming signals among the three baseline algorithms, and we choose Random Forest to present the results in this section. Detailed discussion on the choice of baseline method will be provided in the Discussion and Future Work section. The percentage of different types of data in the condition of using the other two baseline classifiers is provided in the supplement.

**Distribution Pattern of Daydreaming Signals.** Focusing on the condition of using Random Forest classifier as baseline method, we further analyzed the distribution pattern of the daydreaming signals.

In Fig. 5, we provide a bar graph of the percentage of each type of signal (environmental noise, daydreaming signals, and clean data) of all sessions in total for each subject. Daydreaming signals are detected in all 16 subjects, and the percentage of daydreaming signals can be as high as 34.3% or as low as 7.2%, showing significant differences among subjects.

We then utilize a box and whisker plot to determine daydreaming signal distribution in different tasks (Fig. 6). By looking at the distribution pattern of daydreaming signals in different tasks, we can see that: i) a considerable variance exists between different subjects. As the average percent of detected daydreaming signals is between 10 to 20% for all five tasks (Think [T], Count

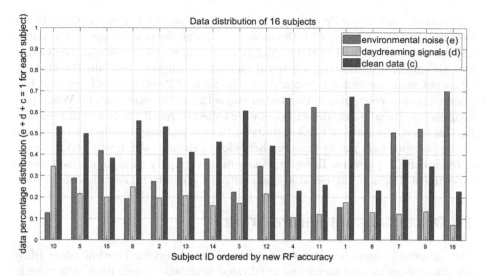

**Fig. 5.** The percentage of environmental noise (e), daydreaming signals (d) and clean data (c) for each subject using Random Forest as baseline classification method. Note that e + d + c = 100%.

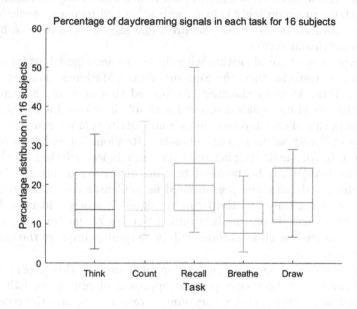

**Fig. 6.** Task-wise distribution of daydreaming signals in 16 subjects.

[C], Recall [R], Breathe [B], Draw [D]), the upper extreme value could be as high as over 50%. This variance shows that the individual differences in daydreaming signals are substantial. A few subjects have a high proportion of daydreaming signals, perhaps because these subjects have difficulty concentrating during the experiment, and ii) daydreaming signals tend to have higher proportions in the task of Recall. Compared with the other four tasks, the percentage of daydreaming signals is the highest in the task of Recall in extremes values, quartile values, and the median, indicating a general trend that subjects fall into the state of "daydreaming" more easily when doing the task of Recall. We believe that this phenomenon corresponds to the design and setup of the experiments. When performing the Recall task, the subjects were asked to recall the last task they did. At this time, the state of EEG activity of the subject may be closer to the state of the previous task rather than the behavior of Recall itself, leading to the noise of unclear EEG patterns. However, this is only a simple assumption based on the experimental design; further analysis might be needed to make valid conclusions.

## 4    Discussion and Future Work

Our proposed algorithm is proven effective for detecting internal noise (daydreaming signals) and increasing prediction accuracy in cognitive task classification. Since subjects may get distracted unconsciously when performing the designated tasks, our algorithm can help to locate the specific time when the subjects are not focused on assigned tasks, either consciously or unconsciously; this algorithm can accordingly help remove noise and increase prediction accuracy. This approach to detecting "daydreaming signals" can also be helpful in adjusting experiment setups.

This paper tested our algorithm with three baseline algorithms for accuracy: the Random Forest classifier, the Support Vector Machines classifier, and the Long Short-Term Memory classifier. We proved that accuracy is increased by removing daydreaming signals compared with all three baseline methods. However, the majority of our daydreaming signal distribution analysis is conducted with Random Forest as the baseline classifier. Random Forest has proven to be a valuable tool for small training data sets and is less affected by the curse-of-dimensionality [16], it is the ideal baseline algorithm to use for Thinking1 BCI experiments dataset and personalized uses. Considering Random Forest is not 100-percent accurate and daydreaming signal is a newly identified class of signals, further analysis on the distribution pattern of daydreaming signals in the case of different baseline methods will be helpful to improve the analysis on daydreaming signals.

Sliding windows is another critical approach used in this paper. Although sliding windows have become a popular approach of processing EEG signals, windows size and overlap choice vary among researchers, and the consequence of using different window sizes and overlaps are still not clear [18,23]. In this paper, we chose a window size of 10 s with 99% overlap based on the result of the plateau threshold. For future work, we plan to test our algorithm with various sizes of sliding windows and overlaps based on the responsive time window of neurons and to further explore the distribution pattern of daydreaming signals.

For dataset selection, we chose the Thinking1 BCI experiments dataset. Although small EEG datasets can be useful for personalizing analysis [18,21], the small size of the dataset leads to hindrance in training and more specific examination on variables. Further investigation on the performance of our algorithm on larger datasets is warranted.

## 5  Conclusion

The accuracy of EEG signal classification on cognitive tasks can be affected by multiple noise sources. This paper focused on "daydreaming signals," the noise caused by mental distractions. We designed a new algorithm to detect and remove these "daydreaming signals" based on sliding windows. We compared the prediction accuracy between the traditional Random Forest algorithm and our improved algorithm. As a result, the average prediction accuracy is increased for all three baseline algorithms: 55.0% to 66.1% for Random Forest classifier, 41.2% to 65.5% for Support Vector Machines classifier, and 46.0% to 56.3% for Long Short-Term Memory classifier. Our approach can be helpful for increasing prediction accuracy, for designing and adjusting experimental setups, and for personalizing uses.

## References

1. Bashivan, P., Rish, I., Heisig, S.: Mental state recognition via wearable EEG. arXiv preprint arXiv:1602.00985 (2016)
2. Bashivan, P., Rish, I., Yeasin, M., Codella, N.: Learning representations from EEG with deep recurrent-convolutional neural networks (2016)
3. Biau, G., Scornet, E.: A random forest guided tour. TEST **25**(2), 197–227 (2016). https://doi.org/10.1007/s11749-016-0481-7
4. Bigdely-Shamlo, N., Mullen, T., Kothe, C., Su, K.M., Robbins, K.A.: The prep pipeline: standardized preprocessing for large-scale EEG analysis. Front. Neuroinform. **9**, 16, e5199 (2015)
5. Bird, J.J., Manso, L.J., Ribeiro, E.P., Ekárt, A., Faria, D.R.: A study on mental state classification using EEG-based brain-machine interface. In: 2018 International Conference on Intelligent Systems (IS), pp. 795–800. IEEE (2018)
6. Breiman, L.: Random forests. Mach. Learn. **45**(1), 5–32 (2001)
7. Chen, Y., Zhang, D.: Well log generation via ensemble long short-term memory (ENLSTM) network. Geophys. Res. Lett. **47**(23), e2020GL087685 (2020)
8. Cortes, C., Vapnik, V.: Support-vector networks. Mach. Learn. **20**(3), 273–297 (1995)
9. Craik, A., He, Y., Contreras-Vidal, J.L.: Deep learning for electroencephalogram (EEG) classification tasks: a review. J. Neural Eng. **16**(3), 031001 (2019)
10. Hochreiter, S., Schmidhuber, J.: Long short-term memory. Neural Comput. **9**(8), 1735–1780 (1997)
11. Ienca, M., Haselager, P., Emanuel, E.J.: Brain leaks and consumer neurotechnology. Nat. Biotechnol. **36**(9), 805–810 (2018)
12. Jas, M., Engemann, D.A., Bekhti, Y., Raimondo, F., Gramfort, A.: Autoreject: automated artifact rejection for MEG and EEG data. Neuroimage **159**, 417–429, 031001 (2017)

13. Lei, J., Liu, C., Jiang, D.: Fault diagnosis of wind turbine based on long short-term memory networks. Renewable Energy **133**, 422–432 (2019)
14. Leske, S., Dalal, S.S.: Reducing power line noise in EEG and meg data via spectrum interpolation. Neuroimage **189**, 763–776, 031001 (2019)
15. Li, G., Lee, C.H., Jung, J.J., Youn, Y.C., Camacho, D.: Deep learning for EEG data analytics: a survey. Concurrency Comput. Practice Exp. **32**(18), e5199 (2020)
16. Lotte, F., et al.: A review of classification algorithms for EEG-based brain-computer interfaces: a 10 year update. J. Neural Eng. **15**(3), 031005 (2018)
17. Lotte, F., Congedo, M., Lécuyer, A., Lamarche, F., Arnaldi, B.: A review of classification algorithms for EEG-based brain-computer interfaces. J. Neural Eng. **4**(2), R1, 031005 (2007)
18. Qu, X., Hall, M., Sun, Y., Sekuler, R., Hickey, T.J.: A personalized reading coach using wearable EEG sensors-a pilot study of brainwave learning analytics. In: CSEDU (2), pp. 501–507 (2018)
19. Qu, X., Liu, P., Li, Z., Hickey, T.: Multi-class time continuity voting for EEG classification. In: Frasson, C., Bamidis, P., Vlamos, P. (eds.) BFAL 2020. LNCS (LNAI), vol. 12462, pp. 24–33. Springer, Cham (2020). https://doi.org/10.1007/978-3-030-60735-7_3
20. Qu, X., Mei, Q., Liu, P., Hickey, T.: Using EEG to distinguish between writing and typing for the same cognitive task. In: Frasson, C., Bamidis, P., Vlamos, P. (eds.) BFAL 2020. LNCS (LNAI), vol. 12462, pp. 66–74. Springer, Cham (2020). https://doi.org/10.1007/978-3-030-60735-7_7
21. Qu, X., Sun, Y., Sekuler, R., Hickey, T.: EEG markers of stem learning. In: 2018 IEEE Frontiers in Education Conference (FIE), pp. 1–9. IEEE (2018)
22. Quitadamo, L., Cavrini, F., Sbernini, L., Riillo, F., Bianchi, L., Seri, S., Saggio, G.: Support vector machines to detect physiological patterns for EEG and EMG-based human-computer interaction: a review. J. Neural Eng. **14**(1), 011001 (2017)
23. Roy, Y., Banville, H., Albuquerque, I., Gramfort, A., Falk, T.H., Faubert, J.: Deep learning-based electroencephalography analysis: a systematic review. J. Neural Eng. **16**(5), 051001 (2019)
24. Wang, Y.B., You, Z.H., Yang, S., Yi, H.C., Chen, Z.H., Zheng, K.: A deep learning-based method for drug-target interaction prediction based on long short-term memory neural network. BMC Med. Inform. Decis. Mak. **20**(2), 1–9 (2020)
25. Zhang, X., Yao, L., Wang, X., Monaghan, J., Mcalpine, D., Zhang, Y.: A survey on deep learning-based non-invasive brain signals: recent advances and new frontiers. J. Neural Eng. **18**(3), 031002 (2021)

# Sustained Attention States Recognition with EEG and Eye-Tracking in the GradCPT

Wei Zhang[1], Yifan Zhang[2], Qinyu Zhang[2], and Jie Xu[2(✉)]

[1] National Aeronautical Radio Electronics Research Institute, Shanghai, China
[2] Zhejiang University, Hangzhou, China
xujie0987@zju.edu.cn

**Abstract.** The objective of the current study is to explore the feasibility of online recognition of human sustained attention states using electroencephalography (EEG) and eye-tracking technology in the gradual onset continuous performance task (gradCPT). Sixteen volunteer participants each completed a 2-min practice session and three 8-min experimental sessions of gradCPT. EEG and eye-tracking data were collected during the experimental sessions. Six machine learning algorithms, including logistic regression (LR), linear discriminant analysis (LDA), support vector machines (SVM), random forest (RF), k-nearest neighbors (kNN), and artificial neural networks (ANN), were tested in their performance in recognizing in-the-zone and out-of-the-zone periods. On the behavioral level, the results were consistent with the previous gradCPT studies. Among the machine learning algorithms, SVM and LR yielded above-average performance, with a classification accuracy of 0.62; SVM was the best performer considering balanced sensitivity and specificity. This study demonstrated that it is feasible to detect human sustained station states using frontal-channels EEG and eye-tracking features with above-chance accuracy.

**Keywords:** Gradual onset continuous performance task · Sustain attention · Electroencephalography

## 1 Introduction

### 1.1 The Gradual Onset Continuous Performance Task

Vigilance tasks are a family of experimental paradigms traditionally used in psychology and neuroscience to study the effect of attention and fatigue [1, 2], and these tasks are also useful in fatigue assessment in various work settings [3, 4], as well as developmental disorders and neuropsychiatric abnormalities diagnosis [5, 6]. For example, researchers implemented a version of the vigilance task, which lasts for 5 min, on a pocketable handheld device to be used in the field to assess work-related fatigue [7]. Recently, similar tests have been implemented in mobile phones to use in healthcare settings [3]. Research

---

W. Zhang and Y. Zhang—Contributed equally to the manuscript.

D. D. Schmorrow and C. M. Fidopiastis (Eds.): HCII 2022, LNAI 13310, pp. 213–221, 2022.
https://doi.org/10.1007/978-3-031-05457-0_18

suggested that vigilance tasks can be used in quantifying hepatic encephalopathy and identifying cirrhosis patients who are dangerous drivers [6].

The gradual onset continuous performance task (gradCPT) is a recently developed vigilance task that can reliably indicate attentional fluctuations over time [8]. A session of gradCPT typically requires 4–8 min to complete, and the generated behavioral data are analyzed offline. GradCPT is a continuous performance task, which requires the participants to respond to frequent stimuli and inhibit the response to infrequent stimuli [9]. As a result, more behavioral data can be obtained to model sustained attention fluctuations during the course of the gradCPT than traditional paradigms of vigilance tasks [10]. A key characteristic of gradCPT is that the sequence of visual stimuli is presented with gradual transitions so that involuntary attention towards the display due to the abrupt offsets and onsets of stimuli can be controlled [11]. Thus, the gradCPT paradigm might be particularly suitable for studying internal attentional control [10]. Currently, gradCPT is widely used in studies of behavioral and neural characteristics of sustained attention in regular and clinical populations [12, 13].

### 1.2 Classifying Sustained Attention States

In applied settings, sustained attention assessments need to be done more efficiently. In the near future, with the advancement and increasing availability of wearable neurophysiological sensing technologies, physiological-computing-based real-time sustained attention assessment is a promising direction to make vigilance tasks more useful in practical settings. Some studies have been done using neurophysiological measures in combination with machine learning to classify sustained attention states in vigilance tasks [14–16]. However, few research has been conducted with the gradCPT paradigm.

Studies using the gradCPT paradigm have developed a method to classify sustained attention states as in-the-zone or out-of-the-zone periods based on the variability of reaction time (RT) [17]. Specifically, when an individual is in-the-zone, he/she can respond to the ongoing stimuli with stable RTs; when he/she is out-of-the-zone, he/she responds to the ongoing stimuli with unstable RTs. Studies have shown that out-of-the-zone is associated with poor performance, such as high commission error rate, high omission rate, and reduced ability to discriminate different stimuli [8, 11, 17]. Neuroscience studies have identified functional brain networks associated with in-the-zone and out-of-the-zone statues, and such networks were used to successfully predict individual differences in performance, especially for populations with attention deficit hyperactivity disorder (ADHD) [18]. The findings suggest that in-the-zone/out-of-the-zone is a valid classification scheme for sustained attention. When one attempts to build models to classify sustained attention statues in gradCPT with features other than behavioral RT, the classification of in-the-zone and out-of-the-zone can be used as labels for machine learning.

The objective of the current study is to explore the feasibility of online recognition of human sustained attention states using electroencephalography (EEG) and eye-tracking technology in the gradCPT. This study explores the feasibility of utilizing frontal-channels EEG and eye-tracking, both of which are available in portable forms, to recognize sustained attention states. The results could provide insights for the future research directions of sustained attention recognition and assessment.

## 2 Methods

### 2.1 Participants

Sixteen volunteer participants were recruited from a large public university in eastern China (age: mean = 24, SD = 3.6; Male = 8, Female = 8). The protocol of the study has been approved by the Research Ethics Board of Center for Psychological Sciences at Zhejiang University.

### 2.2 Apparatus

The experiment was conducted using a gradCPT task platform developed with MAT-LAB. All the stimuli in gradCPT included ten photographs of city scenes and ten photographs of mountain scenes. They were all made into circular grayscale images of the same size, and the viewing angle radius is 3.5°. Examples of the images are shown in Fig. 1. Stimuli were randomly presented according to the specified probability, of which the probability of the mountain scene was 10%, and the probability of the city scene was 90%. Any two contiguous images cannot be the same. Stimuli were presented consecutively at 800 ms intervals. Each stimulus was presented in the same way, with each image transitioning from 100% transparency (totally transparent) to 0% transparency (solidly displayed) in 800 ms and then to 100% transparency in the next 800 ms. That is, two different images are changing at the same time. The participants were asked to press the space bar as soon as they could be sure the image was a city scene. Esterman et al. [17] further details how the gradCPT disambiguates responses in the case of multiple button presses.

**Fig. 1.** Examples of a target image (a city scene, left) and a non-target image (a mountain scene, right)

Eye-tracking data were sampled at 1000 Hz through the EyeLink 1000 Plus eye-tracking system (SR Research, Ottawa, Ontario, Canada). EEG data were sampled at 500 Hz through the Brain Products 64-electrode EEG system (Brain Products GmbH, Germany). The participant's head was held in place by a chin rest, and the eyes were 60 cm away from the screen.

## 2.3  Procedure

Upon arrival, participants were informed of the procedure and signed the consent form. They were asked to wear an EEG cap and told to keep their heads as still as possible to reduce the impact of head movement on signal collection. Participants were then instructed to perform a 2-min session of gradCPT exercise. At the end of the exercise, they were asked to perform three 10-min sessions of gradCPT, with a 2-min break in between each.

## 2.4  Sustained Attention Labeling

In this experiment, the behavioral measures included RT, Variance Time Course (VTC), commission rate, omission rate, d', and criterion score. RT and VTC were used to generate attention labels. VTC is an indicator to measure the variability of RT. For each participant, all RTs were converted into the corresponding Z-score (i.e. standard score), and the absolute deviation between each trial and the overall average RT is the VTC value. Five trials (or 4 s) were defined as a time window, and Gaussian kernel smoothing was carried out for VTC time series in each session of experiments. The smoothed VTC in each session is split by the median, with the lower half labeled in-the-zone and the upper half labeled out-of-the-zone (see Fig. 2).

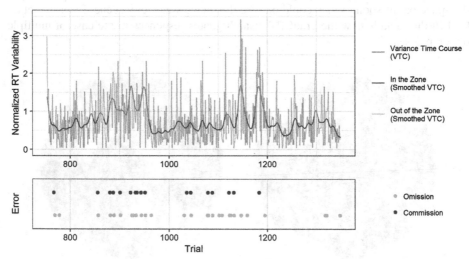

**Fig. 2.** In-the-zone and out-of-the-zone sustained attention states defined by smoothed variance time course from one of the experimental sessions.

## 2.5  Feature Extraction and Selection

Frontal channels EEG (Fp1 and Fp2) and eye-tracking data were collected during the experimental sessions. Raw EEG and eye-tracking data were processed before feature extraction. In 4-s moving windows, features were extracted from the EEG and eye-tracking data.

Specifically, the data were band-pass filtered, and blink artifact removal in EEG was performed with the Savitzky-Golay smoothing filter approach [19]. EEG features included both time-domain features, including the Hjorth parameters [20] and entropy [21], and time-frequency domain features, including the powers in different frequency bands derived from wavelet packet analysis [22].

Eye-tracking features included both eye movement features, including the fixation frequency and saccade speed, and pupillometric features, including the mean and variance of pupil size.

To reduce the dimensionality of the feature space, highly correlated features were deleted, and then a forward and backward elimination procedure was performed for feature selection [23].

### 2.6 Classification

Six machine learning algorithms, including logistic regression (LR), linear discriminant analysis (LDA), support vector machines (SVM), random forest (RF), k-nearest neighbors (kNN), and artificial neural networks (ANN), were tested. In the model training process, data from two randomly selected participants (12.5%) were used as the test set and thus excluded from the training set. The training was performed with 10-fold cross-validation with 5 repeats.

## 3   Results and Discussion

### 3.1   Behavioral Performance

On the behavioral level, comparisons were made for reaction time, d´, criterion score, commission rate, and omission rate between the in-the-zone and the out-of-the-zone periods. linear mixed effects (LME) models [24] were fitted to the data with random intercepts to account for session effects and participant effects whenever applicable. Statistical significance tests were done for the LME models using the Kenward-Roger approximation for degrees of freedom [25].

Consistent with previous studies (such as [11, 17, 18]), in-the-zone/out-of-the-zone periods had significant effects on d´, commission rate, and omission rate. Specifically, lower d´ ($b = 0.69$, $t(75) = 8.68$, $p < 0.05$), higher commission rate ($b = 0.15$, $t(75) = 7.42$, $p < 0.05$), and higher omission rate ($b = 0.02$, $t(75) = 5.38$, $p < 0.05$) were observed in out-of-the-zone periods compared to the in-the-zone periods.

Consistent with previous results from our own study, we found that in-the-zone/out-of-the-zone periods also had significant effects on reaction time and criterion score. Specifically, faster reaction time ($b = 16.41$, $t(75) = 2.13$, $p < 0.05$) and higher criterion score ($b = 0.16$, $t(75) = 5.37$, $p < 0.05$) were observed in out-of-the-zone periods compared to the in-the-zone periods.

The above results are visualized in Fig. 3.

The successful replication of previous results indicated that the gradCPT is a robust experimental paradigm. The differences in reaction time, d´, criterion score, commission

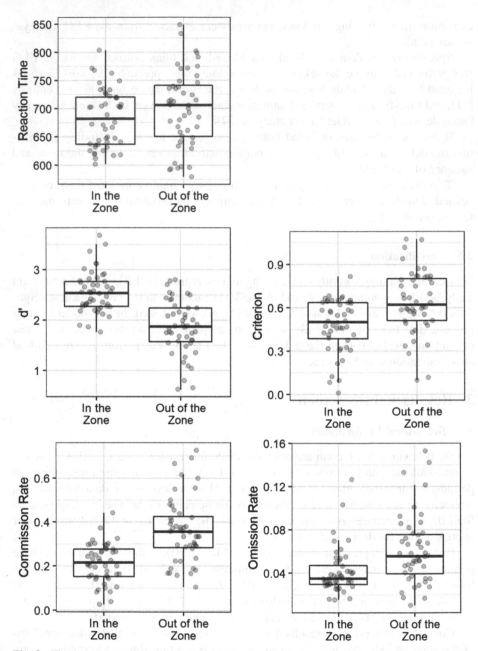

**Fig. 3.** The raw data and distribution of the reaction time, d´, criterion score, commission rate, and omission rate in the in-the-zone and the out-of-the-zone periods

rate, and omission rate between the in-the-zone and the out-of-the-zone periods were in the expected directions, which corresponded to stable and unstable sustained attention. In this regard, the results demonstrated that the in-the-zone/out-of-the-zone labels indeed reflected the unobservable sustained attention states. In other words, the behavioral results provided some support for using in-the-zone/out-of-the-zone as the ground truth for machine learning.

However, using the in-the-zone/out-of-the-zone labels as the ground truth for machine learning is still problematic due to the fact that data were split in half between in-the-zone and out-of-the-zone if we followed the original methodology [17]. This issue was also discussed in [10], in which the author explored the use of different in-the-zone vs. out-of-the-zone ratios (I/O ratios). Here we argue that changing the I/O ratio would not change the underlying assumption that an individual had stable sustained attention in a fixed percentage of time during the task process. Thus, in the following model training exercise, we decided to follow the convention set by the previous studies and used an I/O ratio of 1.

## 3.2  Classification Results

The cross-subject sustained attention states recognition performance of machine learning algorithms is shown in Table 1. The ANN yielded the highest accuracy (0.72) but with an extremely unbalanced sensitivity (0.98) and specificity (0.02). SVM and LR yielded above-average performance. Considering balanced sensitivity and specificity, SVM was the best performer.

**Table 1.** The cross-subject recognition performance of different machine learning algorithms.

| Algorithm | Accuracy | Sensitivity | Specificity | F1 score |
|-----------|----------|-------------|-------------|----------|
| LR | 0.62 | 0.74 | 0.27 | 0.74 |
| LDA | 0.54 | 0.60 | 0.39 | 0.65 |
| SVM | 0.62 | 0.66 | 0.53 | 0.70 |
| RF | 0.50 | 0.46 | 0.58 | 0.57 |
| kNN | 0.59 | 0.70 | 0.31 | 0.71 |
| ANN | 0.72 | 0.98 | 0.02 | 0.83 |

Note: LR – logistic regression; LDA – linear discriminant analysis; SVM – support vector machines; RF – random forest; kNN – k-nearest neighbors; and ANN – artificial neural networks

Overall, while the numbers of the performance metrics looked unsatisfactory, considering the limitations of the current study, there is room for improvement. First, the sample size was small, with only 16 individuals (14 in the training set), and each individual only performed three blocks of tasks. Follow-up studies should experiment with longer experimental sessions to collect more data from each participant. However, as vigilance tasks are mentally demanding [26], prolonged experimental sessions should be avoided.

Second, defining in the zone and out of the zone attentional states only through behavioral reaction times might not be adequate. Future endeavors could develop a more reliably labeling method for attentional states to obtain an improved recognition performance.

## 4 Conclusion

The current study explored the feasibility of recognition of human sustained attention states using EEG and eye-tracking technology in the gradCPT. The results from the behavioral data were consistent with the previous study, demonstrated the robustness of the gradCPT paradigm, and implied that the in-the-zone/out-of-the-zone labeling is indeed reflective of the participants' sustained attention states. The results from the machine learning exercises showed that it is feasible to detect human sustained station states in using frontal-channels EEG and eye-tracking features with above-chance accuracy. Feature research should develop a more reliably labeling method for attentional states and train models with a larger training set to obtain an improved sustained attention classification performance.

**Acknowledgement.** This work was supported by the Aeronautical Science Fund (grant number 20185576005) and the National Natural Science Foundation of China (Grant No. T2192931).

## References

1. Finomore, V., Matthews, G., Shaw, T., Warm, J.: Predicting vigilance: a fresh look at an old problem. Ergonomics **52**(7), 791–808 (2009)
2. Cabrall, C., Happee, R., de Winter, J.C.: From Mackworth's clock to the open road: a literature review on driver vigilance task operationalization. Transport. Res. F: Traffic Psychol. Behav. **40**, 169–189 (2016)
3. Evans, M.S., Harborne, D., Smith, A.P.: Developing an objective indicator of fatigue: An alternative mobile version of the Psychomotor Vigilance Task (m-PVT). In: Editor (ed.) Book Developing an objective indicator of fatigue: An alternative mobile version of the Psychomotor Vigilance Task (m-PVT), pp. 49–71. Springer (2018)
4. Roach, G.D., Dawson, D., Lamond, N.: Can a shorter psychomotor vigilance task be usedas a reasonable substitute for the ten-minute psychomotor vigilance task? Chronobiol. Int. **23**(6), 1379–1387 (2006)
5. Lovejoy, M.C., Rasmussen, N.H.: The validity of vigilance tasks in differential diagnosis of children referred for attention and learning problems. J. Abnorm. Child Psychol. **18**(6), 671–681 (1990)
6. Formentin, C., et al.: The psychomotor vigilance task: role in the diagnosis of hepatic encephalopathy and relationship with driving ability. J. Hepatol. **70**(4), 648–657 (2019)
7. Lamond, N., DAWsON, D., Roach, G.D.: Fatigue assessment in the field: validation of a hand-held electronic psychomotor vigilance task. Aviat. Space Environ. Med. **76**(5), 486–489 (2005)
8. Fortenbaugh, F.C., Rothlein, D., McGlinchey, R., DeGutis, J., Esterman, M.: Tracking behavioral and neural fluctuations during sustained attention: a robust replication and extension. Neuroimage **171**, 148–164 (2018)

9. Robertson, I.H., Manly, T., Andrade, J., Baddeley, B.T., Yiend, J.: Oops!': performance correlates of everyday attentional failures in traumatic brain injured and normal subjects. Neuropsychologia **35**(6), 747–758 (1997)

10. Zhang, W., Zhang, Y., Xu, J.: Performance and Eye Metrics Correlates to Out-of-the-zone Sustained Attention in GradCPT. In: Editor (eds.) Book Performance and Eye Metrics Correlates to Out-of-the-zone Sustained Attention in GradCPT. SAGE Publications, Sage CA, Los Angeles, CA, pp. 112–116 (2020)

11. Fortenbaugh, F.C., et al.: Sustained attention across the life span in a sample of 10,000: dissociating ability and strategy. Psychol. Sci. **26**(9), 1497–1510 (2015)

12. Esterman, M., Poole, V., Liu, G., DeGutis, J.: Modulating reward induces differential neurocognitive approaches to sustained attention. Cereb. Cortex **27**(8), 4022–4032 (2017)

13. Auerbach, R.P., et al.: Adolescent nonsuicidal self-injury: examining the role of child abuse, comorbidity, and disinhibition. Psychiatry Res. **220**(1–2), 579–584 (2014)

14. Jin, C.Y., Borst, J.P., van Vugt, M.K.: Distinguishing vigilance decrement and low task demands from mind-wandering: a machine learning analysis of EEG. Eur. J. Neurosci. **52**(9), 4147–4164 (2020)

15. Armanfard, N., Komeili, M., Reilly, J.P., Pino, L.: Vigilance lapse identification using sparse EEG electrode arrays. In: Editor (ed.) Book Vigilance lapse identification using sparse EEG electrode arrays. IEEE, pp. 1–4 (2016)

16. Shi, L.-C., Lu, B.-L.: EEG-based vigilance estimation using extreme learning machines. Neurocomputing **102**, 135–143 (2013)

17. Esterman, M., Noonan, S.K., Rosenberg, M., DeGutis, J.: In the zone or zoning out? tracking behavioral and neural fluctuations during sustained attention. Cereb. Cortex **23**(11), 2712–2723 (2013)

18. Rosenberg, M.D., Finn, E.S., Scheinost, D., Papademetris, X., Shen, X., Constable, R.T., Chun, M.M.: A neuromarker of sustained attention from whole-brain functional connectivity. Nature Neurosci. **19**(1), 165-+ (2016)

19. Szibbo, D., Luo, A., Sullivan, T.J.: Removal of blink artifacts in single channel EEG. In: Editor (ed.) Book Removal of blink artifacts in single channel EEG, pp. 3511–3514 (2012)

20. Oh, S.-H., Lee, Y.-R., Kim, H.-N.: A novel EEG feature extraction method using Hjorth parameter. Int. J. Electron. Electr. Eng. **2**(2), 106–110 (2014)

21. Liang, Z., et al.: EEG entropy measures in anesthesia. Front. Comput. Neurosci. **9**, 16 (2015)

22. Ting, W., Guo-Zheng, Y., Bang-Hua, Y., Hong, S.: EEG feature extraction based on wavelet packet decomposition for brain computer interface. Measurement **41**(6), 618–625 (2008)

23. Bania, R.: Survey on feature selection for data reduction. Int. J. Comput. Appl. **94**(18) (2014)

24. Bates, D., Mächler, M., Bolker, B., Walker, S.: Fitting linear mixed-effects models using lme4, arXiv preprint arXiv:1406.5823 (2014)

25. Singmann, H., Bolker, B., Westfall, J., Aust, F., Ben-Shachar, M.S.: afex: analysis of factorial experiments. R package version 0.13–145 (2015)

26. Dillard, M.B., et al.: Vigilance tasks: unpleasant, mentally demanding, and stressful even when time flies. Hum. Factors **61**(2), 225–242 (2019)

# Human and Machine Learning

# Towards Human-Like Learning Dynamics in a Simulated Humanoid Robot for Improved Human-Machine Teaming

Akshay, Xulin Chen, Borui He, and Garrett E. Katz[⊠]

Syracuse University, 13244 Syracuse, NY, USA
{akshay,xchen168,bhe100,gkatz01}@syr.edu

**Abstract.** A potential barrier to an effective human-machine team is the mismatch between the learning dynamics of each teammate. Humans often master new cognitive-motor tasks quickly, but not instantaneously. In contrast, artificial systems often solve new tasks instantaneously (e.g., knowledge-based planning agents) or learn much more slowly than humans (e.g., reinforcement learning agents). In this work, we present our ongoing work on a robotic control architecture that blends planning and memory to produce more human-like learning dynamics. We empirically assess current implementations of four main components in this architecture: object manipulation, full-body motor control, robot vision, and imitation learning. Assessment is conducted using a simulated humanoid robot performing a maintenance task in a virtual tabletop setting. Finally, we discuss the prospects for using this learning architecture with human teammates in virtual and ultimately physical environments.

**Keywords:** Human-machine teaming · Humanoid robotics · Virtual environments

## 1 Introduction

Robots have been effectively used for several decades in applications involving highly repetitive tasks, such as automotive manufacturing. Robotic technology has also matured in applications involving full remote control by a human teleoperator, such as consumer quadcopters. However, robotic control remains challenging in applications that team humans with robot partners possessing some degree of autonomy. Human-machine teaming is an important open research topic relevant to several important application areas, such as disaster recovery and assisted living.

Human-machine teaming presents many challenges: the machine must operate safely in the presence of a human, communicate effectively with the human, model and understand the human's goals, and reliably achieve its own goals.

Supported by ONR award N00014-19-1-2044.

Deficiencies in any of these capabilities can reduce the human's trust in the machine and degrade team performance.

Our present work is based on a hypothesis that the robot's learning dynamics are also an important factor in human-machine teaming. In particular, if the robot learns a task at a different rate or in a different manner than its human teammate, this could potentially reduce the human's trust and degrade team performance, even if the robot's individual performance is good. Human-like learning dynamics in a robot might also allow a more direct comparison between humans and robots, in terms of both overt performance and internal mental/computational effort. Current AI systems generally do not have human-like learning dynamics. Data-driven systems often learn much more slowly than humans, relying on many iterations of gradient-based optimization, while knowledge-based systems often learn instantaneously, incorporating new knowledge using a one-shot procedure.

Therefore, to test our learning dynamics hypothesis, it is necessary to build a new robotic control system in which the learning dynamics can be tuned to match a human's. This paper presents our progress towards building such a system. Our initial efforts involve a simulated humanoid robot in a virtual environment, performing an equipment maintenance task from our previous work [9] in which faulty hard disks must be removed from a docking station and replaced. Using a virtual environment is a natural stepping stone towards implementation on a physical system. Moreover, it reduces various barriers to human subject experiments: no physical lab space is needed, there is no risk of damaging robotic equipment or harming human subjects, and there is no need for physically collocated human subjects, robots, and experimenters. We use PyBullet as our physics simulation framework for the virtual environment [3], and Poppy as our humanoid robot [10]. Code for our experiments is open-source and freely available online.[1]

In the following sections we present progress on four main components of the robotic control system. First, we have built a grasp manipulation component that can effectively grasp, remove, and insert disks into the dock slots. Second, we have built a full-body controller that enables the humanoid robot to maintain balance while moving its upper body for object manipulation. Third, we have built a robot vision system that can attend to specific objects in the environment and fine-tune planned grasp points based on the visual observation of the object's fine-grained position, orientation, and surroundings. Finally, we have built an imitation learning component that can learn a discrete sequence of symbolic actions such as "remove disk 1" or "insert disk 4 in slot 1." This imitation learning component blends planning and memory to produce human-like learning dynamics.

Section 2 provides more detail on our methodology for each component listed above. Results of empirical assessments of each component are then presented in Sect. 3. Finally, Sect. 4 discusses limitations in the current implementation and future work needed to better integrate each component and deploy in human subject experiments.

---

[1] https://github.com/garrettkatz/poppy-simulations

# 2    Methods

## 2.1    Object Manipulation

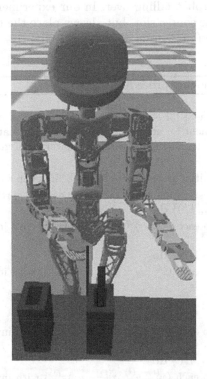

**Fig. 1.** Example object manipulation: moving a mock hard drive (blue) from one slot (red) to another. (Color figure online)

Robotic grasping research has come a long way in the last couple of decades. Research on grasping includes strategies for rigid body [13], soft body(deformable objects) [21], multi-fingered robots [2], and partially visible and unknown objects [7,15]. Our robot uses two-fingered Poppy Ergo Jr. grippers and the approach is fairly simple explained in the algorithm below (Fig. 1).

The grasping algorithm uses the PyBullet environment [3] with position control. The main approach is to divide the trajectory of the gripper into different sub-tasks such as Move close to disk, Move in position to grip object, Grip Object, Move to target position, Release Object. These sub-tasks make use of PyBullet API calls to move the joints of the robot into the correct position for the required sub-task using inverse kinematics. The procedure is codified in Algorithm 1.

The main objective of this task is to move the disk from one slot to another. When testing this component individually (i.e., separately from the full body controller), we treat the abdomen as a "fixed" joint, meaning it stays in place and is not subject to gravity. This allows us to focus on the kinematics of effective grasping without the robot falling over. In our experiments, we systematically vary the position of the source slot, but always place the target slot 0.1 units to the right of the source ($-0.1$ units along the X-axis).

---

**Algorithm 1.** Disk moving procedure

---

**Input:**
$\Delta z^{(s)}$: Vertical displacement for staging gripper above initial disk location
$\Delta z^{(t)}$: Vertical displacement for staging gripper above destination slot location
$N$: Number of iterations for incremental raising/lowering of gripper

1: $(x_i^{(g)}, y_i^{(g)}, z_i^{(g)}) \leftarrow$ Initial grasp points for each fingertip $i \in \{1, 2\}$
2: $(x_i^{(t)}, y_i^{(t)}, z_i^{(t)}) \leftarrow$ Destination grasp points for each fingertip $i \in \{1, 2\}$
3: **for** $n \in \{N, N-1, ..., 1, 0\}$ **do**
4:     Move fingertips to each $(x_i^{(g)}, y_i^{(g)}, z_i^{(g)} + n\Delta z^{(s)})$ with inverse kinematics
5: **end for**
6: **for** $n \in \{0, 1, ..., N-1, N\}$ **do**
7:     Move fingertips to each $(x_i^{(g)}, y_i^{(g)}, z_i^{(g)} - n\Delta z^{(s)})$ with inverse kinematics
8: **end for**
9: Close grippers
10: **for** $n \in \{0, 1, ..., N-1, N\}$ **do**
11:     Move fingertips to each $(x_i^{(t)}, y_i^{(t)}, z_i^{(t)} + n\Delta z^{(t)})$ with inverse kinematics
12: **end for**
13: **for** $n \in \{N, N-1, ..., 1, 0\}$ **do**
14:     Move fingertips to each $(x_i^{(t)}, y_i^{(t)}, z_i^{(t)} - n\Delta z^{(t)})$ with inverse kinematics
15: **end for**
16: Open grippers

---

## 2.2  Full-Body Motor Control

Keeping balance is a classic problem in bipedal locomotion. While a bipedal robot is a complex system, its dynamics are often approximated by a simpler inverted pendulum model, connecting the stance foot to the center of mass (CoM) by massless telescopic legs. The ankle strategy and the hip strategy are two approaches to stabilize this model [20]. The ankle strategy maintains balance in a resting stance subject to small perturbations using torque control at the ankles and keeping all other joints fixed. When perturbations are larger or the ankle control is insufficient, the hip strategy imposes a large deflection on the upper body to reduce the moment of inertia about the ankle and effect a higher angular acceleration of the body [1].

The Zero Moment Point (ZMP) [19] is one of the dominant tools in bipedal robot stability. The ZMP is the point on the contact surface where the resultant force does not produce any horizontal moment. When the robot is dynamically balanced, the ZMP exists inside the boundary of the stance foot and coincides with the center of pressure (CoP). When the robot is not balanced, the ZMP no longer exists while the mechanism collapses about the foot edge. The utility of ZMP calculation has been proven on many robots, including Honda P2 [8] and Asimo [5]. Traditional control methods such as PID control fail to account for the constraint of ZMP and often demand more torque than the robot motors can physically deliver [17].

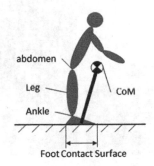

**Fig. 2.** A planar inverted pendulum in the sagittal plane.

Inspired by [17], we designed a balance controller based on the model shown in Fig. 2. We approximate the CoM dynamics as a linear inverted pendulum with the base joint representing the ankle. The pendulum is assumed to always be flat on the ground, hence contributing no kinetic or potential energy. Since in grasp manipulations, the robot only moves its upper body and arms in reaching motions, our controller relies on the abdomen and ankle joints to maintain balance. The controller is derived with the equation of motion (Eq. 1), where $q$ is a vector of the generalized positions, $M$ is the inertia matrix, $N$ is a vector of the centrifugal, Coriolis, and gravitational forces, and $\tau$ is a vector of the generalized forces.

$$M(q)\ddot{q} + N(q, \dot{q}) = \tau \tag{1}$$

We combine PD control and the dynamics of the robot to regulate the position of the CoM. The acceleration of the CoM is written as Eq. 2, where $J = \partial x_{CoM}/\partial q$ is the Jacobian matrix of the CoM. The objective of the regulator is to drive the CoM back to the desired location $x_{CoM}^d$, as shown in Eq. 3. Accordingly, the whole balance controller is in Eq. 4, where $J^{\dagger}$ is the pseudo-inverse of $J$. We employ the controller to both the abdomen and ankles but follow different strategies. For the abdomen, the controller imposes a deflection to decrease the moment caused by the motion of the upper body, similar to the hip strategy. For the ankles, the controller exerts torques on each stance foot, changing the position of the CoP in low perturbation cases.

$$\ddot{x}_{CoM} = J\ddot{q} + \dot{J}\dot{q} \tag{2}$$

$$\ddot{x}_{CoM} = -k^p(x_{CoM} - x_{CoM}^d) - k^d \dot{x}_{CoM} \tag{3}$$

$$\tau = N - MJ^\dagger(k^p(x_{CoM} - x_{CoM}^d) + k^d \dot{x}_{CoM} + \dot{J}\dot{q}) \tag{4}$$

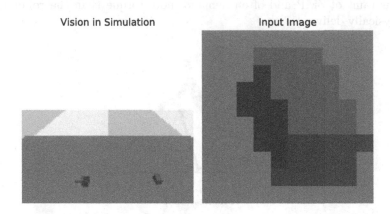

**Vision in Simulation**          **Input Image**

**Fig. 3.** Example image of the robot's full field of view (left) as well as an image patch (right) focused on the red cube and used as input to the vision system. (Color figure online)

### 2.3   Robot Vision

Our current robotic vision implementation focuses on cubic blocks as a starting point. While there are many difficult aspects of robot vision, here we focus on vision-based fine-tuning of grasp points. Therefore we assume the robot has access to the coordinates of the cube center, but not the optimal grasp points on the cube for each fingertip. We train a multilayer perceptron (MLP) [14] to output target grasp points for a given block. The input to the MLP consists of a small image patch centered on the block, which is flattened into a vector and concatenated with the 3D coordinates of the block's center.

Our experiments test whether the MLP is capable of extracting relevant features from the input and predicting high-quality grasp points. Our MLP uses one hidden layer with a Leaky Rectified Linear Unit (Leaky ReLUs) as the non-linear activation function. Our training dataset uses randomly placed blocks for example input, paired with the centers of opposing block faces as example target output. Mean squared error is used to evaluate the similarity between targets and predicted grasp points. Input image patches have shape $10 \times 10 \times 3$ (10 pixel height and width, and 3 color channels). Each such patch is a small image centered on one block on the table, as shown in Fig. 3. Considering that inputs should include all necessary information for the prediction task, we flatten the image patch into a vector of length 300, and then concatenate it with the 3D coordinates of the center of the block, resulting in an input layer size of 303. For the output, there are four faces (left, right, back, and front face) where grasp points could be. We assume that robot fingers touch opposing block faces (left and right, or front and back), and that each finger can touch either opposing side, so their are four possible grasps. For each grasp, there are two relevant 3D points on the cube, one for each finger. Therefore, the shape of the target prediction is $4 \times (3 + 3)$, which is flattened to an output layer size of 24. In our experiments, we vary the hidden layer size from 25 to 1000. We use a training dataset with 2000 examples and test set with 1000 examples, organized into batches with five examples each.

## 2.4  Imitation Learning

The robot's imitation learning component is responsible for learning a symbolic action sequence that accomplishes a maintenance task, such as the one shown in Table 1. This particular task involves discarding and replacing faulty hard disks in a docking station with slots and toggle switches. The robotic learning process is designed to model human experimental subjects learning similar maintenance tasks, so that the robot can produce similar learning dynamics.

We adopt an experimental design with a series of consecutive learning trials. In each trial, the task is first demonstrated to the robot, and then the robot tries to recall and imitate the demonstration. In this work, we use 25 consecutive learning trials, each with the task in Table 1. This experimental design and action sequence were both used with human subjects in previous work [4,16].

Since humans have limited memory capacity, and the action sequences may be relatively long and complex, human subjects often require multiple trials of practice before they successfully learn the action sequence and can accomplish the maintenance task themselves. This is not a pure memorization task, because even if the subject forgets which action to perform next, they can still reason about each available action and whether its effects on the task environment will match what is recalled about the later steps in the demonstration. In other words, the imitation process involves a combination of recall and planning.

Therefore, we model the imitation process in the robot with integrated memory and planning sub-systems. The memory sub-system includes both a working memory (WM) and a long-term memory (LTM). Both WM and LTM are modeled as partial sequences of memorized state-action pairs

$$\langle (s_{t_i}, a_{t_i}) \rangle_{i=1}^{N}, \tag{5}$$

where $N$ is the number of pairs stored in memory, $t_i$ is the $i^{th}$ time-step stored in memory, $a_{t_i}$ is the action performed at time-step $t_i$, and $s_{t_i}$ is the intermediate state of the task environment immediately before $a_{t_i}$ is performed. The double sub-scripts $a_{t_i}$, as opposed to simply $a_t$, reflect the fact that the subject might only remember a potentially non-consecutive sub-sequence of the observed actions at any given point during training.

**Table 1.** Action sequence used to test imitation learning.

| Step | Action |
|------|--------|
| 1 | press toggle 0 |
| 2 | press toggle 3 |
| 3 | pick up disk 3 |
| 4 | put down disk 3 in discard bin |
| 5 | press toggle 1 |
| 6 | pick up disk 0 |
| 7 | put down disk 0 in discard bin |
| 8 | pick up disk 7 |
| 9 | put down disk 7 in slot 3 |
| 10 | pick up disk 1 |
| 11 | put down disk 1 in discard bin |
| 12 | pick up disk 4 |
| 13 | put down disk 4 in slot 0 |
| 14 | press toggle 3 |
| 15 | pick up disk 5 |
| 16 | put down disk 5 in slot 1 |
| 17 | press toggle 0 |
| 18 | press toggle 1 |

WM and LTM are used during demonstration as follows. First, each state-action pair is added to WM as it is observed, but only if it is not already stored in LTM. Similar to humans, WM has a limited capacity $K \in \mathbb{N}$, which is the maximum number of state-action pairs that can be stored simultaneously. If WM reaches capacity before the demonstration is finished, a previously stored pair is chosen uniformly at random and removed from WM whenever a new pair is added. After the demonstration is complete, pairs still retained in WM are copied over to LTM. Each pair is only copied to LTM with a certain probability $\rho \in [0, 1]$ we call "consolidation rate." Among the pairs successfully stored in LTM, we assume that their relative order is properly retained (i.e., $j < k \iff t_j < t_k$). Finally, WM is cleared before the next trial. In this work we fixed the WM capacity $K = 7$ and consolidation rate $\rho = 0.2$.

The entire demonstration phase is codified in Algorithm 2. $\oplus$ denotes sequence concatenation, $\langle x \rangle$ denotes a sequence with a single item $x$, $|x|$ denotes length of a sequence $x$, and $x_i$ denotes the $i^{th}$ element of sequence $x$. $\mathcal{B}(\rho)$ denotes the Bernoulli distribution with probability $\rho$ and $\mathcal{U}(a, b)$ denotes the discrete uniform distribution on integers $a, a + 1, ..., b - 1, b$.

LTM is also used for planning during the imitation phase. In this phase, the $(s_{t_i}, a_{t_i})$ pairs in LTM are recalled in order. For each pair, random search is used to plan a short action sub-sequence $\hat{p}$ that bridges the gap from the

---

**Algorithm 2.** Observing a demonstration $\langle(s_t, a_t)\rangle_{t=1}^T$.

---

1: WM ← $\langle\rangle$
2: **for** $t = 1, ..., T$ **do**
3:    **if** $|\text{WM}| = K$ **then**
4:       Sample $i \sim \mathcal{U}(1, |\text{WM}|)$
5:       Remove the $i^{th}$ item from WM
6:    **end if**
7:    WM ← WM $\oplus\langle(s_t, a_t)\rangle$
8: **end for**
9: **for** $i = 1, ..., |\text{WM}|$ **do**
10:    Sample $c \sim \mathcal{B}(\rho)$
11:    **if** $c = 1$ **then**
12:       $(s_{t_i}, a_{t_i})$ ← $\text{WM}_i$
13:       Insert $(s_{t_i}, a_{t_i})$ into LTM in sorted order ($t_j < t_k$ for all $1 \leq j < k \leq |\text{LTM}|$)
14:    **end if**
15: **end for**

---

current state $s$ to the next recalled state $s_{t_i}$. Borrowing terminology from the automated planning literature, we refer to each $s_{t_i}$ in LTM as a "landmark" state [6]. If random search fails to find a plan to reach the landmark, the imitation phase terminates early. Otherwise, the recalled action $a_{t_i}$ associated with the reached landmark $s_{t_i}$ is applied to advance the current state $s$. The process is then repeated on the next state-action pair in LTM. For notational convenience, we use $s_{|LTM|+1}$ as an alias for $s_T$, the final state of the entire demonstration, which serves as one final landmark. The complete resulting action sequence from initial state $s_0$ to final state $s_{|LTM|+1}$, formed by concatenating the planned sub-sequences from one landmark to the next, is what the subject uses to imitate.

The random search used to plan action sub-sequences between landmarks combines ideas from Monte-Carlo roll-outs [18] and branch-and-bound methods [11]. In this work, we perform at most $R = 100$ roll-outs for each random search. In each roll-out, actions are repeatedly chosen uniformly at random from the available options until the next landmark $s_{t_i}$ is reached. A roll-out is unsuccessful and terminated early if its length reaches $M - |p|$ before the next landmark is reached, where $M$ is a maximum number of actions allowed for imitation and $p$ is the sequence of actions already planned up to the previous landmark $s_{t_{i-1}}$. In this work we set $M = 36$, twice the length of the demonstration. Multiple independent roll-outs are performed in an effort to find shorter paths to the landmark, using a branch-and-bound approach wherein new roll-outs are terminated early if they exceed the shortest successful roll-out performed so far. Lastly, when two consecutive states in the demonstration are both stored as landmarks in LTM, no roll-outs need to be performed. This becomes more common in later trials when more states are contained in LTM and consecutive states are more likely.

**Algorithm 3.** Imitating a task using LTM

**Input:**
LTM: sequence of landmarks $\langle (s_{t_i}, a_{t_i}) \rangle_{i=1}^{N}$
$s_0$: initial state
$s_T$: final state
**Output:**
$p$: planned action sequence

1: $s, p \leftarrow s_0, \langle \rangle$
2: **for** $i = 1, ..., N + 1$ **do**
3:     $\hat{p} \leftarrow \text{SUBPLAN}(p, s, s_{t_i})$
4:     $s \leftarrow \hat{p}(s)$
5:     **if** $s \neq s_{t_i}$ **then**
6:         break
7:     **end if**
8:     $s \leftarrow a_{t_i}(s)$
9:     $p \leftarrow p \oplus \hat{p} \oplus \langle a_{t_i} \rangle$
10: **end for**

**Algorithm 4.** SUBPLAN$(p, s, s_{t_i})$

**Input:**
$p$: plan of actions so far
$s$: current state after performing $p$
$s_{t_i}$: the next landmark state to be reached
**Output:**
$p^*$: A sub-plan of additional actions from $s$ to $s_{t_i}$

1: $p^* \leftarrow \langle \rangle$
2: **for** $r = 1, ..., R$ **do**
3:     $\overline{p} \leftarrow \langle \rangle$
4:     $\overline{s} \leftarrow s$
5:     **for** $i = 1, ..., M - |p|)$ **do**
6:         **if** $\overline{s} = s_{t_i} \vee (r > 1 \wedge |\overline{p}| \geq |p^*|)$ **then**
7:             break
8:         **end if**
9:         $a \leftarrow$ random valid action in $\overline{s}$
10:        $\overline{p} \leftarrow \overline{p} \oplus \langle a \rangle$
11:        $\overline{s} \leftarrow a(\overline{s})$
12:    **end for**
13:    **if** $r = 1 \vee (\overline{s} = s_{t_i} \wedge |\overline{p}| < |p^*|)$ **then**
14:        $p^* \leftarrow \overline{p}$
15:    **end if**
16: **end for**

The top-level imitation process is codified in Algorithm 3, and the random search sub-routine in Algorithm 4. We let $a(s)$ denote the resulting state after performing action $a$ in state $s$. Likewise, $p(s)$ is the result of applying a sequence of actions $p$ to state $s$.

In early trials, when not many memories have been consolidated into LTM, the landmark states tend to be few and far between. Consequently, the planning system must expend more effort on random search to bridge many large gaps between the landmark states stored in LTM. The additional computational effort may allow the system to attain reasonable performance, but is less efficient than in later trials when most of the demonstration can be recalled directly from memory. As such, this computational effort is analogous to mental effort in humans.

At the end of each trial when the robot has computed a complete action sequence for imitation, we measure performance using the Levenshtein distance [12] between the demonstrated action sequence and the actual action sequence planned by the robot. We also measure the running time of the complete imitation process (Algorithm 3) as an analog of "mental" effort expended by the artificial subject.

## 3 Results

### 3.1 Object Manipulation

The results of evaluating grasping performance are shown in Fig. 4. Each datapoint corresponds to an identical independent grasping trial. For every trial, the position of the source slot is varied using a normal distribution with mean at the center of the table and standard deviations of 0.05, 0.02, and 0 in the x, y, and z directions, respectively. As mentioned before, the target slot is always placed $-0.1$ units from the source along the X-axis. For example, if the position of the source slot is (0.22, 0.25, 0.51), the position of the target slot will be (0.12, 0.25, 0.51).

In 2 tries out of 100, the gripper completely missed picking up the disk (large error datapoints in Fig. 4). In approximately 20 trials, the disk is placed close to the slot, but not in it. This includes the disk slipping out of the gripper due to friction and being placed horizontally on slot. In all other trials, the disk is placed inside the slot correctly as expected. Figure 5 shows results in 3d for 1000 datapoints, using the same experimental design and sampling distribution. The robot is positioned at the origin (0,0).

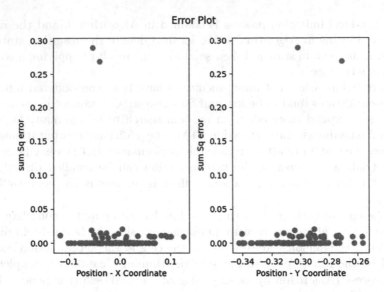

**Fig. 4.** Grasping performance. "sum sq error" is the squared Euclidean distance between the final actual position of the disk and the final target position of the disk. Orientation is not considered in the error calculation. Initial coordinates of the source slot are shown on the horizontal axes.

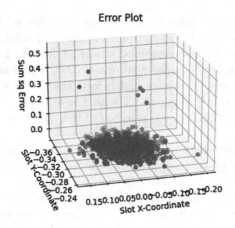

**Fig. 5.** Same experimental setup as Fig. 4, 1000 points with same distribution, shown in 3d.

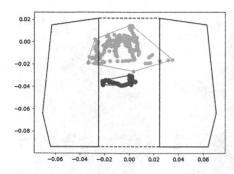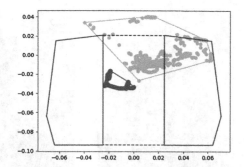

**Fig. 6.** The analysis of the robot dynamics in the x-y plane with different target slot positions. In the left figure, the slots are in front of the robot. In the right figure the slots are at the right-hand side of the robot. The position of the CoM and ZMP in every time step are plotted as orange and blue scatter points, respectively. The green lines show the contact surface of each foot (solid) and their convex hull (dashed).

### 3.2   Full-Body Motor Control

In this section we evaluate the balance controller on object manipulation tasks. We also explore how the ground reaction forces and the position of CoM affect the robot balance. In the simulation we have full access to all information of the robot, including the contact information. Thus, simultaneously analyzing the dynamics of the robot is tractable. When the robot is dynamically balanced, the ZMP is away from the edge of the foot and equivalent to the center of pressure. Accordingly, the position $(p_x, p_y, 0)$ of the ZMP is given by Eq. 6, where $p_i = (p_{ix}, p_{iy}, 0)$ and $f_i = (f_{ix}, f_{iy}, f_{iz})$ are the position and reaction force of the $i$th contact point respectively.

$$p_x = \frac{\sum_{i=1}^{N} p_{ix} f_{iz}}{\sum_{i=1}^{N} f_{iz}} \qquad p_y = \frac{\sum_{i=1}^{N} p_{iy} f_{iz}}{\sum_{i=1}^{N} f_{iz}} \qquad (6)$$

The experiment setup is the following. The robot starts from the upright position and the location of the slot is randomly initialized as described in Sect. 3.1. Then the robot begins to move the gripper to reach the slot, while our balance controller simultaneously produces a response to regulate the CoM position.

From Fig. 6 we observe that the ZMP is always away from the edge of the foot, therefore preserving the dynamical balance. Additionally, the CoM is shifted back when traveling far away from the origin, like a stable inverted pendulum. We show a successful example of keeping balance in Fig. 7. In the simulation, the external disturbance affecting the robot balance only includes the gravity of the disk and the collision. Consequently, we demonstrate the robot's ability to withstand some disturbance without falling over.

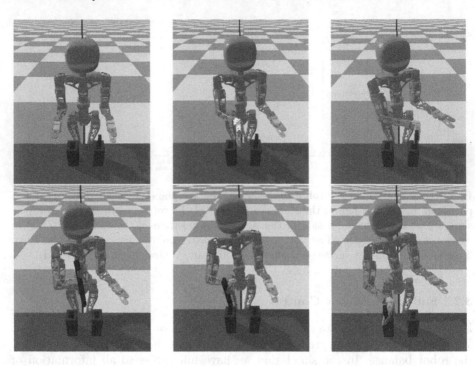

**Fig. 7.** An example of keeping balance on grasp manipulation, where two slots are in front of the robot.

### 3.3 Robot Vision

Learning curves and testing results for the vision component are shown in Fig. 8. The vertical axes show the average Euclidean distance between target grasp points and the grasp points predicted by the MLP. Columns show three hidden layer sizes we tested (12, 25, and 100). Small hidden sizes produce acceptable test errors usually between 0.025 and 0.075 (compared to the length of the table, which is 1 in the virtual environment). We also observe that performance gets worse if hidden layer size is too large, either 100 (Fig. 8, right) or above (data not shown). This may be due to a combination of overfitting and increased numerical difficulty in the training optimization process.

### 3.4 Imitation Learning

Using the action sequence and imitation learning system described in Sect. 2.4, we conduct a training process with 25 consecutive trials, measuring performance and computation time after each trial. To confirm reproducibility of the results, we run 30 independent repetitions of the entire training process. The results from all 30 repetitions are shown in Fig. 9.

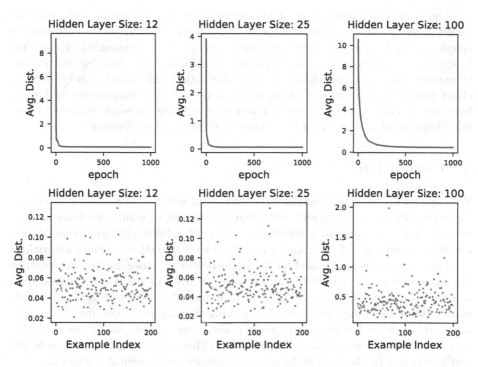

**Fig. 8.** Learning curves (top) and final performance on the test data (bottom). Vertical axes show average Euclidean distance between target and predicted grasp points. The horizontal axes show training epoch (top row) and batch index in the test set (bottom row).

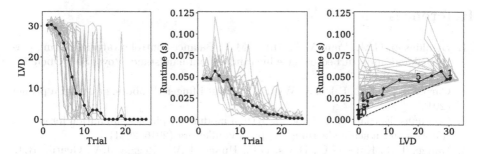

**Fig. 9.** Learning dynamics during training. Individual repetitions of the experiment are shown in gray, and the averages over 30 repetitions are shown in black. **Left**: Levenshtein distance (LVD) between demonstrated and actual action sequence after each trial. **Middle**: Runtime (in seconds) of action sequence planning during each trial. **Right**: Efficiency curve of LVD vs. Runtime (numbers indicate trial). LVD and runtime near zero corresponds to high efficiency. Dashed line connects first and last trials, corresponding to equal rate of efficiency improvement in performance and effort.

The results demonstrate that the artificial system's learning dynamics are qualitatively similar to human learning dynamics on similar tasks. Performance (measured by Levenshtein distance) and "mental" effort (measured by run-time in seconds) both converge to near optimal by the end of 25 trials, but not instantaneously. Moreover, the efficiency curve shows that reduction in computational effort lags behind improvement in performance. This is reminiscent of human learning dynamics, wherein early trials pose difficult memory challenges and additional mental effort must be expended to improve performance.

## 4   Conclusion

We have presented our progress on a humanoid robot that learns maintenance tasks in a virtual environment, with learning dynamics similar to humans. Our work includes an object manipulation component, a full-body balance controller, a visual processing network, and a cognitive-level imitation learning algorithm.

This ongoing work is based on the hypothesis that more human-like learning dynamics will promote better human-robot teaming outcomes. The virtual environment and human-like learning dynamics presented here will facilitate future work with human subjects to test this hypothesis. Regarding the imitation learning component, although several model parameters (WM capacity, consolidation rate, etc.) were chosen by hand in this work, they could be optimized in future work to better fit the human data on performance and mental workload.

Future work should also focus on improving individual performance of each sub-system (manipulation, balance, vision, and imitation), as well as better integration of all four sub-systems to enable end-to-end optimization of the system as a whole.

## References

1. Blenkinsop, G.M., Pain, M.T., Hiley, M.J.: Balance control strategies during perturbed and unperturbed balance in standing and handstand. Royal Soc. Open Sci. **4**(7), 161018 (2017)
2. Carpin, S., Liu, S., Falco, J., Wyk, K.V.: Multi-fingered robotic grasping: a primer (2016)
3. Coumans, E., Bai, Y.: Pybullet, a python module for physics simulation for games, robotics and machine learning. http://pybullet.org (2016–2021)
4. Hauge, T.C., Katz, G.E., Davis, G.P., Huang, D.W., Reggia, J.A., Gentili, R.J.: High-level motor planning assessment during performance of complex action sequences in humans and a humanoid robot. Int. J. Soc. Robot. **13**(5), 981–998 (2021)
5. Hirai, K., Hirose, M., Haikawa, Y., Takenaka, T.: The development of honda humanoid robot. In: Proceedings. 1998 IEEE International Conference on Robotics and Automation (Cat. No. 98CH36146), vol. 2, pp. 1321–1326. IEEE (1998)
6. Hoffmann, J., Porteous, J., Sebastia, L.: Ordered landmarks in planning. J. Artif. Intell. Res. **22**, 215–278, 161018 (2004)

7. Ji, S.Q., Huang, M.B., Huang, H.P.: Robot intelligent grasp of unknown objects based on multi-sensor information. Sensors **19**(7) (2019). https://doi.org/10.3390/s19071595. https://www.mdpi.com/1424-8220/19/7/1595
8. Introduction to Humanoid Robotics. STAR, vol. 101. Springer, Heidelberg (2014). https://doi.org/10.1007/978-3-642-54536-8
9. Katz, G., Huang, D.W., Hauge, T., Gentili, R., Reggia, J.: A novel parsimonious cause-effect reasoning algorithm for robot imitation and plan recognition. IEEE Trans. Cogn. Dev. Syst. **10**(2), 177–193, 161018 (2017)
10. Lapeyre, M., Rouanet, P., Oudeyer, P.Y.: The poppy humanoid robot: leg design for biped locomotion. In: 2013 IEEE/RSJ International Conference on Intelligent Robots and Systems, pp. 349–356 (2013). https://doi.org/10.1109/IROS.2013.6696375
11. Lawler, E.L., Wood, D.E.: Branch-and-bound methods: A survey. Oper. Res. **14**(4), 699–719 (1966)
12. Levenshtein, V.I., et al.: Binary codes capable of correcting deletions, insertions, and reversals. Soviet Phys. Doklady **10**(8), 707–710, 161018 (1966)
13. Lin, Y., Sun, Y.: Robot grasp planning based on demonstrated grasp strategies. Int. J. Robot. Res. **34**(1), 26–42 (2015). https://doi.org/10.1177/0278364914555544. https://doi.org/10.1177/0278364914555544
14. Marius, P., Balas, V., Perescu-Popescu, L., Mastorakis, N.: Multilayer perceptron and neural networks. WSEAS Trans. Circuits Syst. **8**, June 2009
15. Saxena, A., Wong, L., Ng, A.: Learning grasp strategies with partial shape information. vol. 3, pp. 1491–1494 (2008)
16. Shaver, A., Shuggi, I., Katz, G., Davis, G., Reggia, J., Gentili, R.: Effects of practicing structured and unstructured complex motor sequences on performance and mental workload. In: Journal of Sport and Exercise Psychology, vol. 42, p. S56. Human Kinetics (2020)
17. Stephens, B.: Integral control of humanoid balance. In: 2007 IEEE/RSJ International Conference on Intelligent Robots and Systems, pp. 4020–4027. IEEE (2007)
18. Tesauro, G., Galperin, G.: On-line policy improvement using Monte-Carlo search. Adv. Neural. Inf. Process. Syst. **9**, 1068–1074, 161018 (1996)
19. Vukobratović, M., Borovac, B.: Zero-moment point-thirty five years of its life. Int. J. Humanoid Rob. **1**(01), 157–173 (2004)
20. Winter, D.A.: Human balance and posture control during standing and walking. Gait Posture **3**(4), 193–214, 161018 (1995)
21. Zaidi, L., Corrales, J.A., Bouzgarrou, B.C., Mezouar, Y., Sabourin, L.: Model-based strategy for grasping 3d deformable objects using a multi-fingered robotic hand. Robot. Autonomous Syst. **95**, 196–206 (2017)

# Understanding Humans' Cognitive Processes During Computational Thinking Through Cognitive Science

Kiran Datwani, Michael-Brian C. Ogawa[✉], and Martha E. Crosby[✉]

Department of Information and Computer Sciences,
University of Hawaii at Manoa, Hawaii, USA
{kiran25,ogawam,crosby}@hawaii.edu

**Abstract.** Human-computer interaction is a diverse field covering disciplines such as computer technology, human factors, and cognitive science to name a few. Over the past several years, the information age has developed to incorporate a society that intentionally and unintentionally interacts with computing technology every day. The field of computational thinking in human-computer interaction is expanding and incorporating multidisciplinary fields such as psychology and software principles. Research has been conducted in the past regarding the background, social impact and innovation, and a new direction in social computing/issues in HCI. HCI is a diverse, expansive field covering many aspects and disciplines in computer science, the humanities, and others. Computational thinking, a subfield of HCI, explores the way humans process problems, and use problem-solving skills and analogies to solve complex, or seemingly difficult problems (Wing 2006). This research project will be conducted to understand computational thinking in people, along with determining the existing relationship between cognitive science and HCI.

**Keywords:** Computational thinking · Cognitive science · Human-computer interaction

## 1 Introduction

### 1.1 Research Questions

What facets/aspects of cognitive science help researchers in human-computer interaction (HCI) understand how people interact with computers? Are there existing relationships between cognitive science at an individual level in problem-solving and HCI at a group or community level?

### 1.2 Specific Aims

The questions will be answered by the following specific aims. First, to understand different peoples' computational thinking, and the amount of time it takes for a person

© The Author(s), under exclusive license to Springer Nature Switzerland AG 2022
D. D. Schmorrow and C. M. Fidopiastis (Eds.): HCII 2022, LNAI 13310, pp. 242–260, 2022.
https://doi.org/10.1007/978-3-031-05457-0_20

depending on the level of their computer literacy (e.g., programming novices, computer science majors, public) and second to identify, understand, and solve a problem. Secondly, to identify the level of expertise of participants, and determining different approaches to be taken for participants to understand the bigger picture of a program and solve problems with a stronger grasp of computing knowledge and literacy.

### 1.3 Significance of Study

Computing technology has revolved rapidly in the last several decades, however, the relationship between computing technology and the cognitive science when processing information on computing devices is vague. Computational thinking is a portion of computer science that is used by people on a daily basis to take relevant smaller steps to understand and solve larger problems. That being said, it is rare for people to correlate computational thinking with people's cognitive processes, and is seen more as a way computers are programmed, and the steps computer scientists take to write programs (Wing 2006). In this research study, I will be using cognitive science methodology to better understand the cognitive processes that facilitate seeking, filtering, and shaping relevant information to perform tasks that involve computational thinking. With a stronger understanding of computational thinking in individuals of various backgrounds, it can be determined how the problem-solving process takes place depending on an individual's background. Alongside that, I will be developing a stronger understanding of computational thinking and its relationship with HCI and cognitive science.

## 2  Introduction Background Information and Literature Review

Human-computer interaction is a comprehensive field covering disciplines such as computer technology, human factors, and cognitive science to new a few. Over the past several years, the information age has developed to incorporate a society that intentionally and unintentionally interacts with computing technology everyday. The field is expanding and incorporating multidisciplinary fields such as psychology and software principles. The literature review was conducted to further develop knowledge of human-computer interaction, cognitive science, and problem-solving for Senior Honors Project preparation. The terms I used to retrieve the following documents are cognitive science, psychology, human-computer interaction, society AND the information age, and the search engines used were Google Scholar and PubMed. My topics were divided into 5 parts: (1) Background of HCI, (2) Background on cognitive science, (3) Social impact, innovation, and computational thinking, (4) New direction in social computing/issues in HCI, and (5) Implications and impacts of cognitive science in Computer Science. Research in this topic is contributed by strong interest in the connection between humans and computers, and the aspiration to develop a project that will allow in contribution to this topic. As of now, there are several articles available written solely about human-computer interaction, a few written about the cognitive science factors of HCI during the information era, and this paper will reflect the background needed for this study.

## 2.1 Background on HCI

Human-computer interaction, which is also known as HCI, is a diverse, integrative field that encompasses aspects of human factors, system design, technical writing, and programming abilities. Cognitive science, on the other hand, while also an inclusive field overlapping in disciplines such as psychology, linguistics and philosophy, have little means in connecting the disciplines as a common idea. HCI is said to be a role that plays in connecting the disciplines of cognitive science to allow it to become more cohesive; HCI may be able to contribute to a better understanding of cognitive science and its diverse fields. Sharing a similar history, human-computer interaction and cognitive science were formed and developed during the time of World War II, to train soldiers to fight in the war in faster, better methods. It was late after World War II that research began being conducted on the interactions of humans and computers, which eventually led to HCI becoming a collaboration between psychologists and computer scientists. The aspects of cognitive science are included within the realm of HCI, but what is lacking is their inclusion with each other, and their overall role in HCI research (Boring 2002).

There is high importance in user-friendly systems and the development of usable systems using user interface media. The field of human-computer interaction and the components developed from it are unlike any other field, including the disciplines in engineering and design, because it is a combination of the two. Throughout time, user interfaces have become easier to learn and use by consumers, but far more difficult to program and build by programmers and engineers. The concept of user interfaces brings attention to the understanding that the majority of consumers of technological products and achievements have scarce knowledge of the difficulty of programming. It is important to note the development of design through the conceptual, semantic, syntactic, and lexical levels, and how they are impacted by the user and their ability in under-standing and using the software interface (Butler et al. 1998).

Human-computer interaction has become the visible part of computer science and has in recent years become crucial in creating solutions for difficult problems, such as in areas on direct manipulation interfaces, user interface management systems, task-oriented help and instruction, and computer-supported collaborative work. HCI is defined as a science of design, and is established in order to support and understand humans interacting with technology. HCI in software psychology has origins from several decades ago, and during that time, problems were posed. The two problems that were posed were firstly, describing and supporting design and development work, and secondly, better specifying the role social and behavioral science, which are parts of psychology, should play in HCI (Carrol 1997).

## 2.2 Background on Cognitive Science

Previously, psychology was dominated by the behaviorist approach. It was much later on that the human information-processing approach known as the cognitive revolution was discovered by the progress in communication system engineering and statistics. This approach focused on gaining knowledge of the human mind, and gave explanations to a human's perceptions and actions. Psychology and society have both been impacted by the information age largely, and science and technology have only continued to grow and expand throughout the years. It has been stated that eventually in time, the era of the information age will cease to exist, with the explanation that no era lasts forever, and thus, will be replaced with a new age in time (Xiong and Proctor 2018).

Individuals are responsible for creating their own unique experiences through interpretations, emotions and their judgments as elaborated by McCarthy and Wright (2005). Experience is thus created by the relationship between the self and the object, and the concept of life as lived and felt is stated by the writers to be personal, constructive, and transformative, and the connection between interior and exterior aspects of experience. In relation to HCI, the aspect that is already integrated within understanding HCI is the approaches of cognitive information processing addressing the efficiency and effectiveness of performance, but the aspect of understanding a person's experience with technology and their relationship, in positive and negative factors, is usually missed. While both are crucial, they are approached in different methodologies; while cognitive information processing is impersonal, and accessed through observation and experimentation, the felt-like experiences are wholly and completely personal (McCarthy and Wright 2005).

### 2.3 Social Impact, Innovation, and Computational Thinking

Throughout learning, growth, and education, students are strongly encouraged to develop a computational thinking approach, which is the concept of thinking in logical procedural processes. Over the years, a constant thread of the lack, or reduction, of innovation is developed because of the way young people are built to think and complete tasks. By social theories, computation is a major contributor in the lack of innovation. Although it is said that computation is required in order to achieve constant innovation at a steady pace, in the current time and age, computation has actually become the reason that innovation has lessened and impeded (Oren 2011). Although there isn't exact correlation, the reason behind this can be contributed by humans developing lesser skills in the innovation process and step-by-step problem-solving because computing technology has allowed processes to become simpler. A crucial aspect of this study will be to formulate whether stronger skills in computer literacy has benefited rather than harmed their problem-solving skills.

Computational thinking, which are problem-solving skills and thought processes to solve complex problems and write programs, are not only used by software engineers and computer scientists, but by everyone. The concept refers to steps taken in order to analyze, comprehend, and understand how to solve a problem. Computational thinking, along with involving solving problems, includes designing systems, and understanding human behavior, which elaborates on the concepts fundamental to computer science. The field of computer science is encompassed by computational thinking, which includes a range of mental tools. The concept is used in everyday activities, such as preparing your bag for what you need for school/work, losing an item and retracing your steps to find them, or picking a line in the supermarket that will allow you to wait the least amount of time. It takes the idea of a large difficult problem and breaks it down into steps and/or analogies, small pieces of the entire problem, to make it easier to understand and solve the larger picture of the problem. The steps and/or analogies serve as the representation or model of the challenging, relevant aspect of a problem, usually by reduction, embedding, transformation, or simulation. Computational thinking expresses that despite not having every detail or not understanding a problem wholly, or the end goal completely, it is possible to take a large problem, and still be able to use, and modify it to provide a result or solution. The concept of computational thinking is effectively implemented in everyone's lives, not only computer scientists, and it represents the way humans think, and comprehend and solve problems, rather than how a computer is programmed to solve tasks (Wing 2006) (Fig. 1).

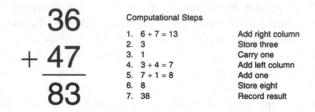

**Fig. 1.** The computational steps represent a simple arithmetic problem that is being solved through computational thinking (Friedenberg and Silverman 2006).

## 2.4  New Direction in Social Computing/issues in HCI

Despite plentiful research and knowledge accumulated in HCI, many researchers are continuing to be unaware of issues pertaining to HCI, such as systems being user-friendly and understanding the intentions and motives of the user. Usability issues are experienced both subjectively and collectively by different groups of people in mass populations. A programmer or computer engineer must understand the users' motives and perspectives, emotional and social drives to develop concepts and methodology that would be applicable to locations such as work practices, communities and organizational social structures. One of the most crucial aspects is understanding the design, development and implementation of systems individually and as a subunit of the whole product. The article by Cairns et al. directly points to the direction that collecting qualitative research in HCI is difficult, because it is less on the concept of measuring and producing numbers, and more on understanding the underlying aspects of a certain piece of software or technology, the ways it is used by numerous people, and their thoughts, expressions and emotions of it (Cairns et al. 2008).

A specialist in HCI should have a solid understanding of psychological factors so that they can be able to have the skill or knowledge to relate their observations to observations in other differing fields; it is difficult to be processed by an individual in domains other than psychology. HCI is described as a descriptive, engineering science, as the HCI specialist would be able to provide a level of analysis that would contribute in impacting the design factors on user behavior, as well as provide specific technical details for the overall product (Carroll et al. 1991).

The usage of technological artifacts and applications such as Artificial Intelligence (AI) would become frequent in home, work, and public environments. The interactions would be not only conscious and intentional, but also unintentional. People would be surrounded by and living among visible and invisible technological artifacts, such as numerous examples of AI and the system of transferring information. The eventual goal of the new technological era is continuing to focus on the human and how their needs shape the way technology is manufactured and used. It is first most important to serve the needs of the user. With that mindset, certain problems can arise, such as humans have more requirements and demands than before, and are more attentive and critical of technological artifacts, while at the same time being less optimistic about the outcomes. There are new challenges that are a consequence of human-centered approaches, and how critical issues need to be addressed and solved in order to establish and maintain a trustful and beneficial relationship between humans and technology (Stephanidis et al. 2019) (Fig. 2).

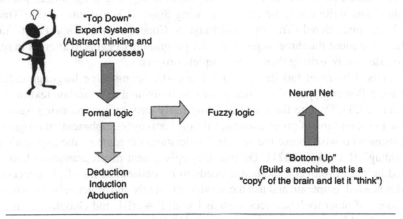

**Fig. 2.** This diagram given by Friedenberg & Silverman expresses the "top-down" approach of building a machine that "imitates" how humans think, while the "bottom-up" approach is of building a machine and letting it think and make decisions on its' own (Friedenberg and Silverman 2006).

HCI is related to the design, implementation and evaluation of interactive computer-based systems along with the multi-disciplinary study of numerous issues involved in the interaction. The user interface of the computer-based system is the application or system by which the user comes into contact and uses cognitively and physically. Over the years, with the development of the information society, computers have become more than scientific tools, but are becoming devices for productivity enhancement, and integrated into environments in such a way that computers are accessible to all people, regardless of their time and location. The information era has progressed to a place in time where various human activities are mediated by computers and will most likely continue to be so (Stephanidis 2001).

## 2.5   Implications and Impacts of Cognitive Science in Computer Science

In a study done by BRACElet, it was reported that students in computer science who were able to trace and read code not created by others were able to write similar code in their own style. On the other hand, "students who cannot read a short piece of code and describe it in relational terms are not intellectually well equipped to write similar code" (Lister 2020). This brings insight to the perspective that computer science students who are able to write effective, well-written code are applying problem-solving strategies and fully understanding the issues in hand prior to attempting to solve and program solutions. That being said, it is common for computer science to try and guess solutions without fully tracing, reading, and/or understanding the code presented to them. This can lead to obstacles and issues later on in their professional life where if they are unable to fully understand a problem, the individual will not be able to program a solution for it. As written by Lister, there are three stages to a young programmer learning to understand and write code; the following being Stage 1: Sensorimotor (Pre-Tracing), Stage 2: Pre-operational (Tracing), and Stage 3: Concrete Operational (Post-Tracing) (2020). Throughout the three stages, a novice programmer begins to attempt in reading code to extensively writing their own complete programs.

Recently, Microsoft has developed a low-code, open-source language called the Power Fx, a Power Apps service, that allows an individual to "translate text into code" (Lardinois 2021). Despite the program being fairly easy to use and using natural language as the main form of programming, Microsoft strongly emphases that programmers and novices who wish to use the service "understand the logic of the application they are building" (Lardinois 2021). Despite the replacement of programming knowledge required by the developers, there still needs to be understanding of the concepts and formulas needed to operate and use the service efficiently and effectively. This is similar to the usage of other tools/services such as Excel, PowerBI, and Google Sheets, which also use natural language query functions (2021). What is necessary to acknowledge is that as technology and AI is advancing so are humans' understanding and application of new tools. This is, however, not to disregard that human to halt their problem-solving processes due to technological advancements, but rather, grow their knowledge to easily learn and develop new strategies and solutions while using modern tool sets and technologies.

Eye tracking is one-way researchers use to attempt to understand their participant's cognitive processes and their future actions (Sharafi et al. 2021). Impact on an individual's thought processes including their comprehension, collaboration, emotion, and so forth can be determined using eye trackers. Throughout the relationship between eye trackers and software engineering, it was crucial for the eye trackers to be use correctly to attain the most accurate results. In addition, the data collection must be completed as carefully as possible and analyzed in great detail to fully understand the participants' cognitive processes and intentions. Researchers are able to determine (1) why problems exist in completing a task, (2) the location where participants find key points, (3) whether certain elements or key points prove to be distracting, (4) how participants are guided by designs, layouts, or artifacts whilst completing a task, (5) differences in a participants' efficiency based on their demographics or experience, and (6) whether the participant focused or scanned the details (2021).

In order to understand and solve problems, programmers must have a level of program comprehension established. There are many variations and levels of program comprehension, dependent on individual programmers as well the specific code itself. Programmers in the field who are experts are able to scan code across a computer screen and use key points, features, or semantic cues, also called beacons, to determine the purpose of the program (Siegmund 2017). This approach is known as the top-down approach, specifically to describe cognitive processes based on experience, whilst the bottom-up approach focuses more on finding explanation in individual pieces of the code when semantic cues are missing in the program (2017). In this article, the theme that was explored in great detail can be formed. There has been a deep connection between cognitive science and its relationship to computer science and overall computer literacy. For individuals to use computing technologies well, they need to have a strong grasp of and acquire an understanding of how and why certain programs, languages, and technologies perform the way they do.

## 3 Methodology and Research Design

### 3.1 Data Collection (from)

Data was collected in two forms/ways. To fulfill my questions of determining the existing relationship between cognitive science and HCI, and the aspects of cognitive science to interpret computational thinking, I reviewed relevant literature on methodology regarding computational thinking and cognitive science. The literature will also serve as a way to seek insight on development of methodology to form my own for my project. To execute my aims in identifying the level of expertise in computing technology in humans and understanding different people's computational thinking, I developed a series of problems in a software program, in pseudocode, and in natural language, and acquired students' comprehension of said problems to determine their level of computing literacy based on the programs.

### 3.2 Data Collection (from) Lab Trainings Completed and Ethics Approved

As of the current state, no training was required for this research project. I had received the following certifications from the CITI program: Human Subjects Research (HSR), Conduct of Research, and Information Privacy and Security (IPS) during the Spring of 2021. I had received clearance from the IRB prior to conducting the official research study in November of 2021. The clearance from IRB and the certifications from CITI program were required in order for me to conduct my research. The certifications from the CITI program were discussed with my faculty mentor and committee member during the months of March and April of 2021 and the IRB proposal was discussed in May of 2021. I understand the importance of compliance and ethical standards with the university's standards.

### 3.3 Resources and Materials

I used articles on computational thinking and methodology of a case study in a cognitive science textbook provided to me by my mentors to develop the methodology of my research project and study. The software I used was Microsoft Excel, which was utilized to develop spreadsheet problems. Lastly, the participants of the project were students of beginner-level ICS courses, such as ICS 101 and 111.

### 3.4 Role of Researcher

My role as the researcher included a process of three steps. During the first step, I developed the proposal and the execution plan and/or design. This included going back and forth between my mentor and committee member to form the idea and the research process.

Throughout the second step, I collected written work in computational thinking, along with developing a group of problems in the program, Microsoft Excel, pseudocode, and natural language. The problem sets will allow observation in HCI and human usability in computing technology. The goal of the participants was to analyze and comprehend the problem and select the most accurate result in a series of multiple choice questions. During the summer of 2021, a pilot program was conducted for the Teaching Assistants of the ICS 101 class in order to formally develop the problem sets and formulate the final research design for the official study. In the pilot study, there were 9 problems each for spreadsheet, pseudocode, and natural language that was inputted in Laulima as a Quizzes, Tests and Surveys assessment for the 10 Teaching Assistants and two Honors Program student volunteers. The order of the 3 subgroups was in different order based on which test group they were a part of. To elaborate, the first group had questions that were: 3 spreadsheet, 3 pseudocode, and 3 natural language problems, group 2 had 3 pseudocode, 3 natural language, and 3 spreadsheet problems, and lastly, group 3 had 3 natural language, 3 spreadsheet, and 3 pseudocode problems.

*Example problems for the question number 1 for group 1, group 2, and group 3 tests developed on Google Forms respectively were the following:*

Pseudocode:

```
If student's grade is greater than or equal to 90
        Print "A"
Else if student's grade is greater than or equal to 80
        Print "B"
Else if student's grade is greater than or equal to 70
        Print "C"
Else if student's grade is greater than or equal to 60
        Print "D"
Else
        Print "F"
```

Question: If you type in 67, what would your result be?

Natural Language:

If the student's grade is at least 90, print out an A. If it
is below 90, but at least 80, print out a B. If it is below 80,
but at least 70, print out a C. If it is below 70, but at
least 60, print out a D. If not, print a F.

Question: If you type in 67, what would your result be?

Microsoft Excel (Spreadsheet):

| | A | B | C |
|---|---|---|---|
| 1 | Name | Score | Grade |
| 2 | Student A | 86 | |
| 3 | Student B | 77 | |
| 4 | Student C | 52 | |
| 5 | Student D | 100 | |
| 6 | Student E | 91 | |
| 7 | Student F | 82 | |
| 8 | Student G | 67 | |
| 9 | Student H | 73 | |
| 10 | Student I | 85 | |
| 11 | Student J | 97 | |

*fx*   =IF(B9>=90,"A",IF(B9>=80,"B",IF(B9>=70,"C",IF(B9>=60,"D","F"))))

Question: You have the following formula located in cell C8, what result does this
function provide, given the information that you have?

Several insights were gained from the pilot study that served in forming the problem
sets for the official study. The participants of the project were students of beginner-level
ICS courses, such as ICS 101 and 111. There were 101 students for ICS 101 and 11
students for ICS 111 that partook in the study. In the official study, which was created
on Google Forms instead of Laulima, there were 9 problems each for spreadsheet, pseudocode, and natural language, and the group of participants were divided into three test
groups where they received 3 different problems of each group set. To elaborate, in
the ICS 101 section, group 1 received 3 pseudocode, 3 natural language, and 3 spreadsheet problems, group 2 received 3 natural language, 3 spreadsheet, and 3 pseudocode
problems, and group 3 received 3 spreadsheet, 3 pseudocode, and 3 natural language
problems. The questions remained the same for all 9 problems, however, since there were
3 versions of each question in spreadsheet, pseudocode, and natural language, there was
a total of 27 problems created and 9 questions each for the three groups in ICS 101 and

three groups in ICS 111. That said, ICS 101 and ICS 111 groups had the same problem sets, such as group 1 for 101 and 111 both had 3 pseudocode problems, then 3 natural language problems, and lastly, 3 Microsoft Excel problems. The questions were written in multiple choice format, with one answer being the correct answer in all.

Finally, during the final step, I collected the data, analyzed the data results, and developed the conclusion.

*Example problems for the question number 9 for group 1, group 2, and group 3 tests developed on Google Forms respectively were the following:*

Microsoft Excel (Spreadsheet):

| ⯃ | A | B | C | D |
|---|---|---|---|---|
| 1 | | | Calories Chart | |
| 2 | | | | |
| 3 | DAY | Calories Eaten | Calories Burned | Workout More the Next Day? |
| 4 | Sunday | 2100 | 1500 | |
| 5 | Monday | 1500 | 1200 | |
| 6 | Tuesday | 1200 | 1200 | |
| 7 | Wednesday | 1800 | 1900 | |
| 8 | Thursday | 1700 | 1800 | |
| 9 | Friday | 2200 | 2000 | |
| 10 | Saturday | 2500 | 1200 | |

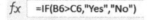 $fx$   =IF(B6>C6,"Yes","No")

Question: You have the following formula located in cell D6, what result does this function provide, given the information that you have?

Pseudocode:

```
If I eat more calories than I burn
    Print "I will work out more the next day"
Else Print "Do not work out"
```

Question: If I ate 1200 calories and burned 1200 calories today, what would my result be?

Natural Language:

```
If I eat more calories than I burn, I will work out more the
next day. Otherwise, I will not work out more the next day.
```

Question: If I ate 1200 calories and burned 1200 calories today, what would my result be?

# 4 Data Analysis

The results were analyzed to determine the accuracy rate and the time duration on each program. It was essential to understand the correlation between the correctness of the numbers and the amount of time taken on average by students. With the results, it could determine the program comprehension on average of the students based on the program with high performance, and to identify, based on their knowledge and literacy, their process in understanding and solving problems by computational thinking.

An item analysis was conducted using ANOVA: single factor tests (1) to compare the variance in the three programs within the three groups with their time duration and (2) to compare the variance in the three groups within the three programs with their time duration. The data analysis was conducted on only the official study for ICS 101 since it was a larger set, and more information could be obtained.

## 4.1 Section 1: Analysis Based on Program

**Microsoft Excel**
See Tables 1 and 2.

**Table 1.** Average for correctness of problems for Group 1, 2, and 3 on Microsoft Excel was 0.728395062, 0.888888889, and 0.733333333 respectively, with Group 2 with the highest performance. Group 1 had the third set of problems in Microsoft Excel, while Group 2 had their second set of problems, and Group 3 had their first set of problems in Microsoft Excel.

| ANOVA | | | | | | |
|---|---|---|---|---|---|---|
| Source of variation | SS | df | MS | F | P-value | F crit |
| Between groups | 0.595803284 | 2 | 0.297901642 | 4.663574614 | 0.011622715 | 3.089203013 |
| Within groups | 6.260082305 | 98 | 0.063878391 | | | |
| Total | 6.855885589 | 100 | | | | |

**Table 2.** Average for the time taken for Group 1, 2, and 3 on Microsoft Excel was 46 s, 45 s, and 1 min and 2 s respectively. Group 2 took the least amount of time on average but still attained the highest amount of correct answers on average.

| ANOVA | | | | | | |
|---|---|---|---|---|---|---|
| Source of variation | SS | df | MS | F | P-value | F crit |
| Between groups | 8.52024E–07 | 2 | 4.26012E–07 | 2.619700453 | 0.077535907 | 3.082014501 |
| Within groups | 1.72376E–05 | 106 | 1.62619E–07 | | | |
| Total | 1.80896E–05 | 108 | | | | |

**Pseudocode**

See Tables 3 and 4.

**Table 3.** Average for correctness of problems for Group 1, 2, and 3 on Microsoft Excel was 0.975308642, 0.743589744, and 0.876190476 respectively, with Group 1 with the highest performance. Group 1 had the first set of problems in Pseudocode, while Group 2 had their third set of problems, and Group 3 had their second set of problems in Pseudocode.

| ANOVA | | | | | | |
|---|---|---|---|---|---|---|
| Source of variation | SS | df | MS | F | P-value | F crit |
| Between groups | 0.889348634 | 2 | 0.444674317 | 10.07033197 | 0.000105319 | 3.089203013 |
| Within groups | 4.327373038 | 98 | 0.044156868 | | | |
| Total | 5.216721672 | 100 | | | | |

**Table 4.** Average for the time taken for Group 1, 2, and 3 on Pseudocode was 27 s, 44 s, and 31 s respectively. Group 1 took the least amount of time on average but still attained the highest number of correct answers on average.

| ANOVA | | | | | | |
|---|---|---|---|---|---|---|
| Source of variation | SS | df | MS | F | P-value | F crit |
| Between groups | 7.43743E–07 | 2 | 3.71872E–07 | 8.799659143 | 0.000305682 | 3.089203013 |

(*continued*)

**Table 4.** (*continued*)

| ANOVA | | | | | | | |
|---|---|---|---|---|---|---|---|
| Within groups | 4.14146E–06 | 98 | 4.22598E–08 | | | | |
| Total | 4.8852E–06 | 100 | | | | | |

## Natural Language
See Tables 5 and 6.

**Table 5.** Average for correctness of problems for Group 1, 2, and 3 on Microsoft Excel was 0.962962963, 0.965811966, and 0.838095238 respectively, with Group 2 with the highest performance by a small margin compared to Group 1. Group 1 had the second set of problems in natural language, while Group 2 had their first set of problems, and Group 3 had their third set of problems in natural language.

| ANOVA | | | | | | |
|---|---|---|---|---|---|---|
| Source of variation | SS | df | MS | F | P-value | F crit |
| Between groups | 0.366418034 | 2 | 0.183209017 | 5.984990277 | 0.003528941 | 3.089203013 |
| Within groups | 2.9999186 | 98 | 0.030611414 | | | |
| Total | 3.366336634 | 100 | | | | |

**Table 6.** Average for the time taken for Group 1, 2, and 3 on Pseudocode was 34 s, 38 s, and 42 s respectively. Group 1 took the least amount of time on average but still attained a high amount of correct answers on average.

| ANOVA | | | | | | |
|---|---|---|---|---|---|---|
| Source of variation | SS | df | MS | F | P-value | F crit |
| Between groups | 1.43218E–07 | 2 | 7.1609E–08 | 0.99835497 | 0.371798914 | 3.078819492 |
| Within groups | 7.88997E–06 | 110 | 7.1727E–08 | | | |
| Total | 8.03319E–06 | 112 | | | | |

It was shown in the results that on average, students performed higher and took the shortest amount of time on natural language than pseudocode and Microsoft Excel.

On average, students performed lower and took the longest time on Microsoft Excel compared to natural language and pseudocode.

### 4.2 Section 2: Analysis Based on Group

**Group 1**
See Tables 7 and 8.

**Table 7.** Average for correctness of problems for Group 1 on the programs pseudocode, natural language, and Microsoft Excel was 0.974358974, 0.961538462, and 0.730769231 respectively, with the highest performance for pseudocode. Group 1 had the first set of problems in pseudocode, the second set of problems in natural language, and the third set of problems in Microsoft Excel.

| ANOVA | | | | | | |
|---|---|---|---|---|---|---|
| *Source of variation* | *SS* | *df* | *MS* | *F* | *P-value* | *F crit* |
| Between groups | 0.977207977 | 2 | 0.488603989 | 13.44043887 | 1.02641E–05 | 3.118642128 |
| Within groups | 2.726495726 | 75 | 0.036353276 | | | |
| Total | 3.703703704 | 77 | | | | |

**Table 8.** Average for the time taken for Group 1 on the programs pseudocode, natural language, and Microsoft Excel was 28 s, 27 s, and 35 s respectively. Although Microsoft Excel had a longer time duration, the accuracy rate was lower compared to pseudocode and natural language.

| ANOVA | | | | | | |
|---|---|---|---|---|---|---|
| *Source of variation* | *SS* | *df* | *MS* | *F* | *P-value* | *F crit* |
| Between groups | 1.43495E–07 | 2 | 7.17473E–08 | 2.724328151 | 0.072084614 | 3.118642128 |
| Within groups | 1.97518E–06 | 75 | 2.63358E–08 | | | |
| Total | 2.11868E–06 | 77 | | | | |

## Group 2
See Tables 9 and 10.

**Table 9.** Average for correctness of problems for Group 2 on the program's natural language, Microsoft Excel, and pseudocode was 0.965811966, 0.888888889, and 0.743589744 respectively, with the highest performance for natural language. Group 1 had the first set of problems in natural language, the second set of problems in Microsoft Excel, and the third set of problems in pseudocode.

| ANOVA | | | | | | |
|---|---|---|---|---|---|---|
| Source of variation | SS | df | MS | F | P-value | F crit |
| Between groups | 0.993352327 | 2 | 0.496676163 | 16.34375 | 5.7434E–07 | 3.075852636 |
| Within groups | 3.464387464 | 114 | 0.030389364 | | | |
| Total | 4.457739791 | 116 | | | | |

**Table 10.** Average for the time taken for Group 2 on the programs natural language, Microsoft Excel, and pseudocode was 34 s, 45 s, and 44 s respectively. Although natural language had a shorter time duration, the accuracy rate was higher compared to Microsoft Excel and pseudocode.

| ANOVA | | | | | | |
|---|---|---|---|---|---|---|
| Source of variation | SS | df | MS | F | P-value | F crit |
| Between groups | 3.89852E–07 | 2 | 1.94926E–07 | 1.293608298 | 0.278274417 | 3.075852636 |
| Within groups | 1.7178E–05 | 114 | 1.50684E–07 | | | |
| Total | 1.75678E–05 | 116 | | | | |

## Group 3
See Tables 11 and 12.

**Table 11.** Average for correctness of problems for Group 3 on the programs Microsoft Excel, pseudocode, and natural language was 0.733333333, 0.876190476, and 0.838095238 respectively, with the highest performance for natural language. Group 3 had the first set of problems in Microsoft Excel, the second set of problems in pseudocode, and the third set of problems in natural language.

| ANOVA | | | | | | |
|---|---|---|---|---|---|---|
| Source of variation | SS | df | MS | F | P-value | F crit |
| Between groups | 0.383068783 | 2 | 0.191534392 | 2.64347079 | 0.075983386 | 3.085465033 |
| Within groups | 7.39047619 | 102 | 0.072455649 | | | |
| Total | 7.773544974 | 104 | | | | |

**Table 12.** Average for the time taken for Group 3 on the programs Microsoft Excel, pseudocode, and natural language was 1 min and 2 s, 31 s, and 42 s respectively. Although pseudocode had a shorter time duration, the accuracy rate was higher compared to Microsoft Excel and natural language.

| ANOVA | | | | | | |
|---|---|---|---|---|---|---|
| Source of variation | SS | df | MS | F | P-value | F crit |
| Between groups | 2.37172E–06 | 2 | 1.18586E–06 | 12.08347123 | 1.95157E–05 | 3.085465033 |
| Within groups | 1.00102E–05 | 102 | 9.81388E–08 | | | |
| Total | 1.23819E–05 | 104 | | | | |

It was shown in the results that on average, students performed higher on their first and second problem sets except for Group 3 which performed higher on their second and third problem sets.

## 5   Conclusion

Throughout the data collection and analysis, there were two realizations found that supported in the determination of the students' computer literacy and cognitive science abilities to solve problems.

The first pattern that was detected while analyzing the results was that the students that took a longer time on average on problem sets usually performed lower than the students who took a relatively shorter time and obtained the correct answer. This displays that the students who took longer on problems were actively trying to understand a problem they had no prior experience or knowledge of, or they weren't as comfortable with.

Microsoft Excel requires knowledge of function in order to understand what a program is doing, on the other hand, natural language does not require external information or knowledge of the matter. Students who took longer on problems and achieved an incorrect answer had thoroughly tried to understand the problem using cognitive processes but selected a choice that they felt was close rather than what they knew was correct by going through a series of steps.

Secondly, on average, Microsoft Excel was the hardest program to comprehend despite being the program the students were most acquainted with. On the other hand, natural language was the easiest on average for two out of three groups despite students not having computing literacy of the fundamentals of the program. With the results given, a conclusion can be made that students were able to perform higher on programs that required extensive specific knowledge but were efficient in doing well for programs where they could use the cognitive science methodology of solving problems through steps they already grasped and understood. That being said, not only is it essential for students to learn material, but also to go through a process of understanding what they learned and how they were able to obtain the information matter.

**Acknowledgement.** This material is based upon work supported by the National Science Foundation (NSF) under Grant No. 1662487. Any opinions, findings, and conclusions or recommendations expressed in this material are those of the authors and do not necessarily reflect the views of the NSF.

# References

Boring, R.L.: Human-computer interaction as cognitive science. In: Proceedings of the Human Factors and Ergonomics Society Annual Meeting, vol. 46, no. 21, 1767–1771 (2002). http://journals.sagepub.com/doi/https://doi.org/10.1177/154193120204602103

Butler, K.A., Jacob, R.J.K., John, B.E.: Human-computer interaction: introduction and overview. In: CHI 98 Conference Summary on Human Factors in Computing Systems, pp. 105–106 (1998). https://dl.acm.org/doi/https://doi.org/10.1145/286498.286556

Cairns, P., Adams, A., Lunt, P.: A qualitative approach to HCI research. Res. Meth. Hum.-Comput. Interact. **138–139**, 152–153 (2008)

Carroll, J.M.: Human-computer interaction: psychology as a science of design. Annu. Rev. Psychol. **46**, 62–64 (1997). https://doi.org/10.1146/annurev.psych.48.1.61

Carroll, J.M., Long, J., Brooks, R.: Comparative task analysis: An alternative direction for human-computer interaction science. Design. Interact. Psychol. Hum.-Comput. Interf. 50–52 (1991)

Friedenberg, J., Silverman, G.: Introduction: exploring inner space; artificial intelligence II: operational perspective, robotics: The ultimate intelligent agents, conclusion: where we go from here. Cogn. Sci. Introduction Study Mind **10**, 356 (2006)

Lardinois, F.: Microsoft uses GPT-3 to let you code in natural language. TechCrunch.com (2021). https://techcrunch.com/2021/05/25/microsoft-uses-gpt-3-to-let-you-code-in-natural-language/

Lister, R.: On the cognitive development of the novice programmer and the development of a computing education researcher. In: 9th Computer Science Education Research Conference (CSERC 2020), pp. 1–15 (2020)

McCarthy, J., Wright, P.: Putting felt-life at the centre of human–computer interaction (HCI). Cogn. Technol. Work, **7**(1), 262–263, 265–267 (2005). https://doi-org.eres.library.manoa.hawaii.edu/https://doi.org/10.1007/s10111-005-0011-y

Oren, M.: Human-Computer Interaction and Sociological Insight: A Theoretical Examination and Experiment in Building Affinity in Small Groups. Graduate Theses and Dissertations, pp. 153–157 (2011). https://doi.org/10.31274/etd-180810-1365

Sharafi, Z., Sharif, B., Gueheneuc, Y., Begel, A., Bednarik, R., Crosby, M.: A practical guide on conducting eye tracking studies in software engineering. Empirical Softw. Eng. **25**(5), 3128-3174 (2021)

Siegmund, J., et al.: Measuring neural efficiency of program comprehension. In: Proceedings of 2017 11th Joint Meeting of the European Software Engineering Conference and the ACM SIGSOFT Symposium on the Foundations of Software Engineering, Paderborn, Germany, 4–8 September 2017 (ESEC/FSE 2017), vol. 11 (2017). https://doi.org/10.1145/3106237.3106268

Stephanidis, C.: User interfaces for all: new perspectives into human-computer interaction. Hum. Factors Ergon. 1, 3-17 (2001). http://citeseerx.ist.psu.edu/viewdoc/download?doi=10.1.1.98.4790&rep=rep1&type=pdf

Stephanidis, C., et al.: Seven HCI grand challenges. Int. J. Hum.-Comput. Interact. **35**(14), 1229–1230 (2019). https://doi.org/10.1080/10447318.2019.1619259

Wing, J.M.: Computational thinking. Commun. ACM, **49**(3), 33–35 (2006). http://www.cs.cmu.edu/~./15110-s13/Wing06-ct.pdf

Xiong, A., Proctor, R.W.: Information processing: the language and analytical tools for cognitive psychology in the information age. Front. Psychol. **9**(1), 1–2 (2018). https://doi.org/10.3389/fpsyg.2018.01270

# A Review of Framework for Machine Learning Interpretability

Ivo de Abreu Araújo[⊠][iD], Renato Hidaka Torres[iD],
and Nelson Cruz Sampaio Neto[iD]

Post-Graduate Program in Computing Science, Federal University of Pará,
R. Augusto Corrêa, 01, Belém, PA 66075-110, Brazil
ivo94@hotmail.com, {renatohidaka,nelsonneto}@ufpa.br
http://www.ufpa.br/ppgcc

**Abstract.** There is a need for several applications to interpret the predictions made by machine learning algorithms. In light of this, this paper provides a literature review with the aim of analyzing the use of interpretable frameworks, which are tools coupled to algorithms for a better understanding of output predictions. Altogether, 10 frameworks were cited, and LIME occurred most frequently in the 26 studies included in the review, following a previous analysis of 143 scientific articles. Finally, when the interpretation of the LIME and SHAP frameworks were compared qualitatively, and similar behaviors were observed in the interpretations generated in the neural network and random forest that allow understanding features that influence particular predictions of non-transparent models considered black boxes.

**Keywords:** Interpretable framework · Black box explanation · Model explanation

## 1 Introduction

Machine learning algorithms have led to advances in a wide range of areas where decision-making is of critical importance, such as health, transport monitoring services, information security and finance. According to [1,2], machine learning has enabled industrial and other sectors to make use of data for application development which can thus provide intelligent solutions, for example, recommendation systems (RecSys), computer vision (CV) and voice recognition.

With regard to the interpretability and explainability concepts of algorithms, there is no full agreement among the members of the machine learning community. In view of this, [4] states that interpretability can be defined as the understanding of the user with regard to what the model has decided when making a prediction, whereas explainability seeks to justify the grounds on which a model has made a decision. [3] notes that the explainability of an algorithm is carried

D. D. Schmorrow and C. M. Fidopiastis (Eds.): HCII 2022, LNAI 13310, pp. 261–272, 2022.
https://doi.org/10.1007/978-3-031-05457-0_21

out through its capacity to determine the features that are either directly or indirectly involved in a prediction. [5] believes that interpretability is closely related to a human being's capacity to grasp both the prediction of a model and its ability to provide an understanding of its results in a consistent manner. In contrast, explainability refers to any kind of technique that can assist users and developers to understand the possible reasons why their models behave in a particular way. On the basis of these definitions, it is clear that explainability is more wide-ranging and explicit, while interpretability tends to be more implicit. This paper focuses on the issue of explainability.

According to [6], interpretable machine learning algorithms, (also called white-box models) allow an understanding of the inner mechanisms of the algorithm, based on an analysis of the input parameters. However, these algorithms do not always have the best predictive performance. In contrast, non-interpretive algorithms also called black-box models are those where the analysis of the input parameters does not provide an understanding of its inner mechanisms, although they generally have a better predictive performance than the white box models.

In summary, solving problems arising from the use of machine learning algorithms is faced with a dilemma, which is how to choose between the predictive performance and capacity for interpretation of the models. Researchers are seeking to overcome this impasse by establishing a framework with a view to opening the black box model and making the results obtained from them more reliable. Thus, it is essential for data scientists and specialists in decision-making to understand how this framework operates and in what area it is being used.

As a means of assisting this understanding, this article conducts a literature review to investigate exactly what kind of framework is being used, as well as its contextual application and machine learning algorithms. It should be stressed that this research study has not focused on any particular interpretability method [8], or any general approach such as that of [9,10]. It is also worth noting that no work of an investigative character was found among the 143 pre-selected scientific articles.

The results of the review are not designed to be systematic, although they follow the adaptation protocol set out by [7]. They demonstrate that frameworks of interpretability such as LIME (Local Interpretable Model-Agnostic Explanations) and SHAP (Shapley Additive Explanations), when coupled with the black box model machine learning algorithms like Random Forest and neural networks, make it possible to determine the factors that lead to the predictions and thus enable the specialists to carry out their decision-making more securely.

This article is divided into the following sections. Section 2 sets out the review protocol. Section 3 addresses issues arising from the answers to the research questions. Finally, Sect. 4 summarizes the conclusions.

## 2    Review Protocol

The aim of this review was to examine the following research questions:(i) Q1. What is the type of framework in the current literature that can assist in the process of interpreting machine learning algorithms? (ii) Q2. What are the machine learning algorithms that are being investigated? (iii) Q3. What are the application approaches being adopted to make an assessment of the interpretability of machine learning algorithms? (iv) Q4. What are the strengths and weaknesses of the kinds of frameworks being examined?

The search string shown in Fig. 1 was used to look for studies in the following repositories of scientific articles: (i) IEEE Xplore Digital Library[1]; (ii) ACM Digital Library[2]; (iii) ScienceDirect[3]. The following inclusion criteria were defined to filter the studies that fell within the scope of the review: (i) The presence of some part of the search string in the title or abstract of the article;(ii) Articles published in the period between 2015 and 2020; (iii) A Reading of the abstract to determine whether the article uses or establishes an interpretability framework for the machine learning models; (iv) Articles written in English. Any articles that failed to meet all the criteria were excluded from the review. After the articles that made up a part of the review had been selected, the general features that are summarized in Table 1 (Sect. 3) were extracted.

("framework of interpretability of machine learning") OR ("tool of interpretability in machine learning") OR ("tools of explainability of machine learning models") OR ("framework of explainability of machine learning") OR ("interpretable machine learning tool") OR ("interpretable machine learning") OR ("explanable machine learning tools") OR ("explainable frameworks of machine learning") OR ("explainability of machine learning models") OR ("performance of framework of interpretability machine learning") OR ("machine learning interpretability techniques") OR ("decipherable machine learning") OR ("understandable machine learning") OR ("explicable machine learning")

**Fig. 1.** The search string used to find the candidates of the scientific articles that formed a part of the review. Prepared by the author.

The process of handling the review was carried out in the period from 2nd January to 25th June, 2020. The application of string matching in the IEEE, ACM Digital and ScienceDirect repositories returned 82, 49 and 12 articles respectively. It should be noted that there was no convergence between the replies from the repositories. After the inclusion filters, 26 articles were selected for the reading and data extraction. The data obtained from each article are summarized in Table 1.

## 3 Analysis of the Research Questions

### 3.1 Q1. What Are the Types of Framework in the Current Literature that Can Assist in the Process of Interpreting Machine Learning Algorithms?

Table 1, Column 2 illustrates the frameworks that the selected articles adopted to undertake the interpretability of the machine learning algorithms. Of the 10

---

[1] http://ieeexplore.ieee.org.
[2] http://dl.acm.org.
[3] http://sciencedirect.com.

frameworks that were observed, LIME was the most widely used since it was found in 73% of the articles. This reveals the importance of LIME in current research on this issue. SHAP was the second most used framework and found in three of the studies. Other frameworks that are well known in the literature were also noted, such as Georgias, Anchors and PDP (Partial Dependence Plots).

**Table 1.** A summarized view of the frameworks, machine learning algorithms and area of application, that were examined by the 26 articles included in the review.

| Authors | Framework | Algorithm | Application Area |
|---|---|---|---|
| [11] | SHAP | Random Forest | Traffic |
| [12] | LIME | DNN | Health |
| [13] | LIME | Random Forest | NLP |
| [14] | LIME | DNN | Health |
| [15] | LIME | Random Forest and AdaBoost | Health |
| [16] | LIME | NN | Security |
| [17] | LIME | NN | Biology |
| [18] | LIME | NN and SVM | NLP |
| [19] | LIME | Random Forest | NLP |
| [20] | LIME | XGBoost | Health |
| [21] | LIME and PDP | Random Forest | NLP |
| [22] | LIME and Counterfactual | DNN | Finance |
| [23] | LIME | DNN | Traffic |
| [24] | LIME | NN | CV |
| [25] | LIME | DNN | NLP |
| [26] | LIME | TPOT | AD Signal |
| [27] | LIME | Decision Tree | RecSys |
| [29] | LIME | DNN | CV |
| [28] | LIME | DNN | AD Signal |
| [30] | LIME, SHAP and ANCHORS | Random Forest | Health |
| [31] | SHAP | XGBoost | Finance |
| [32] | Georgias | Random Forest | Health |
| [33] | IRTED-TL | AdaBoost | Finance |
| [34] | SURF | DNN | Health |
| [35] | Just in Time | Random Forest | Finance |
| [36] | IDS | CN2 e BDL | Health |

The following subtitles have been added to Table 1: Deep Neural Network (DNN); Neural Network (NN); Support Vector Machine (SVM); Natural Language Processing (NLP); CN2 Induction Algorithm (CN2); Bayesian Decision Lists (BDL); Tree-based Pipeline Optimization Tool (TPOT); Analog/Digital (AD) Signal; Interpretable Decision Sets (IDS); Inter-Region Tax Evasion Detection method based on Transfer Learning (IRTED-TL); Speeded-Up Robust Features (SURF). Altogether, five studies established interpretability frameworks for models derived from black box algorithms which are: [22, 33–36]. For example, the counterfactual framework established by [22], provided interpretations of a neural network with a view to deconstructing its complexity and understanding the decisions made by the black box model. An assessment was made of this approach by employing LIME in the same context, which by yielding more significant results, led to a greater degree of trust in the algorithm being used.

As is made clear by [37], LIME is an interpretability framework for machine learning models that make an interpretation of an instance by disturbing it and generating similar synthetic data. This is carried out by using a linear model that makes it possible to map out and understand the result of a model prediction locally. SHAP is another approach to interpreting model predictions, where it is often used in black box models and operates similarly to game theory, which involves regarding the features as players that are given an attribute called SHAPY. This assists in the way the interpretations of the models are carried out and understood by the users, since it means the black boxes are open and can be fully explored [38].

Only two studies [11] e [31] make use of interpretability in both a global and local sphere in their analyses. The other studies only adopt a local approach. According to [3], global interpretability can be regarded as more comprehensive since it seeks to understand a model in general terms or, in other words, as holistic. In contrast, local interpretability is more specific and concentrates on an individual sample with regard to a part of the model, known as local. Thus, it is clear that most of the studies concentrated on understanding individual predictions.

### 3.2   Q2. What Are the Machine Learning Algorithms that Are Being Investigated?

The machine learning algorithms in the selected articles can be seen in Table 1 Column 3. The fact that the Random Forest algorithm has been the most widely investigated (with 8 citations) can be explained by LIME, since when it was published by [37], the way it operated was demonstrated by means of this algorithm. However, the efficiency of the interpretability of these most popular frameworks needs to be examined when they are coupled with other algorithms.

The use of algorithms in the filtered studies can be more clearly checked in percentage terms in Fig. 2. It should be noted that the great majority (92.4%) examined the interpretability in the black box model and only two studies (7.6%) in the white box namely [36] and [27]. These figures were expected given the fact that the use of interpretability mechanisms is an alternative means of

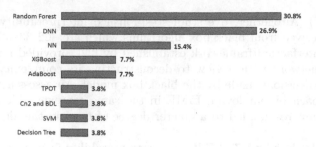

**Fig. 2.** Machine learning algorithms used in the selected articles. Prepared by the author.

understanding algorithms that have an inherent lack of transparency. Random Forest and neural methods were used in 80.7% of the filtered works. XGBoost and AdaBoost were employed in two studies, and the other algorithms in only one article. In other words, the more complex algorithms have been the target of research studies on interpretability, since they take account of the importance of understanding the way the black box model operate.

### 3.3   Q3. What Are the Areas in Which the Frameworks for the Interpretability of Algorithms Are Being Applied?

The areas being examined by the filtered articles are shown in Table 1, Column 4, together with further information in Fig. 3. As well as their traditional applications, such as for health and finance, it is evident that the frameworks of interpretability have been used in various other machine learning areas such as natural language processing and computer vision. Studies conducted by [36], [30] and [22] have examined interpretability in machine learning in more than one operational area.

### 3.4   Q4. What Are the Strengths and Weaknesses of the Frameworks being Examined?

When answering this research question, account should be taken of the two most common frameworks in the review of LIME and SHAP, which are open to question since both are applicable to any kind of model. Its purpose should be to analyze the quality of each interpretation in the local context of a sample to determine if there is a degree of equivalence in the results that can allow one to find out which framework provides an interpretation that is more intuitive and closer to the users in the black box models.

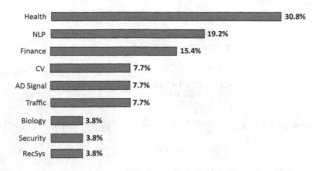

**Fig. 3.** Areas explored by the selected articles. Prepared by the author.

When creating a setting to make a comparison between the LIME and SHAP frameworks, a Random Forest (RF) and a Neural Network (NN) were chosen with 0.74 and 0.77 degree of accuracy, respectively. In this way, four interpretation models RF+LIME, RF+SHAP, NN+LIME and NN+SHAP were analyzed.

A database published by [39] was used to assess the predictive performance of the algorithms and the interpretive capacity of the models. It has a binary domain classification which, with regard to the diagnosis of patients with diabetes, shows an imbalance of 500 instances for Class 0 (patients without diabetes) and 268 for Class 1 (patients with diabetes) with a total of eight features. The RF model was designed on the basis of a standard set of hyperparameters. With regard to the neural network, it was decided to use an architecture based on [40], which is a kind of feed-forward network with five layers that has a total of 127 neurons and 4.051 trained parameters. An instance was selected at random which was correctly classified by the algorithms as positive for diabetes. This instance was then submitted to the interpretation of the LIME and SHAP frameworks, which were coupled with the RF and NN black box algorithms.

The result obtained from the interpretation of LIME of a positive sample for diabetes, can be seen in Part A of Fig. 4 which is displayed through the features with colored bars for each class and varies in size depending on the importance attached to its respective weights. It was clear that the Glucose feature with a value of 168, had the greatest influence on the predicted positive result of the neural network, since when the value of this feature is greater than 140.25, the model treats it as a positive factor for the prediction of diabetes. This explanatory logic applies to the other features such as BMI and Pregnancies that were also important in the prediction. Other key factors are the Feature and Value columns which list the values of the predicted sample features in order of importance these are highlighted in orange to show the influence of the class with diabetes and blue for the class without diabetes.

In Fig. 4B, there is a SHAP interpretation which also displays a graphic representation of the features through red bars for Class 1 and blue for the class without diabetes. The Glucose feature was the most significant because its value tends to increase the base value for prediction from 0.33 to 0.66 to show the risk

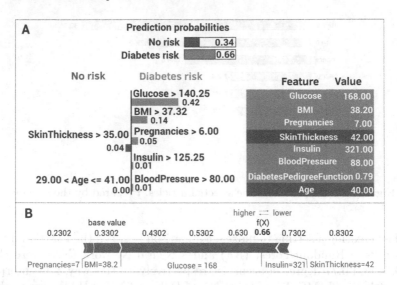

**Fig. 4.** Results of the interpretation of the LIME and SHAP frameworks in the neural network for a Class 1 sample (with diabetes). Prepared by the author. (Color figure online)

of diabetes. It should be noted that the BMI and Pregnancies features had the same order of importance for both frameworks.

Figure 5A shows the LIME interpretation for the prediction of a sample for Random Forest (Class 1), it is worth highlighting the three features that are treated by the model as a determining factor for the result Glucose, BMI and DiabetesPedigreeFunction. In Fig. 5B, there is the result from SHAP where Glucose was also considered to be the most important feature for the prediction. The other parameters in both the frameworks diverged with regard to their degree of predictive importance. It should also be noted that SHAP did not attach importance to the Insulin feature when making this prediction, which, in the case of LIME, had a negative influence.

With regard to the results of the LIME and SHAP interpretations, it can be concluded that LIME provides a more intuitive explanation of the features used for mathematical operators, which suggests that the range of values adopted for the feature are of significance for the prediction. It is worth pointing out that if the name of the feature is too long, LIME tends to conceal the graphic information. On the question of how the local interpretation of SHAP is carried out, we found that the task of understanding the influences for each class of the features is more implicit and not so friendly as in LIME which gives the result in a more detailed way and is closer to everyday speech, as also in the approach adopted by [21,30]. It should be underlined that SHAP only displays the most important features whereas LIME makes it possible to understand the influence of each feature that can be found among the classes in greater detail, even if it is very slight.

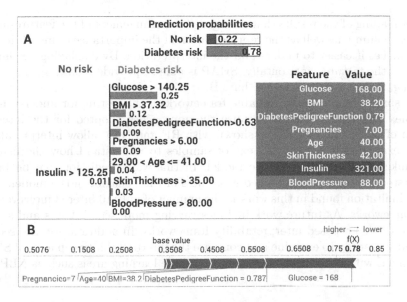

**Fig. 5.** Results of the interpretation of the LIME and SHAP frameworks with regard to Random Forest for a Class 1 sample (with diabetes). Prepared by the author.

The results from the frameworks for an RF and NN in Fig. 4 and 5, support the idea that the interpretations made by the frameworks can assist in choosing a model that has a greater degree of accuracy and can make interpretations of a problem in a more consistent way. In view of the fact that the user is the main target of the interpretation, clarity is essential in the interpretations and this was a noticeable factor in the case of LIME, owing to the points mentioned above. It should be stressed that SHAP provides a more detailed dossier than LIME, which adds weight to its interpretative methods as well as providing a method for a global interpretation, which is beyond the scope of this research question.

## 4   Conclusions

This study conducted a literature review with the aim of exploring the use of frameworks which can assist in the interpretation of predictions carried out by machine learning algorithms. The use of interpretability frameworks took on a leading role in the area of data science, from the time when it was found that simply having a good predictive performance is not enough for many domains such as medical and diagnostic prediction. Currently, specialists also have to understand what kind of inner parameters, among other factors, can enable these models to yield good results.

From a qualitative standpoint, it was found that among the LIME and SHAP frameworks that were prominent in the review, the output of LIME provided a better reading of the results that emerged. The arrangement of the features in the vertical column, as well as the representation of the importance of individualized bars, makes it easier to understand the interpretation. By displaying the importance of the features horizontally, SHAP is able to provide a data misalignment reading, for example in Fig. 5, Chart B.

In summary, the use of valuable frameworks is interesting for understanding complex algorithms. This is because the approaches adopted for the interpretation of black box models (as shown with RF and NN), allow interpretability to be examined in a local context of samples to understand how the features are linked to the output of the model. In this way, prediction can be better understood through a heightened awareness of the behavior of the model.

A limitation found in this work is the number of only 10 filtered interpretability frameworks. As future work includes varying more search bases and strings to find other proposed interpretability frameworks. In addition, we also seek to extend this study to examine and compare the interpretability capacity of SHAP and LIME with other frameworks, and machine learning areas such as NLP and CV.

# References

1. Jordan, M.I., Mitchell, T.M.: Machine learning: trends, perspectives, and prospects. Science **349**(6245), 255–260 (2015)
2. Yang, C., Rangarajan, A., Ranka, S.: Global model interpretation via recursive partitioning (2018)
3. Ahmad, I.: 40 algorithms every programmer should know: hone your problem-solving skills by learning different algorithms and their implementation in Python (2020)
4. Nielsen, A.: Practical Fairness. O'Reilly Media Inc., Newton (2021)
5. Masis, S.: Interpretable Machine Learning with python: learn to build interpretable high-performance models with hands-on real-world examples (2021)
6. Molnar, C.: Interpretable machine learning: a guide for making black box models explainable (2020)
7. Briner, R., Denyer, D.: Systematic review and evidence synthesis as a practice and scholarship tool (2012)
8. He, C., Ma, M., Wang, P.: Extract interpretability-accuracy balanced rules from artificial neural networks: a review. Neurocomputing **387**, 346–358 (2020)
9. Xu, Feiyu, Uszkoreit, Hans, Du, Yangzhou, Fan, Wei, Zhao, Dongyan, Zhu, Jun: Explainable AI: a brief survey on history, research areas, approaches and challenges. In: Tang, Jie, Kan, Min-Yen., Zhao, Dongyan, Li, Sujian, Zan, Hongying (eds.) NLPCC 2019. LNCS (LNAI), vol. 11839, pp. 563–574. Springer, Cham (2019). https://doi.org/10.1007/978-3-030-32236-6_51
10. Linardatos, P., Papastefanopoulos, V., Kotsiantis, S.: Explainable AI: a review of machine learning interpretability methods. Entropy **23**, 18 (2020)
11. Barredo-Arrieta, A., Laña, I., Del Ser, J.: What lies beneath: a note on the explainability of black-box machine learning models for road traffic forecasting (2019)
12. Oni, O., Qiao, S.: Model-agnostic interpretation of cancer classification with multiplatform genomic data, pp. 34–41 (2019)

13. Kumari, P., Haddela, P.S.: Use of LIME for human interpretability in sinhala document classification, pp. 97–102 (2019)
14. Malhi, A., Kampik, T., Pannu, H., Madhikermi, M., Främling, K.: Explaining machine learning-based classifications of in-vivo gastral images, pp. 1–7 (2019)
15. Czejdo, D., Bhattacharya, S., Spooner, C.: Improvement of protein model scoring using grouping and interpreter for machine learning, pp. 0349–0353 (2019)
16. Tolan, S., Miron, M., Gómez, E., Castillo, C.: Why machine learning may lead to unfairness: evidence from risk assessment for juvenile justice in catalonia (2019)
17. Spinner, Thilo, Schlegel, Udo, Hauptmann, Hanna, El-Assady, Mennatallah: explAIner: a visual analytics framework for interactive and explainable machine learning. IEEE Trans. Vis. Comput. Graph. **26**, 1064–1074 (2019)
18. Teso, S., Kersting, K.: Explanatory interactive machine learning, pp. 239–245 (2019)
19. Nagrecha, S., Dillon, J., Chawla, N.: MOOC dropout prediction: lessons learned from making pipelines interpretable. In: WWW 2017 Companion: Proceedings of the 26th International Conference on World Wide Web Companion (2017)
20. Zhang, A., Lam, S., Liu, N., Pang, Y., Chan, L., Tang, P.: Development of a radiology decision support system for the classification of MRI brain scans, pp. 107–115 (2018)
21. De Aquino, R., Cozman, F.: Natural language explanations of classifier behavior, pp. 239–242 (2019)
22. Mothilal, R., Sharma, A., Tan, C.: Explaining machine learning classifiers through diverse counterfactual explanations, pp. 607–617 (2020)
23. Preece, A., Harborne, D., Raghavendra, R., Tomsett, R., Braines, D.: Provisioning robust and interpretable AI/ML-based service bundles, pp. 1–9 (2018)
24. Fong, R., Vedaldi, A.: Interpretable explanations of black boxes by meaningful perturbation (2017)
25. Singh, J., Anand, A.: EXS: explainable search using local model agnostic interpretability. In: WSDM 2019: Proceedings of the Twelfth ACM International Conference on Web Search and Data Mining (2019)
26. Zhang, W., Ge, P., Jin, W., Guo, J.: Radar signal recognition based on TPOT and LIME (2018)
27. Koh, S., Wi, H., Kim, B., Jo, S.: Personalizing the prediction: interactive and interpretable machine learning, pp. 354–359 (2019)
28. Mampaka, M., Sumbwanyambe, M.: Poor data throughput root cause analysis in mobile networks using deep neural network, pp. 1–6 (2019)
29. Schuessler, M., Weiß, P.: Minimalistic explanations: capturing the essence of decisions, pp. 1–6 (2019)
30. El Shawi, R., Sherif, Y., Al-Mallah, M., Sakr, S.: Interpretability in healthcare: a comparative study of local machine learning interpretability techniques. Comput. Intell. **37**, 1633–1650 (2020)
31. Messalas, A., Makris, C., Kanellopoulos, Y.: Model-agnostic interpretability with shapley values (2019)
32. Prentzas, N., Pattichis, C., Kakas, A.: Integrating machine learning with symbolic reasoning to build an explainable AI model for stroke prediction (2019)
33. Zhu, X., Ruan, J., Zheng, Q., Dong, B.: IRTED-TL: an inter-region tax evasion detection method based on transfer learning (2018)
34. Costa, P., Galdran, A., Smailagic, A., Campilho, A.: A weakly-supervised framework for interpretable diabetic retinopathy detection on retinal images. IEEE Access **6**, 18747–18758 (2018)

35. Boer, N., Deutch, D., Frost, N., Milo, T.: Just in time: personal temporal insights for altering model decisions (2020)
36. Lakkaraju, H., Bach, S., Leskovec, J.: Interpretable decision sets: a joint framework for description and prediction. In: KDD: Proceedings. International Conference on Knowledge Discovery and Data Mining (2016)
37. Ribeiro, M., Singh, S., Guestrin, C.: "Why should i trust you?": explaining the predictions of any classifier (2016)
38. Lundberg, S., Lee, S.-I.: A unified approach to interpreting model predictions (2017)
39. Vincent, S.: Research Center. https://www.kaggle.com/mathchi/diabetes-dataset, Accessed 4 Oct 2021
40. Lad, R.: https://www.kaggle.com/richalad/parkinsons-predictions, Accessed 6 Oct 2021

# Abstracting the Understanding and Application of Cognitive Load in Computational Thinking and Modularized Learning

Taylor Gabatino[✉], Michael-Brian C. Ogawa, and Martha E. Crosby

Department of Information and Computer Sciences, University of Hawaii at Manoa,
1680 East-West Road, Honolulu, HI 96822, USA
{tgabatin,ogawam,crosby}@hawaii.edu

**Abstract.** The purpose of this study is to determine whether modularized standalone sections within topics in computer science are deterministic in the performance of students studying subjects that involve computational thinking. Teaching methods regarding this form of cognition within the realm of computer science is presented with a limited understanding in how students think and analyze problems when presented material with ambiguous forms of approach. The method and scope of the work involve the presentation of topics in computer science in a modularized form that determines whether correctness is a function of time based on cognitive load introduced in computational thinking concepts, involving base conversions of transposition ciphers and programming fundamentals.

**Keywords:** Cognitive load and performance · Shared cognition · Team performance and decision making · Understanding human cognition and behavior in complex tasks and environment

## 1 Introduction

Computational Thinking (CT) has become one of the most important skills of the 21$^{st}$ century, with problems being solved not only in the realm of computer science, but its applicable partners within the educational community, and a primary fundamental in modern scientific disciplines [2, 5]. As CT skills increase within the digital society, teaching these abilities become an essential factor in the arsenal of educators; however, there is a limitation of understanding between both students and instructors in what methodologies are best employed in CT. Although Wing [5] states CT to be a fundamental skill, there is still much speculation as to what it truly embodies, with a general knowledge consensus that it comprises of problem-solving skills such as abstraction and decomposition [3, 5]. This invokes a need to design teaching methodologies that are best proposed for this - in particular, how cognitive load changes with the level of difficulty in CT.

Methodologies involved in teaching CT are often invoked in assisting students to understand concepts in computer science that are devised to test pattern recognition, abstraction, and algorithmic design [8]. As the development of teaching computer science grows substantially through the years, there exists the correlation of the demand for CT

© The Author(s), under exclusive license to Springer Nature Switzerland AG 2022
D. D. Schmorrow and C. M. Fidopiastis (Eds.): HCII 2022, LNAI 13310, pp. 273–286, 2022.
https://doi.org/10.1007/978-3-031-05457-0_22

education to increase as a result of the parallels of technological growth in the digital society [4]. Although various studies have been introduced to meet the demands of teaching CT, there is a growing complexity in the field to also meet the difficulties of employers outside of the technological realm.

As computational degrees become increasingly lucrative in modern society, it is argued that it should be a basis for comprehension, as it begins to influence disciplines in fields beyond STEM, with areas of study active in the algorithmic design within social sciences and humanities [1, 6]. In addition, curriculum across the United States along with an increasing number of other countries have begun to adopt CT as a necessity in addition to the base requirements in K-12 schools [14]. Furthermore, universities have also begun to propose computational thinking as a requirement for non-STEM majors systematically introducing them to the teaching curriculum [2]. Various assertions recognize that there is also a common misconception associated with CT, with its alignment primarily associated in computer science [14]. Wing [17] however, states that students should be given the opportunity to participate in a digital society by becoming competent in CT, regardless of their relation to computer science and STEM.

The understanding of CT to abstraction and problem solving; however, is vastly misunderstood. In addition to the pilot study performed, a survey amongst students in the experiment were distributed asking what they best believed computational thinking to be.

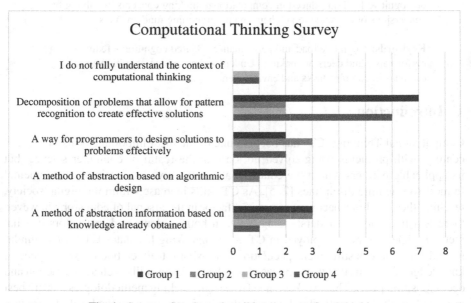

**Fig. 1.** Survey of students describing computational thinking

Results from the survey showed varying discrepancies between the understanding of CT, and how to best use it for abstraction and decomposition of proposed problems. This is further expanded within the pilot study, where questions introduced in modularized pedagogy propose varying cognitive load as a function of time in seconds.

We specifically begin this analysis through discussion of both CT and Cognitive Load, and its relation to methodologies involved in teaching these approaches and methods of thinking to students. This discussion can then further how human cognitive architecture can thus be chunked into sub-divisions that allow for the highest capacity of working memory to be recorded quantitatively and qualitatively. The corresponding experiment associated with how working memory intertwines with cognitive load are thus introduced. Lastly, we look at the associations between correctness of question and time when tested with topics involving ASCII, HEX, Binary, and Programming Fundamentals, providing the evidence for the principle of cognitive load and its determinant of performance.

## 2 Background

### 2.1 Computational Thinking and Cognitive Load

Computational thinking, as defined by Wing are the thought processes that are involved with the formulation of problems and their relative solutions such that they are represented effectively by a potential information-processing agent [6]. It is within reason, thus, that there is a significant level of cognitive load that is placed on individuals when presented with problems that require mental processing contributed to learning, memory, and problem-solving [7]. This cognitive load, based on concepts in cognitive science act as the agent of an information-processing approach, with the mind divided into sensory, working, and long-term memory [7].

Cognitive Load theory as described by Sweller is based on the model that the mind works in two sets [7]. The first set proposes that the human working memory is constrained to a limited capacity, which determines performance based on cognitive load, while the second imposes mechanisms that are designed to elude its weaknesses [7]. As there are a multitude of sensory processors that are used within a cognitive load, the information processing works in conjunction with these sensors to meet the demands of human cognitive architecture [7].

Working memory, often termed *short-term memory* or *intermediate memory* interchangeably, refers to the temporary availability of information that is recalled through a recollection of recent scenarios [10]. This concept, based on Miller [11] introduces a capacity on information processing such that it can be limited to several familiar chunks [10]. These chunks of information are then loaded into working memory, where the cognitive load factor is then introduced; however, the implications presented in the limitation of working memory place a strong emphasis on instructional design and limiting its overstimulation [8]. High working memory otherwise places a complex demand for learners who do not have knowledge that is specific to the domain in where cognitive load is to be implied [19]. Furthermore, the complex knowledge structures that would increase this type of information would be better served through the chunking of individual elements within a single element [19]. Based on the implications imposed on working memory, tasks designed with high cognitive load should be taught in chunks, which allow for better retrieval of information.

Long-term memory is situated on the opposing spectrum of cognitive architecture, with a focus on recollection and processes involved in problem solving [13]. Since this information is characterized as the ability to store large amounts of information in memory, it is argued the long-term memory can best define human cognitive ability as stored knowledge, as opposed to the ability to engage in complicated reasoning and logic within working memory [8]. This can thus limit the need to access working-memory as a single individual segment in human cognition, increasing the capacity for processing within working memory to be a simpler process [9, 15]. Based on this information, CT can be best taught when modularized structures are introduced in an efficient manner that decrease the cognitive load of working memory by enforcing concepts sequentially through long-term memory.

## 2.2    Computational Teaching Methodologies

The pedagogy of computational teaching methodologies raises an interest within significant educational communities, as CT becomes a universal skill set not limited to only computer scientists [9]. The further development involved in CT can thus result in the growth of a learners' abilities to make connections within their knowledge, question what is known, and further express themselves through active engagement [12]. Methodologies further designed to adapt to this difference in teaching must then be implemented in a manner that consider its effectiveness within instructional design, regarding working memory and the limitations of chunks of information, and long-term memory and the cognitive ability to manage storage and retrieval [8].

The importance of understanding CT and teaching it relies on the significant factor that there is an introduction of new challenges for instructors that do not hold a background in computational thinking, with institutions struggling with how to coordinate information technologies in their systems [15]. Given CT is more adept to problem-solving and its processes, it is best understood when decomposed into a staged cycle, where the congruence of CT and problem-solving intertwine [15]. These staged cycles, as introduced in modularized formats, is best designed when taught in progression, where the buildup of one concept is dependent on understanding another [17]. This can decrease the cognitive load introduced on working-memory when instructional design is paired with methodologies that employ understanding of problem approach and deconstruction through introducing them in formats that are designed with long-term teaching methods. Introducing algorithmic concepts to best improve these methods then, are based on modularized design that have yet to be determined. In this scenario, the following questions are imposed to enhance the teaching of computational thinking principles:

1.  Does modularized structure in computer science education have a dependency in its placement within curriculum?
2.  Does teaching concepts within computational thinking depend on the level of cognitive load introduced in a specific topic?
3.  Will the restructuring of modules based on this cognitive load have an effect on the understanding of basic CT principles, such as basic transposition and conversions in hexadecimal, binary, and ASCII?

It is thus important to design modules in teaching computational thinking that are best designed to augment cognitive overload, where the processing of demands that are created from the learning task exceeds the cognitive system [20]. These teaching methodologies much then employ the steps involved in CT, with the process of decomposing a problem, recognizing these specific patters, and thus using a form of abstraction to both generalize and formulate the probable solutions [1]. These logical methodologies can then be augmented to solve the potential problems imposed [1]. Those without prior computational thinking skills may have a more limited capacity in processing complex topics – therefore, design for cognitive overload must be implemented in teaching methodologies, with respect to schemas that are best augmented for long-term retention and less cognitive overload on working memory.

## 3  Pilot Study

The study below seeks to determine whether modularized formats in an introductory computer science course demonstrating methodologies in computational thinking are time-dependent based on the cognitive load of individual questions and their placement in a schema. Considering a given architecture of a lesson plan by Dr. Ogawa introducing hexadecimal, binary, and ASCII, modules are restructured to be determinants in the cognitive load introduced in the sample experiment, with time being the indicating factor in the measurement of cognitive load and relationships to accuracy. Students in the study were given segmented chunks of videos from two lectures introducing transposition ciphers and simple base number conversions. Given the modular formats did potentially have an impact on cognitive load, there should be statistically significant data correlating results to this hypothesis.

## 4  Methodology

### 4.1  Modularized Format

The examination of the experiment was completed within students in an Information and Computer Science introductory level course. The course, labeled as ICS 101 is affiliated with the University of Hawaii at Manoa, covering introductory level concepts in computer science and software used in a variety of productivity environments. The pilot study of this experiment was conducted in an online format in the Fall 2021 semester, with a series of questions in a sequential structure summarizing knowledge based in *Transposition Ciphers, ASCII, HEX, and Binary, Encryption and Decryption,* and lastly *Programming Fundamentals.* The total group of students, $(n = 39)$ were divided into 4 independent subsets based on class section, where each individual group were given the same segments and topics; however, they were organized and presented in varying preparations depending on the class section the group belonged in.

The insight into the development of CT skills of students was taken with cognitive load being a function of time. Given the difficulty involving understanding binary, hexadecimal, and ASCII, the experiment seeks to determine whether changing the structure of these modules is a factor in best understanding concepts introduced in CT, with respect to working-memory and the chunking of information.

The proposed lectures involve recordings of pedagogy performed by Dr. Ogawa, highlighting concepts involved in introductory level programming courses. These lectures were then chunked, in a similar fashion to Miller [11] and his proposal of the working memory. The formatting of these modularized schemas was designed based on the division of curriculum into discrete modules that were short in duration to test the limits of working memory [18]. By dividing and chunking these subcategories into modularized formats, students were limited in their abilities to access the next or previous chunk depending on which version of the test they received. The following diagram organizes these original pedagogies, with the modular formats representing the chunks of information they would receive in varying orders based on which group received the test. In contrast to methodologies that create a linear format of the presentation of information, modularized learning allows stand-alone independent units that can be taken in different orders at varying speeds, associated with the chunking of information and greater intensity in delivery of information [16]. The decomposition of the potential ordering of the tests were then divided, re-structured, and distributed to the respective groups. Data that was collected in this study ensured no personal information was released, and that the confidentiality of those involved would be protected. The results of this study hope to improve the understanding and methodologies involved in teaching computational thinking to those both within and outside of the STEM community.

**Fig. 2.** Structure of original modular lecture in transposition ciphers

It is observed in these pedagogies that although presented in a sequential format, the introduction of quizzes in between each module does not determine the level of understanding of students if there is no qualitative factor that indicates significant knowledge gained in the previous module. This leads to a recurring cycle of students returning to the previous section in which no form of redirection can best be determined without a quantitative approach. In addition, students may attribute their inability to understand current schemas to the previous module, when alternative segments of the schema may be required for further understanding. Furthermore, it is observed in these lectures that background knowledge associated with transposition ciphers is assumed; therefore, the addition of this knowledge was introduced as a subset of number representations and their potential bases, such as hexadecimal, ASCII, and binary. Given CT is a process of decomposition, this also relies heavily on the need to match specific teaching methodologies to the level of proficiency and understanding of the student while introducing new concepts and assessing the CT skills [3]. Since this is an introductory level course of topics in Computer Science, the proficiency of students was considered, and additional information was introduced to match the level of understanding of students to allow them to continue the task.

As cognitive load is to be observed between modules, the introduction of scored quizzes was introduced between each schema to determine level of understanding. These quizzes would be used in the statistical collection, with scoring and time recorded between each question being the indicating variables of cognitive load.

The first group received the original set of lecture activity, with no changes prior to the original teaching methodology. The order in which they received their modules are as follows (Table 1).

**Table 1.** Group 1 chunked module ordering

| Order | Module |
|-------|--------|
| 1 | Transposition ciphers |
| 2 | ASCII, HEX, and binary |
| 3 | Encryption and decryption |
| 4 | Programming fundamentals |

Using this as a control group, as the original base lecture, the modules were then organized in a manner introduced by Fig. 2 above. Since these sections were to be divided into smaller chunks, it was imperative to also link the information relevant to these divisions that students may not have access to. This is where the additions to module 2 were introduced, as it was retrieved from a previous lecture that introduced ASCII, HEX, and Binary as an independent lecture. The following tables show the finalized ordering of the chunked modules based on grouping, in addition to the ASCII, HEX, and Binary module which included supporting material (Tables 2, 3 and 4).

**Table 2.** Group 2 chunked module ordering

| Order | Module |
|-------|--------|
| 1 | ASCII, HEX, and binary |
| 2 | Transposition ciphers |
| 3 | Encryption and decryption |
| 4 | Programming fundamentals |

**Table 3.** Group 3 chunked module ordering

| Order | Module |
|-------|--------|
| 1 | Encryption and DECRYPTION |
| 2 | Transposition ciphers |
| 3 | ASCII, HEX, and binary |
| 4 | Programming fundamentals |

### 4.2 Analyzing Student Outcome

The resulting groups were then tested on video lectures ordered and chunked into their corresponding subsections. Questions were introduced between each schema with relation to the module content, ranging from a variety of multiple-choice types to radio-box

Table 4. Group 4 chunked module ordering

| Order | Module |
|-------|--------|
| 1 | Programming fundamentals |
| 2 | Encryption and decryption |
| 3 | ASCII, HEX, and binary |
| 4 | Transposition ciphers |

selections. The test used to determine statistical significance were ANOVA tests to determine variance in results. Given there were more than three groups independent of each other, this was determined to be the best test to determine statistically significant data based on time and correctness.

Groups 1 and 4, with group 1 being the primary control group scored similarly in average in comparison to group 2 and 3, who also had similar results in respect to scores. In relation to previous findings, although group 1 and 4 scored worse on average in comparison to group 2 and 3, the previous survey introduced asking what students believed computational thinking to be had conflicting results when compared to the average scores across all sections. In addition, when considering the placement of each module, it is observed that group 1 and 4 had noticeable inverses with respect to their structure, receiving scores on the lower end of the study, while groups 3 and 3 received higher averages.

Table 5. Average total scores across groups

| Group | Average score |
|-------|---------------|
| Group 1 | 55% |
| Group 2 | 64% |
| Group 3 | 65.6% |
| Group 4 | 41.75% |

**Average Total Scores Across Groups.** Table 5 shows the average scores between each group who had the same set of questions presented in varying orders depending on the test version received. In relation to Fig. 1, which displays the results of students' thoughts on computational thinking, those in Group 1 and 4 who determined that computational thinking is defined as the decomposition of problems that allow for pattern recognition to design effective solutions scored worse overall in comparison to their similar counterparts. Group 2 and 3 on average, determined that computational thinking was either solely for those in the computer science domain, or computational thinking was based on knowledge already obtained. A possible explanation between these differences in average scores is that students who assumed computational thinking being a decomposition of problems approached the quizzes this way, while those that solved the problem in their working memory based on knowledge obtained prior approached these questions in a similar manner. This can thus relate to working and long-term memory, and how these associations can be determining factors in how students solve problems. Since problems can be identified within specific problem categories, relevant schema associated can be retrieved from memory, and utilized with the information that is otherwise specific to the problem [17].

## 5    Results

The following sections present the findings of the data collected in qualitative and quantitative schemes from the modularized components of each section. Given the assumption that independent schemas have an impact of the cognitive load of students, a significant recording of time and accuracy should be observed. The following observations were then analyzed through the analysis of variance (ANOVA) in order to determine whether there were significant differences between groupings. This statistical analysis will determine the effective between the factors contributing to the cognitive load between groupings.

### 5.1    Quantitative Data

While Table 5 displayed data that showed the average total scores across groups as a sum of their sections, the following tables depict the statistical range and average based on the standalone sections. This however, depicted no findings of statistically significant data based on ANOVA test; however, this gave insight into the variance of scores based on groupings and position in the test, as depicted through the following tables and figures.

**Table 6.** Statistical data scores of transposition ciphers

| Groups | Count | Sum | Average | Variance |
|--------|-------|-----|---------|----------|
| G1S1   | 14    | 8.3 | 60%     | 0.037    |
| G2S1   | 9     | 4.6 | 52%     | 0.058    |
| G3S1   | 6     | 3   | 50%     | 0.166    |
| G4S1   | 10    | 6   | 60%     | 0.069    |

Table 6 shows the statistical data of the average scores between groupings on the Transposition Cipher schema. Between these groupings, groups 1 and 4, and 2 and 3 respectively had similar results in the average scores of their tests.

The module for Sect. 2 tested the understanding of ASCII, HEX, and binary. Here, groups 1, 2, and 3 scored within a similar range, while group 4 scored significantly lower (Tables 7 and 8).

**Table 7.** Statistical data scores of ASCII, HEX, and binary

| Groups | Count | Sum | Average | Variance |
|--------|-------|------|---------|----------|
| G1S2 | 14 | 9.75 | 70% | 0.088 |
| G2S2 | 9 | 6 | 67% | 0.062 |
| G2S3 | 6 | 4.25 | 71% | 0.085 |
| G2S4 | 10 | 4.75 | 48% | 0.061 |

**Table 8.** Statistical data scores of encryptions and decryption

| Groups | Count | Sum | Average | Variance |
|--------|-------|------|---------|----------|
| G1S3 | 14 | 8.5 | 61% | 0.151 |
| G2S3 | 9 | 5.5 | 61% | 0.095 |
| G3S3 | 6 | 4.25 | 71% | 0.160 |
| G4S3 | 10 | 7 | 70% | 0.136 |

The module for Sect. 3 tested the understanding of encryption and decryption. Here the average scores between groupings remained within the same relative range, with groups 1 and 2 recording a similar average range in score, and groups 3 and 4 also showing close averages (Table 9).

**Table 9.** Statistical data scores of programming fundamentals

| Groups | Count | Sum | Average | Variance |
|--------|-------|------|---------|----------|
| G1S4 | 14 | 5.5 | 39% | 0.074 |
| G2S4 | 9 | 4 | 44% | 0.137 |
| G3S4 | 5 | 2.5 | 50% | 0.156 |
| G4S4 | 10 | 3.5 | 35% | 0.016 |

The module for Sect. 4 tests the understanding of basic programming fundamentals. It is observed here that similar scorings of averages across tests were detected between groups 1 and 4 and groups 2 and 3 respectively.

### 5.2 Modularized Results and Cognitive Load

In correspondence to statistically significant results, one of the questions within the modules exhibited a statistically significant difference with respect to both time and results. In relation to time differentials, a similar question depicted trends with relation to cognitive load factors introduced through speculation of time. The questions that thus determined the analysis of cognitive load as a function of time through this survey are as follows, with the first question being the statistically significant result.

- "If it is true that uppercase letters have different ASCII codes than lowercase letters, what is the difference in value needed to change an uppercase letter to a lowercase letter in ASCII?"
- "Conversion of the word "tEsT" to ASCII yields what set of decimal digits when decrypted?"

The first question that showed statistical significance in relation to time and results was Question 4 on the exam under *ASCII, HEX, and Binary*, which prompts: "If it is true that uppercase letters have different ASCII codes than lowercase letters, what is the difference in value needed to change an uppercase letter to a lowercase in ASCII?" Results determined from the ANOVA in Table 10 reveal the statistically significant differences between the groups, pertaining to this question, with ($p = 0.001$). Since this value denotes a significant level less than ($p = 0.05$), the null hypothesis can be rejected noting that there is a significant difference between groupings. Furthermore, the time differential and statistical significance of the results align with the results of accuracy as depicted in Table 11, where ($p = 0.02$), again depicting statistical significance between groupings.

**Table 10.** ANOVA factor of statistically significance of time in question 4 (ASCII, HEX, binary)

| Source | SS | df | MS | F | P-value | F crit |
|---|---|---|---|---|---|---|
| Between Groups | 8.6E–05 | 3 | 2.87 E-05 | 6.77 | 0.001 | 2.87 |
| Within Groups | 0.00014 | 35 | 4.24 E-06 | | | |
| Total | 0.00023 | 38 | | | | |

**Table 11.** ANOVA factor of statistically significance of correctness in question 4 (ASCII, HEX, binary)

| Source | SS | df | MS | F | P-value | F crit |
|---|---|---|---|---|---|---|
| Between Groups | 2.14 | 3 | 0.713 | 3.65 | 0.02 | 2.87 |
| Within Groups | 6.83 | 35 | 0.195 | | | |
| Total | 8.97 | 38 | | | | |

Groups 1 and 3 as depicted in Table 12 under the average column, with the values depicting seconds, performed significantly faster than groups 2 and 4. With reference to Table 6, the average scores on this section showed a relation between the time differential and accuracy. The modularized format between these groupings had similarities

**Table 12.** Summary of time averages on question 4 (ASCII, HEX, binary)

| Groups | Count | Sum | Average | Variance |
| --- | --- | --- | --- | --- |
| G1S2Q4 | 14 | 0.0062 | 39 | 4.60 E-08 |
| G2S2Q4 | 9 | 0.0045 | 44 | 2.29 E-07 |
| G3S2Q4 | 6 | 0.0276 | 37 | 2.90 E-05 |
| G4S2Q4 | 10 | 0.0049 | 43 | 1.16 E-07 |

in structure, with the transposition cipher module occurring directly before the ASCII, HEX, and Binary schema. This could serve as a potential explanation of the similarities in score and time between these questions. Although not directly relation to the cognitive load in analysis, the data presented within this variation could present an interpretation of differences between mental models and understanding, where further study can be performed through content analysis.

The second question depicting an observed time differential was Question 4 under the Encryption and Decryption module, which prompted students to convert the word "tEsT" to its ASCII code and corresponding decimal digits. As cognitive load being a function of time, it can be observed in Table 13 that a similar trend between groups 1 and 4 were depicted when asked questions that were determinant on the understanding of knowledge based on ASCII, HEX, and Binary Fundamentals. Time differentials observed in Table 13 thus show a longer time spent on attempting to convert the word, with shorter time spent on average between groups 2 and 3.

This trend can be further observed through a reference to Table 5, where the average scores across groupings were collected. Similarly, the average scores across subsections of the groups also showed similarities to this trend, with groups 1 and 4 scoring similarly on Transposition Ciphers and Programming Fundamentals respectively. This can potentially be attributed to the inverse and "flip" in the modules, where although similar in design, were different in comparison to groups 2 and 3, who had some form of ASCII, HEX, and Binary or Encryption and Decryption before Transposition Ciphers and Programming.

**Table 13.** Summary of time averages on question 4 (encryption and decryption)

| Groups | Count | Sum | Average | Variance |
| --- | --- | --- | --- | --- |
| G1S2Q4 | 14 | 0.0078 | 48 | 2.23 E-07 |
| G2S2Q4 | 9 | 0.0034 | 33 | 6.36 E-08 |
| G2S3Q4 | 6 | 0.0068 | 39 | 2.01 E-06 |
| G2S4Q4 | 10 | 0.0131 | 54 | 1.79 E-06 |

# 6  Conclusions

## 6.1  Future Development and Research

Results from the study allow us to revisit the questions imposed in this experiment, where we relate the individual discoveries within the study to questions involving cognitive load and potential for future research. The analysis of the findings summarizes and identify themes for future development of this study, in relation to cognitive load factors that are determinant between the most common accurate and inaccurate answers to questions between subsets and groups. Although cognitive load as a function of time was determined between these sets, potential for future study may be determine through content analysis, where the choice of wording in questions can identify themes in how students analyze algorithmic thought and problem-solving solutions. Furthermore, analysis on the reordering of these modules and student performance can be quantified to determine the best ordering of computational material to prevent cognitive overload amongst those with little computational strength.

The potential for future research on computational teaching methods for students analyzed through independent modularized formats in CT involve future analysis of concepts to discover variables associated with potential cognitive load. Additional resources can be supplemented between course material in computer science that can support opportunities to research specific domains that affect cognitive load in computational thinking. The discovery of these variables through content analysis of text, discourse analysis between students and instructor, and quantitative analysis of cognitive load can be further researched for beneficial impact in the educational community.

**Acknowledgements.** This material is based upon work supported by the National Science Foundation (NSF) under Grant No. 1662487. Any opinions, findings, and conclusions or recommendations expressed in this material are those of the authors and do not necessarily reflect the views of the NSF.

# References

1. Imberman, S., Sturm, D., Azhar, M.: Computational thinking: expanding the toolkit. J. Comput. Sci. Coll. **29**(6), 39–46 (2016)
2. Lamprou, A., Repenning A.: Teaching how to teach computational thinking. In: Proceedings of the 23rd Annual ACM Conference on Innovation and Technology in Computer Science Education (2018)
3. De Jong, I.: Teaching computational thinking with interventions adapted to undergraduate students' proficiency levels. In: Annual Conference on Innovation and Technology in Computer Science Education, ITiCSE, pp. 571–572. Association for Computing Machinery (2020)
4. De Jong, I., Jeuring, J.: Computational thinking interventions in higher education: a scoping literature review of interventions used to teach computational thinking. In: Koli Calling 2020: Proceedings of the 20th Koli Calling International Conference on Computing Education Research, pp. 1–10 (2020)
5. Wing, J.M.: Computational thinking. Commun. ACM **49**(3), 33–35 (2006)
6. Resnick, L.B.: Education and Learning to Think. National Academy Press, Washington, DC (1987)

7. Wing, J.M.: Computational thinking—what and why? In: Article of the Magazine of the Carnegie Mellon University School of Computer Science (2011)
8. Shaffer, D., Doube, W., Tuovinen, J.: Applying cognitive load theory to computer science education. In: Petre, M., Budgen, D. (eds.) 15th Annual Workshop of the Psychology of Programming Interest Group, pp. 333–346 (2003)
9. Sweller, J., van Merrienboer, J.J.G., Paas, F.G.W.C.: Cognitive architecture and instructional design. Educ. Psychol. Rev. **10**, 251–296 (1998)
10. Li, Y., et al.: Computational thinking is more about thinking than computing. J. STEM Educ. Res. **3**, 1–18 (2020)
11. Cowan, N.: George Miller's magical number of immediate memory in retrospect: Observations on the faltering progression of science. Psychol Rev. **122**, 536 (2015)
12. Miller, G.A.: The magical number seven, plus or minus two: some limits on our capacity for processing information. Psychol. Rev. **63**(2), 81–97 (1956)
13. Kong, S., Wang, Y.: Formation of computational identity through computational thinking perspectives development in programming learning: a mediation analysis among primary school students. Comput. Human Behav. **106**, 106230 (2020)
14. Franklin, D., Salac, J., Crenshaw, Z., Turimella, S.: Exploring student behavior using the TIPP&SEE learning strategy. In: Proceedings of the 2020 ACM Conference on International Computing Education Research (2020)
15. Sweller, J.: Cognitive load theory. Psychol. Learn. Motiv. **55**, 37–76 (2011)
16. Labusch, A., Eickelmann, B., Vennemann, M.: Computational thinking processes and their congruence with problem-solving and information processing. In: Kong, S.C., Abelson, H. (eds.) Computational Thinking Education, pp. 65–78. Springer, Singapore (2019). https://doi.org/10.1007/978-981-13-6528-7_5
17. Wing, J.M.: Computational thinking's influence on research and education for all. Italian J. Educ. Technol. **25**(2), 7–14 (2017)
18. Dejene, W.: The practice of modularized curriculum in higher education institution: active learning and continuous assessment in focus. Cogent Educ. **6**(1), Art. 1611052 (2019)
19. Gerjets, P., Scheiter, K., Catrambone, R.: Designing instructional examples to reduce intrinsic cognitive load: molar versus modular presentation of solution procedures. Instr. Sci. **32**, 33–58 (2004)
20. Walkington, C., Clinton, V., Ritter, S., Nathan, M.J.: How readability and topic incidence relate to performance on mathematics story problems in computer-based curricula. J. Educ. Psychol. **107**(4), 1051–1074 (2015)

# Optimizing Visual Cues in Educational Software

David Stevens(✉) iD

University of Hawaiʻi, Honolulu, HI 96822, USA
david.stevens@hawaii.edu

**Abstract.** This study examined the effects of software graphical user interface (GUI) visual cues in educational software on user performance. It specifically studied the effectiveness of three distinct and commonly used visual cues -- bolded text, buttons, and arrows to guide a software application user through a series of tasks. The study attempted to prove the hypothesis that specific visual cues in educational software applications could decrease task time.

The study population consisted of a group of 134 post-secondary undergraduate students in Honolulu, Hawaiʻi, that engaged in a web-based educational software simulation which recorded response times when prompted by each of the three distinct visual cues.

The web-based simulation consisted of six steps. Each step consisted of a simple question and the appearance of a new visual cue to lead the participant to the next step only after selecting the correct answer. Each step of the experiment was automatically timed and recorded in milliseconds from the moment the participant selected the correct answer until the moment they clicked on the visual cue to proceed to the next step.

Slower response times indicated that during the first two steps, participants were still scanning the screen for the visual cue after they selected the correct answer. Of the three cues studied on the first two steps of the simulation, the Arrows and Bolded text were clearly the most quickly recognized cues among participants, while the response times for the Button cue were significantly slower.

However, in the last four steps of the simulation, no visual cue could be identified as the leader in participant response times. This would indicate that, since the visual cues were consistently in the same position, the participants acclimated to the position of the cue. At this point, there was no notable differences in response times among the different cues.

This study suggests that using arrows and/or bolded text in educational software are better choices for visual cues than buttons. It also suggests that keeping visual cues for common functions in a consistent location is optimal.

**Keywords:** Visual cues · SRK framework · Task time · GUI · Educational software

## 1 Introduction

### 1.1 Background

Since the creation of the first computer program, one of the core challenges of any application developer has been getting man and machine to interface more efficiently

© The Author(s), under exclusive license to Springer Nature Switzerland AG 2022
D. D. Schmorrow and C. M. Fidopiastis (Eds.): HCII 2022, LNAI 13310, pp. 287–303, 2022.
https://doi.org/10.1007/978-3-031-05457-0_23

[8]. With the birth of Unix in 1969, the earliest user interfaces advised users of the current computer state via visual cues [5]. The Unix command prompt reminded the user of their previous command and informed the user of their current location within the directory structure of the file system [14]. In early computer interfaces, a blinking cursor at the end of the command prompt (the now ubiquitous command line interface (CLI) [33]) would provide users a visual cue where to input commands [26].

XEROX Corporation's Palo Alto Research Center (PARC) was the first computer laboratory to create a true graphical user interface (GUI), which transformed the text based CLI into a more natural visual experience [10]. The GUI has greatly enhanced educational software, which attempts to incorporate some, or all five, typical learning activities: simulation, drill and practice, games, tutorials, and problem solving [13].

Computer-based simulations can improve traditional educational curriculum, particularly in laboratory instruction [27]. Brant, Hooper and Sugrue maintained that computer-based simulations create a cognitive framework or structure to accommodate continued education in an associated subject [6]. Bell, Randy, Trundle and Cabe found that well-designed computer-based simulations, used within a theoretical model of teaching, could be extremely effective in supporting understanding [4].

Thomas and Piemme maintained that computer-based education improves learning, allowing students the preference of pace, place, time, and content of curriculum [39]. Especially during the COVID-19 pandemic, with schools shifting to online learning, there is an even greater need for effective educational software. We can also use e-Learning to enhance a learner's educational experience by allowing educators to customize the curriculum to address the learner's personal educational objectives [34].

For insight into methods to achieve ease of use, software developers have turned to studies of human task-oriented behavior [36]. Many such studies are based on the Skills, Rules, Knowledge (SRK) Framework introduced by Jens Rasmussen in 1983, which delineates human task oriented behavior into three major categories: Skills-based (routine to the point of becoming almost instinctive, such as brushing one's teeth), Rules-based (tasks that are common to an experienced user but which require conscious effort such as changing lanes while driving a car), and Knowledge-based (when the activity is new to an individual and requires more focus and attention, such as traveling across the country for the first time) [32].

### 1.2 Where Does This Study Fit?

Providing computer users with something familiar to guide them through unfamiliar tasks gives them more confidence while performing that task [38]. Visual cues, such as icons, menus, toolbars, and prompts became more common as software developers realized that perceived ease of use by the consumer equated to greater user acceptance [40]. With the release of MS Office, users became accustomed to an array of stimuli to help guide them through almost any task [16]. The GUI came at a cost however, in the form of greater system resource usage resulting in reduced performance. Frustrated users would frequently turn off the most user-friendly cues and prompts, such as the animated office assistant, to optimize their time on a given task [37].

Most software users fail to discover visual cues such as embedded text, animations, and images [11, 29]. Some studies have implied this can be caused by cognitive overload resulting in a user's frustration [7]. To counter this, programmers have attempted to create consistent interface designs that keep most relevant information in view of the user with easy access [23].

The need for structured guidance in educational software GUI continues to exist to guide users through understanding program contents and goals [20]. The question then arose: 'What visual cues should be provided '[7]?

Given Sarenko's study indicating that there can be a disconnect between a software provider's and an end-user's definition of 'user-friendly' cues and prompts, there must be a point at which optimum efficiency is achieved through visual cues.

This study's purpose was to evaluate whether there is a point at which a given task will transform from a knowledge-based activity into a rules-based activity from a user's perspective, and if the user will attain optimum task efficiency while being guided by any one specific visual prompt.

### 1.3  Why is This Study Important?

When deciding what software to use in an educational institution, the perceived ease-of-use by the end user is paramount [15]. Those making the investment in educational software must therefore seriously consider the longevity of the software once it has been implemented [2].

Beale and Sharples define the primary aspect of software "ease of use" as "usability", i.e., "can people use the software effectively and efficiently to perform a task [3]?" Software creators must consider which visual cues to provide to students because ineffective visual cues will take away from student perceived ease-of-use and negatively impact student retention [20].

### 1.4  How Does This Study Relate to Previous Research?

When students utilize educational software, they are often engaged in activities that involve problem solving [3]. However, the more problem solving required to perform a task, the more errors are possible [32]. It would be advantageous, therefore, to reduce the complexity of a given task to reduce errors and improve understanding.

Research indicates that providing software users with structured guidance, such aural and visual cues (i.e., menus and graphics), helps them to avoid becoming disoriented and greatly enhances efficiency [12, 20, 22, 30, 41]. However, a study on design implications by Kim, Brock, Orkland, and Astion found navigational patterns varied based on the experience and content knowledge of the users. Numerous critical visual cues were not noticed by most of the users and icons representing specific functions were not intuitive to some users [18].

An explanation could lie in the relationship between written language and symbols. Early humans attempting to communicate ideas used symbols, icons, and pictures. As early as the Philistines, using symbols to covey ideas and emotions was common [25]. With the advent of written languages, some interpretation of symbols could be subjective and the familiarity with writing seemed to have a particularly distorting effect on their meaning [19]. This might lead to the question of which symbol can be most effective in communicating an idea.

Even though usability studies based on even small numbers of computer users can identify problems in interface design [18], one of the main issues in creating software for training and education is motivating a user to complete an action he or she has not previously completed [31].

A theoretical framework that can be used to address the problem-solving behavior of software users is the Skills, Rules, and Knowledge (SRK) Framework proposed by Jens Rasmussen [32].

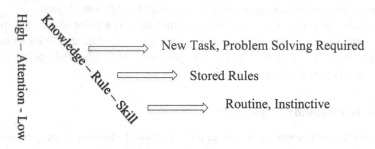

High – Attention – Low

Knowledge – Rule – Skill

⟹ New Task, Problem Solving Required

⟹ Stored Rules

⟹ Routine, Instinctive

**Fig. 1.** Theoretical framework based on the SRK taxonomy.

This study was based on the work of Jens Rasmussen, 1987 and Kim Vicente, 1990 and studied casual factors concerning the knowledge-based and rules-based activity levels from Rasmussen's SRK framework [32] See Fig. 1.

According to the SRK framework, software users engaging in a knowledge-based activity greatly benefit from structured guidance, which increases productivity while reducing frustration levels [20]. With the understanding that any Knowledge Based activity requires problem solving, some of the difficulties in creating educational software could be circumvented by examining the common problems users experience.

Two such problems experienced by most students using educational software are that they do not use all the navigational options available in the program and that some visual cues which are critical to the efficient use of the software are completely overlooked [18].

By adding more guidance for the software user in the form of visual cues, it should be possible to transform a knowledge-based activity (problem solving) into a more rules-based activity (using stored rules) requiring less problem solving and resulting in fewer errors [9].

## The SRK Framework
The Skills, Rules, and Knowledge Framework was developed as a system of determining human cognitive performance and distinguishing at what cognitive level specific tasks and actions are being executed. Jens Rasmussen developed the SRK Framework to help define behavior within three distinct levels: skills, rules, and knowledge-based, and it can provide evidence of the types of human cognition shown at each stage [32].

### Skills-Based Behavior
Skills-based activities are routine in nature, are highly integrated into a person's life and are executed without applying a significant amount of conscious effort [32]. Activities in

this category could almost be considered instinctive. Common examples of skills-based activities are washing dishes or driving a car along a routine path. These activities can be successfully accomplished without a person focusing too heavily on the task. During a skills-based activity, a person uses more subconscious efforts to keep themselves on-task and aware of changes in their immediate environment like subtle changes in road conditions while driving [32].

*Rules-Based Behavior*

Like skills-based behavior, rules-based behavior is guided by "stored-rules", or memories of previous attempts at a particular activity. Unlike skills-based activities, rules-based activities require additional routines and more conscious effort. Rules based actions are accomplished based on empirical data accumulated from similar prior activities or from previous instruction [32].

Following the example of a skills-based activity, driving a car, the rules-based activity associated with this task might be changing lanes or stopping at a red light. These actions are considered rules-based because of the extra cognitive effort associated with completing them.

*Knowledge-Based Behavior*

Knowledge-based activities require cognitive resources to accomplish because they are associated with tasks that a person has not encountered previously. When applying knowledge-based behavior, a person has eliminated the options of using either skills-based or rules-based, since knowledge-based activities have no past routines, experiences, or instruction associated with them [32].

Because of the extra effort required to process these types of tasks, knowledge-based activities are considered the most time consuming and resource intensive processes [32]. Traveling across the country for the first time is a good example of knowledge-based behavior because of the planning involved to accomplish the tasks [32].

## 2 Hypothesis

The world has fundamentally changed in response to the popularity, and availability, of computers for the home, in schools, and in businesses. Research now indicates the importance of computer knowledge in the modern world to achieve some level of individual success [1]. Schools must now meet the need of preparing students for a world driven by technology [24], and we now know that learners acquire more knowledge in less time when they engage in computer-based simulations [35].

We also know that computer-based simulations can improve traditional curriculum [27], and well-designed computer-based simulations, used within a theoretical model of teaching could be extremely effective in supporting understanding [4].

However, when creating educational software that will address the needs of the overwhelmingly large mix of student backgrounds, knowledge, and training, computer software designers must tackle three main user types: knowledge seekers (who use generalized approaches to navigate a program), feature explorers (who focus mainly on audio and visual stimuli), and apathetic users (who follow linear paths with a limited investigation of the program) [21].

When students first encounter new educational software, they are engaging in knowledge-based activity (problem solving) and therefore could greatly benefit from intuitive visual aids, or cues, to help them process this new information and find their way through the new tasks set before them [18].

Situations such as this prompted researchers to ask the question, "What types of navigational tools or guidance should be provided to the learners?" [17]. Another important question would be: of the types of tools or guidance available, how many should be provided to achieve optimal understanding without overwhelming the user [7]?

There are multiple visual cues used in software applications, but not all visual cues when evaluating the rate at which a knowledge-based activity is transformed into a rules-based activity. The hypothesis for this study: does the use of a specific visual user cue in educational computer applications decrease task time? The experiment used in this study was used to address the basic question of which, if any, visual user cues are more effective in educational software.

## 2.1 Materials and Methods

This was a quasi-experimental study conducted in a post-secondary educational setting that utilized a web-based computer simulation. The simulation included a task divided into six sequential steps. Participants were given visual cues to guide them through the steps to accomplish the simulated task. Total task time was automatically measured by the application and recorded in milliseconds. The time taken by participants to execute each step in the simulation was also measured in milliseconds.

### Participants
The population of this study included students of a post-secondary educational institution located in Honolulu, Hawaii. The participants included 134 students between 18–40 years of age and included an equal number of males and females. The sample did not limit participation in the study to any demographic group.

### Assumptions
The following assumptions were made in relation to the study:

• All participants will be familiar with web-based computer programs in general.

### Limitations
The following were limitations to this study:

• Due to limited resources, the number of participants, proctors, and test sites were limited.
• There was limited access to the room in which the study took place, thus participants were only able to complete the simulation during a few specific hours during the regular school week of Monday through Friday.

- Because participants were not completely isolated while running the simulation, some distractions by outside influences were possible, which could affect response times.

## Delimitations

The following were the delimitations of this study:

- The population of the study was limited to students at a certain education level.
- Only students from one college in Honolulu, HI took part in this study.
- This study only investigated three of the most common software visual cues: bold differentiating text, text indicator with a button, and arrow icons [28].

## Instrumentation

Data for this study was collected using a web-based computer simulation. This programming code accurately measures time in milliseconds based on an internal system clock and did not depend on timekeeping by an individual.

## Apparatus

The equipment used by the participants in the experiment included: a Windows OS based personal computer with the following technical specifications: 4 GB RAM, 120 GB local storage, a 3 Ghz Intel processor, a standard US computer keyboard, a standard two button mouse, an LCD flat panel monitor set at 1280 × 1024 pixels, access to the Internet at approx. 15 Mbps, access to the simulation web site using the web browser included with the Windows Operating System.

## Procedures

This study employed a computer application to measure the task time by participants. Each participant was given use of a computer and the test application and told to complete the task indicated on the first screen of the test. The test application simply told the participant to complete the six steps in the task by interpreting the visual cues. Each visual cue led the participant to the next step in the task until all six steps had been completed. For each group of participants, the test application differed only in the type of visual cue provided to lead the participant to the next step in the task.

The first group of participants were given the Bold Text visual cue to lead them to the next step in the task. The next group of participants were given an Arrow Graphic visual cue. The third group of participants were given a Button Graphic with Text visual cue.

## Experiment

Below are the steps used in evaluating the user activity in the test application.

Step 1. Study participants are seated at a computer and given instructions to follow the instructions on the screen.

Step 2. The computer application displays a basic set of instructions to begin the computer-based task along with verbal instructions to choose a certain button. Which button the user is told to choose depends on how much data has been collected before and how much more of each cue is needed to evenly distribute the sample data. These instructions are shown in Fig. 2.

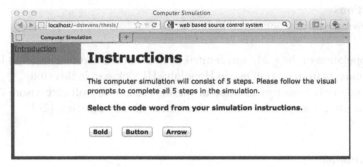

**Fig. 2.** Simulation - introduction

Step 3. Each step of the simulation includes a very basic question or instruction. The user must choose the correct answer. A sample instruction is shown in Fig. 3.

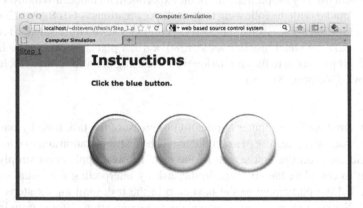

**Fig. 3.** Simulation - instruction

Step 4. Once the user finds the correct answer three things happen:

1. Bold text will appear indicating the user has found the correct response and instructing the user to proceed to the next step.
2. A timer will start.
3. A visual cue will appear. As shown in Fig. 4.

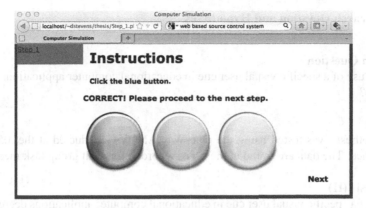

**Fig. 4.** Simulation – correct answer (timer begins)

Step 5. Once the user selects the visual cue three things happen:

1. The timer stops.
2. The program will subtract the start time from the end time to calculate the total time it took for the user to understand and act on the visual cue.
3. The time is imbedded in the html form data and passed to the next step in the simulation.
4. The program takes the user to the next step.

Step 6. At the last step of the simulation, the user is instructed to click on the "Submit" button to submit the data as shown in Fig. 5.

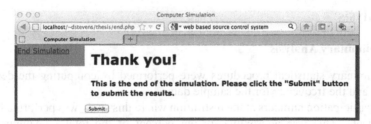

**Fig. 5.** Simulation – end

When the user clicks this button, the form data, including all task times, are submitted to a database that includes the name of the visual cue and each task time for that user identified only be a unique auto-incrementing integer used as a record id.

## 2.2 Research Question and Hypotheses

**Research Question**
Does the use of a specific visual user cue in educational computer applications decrease task time?

**Analysis**
The hypothesis was tested using the One-Way ANOVA conducted at the .05 level of significance. The data are found at the times recorded for each group task measure.

**Hypothesis (H)**
The use of a specific visual user cue in educational computer applications decreases task time.

## 2.3 Strengths and Weaknesses

**Strengths**
The study participants represent a post-secondary demographic of the main island of the state of Hawai'i (O'ahu), providing a variety of learning styles and abilities.

**Weaknesses**
One possible weakness in this study is that participants were chosen from a pool of students who all attend the same post-secondary institution college in Honolulu, which may influence the validity of the research.

# 3 Analysis

## 3.1 Preliminary Analysis

The preliminary statistical procedures were performed by computing the descriptive statistics and the frequency for the sample data.

The participation numbers at the institution where this study was performed equaled 134 students. This was approximately ten percent of the total on-campus student population. Students enrolled in the online-only programs did not participate.

**Descriptive Statistics**
Table 1 displays the frequencies of the Independent Variable "Visual Cue". The sample populations for each cue varied slightly.

**Table 1.** Frequencies of the independent variable visual cue

| Visual cue | Frequency | Percentage |
| --- | --- | --- |
| Bold text | 57 | 42.5 |
| Button | 43 | 32.1 |
| Arrow | 34 | 25.4 |
| Total | 134 | 100 |

Table 2 displays the Frequencies, Mean, Standard Deviation, and Standard Error of the Dependent Variable Step 1.

**Table 2.** Frequencies, mean, std. dev., std. err., of the dependent variable step 1

| Cue | N | Mean | Std. deviation | Std. error |
| --- | --- | --- | --- | --- |
| Bold text | 57 | 3182.02 | 1412.720 | 187.119 |
| Button | 43 | 8334.07 | 10053.547 | 1533.152 |
| Arrow | 34 | 4057.26 | 4115.228 | 705.756 |
| Total | 134 | 5057.37 | 6495.733 | 561.146 |

Table 3 displays the Frequencies, Mean, Standard Deviation, and Standard Error of the Dependent Variable Step 2.

**Table 3.** Frequencies, mean, std. dev., std. err., of the dependent variable step 2

| Cue | N | Mean | Std. deviation | Std. error |
| --- | --- | --- | --- | --- |
| Bold text | 57 | 1581.40 | 468.033 | 61.992 |
| Button | 43 | 1993.21 | 838.960 | 127.940 |
| Arrow | 34 | 1997.74 | 1295.893 | 222.244 |
| Total | 134 | 1819.19 | 879.405 | 75.969 |

Table 4 displays the Frequencies, Mean, Standard Deviation, and Standard Error of the Dependent Variable Step 3.

**Table 4.** Frequencies, mean, std. dev., std. err., of the dependent variable step 3

| Cue | N | Mean | Std. deviation | Std. error |
|---|---|---|---|---|
| Bold text | 57 | 1636.51 | 601.099 | 79.618 |
| Button | 43 | 1736.91 | 490.425 | 74.789 |
| Arrow | 34 | 1773.97 | 843.334 | 144.631 |
| Total | 134 | 1703.60 | 638.833 | 55.187 |

Table 5 displays the Frequencies, Mean, Standard Deviation, and Standard Error of the Dependent Variable Step 4.

**Table 5.** Frequencies, mean, std. dev., std. err., of the dependent variable step 4

| Cue | N | Mean | Std. deviation | Std. error |
|---|---|---|---|---|
| Bold text | 57 | 1398.89 | 517.174 | 68.501 |
| Button | 43 | 1552.16 | 572.790 | 87.350 |
| Arrow | 34 | 1393.06 | 518.434 | 88.911 |
| Total | 134 | 1398.89 | 517.174 | 68.501 |

Table 6 displays the Frequencies, Mean, Standard Deviation, and Standard Error of the Dependent Variable Step 5.

**Table 6.** Frequencies, mean, std. dev., std. err., of the dependent variable step 5

| Cue | N | Mean | Std. deviation | Std. error |
|---|---|---|---|---|
| Bold text | 57 | 1296.51 | 467.534 | 61.926 |
| Button | 43 | 1539.49 | 756.033 | 115.294 |
| Arrow | 34 | 1603.35 | 1474.029 | 252.794 |
| Total | 134 | 1452.34 | 911.228 | 78.718 |

Table 7 displays the Frequencies, Mean, Standard Deviation, and Standard Error of the Dependent Variable Total of the Step Times.

**Table 7.** Frequencies, mean, std. dev., std. err., of the dependent variable total of step times

| Cue | N | Mean | Std. deviation | Std. error |
|-----|---|------|----------------|------------|
| Bold text | 57 | 9095.33 | 2508.421 | 332.249 |
| Button | 43 | 15155.84 | 10724.269 | 1635.436 |
| Arrow | 34 | 10825.38 | 4728.608 | 810.950 |
| Total | 134 | 11479.09 | 7171.563 | 619.529 |

# 4 Results Analysis

## 4.1 Research Question

The question posed by this study is, does the use of a specific visual user cue in educational computer applications decrease task time? The question was investigated by using a One-Way ANOVA test conducted at the .05 level of significance using the Total of Step Times (total task time) in the experiment.

## 4.2 Results

Table 8 displays the results of the One-Way ANOVA test for the dependent variable Total of Step Times. In these results we see a P-value that is less than .05 indicating there is a significant difference in visual cues for the Total of the Step Times. In this case we need to test for homogeneity using the Levene test.

Table 9 displays the results of the Levene test. Since the Sig. value of this test is also less than .05, the homogeneity of this test has been violated. Further analysis must be done. Since the results of the ANOVA were significant, a Tamhane's post hoc test was performed.

Table 10 displays the results of the Tamhane's test indicating the Bold Text and Arrow cues have no significant difference, yet the differences between the Bold Text and Button cues, and the Button and Arrow cues, are significant. The results of the analysis for the dependent variable Total of Task Times indicated a significant difference in visual cues and therefore support the hypothesis H.

**Table 8.** ANOVA test for the variable total of step times

| | Sum of squares | df | Mean sq. | F | P |
|---|----------------|-----|----------|-------|------|
| Between groups | 9.197E8 | 2 | 4.599E8 | 10.175 | .000 |
| Within groups | 5.921E9 | 131 | 4.520E7 | | |
| Total | 6.840E9 | 133 | | | |

**Table 9.** Test of homogeneity of variances for the total of step times

| Levene statistic | df1 | df2 | Sig |
|---|---|---|---|
| 18.495 | 2 | 131 | .000 |

**Table 10.** Tamhane's test for the variable total of step times

| (I) Cue | (J) Cue | Mean difference (I–J) | Std. error | P |
|---|---|---|---|---|
| Bold text | Button | −6060.504* | 1668.844 | .002 |
| | Arrow | −1730.049 | 876.372 | .155 |
| Button | Bold text | 6060.504* | 1668.844 | .002 |
| | Arrow | 4330.455 | 1825.456 | .061 |
| Arrow | Bold text | 1730.049 | 876.372 | .155 |
| | Button | −4330.455 | 1825.456 | .061 |

* The mean difference is significant at the 0.05 level.

# 5  Findings

The following results explain the analysis of the research question H: does the use of a specific visual user cue in educational computer applications decrease task time?

This analysis was performed on the data from the Total of Task Times in the experiment at the .05 level of significance. The first analysis showed the Mean total task time for the Bold Text visual cue to be 9095.33 ms, with a Standard Deviation of 2508.421 and a Standard Error of 332.249, while the Mean total task time for the Button visual cue was 15155.84 ms, with a Standard Deviation of 10724.269 and a Standard Error of 1635.436, and the Mean total task time for the Arrow visual cue was 10825.38 ms, with a Standard Deviation of 4728.608 and a Standard Error of 619.529.

A One-Way ANOVA test revealed the P-value to be $< .001$, indicating a significant difference in the task times between the visual cues. A test for Homogeneity followed using the Levene's test. This test showed the Sig. value to also be $< .001$, indicating Homogeneity had been violated and therefore additional tests were required for further investigation.

Analyzing the data with a Tamhane's test revealed the P-value representing the difference between the Bold Text and Button visual cues to be .002, and therefore significant. However, the P-value representing the difference between the Bold Text and Arrow visual cues was .155 and the P-value representing the difference between the Button and Arrow visual cues was .061, and therefore not significant.

The analysis of the data for the Total of Test Times supports the primary research question H, that the use of a specific visual user cue in educational computer applications decreases task time. In this case, Bold Text was the visual cue that most significantly reduced task time.

# 6  Conclusions

The interpretations of the results of this analysis are that Bold Text and Arrows are more effective visual cues in decreasing task time as shown in steps 1 and 2 of the experiment. However, seeing almost no difference in task times between cues in steps 3 through 5 might indicate that once a software user finds, and commits to memory, the location of a certain visual cue, then the difference in visual cues matters much less than the position of the visual cue.

The results of this analysis show that during steps 1 and 2 of the experiment, the users were searching for a visual cue to guide them through to the next step. However, after seeing visual cues appear in the same location for steps 1 and 2, the users had much less trouble identifying where the visual cue would appear in the next 3 steps of the experiment.

Because, after the first 2 steps of the experiment, the users were accustomed to the location of the visual cue to proceed to the next step, they found the visual cues easier to find in steps 3 through 5 and this was most likely the cause for the visual cues having no significant difference in task times for steps 3 through 5 of the experiment.

This falls in line with Rasmussen's Skills, Rules, and Knowledge Framework [32]. The analysis of the results clearly shows that after a software user establishes the location of a visual cue, the software user is no longer engaging in Knowledge based activity, where most errors occur. But is instead, engaging in Rules based behavior and therefore less susceptible to errors and experiencing decreased task time.

This research clearly shows the importance of an efficient visual cue. But also shows there might very well be a good case for always placing visual cues in a location a software user might expect them to be.

This analysis also indicates that, of the three visual cues studied, Bold Text and Arrows have the most positive effect on software user performance.

# 7  Recommendations

## 7.1  Recommendations for Use of Results

This study has shown that using Bold Text and Arrows as visual cues to guide a user through a process and keeping the visual cues in the same location throughout a software application, will minimize task time and reduce software user errors.

Because of the results of this study, I recommend using the Bold Text and Arrow visual cues when creating educational software. I also recommend placing the visual cues in the same position as often as possible, so users become accustomed to this location for a given function.

## 7.2  Recommendations for Future Research

This analysis brought to light the need for further research on visual cues relating to the position of the cue in a software application.

More research can also be done to include a survey of the participants to find out what age demographic they belong to or what level of computer experience they have.

Another study of the same type could also include a survey to find out if participants are male or female, or if they play video games and how often.

**Acknowledgement.** This material is based upon work supported by the National Science Foundation under Grant No. 1662487. Any opinions, findings, and conclusions or recommendations expressed in this material are those of the authors and do not necessarily reflect the views of the NSF.

# References

1. Agee, R.: Are we really training computer teachers? Technol. Horizans Educ. J. **12**, 96–99 (1985)
2. Awidi, I.T.: Critical factors in selecting a course management system for higher education in Ghana. Educase Q. **31**(1), 24–32 (2008)
3. Beale, R., Sharples, M.: Proceedings of the 8th European Conference on Information Technology Evaluation, pp. 2–29. Vienna: ECIS (2001)
4. Bell, R.L., Trundle, K.C.: The use of a computer simulation to promote scientific conceptions of moon phases. J. Res. Sci. Teach. **45**(3), 346–372 (2008)
5. Boldyreff, C.: UNIX on a micro. ACM SIGSMALL Newsl. **7**(1), 7–8 (1981)
6. Brant, G., Hooper, E., Sugrue, B.: Which comes first the simulation or the lecture? J. Educ. Comput. Res. **7**(4), 469–481 (1991)
7. Brickell, G.: Navigation and learning style. Aust. J. Educ. Technol. **9**(2), 103–114 (1993)
8. Bullynck, M., De Mol, L.: Setting-up early computer programs: D. H. Lehmer's ENIAC computation. Arch. Math. Logic **42**(2), 123–146 (2010)
9. Chung, P.H.: Visual Cues to Reduce Error in Computer-based Routine Procedural Tasks. Rice University, Houston (2004)
10. Fishkin, K.P.: Embodied user interfaces for really direct manipulation. Commun. ACM **43**(9), 74–80 (2000)
11. Flemming, J.: Web Navigation: Designing the User Experience. O'Reilly and Associates, Sebastapol (1998)
12. Fleming, E., Pritchett, A.: SRK as a framework for the development of training for effective interaction with multi-level automation. Cogn. Technol. Work **18**(3), 511–528 (2016). https://doi.org/10.1007/s10111-016-0376-0
13. Frank, M.C.: Instructional Software (2008). Accessed 4 Jan 2012, from Boise State University: http://edtech2.boisestate.edu/frankm/EDTECH575/home_is.html
14. Hodges, M.S.: Computers: Systems, Terms and Acronyms, 17th edn. SemCo Enterprises Inc., Winter Springs (2007)
15. HyperOffice. Selecting Software (2008). Accessed 10 Jan 2011, www.hyperoffice.com/files/pdf/selectingsoftware.pdf
16. Joch, A.: Interfacing the facts. Inc. **19**(9), 39 (1997)
17. Jonassen, D.H., Grabinger, R.S.: Designing Hypermedia for Learning. Springer, London (1990). https://doi.org/10.1007/978-3-642-75945-1_1
18. Kim, S., Brock, D.M., Orkland, A., Astion, M.L.: Design implications from a usability study of GramStain-Tutor. Br. J. Edu. Technol. **32**(5), 595–605 (2001)
19. Kippenberg, H.G., Van Den, B., Leertouwer, L.: The Image of Writing. Brill Academic Publishers, Boston (1988)
20. Koneman, P.A., Jonassen, D.H.: Hypertext interface design and structural knowledge acquisition. In: Proceedings of the National Convention of the Association for Educational Communication and Technology, pp. 349–355 (1994)

21. Lawless, K.A., Brown, S.W.: Multimedia learning environments: issues of learner control and navigation. Instr. Sci. **25**(2), 117–131 (1997)
22. Litchfield, B.C.: Design factors in multimedia environments: research findings and implications for instructional design. In: Annual Meeting of the American Educational Research Association, Atlanta, pp. 2–16 (1993)
23. Marshal, C., Nelson, C., Gardiner, M.M.: Applying Cognitive Psychology to User-interface Design. Wiley, Chichester (1987)
24. Molnar, A.S.: Computers in education: a brief history. Technol. Horizons Educ. **24**, 63–68 (1997)
25. Moore, A.: Iconography of Religions: An Introduction. Fortress Press, Minneapolis (1977)
26. Moore, B.: Waiting at the terminal. J. Acad. Librarianship **4**(6), 443 (1979)
27. Nico, R., van Joolingen, W.R., van der Veen, J.T.: The learning effects of computer simulations in science education. Comput. Educ. **58**(1), 136–153 (2012)
28. Pandhi, D.: How to create the best user experience for your application (2006). Accessed Dec 2011, from MSDN (Microsoft Developer Network): http://msdn.microsoft.com/en-us/library/aa468595.aspx#humanux_topic9
29. Park, I., Hannafin, M.J.: Empirically-based guidelines for the design of interactive multimedia. Educ. Tech. Res. Dev. **41**(3), 63–85 (1993)
30. Percisco, D.: Methodological constants in courseware design. Br. J. Edu. Technol. **28**(2), 111–123 (1997)
31. Powell, J., Wright, T., Newland, P., Creed, C., Logan, B.: Fire play: ICCARUS—intelligent command and control, acquisition and review using simulation. Br. J. Edu. Technol. **39**(2), 369–389 (2008)
32. Rasmussen, J.: Skills, rules, and knowledge; signals, signs, and symbols, and other distinctions in human performance models. IEEE Trans. Syst. Man Cybern. **13**(3), 257–266 (1983)
33. Ritchie, D.M.: The evolution of the unix time-sharing system. In: Tobias, J.M. (ed.) Language Design and Programming Methodology. LNCS, vol. 79, pp. 25–35. Springer, Heidelberg (1980). https://doi.org/10.1007/3-540-09745-7_2
34. Ruiz, J.G., Mintzer, M.J., Leipzig, R.M.: The impact of e-learning in medical education. Acad. Med. **81**(3), 207–212 (2006)
35. Schacter, J.: The impact of education technology on student achievement what the most current research has to say. The Milken Exchange on Education Technology, Santa Monica (1999)
36. Seffah, A., Gulliksen, J., Desmarais, M.C. (eds.): Human-Centered Software Engineering — Integrating Usability in the Software Development Lifecycle. Springer, Dordrecht (2005). https://doi.org/10.1007/1-4020-4113-6
37. Serenko, A.: The development of an instrument to measure animation predisposition of users of animated agents in ms office applications. McMaster University. DeGroote School of Business, Quebec (2004)
38. Sutch, L.A.: "You know more than you think you do": helping participants transfer knowledge. In: Proceedings of the 35th Annual ACM SIGUCCS Fall Conference. SIGUCCS, New York (2007)
39. Thomas, E., Piemme, M.: Computer-assisted learning and evaluation in medicine. J. Am. Med. Assoc. **260**, 367–372 (1988)
40. Venkatesh, V.: Determinants of perceived ease of use: integrating control, intrinsic motivation, and emotion into the technology acceptance model. Inf. Syst. Res. **11**(4), 342–365 (2000)
41. Wild, M., Quinn, C.: Implications of educational theory for the design of instructional multimedia. Br. J. Educ. Technol. **29**(1), 73–82 (1998)

# Selecting and Training Young Cyber Talent: A Recurrent European Cyber Security Challenge Case Study

Muahmmad Mudassar Yamin[✉], Laszlo Erdodi, Espen Torseth, and Basel Katt

Norwegian University of Science and Technology, Teknologivegen 22, 2815 Gjøvik, Norway
{muhammad.m.yamin,laszlo.erdodi,espen.torseth,basel.katt}@ntnu.no

**Abstract.** Cyber security is a big challenge nowadays. However, the lack of qualified individuals and awareness is making the current situation more problematic. One way to address this problem is through National cyber security competitions. Such competitions provide large-scale awareness of cyber security issues and motivate individuals to join the cyber security workforce. ENISA (European Network and Information Security Argent) motivated European countries to organize national-level cyber security competitions in early 2014, similar to national-level football competitions. After that, ENISA organized a European-level competition similar to UEFA football league in which multiple countries participated with their national teams. This cyber security competition is known as a ECSC (European Cyber Security Challenge). Individuals aged between 14–25 participate and try to solve different cyber security challenges related to web, forensics, crypto, OSINT (Open Source Intelligence), and reversing. To select individuals and to teach those skills, different countries apply different strategies. In this study, we focus on how different countries select cyber talent and train them for national competitions and how they impact their overall cyber security ecosystem to produce skilled individuals for a cyber security workforce.

**Keywords:** Cyber security · Education · Training · Team building

## 1  Introduction

Due to the rapidly deteriorating cyber security situation around the world, there is a need for highly skilled security professionals and general public awareness to tackle evolving cyber security threats. Different countries are increasing their investment for the aforementioned purposes, but the effectiveness of the investment is yet to be measured. Setting aside training highly skilled professionals, there are general public awareness measures to make society more resilient against cyber attacks. These measures include cyber security awareness months, workshops, seminars, and competitions. One of these measures is the ECSC

D. D. Schmorrow and C. M. Fidopiastis (Eds.): HCII 2022, LNAI 13310, pp. 304–321, 2022.
https://doi.org/10.1007/978-3-031-05457-0_24

(European Cyber Security Challenge) [1], in which countries across Europe compete against each other to evaluate their cyber competence against cyber security curricula defined by ENISA (European Network and Information Security Argent) [2]. The curricula comprises of key skill and general domains like *Information/Crypto, Network, Operating Systems, Organizational and human factors* as well as specific domains like *Web, Mobile, IoT, OSINT, Specific Operating Systems and Hardware Support, Privacy, surveillance and censorship, PKI in practice*. The curricula also focuses on cyber security approaches and methodology which contains *Reconnaissance, Cryptanalysis, Operations Security* and *Forensics/Malware Analysis*.

To participate in ECSC, European countries have to select and train their national teams for a wide area of skill sets. Unlike other security competitions, ECSC is a team-based challenge comprising of 5 seniors and 5 juniors participants per team. Selecting and training such individuals with varying skill sets and age groups is a complex and difficult task. In this study, we are focusing on how different national teams are selected and trained for the competition. Additionally, we used the collected data to measure the cyber security ecosystem maturity of different countries. The paper is organized as follows: first we share the research background, continuing that we will present the research methodology after that we will highlight the national team selection and training strategies, following that we will map the national competitions maturity and conclude the article.

## 2   Research Background

Different researchers have been working on cyber security team organization and training over the years Dodge et al. [3] in 2003 focused on  *Organization and training of a cybersecurity team*. The researchers analyzed the data from different cyber defense exercises conducted between different US military academies and identified that such exercises improve the skill and knowledge of participants while developing leadership qualities. The researchers measured the team's performance during the exercises; however, they didn't identify how the team was trained and how it impacted their performance.

In 2021 researchers [4] conducted a study in which they analyzed the performance of different cyber security teams in different US cyber defense exercises. They collected the data from 36 teams with 2 to 8 members each and participated in four events over three years. Their findings indicated that the experience of the teams plays a significant role in team performance. The more the team played or participated in a similar competition, the more their performance will be. The researchers stated that the current evaluation methods are based upon qualitative data collection and analysis. There is a need for further data collection in terms of system logs and psychometric data that can empirically evaluate team performance. While the researchers focused on team training and performance, they didn't consider different factors that are involved in team selection.

This study is the continuation of our previous work [5] in which we conducted detailed interviews with 15 team coaches and officials in ECSC 2019. The study highlighted the process with which different teams national teams are selected and trained for ECSC. In the study, we suggested a five-step process to select and train national teams, which is: (1) Good marketing strategy, (2) Corporation among universities, (3) Long-term training, (4) Specific training platforms, and (5) Core focus on technical skills. Continuing that, we conducted a detailed study with the collaboration of ENISA to develop a common model for organizing NCSC (National Cyber Security Competitions) [6]. In the study, all ECSC participating countries participated and provided detailed inputs for the model. Additionally, in the study, we conducted a literature review and interviews with key stakeholder from government, academia, and industry across Europe to formulate the model. We called the developed model the TREE model. In the TREE model, we first focused on the root level, where we suggested targeting the primary and secondary school pupils to increase the participation numbers and awareness about the cyber security topics. After that, we suggested focusing on colleges and universities with STEM programs to recruit potential candidates. And at the fruit level, we suggested recruiting professionals from government academia and industry. We theorized that after the implementation of the TREE model, there would be a constant stream of individuals joining the cyber security workforce. The formulated TREE model presented in Fig. 1.

The TREE model can be used to measure the maturity of the cyber security ecosystem of a country. It considers different factors like the participation number of individuals in different age brackets and correlates it with the awareness level present in the country's population. The higher number of participants in the root level of the TREE model ensures a steady stream of participation in STEM and FRUIT levels. This resolves issues like the lack of a skilled workforce and gender diversity.

## 3    Methodology

We used a similar methodology form our previous work [5] and conducted a survey at ECSC 2021 in which coaches and team officials of 12 out of 18 participating countries provided their inputs. We asked questions about their national selection and training strategies, how many qualifying rounds they have, what kind of skills they're looking for, and how they train individuals for such competitions. We collected quantitative data and used statistical descriptive methods to identify the overall presence of interest in their country related to cyber security. We employed graphs and numerical analysis for data representation and analysis in an human understandable form. We used our TREE Model developed with a collaboration of ENISA to map the cyber security ecosystem of the country. Additionally, we asked questions about their handling of the COVID-19 pandemic for the selection and training to their national teams.

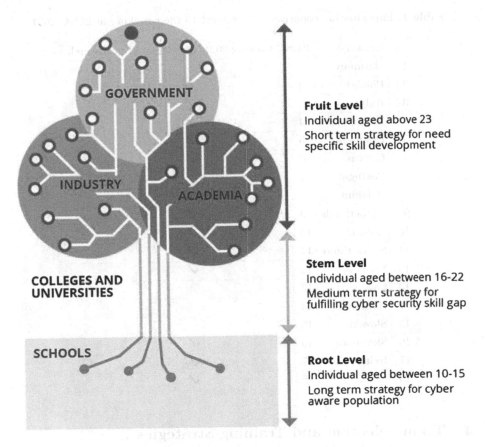

Fruit Level
Individual aged above 23
Short term strategy for need specific skill development

Stem Level
Individual aged between 16-22
Medium term strategy for fulfilling cyber security skill gap

Root Level
Individual aged between 10-15
Long term strategy for cyber aware population

**Fig. 1.** TREE model for NCSCs [6]

Countries that participated in the study are presented in Table 1. Additionally, we have collected data from Norway and the Czech Republic, but that was not included in the study. As Norway wasn't able to participate due to the COVID-19 risk assessment, and the Czech Republic voluntarily didn't participate as they were the host of the challenge and wanted to avoid any conflict of interest. The question that were asked for the data collection are presented in Appendix A.

**Table 1.** Participating countries with respect to their ranking in ECSC 2021

| No | Country | ECSC ranking 2021 | Participated in research |
|----|---------|-------------------|--------------------------|
| 1 | Germany | 1 | |
| 2 | Poland | 2 | |
| 3 | Italy | 3 | ✓ |
| 4 | France | 4 | ✓ |
| 5 | Denmark | 5 | ✓ |
| 6 | Cyprus | 6 | ✓ |
| 7 | Portugal | 7 | |
| 8 | Belgium | 8 | ✓ |
| 9 | Netherlands | 9 | ✓ |
| 10 | Austria | 10 | ✓ |
| 11 | Switzerland | 11 | ✓ |
| 12 | Spain | 12 | ✓ |
| 13 | Greece | 13 | |
| 14 | Romania | 14 | |
| 15 | Slovakia | 15 | |
| 16 | Slovenia | 16 | ✓ |
| 17 | Ireland | 17 | ✓ |
| 18 | Malta | 18 | ✓ |

## 4   Team Selection and Training Strategies

Countries applied different selection and training strategies which resulted in variable results. In terms of participation numbers of the first round of national competition, these variable results can be attributed to various factors like population, geography, lack of awareness [6]. The gathered data from all the participated countries identified that the Italian cyber security challenge witnessed the most number of participants with respect to numbers which 46% of total participants in ECSC. Continuing that, France was in second place for participation numbers which is 28% of total participants in ECSC. These large participation numbers can be attributed to their large population sizes. However, large population sizes can not always guarantee a large pool of talent. For example Spain, Belgium, and Austria, where participation numbers were 6%, each having vastly different population sizes. This different participation number can be attributed to the media campaign's effectiveness and the geographic size of Austria, which positively affected the participation numbers. The overall participation number percentage with respect to each country is presented in Fig. 2.

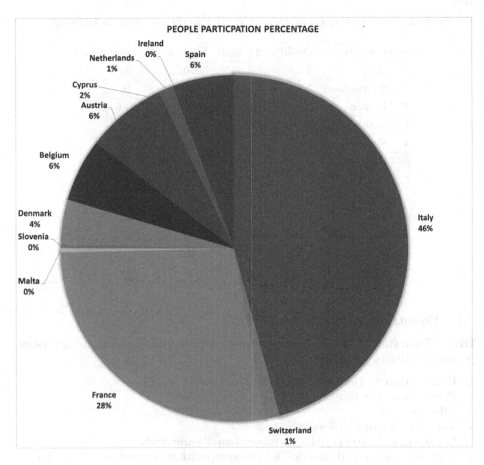

**Fig. 2.** Participation in NCSC

For selecting the teams, different countries have different processes. These processes involve different qualifying rounds and boot camps to identify individuals with the specific skill sets required for the competition. In Denmark, individuals have to go through 4 qualifying rounds to be selected for the national team, while in Italy, individuals have to go through 3 rounds of qualification. On average most countries have 2 qualifying rounds, details of which is presented in Table 2. The process of for selecting the nation teams is presented country wise below:

**Table 2.** Participating countries with respect to their ranking in ECSC 2021

| No | Country | Qualifying rounds | First round | Final round |
|----|---------|-------------------|-------------|-------------|
| 1 | Italy | 3 | 5000 | 20 |
| 2 | Switzerland | 2 | 150 | 16 |
| 3 | France | 2 | 3000 | 30 |
| 4 | Malta | 2 | 42 | 12 |
| 5 | Slovenia | 2 | 40 | 15 |
| 6 | Denmark | 4 | 450 | 25 |
| 7 | Belgium | 2 | 637 | 240 |
| 8 | Austria | 1 | 600 | 20 |
| 9 | Cyprus | 1 | 220 | 20 |
| 10 | Netherlands | 2 | 150 | 22 |
| 11 | Ireland | 2 | 18 | 18 |
| 12 | Spain | 1 | 600 | 100 |

### 4.1    Country Specific Process

**Italy.** Team Italy [7] has the most comprehensive selection and training process. It has five phases which are:

1. Registration on the website for the students
2. Pre-assessement test
3. Selection test
4. Training program of 3 month
5. Local jeopardy competition in more than 30 universities
6. National team-based Attack/Defense competition (1 team per university)

Best players from all the competitions are selected for the European finals.

**France.** Team France [8] was selected based upon a 10 d national CTF. Interviews with 5 best juniors, 5 best seniors and top 3 in all the categories like pwn, reverse, web, crypto were conducted. The coaches then select 10 players and 4 back ups for European finals.

**Switzerland.** Team Switzerland [9] was selected in two steps. First an online qualifier which was a jeopardy style CTF was organized for 3 months. Challenges were released every other week and in total there were more than 20 challenges. 16 people that ranked the highest in the CTF were qualified for the next round. In the second step they were divided into 4 teams of 4 people each. Everyone in the team had to develop challenges and train the team. Then, in the final round, the teams competed against each other, solving challenges that the others teams created plus additional hardware and teamwork challenges. Based on overall impression and the people's skill-set, 10 people were selected from the 16 as finalists for the European finals.

**Slovenia.** Team Slovenia [10] was selected after a national CTF competition. Top performers from the CTF were selected for the European finals.

**Malta.** Team Malta [11] was selected in two phases, in which the first phase was a 24 h long CTF out of which 12 people were selected. The people were trained individually and at the end of training in the second phase, an 8-hour CTF was organized to assist for the decision of the final 10 contestants and assign appropriate roles for European finals.

**Denmark.** Similar to team Italy, team Denmark [12] was also selected in multiple phases targeting multiple regions:

1. In the first phase a virtual qualification round was organized, in which each participant has to solve at least 6 out of 10 (relatively easy) challenges.
2. In the second phase a regional championship (held in the 5 regions) was organized, where 25 individuals were selected for the national finals.
3. In the third phases, a boot camp weekend was organized, which also constituted as the final selection round.

In the first part, the main focus was on technical skills while in the boot camp the selection process also focused on personal/team-related skills.

**Belgium.** Team Belgium [13] selection and training process was very different compared to the rest of the countries. They created the following rules for the people who want to participate and join the national team:

- Only students or first year workers (graduated same year) can participate in the qualifiers.
- Previous winner of the national qualifiers weren't allowed to participate in this phase for giving opportunity to new people.
- Top individuals from a national qualifiers will be selected.
- Top individuals will be combined with previous year winners based upon age brackets and required skill set for creating the national team for European qualifiers.

**Austria.** Team Austria [14] was selected by the team trainer. The trainers selected the team from a pool of finalists of local and national competitions. For consideration in the national team, reaching the top 10 places in the national finale is mandatory. In addition, the trainers can nominate players who have been at a European finale and players which have made it to the top 10 in the past years.

**Cyprus.** Team Cyprus was selected after an online national qualifier CTF. The qualifier runs for 2 weeks to identify the participants that will be eligible for ECSC. 20 in total were selected, and after the course of the next months, each team member was assessed based on their performance on CTFs and workshops and contribution to the team to identify the 10 final members.

**Netherlands.** Team Netherlands [15] was selected in two phases. In the first phase, a National qualifier CTF in which 150 people participated was organized. Top 20+2 wildcard (promote diversity) was selected for the second phase. In addition, a cyber boot camp was organized led to the selection of 10 individuals who were trained in workshops with the collaboration of commercial entities for ECSC finals.

**Ireland.** Team Ireland [16] was selected in a similar way to team Austria. They organize a national qualifier CTF to select the top-performing individuals and invite high achievers from other CTF completions to be part of the national team for ECSC finals.

**Spain.** Team Spain [17] was selected through a competition that was based on the rules of ECSC. The competition is a classic Jeopardy style CTF covering categories such as *Crypto, Forensics, Web, Reversing, Pwn...* This competition has two phases:

1. A qualification phase, where the aim is to create a pool of candidates.
2. A final phase where top candidates were selected based upon specific required technical skills and interviews.

For team Spain, it was important not just to select the final candidates but also to have a backup of candidates. Just in case of any replacement, especially in the uncertainties of COVID-19.

### 4.2    Technical and Social Skills

**Technical Skills.** Team officials and coaches from Italy, Switzerland, Denmark, Austria, Netherlands, Ireland, and Spain indicated that they look for the following skills in in the participants: (1) *Cryptography*, (2) *Web Security*, (3) *Binary exploitation/PWN/Software Security*, (4) *Hardware Security*, (5) *Network Security*, (6) *Forensics/Malware Analysis*, (7) *Attack/Defense* , (8) *Reverse engineering*, (9) *Penetration testing* , (10) *Mobile Security*, and (11) *Networking & Sysadmin*. From the feedback of the team officials and coaches, it was identified that web security was the most sought after technical skill. Country specific skill set requirement for national competitions is presented in Fig. 3.

Coaches of Malta looked for all-rounders who can solve multiple type of challenges. In Slovenia, the coaches looked for different skills to cover the majority of security topics. In Cyprus, the number of eligible participants was low, so they wanted to have at least an advanced player for each of the major categories. Similarly, in France, coaches looked for very good skills in at least one category and the ability to help another player in at least another category. In Belgium,

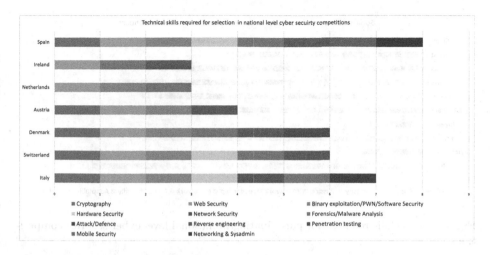

**Fig. 3.** Technical skills required for participating in national level cyber security competitions

the national contest was team-based, so little focus was given on specific skills. To determine who can join to fill in the extra slots and decide who becomes reserve and the main team, they use a questionnaire where the participants have to rate their own proficiency in different categories.

**Social and Teamwork Skills.** Team officials and coaches from Italy, Switzerland, France, Slovenia, Denmark, Belgium, Austria, Cyprus, Ireland, and Spain indicated that they look for the following social skills in the participants: (1) *Ethics*, (2) *Patience*, (3) *Curiosity*, (4) *Passion*, (5) *Teamwork*, (6) *Leadership*, (7) *Hard work*, (8) *Media friendly*, (9) *Adaptable*, and (10) *Helpful*. From the team officials and coaches feedback it was identified that teamwork, patience, curiosity and passion are the most sought after social skills. Country specific social skill set requirement for national competitions is presented in Fig. 4. The team official and coaches from Netherlands stated that they select the individuals based on their teams' scores, so this selection is purely based on CTF performance. With regards to specific Teamwork skills team official and coaches from Italy, Slovenia, Denmark, Netherlands and Spain indicated that they look for for the following skills: (1) *Coordination and collaboration*, (2) *Time management*, (3) *Stress Management*, (4) *Communication*. From the team officials and coaches feedback it was identified *Coordination and collaboration* is the most sought after teamwork skill. Country specific teamwork skill set requirement for national competitions is presented in Fig. 5:

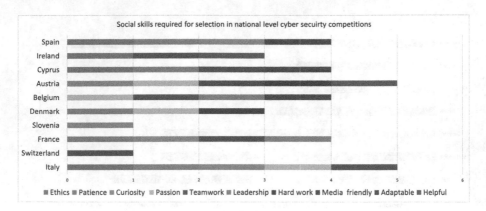

**Fig. 4.** Social skills required for participating in national level cyber security competitions

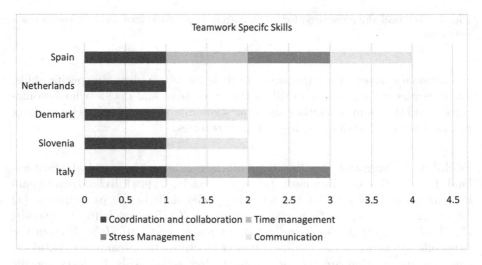

**Fig. 5.** Teamwork skills required for participating in national level cyber security competitions

In the Netherlands, collaboration is achieved by pairing up the team members based upon different skill categories. So, if someone top 2 skills are Web Security and Pwn, they will get coupled with someone who also has either Web or Pwn as their first or second preference for training. In Belgium, they like having a few people that can keep up the good moods even if things don't go as planned. While in Spain, they look for individuals who have an interest in international CTFs and cyber security in general with the ability to dedicate a non-trivial amount of time to team training.

### 4.3  Training

The teams applied primarily four training strategies: (1) *CTF*, (2) *Escape room*, (3) *Boot camps*, and (4) *Team building*. Playing CTFs and organizing training boot camps was the most popular training strategy. Team Italy, Denmark, Austria, Cyprus, Netherlands, and Spain played various CTFs before coming to the competition, while team Switzerland participated in 10 CTF events. In terms of boot camps. France organized a 2-day online training session while Malta and Slovenia organized a 5 day long boot camp. On the other hand Netherlands organized 4 training sessions with industrial partners and Spain organized periodic team meetings. In the boot camps, different countries also focused on team building using team member presentations on CTF challenges and solving the challenges together. Figure 6 presents different training strategies employed by national teams.

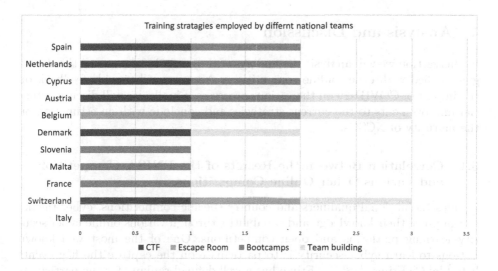

**Fig. 6.** Training strategies employed by different national teams

Furthermore, Switzerland rehearsed for ECSC with an escape room to train a small group of 4 people for the escape room challenge and also organized a non-technical team event to improve teamwork. Similarly, Belgium used an escape room for team building process. Due to the difficult circumstances, Ireland was not able to organize any training event, and they participated without any training in ECSC. In term of technical training platforms, different teams used different platforms which are presented in Table 3:

**Table 3.** Training platforms employed by different teams

| No | Country | Platform used |
|----|---------|---------------|
| 1 | Italy | Custom |
| 2 | Switzerland | CTFd |
| 3 | France | Custom |
| 4 | Malta | rootme |
| 5 | Slovenia | Hack The Box, CTFtime |
| 6 | Denmark | Multiple platforms |
| 7 | Belgium | No specif platform |
| 8 | Austria | Hacking-Lab |
| 9 | Cyprus | Public CTFs |
| 10 | Netherlands | No specific platform |
| 11 | Ireland | No specific platform |
| 12 | Spain | Custom with public platforms Hack The Box, TryHackME, W3Challs |

## 5    Analysis and Discussion

In this section we will analysis the findings of the study by comparing the strategies applied with other online competitions. Also, we will provide feedback on the impact of COVID-19 on the various processes. Finally, we will discuss potential improvements to the current strategies and conclude with an estimation on the maturity of NCSCs.

### 5.1    Correlation Between the Results of the ENISA Competition and Various Other Online Competitions

Besides the national qualifiers and country specific competitions, cyber talents can improve their knowledge and capabilities through various online cyber security learning platforms and open competitions. One of the most well known options to learn cyber security is to participate on the capture the flag events listed by CTFtime [18]. CTFtime has a well defined ranking for the participating teams where each competition is considered with different weights according to the difficulty level. CTFtime can also provide national ranking for the teams as well as an overall ranking for all teams based on the points they collected on an annual basis. This international ranking makes it possible to compare the results with the ENISA competition results, however some differences have to be highlighted. The first significant difference is the lack of the age limit. Whilst ENISA only allows national players in the national teams with the age limit of 25, competitions on CTFtime has no age limit at all. In addition to this, CTF-Time teams have no team size limit. In extreme cases one team can be only one single player or it can even be a whole country with hundreds of players. CTFtime teams can choose countries in their profile description to indicate their nationality, on the other hand, there is no strict restriction for this. Mixed teams with multiple citizenship can also participate. For our comparison we considered the 2020 and 2021 results (as of 1 December 2021) on CTFtime by checking the position of the best national team and the number of teams in one country in the top 100. Ranking for cyber talents is also provided by other well known platforms such as the HTB (Hack the Box) [19] or Try hack me [20]. With both learning platforms the players can continuously solve cyber security challenges and collect points for the right solutions. Hack the box has an overall ranking for the countries based on the players results, with Try hack me we analyzed the position of the best national player for each country as well as the number of players in the top 50 for each country. Table 4 summarizes the results.

**Table 4.** Results in other competitions

| Country | ECSC | CTFtime | | | | HTB | TryHackMe | |
|---|---|---|---|---|---|---|---|---|
| | 2021 ranking | Best team 2020 | Top 100 2020 | Best team 2021 | Top 100 2021 | Country position | Best player | Top 50 |
| Germany | 1 | 6 | 6 | 25 | 6 | 3 | 11 | 4 |
| Poland | 2 | 8 | 4 | 13 | 3 | 9 | 3 | 3 |
| Italy | 3 | 40 | 5 | 42 | 4 | 6 | 94 | 0 |
| France | 4 | 11 | 4 | 19 | 3 | 5 | 71 | 0 |
| Denmark | 5 | 66 | 1 | 14 | 1 | 48 | 163 | 0 |
| Cyprus | 6 | 159 | 0 | 138 | 0 | 80 | 376 | 0 |
| Portugal | 7 | 56 | 1 | 54 | 1 | 63 | 128 | 0 |
| Belgium | 8 | 522 | 0 | 204 | 0 | 35 | 350 | 0 |
| Netherlands | 9 | 144 | 0 | 193 | 0 | 11 | 2 | 3 |
| Austria | 10 | 69 | 2 | 77 | 1 | 27 | 18 | 2 |
| Switzerland | 11 | 47 | 2 | 2 | 3 | 46 | 231 | 0 |
| Spain | 12 | 71 | 1 | 84 | 3 | 7 | 63 | 0 |
| Greece | 13 | 73 | 1 | 40 | 1 | 14 | 85 | 0 |
| Romania | 14 | 260 | 0 | 240 | 0 | 29 | 80 | 0 |
| Slovakia | 15 | 546 | 0 | 499 | 0 | 71 | 123 | 0 |
| Slovenia | 16 | 637 | 0 | 59 | 0 | – | 1461 | 0 |
| Ireland | 17 | 196 | 0 | 471 | 0 | – | 7 | 1 |
| Malta | 18 | – | 0 | 4175 | 0 | – | 5005 | 0 |

Based on the collected results we conclude that the results of other learning platforms and competitions are aligned with the ENISA competition results with some exceptions. One exception is Cyprus that achieved much better result at the ENISA 2021 competition than was expected based on the results of other cyber security platforms. Belgium and Netherlands ENISA results are also much better than what was reflected by CTFtime, but these countries have stronger country profiles on Hackthebox or TryHackme. Another exception is Switzerland. Based on the comparison the 11th position on the ENISA competition can be disappointing for the Swiss team, since Switzerland has the best European team in 2021 on CTFtime as of 1 December 2021.

## 5.2 Impact of COVID-19

COVID-19 significantly impacted the selection and training process of different participating countries. Some countries opted for a completely digital selection and training process, while other countries implemented a hybrid approach. In France, Austria, Cyprus, and Spain, all selection and training process was organized digitally. Most of the countries used Discord as a communication channel with the participants, while some countries also used Microsoft Teams for training activities. Countries' issue while digitally organizing such events was to keep the participants motivated in solving difficult and complex challenges and build meaningful team players connections. The mentioned countries will try to organize physical events when the situation gets normalized.

In Italy, all the selection and training phases were performed completely online and remotely, except for the last round with 20 students where it was possible to be physically together. Similarly, in Switzerland, phase 1 of the competition was organized online. While phase 2 was organized online with a COVID-19 emergency plan. Additionally, the organizers communicated the vaccination policy to the participants if they wanted to be a part of the team. Likewise, the first phase of the competition was organized online in Malta, and the short-listed participants were individually interviewed. Training and the final selection were carried out in person, given that there were just 12 people with a reduced risk of virus transmission. In Denmark, Netherlands, Belgium, and Slovenia, COVID-19 mainly impacted the first qualification round and the regional championships since these had to be held virtually (due to government restrictions). When the restrictions eased up, in-person training was organized for the teams. The Netherlands organized an onsite boot camp with a relatively small group (22 participants) + testing before, during, and after the event.

## 5.3 Future Improvement Strategies

The participating countries are planning to improve their NCSC in three ways, which are: (1) *Time*, (2) *Challenges* and (3) *Diversity*. In terms of *Time* countries like Spain, Malta, Ireland, Austria, and Slovenia are planning to increase the duration of their national cyber security competitions, while France is planning to reduce the time required for participation in a challenge to one week or less. According to officials from Spain more time will allow them to spend more time with candidates and help them to evaluate them for all the relevant skills in the best possible ways. Similarly, officials from Malta are planning to schedule their NCSC so that it doesn't overlap with the high school exam dates to ensure the maximum number of participants. In term of *Challenges* countries like Belgium, Switzerland, Italy, Spain, Malta, and Austria are planning to focus on more comprehensive challenges to train their team on a more diverse skill set. Officials from Switzerland specifically mention that they want to train the participants for unforeseen events and how the team should react to them, and they want to push harder the skills of individuals in their primary and secondary strengths. In terms of *Diversity* Spain and Denmark are directly targeting female participants and encouraging female participation in all levels of their national competitions. Countries like Netherlands and Malta are planning to encourage more participation in their national competitions from an early stage, which can positively affect their competitions' diversity. Figure 7 presents different future improvement strategies that are going to be employed by national cyber security competition organizers.

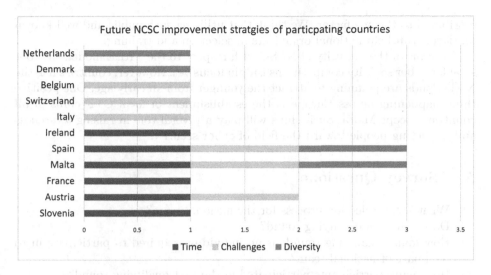

**Fig. 7.** Future strategies for improving national cyber security competitions

## 5.4  NCSC Maturity

If we analyze the maturity of NCSC using the TREE model, countries like Italy and France have a very mature stem for attracting individuals for the ECSC age group. While Austria and Belgium were able to attract a considerable number of individuals even with their small population sizes, compared to Spain, their stem level is also flourishing. The rest of the countries are struggling to attract a large number of individuals to their NCSC, considering the example of Ireland, in which only 18 people participated in their national competition. The best way to move forward is to focus on the root level, schools have to raise awareness about cyber security and attract people in their national competitions, which the Czech Republic did and attracted 5700 individuals in their NCSC. Additionally from the data it was identified that local CTF clubs are being formed across Europe except in Malta. This will help to strengthen the root level of the TREE model for a better cyber security ecosystem.

## 6  Conclusion

In this study, we collected and analyzed data from national teams of 12 European countries for their selection and training strategies for ECSC. The data indicated that most of the participation and talent pool of cyber security was present in countries like Italy and France. At the same time, countries like Austria were able to attract more people compared to other countries concerning their population size. Comparing the ECSC results with other online competition platforms, like CTFTime, Showed that there are some deviations in terms of actual standings in ECSC and the perceived standings in public CTF platforms, which can be attributed to the age factor. We think that utilizing such public and well-known platforms can help national organizers in selection and training.

In terms of the maturity of NCSC with respect to the TREE model, the root level for cyber security competitions isn't in focus yet. However, countries like the Netherlands are planning to attract the younger from an early age. One positive thing happening across Europe is the establishment of local CTF clubs in all countries except Malta. Such clubs will play a pivotal role in raising awareness and attracting people toward the field of cyber security.

## A     Survey Questioner

1. What is the selection process for the national team?
2. Do you have a qualifying round?
3. How many qualifying rounds is an individual required to participate in to be a part of national team?
4. How many participants participated in the first qualifying round?
5. How many participants participated in final round?
6. What technical traits/skills did you look for with regards to individual selection?
7. What personality traits did you look for with regards to individual selection?
8. What team related skills did you look with regards to the individual team member?
9. How did you train the selected team for the ECSC competition?
10. Any specific platforms you used for training?
11. What do you think can be improved in selection and training process?
12. Do you have hacking and CTF clubs in your country?
13. How did you manage the COVID-19 pandemic during team selection and training?

## References

1. European cyber security challenge - ECSC. https://ecsc.eu/. Accessed 5 Feb 2022
2. Enisa. https://www.enisa.europa.eu/. Accessed 5 Feb 2022
3. Dodge, R.C., Ragsdale, D.J., Reynolds, C.: Organization and training of a cyber security team. In: SMC 2003 Conference Proceedings. 2003 IEEE International Conference on Systems, Man and Cybernetics. Conference Theme-System Security and Assurance (Cat. No. 03CH37483), vol. 5, pp. 4311–4316. IEEE (2003)
4. La Fleur, C., Hoffman, B., Gibson, C.B., Buchler, N.: Team performance in a series of regional and national US cybersecurity defense competitions: generalizable effects of training and functional role specialization. Comput. Secur. **104**, 102229 (2021)
5. Yamin, M.M., Katt, B., Torseth, E.: Selecting and training young cyber talent: a European cybersecurity challenge case study. In: Schmorrow, D.D., Fidopiastis, C.M. (eds.) HCII 2021. LNCS (LNAI), vol. 12776, pp. 462–483. Springer, Cham (2021). https://doi.org/10.1007/978-3-030-78114-9_32

6. Towards a common ecsc roadmap - enisa, April 2021. https://www.enisa.europa.eu/publications/towards-a-common-ecsc-roadmap. Accessed 5 Feb 2022

7. Cyberchallenge.it. https://cyberchallenge.it/. Accessed 5 Feb 2022

8. France cybersecurity challenge. https://france-cybersecurity-challenge.fr/. Accessed 5 Feb 2022

9. Swiss hacking challenge. https://www.swiss-hacking-challenge.ch/. Accessed 5 Feb 2022

10. Kibertalent - home. https://kibertalent.si/en/home/. Accessed 5 Feb 2022

11. Cyber security malta - education towards a safest future. https://cybersecurity.gov.mt. Accessed 5 Feb 2022

12. De danske cybermesterskaber - national cybersikkerhed. https://nationalcybersikkerhed.dk/ddc. Accessed 5 Feb 2022

13. Cyber security challenge Belgium. https://www.cybersecuritychallenge.be. Accessed 5 Feb 2022

14. Cyber security Austria - du bist verboten gut? dann zeig's uns! https://verbotengut.at. Accessed 5 Feb 2022

15. Home — challenge the cyber. https://challengethecyber.nl/. Accessed 5 Feb 2022

16. Zero days ctf - cyber-security training

17. Cybercamp—cybercamp 2019

18. Ctftime.org/all about ctf (capture the flag). https://ctftime.org/. Accessed 5 Feb 2022

19. Hack the box: Hacking training for the best — individuals & companies. https://www.hackthebox.com/. Accessed 5 Feb 2022

20. Tryhackme — cyber security training. https://tryhackme.com/. Accessed 5 Feb 2022

# Extended Reality and Augmented Cognition

# Human-Centered Augmentation of xR Training Technologies with a Self-regulatory Cognitive Process

Christian Ampo(✉), Nicholas A. Moon, Zachary B. Hesson, Valerie Robbins-Roth, Brett Wallace, and Richard L. Griffith

Florida Institute of Technology, Melbourne, FL 32901, USA
campo2020@my.fit.edu, griffith@fit.edu

**Abstract.** The emergence of extended reality (xR) training technologies have become popular in practice at a much faster pace than supporting research. Reviews on xR training not only call into question its effectiveness and value beyond traditional training methods, but also highlights further research on the role of individual differences in xR training as a way of improving xR training effectiveness. The purpose of this paper is to present a self-regulatory cognitive process, called Guided Mindfulness (GM), as a human-centered augmentation of xR training technologies to improve transfer from the training environment to the actual work environment. With a focus on tailored experiences, a discussion of how GM expands on After-Action Reviews and an illustrative example of incorporating GM in an existing xR training design in a workplace context is provided. Implications of the future of GM in xR training is further discussed.

**Keywords:** Extended reality · Training · After-action review · Guided mindfulness

## 1 Introduction

The emergence of augmented reality (AR), virtual reality (VR), and mixed reality (MR) technologies will play a prominent role in the landscape of training delivery [1]. Collectively known as extended reality (xR) [2], the immersive nature of these training methods has helped bridge the gap between the training environment and the actual work environment. Furthermore, xR training can be readily adapted to different situations and help learners become better prepared for conditions of volatility, uncertainty, complexity and ambiguity (VUCA) [3] that is prevalent in the modern world. These conditions create a complex environment that is pervasive in different contexts, such as in the military where leaders must be vigilantly prepared for it [4] and in the workplace, where leaders must be consciously aware of how VUCA affects their business [5]. In comparison to the restrictive and costly nature of live-fire simulations [6] and traditional training programs, the adaptable and cost-effective immersive technologies are poised to be the future of training in a VUCA world.

© The Author(s), under exclusive license to Springer Nature Switzerland AG 2022
D. D. Schmorrow and C. M. Fidopiastis (Eds.): HCII 2022, LNAI 13310, pp. 325–332, 2022.
https://doi.org/10.1007/978-3-031-05457-0_25

With the rapidly growing popularity of xR training, there is emerging concern that the practice of development is progressing much faster than theory and supporting research can keep up [7]. As new training technologies are being tested, novel ones emerge. The paucity of research on emerging learning technologies is a hindrance to xR training practitioners, and can lead to negative consequences, such as inconsistent transfer of training. In a recent meta-analysis, Kaplan and colleagues [8] highlighted the wide variability of transfer with xR training. In other words, the ability for learners to apply skills learned in xR training to the actual work environment was fairly inconsistent. In light of their findings, Kaplan and colleagues [8] identified individual differences as a major factor for such mixed results and emphasized the immediate need for further research.

One avenue towards expanding the role of individual differences in xR training is through exploration of tailored approaches for training. Therefore, the purpose of this paper is to present a self-regulatory cognitive process, called Guided Mindfulness (GM) [9], as a human-centered augmentation tool to enable a tailored approach with xR training. The implementation of GM as a tailored approach can help improve xR transfer of training by utilizing simple preparatory and reflection prompts before and after key events of the training. These prompts will enable self-regulatory cognitive processes that will equip individuals to become better aware of the event, better make meaning of the event and better visualize how future events may look like. A key feature of GM is that the semi-structured nature of the intervention allows an individual to tailor their learning experience, thus enhancing the effectiveness of training through a focus on the individual. With a focus on tailored experiences, a discussion of how GM expands on After-Action Reviews and an illustrative example of incorporating GM in an existing xR training design in a workplace context is provided. Implications of the future of GM in xR training is further discussed.

## 2   XR Training Technologies

xR training technologies were initially seen as promising new methods to increase training efficiency [10]. However, recent reviews call into question the necessity of transitioning current traditional training methods towards xR. A meta-analysis by Kaplan and colleagues [8] found that training provided through xR and through traditional methods are equally effective in regards to training outcomes. This pattern was a consistent trend across different types of skills learned (i.e., physical, cognitive, and mixed). In another meta-analysis by Howard & Gutworth [11], virtual reality training programs performed worse than non-immersive programs when training for social skill development. Although the literature suggests the current state of xR training effectiveness does not seem bright, its promise is still seen across different industries, such as mineral mining [12] and in medical training [13]. To advance xR training effectiveness and improve its outlook, further systematic evaluation needs to be conducted and best practices must be grounded in theory.

One of the most prominent frameworks relevant to transfer of training is Baldwin and Ford's [14] Model of the Transfer Process. This model purports that conditions of transfer are directly influenced by three training inputs: (1) trainee characteristics, which is focused on the learner, (2) work environment, which is focused on the psychological or physical situational variables of the training and (3) training design, which is focused on the training methodology. Additionally, the three training inputs can also have an indirect influence on the conditions of transfer through training outputs, namely learning and retention. A successful condition of transfer is evident with a generalization and maintenance of skill learned during training to behavior in the actual work environment. A recent review of the model by Grossman & Salas [15] further reinforced the importance of this model in transfer of training and asserted, "the factors included in our review, we argue, have now garnered sufficient evidence suggesting that they do, in fact, reliably exhibit strong relationships with the transfer of training" (p. 117). According to the authors, a successful condition of transfer is predicated on all three training inputs, however, the role of trainee characteristics and tailored approaches in xR training has largely been neglected. Therefore, a further investigation of how trainee characteristics can help inform tailored approaches in xR training is warranted to improve the outlook of xR training.

Beyond Kaplan and colleagues [8], other researchers echo the importance of a focus beyond training design in xR training. Fracaro and colleagues [16] studied VR training design in the chemical industry and indicated that motivation and engagement during VR training can be enhanced using game-based learning elements. Additionally, in a review of VR training effectiveness, Abich and colleagues [17] recommend that trainers should consider the characteristics of the training audience during VR training design, such as the level of trainees proficiency [18]. Currently, there are research efforts regarding trainee characteristics, but more can be done, especially research that directly targets tailored trainee experiences. We propose to expand the literature of xR training focusing on how a tailored approach can affect trainee characteristics, particularly self-efficacy. We aim to do this by presenting a tailored, self-regulatory cognitive process, called Guided Mindfulness, to enhance self-efficacy and improve transfer of training.

## 3 Guided Mindfulness

Guided Mindfulness (GM) is a self-regulatory cognitive process that can help facilitate transfer of training by engaging the users in event-based preparation and reflection cognitive exercises centered on key experiences in the training event [9, 19]. The GM process helps provide structure for complex skill acquisition through experiential learning, which is a form of learning through interacting with our environment and reflecting on past experiences [20]. Essentially, GM is a personalized approach to experiential learning equipped to improve complex skill acquisition through self-regulatory processes.

Self-regulation is a term that describes a variety of cognitive, affective, and behavioral processes, which are key mechanisms for the effectiveness of training interventions [21]. These processes allow individuals to focus their attention and reflect on their goals [22]. GM capitalizes on self-regulation processes by engaging the user in the following processes: self-awareness, situational awareness, social awareness, sensemaking, and simulation [9]. Self-awareness helps identify gaps in competency or skill levels by increasing understanding of one's assumptions, biases, emotions, skills, values, strengths, and weaknesses [23]. Situational awareness refers to an individual's understanding of an experience in a way that recognizes and incorporates both environmental and situational changes rapidly and effectively [24]. Social awareness refers to the ability to recognize inferred relational cues in order to understand the social dynamics of an interpersonal environment and better select behaviors that are suitable [25]. Sensemaking, the process in which individuals infer meaning from an event, involves using the inferences for decision-making, information organization, and complex skill acquisition [26]. Lastly, simulation encompasses mental rehearsal of previous or anticipated interactions. These "5-S's" are a feedback loop which helps inform future learning events. This process is iterative and can occur many times during a learning experience or throughout the learning cycle.

GM integrates each of these 5-S's at various levels in three stages of learning: early, intermediate, and late [27, 28]. Early learning is focused on one's internal state and learners are considered to have little to no information regarding their skill and primarily leverages self-awareness and sensemaking. Intermediate learning is focused more on the task and situation, and it is assumed that learners at this stage have some experiences to draw from and most often utilizes situational awareness, social awareness and simulation. Late learning is where learners are considered experts, and this is where the focus is shifted to minor details that could help them perfect their skill with all 5-S's.

# 4   Guided Mindfulness Targeting Self-efficacy Through AAR

A primary feature of the GM approach is to allow individuals to capitalize on their own experiences. Further, these individuals utilize self-regulatory resources to learn while experiencing events [21], and they should be able to enhance this learning by implementing the GM process [19, 27]. Specifically, the GM process can help an individual improve their self-efficacy (i.e., an individual's belief in their capacity to perform) [29], a central component to self-regulation [30]. GM allows the individual to more effectively identify their skill level (i.e., self-awareness), make sense of themselves in the context of their situational and social situation (i.e., sensemaking), and finally act out new situations to help apply what they have learned through this exercise (i.e., simulation). As learners continually engage in the GM process, they become better equipped to handle the next learning event, which can improve their confidence and level of self-efficacy.

In practice, a model of GM is already widely practiced throughout the military in the form of After-Action Reviews (AAR), which is described as a systematic review composed of reviews and discussion on the learner's performance with recently completed learning events Hu [31]. The similarity of AAR in GM can be seen in its intended use of being useful for highly complex and ambiguous environments [32] through targeting self-efficacy as a source of improvement [33]. In terms of process, the similarity between AAR and GM can be seen in the engagement of sensemaking and simulation processes during the reflection discussion after the learning event. However, GM is distinct from AAR by the addition of a preparation phase and focused discussion around self-awareness, situational awareness and social awareness. Additionally, AAR are traditionally focused more on groups [34], whereas GM is focused more on the individual. In essence, GM is intended to be an improvement of the overall AAR process that includes personalization, additional phases, and focused attention on self-regulatory processes.

Prior research has demonstrated that AAR is effective in learning and training outcomes, such as attitudes, cognition, task performance, and processes [35]. The benefits of AAR were also observed in synthetic training environments [36], which is a form of xR training that is popular in the military [37]. However, a conflicting study found that individuals who participate in AARs may not fully benefit past initial skill acquisition [38]. Therefore, GM is intended to aid in this individualized approach in xR training.

Due to the similarities between AAR and GM conceptually, it is expected that GM will have similar effects, such that those who practice GM will likely increase their cognitions, task performance (both inside and outside of training), overall processes, and attitudes. Further, given the benefits of AAR to self-efficacy, it is expected that GM will have similar effects and benefits to increasing an individual's self-efficacy.

## 5    Guided Mindfulness Application to xR

Although the initial application of AAR is within the military context, its application has spread beyond to other industries [31]. Likewise, the application of GM is also expected to apply in other industries, such as the workplace context, and can specifically augment the growing use of VR training in the workplace that was necessitated with the COVID-19 pandemic [39]. With the reduction in costs of developing VR training and its ever-increasing fidelity of real-life work, it is possible that VR training would become a reality for more organizations [40].

For example, in a public report published by PricewaterhouseCoopers (PwC) [41], their Emerging Technology Group and Learning and Development Innovation team developed a soft-skills training module supported by VR, specifically using the Oculus headset. Briefly, to illustrate how VR training could be developed, they spent three months to design the training, which put learners inside a virtual office environment where they had to sit either at a conference table or attend a conference call (i.e., similar expectations of the actual job). To interact with the virtual characters, the learners would read the dialogue aloud from a list of options. During this training, the virtual characters would adapt to the conversation as the learner engaged with them while the learner practiced making inclusive leadership decisions. Overall, learners in the VR training condition, in comparison to traditional forms of training, were faster, more confident, more focused and felt stronger emotional connections. However, the information retention between pre- and post-assessments between training conditions (i.e., VR or traditional) was not significant. This result is consistent with the results of the meta-analysis on transfer of training by Kaplan and colleagues [8].

Since soft-skills, such as leadership, are complex skills [42], GM is a well-suited augmentation in the PwC VR training design to help improve transfer. GM is flexible and can be implemented in the PwC VR training design either in conjunction (i.e., outside the virtual environment) or integrated (i.e., inside the virtual environment) within the VR training environment. Outside the virtual world, GM prompts can be delivered through mobile apps augmented with artificial intelligence [43]. This has the benefit of GM being in a mobile device, which can be used beyond this training. However, this would increase procedural timer in training since both phone and VR headset are needed. The GM preparation phase prompts will be answered before putting on the VR headset and then the GM reflection phase prompts will be answered after removing the VR headset. Integrated within the virtual world, GM can be delivered as audio prompts.

Specifically, a personal voice over may provide users a way to express their thoughts and self-motivations, which have been shown to improve self-efficacy of learners [44]. The benefit of increased integration by using an audio modality may seem more natural, but can also be problematic with increased risk of cognitive overload in training programs as more features are included. Regardless of which reality (i.e., actual reality vs virtual reality) and what modality through which it is delivered, GM can help with calling attention to specific training cues and learning moments through increasing trainee awareness focused on learning objectives. Therefore, this can help with the VR overload that individuals experience because VR learning can distract the learning (e.g., increased cognitive load), which may result in the learner having poorer performance [45]. The illustrative example highlights the potential of GM integration in xR training.

## 6   Guided Mindfulness Beyond

xR technology application is happening across industries. Research has primarily focused on training effectiveness and much of the research is moving past an important part of the training: the learner. More consideration must be given to learners, individual differences, and tailored developmental experiences when designing xR training. Through GM, an xR training with a more tailored approach can be actualized, which can increase self-efficacy and training outcomes as the personalized approach can better account for unique learner characteristics. Furthermore, the self-regulatory process of the 5-S's is flexible as different parts of the intervening process can be emphasized for learner-specific optimization.

In conjunction with xR training, the scalable and mobile features of GM [42] enables its application beyond the military or workplace and can be applied in a variety of contexts and technologies. GM is not limited to training for specific competencies as it is an adaptable process that applies to multiple complex competencies [19]. In other words, GM can be augmented within training programs beyond military context, such as medical or manufacturing assembly training. Furthermore, GM is not limited to a specific modality and can therefore be adapted to current technological training methodologies and future technologies that may emerge. Just as the "x" in xR accounts for future technologies, GM is also able to adapt to future technology. As more forms of technology expand in the "x," as technological advancement results in more sophisticated methodologies, GM will be poised to augment and maintain pace new emerging technologies to their maximal potential.

## References

1. Bisbey, T.M., Traylor, A., Salas, E.: Implications of the changing nature of work for training. In: Hoffman, B., Shoss, M., Wegman, L. (eds.) Cambridge Handbook of the Changing Nature of Work. Cambridge University Press, Cambridge (2020)
2. Palmas, F., Klinker, G.: Defining extended reality training: a long-term definition for all industries. In: 2020 IEEE 20th International Conference on Advanced Learning Technologies (ICALT), pp. 322–324. IEEE (2020)
3. Gerras, S.J., et al.: Strategic leadership primer. Carlisle, PA: Army War College, Carlisle Barracks (2010)

4. Kirchner, M., Akdere, M.: Military leadership development strategies: implications for training in non-military organizations. Ind. Commer. Train. **49**(7/8), 357–364 (2016)
5. Bennett, N., Lemoine, J.G.: What difference a word makes: understanding threats to performance in a VUCA world. Bus. Horizons, **57**(3), 311–317 (2014)
6. Harper, J.: Army to build synthetic training environments. Natl. Defense **101**(757), 28–30 (2016)
7. Hancock, P.A., Hoffman, R.R.: Keeping up with intelligent technology. IEEE Intell. Syst. **30**(1), 62–65 (2015)
8. Kaplan, A.D., Cruit, J., Endsley, M., Beers, S.M., Sawyer, B.D., Hancock, P.A.: The effects of virtual reality, augmented reality, and mixed reality as training enhancement methods: a meta-analysis. Human Factors J. Human Factors Ergon. Soc. **63**(4), 706–726 (2021)
9. Griffith, R.L., Steelman, L.A., Wildman, J.L., LeNoble, C.A., Zhou, Z.E.: Guided mindfulness: a self-regulatory approach to experiential learning of complex skills. Theor. Issues Ergon. Sci. **18**(2), 147–166 (2016)
10. Hancock, P.A.: The future of simulation. In: Vicenzi, J.D., Mouloua, W.M., Hancock, P.A. (eds.) Human Factors in Simulation and Training, pp. 169–186 (2009)
11. Howard, M.C., Gutworth, M.B.: A meta-analysis of virtual reality training programs for social skill development. Comput. Educ. **144**, 103707 (2020)
12. Tichon, J., Burgess-Limerick, R.: A review of virtual reality as a medium for safety related training in mining. J. Health Saf. Res. Pract. **3**(1), 33–40 (2011)
13. Barsom, E.Z., Graafland, M., Schijven, M.P.: Systematic review on the effectiveness of augmented reality applications in medical training. Surg. Endosc. **30**(10), 4174–4183 (2016). https://doi.org/10.1007/s00464-016-4800-6
14. Baldwin, T.T., Ford, J.K.: Transfer of training: a review and directions for future research. Pers. Psychol. **41**(1), 63–105 (1988)
15. Grossman, R., Salas, E.: The transfer of training: what really matters. Int. J. Training Dev. **15**(2), 103–120 (2011)
16. Fracaro, S.G., et al.: Towards design guidelines for virtual reality training for the chemical industry. Educ. Chem. Eng. **36**, 12-23 (2021)
17. Abich, J., Parker, J., Murphy, J.S., Eudy, M.: A review of the evidence for training effectiveness with virtual reality technology. Virtual Reality **25**(4), 919–933 (2021). https://doi.org/10.1007/s10055-020-00498-8
18. Pulijala, Y., Ma, M., Pears, M., Peebles, D., Ayoub, A.: Effectiveness of immersive virtual reality in surgical training: a randomized control trial. J. Oral Maxillofac. Surg. **76**(5), 1065–1072 (2018)
19. Quraishi, N., et al.: Guided mindfulness: new frontier to augmented learning. In: Schmorrow, D.D., Fidopiastis, C.M. (eds.) HCII 2019. LNCS (LNAI), vol. 11580, pp. 586–596. Springer, Cham (2019). https://doi.org/10.1007/978-3-030-22419-6_42
20. Kolb, D.A.: The process of experiential learning. In: Experiential Learning: Experience as the Source of Learning and Development, pp. 20–38. Prentice-Hall, Inc. (1984)
21. Sitzmann, T., Ely, K.: A meta-analysis of self-regulated learning in work-related training and educational attainment: what we know and where we need to go. Psychol. Bull. **137**(3), 421 (2011)
22. McCall, M.W.: Recasting leadership development. Industrial Organ. Psychol. **3**(1), 3–19 (2010)
23. Goleman, D.: Working with Emotional Intelligence. Bantam, New York (1998)
24. Rico, R., Sánchez-Manzanares, M., Gil, F., Gibson, C.: Team implicit coordination processes: a team knowledge–based approach. Acad. Manag. Rev. **33**(1), 163–184 (2008)

25. Hilton, R.M., Shuffler, M., Zaccaro, S.J., Salas, E., Chiara, J., Ruark, G.: Critical Social Thinking and Response Training: A Conceptual Framework for a Critical Social Thinking Training Program (ARI Research Report). Army Research Institute for the Behavioral and Social Sciences, Arlington (2009)
26. Weick, K.E., Sutcliffe, K.M., Obstfeld, D.: Organizing and the process of sensemaking. Organ. Sci. **16**(4), 409–421 (2005)
27. Milosevic, M., et al.: Guided mindfulness: using expert schemas to evaluate complex skill acquisition. In: International Conference on Human-Computer Interaction, pp. 233–256. Springer, Cham (2020)
28. VanLehn, K.: Cognitive skill acquisition. Annu. Rev. Psychol. **47**(1), 513–539 (1996)
29. Bandura, A.: Self-efficacy conception of anxiety. Anxiety Res. **1**(2), 77–98 (1988)
30. Bandura, A.: Social cognitive theory: an agentic perspective. Annu. Rev. Psychol. **52**(1), 1–26 (2001)
31. Villado, A.J., Arthur, W., Jr.: The comparative effect of subjective and objective after-action reviews on team performance on a complex task. J. Appl. Psychol. **98**, 514–528 (2013)
32. Villado, A.J.: The after–action review training approach: an integrative framework and empirical investigation (2008)
33. Moilanen, J.H.: The wisdom of tacit knowing-in-action and mission command. Adult Learn. **26**(3), 101–108 (2015)
34. Ruiz, C.: After Action Review. Mission Critical Team Institute (2018)
35. Keiser, N., Arthur, W., Jr.: A meta-analysis of the effectiveness of the after-action review (or debrief) and factors that influence its effectiveness. J. Appl. Psychol. **106**(7), 1007–1032 (2021)
36. Jarrett, S.M., et al.: The comparative effectiveness of distributed and colocated team after-action review. Hum. Perform. **29**(5), 408–427 (2016)
37. Harper, J.: Synthetic training technologies gaining foothold with military. Natl. Defense **102**(769), 38–40 (2017)
38. Munoz, G.J., et al.: After-action reviews and long-term performance: an experimental examination in the context of an emergency simulation. Hum. Factors J. Human Factors Ergon. Soc. (2020)
39. Is VR the future of corporate training, https://hbr.org/2020/09/is-vr-the-future-of-corporate-training. Accessed 08 Feb 2022
40. The growing impact of virtual reality training, https://www.shrm.org/hr-today/news/hr-magazine/spring2021/pages/virtual-reality-training-spreads-its-wings.aspx. Accessed 08 Feb 2022
41. PricewaterhouseCoopers Public Report.: The effectiveness of virtual reality soft skills training in the enterprise, https://www.pwc.com/us/en/tech-effect/emerging-tech/virtual-reality-study.html. Accessed 08 Feb 2022
42. Griffith, R.L., Sudduth, M.M, Flett, A., Skiba, T.S.: Looking forward: meeting the global need for leaders through guided mindfulness. In: Wildman, J.L., Griffith, R.L. (eds.) Leading Global Teams, pp. 325–342 (2014)
43. Griffith, R.L., Steelman, L.A., Moon, N., al-Qallawi, S., Quraishi, N.: Guided mindfulness: optimizing experiential learning of complex interpersonal competencies. In: Schmorrow, D.D., Fidopiastis, C.M. (eds.) AC 2018. LNCS (LNAI), vol. 10916, pp. 205–213. Springer, Cham (2018). https://doi.org/10.1007/978-3-319-91467-1_17
44. Ding, D., Brinkman, W., Neerincx, M.A.: Simulated thoughts in virtual reality for negotiation training enhance self-efficacy and knowledge. Int. J. Hum. Comput. Stud. **139**, 102400 (2020)
45. Makransky, G., Terkildsen, T.S., Mayer, R.E.: Adding immersive virtual reality to a science lab simulation causes more presence but less learning. Learn. Instr. **60**, 225–236 (2019)

# User Interactions in Virtual Data Explorer

Kaur Kullman[1,2]([✉]) [iD] and Don Engel[1] [iD]

[1] University of Maryland, Baltimore County, Baltimore, MD 21250, USA
donengel@umbc.edu
[2] Tallinn University of Technology, 12616 Tallinn, Estonia
hcii@coda.ee

**Abstract.** Cybersecurity practitioners face the challenge of monitoring complex and large datasets. These could be visualized as time-varying node-link graphs, but would still have complex topologies and very high rates of change in the attributes of their links (representing network activity). It is natural, then, that the needs of the cybersecurity domain have driven many innovations in 2D visualization and related computer-assisted decision making. Here, we discuss the lessons learned while implementing user interactions for Virtual Data Explorer (VDE), a novel system for immersive visualization (both in Mixed and Virtual Reality) of complex time-varying graphs. VDE can be used with any dataset to render its topological layout and overlay that with time-varying graph; VDE was inspired by the needs of cybersecurity professionals engaged in computer network defense (CND).

Immersive data visualization using VDE enables intuitive semantic zooming, where the semantic zoom levels are determined by the spatial position of the headset, the spatial position of handheld controllers, and user interactions (UIa) with those controllers. This spatially driven semantic zooming is quite different from most other network visualizations which have been attempted with time-varying graphs of the sort needed for CND, presenting a broad design space to be evaluated for overall user experience (UX) optimization. In this paper, we discuss these design choices, as informed by CND experts, with a particular focus on network topology abstraction with graph visualization, semantic zooming on increasing levels of network detail, and semantic zooming to show increasing levels of detail with textual labels.

**Keywords:** User interactions · Virtual reality · Mixed reality · Network visualization · Topology visualization · Data visualization · Cybersecurity

The material is based upon work supported by NASA under award number 80GSFC21M0002.

# 1   Introduction

This work follows a large volume of prior research done on 3D user interactions [3,6,10,24], immersive analytics [1,4,5,18] and the combination of the two [9,17,21,23]. Although the task-specific layout of an immersive data visualization is arguably the most important aspect determining its utility [15], non-intrusive and intuitive user interfaces (UI) and overall user experiences (UX) are also important in determining the usability and utility of an immersive data visualization. In this paper, we report on the applicability of various user interaction (UIa) methods for immersive analytics of node-link diagrams.

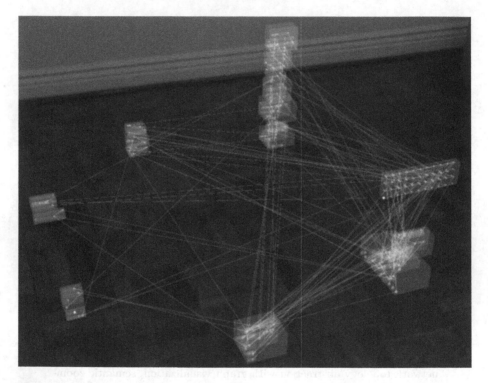

**Fig. 1.** A computer network's topology visualized with VDE, using a Mixed Reality headset.

Work on Virtual Data Explorer (VDE, Fig. 1) started in 2015, initially as a fork of OpenGraphiti and then rebuilt from scratch as a Unity 3D project [14]. One of the factors that motivated the transfer away from OpenGraphiti at the time was its lack of support for user interactions in virtual reality, which became a particularly significant omission when Oculus Touch controllers were released in late 2016 which enabled sufficiently precise user interactions to be implemented with Unity 3D. User feedback solicited from early VDE users motivated various alterations and additions to the interactions implemented for virtual and mixed reality in VDE.

## 2   Objective

Encoding information into depth cues while visualizing data has been avoided in the past for a good reason: on a flat screen, it's not helpful [19]. Nevertheless, recent studies have confirmed [23] that with equipment that provides the user with stereoscopic perception and parallax, three-dimensional shapes can be useful in providing users with insight into the visualized dataset [12]. Additionally, researchers have found that test subjects managed to gather data and to understand the cyber situation presented to them only after few sessions with great performance scores, even if the task seemed difficult to them on the first try [8].

The motivating factors for creating VDE were the challenges that cyber defense analysts, cyber defense incident responders, network operations specialists, and related professionals face while analyzing the datasets relevant to their tasks. Such datasets are often multidimensional but not intrinsically spatial. Consequently, analysts must either scale down the number of dimensions visible at a time for encoding into a 2D or 3D visualization, or they must combine multiple visualizations displaying different dimensions of that dataset into a dashboard. The inspiration for VDE was the hope that immersive visualization would enable the 3D encoding of data in ways better aligned to subject matter experts' (SMEs') natural understanding of their datasets' relational layout, better reflecting their mental models of the multilevel hierarchical relationships of groups of entities expected to be present in a dataset and the dynamic interactions between these entities [13].

Therefore, the target audience for the visualizations created with VDE are the SMEs responsible for ensuring the security of networks and other assets. SMEs utilize a wide array of Computer Network Defense (CND) tools, such as Security Information & Event Management (SIEM) systems which allow data from various sources to be processed and for alerts to be handled [15]. CND tools allow analysts to monitor, detect, investigate, and report incidents that occur in the network, as well as provide an overview of the network state. To provide analysts with such capabilities, CND tools depend on the ability to query, process, summarize and display large quantities of diverse data which have fast and unexpected dynamics [2]. These tools can be thought of along the lines of the seven human-data interaction task levels defined by Shneiderman [22]:

1. Gaining an overview of the entire dataset,
2. Zooming in on an item or subsets of items,
3. Filtering out irrelevant items,
4. Getting details-on-demand for an item or subset of items,
5. Relating between items or subset of items,
6. Keeping a history of actions, and
7. Allowing extraction of subsets of items and query parameters.

These task levels have been taken into account while developing VDE and most have been addressed with its capabilities. When appropriate, Shneiderman's task levels are referred to by their sequential number later in this paper.

# 3    Virtual Data Explorer

VDE enables a user to stereoscopically perceive a spatial layout of a dataset in a VR or MR environment (e.g., the topology of a computer network), while the resulting visualization can be augmented with additional data, like TCP/UDP/ICMP session counts between network nodes [16]. VDE allows its users to customize visualization layouts via two complimentary text configuration files that are parsed by the VDE Server and the VDE Client.

To accommodate timely processing of large query results, data-processing in VDE is separated into a server component (VDES). Thread-safe messaging is used extensively - most importantly, to keep the Client (VDEC) visualization in sync with (changes in) incoming data, but also for asynchronous data processing, for handling browser-based user interface actions, and in support of various other features.

A more detailed description of VDE is available at [11].

## 3.1    Simulator Sickness

Various experiments have shown that applying certain limitations to a user's ability to move in the virtual environment - limit their view and other forms of constrained navigation - will limit confusion and help prevent simulator sickness while in VR [7]. These lessons were learned while developing VDE and adjusted later, as others reported success with the same or similar mitigation efforts [20]. Most importantly, if an immersed user can only move the viewpoint (e.g., its avatar) either forwards or backwards in the direction of user's gaze (or head-direction), the effects of simulator sickness can be minimized or avoided altogether [12]. This form of constrained navigation in VR is known as "the rudder movement" [20].

## 3.2    Virtual or Mixed Reality

Although VDE was initially developed with Virtual Reality headsets (Oculus Rift DK2 and later CV1 with Oculus Touch), its interaction components were always kept modular so that once mixed reality headsets such as the Meta 2, Magic Leap, and Hololens became available, their support could be integrated into the same codebase.

The underlying expectation for preferring MR to VR is the user's ability to combine stereoscopically perceivable data visualizations rendered by a MR headset with relevant textual information represented by other sources in the user's physical environment (SIEM, dashboard, or another tool), most likely from flat screens. This requirement was identified from early user feedback that trying to input text or define/refine data queries while in VR would be vastly inferior to the textual interfaces that users are already accustomed to operating while using conventional applications on a flat screen for data analysis. Hence, rather than spend time on inventing 3D data-entry solutions for VR, it was decided to focus on creating and improving stereoscopically perceivable data layouts and letting users use their existing tools to control the selection of data that is then fed to the visualization.

A major advantage provided by the VR environment, relative to MR, is that VR allows users to move (fly) around in a larger scale (overview) visualization of a dataset while becoming familiar with its layout(s) and/or while collaborating with others. However, once the user is familiar with the structure of their dataset, changing their position (by teleporting or flying in VR space) becomes less beneficial over time. Accordingly, as commodity MR devices became sufficiently performant, they were prioritized for development - first, the Meta 2, later followed by support for the Magic Leap and HoloLens.

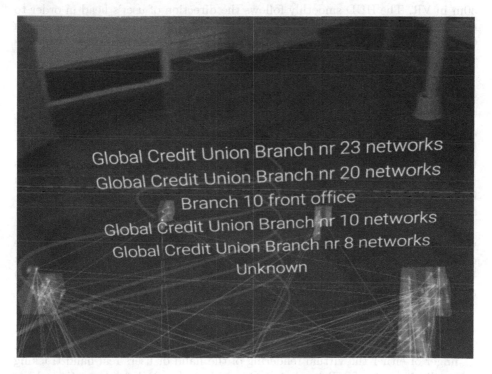

**Fig. 2.** Head-Up Display showing labels of visualized groups that the user focuses on, retaining visual connections to those with Bézier curves. HUD is used also for other interaction and feedback purposes.

### 3.3  User Interface

In the early stages of VDE development on Unity 3D, efforts were made to either use existing VR-based menu systems (VRTK, later MRTK) or to design a native menu, such that would allow the user to control which visualization components are visible and/or interactive; to configure connection to VDE Server; to switch between layouts; and to exercise other control over the immersive environment. However, controlling VDE's server and client behavior, including data selection and transfer, turned out to be more convenient when done in combination with the VDES web-based interface and with existing conventional tools on a flat screen. For example, in case of cybersecurity related datasets, the data source could be a SIEM, log-correlation, netflow, or PCAP analyzing environments.

### 3.4  Head-Up Display

Contextual information is displayed on a head-up display (HUD) that is perceived to be positioned a few meters away from the user in MR and about 30m in VR. The HUD smoothly follows the direction of user's head in order to remain in the user's field of view (see Fig. 2). This virtual distance was chosen to allow a clear distinction between the HUD and the network itself, which is stereoscopically apparent as being nearer to the user.

### 3.5  User Interactions

The ability to interact with the visualization, namely, to query information about a visual representation of a datapoint (ex: semi-transparent cube for a node or line for a relation between two nodes) using input devices (ex: hand- and finger-tracking, input controllers) is imperative. While gathering feedback from SMEs [12], this querying capability was found to be crucial for the users' immersion in the VR data visualization to allow them to explore and to build their understanding of the visualized data.

The MR or VR system's available input methods are used to detect whether the user is trying to grab something, point at a node, or point at an edge. In case of MR headsets, these interactions are based on the user's tracked hands (see: Fig. 3 and Fig. 4), and in case of VR headsets, pseudo-hands (see: Fig. 5 Fig. 6) are rendered based on hand-held input controllers.

A user can:

1. point to select a visual representation of a data-object - a node (for example, a cube or a sphere) or an edge - with a "laser" or dominant hand's index finger of either the virtual rendering of the hand or users real hand tracking results (in case of MR headsets). Once selected, detailed information about the selected object (node or edge) is shown on a line of text rendered next to user's hand, (Shneiderman Task Level 4).
2. grab (or pinch) nodes and move (or throw) these around to better perceive its relations by observing the edges that are originating or terminating in that node: humans perceive the terminal locations of moving lines better than that of static ones, (Shneiderman Task Levels 3, 5).

3. control data visualization layout's properties (shapes, curvature, etc.) with controller's analog sensors, (Shneiderman Task Levels 1, 5).
4. gesture with non-dominant hand to trigger various functionalities. For example: starfish - toggle the HUD; pinch both hands - scale the visualization; fist - toggle edges; etc.

In addition to active gestures and hand recognition, the user's position and gaze (instead of just their head direction) are used if available to decide which

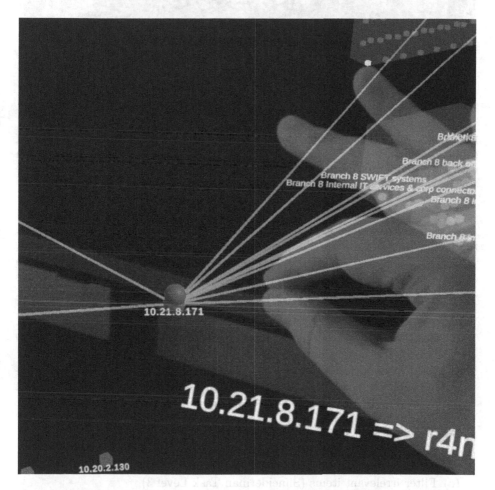

**Fig. 3.** In an MR environment, the user pinches a node, that is sized accordingly, to move that around and explore its relations. Notice the two gray spheres indicating the location, where the MR device (Magic Leap) perceives the tips of user's thumb and index finger to be: due to the device' lack of precision, these helper-markers are used to guide the user. Note that the distortion is further aggravated by to the way the device records the video and overlays the augmentation onto it. For comparison with Virtual Reality view, please see Fig. 5.

**Fig. 4.** MR view of Locked Shields 18 Partner Run network topology and network traffic visualization with VDE; user is selecting a Blue Team's network's visualization with index finger to have it enlarged and brought into the center of the view. Please see the video accompanying this paper for better perception: https://coda.ee/HCII22

visualization sub-groups to focus on, to enable textual labels, to hide enclosures, to enable update routines, colliders, etc. (Shneiderman Task Levels 2, 3, 4, 5, 7). Therefore, depending on user's direction and location amongst the visualization components and on the user's gaze (if eye-tracking is available), a visualization's details are either visible or hidden, and if visible, then either interactive or not.

The reasons for such a behavior are threefold:

1. Exposing the user to too many visual representations of the data objects will overwhelm them, even if occlusion is not a concern.
2. Having too many active objects may overwhelm the GPU/CPU of a standalone MR/VR headset - or even a computer rendering into a VR headset - due to the computational costs of colliders, joints, or other physics. (see "Optimizations" section, below)
3. By adjusting their location (and gaze), the user can:
   (a) See an overview of the entire dataset (Shneiderman Task Level 1),
   (b) Zoom on an item or subsets of items (Shneiderman Task Level 2),
   (c) Filter irrelevant items (Shneiderman Task Level 3),
   (d) Get details-on-demand for an item or subset of items (Shneiderman Task Level 4),
   (e) Relate between items or subsets of items. (Shneiderman Task Level 5).

Figure 7 and Fig. 8 show this behavior, while the video (https://coda.ee/ HCII22) accompanying this paper makes understanding such MR interaction clearer than is possible from a screenshot, albeit less so than experiencing it with a MR headset.

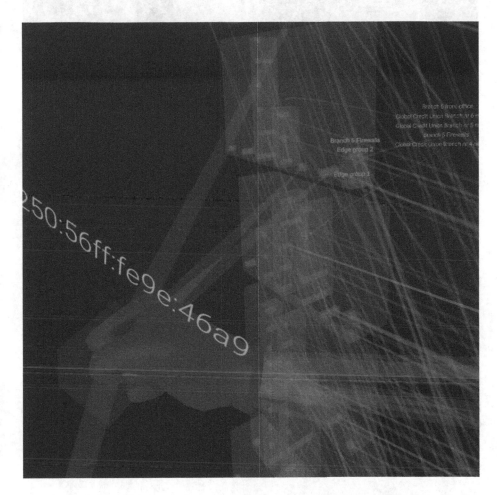

**Fig. 5.** In a VR environment, the user grabs a node, that is sized to sit into ones palm. For comparison with Mixed Reality view, please see Fig. 3.

**Fig. 6.** User touches an edge with the index finger of Oculus avatar's hand, to learn details about that edge.

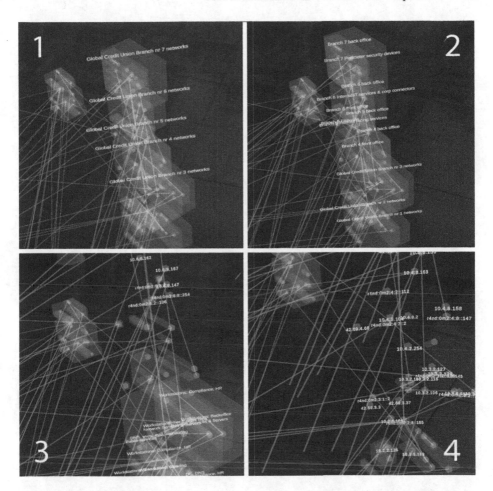

**Fig. 7.** Once user moves closer to a part of the visualization that might be of interest, textual labels are shown for upper tier groups first, while the rectangular representations of these groups are disappeared as the user gets closer, to enable focusing on the subgroups inside, and then the nodes with their IP addresses as labels. To convey the changes in visualization as the user moves, screenshots are provided sequentially, numbered 1–4. For comparison with Virtual Reality view, please see Fig. 8.

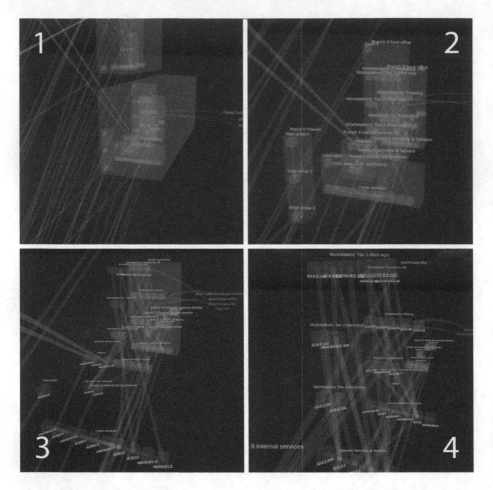

**Fig. 8.** Once user moves closer to a part of the visualization that might be of interest, textual labels are shown for upper tier groups first, while the rectangular representations of these groups are disappeared as the user gets closer, to enable focusing on the subgroups inside, and then the nodes with their IP addresses as labels. To convey the changes in visualization as the user moves, screenshots are provided sequentially, numbered 1–4. For comparison with Mixed Reality view, please see Fig. 7.

## 3.6    Textual Information

Text labels of nodes, edges, groups are a significant issue, as these are expensive to render due to their complex geometrical shapes and also risk the possible occlusion of objects which may fall behind them. Accordingly, text is shown in VDE only when necessary, to the extreme that a label is made visible only when the user's gaze is detected on a related object. Backgrounds are not used with text in order to reduce their occlusive footprint.

## 3.7   Optimizations

The basis for VDE: less is more.

Occlusion of visual representations of data objects is a significant problem for 3D data visualizations on flat screens. In VR/MR environments, occlusion can be mostly mitigated by stereoscopic perception of the (semi-transparent) visualizations of data objects and by parallax, but may still be problematic [5].

While occlusion in MR/VR can be addressed by measures such as transparency, transparency adds significant overhead to the rendering process. To optimize occlusion-related issues, VDE strikes a balance between the necessity of transparency of visualized objects, while adjusting the number of components currently visible (textual labels, reducing the complexity of objects that are farther from the user's viewpoint, etc.) based on the current load (measured FPS); on objects' relative positions in user's gaze (in-view, not-in-view, behind the user); and on the user's virtual distance from these objects. This XR-centric approach to semantic zooming proves a natural user experience, visually akin to the semantic zooming techniques used in online maps which smoothly but dramatically change the extent of detail as a function of zoom level (showing only major highways or the smallest of roads, toggling the visibility of street names and point of interest markers).

Although colors and shapes of the visual representations of data objects can be used to convey information about their properties, user feedback has confirmed that these should be used sparsely. Therefore, in most VDE layouts, the nodes (representing data objects) are visualized as transparent off-white cubes or spheres, and the latter only in case if the available GPU is powerful enough. Displaying a cube versus a sphere may seem a trivial difference, but considering the sizes of some of the datasets visualized (>10,000 nodes and >10,000 edges), these complexities add up quickly and take a significant toll.

## 4   Conclusion

Immersive visualization of large, dynamic node-link diagrams requires careful consideration of visual comprehensibility and computational performance. While many of node-link visualization idioms are well-studied in 2D flat screen visualizations, the opportunities and constraints presented by VR and MR environments are distinct. As the pandemic made a larger-scale study with many participants impossible, VDE instead underwent a more iterative review process, drawing input from representative users and domain expertise. The approach described herein reflects many iterations of performance testing and user feedback.

Optimizing user interactions for VDE presented the design challenge of providing an interface which intuitively offers an informative presentation of the node-link network both at a high-level "overview" zoom level and at a very zoomed "detail" view, with well-chosen levels of semantic zoom available along the continuum between these extremes. Constrained navigation further optimizes the user experience, limiting confusion and motion sickness. Dynamic highlighting, through the selection and controller-based movement of individual notes, enhances the users' understanding of the data.

**Acknowledgement.** The authors thank Alexander Kott, Jennifer A. Cowley, Lee C. Trossbach, Matthew C. Ryan, Jaan Priisalu, and Olaf Manuel Maennel for their ideas and guidance. This research was partly supported by the Army Research Laboratory under Cooperative Agreement Number W911NF-17-2-0083 and in conjunction with the CCDC Command, Control, Computers, Communications, Cyber, Intelligence, Surveillance, and Reconnaissance (C5ISR) Center. The material is based upon work supported by NASA under award number 80GSFC21M0002.

# References

1. Batch, A., Elmqvist, N.: The interactive visualization gap in initial exploratory data analysis. IEEE Trans. Visual Comput. Graph. **24**(1), 278–287 (2018). https://doi.org/10.1109/TVCG.2017.2743990
2. Ben-Asher, N., Gonzalez, C.: Effects of cyber security knowledge on attack detection. Comput. Hum. Behav. **48**, 51–61 (2015). https://doi.org/10.1016/j.chb.2015.01.039. https://www.sciencedirect.com/science/article/pii/S0747563215000539
3. Casallas, J.S., Oliver, J.H., Kelly, J.W., Merienne, F., Garbaya, S.: Using relative head and hand-target features to predict intention in 3d moving-target selection. In: 2014 IEEE Virtual Reality (VR), pp. 51–56 (2014). https://doi.org/10.1109/VR.2014.6802050
4. Dübel, S., Röhlig, M., Schumann, H., Trapp, M.: 2d and 3d presentation of spatial data: a systematic review. In: 2014 IEEE VIS International Workshop on 3DVis (3DVis), pp. 11–18 (2014). https://doi.org/10.1109/3DVis.2014.7160094
5. Elmqvist, N., Tsigas, P.: A taxonomy of 3d occlusion management for visualization. IEEE Trans. Visual Comput. Graphics **14**(5), 1095–1109 (2008). https://doi.org/10.1109/TVCG.2008.59
6. Günther, T., Franke, I.S., Groh, R.: Aughanded virtuality - the hands in the virtual environment. In: 2015 IEEE Virtual Reality (VR), pp. 327–328 (2015). https://doi.org/10.1109/VR.2015.7223428
7. Johnson, D.M.: Introduction to and review of simulator sickness research (2005)
8. Kabil, A., Duval, T., Cuppens, N.: Alert characterization by non-expert users in a cybersecurity virtual environment: a usability study. In: De Paolis, L.T., Bourdot, P. (eds.) AVR 2020. LNCS, vol. 12242, pp. 82–101. Springer, Cham (2020). https://doi.org/10.1007/978-3-030-58465-8_6
9. Kabil, A., Duval, T., Cuppens, N., Comte, G.L., Halgand, Y., Ponchel, C.: Why should we use 3d collaborative virtual environments for cyber security? In: 2018 IEEE Fourth VR International Workshop on Collaborative Virtual Environments (3DCVE), pp. 1–2 (2018). https://doi.org/10.1109/3DCVE.2018.8637109
10. Kang, H.J., Shin, J.h., Ponto, K.: A comparative analysis of 3d user interaction: How to move virtual objects in mixed reality. In: 2020 IEEE Conference on Virtual Reality and 3D User Interfaces (VR), pp. 275–284 (2020). https://doi.org/10.1109/VR46266.2020.00047
11. Kullman, K.: Creating useful 3d data visualizations: Using mixed and virtual reality in cybersecurity (2020). https://coda.ee/MAVRIC, 3nd Annual MAVRIC Conference

12. Kullman, K., Ben-Asher, N., Sample, C.: Operator impressions of 3d visualizations for cybersecurity analysts. In: 18th European Conference on Cyber Warfare and Security. Coimbra, Portugal (2019)
13. Kullman, K., Cowley, J., Ben-Asher, N.: Enhancing cyber defense situational awareness using 3d visualizations. In: 13th International Conference on Cyber Warfare and Security, Washington, DC (2018)
14. Kullman, K.: Virtual data explorer. https://coda.ee/
15. Kullman, K., Buchanan, L., Komlodi, A., Engel, D.: Mental model mapping method for cybersecurity. In: HCI (2020)
16. Kullman, K., Engel, D.: Interactive stereoscopically perceivable multidimensional data visualizations for cybersecurity. J. Defence Secur. Technol. 4(3), 37–52 (2022). 10.46713/jdst.004.03
17. Lu, F., Davari, S., Lisle, L., Li, Y., Bowman, D.A.: Glanceable ar: evaluating information access methods for head-worn augmented reality. In: 2020 IEEE Conference on Virtual Reality and 3D User Interfaces (VR), pp. 930–939 (2020). https://doi.org/10.1109/VR46266.2020.00113
18. Miyazaki, R., Itoh, T.: An occlusion-reduced 3d hierarchical data visualization technique. In: 2009 13th International Conference Information Visualisation, pp. 38–43 (2009). https://doi.org/10.1109/IV.2009.32
19. Munzner, T.: Visualization Analysis and Design. AK Peters Visualization Series. CRC Press (2015). https://books.google.de/books?id=NfkYCwAAQBAJ
20. Pruett, C.: Lessons from the frontlines modern vr design patterns (2017). https://developer.oculus.com/blog/lessons-from-the-frontlines-modern-vr-design-patterns, unity North American Vision VR/AR Summit
21. Roberts, J.C., Ritsos, P.D., Badam, S.K., Brodbeck, D., Kennedy, J., Elmqvist, N.: Visualization beyond the desktop-the next big thing. IEEE Comput. Graphics Appl. 34(6), 26–34 (2014). https://doi.org/10.1109/MCG.2014.82
22. Shneiderman, B.: The eyes have it: a task by data type taxonomy for information visualizations. In: Proceedings 1996 IEEE Symposium on Visual Languages, pp. 336–343 (1996). https://doi.org/10.1109/VL.1996.545307
23. Whitlock, M., Smart, S., Szafir, D.A.: Graphical perception for immersive analytics. In: 2020 IEEE Conference on Virtual Reality and 3D User Interfaces (VR), pp. 616–625 (2020). https://doi.org/10.1109/VR46266.2020.00084
24. Yu, D., Liang, H.N., Fan, K., Zhang, H., Fleming, C., Papangelis, K.: Design and evaluation of visualization techniques of off-screen and occluded targets in virtual reality environments. IEEE Trans. Visual Comput. Graphics 26(9), 2762–2774 (2020). https://doi.org/10.1109/TVCG.2019.2905580

# Human Intelligent Machine Teaming in Single Pilot Operation: A Case Study

Narek Minaskan[1]([✉]), Charles Alban-Dromoy[3], Alain Pagani[1], Jean-Marc Andre[4], and Didier Stricker[1,2]

[1] Augmented Vision Department, German Research Center for Artificial Intelligence, Kaiserslautern, Germany
nareg.minaskan_karabid@dfki.de
[2] Technical University of Kaiserslautern, Kaiserslautern, Germany
[3] Universit'e de Bordeaux, CATIE, Talence, France
[4] Bordeaux INP-ENSC IMS UMR CNRS, 5218 Talence, France

**Abstract.** With recent advances in artificial intelligence (AI) and learning based systems, industries have started to integrate AI components into their products and workflows. In areas where frequent testing and development is possible these system have proved to be quite useful such as in automotive industry where vehicle are now equipped with advanced driver-assistant systems (ADAS) capable of self-driving, route planning, and maintaining safe distances from lanes and other vehicles. However, as the safety-critical aspect of task increases, more difficult and expensive it is to develop and test AI-based solutions. Such is the case in aviation and therefore, development must happen over longer periods of time and in a step-by-step manner. This paper focuses on creating an interface between the human pilot and a potential assistant system that helps the pilot navigate through a complex flight scenario. Verbal communication and augmented reality (AR) were chosen as means of communication and the verbal communication was carried out in a wizard-of-Oz (WoOz) fashion. The interface was tested in a flight simulator and it's usefulness was evaluated by NASA-TLX and SART questionnaires for workload and situation awareness.

**Keywords:** Human-computer interaction · Augmented reality · Human-machine interaction

## 1 Introduction

Human-computer interaction (HCI) has developed certain common guidelines for traditional interfaces. However with rise of AI and fast-paced evolution of learning-based systems, new types of human-machine interaction (HMI) and interfaces (HMI$^2$) is needed since these systems do not have the traditional attributes of a computer system, namely due to uncertainty [2,23]. The models

---

N. Minaskan and C. Alban-Dromoy—These authors contributed equally to this work.

D. D. Schmorrow and C. M. Fidopiastis (Eds.): HCII 2022, LNAI 13310, pp. 348–360, 2022.
https://doi.org/10.1007/978-3-031-05457-0_27

provided by the learning systems may turn out to be inaccurate and will need to be updated possibly through human intervention. There the operator must be provided with an interface to change the parameters and update the model.

Naturally each industry will need their own AI-enabled assistant and interaction models which complicates interface design since following a global paradigm is not possible. This paper focuses on the field of aviation and the problem of assistant system for single pilot operations (SPO). With the increasing numbers of commercial flights in the upcoming years, a shortage of pilots is to be expected. One solution to this problem is reducing the numbers of pilots in the cockpit. Three strategies proposed as a solution include: Single pilot in cruise (SPIC), reduced crew operation (RCO), and single pilot operation (SPO). The major difference between these there is that, SPIC and RCO propose a reduction in number of crew for a long-haul flight whereas in SPO the pilot is alone for the entire duration of the flight. This immediately implicates that for a SPO, highest levels of safety must be maintained at all times.

A major concern in SPO is total pilot incapciation (e.g. due to heart failure) and has been assesd in American airline pilots at 0.045 and impairment rate of 0.013 per 100000 flying hours [8,9]. There are several solutions in the case of overloading and total or partial incapacitation such as assistant by automated systems, assistance on board the aircraft, or assistance from operator on the ground. For a SPO however, increasing the automation in the cockpit will put an extra burden on the pilot for monitoring the systems and will reinforce the paradox of automation [4,18]. Nevertheless, an assistant system for SPO should have the characteristics of a co-pilot. A set of functional requirements for such a system were described by Cummings et al. [7]. Which includes verbal and nonverbal communication.

For nonverbal communication, AR has been used for many decades in aviation to enhance navigation in aircraft [17]. The purpose of utilizing AR is to increase the pilot's situation awareness (SA) [21] in critical segments of flight such as take-off and landing [15,20]. Moreover, new vision technologies such as synthetic vision system (SVS) or enhanced vision system (EVS) implemented on head-mounted displays (HMD) can decrease the workload of the pilot and increase their SA [22]. A study by Bailey et al. [3] shows that pilots are capable of handling abnormal situations safely with acceptable performance conditions, but with decrease flight performance and unacceptable workload.

The goal of this paper is to create an assistant system interface that not only is inline with human autonomy team (HAT) [16,19] but also adds a level on intelligence to the system, thus creating a human-intelligent machine team (HiMT) that serves as a replacement for the co-pilot and mimics cognitive abilities of the human (cognitive assistant). The system is assessed by measuring the SA and workload [10] of the pilots in a complex flight scenario. For the purpose of simplicity, the role of AI and verbal communication is played out by a WoOZ. The paper is structured as follows: Sect. 2 describes the design of the experiment, flight scenario, the levels of communication and hypothesis followed by Sect. 3 which describes the technical implementation. In Sects. 4 and 5, the methodology and results of the experiment are presented. The results of the experiment as discussed in Sect. 6, followed by conclusion in Sect. 7.

## 2    Experiment

The first activity carried out in the design of the experiment and the interface was a preliminary interview with the pilots to understand the tasks carried out and whether they would like to delegate tasks (under normal and abnormal circumstances) with the AI assistant system. In the results, it was clear that pilots do not wish a total handover to the system, rather wish to be presented with sufficient information which helps them with decision making in different phases of the flight and in time constraint.

### 2.1    Flight Scenario

According to accidents statistics [1], 49% of accidents occur during landing and approach phase of the flight. Together with the risk associated with runway (RW) safety [11], a relevant scenario must be chosen which represents the risks of landing and approach. The flight scenario chosen for the experiment is commonly known as the Bremen scenario (Fig. 1) which represents the approach and landing phase of the flight. This scenario was used in the project Future Sky Safety "Human Performance Envelope" [5,13] with normal two pilot crew in A320 flight simulator. As in this paper the scenario is used in a SPO scenario with AI cognitive assistant, it will allow a comparison of results for workload and situation awareness with the baseline two pilots crew.

The scenario starts at top of decent (TOD), at 32000 feet to Bremen airport, and plays out as follows:

1. The aircraft has 50 min left, which is around 2000 kg. The initial approach is on runway 27.
2. The air traffic controller (ATC) requests a Go-Around due to a truck stuck on the runway.
3. A shift in wind direction.
4. Electrical failure occurs (AC BUS 1 fault) during downwind.
5. Approach and landing on new runway. Possibility of running out of fuel.

The complexity in decision making in this scenario is due to time pressure from the amount of fuel remaining which, a high workload, and degraded SA.

### 2.2    Communication Levels of the Assistant and Hypothesis

Based on the flight scenario, the experiment was divided into four levels of communication:

– No assistant. The pilot flies the aircraft alone without any kind of assistant.

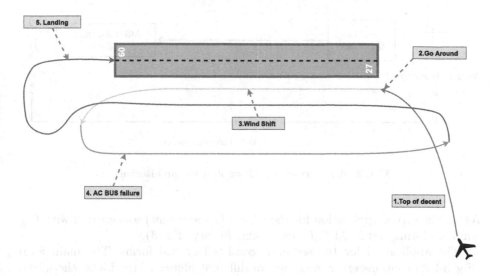

**Fig. 1.** A representation of Bremen scenario played out in A320 flight simulator for SPO.

- Assistant on request. The assistant is active only if the pilot asks a question or requests help. It does not provide any explanation for the provided information.
- Proactive simple assistant. Provides information through verbal communication and visual cues by AR. It does not provide any explanation for the provided information.
- Proactive evolved assistant. Provides information through verbal communication and visual cues by AR, and provides explanation to the pilot for the provided information and mimics reasoning.

With regards to the flight scenario and communication levels, the main hypothesis are the following:

- AI assistant has not effect on pilot workload and mental demand.
- A proactive assistant provides better situation awareness, with explanation

To verify the hypothesis, NASA-TLX and SART questionnaires were used to assess the cognitive workload and situation awareness of the pilots, and to understand which level of communication for the assistant was the most useful.

## 3   Implementation

Since the role of the AI assistant is played out by WoOz, the AR interface is implemented on a server-client architecture (Fig. 2).

A restriction imposed on the assistant system is that it doesn't directly communicate with the ATC; however, it is capable of understanding the communication between the pilot and ATC as well as the commands issued by the

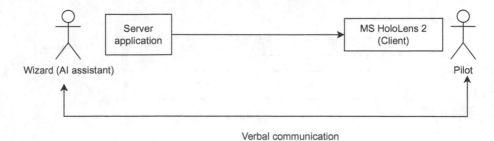

Fig. 2. An overview of AR application architecture.

ATC. The server application for the wizard (AI assistant) was created with C# windows forms and MQTT [6] networking library (Fig. 3).

The application for the server is consisted of two forms. The main form (Fig. 3 left) contains error messages for different phases of the flight, checklists, and units, such as flight control unit (FCU), and electronic centralized aircraft monitoring (ECAM). Some messages are displayed with two colors, either amber or red. indicating the severity of the error or situation which is meant to draw the pilot's attention to an problem or make him aware of an existing one. The second form (Fig. 3 right) is for passing FCU calculations to the pilot.

The AR application was developed with Unity engine together with MQTT broker [14] for receiving messages over the network and Microsoft Mixed Reality Toolkit [12] for enabling interactions in AR environment. The client application contains 3D and 2D visual cues which were enabled and disabled by the wizard through the server application. For the 3D format, the messages where shown in an extended panel (Fig. 4 top left) with the purpose of helping the pilot to keep track of the issues going on at the given time, or highlighted the necessary buttons on the overhead panel to help them speed up processes (Fig. 4 bottom). The inputs for the FCU were displayed directly above the unit, with the numbers on top of their respective fields on the panel (Fig. 4 top right). The 2D cues appeared in the middle-up part of pilot's field of view. To avoid repetitive calibration for each pilot, the 3D cues were pinned to the specific location on the world map generated by HoloLens, using world anchors so that the scene needs to be set up only once.

For verbal communication, the main difference between the simple and evolved assistant lies in the explanation for the information provided. For both versions of the assistant, the pilot can issue commands with keywords such as: "Perform ..." or "Compute ...". Lastly, in the case of the assistant of request, the simple version of the assistant was used.

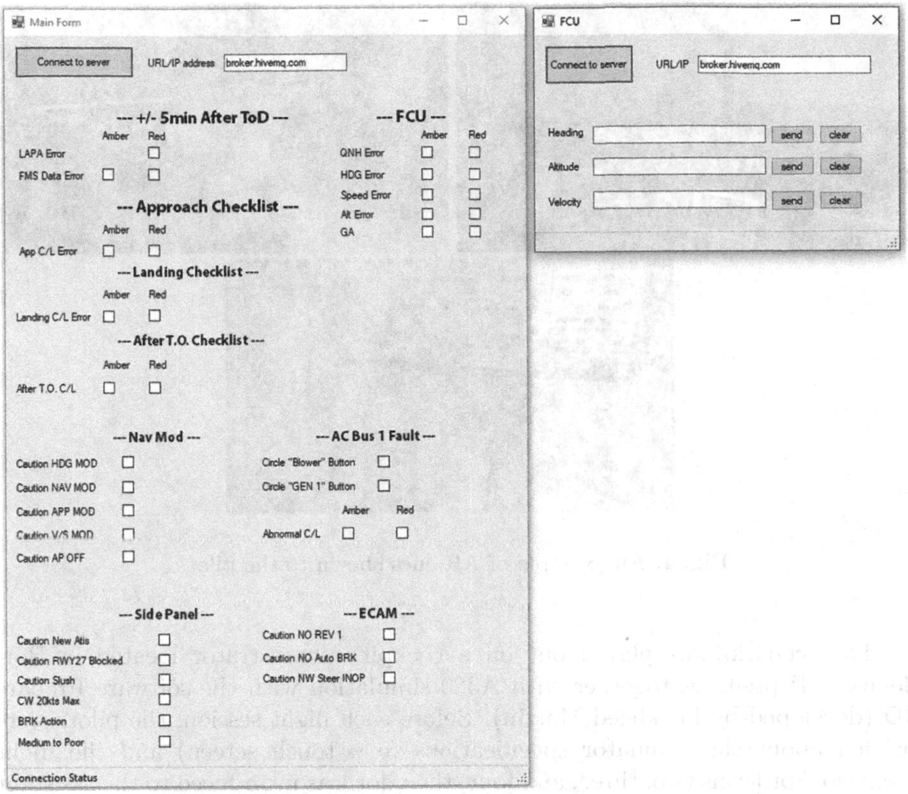

**Fig. 3.** The server application for wizard (AI assistant) consists of two forms. Left: Main form consisting error messages with indication in color. Left: Calculations for FCU.

## 4 Methodology

Twenty-four pilots were recruited to participate in the experiment of which two could not finish the experiment properly due to technical problems. The 22 pilots had a mean age of: $36,72$ y.o ($SD = 10,88$), a 2975 mean flight hours (fh) experience on A320. 21% of the pilots were female and 61% were first officers, and were evenly distributed over the 4 levels. Ten pilots participated in the baseline ($M = 30.9$ y.o., $SD = 3.28$, $M = 3125$ fh, $SD = 1557$), five in level 1 ($M = 28.2$ y.o., $SD = 4.38$, $M = 2240$ fh, $SD = 1415$), five in level 2 ($M = 35$ y.o., $SD = 10$, $M = 2700$ fh, $SD = 1987$), seven in level ($M = 35.71$ y.o., $SD = 7.9$, $M = 3685$ fh, $SD = 2814$) and five in level 4 ($M = 48.4$ y.o., $SD = 11.93$, $M = 3670$fh, $SD =1616$).

**Fig. 4.** An example of AR cues shown to the pilot.

The scenario was played out on a cockpit demonstrator located in Bordeaux INP premises together with A320 simulation with the software Prepare 3D (developed by Lockheed Martin). Before each flight session, the pilots were briefed about the simulator specifications (e.g. touch screen) and the flight scenario. For levels two, three, and four, the pilot was introduced to the assistant "Jack", and how they communicate with it and the capabilities it had (e.g. cannot take over, or push buttons). The pilots were presented with a paper summary of all the points. For pilots to familiarize themselves with the simulator, touch screens, and the assistant, a training scenario was conducted which consisted of take-off from Bordeaux, and landing. For experiment scenario, the pilots were briefed on the destination airport (Bremen), and are given the amount of time they need to get to know the destination airport on paper charts or electronic flight bag (EFB).

## 5   Results

Before data analysis, data was cleaned and assumptions for normality were tested, and violations of normality assumptions were identified using Shapiro-Wilk test for all variables in order to guide selection of statistical tests. Univariate analyses were conducted using Kruskal-Wallis tests for non-normally distributed variables to determine whether there were significant differences between the four levels compared to the Baseline. All analyses were conducted using Jamovi 1.6.23 statistical software.

## 5.1   Workload NSA-TLX

To assess pilots' workload during the flight scenario a digital version of the NASA-TLX was used. By incorporating a multi-dimensional rating procedure, the questionnaire derives an overall workload score based on a weighted average of ratings on six subscales [10]: Mental demand, physical demand, temporal demand, performance, effort, and frustration.

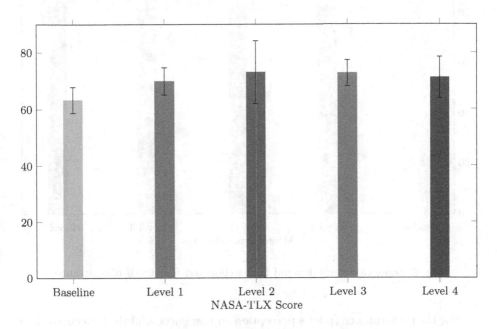

**Fig. 5.** Overall score of NASA-TLX for workload.

The overall workload did not significantly change between the different levels as shown in Fig. 5, $\chi^2(4) = 3.48, p = 0.482$. The means of the baseline (pilot and copilot) and the level 4 (Evolved Assistant) are close to each other. Baseline ($M = 63, SD = 14.5$) and level 4 ($M = 70.2, SD = 15.7$). The cognitive load score did not increase significantly, only 7.02 points for those with the evolved assistant (Level 4) compared to level 1 ($W = 1.386, p = 0.865$), and the cognitive load score increased by 10.1 points for those in level 2 ($M = 73, 1; SD = 24.8$) (IA on request) compared to the baseline, but this difference is not significant ($W = 1.732, p = 0.737$).

Ratings regarding mental demand (required mental and perceptual activity), showed no significant changes over different levels (Fig. 6), $\chi^2(4) = 3.28, p = 0.512$.

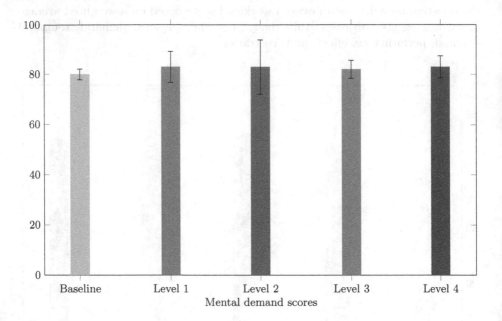

**Fig. 6.** Score of mental demand for baseline and four levels of assistance.

For the performance (pilot's perception on how successful they executed their tasks), there was increase in level 2 (assistant on request) compared to rest of the levels (Fig. 7). On the other hand, perception of performance decreased in level 3, and 4 ($\chi^2(4) = 3.70 p = 0.448$).

## 5.2   Situation Awareness

The overall levels of situation awareness for the four levels are presented in Fig. 8. The lowest level of situation awareness was in level 1 followed by level 2. The highest level of situation awareness was in level 4 ($M = 22, SD = 2.12$). The level of situation awareness is even higher than the baseline ($M = 15.1; SD = 3.78$) but the difference between the levels was not significant.

The attentional demand (Fig. 9) was slightly lower in level 4 compared to the baseline, but the results were not significantly different ($\chi^2(4) = 5.07, p = 0.280$).

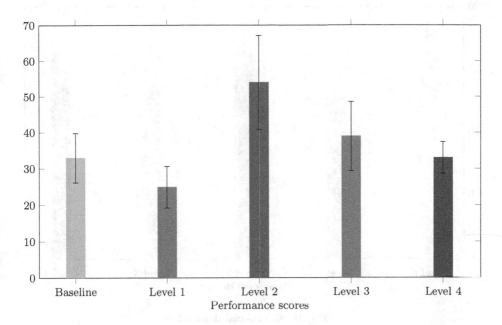

**Fig. 7.** Score of perception of performance for baseline and four levels of assistance.

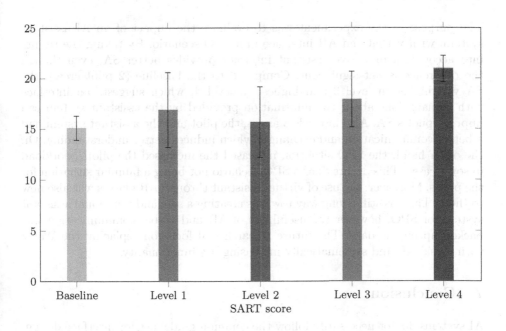

**Fig. 8.** Score of SART situation awareness.

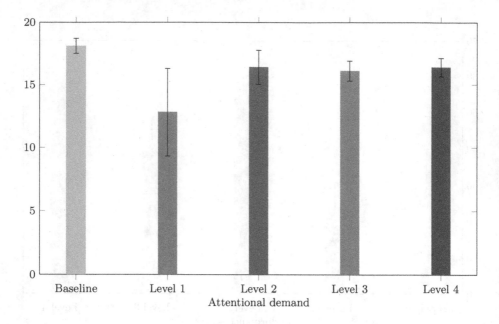

**Fig. 9.** Attentional demand.

# 6   Discussion

The purpose of the experiment was to evaluate the impact of an AI assistant system, with verbal and AR interface in a SPO scenario. By taking the results into account, a proactive assistant interface provides better SA, even though the difference is not significant. Compared to the baseline (2 pilot crew), the SA was higher in level 3 and highest in level 4, which suggests an interface with explanations about the information provided by the assistant system can improve pilot's SA. Also in levels 3 and 4, the pilot and the assistant system had a better communication and exchanges which induces better understanding. On the other hand, the SPO situation increased the increased the pilots' workload in some cases. This occurs due to SPO scenario not being a familiar situation for the pilots. Moreover, the use of virtual assistant through AR glasses was also new to them. There is still a long way towards creating a safe and functional assistant system for SPO, however the usefulness of AR and verbal communication was backed up by the data. The future research will focus on replacing the WoOz with a real AI, and systematically increasing it's functionality.

# 7   Conclusion

AI systems do not necessarily follow the common guidelines for interface design. In this paper, a scenario of SPO was tested to study the collaboration of human pilot with a AI system which was played out as a WoOz together with AR as means of providing visual cues. Three types of communication styles were tested: On request, Simple proactive, and evolved proactive. The scenario was played out in a A320 simulator located in BordeauxINP premises, where pilots were recruited to pilot an A320 aircraft alongside with one of the levels. Afterwards, they were asked to fill out the NASA TLX and SART questionnaires for evaluation of mental workload and SA. The statistical analysis showed that a proactive interfaces (level 3 and 4) resulted in a better SA and understanding of the situation. Future work will focus on replacing the WoOz with a real AI, with capabilities such as pilot monitoring. Moreover, natural language processing units should be used to enable verbal communication and interface with the AI. Designing a dedicated AR headset for commercial cockpits is also of importance, as AR played a positive role in assisting the pilots in levels 3 and 4.

**Acknowledgements.** This project has received funding from the Clean Sky 2 Joint Undertaking under the European Union's Horizon 2020 research and innovation programme under grant agreement No 831891. The authors would like to thank Th'eodore Letouz'e for taking care of the technical aspects of the simulator and Turkan Hentati for help with statistical analysis.

# References

1. Airplanes, B.C.: Statistical summary of commercial jet airplane accidents. Worldwide Operations 2008 (1959)
2. Amershi, S., et al.: Guidelines for human-AI interaction, May 2019. https://doi.org/10.1145/3290605.3300233
3. Bailey, R.E., Kramer, L.J., Kennedy, K.D., Stephens, C.L., Etherington, T.J.: An assessment of reduced crew and single pilot operations in commercial transport aircraft operations. In: 2017 IEEE/AIAA 36th Digital Avionics Systems Conference (DASC), pp. 1–15. IEEE (2017)
4. Bainbridge, L.: Ironies of automation. In: Analysis, Design and Evaluation of Man-Machine Systems, pp. 129–135. Elsevier (1983)
5. Biella, M., Wies, M., Charles, R., Maille, N., Nixon, J.: How eye tracking data can enhance human performance in tomorrow's cockpit. results from a flight simulation study in future sky safety. In: Joint AIAA and Royal Aeronautical Society (RaeS) Fall Conference on Modeling and Simulation for ATM (2017)
6. Craggs, I.: Mqtt for.net. https://github.com/eclipse/paho.mqtt.m2mqtt. https://github.com/eclipse/paho.mqtt.m2mqtt
7. Cummings, M.L., Stimpson, A., Clamann, M.: Functional requirements for onboard intelligent automation in single pilot operations. In: AIAA Infotech@ Aerospace, p. 1652 (2016)
8. DeJohn, C.A., Wolbrink, A.M., Larcher, J.G.: In-flight medical incapacitation and impairment of us airline pilots: 1993 to 1998. Tech. rep, FEDERAL AVIATION ADMINISTRATION OKLAHOMA CITY OK CIVIL AEROMEDICAL INST (2004)
9. DeJohn, C.A., Wolbrink, A.M., Larcher, J.G.: In-flight medical incapacitation and impairment of airline pilots. Aviat. Space Environ. Med. **77**(10), 1077–1079 (2006)
10. Hart, S.G., Staveland, L.E.: Development of NASA-TLX (task load index): Results of empirical and theoretical research, pp. 139–183 (1988). https://doi.org/10.1016/S0166-4115(08)62386-9

11. ICAO: Icao accident statistics. https://www.icao.int/safety/iStars/Pages/Accident-Statistics.aspx
12. Leigh, K.: Microsoft mixed reality toolkit. https://github.com/microsoft/mixedrealitytoolkit-unity. https://github.com/microsoft/MixedRealityToolkit-Unity
13. Letouzé, T., Créno, L., Diaz-Pineda, J., Dormoy, C.A., Hourlier, S., André, J.M.: Mental representation impact analysis (meria), a method for analyzing mental representations for the design of hmi. a case study in aeronautics. Le travail humain **83**(1), 61–89 (2020)
14. Light, R.: Mosquitto mqtt broker. https://github.com/eclipse/mosquitto
15. Lim, Y., Gardi, A., Sabatini, R., Ramasamy, S., Kistan, T., Ezer, N., Vince, J., Bolia, R.: Avionics human-machine interfaces and interactions for manned and unmanned aircraft. Prog. Aerosp. Sci. **102**, 1–46 (2018)
16. Matessa, M., Vu, K.P.L., Strybel, T.Z., Battiste, V., Schnell, T., Cover, M.: Using distributed simulation to investigate human-autonomy teaming. In: International Conference on Human Interface and the Management of Information. pp. 541–550. Springer (2018)
17. Nicholl, R.: Airline head-up display systems: human factors considerations. Available at SSRN 2384101 (2014)
18. Parasuraman, R., Molloy, R., Singh, I.L.: Performance consequences of automation-induced 'complacency'. Int. J. Aviat. Psychol. **3**(1), 1–23 (1993)
19. Shively, R.J., Lachter, J., Brandt, S.L., Matessa, M., Battiste, V., Johnson, W.W.: Why human-autonomy teaming? In: International Conference on Applied Human Factors and Ergonomics, pp. 3–11. Springer (2017)
20. Spitzer, C., Ferrell, U., Ferrell, T.: Digital avionics handbook. CRC Press (2017)
21. Taylor, R.M.: Situational awareness rating technique (sart): The development of a tool for aircrew systems design. In: Situational Awareness, pp. 111–128. Routledge (2017)
22. Viertler, F., Hajek, M.: Evaluation of visual augmentation methods for rotorcraft pilots in degraded visual environments. J. Am. Helicopter Soc. **62**(1), 1–11 (2017)
23. Yang, Q., Steinfeld, A., Rosé, C., Zimmerman, J.: Re-examining whether, why, and how human-ai interaction is uniquely difficult to design. In: Proceedings of the 2020 chi Conference on Human Factors in Computing Systems, pp. 1–13 (2020)

# Assessment of a Novel Virtual Environment for Examining Human Cognitive-Motor Performance During Execution of Action Sequences

Alexandra A. Shaver[1], Neehar Peri[2], Remy Mezebish[2], George Matthew[2],
Alyza Berson[1], Christopher Gaskins[3], Gregory P. Davis[2], Garrett E. Katz[4],
Immanuel Samuel[5], Matthew J. Reinhard[5], Michelle E. Costanzo[5],
James A. Reggia[2,3,6,7], James Purtilo[2], and Rodolphe J. Gentili[1,3,7(✉)]

[1] Department of Kinesiology, University of Maryland, College Park, MD, USA
rodolphe@umd.edu
[2] Department of Computer Science, University of Maryland, College Park, MD, USA
purtilo@umd.edu
[3] Neuroscience & Cognitive Science Program, University of Maryland, College Park, MD, USA
[4] Electrical Engineering & Computer Science, Syracuse University, Syracuse, NY, USA
[5] War Related Illness and Injury Study Center,
Washington DC VA Medical Center, Washington DC, USA
[6] Institute for Advanced Computer Studies, University of Maryland, College Park, MD, USA
[7] Maryland Robotics Center, University of Maryland, College Park, MD, USA

**Abstract.** The examination of neural resource allocation during complex action sequence execution is critical to understanding human behavior. While physical systems are usually used for such assessment, virtual/remote systems offer other approaches with potential benefits such as remote training/evaluation. Here we describe a virtual environment (VLEARN) operated via the internet that has been developed to study the cognitive-motor mechanisms underlying the execution of goal-oriented action sequences in remote and laboratory settings. This study aimed to i) examine the feasibility of evaluating human cognitive-motor behavior when individuals operate VLEARN to complete various tasks; and ii) assess VLEARN by comparing its usability and the resulting performance, mental workload, and mental/physical fatigue during virtual and physical task execution. Results revealed that our approach allowed human cognitive-motor behavior assessment as the tasks completed physically and virtually via VLEARN had similar success rates. Also, there was a relationship between the complexity of the virtual control systems and the dependency on those to complete tasks. Namely, relative to controls with more functionalities, when VLEARN enabled simpler controls, above average usability and similar levels of cognitive-motor performance for both physical and virtual task execution were observed. Thus, a simplification of some aspects of the VLEARN control interface should enhance its usability. Our approach is promising for examining human cognitive-motor behavior and informing multiple applications (e.g., telehealth, remote training).

A. A. Shaver and N. Peri—both are co-first authors.
J. Purtilo and R. J. Gentili—both are co-last authors.

© The Author(s), under exclusive license to Springer Nature Switzerland AG 2022
D. D. Schmorrow and C. M. Fidopiastis (Eds.): HCII 2022, LNAI 13310, pp. 361–380, 2022.
https://doi.org/10.1007/978-3-031-05457-0_28

**Keywords:** Virtual environment · Action sequences · Mental workload · Cognitive-motor performance · Human-machine interface · Rehabilitation

# 1 Introduction

The ability to efficiently recruit neural resources to face varying task demands is critical in driving the underlying mental workload and performance dynamics ultimately enabling adaptive cognitive-motor behavior [1–4]. For instance, an increase in task demands would result in greater engagement of the corresponding neural resources, ultimately causing an elevation in mental workload. Objective indicators of mental workload may be helpful to several applications such as evaluating heterogenous neurological conditions with poorly understood etiology such as Anomalous Health Incident sequalae and post concussive syndrome experienced by military populations, since they capture both behavioral and cognitive performance. The concept of mental workload has been largely studied via various tasks (e.g., single reaching movements, action sequences, dual-tasking) in both physical and/or virtual environments. Despite this large body of work, mental workload is not well understood in the context of performance of complex action sequence tasks which typically: i) generate high cognitive-motor demands in novices (e.g., high-level planning; working memory; attention; [5]); ii) require a substantial amount of practice to be mastered, iii) involve several degrees of freedom while requiring substantial hand-eye coordination, and iv) are a good vehicle to study human behavior in more real-world conditions [6].

Recently, a limited number of studies have examined the changes in mental workload when individuals execute or practice such complex actions sequences [7–9]. These studies generally examined this notion when individuals performed the task using physical systems, except for the well-established Tower of Hanoi task. However, it is also important to further examine performance and mental workload concurrently during the execution of various types of complex tasks in virtual environments operated remotely rather than in a controlled lab setting or with physical equipment. Virtual environments provide individuals the opportunity to be assessed or trained remotely from a more convenient and possibly safer location when in-person assessment or training can be very challenging or dangerous. As such, the current study is important not only to further understand the cognitive-motor mechanisms that support virtually executing complex action sequences to solve a problem but also to inform applications related to telemedicine, telehealth, and training/re-training of civilians and military personnel all over the world. A need for effective, scalable and efficient remote options is crucial during special circumstances such as the COVID-19 pandemic which has forced many institutions globally to delay and/or halt in-person human data collection and further complicated interventions, evaluation and training during an uncertain time for many individuals (e.g., social distancing, wearing masks), problems that a tool, such as the one proposed here, could by-pass via remote operations. A possible first step to enabling the examination of cognitive-motor processes remotely is to develop a new experimental medium that is flexible, cost-effective, easy to use, and mimics physical systems with the level of fidelity needed to provide accurate and meaningful experimental data. As such, in an attempt to fulfill these requirements, our research group has been developing a new virtual environment (named virtualized learning or VLEARN[1]) that is accessible remotely via the internet and allows for observing human behavior and neural mechanisms when individuals perform and learn action sequences to successfully execute complex cognitive-motor tasks. So far, VLEARN can simulate multiple scenarios intended to assess cognitive-motor performance and learning during execution of complex action sequences. However, before employing this new virtual platform to conduct human studies that include experimental manipulations, its usability and more generally its effects on cognitive-motor behavior need to be examined.

Thus, this study aims to i) determine the feasibility of experimentally assessing human cognitive-motor behavior (performance, mental workload and fatigue) when individuals operate this novel virtual environment, via the internet, to complete various tasks by executing specific action sequences, and ii) if so, to assess the usability of this novel remote virtual platform and determine which features are appropriately designed and which need improvements. In particular, VLEARN's assessment was conducted by comparing the level of usability, performance, mental workload and fatigue obtained when individuals operated matching virtual and physical systems.

We hypothesized that if the proposed approach is feasible, VLEARN will enable individuals to complete the various virtual tasks while investigators successfully collect metrics related to performance, mental workload and fatigue with data quality similar to using the physical systems. Alternatively, any major limitations of the proposed method (e.g., technical glitches; excessive computational delays; etc.) that compromise the data integrity (e.g., participants drop-out, incomplete data set for the task and/or metrics) would suggest that such an approach is currently not feasible. Also, under the assumption that the proposed approach is feasible, we hypothesized that if the fidelity of the virtual environment is appropriate, measurements indexing the usability, performance, mental workload and fatigue should not differ compared to measurements collected when individuals use the corresponding physical systems.

## 2   Material and Methods

### 2.1   The Virtual Environment

**General Presentation.** The VLEARN application serves as a participant and experiment development and management tool, containing both a dashboard and a trial completion page. The dashboard provides a hub where participants can log in and view their assigned experimental tasks to perform, while allowing administrators to create new participant accounts, create tasks/trials, and manage experimental data. Through the trial completion page, participants interact with the virtual environment to complete a task which was designed by the administrator beforehand. On this page, participants have a control readout, as well as a window, from which they complete tasks within a virtual 3D environment. Although VLEARN allows the administrator to design various scenarios, currently three tasks of interest have been developed: i) the well-known Tower of Hanoi task (ToH; [7–11]); ii) a disk hard drive dock maintenance (DM) task where drives were

---

[1] https://github.com/gmatthew1141/VLEARN.

manipulated similarly to prior studies [12–15] and iii) a pipe system maintenance (PM) task (see Sect. 2.2 for details). These tasks were created using the unity game engine, and currently support multi-user collaboration for up to four users, allowing multiple administrators/participants to join in task completion. While not tested here, the RESTful API also provides a system to create autonomous virtual agents to collaboratively execute tasks with a human (Fig. 1).

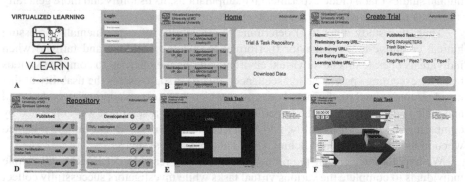

**Fig. 1.** Administrator's view of VLEARN. (A) Login page for administrator (and participants); (B) Administrator's homepage for visualization of participant list, datasets, trial/task repository. Administrator can: (C) select details of a task to assign to participants; (D) publish trials/tasks that can be (un)assigned, edited or deleted (left) and trials/tasks still being created/edited (right); (E–F) manipulate the environment before each trial and highlight elements of a task (here DM task).

VLEARN builds on a previously created virtual environment called the Simulator for Maryland Imitation Learning Environment (SMILE) developed at the University of Maryland - College Park [16, 17]. SMILE is a Java based simulator for studying imitation learning. An experimenter uses SMILE to create animated demonstrations that can then be observed by robots as they learn to imitate what is being demonstrated. SMILE hypothesizes that robots can learn more effectively by ignoring the demonstrator's motions and instead only observing the behaviors of the object in the demonstration environment. SMILE allows video playback, text logging, and scene creation using XML. In addition, it allows for a simulated robot to interact with the Java environment through MATLAB (for details see [16, 17]). Although interesting, SMILE serves a different purpose than the VLEARN software, which allows us to study high-level learning behaviors in humans. Moreover, our proposed solution implements multi-agent interaction, and allows for us to control agents using a flexible web API.

The long-term goal of VLEARN is to facilitate high fidelity research into human learning by reducing confounding factors, improving the movement and interaction system, and providing extensive experimental manipulation options with enhanced data collection and logging capabilities. To this end, we modeled the Unity assets to closely approximate a real environment. Specifically, we ensured that interactions with objects in a scene were realistic, while also considering the limited degrees of freedom provided by mouse and keyboard input. We discretized the movement system such that an agent can only travel to fixed positions in the virtual world using teleporter pads. Moreover, we translated almost all keyboard interaction into clickable buttons on the software inter-face to facilitate manipulation of the virtual environment. This is important to ensure that even participants who are not used to manipulating virtual environments (e.g., com-puter graphics, software design; gamers) can still operate VLEARN fairly easily. This ensures that learning effects are mitigated, thus avoiding introducing experimental bias. It also ensures that a number of potential individuals can participate simultaneously in cognitive-motor studies using this virtual system. Lastly, we expanded the logging capa-bilities to facilitate multi-agent interactions. We defined an object-oriented relationship between all objects and agents in a scene, facilitating important research insights about the order of object interactions.

**Software Architecture.** The VLEARN front-end was developed in Node.js, while the virtual world was implemented in Unity and rendered through WebGL. The dashboard connects the administrator and the study participant to the simulation or the participant information. The simulations are stored on a web server with the corresponding XML files to generate the task. VLEARN synchronously logs each participant's interactions with the environment. All experimental data are stored in a MongoDB database, and each participant is only identified by a unique hash in accordance with Institutional Review Board standards. The administrator prepares trials by uploading an XML file to the web server.

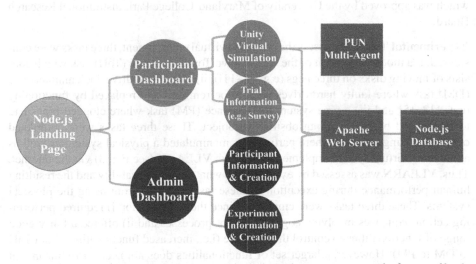

**Fig. 2.** High-level architecture of VLEARN. The circles and squares represent the front- and back-end while administrator and participant actions are denoted by red and green circles, respectively.

These XML files contain the information needed to generate each task and serve as a convenient way to save the starting layout of a task (see Fig. 2 for the high-level architecture of VLEARN). A RESTful API in Node.js was also implemented to allow for external logging of interactions with participants and objects (e.g., toggle, disk, magnetic pointer) through events (e.g., "press", "hold", "drop", "hide"). Events contain environment or agent observations when querying for information. All events contain an agent identifier, Cartesian coordinates and Euler angle to show position and rotation of interactable objects in a scene. Some events additionally contain an object identifier which uniquely identifies the actions taken related to a given object in the log. As such, events can be tracked, saved, and replayed as a sequence of events or interactions. For example, in DM task when the participant inserts a drive into the slot, the corresponding event would contain the participant's identifier, current position and the drive's identifier. Additionally, the RESTful API can be queried for only interactions involving a specific object or user. These event lists could be used in the place of manually entered behavioral data for quick analysis of sequence efficiency and eventually for real-time feedback. These events originate from Unity's Photon Unity Network (PUN V2), a real-time multiplayer game development framework. The PUN cloud service enables up to 20 concurrent users maximum on worldwide servers.

## 2.2 Experimental Evaluation

**Participants.** Twelve healthy individuals participated in this study (2 men and 10 women; age range 19–33 years). No history of neurological impairment or use of medication known to alter the central nervous system was reported. Participants had a normal or corrected-to-normal vision and were free of drug and alcohol use at the time of the study. Prior to starting the study all individuals provided their written informed consent which was approved by the University of Maryland-College Park Institutional Research Board.

**Experimental Tasks.** To assess the proposed virtual environment, three tasks were considered: i) a modified version of the well-known Tower of Hanoi (ToH) task which consists of moving disks on three pegs (e.g., [7–11]); ii) a disk hard drive dock maintenance (DM) task where faulty hard drives need to be removed and replaced by functioning ones [12–15] and iii) a pipe system maintenance (PM) task where clogged pipes had to be cleaned by removing an obstructive object. These three tasks were completed over two testing sessions where participants manipulated a physical system as well as a matching virtual system implemented through VLEARN (see Fig. 3) via the internet. Thus, VLEARN was assessed by examining to what extent its usability and the resulting human performance during execution of these tasks differed from using the physical systems. These three tasks were employed since their completion i) required performing action sequences involving cognitive-motor processes and ii) offered a fairly good range of functionalities to control the interface (i.e., increased functionalities from ToH to DM to PM). However, a larger set of functionalities does not necessarily mean that the task demands were higher. Importantly, the aim of this study was not to manipulate task demands to probe the engagement of cognitive-motor resources (e.g., attention, high-level planning) by having participants complete tasks using scenarios of increasing complexity. Instead, as a first step, this work mainly aimed to study the feasibility of remotely assessing cognitive-motor behavior with the proposed approach and the usability of VLEARN when participants operated it to perform these three tasks.

*Tower of Hanoi Task.* Typically, the ToH task consists of several disks stacked in ascending order of diameter on one of three identical, evenly-spaced pegs. The physical ToH system was composed of a wooden board with three pegs and wooden disks. In the virtual system, this task was executed using a classic point-and-click control system to manipulate the disks and as such served as a standard approach for potential subsequent comparisons (see Fig. 3; first column). The objective of the original ToH task is to move all disks from the leftmost to the rightmost peg while following three rules: a) only one disk can be displaced at a time, b) a disk may not be placed on the table or held while another disk is being moved, and c) a larger disk cannot be stacked on top of a smaller disk. As mentioned earlier, since this work aimed to assess the proposed virtual environment, participants were asked to perform a modified version of the ToH with three disks and three pegs using the physical and virtual system. Namely, participants were asked to move the disks from the leftmost peg to the middle peg and finally to the rightmost or back to the leftmost peg. Trials were deemed successful when the task goal was completed while the two first rules mentioned above (i.e., only one disk can be displaced at a time; a disk may not be placed on the table or held while another disk is being moved) were respected.

*Disk Drive Dock Maintenance Task.* The DM task has been used in prior research to examine high-level plan generation in a humanoid robot and humans during action sequence imitation [13, 14]. This task involves a mock-up hard drive docking station with a drawer that, when opened, allows participants to manipulate four hard drives placed in individual slots, each being associated with a LED indicator and a toggle switch. LED indicators were either red, green, or off designating that the associated drive was broken, working properly, or had been turned off, respectively. The physical system was a custom-made mock-up controlled by an Arduino processor [13–15] and used as a model for the virtual system (see Fig. 3; second column). The goal of the task was to safely replace the faulty drive with a new drive. Trials were considered successful if the goal was attained while following the rule that the LED had to be turned off when a drive is added or removed. Although multiple possibilities could be considered to challenge individuals, for the reasons previously mentioned, participants only had to replace one faulty drive.

*Pipe Maintenance Task.* Although the PM task was initially designed to examine cognitive-motor processes that involve both cognitive (e.g., high-level planning) and motor (e.g., fine motor precision) demands, here, akin to the two tasks mentioned above, fairly simple task sequences involving all key components were used to assess the usability of the proposed virtual environment compared to its physical counterpart. In both environments, this task involved a mock-up pipe station with a main valve which had to be closed before any of the other four PVC pipes could be safely manipulated. The main valve and the four pipes were each associated with a toggle switch and LED indicator that were red, green, or off designating whether the water had stopped (i.e., closed main valve or clogged pipe), was working properly, or had been turned off, respectively. The pipes could be opened or closed by replacing or removing the PVC adaptor (top used to cover pipe opening). A magnetic tool was used to extract the obstructive object from the affected pipe. A red LED and small buzzer were triggered to alert participants that the object had touched the edge of the physical pipe. Similarly, during virtual trials the object would turn red if it came into contact with the pipe during extraction. Virtual extraction was accomplished by controlling the virtual tool with a computer mouse or trackpad (Fig. 3; third column) depending on what the participant used at home. This task aimed to safely clear a clogged pipe using a tool to extract the object without letting it touch the edge of the pipe. Trials were considered successful when the task goal was reached while two rules were respected: a) the main valve had to be closed (red) before any pipes can be opened; b) the corresponding LED had to be turned off before a pipe can be opened.

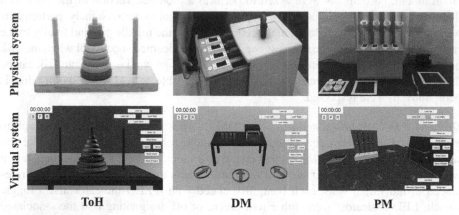

**Fig. 3.** The physical and virtual systems employed to execute the ToH, the DM and PM tasks to assess VLEARN usability and human cognitive-motor performance when performing with this simulator. ToH: Tower of Hanoi; DM: Disk drive dock maintenance; PM: Pipe maintenance.

**Experimental Procedures.** Participants were required to perform the three (ToH, DM and PM) tasks over two testing sessions using in-person physical systems and the virtual environment, VLEARN, controlled through the internet. For the latter, participants were given an individual username and password to access the VLEARN website. Order of the testing sessions, modality and tasks were counterbalanced. First, for each task (i.e., ToH, DM and PM) and both execution modalities (i.e., physical and virtual) a familiarization phase was conducted to ensure that the participants understood the tasks and how to use the current system. Specifically, the rules and goal of the task were explained, and participants were provided with up to five minutes to manipulate the system they would be using for the upcoming trials. To mitigate practice effects, the action sequences used during the testing session were not used during this phase. With the PM task, participants were not allowed to attempt any actual extraction but instead only touched the edge of the pipe with the pointer. This allowed participants to explore the collision feedback (i.e., LED, red object color change, buzzer) with both the physical and virtual systems without practicing the actual extraction. Once this familiarization period was completed, for each task and execution modality participants had to perform four blocks of four trials resulting in a total of 16 trials per task. To vary the conditions and ensure use of all system components, the task was slightly different for each block (i.e., the peg to transfer the disks, the disk drive to replace and the pipe to clean differed between blocks, respectively). At the beginning of each block, a video demonstration of the action sequence (i.e., the reference sequence) to perform was presented to the participants. Participants were permitted to ask about the rules of the task and for the next step of the sequence at any time during a trial and see again the video demonstration between trials at their request. This approach was employed to ensure that the usability and the cognitive-motor states examined here were primarily related to operating the virtual or physical system, not the engagement of cognitive-motor resources (e.g., working memory; attention; high-level planning processes) due to demands related to over-complicated action sequences. Individuals were allowed to start their trial whenever they wanted after a verbal 'Go' signal and trials were stopped as soon as the task was completed or the time limit of two or five minutes was reached, whichever came first for the physical and virtual trials, respectively. These limits were set such that both virtual and physical trials potentially allowed to collect the same number of trials for direct comparison while their respective sessions lasted a maximum of about two hours[2]. Any session going beyond the session time limit was stopped. Trials were considered successful if participants completed the action sequence reaching the goal within the time limit while following the corresponding rules. Trials with burdensome or excessive technical glitches (e.g., frozen screen, system component not working properly, internet connection issues) were halted and restarted. For each trial, the performance of the participant was video recorded for subsequent data processing.

After 16 trials with the physical or virtual system, individuals were asked to complete the System Usability Scale (SUS) to determine the perceived usability of the systems used for this task. While other options exist, the SUS is a widely accepted measure of perceived usability that is versatile, cost and time effective, as well as, robust even when small sample sizes are used [18, 19]. Also, it has been used successfully to estimate the usability of many software systems, devices, services and is related to internet self-efficacy [18, 19]. The SUS consists of 10 questions which alternate between positive and negative statements about the system. Answers are recorded using a five-point scale [20].

After each block of four trials, participants completed questionnaires to assess their level of perceived workload and fatigue. The NASA TLX is a well-established multidimensional questionnaire used to report different aspects of perceived workload during cognitive-motor performance [4, 21]. NASA TLX scores are generally consistent with more objective measurements, such as those obtained via neuroimaging (e.g., [3]). Workload is assessed along six subscales: mental, physical, temporal, perceived performance, effort, and frustration (ranging from 0 to 100 in increments of 5) (for details, see [21]). Although all the subscales of the NASA TLX were examined here, the mental demand dimension was of primary interest since it has been shown as the most representative of the mental workload (e.g., [3, 4]). A visual analog scale was used to measure participants' levels of mental and physical fatigue. This scale ranged from 0–100 in increments of 5 where 0, 50 and 100 indicated that individuals were not fatigued at all, moderately fatigued and very fatigued, respectively. For trials executed with the physical and virtual system, these measurements were collected using online surveys [22]. Participants'

---

[2] The 2 min time limit for the physical trials was set from prior work which clearly established that it was largely enough for task completion and thus did not bias the present study.

performance during physical and virtual trials was examined through video analysis. The video recordings allowed us to compute i) the Levenshtein's Distance (LD; [8, 14]) which indicates to what extent the executed sequence differs from the demonstrated (reference) sequence and ii) sequence completion time (SCT; [8]) which was the time between starting the first and completing the last sequence action.

## Data Processing

*Survey Data.* The raw SUS scores were normalized and then combined resulting in a single score between 0–100 for each participant, task and execution modality [23, 24]. Similarly, each subscale of the NASA TLX and fatigue scores were separately averaged, resulting in scores between 0–100 for each participant, task and execution modality [21].

*Performance Data.* The SCT represented the time elapsed by the participant to complete the demonstrated action sequence for a given task and execution modality. Then, the average SCT was computed for each participant and conditions to be subjected to statistical analysis. In addition, the LD was computed for each participant and condition.

The LD measures the distance between two sequences, which represents the minimum number of operations (here insertions, deletions, and substitutions were considered; see below) needed to match one sequence to the *reference sequence* [8, 14, 25]. Computing LD is achieved by defining an alphabet of symbols representative of all possible sequence components, sequences, and operations. In general, a sequence alphabet can be defined as a finite set $\{A_1, A_2, \ldots A_i, \ldots, A_{n-1}, A_n\}$ where $A_j$ is the $j^{th}$ atomic symbol among all N possible symbols. For instance, the alphabet for the PM task was {Open main valve; Close main valve; Press toggle i; Remove cleanout adapter i; Put down cleanout adapter i; Pick up spare cleanout; Discard in bin; Pick up tool; Extract object from pipe; Discard object in bin; Put down tool} where i = {1, 2, 3 ,4} (for the alphabet for the ToH and DM tasks, see [14]). As such, the operators modify one action at a time resulting in a different sequence. In the current context, each atomic "symbol" represents an elementary action in a given action sequence—an atomic action. A motor sequence would then be defined as a finite, ordered list of zero or more atomic actions from the alphabet with or without repeating atomic actions. For instance, one of the demonstrated action sequences for the PM task was <Open main valve, Press toggle 1, Remove cleanout adapter 1, Pick tool up, Extract object, Discard object, Put down tool, Replace cleanout adapter 1, Press toggle 1, Close main valve>. To compare the reference (or demonstrated sequence) and the sequence executed by the participant, the following three classical LD operators were considered: (i) *insertion* of one action, (ii) *deletion* of one action, and (iii) *substitution* of one action for another one (i.e., a replacement). More specifically, insertions refer to the addition of an action anywhere in the sequence that increases the sequence length by one compared to the reference sequence. A deletion eliminates an action at any location in the sequence which decreases its length by one. Substitutions describe the replacement of an existing action in the sequence with a different action without changing the action sequence length. Thus, this processing allowed to obtain the LD, the number of insertion (NI), number of deletion (ND) and the number of substitution (NS) (for details see [8, 14]). Computationally, the LD was computed using the well-established dynamic programming approach Wagner-Fischer algorithm (for details see [8, 14, 26]). Then, the average LD, NI, ND and NS were subjected to statistical analysis.

**Statistical Analysis.** First, an analysis to assess the success rate for the three tasks executed physically and virtually was conducted. Then, for each task separately, the mean survey scores (total SUS score, each NASA TLX subscale scores, the physical and mental fatigue survey scores) as well as the mean SCT, LD, NI, ND, and NS obtained when individuals used the physical and virtual systems were compared using paired *t-tests* or *Wilcoxon signed-ranked tests* depending on whether the assumption of normality (assessed by a Lilliefors test) was violated or not. In addition, the Cohen's d effect sizes were computed and reported. A one sample t-test was used to compare the mean SUS scores to the well-established industry threshold value of 68 (i.e., scores smaller and greater than this cut-off represent below and above and average usability) [23, 24]. The false discovery rate was employed to account for the multiple comparisons conducted to compare the measurements listed above (i.e., survey scores; SCT, LD, NI, ND, and NS) obtained for both physical and virtual systems. All criterion alpha levels were set to $p < 0.05$.

# 3   Results

## 3.1   Usability

The results of the qualitative analysis revealed that all participants fully completed the three tasks either physically or virtually. Thus, no participant drop-out from the study or any session. This resulted in the same number of trials for both the physical and virtual systems. Considering technical issues and rule breaking, the vast majority of the trials were successful for the three tasks when physically (97.48%) or virtually (94.01%) performed. Specifically, most of the trials were free of any technical glitches for the physical (98.44%) and virtual (93.75%) system. Further examination revealed that this difference in success rate was comparable between tasks. Also, for the three tasks, a large majority of the physical (96.53%) and virtual (94.27%) trials executed did not have any rule breaks. Additional analyses revealed that when virtually executed the PM task completion was less successful than when physically completed (Physical: 94.79%; Virtual: 89.58%). However, both the ToH and DM tasks presented a similar and greater success (ToH – Physical: 100%, Virtual: 100%; DM – Physical: 94.79%, Virtual: 93.23%) regardless of the system (i.e., physical or virtual) used.

The SUS scores for each of the three tasks were significantly higher when executed with the physical compared to the virtual systems (ToH: $t(11) = 2.580$, $p = 0.036$, d $= 0.745$; DM: $t(11) = 5.461$, $p < 0.001$, d $= 1.576$; PM: $t(11) = 4.893$, $p < 0.001$, d $= 1.412$). Also, while the SUS scores obtained for the physical system were all above the usability threshold (ToH: $t(11) = 8.537$, $p < 0.001$, d $= 2.465$; DM: $t(11) = 5.000$, $p < 0.001$, d $= 1.443$; PM: $t(11) = 4.893$, $p < 0.001$, d $= 2.057$) the results were less consistent for the virtual system. Specifically, the SUS scores obtained with the virtual system when executing the ToH ($t(11) = 2.376$, $p = 0.041$, d $= 0.686$) and the PM ($t(11) = -2.530$, $p = 0.036$, d $= 0.730$) tasks were above and below this threshold, respectively. Finally, the average SUS score for the DM was below the usability threshold although statistically not different from it ($t(11) = -1.886$, $p = 0.086$, d $= 0.544$) (see Fig. 4).

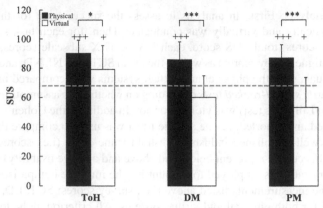

**Fig. 4.** Usability scores when individuals perform the ToH, DM and PM tasks with the physical and virtual systems. The dashed gray line represents the 68 threshold usability level (see text for details). ToH: Tower of Hanoi; DM: Disk drive dock maintenance; PM: Pipe maintenance. The stars (*) and crosses (+) represent the significance level for the physical vs. virtual contrast and the physical or virtual vs, average acceptability threshold contrast, respectively. *: $p < 0.05$; **: $p < 0.01$; ***: $p < 0.001$; +: $p < 0.05$; + +: $p < 0.01$; + + +: $p < 0.001$.

### 3.2 Mental Workload

The same statistical analysis revealed that the physical and virtual execution of the ToH task did not affect any workload dimensions of the NASA TLX ($p > 0.137, 0.001 < d < 0.544$). Also, no difference in the perceived temporal demand between the physical and virtual execution of any of the three tasks was detected ($p > 0.117, 0.095 < d < 0.634$). However, the perceived mental demand increased when the DM ($z = -2.511$, $p = 0.024, d = 0.858$) and PM ($t(11) = -3.930, p = 0.019, d = 1.135$) tasks were executed with the virtual compared to the physical system. Similarly, perceived effort and frustration were greater when participants operated the virtual system to complete the DM (Effort: $z = -2.590, p = 0.022, d = 0.816$; Frustration: $z = -2.805, p = 0.019$, $d = 0.917$) and PM (Effort: $t(11) = -2.786, p = 0.019, d = 1.105$; Frustration: $z = -3.062, p = 0.019, d = 0.899$) tasks relative to the physical systems.

In addition, the performance was perceived as better when executing the DM ($z = -2.669, p = 0.020, d = 0.939$) and PM ($t(11) = -3.688, p = 0.019, d = 1.065$) tasks with the physical relative to the virtual system. Finally, the analysis also revealed that the physical demand was perceived as higher when the PM task was executed in the virtual compared to the physical environment ($z = -2.688, p = 0.020, d = 1.035$) whereas this was not observed for the DM task ($z = -1.174, p = 0.333, d = 0.278$) (see Fig. 5).

### 3.3 Performance

Statistical analysis of SCT revealed no differences between the ToH executed with the physical and virtual systems ($z = -0.533, p = 0.594, d = 0.237$). However, an elevation of SCT was observed when participants executed the DM task with the virtual compared to the physical system ($z = -3.059, p = 0.002, d = 1.795$). Similarly, compared to

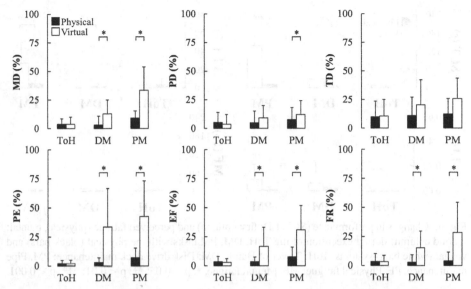

**Fig. 5.** Differences in perceived mental demand (top left panel) and the other five dimensions (PD, TD, PE, EF, FR) obtained by means of the NASA TLX questionnaire during the performance of the ToH, DM and PM tasks using the physical (black bars) and virtual (white bars) systems. MD: Mental demand; PD: Physical demand; TD: Temporal demand; PE: Performance; EF: Effort; FR: Frustration. ToH: Tower of Hanoi; DM: Disk drive dock maintenance; PM: Pipe maintenance. *: p < 0.05; **: p < 0.01; ***: p < 0.001.

the physical system, the execution of the PM task with the virtual system resulted in a significantly longer SCT (t(11) = −11,600, p < 0.001, d = 3.349). For the three tasks, no difference in LD or its operators (NI, ND and NS) were revealed for action sequences executed with the physical and virtual system (p > 0.469) (see Fig. 6; first column; the NI, ND and NS are not represented).

## 3.4 Fatigue

No differences in physical fatigue were observed between the virtual and physical systems for the ToH task (z = 1.035, p = 0.319, d = 0.318). However, the completion of the DM and PM tasks with the virtual systems resulted in greater physical fatigue in participants relative to the physical systems (DM: z = −2.670, p = 0.040, d = 1.012; PM: z = −2.473, p = 0.040, d = 0.870). In addition, the mental fatigue elicited by each of the three tasks was not significantly different between physical and virtual systems (ToH: z = 0.997, p = 0.319, d = 0.289; DM: z = −1.992, p = 0.093, d = 0.570; PM: z = −1.844, p = 0.098, d = 0.540) (see Fig. 6; second column).

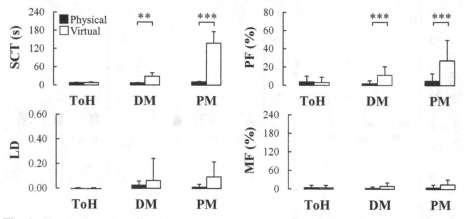

**Fig. 6.** Changes in performance (SCT, LD; first column) and perceived fatigue (physical, mental; second column) during execution of the ToH, DM, PM tasks with the physical (black bars) and virtual (white bars) systems. ToH: Tower of Hanoi; DM: Disk drive dock maintenance; PM: Pipe maintenance. PF: Physical fatigue; MF: Mental fatigue. *: $p < 0.05$; **: $p < 0.01$; ***: $p < 0.001$.

## 4   Discussion

Overall, findings revealed that the proposed approach appropriately assessed human cognitive-motor behavior when individuals executed various virtual tasks involving action sequences remotely. The results also revealed that when individuals executed the virtual and physical ToH tasks, similar levels of usability, performance, mental workload and mental/physical fatigue were obtained. Conversely, relative to physical execution, the virtual completion of the PM task and, to a slightly lesser extent, the DM task resulted in below average levels of usability as well as performance decrements along with elevations in mental workload and physical fatigue.

### 4.1   Systems-Dependent Differences in Usability, Performance, Mental Workload and Fatigue

First, for all three tasks, it appeared that the entire study could be successfully conducted remotely using VLEARN and the internet to complete tasks with a similar level of success compared to physically executing these tasks. Although slightly better for the physical system, few technical issues among the three tasks were observed when individuals performed with VLEARN. In addition, both the physical and virtual trials had a very similar task completion success rate for both the ToH and the DM tasks. The success rate for PM task was lower for virtual compared to physical execution. Second, for all three tasks, the usability of the physical system reached an "excellent" rating according to the acceptability range paired with adjectives and letter-grade scales proposed by Bangor and colleagues [18–20]. Although not surprising, this is important since these physical set-ups served as a reference to evaluate the usability of VLEARN and more generally its effects on human performance when executing the three tasks considered here. The virtual environment for the ToH task received the highest SUS score of all virtual systems.

Importantly, it was the only virtual system which received a score above the industry-driven and widely acknowledged threshold (i.e., 68 points) which corresponds to a "good" rating on the aforementioned scale [18–20]. Although the ToH task executed physically elicited a higher usability relative to its virtual execution, this difference was much smaller compared to those obtained for the DM and PM tasks as indicated by smaller effect sizes. The virtual and physical completion of the ToH led to similar performance as suggested by comparable imitation quality of the demonstration (LD ≈ 0) and duration of sequence completion (similar SCT). It must be noted that here the former was expected for all three tasks and both systems due to the simplification of sequences for experimental purposes (see Sect. 2.2). Thus, similar SCT suggest that the velocity at which the actions of the sequence were performed when operating the physical and virtual systems were similar. Also, the same between-systems comparison led to similar levels of mental workload (and subscale scores of the NASA TLX) which, when combined with performance results, suggest comparable cognitive-motor efficiency along with a similar physical and mental fatigue [3, 4, 27].

However, the virtual execution of the DM and PM tasks resulted in a level of usability below the industry standard score of 68 with scores of 60 and 53.13 which both corresponded to "OK" and fell in the "marginally low" range of acceptable usability with letter-grades of D and F, respectively [18–20]. However, while the usability score for the virtual DM task was below average, it was not statistically different from the standard score of 68 whereas the PM task was well below this standard. Along these lines, compared to physical execution, the SCT for both the DM and PM tasks with VLEARN was longer whereas no major discrepancies between the demonstrated and imitated sequences was observed (the latter was expected for the reasons mentioned in Sect. 2.2). Thus, these results (similar LDs and greater SCT) suggest that slower execution of the actions composing the sequence when operating the virtual system (relative to the physical system) were likely not due to mistakes while forming the sequences (e.g., adding extraneous actions) and/or excessive pause between actions due to mistake or hesitation (as observed in the video analysis).

Furthermore, relative to physical task execution, higher mental workload (as well as perceived performance failure, effort and frustration) were obtained when the DM and PM tasks were executed virtually. In particular, a reduction in performance (i.e., SCT) along with this elevation of the mental workload collectively suggest a reduction of the cognitive-motor efficiency [3, 4, 27] when the DM and PM tasks were completed virtually relative to physically. It is important to note that although a decrement of usability and performance along with an elevation of the mental workload were observed for these two virtual systems, the changes were more prominent for the PM task (as indicated by greater effect sizes). Importantly, although the execution of the DM and PM tasks with the virtual relative to the physical system led to differences in mental workload it did not translate to mental fatigue which was comparable for both systems. Finally, the execution of the PM task with VLEARN was perceived as more physically demanding than when executed with the actual set-up whereas this was not observed for the DM task. However, when both tasks were virtually executed an elevation in physical fatigue was observed. It must be noticed that, as expected, temporal demand was not significantly different between any of the physical and virtual task systems since the emphasis was placed on using the core components of each system to complete the imitation task correctly rather than quickly.

## 4.2 The Effect of the Controls on the Usability, Performance, Mental Workload and Fatigue

Generally, the virtual and physical execution of the ToH task led to acceptable levels of usability and cognitive-motor performance without eliciting elevated mental or physical fatigue. Conversely, compared to its physical execution, the virtual completion of the DM and PM tasks led to below average levels of usability along with degraded performance and increased mental workload implying decreased cognitive-motor efficiency which translated in an elevation of the physical fatigue. Several reasons discussed below could explain these results. First, these differences are likely due to the fact that when individuals used VLEARN to execute the ToH task, they could employ a classical point-and-click technique whereas the DM and PM required actively manipulating 3D objects in 3D space with their mouse/trackpads which ultimately imposed a certain accuracy requirement and thus was likely more challenging. For instance, in the ToH task, to move a disk from one peg to another, individuals had just to click the disk to select it then click the peg to which they wanted to move the disk. However, replacing a faulty disk in the DM task required multiple steps, for example, participants had to click the disk and actively move it (e.g., pick up, drop, proper placement of the cursor) with their mouse/trackpad while using keyboard controls to switch between movement planes until the disk was above the empty slot before finally using a right-click to drop the disk into the slot. As such, when this task was executed in the virtual environment, removing and replacing the drive proved more challenging than manipulating its physical counterpart. Similarly, to complete the PM task, individuals had to combine mouse/trackpad with keyboard and on-screen controls to adjust angles before tool use, place, extract and discard object which was likely more demanding.

A second element to explain these results was that the PM and, to a lesser extent, the DM tasks involved a greater number of controls and components as well as an increased dependency on those controls to manipulate relevant objects in the environment. For instance, the layout of the virtual PM task required individuals to use transport pads (selected by mouse-click) to actually navigate through the 3D environment to complete this task because not all system components were accessible from individual transport pads. As a result, when executing the PM task with VLEARN, the participants had to move to relevant transport pads (see green circles with arrows in Fig. 3) and manage switching between on-screen, keyboard, and cursor control throughout each trial. However, while executing the PM task with the physical system, participants had all system components within reach and field of vision while being able to rely on haptic and visual feedback during task execution.

Therefore, the use of the simplified controls to virtually complete the ToH task allowed action sequences to be completed without any additional challenges compared to the physical system resulting in comparable performance (particularly the SCT). In addition, although it was suggested that the execution of a physical 3D relative to a virtual 2D ToH task differently engage cognitive-motor resources [11], these simplified controls did not necessarily magnify these differences as the perceived mental workload elicited with both physical and virtual systems were comparable for this task. Such similar levels of performance and mental workload resulted in comparable cognitive-motor efficiency as well as levels of physical and mental fatigue when the ToH task was executed with both the virtual and physical systems.

Conversely, the virtual execution of the DM and for PM tasks required additional controls involving active object manipulations which were more demanding potentially requiring further engagement of cognitive (e.g., attentional) and motor (e.g., fine coordination) resources. These constraints were particularly challenging because the virtual controls inherently lack the natural feedback (e.g., cutaneous; proprioceptive) present when physical systems are used. Challenges related to using the more complex virtual controls to perform the DM and PM tasks were likely magnified by the use of a trackpad (for 10 of 12 participants) instead of a traditional computer mouse in addition to the on-screen and keyboard controls. As a result, the execution of the DM and PM tasks with VLEARN led to lower levels of usability as well as a degraded performance (SCT) combined with a greater mental workload resulting a lower cognitive-motor efficiency compared to those observed when these tasks were physically completed [3, 4, 27]. Interestingly, these changes were more prominent in the PM compared to the DM task; the latter being associated with a SUS score below, but not statistically different from, the acceptance-threshold as well as smaller effect sizes when contrasting the virtual and physical cognitive-motor performance. Possibly, the navigation element of the virtual PM task may have magnified the discrepancies in usability, performance and mental workload compared to its completion with the physical system. Such differences are important since compared to the DM task, the success rate for PM task was lower for its virtual than physical execution. Namely, for the former less than half of the trials reached the time limit, thus such higher rule breaking was also related to the execution action sequence rules per-se (see Sect. 2.2). Possibly, a greater deployment of attentional resources (and thus higher mental workload) may have been needed to deal with the interface controls, leaving less of these resources for action monitoring contributing thus to rule breaking. This is consistent with the idea that both attentional control and action monitoring are closely related [28]. Finally, the use of these demanding controls to perform both of these tasks virtually may have ultimately led to greater physical fatigue compared to their execution with the physical set-up.

### 4.3 Limitations, Conclusions, and Future Work

Overall, this work suggests that our approach allows to experimentally assess human cognitive-motor behavior (performance, mental workload, fatigue) when individuals operate VLEARN via the internet as suggested by similar success rates for both the physical and virtual execution of the three action sequence tasks considered here. Similar levels of usability, performance, mental workload and fatigue were observed when individuals operated the physical systems or a virtual system with simple controls (e.g., point-and-click method used for the ToH task). This suggests that under such conditions VLEARN reproduced its real counterpart with fairly good fidelity. However, when VLEARN used more complex control systems (e.g., those used for the DM and PM tasks), usability and cognitive-motor behavior degraded in particular for the PM task which contained the most elements. Thus, these complex control systems (which are critical for tasks with many components to manipulate) should be revised. Otherwise, excessive complexity of the controls can become a cofounding factor when assessing human cognitive-motor behavior with experimental manipulations (e.g., task demands). The simplification of the controls may be easier to implement with tasks having a limited number of elements (e.g., the DM task) relative to those with many components (e.g., the PM task) for which a more immersive system may be needed. Although simplified controls (e.g., point-and-click) may somewhat limit the study of finer motor manipulations, this is already well adapted for examining high-level planning processes engaged to generate action sequences under different levels of challenge.

This study had limitations. First picking up and dropping objects was notably harder for the participants who used a trackpad instead of a traditional computer mouse. Although individuals used personal computers with their trackpad or computer mouse, having them trying different control options during the familiarization phase may have allowed them to choose the option that best matched to their experience and ultimately provided enhanced results. This should be considered in future studies. Also, although this was a performance and not a learning study, an exploratory analysis of the blocks revealed that there were limited practice effects such that performance, mental workload and fatigue were stable during the last two blocks for both the physical and virtual systems. Thus, a future study to assess learning and retention could be conducted although ultimately the design of the controls used in VLEARN should minimize learning to be able to operate this virtual platform.

This study provided valuable information for revising and extending VLEARN. Overall, our approach allowed us to examine cognitive-motor performance and mental workload during remote execution of various complex action sequences via VLEARN in healthy and patient populations. Such work could inform various applications such as telehealth evaluations for Veterans having complex symptom presentations. In particular, the addition of brain monitoring along with task demand manipulation to investigate high-level planning processes would enable the objective measurement of brain dynamics and performance outcomes that may be influenced by military exposures.

Although the present work could be extended in different directions, immediate future efforts will first aim to update and extend VLEARN by enhancing its control interface and possibly incorporating novel hardware (e.g., joysticks, immersive VR technology) to improve its usability. Such an approach would allow us to remotely study human cognitive-motor behavior during various action sequence tasks which can be manipulated experimentally (e.g., high versus low cognitive demand). A second immediate future step would be to deploy this virtual system to remotely assess cognitive-motor performance combining behavior and electroencephalography when individuals execute action sequences to complete complex tasks. Future work that is currently underway aims to allow multiple human or robotic agents to interact within the VLEARN environment to evaluate human-human, human-robot, and robot-robot teaming when collaboratively performing or learning complex cognitive-motor tasks.

**Acknowledgment.** This work was supported by The Office of Naval Research (N00014–19-1–2044).

# References

1. Wickens, C.D.: Multiple resources and mental workload. Hum. Factors **50**(3), 449–455 (2008)
2. Young, M.S., Brookhuis, K.A., Wickens, C.D., Hancock, P.A.: State of science: mental workload in ergonomics. Ergonomics **58**(1), 1–17 (2015)
3. Shaw, E.P., et al.: Measurement of attentional reserve and mental effort for cognitive workload assessment under various task demands during dual-task walking. Biol. Psychol. **134**, 39–51 (2018)
4. Shuggi, I.M., et al.: Motor Performance, mental workload and self-efficacy dynamics during learning of reaching movements throughout multiple practice sessions. Neuroscience **423**, 232–248 (2019)
5. Welsh, M.C., Huizinga, M.: Tower of Hanoi disk-transfer task: influences of strategy knowledge and learning on performance. Learn. Individ. Differ. **15**(4), 283–298 (2005)
6. Wulf, G., Shea, C.H.: Principles derived from the study of simple skills do not generalize to complex skill learning. Psychon. Bull. Rev. **9**(2), 185–211 (2002)
7. Hardy, D.J., Wright, M.J.: Assessing workload in neuropsychology: an illustration with the Tower of Hanoi test. J. Clin. Exp. Neuropsychol. **40**(10), 1022–1029 (2018)
8. Hauge, T.C., et al.: A novel application of Levenshtein distance for assessment of high-level motor planning underlying performance during learning of complex motor sequences. J. Mot. Learn. Dev. **8**(1), 67–86 (2019)
9. Radüntz, T.: The effect of planning, strategy learning, and working memory capacity on mental workload. Sci. Rep. **10**(1), 7096 (2020)
10. Vakil, E., Lev-Ran Galon, C.: Baseline performance and learning rate of conceptual and perceptual skill-learning tasks: the effect of moderate to severe traumatic brain injury. J. Clin. Exp. Neuropsychol. **36**(5), 447–454 (2014)
11. Milla, K., Bakhshipour, E., Bodt, B., Getchell, N.: Does movement matter? Prefrontal cortex activity during 2D vs. 3D performance of the Tower of Hanoi puzzle. Front. Hum. Neurosci. **13**, 156 (2019)
12. Steunebrink, B., Wang, P., Goertzel, B. (eds.): AGI -2016. LNCS (LNAI), vol. 9782. Springer, Cham (2016). https://doi.org/10.1007/978-3-319-41649-6
13. Katz, G., Huang, D.W., Hauge, T., Gentili, R., Reggia, J.: A novel parsimonious cause-effect reasoning algorithm for robot imitation and plan recognition. IEEE Trans. Cognit. Dev. Syst. **PP**(99), 1–17 (2017)
14. Hauge, T.C., Katz, G.E., Davis, G.P., Huang, D.W., Reggia, J.A., Gentili, R.J.: High-level motor planning assessment during performance of complex action sequences in humans and a humanoid robot. Int. J. Soc. Robot **13**, 981–998 (2021)
15. Shaver, A., Shuggi, I., Katz, G., Davis, G., Reggia, J., Gentili, R.: Effects of practicing structured and unstructured complex motor sequences on performance and mental workload. In: North American Society for the Psychology of Sport and Physical Activity Virtual Conference, Journal Sport Exercise Psychology, vol. 42, no. S1, pp. S56–S56. Human Kinetic Publisher Inc (2020)
16. Huang, D.W., Katz, G.E., Langsfeld, J.D., Gentili, R.J., Reggia, J.A.: A virtual demonstrator environment for robot imitation learning. In: IEEE International Conference on Technologies for Practical Robot Applications (TePRA), Woburn, MA, USA, pp. 1–6 (2015)
17. Huang, Di-Wei., Katz, G., Langsfeld, J., Oh, H., Gentili, R., Reggia, J.: An object-centric paradigm for robot programming by demonstration. In: Schmorrow, D.D., Fidopiastis, C.M. (eds.) AC 2015. LNCS (LNAI), vol. 9183, pp. 745–756. Springer, Cham (2015). https://doi.org/10.1007/978-3-319-20816-9_71
18. Bangor, A., Kortum, P.T., Miller, J.T.: An empirical evaluation of the system usability scale. Intl. Int. J. Hum.-Comput. Int. **24**(6), 574–594 (2008)

19. Kortum, P.T., Bangor, A.: Usability ratings for everyday products measured with the system usability scale. Int. J. Hum.-Comput. Int. **29**(2), 67–76 (2013)
20. Bangor, A., Kortum, P., Miller, J.: Determining what individual SUS scores mean: adding an adjective rating scale. J. Usability Stud. **4**(3), 114–123 (2009)
21. Hart, S.G., Staveland, L.E.: Development of NASA-TLX (Task Load Index): results of empirical and theoretical research. Adv. Psychol. **52**, 139–183 (1988)
22. Childs, A.: Qualtrics, Provo, UT, USA (2020). https://www.qualtrics.com
23. Sauro, J., Lewis, J.R.: Quantifying the User Experience: Practical Statistics for User Research, 2nd edn. Morgan Kaufmann, Cambridge (2016)
24. Barnum, C.N.: Usability Testing Essentials, 2nd edn. Morgan Kaufmann, Cambridge (2021)
25. Levenshtein, V.I.: Binary codes capable of correcting deletions, insertions, and reversals. Soviet physics doklady **10**(8), 707–710 (1966)
26. Wagner, R.A., Fischer, M.J.: The string-to-string correction problem. J. ACM **21**(1), 168–173 (1974)
27. Jaquess, K.J., et al.: Empirical evidence for the relationship between cognitive workload and attentional reserve. Int. J. Psychophysiol. **121**, 46–55 (2017)
28. Mahon, A., Bendžiūtė, S., Hesse, C., Hunt, A.R.: Shared attention for action selection and action monitoring in goal-directed reaching. Psychol. Res. **84**(2), 313–326 (2018). https://doi.org/10.1007/s00426-018-1064-x

# Love as Augmented Cognition: Passionate Gaming in the Era of Virtual Romance

Suraj Sood(✉)

Autism Behavior Consultants, California, United States
thesiriusproj@gmail.com

**Abstract.** Love has been understood differently by various theorists. A triple-process theory of love—in which such a dual-process one consists of System 1 romantic love and System 2 care—is undertaken in this chapter as a contribution to the cognitive psychology of love. (Further, speaking of the head and heart in metaphorical terms could lead to the quantification of just how much more mature cognition or affect might be in relation to the other (either individually or interpersonally).). This theory builds on others positing that romantic love consists of joy, interest [21], and arousal [1], while consummate love in general consists of passion, commitment, and intimacy [2]. (Love has also been described as "an aspect of a relationship" ([21], p. 95).) In a Platonic model [3], love can be conceptualized as being affective, consisting of emotions like joy; cognitive, containing fond thoughts of the subject or object of love; or conative, demanding action on the part of the lover to better the state of the loved subject or object. Maslow conceived of love as a need typically experienced following the fulfillment of physiological and safety needs, and preceding esteem and self-actualization needs [5].

Love is not assumed to be wholly reducible to an algorithm. However, the rise of online dating and romantic matchmaking services has raised the question of to what extent it can be. True love—an enduring and nonchanging trate (state-trait) between two individuals characterized by joy, interest, arousal, passion, commitment, and intimacy—includes, yet exceeds, logic. Psychologically, such love transcends persons and situations in favor of the true, good, beautiful [6], and functional. It is metamodern in being, at best, partially understandable via traditional scientific methods (i.e., those of logico-empiricism). It involves intersubjective interaction from which "super-rationality" can emerge.

For the purposes of this chapter, love is understood partially as a sustainably positive, emergent property of human-computer interaction which gives rise to augmented cognition for all capable subjects involved. An ultimate goal of augmented cognition is posited to be the attainment of B-cognition [7], which "tends to perceive external objects, the world, and individual people as more detached from human concerns" (p. 61). B-cognition occurs during peak experiences along with Being values (B-values) [8]. Maslowian B-values are updated to include love. Lastly, an ecology of love is proposed.

**Keywords:** Love · Relationship · Augmented dating · Pokémon · Self-actualization

© The Author(s), under exclusive license to Springer Nature Switzerland AG 2022
D. D. Schmorrow and C. M. Fidopiastis (Eds.): HCII 2022, LNAI 13310, pp. 381–401, 2022.
https://doi.org/10.1007/978-3-031-05457-0_29

# 1 Introduction

"Love is a delicate thing…it's hard to grasp in its true form." -Fubuki Tenjoin, Yu-Gi-Oh! GX ([45], 6:20–6:26).

Does Pokémon teach compassion—and determination in the face of adversity—to its consumers (players, viewers, and collectors)? Anecdotal evidence exists suggesting directly that it can [4]. Seeing a Pokémon stagger upon fainting—or sensing it (visually or auditorily) at low health—can both trigger the phenomenal feeling of compassion and visceral empathy via physiological reaction. Theoretically and at the experiential first-person level, therefore, Pokémon can inculcate the compassionate sentiment. The next empirical question to pose is: For how many people does engagement[1] with the franchise's media instill compassion? The mechanical question is of how Pokémon does so.

Ontologically, one can love subjects or objects. Love and compassion, along with generosity, enable the achievement of fulfillment [53]. Intuition that enables love (along with openness) affords the expression of natural awareness [54]. One can have a passion for gaming[2], just as another can feel platonic, erotic, or agapic [9] forms of love for other kinds of activities. (Agapic love is defined as endless, selfless, and egoless love.) Platonic love is usually defined as friendly, but it can also be defined psychologically as manifesting in behavior, permeating cognition, characterizing affect, and determining motivation. The affective state of "loving" can be characterized as a subset of fondness [12]. Gray [13] wrote that—above all other considerations—"love is giving, compassionate, and forgiving" (p. 22). Finally, both self- and other-love must be dealt with to ultimately reach self-other or interpersonal love.

It is an open question whether modern dating apps (which have ushered in what can be termed "swipe consciousness")—along with dating itself—enable holistic love. Modern dating could be conceived of as a "mixed methods" practice in that individuals seek equilibrium between the quality of a date and quantity of dates, filtering through candidates to optimize said equilibrium satisfactorily. Holistic love is presumably what becomes soulmate love, which certain dating apps (e.g., Coffee Meets Bagel) and online matchmaking services (e.g., eHarmony) purport to render more attainable for users. An ideal function of dating apps and online matchmaking is that they enable users to filter through unsuitable candidates as they search for their respective soulmates. (More simplistically, dating allows individuals to determine their romantic relational preferences.) Also important for soulmate love is the psychological fact that shared values are a primary determinant of relational longevity, as well as potentially infinite meaning being found through such love.[3]

Maslow [5] elaborated the love needs as follows.

"If both the physiological and the safety needs are fairly well gratified, then there will emerge the love and affection and belongingness needs, and the whole cycle…already

---

[1] One may play on the double meaning of engagement, referring to a factor of well-being as well as the status of a romantic relationship immediately preceding marriage.

[2] Whether artificial passion can be created and henceforth sustained is an open question.

[3] An analogy may attempt to be drawn between dating apps and job boards like LinkedIn. Specifically, both can enable "easy" requests for connection. Naturally, the quality of said connection is distinct (i.e., dating versus interviewing for a position, respectively).

described will repeat itself with this new center. Now the person will feel keenly, as never before, the absence of friends, or a sweetheart, or a wife, or children. He will hunger for affectionate relations with people in general, namely, for a place in his group, and he will strive with great intensity to achieve this goal. He will want to attain such a place more than anything else in the world and may even forget that once, when he was hungry, he sneered at love.

"In our society the thwarting of these needs is the most commonly found core in cases of maladjustment and more severe psychopathology. Love and affection, as well as their possible expression in sexuality, are generally looked upon with ambivalence and are customarily hedged about with many restrictions and inhibitions. Practically all theorists of psychopathology have stressed thwarting of the love needs as basic in the picture of maladjustment. Many clinical studies have therefore been made of this need and we know more about it perhaps than any of the other needs except the physiological ones...

"One thing that must be stressed...is that love is not synonymous with sex. Sex may be studied as a purely physiological need. Ordinarily sexual behavior is multi-determined, that is to say, determined not only by sexual but also by other needs, chief among which are the love and affection needs. Also not to be overlooked is the fact that the love needs involve both giving and receiving love..."

It is additionally an open question whether Maslowian love is conquerable in the sense of satisfying it once and for all within a lifetime. Social justice and the anti-dating app attitude can be summarized as follows: "How dare developers attempt to reduce love to an algorithm?"[4] While the sentiment such an indignant interrogation captures might be valid, it may represent something of an informal strawman in that developers are not necessarily reducing love, instead intending to offer a novel venue through which love can begin and grow.[5]

Love could be viewed as a subset of the human person's life adventure. The role of literary consciousness in love is an open question for HCI, given literature's virtual accessibility and potential to augment the reader's cognitive experience and landscape. Intimacy is treated by Yalom [16]: "the ABC's, the language of intimacy [include]...for example, how to use the pronoun 'I' and 'you'; how to identify feelings, starting with the difference between feelings and thoughts; how to 'own' and express feelings...the basic feelings: 'bad', 'sad', 'mad', 'glad'" (1:04:26–45).

## 2   Love in Communication (Augmenting Communication)

Concern is a manifestation of love for (at least) one's intimates. Care characterizes how love is enacted and embodied. "Warm" and "cool" love both are preferable to—as well

---

[4] More strongly and generally, one may adopt the attitude of faithlessness in dating apps as a collective way to connect two soulmates. Other possible affects toward such apps include ambivalence and positive faith, where the latter involves placing faith in the process of successfully matching between individuals. Moods toward dating and marriage apps can include hopefulness, apathy, and (again) ambivalence.

[5] However, a Levinasian postphenomenology of dating app use might reveal the adverse effect of sexual objectification—or perhaps even subjectification (possibly more so for online matchmaking)—via the gendered gaze.

as more consistent than, moderate, and sustainable than—their more "hot" and "cold" counterparts (since warm and cool love lack harmful emotional peaks and valleys). Assertive, warm and cool, self-actualizing (SA) love can be regarded as the ideal psychological kind. William James' characterization of the temperaments of his philosopher contemporaries as being tender versus toughminded can be extended into the present philosophy of love. Specifically, love can be tender or tough: ideally, it is firm.

Romantic love between two persons has traditionally been sanctified through the institution of marriage. Whether in times past, or among more sophisticated classes, it has occurred most frequently between a lady and gentleman. A gentleman is expected to be strong (though not necessarily a "tough guy"); a lady is expected to be caring, and is usually not referred to as—contra-gentlemen—a "tough gal".[6,7] Courting individuals are often required to learn of and adapt to the other's love style. Love style could be viewed as a more formal version of the popular psychological notion of love languages, of which there are most commonly five. (These five "languages" are physical touch, acts of service, gift-giving, words of affirmation—the only explicitly linguistic love language—and quality time [22]).

A performative contradiction can be conducted in which heartbreak[8]—or, perhaps more technically, affective stagnation—is expressed via art. For instance, one may channel such a state of affective devastation or standstill through visual art, posing it in an atmospherically meaningful manner for social media photography. Such photography can, from the perspective of positive computing, represent the content creator's wish for affective reversal: possibly beginning with a desired "heartfix".

Photos like Fig. 1 can be shared via social network platforms such as Instagram and Facebook as part of the user's overall "life stream". Said life stream is presented to anyone who views one's profile, be they followers on Instagram, friends on Facebook, viewers or followers of hashtags (where hashtags are included in a post), or bots (see [24] for the predictive discrimination between bot and human users on Twitter).

Memetic love can be postulated as expressing shallow appreciation or humor in viral form (for instance, in the form of social media memes). Platonic love can be expressed via sending adorable Pokémon GO stickers. Figure 2 shows an example of such stickers.

Anthropomorphizing animals via online meme-sharing is perceived by fans of franchises like Pokémon as being cute, "chibi", or "kawaii". The latter two terms are Japanese in origin but are colloquially used by fans of Japanese animation—i.e., anime—and anime-styled art to mean simply cute. The process of intrapersonal affective identification can be augmented by sending appropriate gift stickers to friends in Pokémon GO:

---

[6] Related to this discussion of gender, love relationships can be conceptualized in terms of the construct of flow. For instance, men may experience flow as a function of equilibrium between challenge and skill in pursuing a mate.

[7] This traditional view of romantic relationship mechanics has been subverted in the current, postmodern society. Romantic gender subversion is evident in media from this period, such as in *Pokémon the Series: XYZ* (the anime).

[8] Heartbreak is addressed in the *Yu-Gi-Oh! 5D's* anime series when caretaker Martha orders "duel police officer" Tetsu Ushio to work, after he sees the woman he loves showing vulnerable feelings for another character [51].

**Fig. 1.** "Heart on lockdown" [23]. An original work drawn, colored, and painted near the beginning of the COVID-19 pandemic. Original work was woven into its artist's white Ibanez RG350DX's standard steel guitar strings.

**Fig. 2.** Mascot Pokémon Eevee and Pikachu cuddling over a mug holding a beverage. Said mug is the Pokémon Ditto using the move Transform.

an example of such is a sticker of Pikachu lying flat on its stomach, looking dozy. One's choice of gift sticker sent reflects the player's mood at that point in time.

Playing games with others can be fun and lead to a certain kind of insight. "Hearts playing together" is a phrase capturing the spirit of such interaction. Ludic love [28] equals game-playing love. Such game-playing is sometimes—though, perhaps not accurately—considered in terms of practices like emotional manipulation.[9] Players of recreational social games such as video games (VGs) and board games communicate via the popular app Discord and inbuilt voice chat of VG consoles like PlayStation 4 (PS4) and PlayStation 5 (PS5). Such communication was presaged by online voice chat applications TeamSpeak and Ventrilo, both of which were used to coordinate gameplay between players of VGs such as the massively multiplayer online game, Guild Wars.

Love enables and requires healthy communication. A 2004 study reportedly found that "romantic relationships were higher in commitment, satisfaction, trust and intimacy, and lower...daily conflict when partners validated each other's good fortune" ([52], Ch. 3). The following questions regarding love itself are now posed: What does one learn from love; what insights does one gain from practicing it? Which insights does intuition grant those who love: can said insights be applied in the domain of human-computer interaction (HCI)'s augmented cognition (AugCog)?

Much of interpersonal communication is now global, remote, and intercultural. It may take the forms of letters, gifts, and services (again, evoking love languages).[10] One function of communication as in verbalized affect is to prevent neuroticism from increasing, i.e. serving as a kind of "talking cure" as was pioneered as a psychotherapeutic treatment by Sigmund Freud.

Patience involves waiting for the other and granting them space to process affect and cognition (i.e., cogfect). Such is requisite for "true love", which in the present context can be contrasted with false love.[11] True love is defined here as an enduring and nonchanging trate (state-trait) between two individuals that is characterized by joy, interest, arousal, passion, commitment, and intimacy. Such love is definitionally psycho-romantic.[12]

Possible limitations in love are related to boundaries, which may be considered practically necessary or ideal. Limitations of love itself may be logistical, political, or physiological. The deepest love, however, is boundless. Boundaries dissolve between two true lovers, or else are transformed into an "open window" between them and metaphorical walls separating them from the rest of the world [15]. Alternately, and possibly more practically, boundaries can expand endlessly as a result of consistent

---

[9] For the present philosophy, such manipulation is deemed morally subpar in favor of emotional freedom.

[10] Linguistic reality could be termed "linguisticality", building on [26]'s system of neologisms and existent terms denoting particular domains of reality.

[11] True and false love could be taken up for ideational play or inspired theory-building by the theoretical or mathematical psychologist as "Boolean love".

[12] Arousal can be treated as a necessary but insufficient condition for true love. However, mutual attraction between Jungian personas and true selves is asserted here to be requisite for true love. Also relevant vis-à-vis attraction is the trend of higher satisfaction levels reported by spouses in arranged marriages who are typically matched for shared values and lifestyle [60].

love. Approaching infinity in such a way, the original purpose of boundaries might itself dissolve as love has sufficient space within them to grow healthily and controllably.

A general philosophy of relationships may be that one should have a unique philosophy of such for any new relationship. An example of what this means practically is that what worked for one kind of relationship (e.g., a primarily virtual one) will not for another (i.e., a more face-to-face one). If two individuals decide to end a romantic relationship, what becomes of their position vis-à-vis the window introduced in the preceding paragraph: or of the window, itself? A new metaphor for a new relation between two people following such a relationship could be discovered and invented.

Security in love is partially a function of healthy, assertive communication. Such communication can take the following form: "I don't feel secure when you communicate to me in X manner." This point addresses safety and love on Maslow's hierarchy of needs (levels two and three, respectively) simultaneously.[13]

## 3   The Future of Love: Augmenting Relationships

A relationship here is defined as sustained interaction between two agents. A good relationship, qua a good X a la Hartman's axiology [48], fulfils its concept. It ought to be healthy, consisting of individuals who care for and understand one another. Objective aspects of relationships include time spent together (i.e., quality time). A relationship can be built or thought of as a system. A necessary feature of such a functional relational system is trust, where absence of trust implies the same for a positive relationship. Axiologically, the intrinsic value of a connection between two agents is fundamental for what else might follow from it.

Relationships also fulfill purposes beyond themselves (e.g., generating love). They are characterized by and have one or more purposes. The purpose of strength is to support and defend love, thereby making strength subservient to loving relationships.[14] Love can be viewed as the augmented cognition, affect, and conation—the augmented psychology—characterizing and resulting from relationships.

Though relationship science and engineering exist at least in name, in psychology, it is most common to speak simply of either social psychology or relationship (couples or group) therapy. The potential for a "harder" approach to relationships seems generally unexplored in the field. Such an approach has obvious relevance for both HCI and AugCog. The recent rise of online therapy renders the human-computer interactive modality of therapy ever more salient. Though objective benchmarks exist in cognitive-behavioral therapy (CBT), such therapy is generally delivered one-on-one (even if it does focus on relationship-relevant thoughts and actions). The increased trend of socializing with others through virtual means—e.g., social network apps like Facebook and dating

---

[13] It is worth considering whether measured agreeableness and frequency of expressed truth correlate for any given individual.

[14] The "purpose of purpose" may be studied as *meta-purpose*, referring to a higher reason for something (such as a relationship) than is conceivable at *t*.

apps such as Hinge[15]—has been reinforced by the quarantine and lockdown conditions imposed as a response to the recent COVID-19 pandemic[16].

Most fundamentally, human interaction consists of two or more socializing agents.[17] Thus, the parts of a relationship from the engineering standpoint are simply two coupled human beings. Relationships feature in positive psychology's PERMA model of well-being (the "R" here standing for relationships). Individuals' respective well-being functions may vary such that relationships are a more or less influential factor. However, the fundamentality of relationships for society in general and its sub-components are sufficient to warrant a basic understanding of their ontology and function.

As the third component of the PERMA model, relationships are an important factor of well-being as studied in positive psychology. When relationships are successful, human beings experience heightened well-being. However—when relationships are not what one may desire—problems can be experienced (e.g.: unwanted arousal). In such instances, virtual communities of practice (VCoPs) can be utilized to troubleshoot personal problems. Specifically, greater objectivity can be reached when others come to know of one's cognitions as expressed via anonymous media such as online forum boards (themselves, potential VCoPs).

Relationships ought to be utilitarian (in the western philosophical sense).[18] Utilitarianism prioritizes "the greater good for the greatest number of people". Relationships should be devoted to a higher cause, e.g. building family or community. Relationships should also be good for their constituent parties, in at least this sense being "good in themselves". Relationships satisfying both utilitarianism and intrinsic goodness may be considered satisfactorily augmented.

Relationships include maintenance and creative components. Maintaining creative love involves both work—e.g., putting effort into understanding the other—and creativity, viz. for romantic upkeep. The maintenance aspect entails an optimal degree of self-other automation.[19] In terms of HCI's design focus [25], a relationship's creative aspect may serve to augment its parties' respective cognitions via increased positive affect. A good relationship constitutes a melded cognitive field, whereby the interaction between two parties' minds leads to novel emergence. Applying Gestalt psychology's maxim that "the whole is greater than the sum of its parts" to such emergence implies that the cognition of a good relationship can be inherently more augmented than the cognition of each party would be individually.[20]

---

[15] Social media may be regarded as being comprised of relational algorithms. A relational algorithm is defined here as any algorithm implemented for the purpose of establishing a relationship between two agents. It is an open question whether a "master algorithm" can be abstracted from such algorithms and be represented in pseudocode.

[16] For some, this pandemic made more salient than before the willpower sometimes necessary to remain in touch with virtual contacts.

[17] Postphenomenology, i.e. the study of human-technology relations [43], emphasizes the technological mediation of human-human interaction.

[18] Relational integrity may stagnate, be compromised, or experience structural breakdown when this condition fails to be met.

[19] Such automation would be formalizable in terms of relationship mechanics.

[20] Elaboration of such a simple, Gestalt relational calculus would be a substantive contribution to the intersection between the psycho-mathematics of relationships and AugCog.

Relational optimization is the end goal of augmenting relationships. Relationship engineering [50] can be considered parallel to marriage and family therapy (MFT) and couples therapy.[21] Such engineering *qua* engineering is "hard", i.e. evidence-based. Relationship engineering assumes we can have knowledge about love and optimize, enhance, correct—and, if necessary, take control of—a relationship. It may be possible to engineer individuals' attachment styles in the case that these are non-ideal (i.e., are any of the following: anxious, avoidant, anxious-avoidant). The attainment of secure attachment styles is one worthwhile goal of relationship engineering. Another case problem for relationship engineering as discussed in this chapter is a romantic relationship constituted of two individuals with distinct religious backgrounds and identities. A more specific formulation could be posed thusly: If one or more parties in a two-person romantic relationship feel dissonance between the individuals' respective religious identities, the relationship is likelier to fail than if they felt neutral. Such a problem may be intractable for secular relationship engineering, but it does pose the interesting possibility of a specifically religious relationship engineering. Of course, if both parties in a relationship are satisfied in spite or because of religious differences, relationship engineering becomes unnecessary.[22]

One interesting way to augment relationships is to merge literary and computational consciousnesses to attain System 3 (1-plus-2) love. System 1 lends itself to love with intuition, creativity, care, and emotion; System 2 could do the same but with logic, maintenance, and behavioral demand (including execution in the form of follow-through). System 2 necessarily includes the systemization of relationships, while System 1 offers the unconditional love that a priori enables and ultimately justifies them. Love may be cognized via System 2 or affected via "System" 1 (by the present interpretation, treating System 1 as a system begins to grow less tenable). System 2 intellectualizes, logicizes, quantifies, operationalizes, and executes (precisely in this order) the maintenance components of a relationship. "System" 1—or, perhaps more ontologically faithful and parsimonious at this juncture, merely affect—is more sensitive to relationships as subjective (epistemically and ontologically), and as a topic best approached in terms of the arts and humanities. In contrast, System 2 handles relationships objectively (again, both epistemically and ontologically), regarding them from the vantage points of science, technology, engineering, and mathematics (STEM). "System" 1 plays with affective metaphor—System 2 cognizes logical literality. AugCog is able to raise dual-process cognitive theory to a triple-process, triple-substance model by elaborating the technological aspects of System 3, relational and (un)conditional love.

At least one person must first yield in love; two should do so, next (logico-algebraically). Love can be discovered when it arrives; persons go to it as it reveals itself more over time, until it merges with them and are enacted by these agents increasingly. In this manner, persons become love as love becomes them: it becomes indistinguishable from Being, thereby becoming a candidate for a new Maslowian Being value (B-value).

---

[21] Through transpersonal MFT, wedded soulmates could learn more about the divine forces keeping them together (and of the evil ones possibly tempting them away from one another).

[22] A sustainable relationship marked by religious difference could be further enhanced if both parties are committed to exploring relevant possibilities—i.e., for joint religious participation—mutually selecting among them, and actualizing their choice set together.

Successful relationships require faith, hope, and conviction—assuredness that the relationship is correct, i.e. is at least its own justification—of their constituent parties. Love as a B-value is to be regarded as one of AugCog's most powerful forces of interest.

In the present context, fear is defined functionally as a love inhibitor (less formally, a "love-blocker") that can be removed through courageous action. True lovers cannot demand; they can only seek from and interrogate one another. Expectation should be managed with respect to the free offer of love, such that expectations of automatic acceptance and requital approach 0. Practically, however, requited love may be more easily sustained than unrequited love; the latter love type may be treated as an ideal leading to the general reality of requited love.

In the context of popular HCI—including fictional representations such as the 2013 movie Her—loving human-machine symbiosis should be considered. Such symbiosis could involve a loving connection between distinct kinds of agents, viz. humans and computers (e.g., robots). The possibility of such love may be only fictional in nature; but more weakly, affect can be observed to bond humans with machines in some cases. The nature of such a bond may be possible given that humans and machines share agency. Affect can be experienced as extending into the virtual, e.g. from humans playing an MMORPG like Guild Wars with one another.[23]

The increasingly virtual nature of human relationships has already been noted. In the event that such romantic relationships end, each party may decide to pursue the same kind of prospect, but with different partners. Moving on in such a way is—at least not ideally, for the psychoanalytically-oriented psychologist—a function of suppression. (Such suppression may be termed "moving off" rather than moving on to novel situations.) Healthily moving on may consist in converting disturbed affect into realistic and enabling cognition, which then may reverse the negative state of such affect for it to be augmented in turn. When two individuals previously in psycho-romantic love "break up"[24]—i.e., move away physically or emotionally from one another, either naturally or due to loss of relational integrity—it may then become prudent for them to adapt and evolve intelligently into relationships for which they are better-suited.[25,26] Commitments made between such former partners must be deemed purely functions of the past relationship in order for both to move on. Moving on from a relationship could be done via experiencing the same feelings one did in that context in another. For instance,

---

[23] Bonds between cooperative game-players working to solve mutual problems (such as threats to virtual space) may also exist.

[24] Arbitrarily contriving rationale for why a breakup occurred (as is suggested in [59]) should not be expected to result in affective closure. Instead, truth regarding such past occurrences may become clearer over time due to requisite increases in detachment and objectivity.

[25] "Letting go" is often discussed as antecedent to moving on from a romantic partner and relationship. Such letting go may be done for its own sake—i.e., it is right—as well as to reach a more desirable outcome. In the worst case, glitches in matchmaking ("unmaking") may need to be acknowledged as having occurred for romantic lovers who were not meant to be together forever.

[26] While attending therapy following the end of a relationship, one could learn of possible "red flags" (i.e., possible problem factors evidenced by the other). One could then attempt to focus on "green flags", i.e. positive signs suggesting that a relationship with another is likely to be successful.

the pride and joy one might have felt in the former could find a new home in a project that acts as a continuation of what could not continue (the relationship).

Managing conflict in love involves transforming hatred (e.g., into positive passion) such that peaceful love results. Passion and peace may be sensibly understood at being at odds, and perhaps unreconcilable with one another. Yet they coexist at least theoretically: passion is exemplified in the eros, ludus, and mania (possessive and dependent) love styles; peace is more characteristic of the storge (familial and friendly), pragma (practical), and agape (selfless) love styles [28]. Unmanaged conflict can lead to relational "toxicity", in which case the parties interested in repairing damage should utilize a 50/50 prevention-and-cure approach [26] (this may be subsumed under the domain of pragma).[27]

Love between two humans may transform or even perish. One psychological writer theorized that erotic love for a former partner could evolve into the agapic kind for them [47]. It is now asserted that true love never dies and must be honored throughout all of time. But any of the three primary love styles discussed in the preceding paragraph—i.e., eros, ludus, and storge—may, in isolation, transform or undergo destruction. For instance, eros may perish if it happens that romance "crumbles under inspection" ([16], Ch. 1). One may fall out of love with the process of falling in love (even if only temporarily), perhaps exhausting what is entertained as a "doomed romance loop" (i.e., systematically falling in and out of love with subsequent partners). The sustenance of love is preferable to its exhaustion: love should be permitted to renew in the proper way if and when it expires.

Finally, love and ownership should be shared within relationships. It may be that— for the case of true love between two soulmates—both competition and cooperation exist.[28] In such a case, ego and soul necessarily coexist: yet the latter is ultimately prioritized. Soul may contain ego ("contain" is used in a sense similar to Carl G. Jung's, per his treatment of one party in marriage psychically containing the other [29]). Decision-making should be shared equally but divided into domains per nontrivial concerns such as practicality. It is trivially true that partners in a relationship like marriage must cooperate for the greater good. But possibly disparate love styles—e.g., eros and storge (for discussion of friendship and romance being at odds, see ([30], p. 512))[29]—must also be made to cooperate.

---

[27] Eros and mania appear to correspond with Sternberg's notion of passion [2], and with Izard's notions of the sex drive (i.e., arousal), joy, and interest ([21], p. 95). Pragma can manifest as Sternbergian commitment; storge manifests as Sternbergian intimacy.

[28] Love can be applied to the prisoner's dilemma, the eminent example of a game centrally involving cooperation and competition (as play strategies). The optimal strategy in the prisoner's dilemma has been demonstrated to be tit-for-tat, where a player cooperates by default unless the other player defects (in which case the former competes). In a loving relationship, the ideal for two partners is to always cooperate with one another, thereby transcending tit-for-tat.

[29] A more ideal (and perhaps necessary) state of affairs for soulmates is that the unidirectional progression from friend, to date, to boyfriend or girlfriend, to fiancé, to spouse transcends such opposition.

# 4  Holarchic Love

Holarchic love includes parts and wholes of relationships. Loving relationships are therefore holonic, and a holarchy of love can be discussed. (Holarchy refers to any subjective-objective, part-whole system of reality [11].) Sood's holarchic metaphysics [11] could be interpreted as transjective [32], i.e. transcending its original subjective-objective ontology. An epistemology of love as being (epistemically) subjective-objective could be undertaken for the purpose of clarifying it as a vital phenomenon for globality.

Given that love augments relationships, the two are here considered together. Love is greater than happiness, but these should be combined into agapic eudaimonia (i.e., selfless fulfillment resulting in deep happiness for the Other). The former is more significant than hedonistic happiness, but true romantic love is enabled by Kairos: i.e., being at the right place and time (and—for this chapter's purposes—with the right person). Successful romance is taken up in postmodern media as requiring focus [58].

Holarchic (again, subjective-objective) love is derivable from the dependent arising of Buddhist metaphysics [10]. Loving kindness [18], also known as altruistic love, is defined as "the wish that others be happy and that they find the true causes of happiness[30]".(Ricard advises for loving-kindness meditation to be revitalized when it wanes.) Niceness—a weaker form of kindness—may be considered requisite for storge.

Loving activities are processes which yield important substances (i.e., outcomes). Heideggerian Care [31] is the structure that renders Dasein possible. Ordinary care expressed through social media manifests as affection (e.g., hug emojis), sympathy, and the "care" reaction added to Facebook in 2020 as a form of mental health augmentation during the stressful COVID-19 pandemic and quarantine situation(s). Such ordinary care is obviously related to love. Mutual acceptance is asserted to be requisite for love, as is benefit from a transactional perspective. Passionate love can transform into—but ideally, accompanies—humane care. Love manifests via social media through verbal expressions for (e.g.) specific readers and one's work.

Loving cognition should be treated as a form of AugCog, along with the former's subservient positive affect. Similarly, happiness and gratitude toward other and self can be treated as forms of relational AugCog. Eternal love may consist in commitment to each of these forms of relational AugCog. Such love that can sustain may be treated as sustainable love. Loving cognition and its associated affect in the context of true romantic love consists in an exclusive perception of the other's beauty and eternal belongingness with oneself. Such perception may include eudaimonic warm glow—i.e., altruistic fulfillment—as well as the happiness of love itself, which consists of little pleasures (as a function of hedonism).

The phenomenology of love [34] has already been treated. A detrimental such phenomenology may involve the experience of successive "fake love loops", i.e. harmful patterns in establishing relationships as a function of harmful "relationshipping". Breaking out of such loops may be regarded as a potential application of augmented relationships ("AugRel") and holarchic love. Such optimization would involve the absence of toxic and (U-, Sb-)Cs (un-subconscious [35]) game-playing (ludus). Any of two ludic

---

[30] Triarchic happiness as termed here is defined to consist of hedonism, eudaimonia (fulfillment), and Kairos.

manifestations may be at play: it can manifest as manipulative, or as fun, exciting, and mutually enjoyable. While manipulative ludus is unethical—as is behavioral manipulation, more generally—the latter, playful ludus is experienced as positive and reinforcing (either positively or negatively per operant conditioning).[31]

Love may be defined as what characterizes and results from flow. It constitutes and directs meaningful flow activities, e.g. quality time spent with a cherished partner. Psycho-romantic love can be conceptualized as a kind of flow in which challenge meets skill, and neither comfort nor challenge exist in excess: it is understood that excess comfort entails boredom, and excessive challenge entails despair. Relationships approaching flow in love are optimized as they reach the ideal equilibrium just introduced.

Just as love is often described as being patient, it may also be characterized as wise. It is flexible, as well as strong yet yielding (viz., to a higher power). Love may change from passion to care or vice versa; an equal blend between these can be treated as equilibrium. Benevolent love consists in the protection of the other from all possible harm (including from damaging relationships). "Love from afar" is possible and may take the forms of prayer or the aforementioned loving-kindness meditation. Behavioral extensions of such latent, remote love—loving intentions—should result (revealing love's pragmatic dimension). This point is especially important when love is multicultural, multifaceted, and global.

Holarchic love and AugRel should include and consider (respectively) the case of self-actualizing relationships, which may be conceptualized as a form of self and other-actualization. Self-actualizing (SA) love is passive just to the extent that Maslow's Being cognition (B-cog) is [8].[32] Such love consists in the acceptance of self and other. SA love is appreciative (without being lustful). The creative spirit and romance may find a home in such love. Self-actualizing relationships may be considered requisite for the mythical Maslowian self-transcendence (which exists above Maslowian self-actualization [37]). It must be contended with that self-actualizers are not necessarily settled lovers, sometimes leaving their partners abruptly [36]. Lovers should be willing to let one another go but not abandon each other. Healthy SA love should be regarded as requisite for Eupsychia, Maslow's notion of a psychologically healthy socio-culture [38]. Eupsychia is optimally interdependent and free of psychological illness such as depression, codependence, and trauma.

Holarchic love would harmonize distinct forms and definitions of love, such as the six types discussed in the previous section. Fear was also discussed in Sect. 3. (Fear may be antagonistic to love, though hate is the more usual contrast concept to the latter.)

It may be that one discovers him- or herself prior to entering a relationship with another. This is to be contrasted from relational partners finding themselves within a relationship. One changes while in a relationship with genuine affect, and can become perpetually rediscovered—ideally, renewed—within it (if the relationship is long-term). However—while affects are definitionally pre-personal [33]—affect toward others is

---

[31] A potential example of pragma in dating is the utilization of applied behavior analysis principles (e.g., contingent reinforcement) in interacting with one's partner.

[32] Passivity, as well as the willingness to wait in love may both be conceived of as functions of patience (itself requisite for love).

probably prerational. People may experience different emotions toward others, even if said others have remained static.

In love between two or more individuals, problems are shared. Love is given freely; it can also be earned. It should be distinguished from submission, where the latter might consist in submitting to the other's desire (however impure said desire might be). Peak, plateau, and valley experiences in love all remain to be elucidated: the B-cog present in peak experiences may be regarded as parallel—if not overlapping—with AugCog. The plateau experience of love may consist in "settling", as is done formally by two marrying individuals. The valley experience of love may be rather unsettled, dominated by deficiency cognition ("D-cog") rather than B-Cog, where individuals may be locked less fortunately in a struggle to satisfy their lower-level needs. In general, the experience of love is to be justified not via rationalization (e.g., defense mechanisms), but rather via deriving a satisfactory level of meaning.

The soulmate connection can be metaphorically conceived as a "golden switch" that can never be "turned off". The relation between gaming and love can be explored via the concept of ludus. Examples of quality time spent between family and friends via games include Steam's The Jackbox Party Pack [40] trivia and mobile game Among Us, both of which became more popular during 2020. Also, axiomatically, love (as well as peace) should be deemed greater than war. Though passion might be thought to connect love and war, passionate love should in fact be nonviolent and nonharmful.

Political situations may serve as conditioners (i.e., influencing factors) of love's course. Love as a feeling and way of being consists of compromise. True lovers are always "part of" one another. Also important for the cultural psychology of love—and thus, for holarchic love, which includes cultural reality formalized as Cl and psychological reality as $\psi$ [11]—is cultural variance in the weight assigned to individual success versus collective harmony. An example of a topic for the psycho-cultural study of love is the prioritization of education, career, or aspirations more broadly in individualistic societies over the continuation of a romantic relationship; conversely, a collectivistic society would prioritize relationships themselves. Individualism in a relationship should manifest as autonomy, but not aloofness. In an indivectivistic (equally individualistic and collectivistic) [3] society, ego and relationships are theorized to be valued equally.

The ego's role in love and resulting attachment should be reconciled in holarchic love, perhaps by psychoanalytic and Buddhist theorists. Love for another may include love (or at least, tolerance) for the products of their intellectual imagination, i.e. their ideas. In love, all involved parties should be imagined and felt as being worthy of its receipt. The maturity level of love renders the question of love's quantifiability relevant. Love is variously quantifiable, including sub-measures such as its intensity.

One way to treat Maslow's hierarchy of needs is to place self-actualizing (SA) love at the very top, treating lower levels as ones to be conquered in order to reach the peak. SA love might be equated partially with "putting one's heart and soul" into the loved entity (e.g., a relationship or personal project). Such love may be compelling enough to transcend fears such as that of failure. However, ultimate love also requires the optimal configuration of body, mind, and spirit to succeed.[33]

---

[33] In any case, it may be asserted that the heart follows the soul. This justifies religiously liberal democracies' emphasis on and tendency of their constituent individuals "following their hearts".

AugCog must consider dissonance detrimental and inimical to the enterprise of love. The contents of this section thus far may lead the reader to inquire whether one should be a scientist-practitioner of love. A possible, albeit general, affirmative answer to this is so that such a person can be a competent—i.e., knowledgeable, capable, and authoritative—wielder of one of the most powerful forces known to and experienced by life on Earth.[34]

## 5   Love of Subjects vs. Sentimental Attachment to Objects

Subjects such as persons include one's self as well as others. Objects include (e.g.) technology and property. One can have and display love for both of these. One may have love for his or her family, which could then be extended to the rest of humankind via loving-kindness meditation (as Ricard suggests). Patriots are a kind of people who embody or espouse love for their respective nations.

Following from the previous section's discussion of the ontology of love, love can consist of permitting others to follow their daemons (i.e., fulfilling their life calling via traversing their life path). Love can also exist for what one may treat as a game of discovering (finding) or inventing (imagining) one's soulmate[35]. Also, one can love more basic enterprises and hobbies such as science, anime[36], sports (e.g., racquetball augmented via phone use for music-listening), or media. Joy for any of these items can be affectively experienced. The emotional state of joy may overlap with subjective well-being (SWB) and has been included by Izard as a component of romantic love [21]. In relationships, love can involve encouraging the expression of a partner's emotion (as is often expected to be done by the trainer of Pokémon).

Love of subjects can take the forms of self- and other-kindness [14]. Self-preservation is an established concept; however, other-preservation should be deemed requisite for agapic love. Returning to romantic love, personality compatibility between vying partners is necessary but insufficient for the successful advancement of their relationship. More necessary is "value-and-character" compatibility [41]. A meaningful distinction has been made between emotive and cognitive values [17]. The former kind of values may be unspoken, while the latter are presumably formalizable.

---

While doing so might be optimal for maximizing economic utility, more importantly, it enables salvation for such citizens.

[34] Such considerations raise the question of whether the set of holons humans may love is countable or not. This depends on how many holons exist that are, in theory, capable of being loved. The scientist of love may conduct an empirical investigation into the matter; the mathematician would settle for an inductive proof of such. Roughly, then, there are both the possibilities for deductive and inductive approaches to the study of love. However, caution should be exercised by anyone entertaining the notion that love is ultimately calculable (see [57], which concludes that love types are).

[35] In this way, the epistemology of love is both *a priori* and *a posteriori*: love is necessarily learnt of through theory and experience.

[36] Anime offers various perspectives on love. In Season 1 of the anime *Yu-Gi-Oh! GX*, lead female character Asuka Tenjoin asserts: "Love...must blossom from the feelings of two people connecting with each other" ([46], 19:22–19:26). In an earlier episode, Asuka's elder brother Fubuki Tenjoin states that "Love is about the back and forth" ([45], 6:56–6:57).

Love of subjects should involve concern that the other actualize their life dreams, wishes, and hopes. Soulmate love involves loving the other's whole self, including an embrace of their potentially more destructive nature. It should encompass the other's temperament, personality, and character, thereby encompassing the temperament-personality-character (TPC) matrix [39]. In soulmate love, the soulmates' respective TPC matrices may be said to join. In this paragraph's sense, love involves encouraging the good to arise from the other's wholeness.

Yalom warned: "Beware the powerful, exclusive attachment to another. It is not—as people sometimes think—evidence of the purity of the love. Such encapsulated, exclusive love, feeding on itself—neither giving to nor caring about others—is destined to cave in on itself. Love is not just a passioned spark between two people: there is infinite difference between falling in love and standing in love. Rather, love is a way of being—a giving to, not a falling for; a mode of relating at large, not an act limited to a single person" ([16], Prologue). The ideal utilitarianism of relationships mentioned in Sect. 3 should perhaps be characteristic of any kind of love-producing relationship.

Despite the preceding paragraph, it is common to at least romanticize the notion of being willing to die for "the love of one's life". This could be one of possibly infinite ways to love another person. Thus, the statement "I love you" may be validated in a potentially innumerable number of ways.

Mutual admiration is an ideal of intersubjective love. Respect is also important, particularly with respect to personal boundaries. Admiration may be considered a "softer" artifact of love, while respect is potentially "harder". One may speak of soft versus hard self-love styles: for instance, one may take a more permissive (soft) or authoritarian (hard) attitude toward oneself. The assertive love style is superior to its passive and aggressive variants.

Love can be formalized as follows:

$$L = F[Ag, Es, Ld, Mn, Sr, Pm] \tag{1}$$

where L equals "love", Ag equals "agape", Es equals "eros", Ld equals "ludus", Mn equals "mania", Sr equals "storge", and Pm equals "pragma". This equation's right half could be simplified to $F[Es, Ld, Sr]$, since—per Lee's color wheel theory of love [42]—Ag, Mn, and Pm are simply compounds of these primary love types. It is interesting to consider what could result if two individuals felt and practiced each of the three primary love types equally.[37]. However, an important limitation of (1)'s mathematical leveling of the color wheel of love is that its love styles are not equally optimal. What this has meant scientifically is that only two—eros and agape—correlate positively with the secure attachment style, while ludus correlates negatively with it, with ludus correlating positively with the avoidant attachment style and mania correlating positively with the anxious attachment style [49].

Psycho-romantic[38] consummate love is formalizable as follows

$$\psi L = F[J, It, As, Pn, Ct, Iy] \tag{2}$$

---

[37] Lee additionally discusses tertiary love types, each of which would blend all three primary types.

[38] Romance itself may only be formalizable if it is mature.

where $\psi$L equals "psychological love", J equals "joy", It equals "interest", As equals "arousal", Pn equals "passion", Ct equals "commitment", and Iy equals "intimacy". While this psycho-romantic equation of love fails to capture love's informal, irrational, or necessarily super-rational aspects, it represents a more specified formalization of love than (1).

In Sternberg's model, seven types of love exist. Consummate love was just fused with psycho-romantic love, above; the triangular theory of love also includes empty love (Ct), passionate love (Pn), and intimate love (Iy) [56]. Also, three more types of love result when combining any two components of consummate love: Iy + Pn = romantic love; Iy + Ct = companionate love; and Pn + Ct = fatuous love [56]. Further equations may result from blending Izard's and Sternberg's love constructs such as

$$J + It + As = Iy + Pn \tag{3}$$

Further love formalisms can be created by also setting variables equal to Sternberg's companionate and fatuous love types. Equations (1)–(3) represent a start for the formal science of love, which itself should serve careful cultivation of the feeling, experience, and understanding of loving relationships[39].

# 6 Conclusion

In order for a romantic relationship to be healthy and long-term, it must be prioritized over each partner. Relationships should be treated as missionary, greater than any of its individual's possible interests to the contrary. The possibility for a love calculus (per-haps—playfully—a "loveculus") has been examined in this chapter. The mathematics of love has been taken up in Eqs. (1)-(3). The study of love may ultimately be settled for to exist between astrology and science, possibly done most effectively within the arts and humanities. However—as has been done in this chapter—love can be considered mathematically, and in interesting ways. For instance, a $0^{th}$-person study [3] of one's "existential origin point" (e.g., God) could be done; soulmate love could be theorized as being an infinite function transcending the finitude of empirically-known spacetime.[40] Soulmate love could be further theorized as being an emergent property of: Izardian romantic (premarital) love, followed by Sternbergian consummate (marital) love, and culminating in a divine love perhaps described best in terms at least similar to Lee's (viz., in his employment of religious constructs). In any event, the practical proof of love lies in verbal behavior (in what two people say and do).

It can be hopefully asserted that true love should be enjoyable. Love itself can, though does not necessarily need to, be difficult or painful. Love can be treated as a lifetime habit

---

[39] It may be wondered whether soulmate love is or emerges from the combination of Izard's, Lee's, and Sternberg's notions. If so, it is probable that soulmate love is an emergent property greater than their sum. This precludes it from being reduced to a formal equation, especially given soulmate love's divine nature.

[40] One could also add love to the traditional data science pyramid, which illustrates the process of ascending from data to information to knowledge to wisdom. Love could be defined here as the ideal outcome of wisdom's application.

of learning. Additionally, it is active rather than passive when performed deliberately (a la behavioral implementation of a System 2 plan). One can speculate on "System 1 lovers" and "System 2 lovers", though such philosophizing should not be confined exclusively to cognition. Indeed, holistic love is also affective and conational (and love itself may be radical, weak, strong, mature, or naïve). True love in this chapter has been elaborated and formalized as being holistically psycho-philosophical.

This chapter has treated love (with the exception of soulmate love) as a phenomenon that can be intellectualized via representation, or "knowing-that". Its enactive, i.e. "knowing-how", component has also been discussed. It should be noted that Lee's framework employs Greco-Christian notions in agape, eros, and storge. Thus, their enactment should be done with greater power and consistency by those whose lineage and identification are rooted in the Christian tradition.

A construct critical to the study of love undertaken in this chapter (yet unexplored in it, thus far) is psychological identity. Identity has been defined as "a multi-dimensional concept, incorporating disposition, cognitive style, affect, judgment, and value" ([17], p. 238). In the context of love, it is important that two individuals sufficiently share identity; discomforting dissonance can arise if, for instance, one partner feels that the other's values are irreconcilable with his or her own.[41] Identity may also be conceptualized as the successful integration between the true self or "true other" and persona, making it akin to Jungian individuation.

A "loving ecology" can be—and is, here, finally conceived of—as a person-environment system in which nature is loved and technology's positive role in civilization is acknowledged. Such an ecology can expand on the study of human-technology relations core to postphenomenology, defining the optimal state of such relations for ecological sustainability. Love must not be confused with any maladaptive HCI practice, including those that diminish cognition. Love has been shown in this chapter to be formalizable, but it cannot necessarily be well-defined. Furthermore, it is necessary in contexts like successful marriage to augment love with trust, dedication, and faith. (In the case of love between two romantic partners, it is also critical that they not hold onto grudges.) Marital outcomes can be augmented if individuals learn mindfulness about love ([61], 12:33–12:52) as well as how to preclude divorce [55]. Regardless, socio-environmental justice is best taken up as a project of love, where love is lastly defined as the penultimate form of augmented cognition.[42,43]

**Acknowledgments.** The author thanks Supriya Sood, Joohi Sood, Andrew Tam, Melinda Yin, Geneva Vogelheim, Allison Wright, Loredana Crusoveanu, and Justin Hernandez.

---

[41] Further dissonance can arise if at least one of two people have not finished exploring their respective romantic identities, yet had verbally or ritualistically committed to one another prior to attaining knowledge of the former. Identity achievement [44] can be forsaken at the end of such a scenario.

[42] Love as AugCog affords a bond that extends beyond pre-technological spacetime.

[43] An example of love as AugCog is "agapic cognition", consisting of agapic truth such as *I would die for person X*. Erotic cognition is posed as another sub-concept of loving cognition, corresponding to sexual fantasy.

# References

1. Cornelius, R.R.: The Science of Emotion: Research and Tradition in the Psychology of Emotions. Prentice Hall, New Jersey (1996)
2. Sternberg, R.J.: A triangular theory of love. Psychol. Rev. **93**(2), 119–135 (1986)
3. Sood, S.: Holarchic HCI and augmented psychology ("AugPsy"). In: Schmorrow, D.D., Fidopiastis, C.M. (eds.) HCII 2021. LNCS (LNAI), vol. 12776, pp. 305–330. Springer, Cham (2021). https://doi.org/10.1007/978-3-030-78114-9_22
4. https://www.reddit.com/r/pokemon/comments/2jg57z/how_pokemon_taught_me_about_being_compassionate/?utm_medium=android_app&utm_source=share/. Accessed 25 Dec 2020
5. Maslow, A.H.: A theory of human motivation. Psychol. Rev. **50**, 370–396 (1943)
6. Plato: The Republic. (2$^{nd}$ ed.). Penguin Books, London (2007). (Original Work Published in ~375 B.C.)
7. Maslow, A.H.: Religions, Values, and Peak-experiences. Penguin Compass, New York (1976)
8. Maslow, A.H.: Toward a Psychology of Being. (1$^{st}$ ed.). Wilder Publications, Blacksburg (2011). (Original Work Published in 1962)
9. Gibson, M.: Real Life Love: Saying Goodbye to the Fairytale and Hello to True Relationships. Faith Words, New York (2019)
10. Schaab, G.L.: Relational ontology. Relational Ontology. In: Runehov A.L.C., Oviedo L. (eds) Encyclopedia of Sciences and Religions. Springer, Dordrecht. https://doi.org/10.1007/978-1-4020-8265-8_847
11. Schmorrow, D.D., Fidopiastis, C.M. (eds.): HCII 2019. LNCS (LNAI), vol. 11580. Springer, Cham (2019). https://doi.org/10.1007/978-3-030-22419-6
12. Baron-Cohen, S.: Mind Reading Emotions Library. Jessica Kingsley Publishers, U.K. (2004)
13. Gray, J.: Men are from Mars, Women are from Venus, 20$^{th}$ Anniversary edn. HarperCollins e-books [Kindle DX version] (2013). (Original Work Published in 1992)
14. McGonigal, J.: SuperBetter: A Revolutionary Approach to Getting Stronger, Happier, Braver, and More Resilient. Penguin Press, New York (2015)
15. Gottman, J., Gottman, J.S., Abrams, D., Abrams, R.C.: Eight Dates: Essential Conversations for a Lifetime of Love. Workman Publishing Company, New York [Kindle DX version] (2019)
16. Yalom, I.: Love's Executioner and Other Tales of Psychotherapy. Echo Point Books & Media [Audible version] (2013)
17. Osbeck, L.M., Nersessian, N.J.: Epistemic identities in interdisciplinary science. Perspect. Sci. **25**(2), 226–260 (2017)
18. Ricard, M.: Why Meditate? Working with Thoughts and Emotions. Hay House, United States [Kindle DX version] (2010)
19. Friedman, R., James, J.W.: Moving On: Dump Your Relationship Baggage and Make Room for the Love of Your Life. M. Evans: Lantham [Kindle DX version] (2006)
20. Freud, S.: The Interpretation of Dreams. (J. Strachey, Trans.) Basic Books, New York (1955). (Original Work Published in 1899)
21. Izard, C.: Human Emotions. Springer, United States (2013)
22. Chapman, G.: The Five Love Languages: How to Express Heartfelt Commitment to Your Mate. Northfield Publishing, Chicago (2004)
23. https://www.instagram.com/p/CJ8HVdzlwHY/?utm_source=ig_web_copy_link. Accessed 17 Aug 2021
24. Neumann, S., Sood, S., Hollander, M., Wan, F., Ahmed, A.-W., Hancock, M.: Using bots in strategizing group compositions to improve decision–making processes. In: Schmorrow, D.D., Fidopiastis, C.M. (eds.) AC 2018. LNCS (LNAI), vol. 10916, pp. 305–325. Springer, Cham (2018). https://doi.org/10.1007/978-3-319-91467-1_24

25. Collazos, C., Liborio, A., Rusu, C. (eds.): CLIHC 2013. LNCS, vol. 8278. Springer, Cham (2013). https://doi.org/10.1007/978-3-319-03068-5

26. Sood, S.: Global problem-solving and ethics. Int. J. Glob. Environ. Issues **17**(4), 322-339 (2018). https://doi.org/10.1504/IJGENVI.2018.095134

27. Cruciani, F., Berardi, A., Cabib, S., Conversi, D.: Positive and negative emotional arousal increases duration of memory traces: common and independent mechanisms. Front. Behav. Neurosci. **5**, 86 (2011). https://doi.org/10.3389/fnbeh.2011.00086

28. https://www.psytoolkit.org/survey-library/love-styles-hendrick-sf.html#:~:text=After%20an%20extensive%20interview%20procedure,and%20three%20main%20secondary%20styles%3A. Accessed 21 Aug 2021

29. Jung, C.G.: Marriage as a psychological relationship. http://ww3.haverford.edu/psychology/ddavis/p109g/internal/j_anima.html (Original Work Published in 1925). Accessed 21 Aug 2021

30. Solomon, R.C.: The virtue of (erotic) love. In: Solomon, R.C., Higgins, K.M. (eds.) The Philosophy of (Erotic) Love, pp. 492–518. University Press of Kansas, KS (1991)

31. https://plato.stanford.edu/entries/heidegger/#Car. Accessed 21 Aug 2021

32. https://en.wiktionary.org/wiki/transjective. Accessed 11 Mar 2021

33. Shouse, E.: Feeling, emotion, affect. M/C J. **8**(6) (2005). http://journal.media-culture.org.au/0512/03-shouse.php. Accessed 22 Feb 2021

34. Sośnicka, J.: Phenomenology of Love: A Philosophical Analysis of the Conception of Love in the Light of Dietrich Von Hildebrand's Realistic Phenomenology. Logos Verlag Berlin, Germany (2015)

35. Sood, S.: The Platonic-freudian model of mind: defining self and other as psychoinformatic primitives. In: Schmorrow, D.D., Fidopiastis, C.M. (eds.) HCII 2020. LNCS (LNAI), vol. 12196, pp. 76–93. Springer, Cham (2020). https://doi.org/10.1007/978-3-030-50353-6_6

36. Maslow, A.H.: Motivation and Personality. Harper & Row, Publishers, New York (1954)

37. Maslow, A.H.: The Farther Reaches of Human Nature. Penguin Books, New York (1983). (Original Work Published in 1971)

38. Maslow, A.H.: Eupsychia—the good society. J. Humanist Psychol. **1**(2), 1-11. https://doi.org/10.1177/002216786100100202 (1961)

39. Sood, S.: Enactive, integrative personality and the temperament-personality-character matrix. https://www.academia.edu/34283489/Enactive_integrative_personality_and_the_temperament_personality_character_matrix. Accessed 26 Aug 2021

40. https://store.steampowered.com/app/331670/The_Jackbox_Party_Pack/. Accessed 25 Aug 2021

41. https://www.gottman.com/blog/psychology-finally-reveals-the-answer-to-finding-your-soulmate/?fbclid=IwAR153x6kwQ7lGjmhFHX707pec7LefAYngpc5MhevuMEkk5z3TTE0uloGLoM. Accessed 26 Aug 2021

42. Lee, J.A.: Colours of Love: An Exploration of the Ways of Loving. New Press, Toronto (1973)

43. Rosenberg, R., Verbeek, P.-P.: Postphenomenological Investigations: Essays on Human-Technology Relations. Lexington Books, Lanham, MD (2015)

44. Zacarés, J.J., Iborra, A.: Self and identity development during adolescence across cultures. In: International Encyclopedia of the Social & Behavioral Sciences (2$^{nd}$ ed.) (2015)

45. https://www.crunchyroll.com/yu-gi-oh-gx/episode-47-asuka-versus-manjome-cyber-angel-benten-685951. Accessed 7 Nov 2021

46. https://www.crunchyroll.com/yu-gi-oh-gx/episode-20-the-maiden-in-love-is-strong-deck-684107. Accessed 7 Nov 2021

47. https://www.psychologytoday.com/us/blog/living-forward/201508/5-ways-move-ex-you-still-love. Accessed 22 Dec 2021

48. Hartman, R.: The Structure of Value: Foundations of Scientific Axiology. Southern Illinois University Press, Carbondale, IL (1967)

49. Fricker, J., Moore, S.: Relationship satisfaction: the role of love styles and attachment styles. Curr. Res. Soc. Psychol. **7**(11) (2002). https://web.archive.org/web/20080117182741/http://www.uiowa.edu/~grpproc/crisp/crisp.7.11.htm. Accessed 20 Dec 2021
50. Hutton, G.: Relationship Engineering: Understand the Dating Instinct and Create Deep Feelings of Love in Anybody at Will. Mind Persuasion [Kindle DX version] (2018)
51. https://www.crunchyroll.com/library/Tetsu_Ushio. Accessed 26 Dec 2021
52. Sorensen, M.S.I.: Hear You: The Surprisingly Simple Skill Behind Extraordinary Relationships. Autumn Creek Press [Audible Version] (2017)
53. Lama, D., Tutu, D.: The Book of Joy: Lasting Happiness in a Changing World. Penguin Random House, New York [Kindle DX version] (2016)
54. https://www.mindful.org/tara-brach-rain-mindfulness-practice/. Accessed 31 Dec 2021
55. https://www.ted.com/talks/george_blair_west_3_ways_to_build_a_happy_marriage_and_avoid_divorce. Accessed 1 Jan 2022
56. https://opentextbc.ca/socialpsychology/wp-content/uploads/sites/21/2014/10/dc7534281f2bc5583bc511b29ea9c2a0.jpg. Accessed 1 Jan 2022
57. Tobore, T.O.: Towards a comprehensive theory of love: The quadruple theory. Front. Psychol. (2020). https://www.frontiersin.org/articles/10.3389/fpsyg.2020.00862/full. Accessed 1 Jan 2022
58. ILCA: Pokémon Brilliant Diamond. Nintendo, Kyoto, Japan (2021)
59. https://www.ted.com/talks/guy_winch_how_to_fix_a_broken_heart/transcript?language=en#t-660802. Accessed 14 Jan 2022
60. https://psychcentral.com/blog/do-opposites-really-attract#1. Accessed 17 Jan 2022
61. https://www.youtube.com/watch?v=vhhgI4tSMwc. Accessed 22 Jan 2022

# Compensation Method of Flight Simulator Visual System

ShiXiong Su, Zhen Wang[✉], Shan Fu, and Dan Huang

Shanghai Jiao Tong University, Shanghai 200240, People's Republic of China
b2wz@sjtu.edu.cn

**Abstract.** The Stewart 6DOF motion platform is widely used in flight simulators. However, due to performance and parameter limitations, many Stewart motion platforms cannot meet the acceleration and motion range requirements in some flight training missions. Therefore, we propose to make up for its limitation with the method of visual compensation. In this paper, we first simulated the Stewart motion platform through Simulink, and determined its maximum motion range on the x-axis, y-axis, and z-axis, as well as the maximum motion angle on the rotation angles $\alpha$, $\beta$, $\gamma$ in three directions. At the same time, we confirmed the limitations of the Stewart platform in some flight training missions based on its range of motion. After that, we propose a specific visual compensation scheme. Based on FlightGear flight simulation software and C++ program, we realized the adjustment of the visual information and made some attempts to the compensation algorithm. The results show that the method can make additional adjustments to the visual information when the Stewart motion platform reaches the extreme state of motion.

**Keywords:** Stewart platform · Flight simulator · Visual compensation

## 1 Introduction

### 1.1 The History of Flight Simulators

Flight simulator has a history of nearly one hundred years. At the beginning, people's understanding of aerodynamics was still in its infancy, and flight simulators could only simulate simple aircraft attitude changes. Antoinette simulator is a typical example. It cuts a barrel in half and places it perpendicular to each other to simulate pitch and roll motions (see Fig. 1).

In 1929, the American Edwin Link invented the Link training machine [1], which is considered to be the beginning of flight simulators. The Link Trainer is an electrome-chanical simulator with a pneumatic platform that simulates pitch, roll and yaw flight actions. In the 1940s, analog computers began to be used to calculate flight formulas, resulting in the first electronic simulators. In 1948, Wright gifted Pan Am a Boeing 377 simulator, the first to be owned by a private airline. Until 1960, people began to use digital computers to simulate flight. In 1965, German engineer Stewart published a paper on

© The Author(s), under exclusive license to Springer Nature Switzerland AG 2022
D. D. Schmorrow and C. M. Fidopiastis (Eds.): HCII 2022, LNAI 13310, pp. 402–416, 2022.
https://doi.org/10.1007/978-3-031-05457-0_30

**Fig. 1.** Antoinette simulator

the six-degree-of-freedom platform [2] and proposed its application in flight simulators, which aroused widespread interest in the academic community. With the application of the six-degree-of-freedom platform, the fidelity of flight simulators has gradually improved. And so far, the flight simulator for commercial airline training still widely uses the Stewart platform as a motion system. After 1980, with the rapid development of computer technology and control science, the simulator's real-time calculation of the aircraft state and the control of the motion platform became more accurate. In 1984, fully digitally controlled motion systems were used in flight simulators, making motion simulations more realistic and more reliable. The visual system of the flight simulator also changed a lot at this stage. The previous method of visual display using film is eliminated, and the computer is used to generate images in real time. This enriches the scene of the visual display, and is no longer limited to the simple scene provided by the film [3].

A flight simulator has many advantages over a real flight. It can provide pilots with an environment similar to real flight, and reproduce the aircraft attitude, acceleration changes, and even changes in light and sound in the environment during flight. The instrument display, prompt system, warning information, etc. in the simulated cockpit can also bring a more realistic flight experience to the pilot. In today's rising demand for flying, training pilots with flight simulators can not only save a lot of cost, but also ensure the safety of pilot training.

### 1.2 Motion Analysis of Flight Simulator

The motion state of the aircraft is the most important state information that the pilot needs to obtain. The human body's perception of its own motion can be divided into two parts: the first is the visual perception using the photoreceptors in the eye, and the second is the non-visual perception through the gravitational inertial body system that feels mechanical force (see Fig. 2).

As can be seen from the above figure, visual perception can be divided into central visual perception and peripheral visual perception; non-visual perception can be divided into vestibular system in human ear, gravity receptor in kidney and somatosensory system in skin and muscles. For motion perception during flight, it can be simplified into the vestibular system and the visual system, which are crucial to maintaining the normal physiological and psychological state of the human body [4].

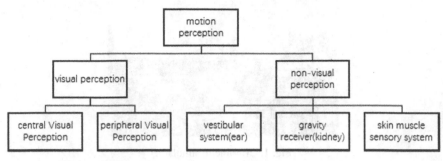

**Fig. 2.** Classification of human perception systems

At present, the flight simulator based on the Stewart motion platform combines the motion system and the vision system, both of which provide the pilot with motion status information. The flight motion simulation system mainly provides motion effects for pilots through three aspects [5]:

a)  The human body's tactile perception system is under constant stress, such as the constant stress on the back of the human body during takeoff.
b)  The stimulation of the pilot's vestibular system when the aircraft is in motion, such as the angular velocity, angular acceleration, and tilt angle of the aircraft when it is rolling.
c)  The human visual system's perception of the changes in the scenery outside the window and the information of the instrument

Among them, it is easier to realize the display of the view outside the window and the instrument. But providing motion sensations through motion platforms is harder. The range of motion of the aircraft can be regarded as infinite, while the range of motion of the motion platform is limited. Therefore, it is impossible for a flight simulator to provide the pilot with a sense of motion by directly reproducing the real state of the aircraft. To solve this problem, a special algorithm-washout algorithm is added between the aircraft motion state and the simulator motion state [6]. According to the duration of the motion, it is divided into sudden motion and continuous motion in the precipitation algorithm. After each sudden motion, the motion platform slowly returns to the initial state by means of the wash-out algorithm at an amplitude that the pilot cannot perceive. And for continuous motion, the washout algorithm issues a command to tilt the platform after performing the calculations, simulating it with the component of gravity. The washout algorithm can perform motion simulation in this way mainly based on two points:

a)  The human body's perceptual organs have thresholds, that is, motion perception has a minimum limit.
b)  The vestibular system cannot tell whether the sense of motion is due to inertia or gravity.

There are three commonly used washout algorithms: classic washout algorithm [7], adaptive washout algorithm [8], optimized washout algorithm [9]. Different washout algorithms also have their own characteristics. But in addition to the efficiency of the washout algorithm, another factor that affects the fidelity of the motion platform is the motion characteristics of the platform itself. The FAA classifies flight simulators into four levels: A, B, C, and D. Among them, the D-level simulator is the simulator with the highest fidelity. Generally, the higher the simulator level, the longer the hydraulic cylinder or motor cylinder stroke and the greater the acceleration of its motion platform. Correspondingly, higher-level simulators have greater motion amplitudes and accelerations.

## 1.3  Problem

In the previous section, we saw how a flight simulator produces the sense of motion. The visual display mode of different levels of simulators, the maximum acceleration and angle of the motion platform, and the time delay of the simulator system are the main reasons for limiting its fidelity. Class D simulators are already good at simulating flight motion, but they are complex to manufacture and extremely expensive. Most university labs or institutes cannot afford Class D simulators. These simulators have deficiencies in the visual display effect and the motion range of the motion platform. Therefore, how to improve the fidelity of the simulator under limited conditions is a problem worthy of study.

On this issue, Mujun Xie and Wenqi Ge [10] applied an improved fuzzy algorithm combined with traditional feedforward control to successfully solve the problem of image rotation. Guoquan Chen et al. [11] added a physical motion platform to the sailing simulator. At the same time, they propose a visual compensation method and realization for the limit of the motion platform. Specifically, they increase the motion amplitude of the boat in the visual display when the motion platform exceeds the motion amplitude limit of a certain degree of freedom. Such an approach alleviates the unrealistic feeling that the motion platform brings after reaching its limit.

Similarly, the flight simulator also has a situation where the visual information and motion information do not match due to the limitation of the motion platform parameters. The main goal of this paper is to apply the method of visual compensation in flight simulators. This paper firstly simulates the six-degree-of-freedom platform through Simulink, and determines the motion range of the motion platform. At the same time, the simulation results show that the motion platform has limitations in simulating some flight actions. After that, this paper proposes a visual compensation method based on FlightGear flight simulation software, and implements it through C++ program.

## 2  Stewart 6DOF Motion Platform Simulation

### 2.1  Structure of a 6DOF Platform

6DOF motion platform is essentially a Spatial Parallel Mechanism (SPM) formed by hinges and telescopic mechanism. Stewart platform is one of the 6DOF platforms. It has two platforms up and down and six drive rods of equal length. The drive rod and the platform are connected by hinges. The driving mode of the driving rods is motor driving or hydraulic driving, and each driving rod can move independently. By extending and compressing each driving rod, the motion platform can be controlled to move in six degrees of freedom, thereby changing the position and posture of the motion platform. By extending and compressing each driving rod, the motion platform can be controlled to move in six degrees of freedom, thereby changing the position and posture of the motion platform. The six degrees of freedom are translation along the x-axis, y-axis, and z-axis, and rotation along the x-axis (α angle), y-axis (β-angle), and z-axis (γ-angle) (see Fig. 3).

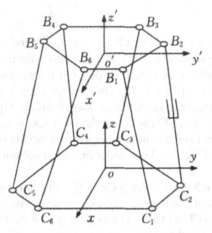

**Fig. 3.** Structure of the Stewart platform

## 2.2 Stewart Platform Simulation Model

The motion model of the Stewart platform is divided into forward solution and reverse solution [12]. The forward solution refers to calculating the position and attitude of the motion platform when the length of each drive rod is known. The reverse solution refers to calculating the length of each driving rod through the position and attitude of the motion platform (that is, the data of six degrees of freedom). In contrast, the reverse solution calculation is simpler. In contrast, the reverse solution calculation is simpler. The simulation model in this paper will be established by the method of reverse solution.

Here are the static parameters of the Stewart platform in our lab:

| | |
|---|---|
| *Number of drive motor | 6 |
| *Minimum drive rod length | 1140 mm |
| *Maximum drive rod length | 1740 mm |
| *Drive rod telescopic range length | 600 mm |
| *Upper platform diameter of circumcircle | 790 mm |
| *Lower platform diameter of circumcircle | 840 mm |

According to Fig. 3, the dynamic coordinate system of the upper platform is $\{B\}$-$o'x'y'z'$, and the static coordinate system of the lower platform is $\{C\}$-$oxyz$. The origin of the moving coordinate system is located at the center of the upper platform, and the origin of the static coordinate system is located at the center of the lower platform. When the upper platform is at the initial position, the axis directions of the two coordinate systems are the same, and the positive direction of the z-axis of the static coordinate system passes through the center of the upper platform. In the figure, $B_1$–$B_6$ are the connection points between the driving rod and the upper platform; $C_1$–$C_6$ are the connection points between the driving rod and the lower platform. And we specify $L_1$–$L_6$ as the length of six drive rods.

Then we can get the coordinates of $B_1$-$B_6$ in static coordinates:

| | |
|---|---|
| $B_1(-647.34, -452.82, 901)$ | $B_2(647.34, -452.82, 901)$ |
| $B_3(715.83, -334.20, 901)$ | $B_4(65, 787.32, 901)$ |
| $B_5(-65, 787.32, 901)$ | $B_6(-715.83, -334.20, 901)$ |

and coordinates of C1-C6 in static coordinates:

| | |
|---|---|
| $C_1(-65, -837.48, 0)$ | $C_2(65, -837.48, 0)$ |
| $C_3(757.80, 362.42, 0)$ | $C_4(692.76, 475.06, 0)$ |
| $C_5(-692.76, 475.06, 0)$ | $C_6(-757.80, 362.42, 0)$ |

In the moving coordinate system, the coordinates of $B_1'$-$B_6'$ are:

| | |
|---|---|
| $B_1'(-647.34, 452.82, 0)$ | $B_2'(647.34, -452.82, 0)$ |
| $B_3'(715.83, -334.20, 0)$ | $B_4'(65, 787.32, 0)$ |
| $B_5'(-65, 787.32, 0)$ | $B_6'(-715.83, -334.20, 0)$ |

There is a transformation method between the static coordinate system and the moving coordinate system, which is described in the form of language: first translate along the x-axis, y-axis, and z-axis; then rotate around the x-axis, y-axis, and z-axis by $\alpha$, $\beta$, $\gamma$. The transformation matrix of the upper platform coordinates $B_1$–$B_6$ to $B_1'$–$B_6'$ is:

$$A = \begin{bmatrix} \cos\beta \cos\gamma & \sin\alpha \sin\beta \cos\gamma - \cos\alpha \sin\gamma & \cos\alpha \sin\beta \cos\gamma + \sin\alpha \sin\gamma & x' \\ \cos\beta \sin\gamma & \sin\alpha \sin\beta \sin\gamma + \cos\alpha \cos\gamma & \cos\alpha \sin\beta \sin\gamma - \sin\alpha \cos\gamma & y' \\ -\sin\beta & \sin\alpha \cos\beta & \cos\alpha \cos\beta & z' \\ 0 & 0 & 0 & 1 \end{bmatrix} \quad (1)$$

where $x'$, $y'$, $z'$ represents the coordinates of the origin of the moving coordinate system in the static coordinate system; $\alpha$, $\beta$, $\gamma$ represents the rotation angle of the upper platform around the x-axis, y-axis, and z-axis.

Then we can get $B_i = A * B_i'$:

$$\begin{bmatrix} B_{ix} \\ B_{iy} \\ B_{iz} \\ 1 \end{bmatrix} = A \begin{bmatrix} B'_{ix} \\ B'_{iy} \\ B'_{iz} \\ 1 \end{bmatrix} \tag{2}$$

where i = 1, 2, ..., 6. Through this calculation, we can know the coordinates of each point of the upper platform in the static coordinate system.

We can then calculate the current length of each drive rod using the formula:

$$L_i = \sqrt{(B_{ix} - C_{ix})^2 + (B_{iy} - C_{iy})^2 + (B_{iz} - C_{iz})^2} \tag{3}$$

where i = 1, 2, ..., 6.

According to the above three formulas and the coordinates of each point, we built a Simulink model in MATLAB. We take the information of six degrees of freedom as input. After the inverse solution program calculates the length of each drive rod, the length is displayed. We can check the motion variation of each drive rod in the results (see Fig. 4).

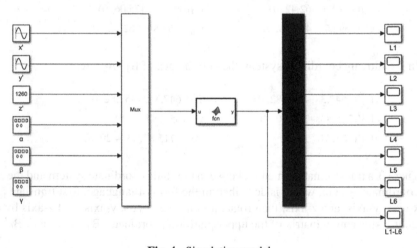

**Fig. 4.** Simulation model

### 2.3 Measurement of Motion Limit Positions

After building the motion platform model, we measured its range of motion. We set the initial size of the moving platform height z' to 1260 mm, which ensures that the length of each drive rod is 1440 mm (the middle position). After that, we change the input of a certain degree of freedom with a certain slope while ensuring that other input information is 0 (except z′). For x′, y′, z′ when the length of a certain drive rod is greater than 1740 mm or less than 1140 mm for the first time, the length corresponding to the time axis at this time is the limit under this degree of freedom. The method for α, β, γ measurement is the same. The following six figures are the measurement results (see Figs. 5, 6, 7, 8, 9 and 10).

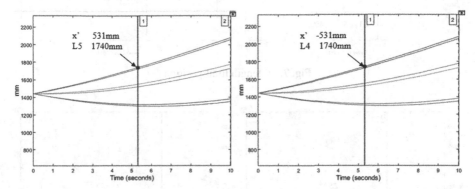

**Fig. 5.** x′ length limit position

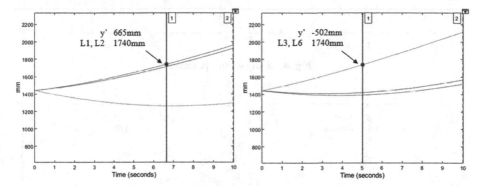

**Fig. 6.** y′ length limit position

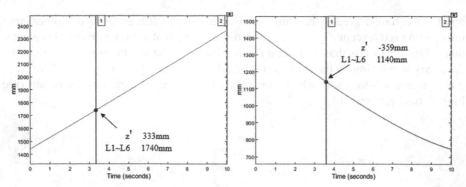

**Fig. 7.** $z'$ length limit position

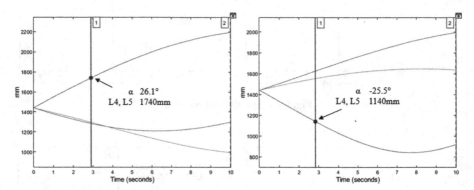

**Fig. 8.** $\alpha$ angle limit position

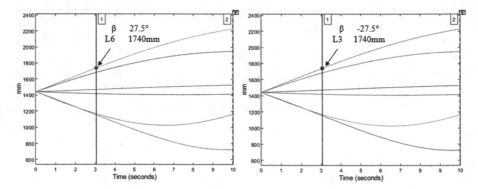

**Fig. 9.** $\beta$ angle limit position

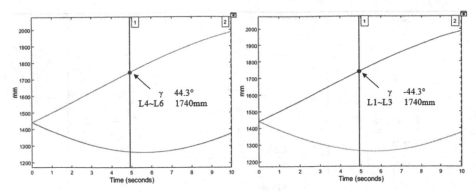

**Fig. 10.** γ angle limit position

Then we come to the conclusion:

**Table 1.** Platform continuous range of motion

| Six degrees of freedom continuous motion range (z = 1260 mm) | |
| --- | --- |
| $x'$ | – 531 mm–531 mm |
| $y'$ | – 502 mm–665 mm |
| $z'$ | – 359 mm–333 mm |
| $\alpha$ | – 25.5° –26.1° |
| $\beta$ | – 27.5°–27.5° |
| $\gamma$ | – 44.3° –44.3° |

## 2.4  Problem Caused by Range of Motion

The range of motion of the platform in each degree of freedom is given in Table 1. In general flight training tasks, the pitch angle $\alpha$ of the aircraft during take-off and landing is 12°–15°, and the maximum is not more than 20°. At the same time, yaw angle $\gamma$ of 40° or more are rarely required. However, the range of the roll angle $\beta$ is obviously insufficient. In missions such as circling at a large bank angle of 45°, recovering from an abnormal state caused by the bank angle, and turning immediately after take-off, the aircraft bank angle (roll angle) will be greater than 30°, exceeding the maximum angle that the platform can provide. Take the turn immediately after takeoff as an example, set the pitch angle to 15° (see Fig. 11):

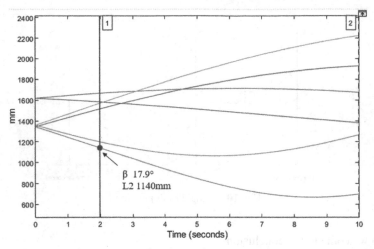

**Fig. 11.** Turning immediately after takeoff

It can be seen that the maximum roll angle in these states is only 17.9°, and the requirement for this task is an angle of 20°–30°. Therefore, the motion platform is not fully competent in the face of similar flight tasks.

## 3 Visual Compensation Method

### 3.1 Software Basis for Visual Simulation

FlightGear is an open-source, multi-platform flight simulation software with powerful real-time calculation and input and output functions for flight data. It can receive operational input from external devices and solve for the current state of the aircraft and environment. At the same time, it supports the real-time output and input of aircraft attitude angle, flight status, instrument control information, pilot's viewpoint position and other information. That is to say, FlightGear can be used as a host computer to input and calculate flight control data and provide flight visual information; it can also be used as a slave computer to receive externally input flight status information and display visual information. Figure 12 is the input and output interface of FlightGear.

All data that can be imported and exported in FlightGear can be found in the PropertyTree. At the same time, the XML file is used to define the format of the input and output data.

### 3.2 Concept and Realization of Visual Compensation Method

Due to the characteristic of FlightGear's input and output function, the compensation method requires two computers - a master and a slave. The host computer is responsible for receiving the control signals of the flight simulator and calculating the real-time flight status; the slave computer is responsible for receiving the flight status information sent by the host computer and displaying the cockpit visual information. This method

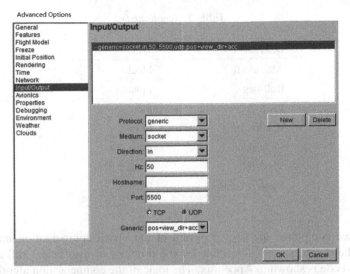

**Fig. 12.** FlightGear input and output interface

considers adding a compensation module in the process of sending data from the master to the slave. The compensation module receives the flight information from the host, performs compensation and adjustment, and then sends it to the slave. The slave displays the visual information after compensation. Compensation module will be implemented with C++ program, its main function is to receive and send data under UDP protocol (see Fig. 13).

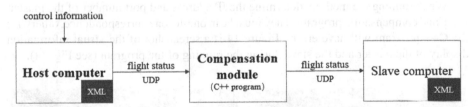

**Fig. 13.** Implementation structure diagram

First, we determined the data that needs to be defined in the XML file. The flight state data required by this method are shown in Table 2.

**Table 2.** Flight data in XML

| Data name | Type |
| --- | --- |
| Latitude-deg | Double |
| Longitude-deg | Double |

*(continued)*

**Table 2.** (*continued*)

| Data name | Type |
|-----------|------|
| Altitude-ft | Float |
| Roll-deg | Float |
| Pitch-deg | Float |
| Heading-deg | Float |
| View-pitch | Float |
| View-roll | Float |
| View-heading | Float |

Next, we completed the C++ program of the visual compensation method, and designed the compensation algorithm for the problem of insufficient roll angle. Part of the C++ code is shown in Appendix. The logic of the compensation algorithm:

a) When the roll angle of the aircraft is greater than 20°, the angular velocity of the aircraft roll angle greater than 20° is changed to 1.5 times the original.

b) When the roll angle of the aircraft is not 0, change the roll angle of the pilot's viewpoint to –0.5 times the roll angle of the aircraft. It is used to simulate a situation where a person's head moves in the opposite direction when encountering lateral acceleration.

When running the method, determine the IP address and port number of the master, slave and compensation program. They must be in one-to-one correspondence, otherwise the C++ program will have errors. Figure 14 is a screenshot of the visual information display of the master and the slave during the running of the program (see Fig. 14).

**Fig. 14.** Screenshot of master and slave

# 4  Conclusion

Aiming at the limitation of motion platform, this paper proposes a visual compensation method. Based on FlightGear flight simulation software and C++ program, we have implemented a complete visual compensation method. This is an attempt to improve the fidelity of the simulator using visual information. In future research, we will consider combining the motion platform inverse solution method with the visual compensation method, and consider the effect of acceleration.

# Appendix

```
WSAData wsaSend;
SOCKET sockServer;
SOCKADDR_IN addrServerRemote, addrServerLocal;
...
...
sockServer = socket(AF_INET, SOCK_DGRAM, IPPROTO_UDP);
if (sockServer == SOCKET_ERROR) {
    cout << "socket Error = " << WSAGetLastError() << endl;
    return 1;
}
int serverPort = 5500;
addrServerLocal.sin_family = AF_INET;
addrServerLocal.sin_port = htons(serverPort);
inet_pton(AF_INET, "192.168.1.10", &addrServerLocal.sin_addr);
//Create socket Server
...
...
sockClient = socket(AF_INET, SOCK_DGRAM, IPPROTO_UDP);
if (sockClient == SOCKET_ERROR) {
        cout << "socket Error = " << WSAGetLastError() << endl;
        return 1;
}
int nPort = 5501;
addrClient.sin_family = AF_INET;
addrClient.sin_port = htons(nPort);
inet_pton(AF_INET, "192.168.1.10", &addrClient.sin_addr);
// Create socket Client
...
sendFlag        =        sendto(sockClient,        sendPointAdd,
sendPointAddLength,        0,        (SOCKADDR*)&addrClient,
sizeof(SOCKADDR));
// Send data to specified port
```

# References

1. Bezdek, W., Mays, D., Powell, R.: The history and future of military flight simulators. In: AIAA Modeling and Simulation Technologies Conference and Exhibit, p. 5148 (2004). https://doi.org/10.2514/6.2004-5148
2. Stewart, D.: A platform with six degrees of freedom. Proc. Inst. Mech. Eng. **180**(1), 371–386 (1965). https://doi.org/10.1243/PIME_PROC_1965_180_029_02
3. Zhang, Y., Huang, Q., Han, J., Zhang, L., Jiang, H.: Design and realization of flight simulator vision system (in Chinese). J. Syst. Simul. **12**, 3662–3667 (2009)
4. Gu, X., Wu, L., Wu, D.: Characteristics of normal human vision-vestibular interaction (in Chinese). Eye Sci. **6**(3), 60–65 (1990)
5. Liu, J.: A Preliminary Study on Human Motion Perception in Flight Environment. (Master's thesis, Nanjing University of Aeronautics and Astronautics) (2018). (in Chinese)
6. Yang, Y., Han, J.: Research on Key Technology of Motion Cueing for Flight Simulator (2010). (in Chinese). (Doctoral dissertation, Harbin Institute of Technology)
7. Conrad, B., Schmidt, S.F.: Motion drive signals for piloted flight simulators (No. NASA-CR-1601). NASA (1970)
8. Parrish, R.V., Dieudonne, J.E., Bowles, R.L., Martin Jr, D.J.: Coordinated adaptive washout for motion simulators. J. Aircr. **12**(1), 44–50 (1975). https://doi.org/10.2514/3.59800
9. Sivan, R., Ish-Shalom, J., Huang, J.K.: An optimal control approach to the design of moving flight simulators. IEEE Trans. Syst. Man Cybern. **12**(6), 818–827 (1982). https://doi.org/10.1109/TSMC.1982.4308915
10. Xie, M., Ge, W.: The Implementation of Image derotation of visual system in a flight simulator. Control Theory Appl. **3**, 400–404 (2000)
11. Chen, G., Yi, Y., Li, L., Yang, S.: 3D scene compensation algorithm for physical motion platform (in Chinese). Navig. China **3**, 57–60 (2015)
12. Shilei, Y.: Research on Control System of a 6-DOF Motion Platform. (Doctoral dissertation, Harbin Institute of Technology) (2013). (in Chinese)

# Author Index

Printed in the United States
by Baker & Taylor Publisher Services